Rail Guide
2015

Colin J. Marsden

First published 2010
Reprinted 2010, 2011, 2012, 2013, 2014
This Fourth Edition first published 2015

ISBN 978 0 7110 3806 6

Published by Ian Allan Publishing.

An imprint of Ian Allan Publishing Ltd, Hersham, Surrey KT12 4RG.

Visit the Ian Allan Publishing website at www.ianallanpublishing.com

Front Cover Top: *Newly converted GB Railfreight Class 73/9 No. 73961 undergoes dynamic testing on the Great Central Railway, piloting 'Peak' No. 45041 at Woodthorpe Bridge on 18 October 2014.* **Lindsay Atkinson**

Front Cover Bottom: *Colas Rail Freight Class 70 No. 70808 stands light loco at Westbury on 23 July 2014.* **CJM**

Back Cover Top: *2014 saw the official opening of the Edinburgh tram system. Tram No. 271 is seen at the St Andrews Square stop, the nearest to Edinburgh Waverley station, on 2 July 2014.* **CJM**

Back Cover Bottom: *Network Rail-operated Class 313 No. 313121 is currently undergoing development work for ERTMS on the Hartford Loop Line. It is seen at Watton-on-Stone.* **Antony Christie**

Acknowledgement – The Author would like to record his thanks to the many railway staff who have provided invaluable information for the production of this book. Also to the many photographers, especially Antony Christie, Nathan Williamson and John Binch, for providing many of the images. I would also like to express my thanks to Keith Ewins and Antony Christie for reading the updated manuscript. **CJM**

Introduction

Welcome to the 2015 edition of the Ian Allan *ABC Rail Guide*, which continues to be the only comprehensive listing of all locomotives, multiple units, coaches and track machines provided by operator. This edition includes the massive number of changes seen in 2014-15.

On the locomotive front, GBRf took delivery of 21 Class 66s, built at the new EMD plant in Muncie, Indiana, USA. These will be the final examples of the current Class 66 design as the power unit does not meet new emissions standards introduced in January 2015. GBRf also started to take delivery of rebuilt Class 73/9s from Brush Traction, which include new diesel prime movers and revised electric equipment. These will be used on general duties as well as on the new Scottish sleeper contract. RVEL has also been busy rebuilding Class 73s for Network Rail.

The expanding Colas Rail Freight business took full delivery of 10 Class 70 diesel-electric locos from General Electric. The company also started to take delivery of 10 Class 60s, purchased from DB-S and given the 'Super 60' overhaul at Toton.

Direct Rail Services received the first order of 10 Class 68 mixed-traffic locos from Vossloh in Spain; the company also extended its fleet size by 10 units as new work flows were identified for the design.

DB-Schenker maintained a status-quo with its main-line traction fleet, but decided to drastically reduce its Class 08/09 shunter fleet, with most yard work now undertaken by road power.

On the multiple unit side, First TransPennine Express and London Midland both introduced 'Desiro' Class 350 sets, while more of the expanding 'Electrostar' product line built by Bombardier were introduced, with examples of Class 377/7 and 387 entering service. Fifth cars also started to be added to TfL Class 378 stock.

The rebuilding of the Class 458 stock for South West Trains continued with a very slow introduction rate. South West Trains also announced that a fleet of 30 five-car Class 707 'Desiro City' sets had been ordered for suburban use.

The highlight of the year was the unveiling of the first Class 700 'Desiro City' for the Thameslink project; this was shown off at Innotrans in Berlin. The unveiling coincided with the announcement of the new Thameslink, Southern and Great Northern franchise. Many other franchise changes have also been seen.

The first of the InterCity replacement stock (IEP) Class 800s was unveiled in Japan towards the end of the year, with the first complete set due in the UK in Spring 2015.

The modernisation and expansion of the Eurostar operation continued, with the unveiling of the first Class 374 at St Pancras in November. These sets are scheduled to be introduced in 2015-16 and will allow Eurostar operations to extend to new cities in Mainland Europe.

The Editor of the *ABC Rail Guide* welcomes correspondence about omissions or corrections or suggestions for further items to be included.

We hope you enjoy following the UK rail scene in 2015, but please always remember to keep safe, do not trespass on the railway and keep an eye open around you; if you see anything suspicious please notify the British Transport Police or a railway official.

Colin J. Marsden
Dawlish, January 2015

Information in Rail Guide 2015 is correct to 15 January 2015

The West Coast Main Line still sees a large number of freight operations operated by all the main UK carriers. A number of these freights use diesel power running under the overhead power lines. On 21 May 2014, Direct Rail Services Class 66/4 No. 66433 heads south at South Kenton with the 12.37 Daventry to Purfleet intermodal service, mainly formed of Stobart vehicles. **CJM**

Train Operators, The Association of Train Operating Companies, and Network Rail welcome rail enthusiasts and photographers, but in today's safety-led railway and with the continued concerns about possible transport terrorism, guidelines are very important and we encourage all to follow these published guidelines as much as possible. They are available to view and download from the National Rail and ATOC websites, but are reproduced in full below to assist you with this information. ■

The Official Railway Enthusiasts Guidelines

■ Network Rail welcomes rail enthusiasts to our stations.

■ The following guidelines are designed to help you to have a safe and enjoyable experience. Please keep them with you when you are at Network Rail-managed stations.

■ You may also wish to take a copy of the Railway by-laws which are available from the Office of Public Sector Information website.

Before you enter the platform

■ When you arrive at a station, please let the staff at the Network Rail Reception Desk know that you are on the station. This will help keep station staff informed so that they can go about their duties without concern as to your reasons for being there.

■ You may require a platform ticket to allow access to platforms.

While you are on the platform

■ You need to act safely and sensibly at all times.
- Stay clear of the platform edge and stay behind the yellow lines where they are provided.
- Be aware of your surroundings.

Please DO NOT:
- Trespass on to the tracks or any other part of the railway that is not available to passengers.
- Use flash photography because it can distract train drivers and train despatch staff and so is potentially very dangerous.
- Climb on any structure or interfere with platform equipment.
- Obstruct any signalling equipment or signs which are vital to the safe running of the railway.
- Wear anything which is similar in colour to safety clothing, such as high-visibility jackets, as this could cause confusion to drivers and other railway employees.
- Gather together in groups at busy areas of the platform (e.g. customer information points, departure screens, waiting areas, seating etc.) or where this may interfere with the duties of station staff.

■ If possible, please try to avoid peak hours which are Monday – Friday 6:00am (06.00) – 10:30am (10.30) and 3:30pm (15.30) – 7:30pm (19.30).

Extra eyes and ears

■ If you see anything suspicious or notice any unusual behaviour or activities, please tell a member of staff immediately.

■ For emergencies and serious incidents, either call:
The British Transport Police on 0800 40 50 40.
The Police on 999, or 101

■ Your presence at a station can be very helpful to us as extra "eyes and ears" and can have a positive security benefit.

Photography

■ You can take photographs at stations provided you do not sell them. However, you are not allowed to take photographs of security-related equipment, such as CCTV cameras.

■ Flash photography on platforms is not allowed at any time. It can distract train drivers and train despatch staff and so is potentially very dangerous.

■ Tripod legs must be kept away from platform edges and behind the yellow lines. On busy stations, you may not be allowed to use a tripod because it could be a dangerous obstruction to passengers.

Railway By-laws

For safety and ease of travel on the railway system (which includes passengers, staff, property and equipment), the by-laws must be observed by everyone. A copy of the by-laws can be obtained at stations or downloaded from the Office of Public Sector Information website.

General

Train operators must put the safety of their passengers and staff first. You may very occasionally be asked by station staff to move to another part of the station or to leave the station altogether. Station staff should be happy to explain why this is necessary. If you are travelling by train, they may ask you to remain in the normal waiting areas with other passengers. If this occurs, please follow their instructions with goodwill as staff have many things to consider, including the safety and security of all passengers, and are authorised to use judgement in this regard.

Below: *At the very end of 2014, a start was made to introduce DRS Class 68s onto the Chiltern Railways loco-hauled duties, replacing DB S Class 67s. On 7 January 2015, Chiltern-liveried No. 68012 stands under the lights at London Marylebone with the 17.50 to Banbury. Note the extra jumper connection on the buffer beam to the left of the electric train supply jumper allowing control of the loco from a DVT.* **Antony Christie**

Contents

Arriva Trains Wales
Trenau Arriva Cymru

Address: ✉ St Mary's House, 47 Penarth Road, Cardiff, CF10 5DJ
✍ customer.relations@arrivatrainswales.co.uk
✆ 0845 6061 660
ⓘ www.arrivatrainswales.co.uk

Managing Director: Ian Bullock
Franchise Dates: 7 December 2003 - October 2018
Principal Routes: Cardiff to Swansea and West Wales
Cardiff Valleys
Cardiff - Hereford - Shrewsbury - Crewe - Manchester Piccadilly
Cardiff - Hereford - Shrewsbury - Chester - Bangor - Holyhead
Manchester - Crewe - Bangor - Holyhead
Shrewsbury - Pwllheli/Aberystwyth
Swansea - Shrewsbury
Depots: Cardiff Canton (CF), Chester (CH), Holyhead* (HD)
Machynlleth (MN), Shrewsbury* (SX) * Stabling point
Parent Company: Deutsche Bahn AG (DB Regio)

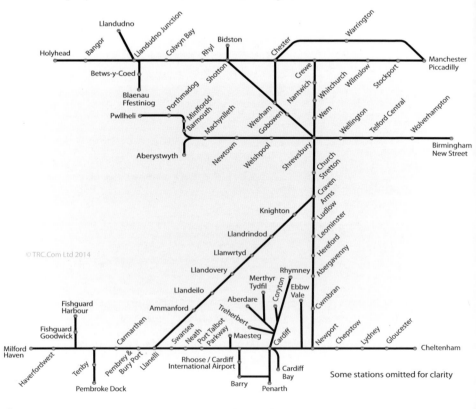

Some stations omitted for clarity

© TRC.Com Ltd 2014

Class 67

Vehicle Length: 64ft 7in (19.68m)
Height: 12ft 9in (3.88m)
Width: 8ft 9in (2.66m)

Engine: EMD 12N-710G3B-EC
Horsepower: 2,980hp (2,223kW)
Electrical Equipment: EMD

Number	Depot	Pool	Livery	Owner	Operator
67001	CE	WAWC	ATW	DBS	DBS/ATW
67002	CE	WAWC	ATW	DBS	DBS/ATW
67003	CE	WAAC	ATW	DBS	DBS/ATW

Right: *Three DB Schenker Class 67s are dedicated to Arriva Trains Wales for use on the Cardiff-Holyhead and North Wales loco-hauled services. Painted in un-branded Arriva turquoise livery, the three locos, Nos. 67001-003, are usually out-based at Cardiff but return to Crewe depot for extended maintenance. These locos operate on the ATW Mk3 loco-hauled trains with a Driving Van Trailer at the remote end. No. 67001 is seen at Newport on 19 June 2014 with the morning southbound train.* **CJM**

Class 142
Pacer

Vehicle Length: 51ft 0½in (15.55m)
Height: 12ft 8in (3.86m)
Width: 9ft 2¼in (2.80m)

Engine: 1 x Cummins LTA10-R per vehicle
Horsepower: 460hp (343kW)
Seats (total/car): 90S, 46S/44S

Number	Formation DMS+DMSL	Depot	Livery	Owner	Operator
142002	55543+55593	CV	ATW	ANG	ATW
142006	55547+55597	CV	ATW	ANG	ATW
142010	55551+55601	CV	ATW	ANG	ATW
142069	55719+55765	CV	ATW	ANG	ATW
142072	55722+55768	CV	ATW	ANG	ATW
142073	55723+55769	CV	ATW	ANG	ATW
142074	55724+55770	CV	ATW	ANG	ATW
142075	55725+55771	CV	ATW	ANG	ATW
142076	55726+55772	CV	ATW	ANG	ATW
142077	55727+55773	CV	ATW	ANG	ATW
142080	55730+55776	CV	ATW	ANG	ATW
142081	55731+55777	CV	ATW	ANG	ATW
142082	55732+55778	CV	ATW	ANG	ATW
142083	55733+55779	CV	ATW	ANG	ATW
142085	55735+55781	CV	ATW	ANG	ATW

Name applied
142072 *Myfanwy*

Operating alongside a Class 143 and 150 fleet, Arriva Trains Wales has a fleet of 15 Class 142 'Pacer' units allocated to Cardiff Canton; these are owned by Angel Trains and are in the process of being repainted into the latest two-tone turquoise livery. Sets Nos. 142073 and 142080 in the older livery are seen at Barry on 19 June 2014 with a Barry Island to Pontypridd service. **CJM**

Arriva Trains Wales

Class 143
Pacer

Vehicle Length: 51ft 0½in (15.55m)
Height: 12ft 2¼in (3.73m)
Width: 8ft 10½in (2.70m)

Engine: 1 x Cummins LTA10-R per vehicle
Horsepower: 460hp (343kW)
Seats (total/car): 92S, 48S/44S

Number	Formation DMS+DMSL	Depot	Livery	Owner	Operator
143601	55642+55667	CV	ATT	BCC	ATW
143602	55651+55668	CV	ATW	PTR	ATW
143604	55645+55670	CV	ATW	PTR	ATW
143605	55646+55671	CV	ATT	PTR	ATW
143606	55647+55672	CV	ATW	PTR	ATW
143607	55648+55673	CV	ATW	PTR	ATW
143608	55649+55674	CV	ATT	PTR	ATW
143609	55650+55675	CV	ATW	CCC	ATW
143610	55643+55676	CV	ATW	BCC	ATW
143614	55655+55680	CV	ATW	BCC	ATW
143616	55657+55682	CV	ATW	PTR	ATW
143622	55663+55688	CV	ATW	PTR	ATW
143623	55664+55689	CV	ATW	PTR	ATW
143624	55665+55690	CV	ATT	PTR	ATW
143625	55666+55691	CV	ATW	PTR	ATW

Name applied

143609	*Sir Tom Jones*

Below: *A fleet of 15 Class 143 'Pacer' sets is operated by Arrive Trains Wales from Cardiff Canton and shares Valley Lines duties with Class 142 and 150 stock. Showing the latest two-tone turquoise livery, set No. 143608 arrives at Radyr on 19 June 2014 with a service bound for Barry Island.* **CJM**

Class 150/2
Sprinter

Vehicle Length: 64ft 9¾in (19.74m)
Height: 12ft 4½in (3.77m)
Width: 9ft 3⅛in (2.82m)

Engine: 1 x NT855R5 of 285hp per vehicle
Horsepower: 570hp (425kW)
Seats (total/car): 128S, 60S/68S

Number	Formation DMSL+DMS	Depot	Livery	Owner	Operator
150208	52208+57208	CV	ATW	PTR	ATW
150213	52213+57213	CV	ATT	PTR	ATW
150217	52217+57217	CV	ATW	PTR	ATW
150227	52227+57227	CV	ATT	PTR	ATW
150229	52227+57227	CV	ATW	PTR	ATW
150230	52230+57230	CV	ATT	PTR	ATW
150231	52231+57231	CV	ATW	PTR	ATW
150235	52235+57235	CV	ATW	PTR	ATW
150236	52236+57236	CV	ATT	PTR	ATW
150237	52237+57237	CV	ATT	PTR	ATW
150240	52240+57240	CV	ATW	PTR	ATW
150241	52241+57241	CV	ATW	PTR	ATW
150242	52242+57242	CV	ATW	PTR	ATW
150245	52245+57245	CV	ATW	PTR	ATW
150250	52250+57250	CV	ATT	PTR	ATW
150251	52251+57251	CV	ATT	PTR	ATW
150252	52252+57252	CV	ATT	PTR	ATW
150253	52253+57253	CV	ATT	PTR	ATW
150254	52254+57254	CV	ATW	PTR	ATW
150255	52213+57255	CV	ATW	PTR	ATW
150256	52256+57256	CV	ATW	PTR	ATW
150257	52257+57257	CV	ATT	PTR	ATW

Number	Formation					Number	Formation			
150258	52258+57258	CV	ATW	PTR	ATW	150279	52270+57279	CV	ATT	PTR	ATW
150259	52259+57259	CV	ATW	PTR	ATW	150280	52280+57280	CV	ATT	PTR	ATW
150260	52260+57260	CV	ATW	PTR	ATW	150281	52281+57281	CV	ATW	PTR	ATW
150262	52262+57262	CV	ATW	PTR	ATW	150282	52282+57282	CV	ATW	PTR	ATW
150264	52264+57264	CV	ATW	PTR	ATW	150283	52283+57283	CV	ATW	PTR	ATW
150267	52267+57267	CV	ATW	PTR	ATW	150284	52284+57284	CV	ATT	PTR	ATW
150278	52278+57278	CV	ATT	PTR	ATW	150285	52285+57280	CV	ATW	PTR	ATW

Right: *By far the largest Arriva Trains South Wales fleet are the 36 members of Class 150/2. Currently these are in the process of refurbishment by LNWR Crewe and are returning to traffic in the revised two-tone turquoise livery, as shown on set No. 150236 arriving at Radyr on 19 June 2014 with its DMSL vehicle nearest the camera. All the ATW Class 150 sets have 2+2 seating in a mix of group and airline style.* **CJM**

Class 153

Vehicle Length: 76ft 5in (23.29m)
Height: 12ft 3⅛in (3.75m)
Width: 8ft 10in (2.70m)

Engine: 1 x NT855R5 of 285hp
Horsepower: 285hp (213kW)
Seats (total/car): 72S

Number	Formation DMSL	Depot	Livery	Owner	Operator	Number					
						153323	52323	CV	ATT	PTR	ATW
						153327	52327	CV	ATT	ANG	ATW
153303	52303	CV	ATT	ANG	ATW	153353	57353	CV	ATT	ANG	ATW
153312	52312	CV	ATT	ANG	ATW	153362	57362	CV	ATT	ANG	ATW
153320	52320	CV	ATW	PTR	ATW	153367	57367	CV	ATW	PTR	ATW

Right: *For rural operations, Arriva Trains Wales has a fleet of eight single-car or 'Bubble car' Class 153s; these are based at Cardiff Canton and can be found over the entire ATW network. Since the demise of the 'Heritage' Class 121 set from the Cardiff Bay 'shuttle' service, a class member is allocated to this duty. Vehicles are mainly painted in the revised two-tone turquoise colours. No. 153353 is seen at Shrewsbury from its small cab end, recognisable by the higher than normal position of the marker light clusters.* **Keith Ewins**

Class 158

Vehicle Length: 76ft 1¾in (23.21m)
Height: 12ft 6in (3.81m)
Width: 9ft 3¼in (2.82m)

Engine: 1 x Perkins 2006-TWH of 350hp per vehicle
Horsepower: 700hp (522kW)
Seats (total/car): 134S, 66S/68S

Number	Formation DMSL+DMSL	Depot	Livery	Owner	Operator	Number					
						158829	52829+57829	MN	ATT	ANG	ATW
						158830	52830+57830	MN	ATT	ANG	ATW
158818	52818+57818	MN	ATT	ANG	ATW	158831	52831+57831	MN	ATT	ANG	ATW
158819	52819+57819	MN	ATT	ANG	ATW	158832	52832+57832	MN	ATT	ANG	ATW
158820	52820+57820	MN	ATT	ANG	ATW	158833	52833+57833	MN	ATT	ANG	ATW
158821	52821+57821	MN	ATT	ANG	ATW	158834	52834+57834	MN	ATT	ANG	ATW
158822	52822+57822	MN	ATT	ANG	ATW	158835	52835+57835	MN	ATT	ANG	ATW
158823	52823+57823	MN	ATT	ANG	ATW	158836	52836+57836	MN	ATT	ANG	ATW
158824	52824+57824	MN	ATT	ANG	ATW	158837	52837+57837	CV	ATT	ANG	ATW
158825	52825+57825	MN	ATT	ANG	ATW	158838	52838+57838	CV	ATT	ANG	ATW
158826	52826+57826	MN	ATT	ANG	ATW	158839	52839+57839	CV	ATT	ANG	ATW
158827	52827+57827	MN	ATT	ANG	ATW	158840	52840+57840	CV	ATT	ANG	ATW
158828	52828+57828	MN	ATT	ANG	ATW	158841	52841+57841	CV	ATT	ANG	ATW

Arriva Trains Wales

Left: Longer-distance ATW services and especially those operated over the Cambrian route are operated by a fleet of 24 two-car Class 158s. All are refurbished and sport the latest ATW livery and are fitted with ERTMS cab signalling. The sets are allocated to both Cardiff Canton and Machynlleth depots. Set No. 158824 is seen on a Holyhead to Cardiff train at Newport on 6 June 2014. **CJM**

Class 175/0
Coradia 1000

Vehicle Length: 75ft 7in (23.06m)
Height: 12ft 4in (3.75m)
Width: 9ft 2in (2.80m)

Engine: 1 x Cummins N14 of 450hp per vehicle
Horsepower: 900hp (671kW)
Seats (total/car): 118S, 54S/64S

Number	Formation DMSL+DMSL	Depot	Livery	Owner	Operator
175001	50701+79701	CH	ATW	ANG	ATW
175002	50702+79702	CH	ATW	ANG	ATW
175003	50703+79703	CH	ATW	ANG	ATW
175004	50704+79704	CH	ATW	ANG	ATW
175005	50705+79705	CH	ATW	ANG	ATW
175006	50706+79706	CH	ATW	ANG	ATW
175007	50707+79707	CH	ATW	ANG	ATW
175008	50708+79708	CH	ATW	ANG	ATW
175009	50709+79709	CH	ATW	ANG	ATW
175010	50710+79710	CH	ATW	ANG	ATW
175011	50711+79711	CH	ATW	ANG	ATW

Left: Eleven two-car Alstom-built Class 175/0s are based at Chester. These together with the three-car version (175/1) form the backbone of long-distance ATW services. Sets have 2+2 seating with good luggage accommodation and sport a main-line interior with external doors feeding a cross walkway rather than direct into the saloon. Set No. 175006 is shown at Newport on a Cheltenham to Cardiff service on 24 July 2013. **CJM**

Class 175/1
Coradia 1000

Vehicle Length: 75ft 7in (23.06m)
Height: 12ft 4in (3.75m)
Width: 9ft 2in (2.80m)

Engine: 1 x Cummins N14 of 450hp per vehicle
Horsepower: 1,350hp (1,007kW)
Seats (total/car): 186S, 54S/68S/64S

Number	Formation DMSL+MSL+DMSL	Depot	Livery	Owner	Op'r
175101	50751+56751+79751	CH	ATW	ANG	ATW
175102	50752+56752+79752	CH	ATW	ANG	ATW
175103	50753+56753+79753	CH	ATW	ANG	ATW
175104	50754+56754+79754	CH	ATW	ANG	ATW
175105	50755+56755+79755	CH	ATW	ANG	ATW
175106	50756+56756+79756	CH	ATW	ANG	ATW
175107	50757+56757+79757	CH	ATW	ANG	ATW
175108	50758+56758+79758	CH	ATW	ANG	ATW
175109	50759+56759+79759	CH	ATW	ANG	ATW
175110	50760+56760+79760	CH	ATW	ANG	ATW
175111	50761+56761+79761	CH	ATW	ANG	ATW
175112	50762+56762+79762	CH	ATW	ANG	ATW
175113	50763+56763+79763	CH	ATW	ANG	ATW
175114	50764+56764+79764	CH	ATW	ANG	ATW
175115	50765+56765+79765	CH	ATW	ANG	ATW
175116	50766+56766+79766	CH	ATW	ANG	ATW

Left: Sixteen members of the Class 175/1 formed as three-car sets are also based at Chester. These main-line sets accommodate 186 standard class passengers in a mix of 2+2 airline and group seats. These sets were built by Alstom at Washwood Heath, UK, as part of the Coradia 1000 product range which also included the streamlined Class 180 sets all originally operated by Great Western. Set No. 175113 is illustrated at Cardiff Central station with a Manchester-bound duty on 24 July 2013. **CJM**

Class AJ1G / RFM

Vehicle Length: 75ft 0in (22.86m)
Height: 12ft 9in (3.88m)
Width: 8ft 11in (2.71m)
Bogie Type: BT10

Number	Type	Depot	Livery	Owner	Operator
10249 (10012)	RFM	CV	ATT	DBR	ATW
10259 (10025)	RFM	CV	ATT	ATW	ATW

Right: *The modernised Arriva Trains loco-hauled fleet now consists entirely of Mk3 stock, all of which has been refurbished, sporting the latest ATW livery. Two catering vehicles are on the books, both RFMs, which in addition to providing catering needs also have first class seating for 24. Viewed from its buffet counter end, car No. 10259 is seen at Newport.* **CJM**

Class AD1H / TSO

Vehicle Length: 75ft 0in (22.86m)
Height: 12ft 9in (3.88m)
Width: 8ft 11in (2.71m)
Bogie Type: BT10

Number	Type	Depot	Livery	Owner	Operator
12176 (11064)	TSO	CV	ATT	ATW	ATW
12177 (11065)	TSO	CV	ATT	ATW	ATW
12178 (11071)	TSO	CV	ATT	ATW	ATW
12179 (11083)	TSO	CV	ATT	ATW	ATW
12180 (11084)	TSO	CV	ATT	ATW	ATW
12181 (11086)	TSO	CV	ATT	ATW	ATW
12182 (11013)	TSO	CV	ATT	ATW	ATW
12183 (11027)	TSO	CV	ATT	ATW	ATW
12184 (11044)	TSO	CV	ATT	ATW	ATW
12185 (11089)	TSO	CV	ATT	ATW	ATW
§ Awaiting conversion					

Below: *Over the last year four extra Mk3 TSO vehicles have been added to the ATW fleet which will be refurbished and introduced on expanded services. The TS vehicles seat 70. Vehicle No. 12176 is illustrated at Newport.* **CJM**

Mk3 Hauled Stock (NPCCS)

Length: 75ft 0in (22.86m)
Height: 12ft 9in (3.88m)
Width: 8ft 11in (2.71m)
Bogie Type: BT7

NZAG - DVT

Number	Depot	Livery	Owner	Operator
82306 (82144)	CV	ATT	ATW	ATW
82307 (82131)	CV	ATT	ATW	ATW
82308 (82108)	CV	ATT	DBR	ATW

Right: *Remote driving controls for the Arriva Trains Wales loco-hauled services are provided by a small fleet of three Mk3 Driving Van Trailers (DVTs). These have been refurbished from their previous Virgin Trains days, but have not been fitted with auxiliary generators. The coaches sport the latest Arriva Trains Wales livery. No. 82308 is seen on the rear of a westbound working at Newport on 19 June 2014.* **CJM**

c2c - Essex / East Thameside

Address: ✉ 10th Floor, 207 Old Street, London, EC1V 9NR
         ✍ c2c.customerrelations@nationalexpress.com
         ✆ 0845 6014873
         ⓘ www.c2c-online.co.uk

Managing Director: Julian Drury
Franchise Dates: 26 May 1996 - 2029
Principal Routes: London Fenchurch Street - Shoeburyness
         Barking - Pitsea via Purfleet
         Ockendon branch
         London Liverpool Street - Barking (limited service)
Depots: East Ham (EM), Shoeburyness*
         * Stabling point
Parent Company: National Express

Note: Under the terms of the new East Thameside franchise, a commitment has been made to introduce 68 new vehicles (17 four-car sets) by 2019. These are likely to be an 'Electrostar'-based product to keep uniformity with the existing fleet.

Passenger Train Operating Companies - c2c

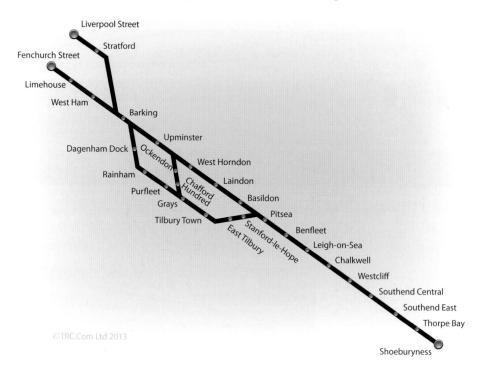

Class 357/0
Electrostar

Vehicle Length: (Driving) 68ft 1in (20.75m) Width: 9ft 2½in (2.80m)
(Inter) 65ft 11½in (20.10m) Horsepower: 2,011hp (1,500kW)
Height: 12ft 4½in (3.78m) Seats (total/car): 282S, 71S/78S/62S/71S

Number	Formation DMSO(A)+MSO+PTSO+DMSO(B)	Depot	Livery	Owner	Op'r	Name
357001	67651+74151+74051+67751	EM	NE2	PTR	c2c	Barry Flaxman
357002	67652+74152+74052+67752	EM	NE2	PTR	c2c	Arthur Lewis Stride 1841-1922
357003	67653+74153+74053+67753	EM	NE2	PTR	c2c	Southend City on Sea
357004	67654+74154+74054+67754	EM	NE2	PTR	c2c	Tony Amos
357005	67655+74155+74055+67755	EM	NE2	PTR	c2c	
357006	67656+74156+74056+67756	EM	NE2	PTR	c2c	Diamond Jubilee 1952 - 2012
357007	67657+74157+74057+67757	EM	NE2	PTR	c2c	
357008	67658+74158+74058+67758	EM	NE2	PTR	c2c	
357009	67659+74159+74059+67759	EM	NE2	PTR	c2c	
357010	67660+74160+74060+67760	EM	NE2	PTR	c2c	
357011	67661+74161+74061+67761	EM	NE2	PTR	c2c	John Lowing
357012	67662+74162+74062+67762	EM	NE2	PTR	c2c	
357013	67663+74163+74063+67763	EM	NE2	PTR	c2c	
357014	67664+74164+74064+67764	EM	NE2	PTR	c2c	
357015	67665+74165+74065+67765	EM	NE2	PTR	c2c	
357016	67666+74166+74066+67766	EM	NE2	PTR	c2c	
357017	67667+74167+74067+67767	EM	NE2	PTR	c2c	
357018	67668+74168+74068+67768	EM	NE2	PTR	c2c	
357019	67669+74169+74069+67769	EM	NE2	PTR	c2c	
357020	67670+74170+74070+67770	EM	NE2	PTR	c2c	
357021	67621+74171+74071+67771	EM	NE2	PTR	c2c	
357022	67672+74172+74072+67772	EM	NE2	PTR	c2c	
357023	67673+74173+74073+67773	EM	NE2	PTR	c2c	
357024	67674+74174+74074+67774	EM	NE2	PTR	c2c	
357025	67675+74175+74075+67775	EM	NE2	PTR	c2c	
357026	67676+74176+74076+67776	EM	NE2	PTR	c2c	
357027	67677+74177+74077+67777	EM	NE2	PTR	c2c	
357028	67678+74178+74078+67778	EM	NE2	PTR	c2c	London, Tilbury & Southend Railway 1854-2004
357029	67679+74179+74079+67779	EM	NE2	PTR	c2c	Thomas Whitelegg 1840-1922
357030	67680+74180+74080+67780	EM	NE2	PTR	c2c	Robert Harben Whitelegg 1871-1957
357031	67681+74181+74081+67781	EM	NE2	PTR	c2c	
357032	67682+74182+74082+67782	EM	NE2	PTR	c2c	
357033	67683+74183+74083+67783	EM	NE2	PTR	c2c	
357034	67684+74184+74084+67784	EM	NE2	PTR	c2c	
357035	67685+74185+74085+67785	EM	NE2	PTR	c2c	
357036	67686+74186+74086+67786	EM	NE2	PTR	c2c	
357037	67687+74187+74087+67787	EM	NE2	PTR	c2c	
357038	67688+74188+74088+67788	EM	NE2	PTR	c2c	
357039	67689+74189+74089+67789	EM	NE2	PTR	c2c	
357040	67690+74190+74090+67790	EM	NE2	PTR	c2c	
357041	67691+74191+74091+67791	EM	NE2	PTR	c2c	
357042	67692+74192+74092+67792	EM	NE2	PTR	c2c	
357043	67693+74193+74093+67793	EM	NE2	PTR	c2c	
357044	67694+74194+74094+67794	EM	NE2	PTR	c2c	
357045	67695+74195+74095+67795	EM	NE2	PTR	c2c	
357046	67696+74196+74096+67796	EM	NE2	PTR	c2c	

Right: The current fleet of 74 four-car 'Electrostar' sets for the c2c service are formed in two sub-classes. Class 375/0 are owned by Porterbrook and Class 375/2 are owned by Angel Trains. The sets are otherwise identical. Painted in the standard white National Express/c2c livery, set No. 375036 passes Shadwell with a Fenchurch Street to Grays service. Several of the '375s' carry cast nameplates to the rear of the cab, above the passenger windows; these are mainly named after staff or to mark events. **CJM**

Passenger Train Operating Companies - c2c

c2c

Class 357/2
Electrostar

Vehicle Length: (Driving) 68ft 1in (20.75m)	Width: 9ft 2½in (2.80m)
(Inter) 65ft 11½in (20.10m)	Horsepower: 2,011hp (1,500kW)
Height: 12ft 4½in (3.78m)	Seats (total/car): 282S, 71S/78S/62S/71S

Number	Formation DMSO(A)+MSO+PTSO+DMSO(B)	Depot	Livery	Owner	Operator	Name
357201	68601+74701+74601+68701	EM	NE2	ANG	c2c	Ken Bird
357202	68602+74702+74602+68702	EM	NE2	ANG	c2c	Kenny Mitchell
357203	68603+74703+74603+68703	EM	NE2	ANG	c2c	Henry Pumfrett
357204	68604+74704+74604+68704	EM	NE2	ANG	c2c	Derek Flowers
357205	68605+74705+74605+68705	EM	NE2	ANG	c2c	John D'Silva
357206	68606+74706+74606+68706	EM	NE2	ANG	c2c	Martin Aungier
357207	68607+74707+74607+68707	EM	NE2	ANG	c2c	John Page
357208	68608+74708+74608+68708	EM	NE2	ANG	c2c	Dave Davis
357209	68609+74709+74609+68709	EM	NE2	ANG	c2c	James Snelling
357210	68610+74710+74610+68710	EM	NE2	ANG	c2c	
357211	68611+74711+74611+68711	EM	NE2	ANG	c2c	
357212	68612+74712+74612+68712	EM	NE2	ANG	c2c	
357213	68613+74713+74613+68713	EM	NE2	ANG	c2c	Upminster IECC
357214	68614+74714+74614+68714	EM	NE2	ANG	c2c	
357215	68615+74715+74615+68715	EM	NE2	ANG	c2c	
357216	68616+74716+74616+68716	EM	NE2	ANG	c2c	
357217	68617+74717+74617+68717	EM	NE2	ANG	c2c	Allan Burnell
357218	68618+74218+74618+68718	EM	NE2	ANG	c2c	
357219	68619+74719+74619+68719	EM	NE2	ANG	c2c	
357220	68620+74720+74620+68720	EM	NE2	ANG	c2c	
357221	68621+74721+74621+68721	EM	NE2	ANG	c2c	
357222	68622+74722+74622+68722	EM	NE2	ANG	c2c	
357223	68623+74723+74623+68723	EM	NE2	ANG	c2c	
357224	68624+74724+74624+68724	EM	NE2	ANG	c2c	
357225	68625+74725+74625+68725	EM	NE2	ANG	c2c	
357226	68626+74726+74626+68726	EM	NE2	ANG	c2c	
357227	68627+74727+74627+68727	EM	NE2	ANG	c2c	Southend United
357228	68628+74728+74628+68728	EM	NE2	ANG	c2c	

Below: *All the Class 357s are based at East Ham depot, where the ongoing high quality of maintenance sees this fleet frequently return the highest availability figure of any UK EMU. The sets have a rather cramped 2+3 passenger interior, but this reflects the nature of the fleet's operations, shifting large numbers of people into and out of the Capital each day. Set No. 357203 is seen on the approaches to London Fenchurch Street.* **CJM**

Chiltern Railways

Passenger Train Operating Companies - Chiltern Railways

Address: ✉ 2nd floor, Western House, Rickfords Hill, Aylesbury, Buckinghamshire, HP20 2RX

🖱 Via website (www.chilternrailways.co.uk)

☎ 08456 005165   ⓘ www.chilternrailways.co.uk

Managing Director: Rob Brighouse

Franchise Dates: 21 July 1996 - 21 December 2021

Principal Routes: London Marylebone - Birmingham Snow Hill

London Marylebone - Aylesbury

London Marylebone - Stratford-upon-Avon

Depots: Aylesbury (AL), Wembley*   * Stabling point

Parent Company: Deutsche Bahn AG (DB Regio)

Class 170s Nos. 170301-170309 due to transfer from First TransPennine Express in spring 2015, to be renumbered 168301-168309 after compatibility modification with existing Class 168s.

Class 121

	Length: 64ft 6in (19.66m)	Engine: 2 x Leyland 150hp
	Height: 12ft 8½in (3.87m)	Horsepower: 300hp (224kW)
	Width: 9ft 3in (2.81m)	Seats (total/car): 65S

Number	Formation DMBS	Depot	Livery	Owner	Operator
121020	55020	AY	BLU	CRW	CRW
121032(S)	55032	AY	ATW	CRW	-
121034	55034	AY	GRN	CRW	CRW

Chiltern Railways

Left: *Chiltern Railways operates a fleet of three 'Heritage' Class 121 'Bubble cars' from Aylesbury depot for use on the Aylesbury to Princes Risborough branch line. In early 2015 the vehicles carried three liveries, green, blue and Arriva Trains. However, the Arriva Trains carriage (55032) is currently not available for use and stored. Green-liveried No. 55034, set No. 121034, is viewed stabled on Aylesbury depot.* **Antony Christie**

Class 165/0 (2-car)
Networker Turbo

Vehicle Length: (Driving) 75ft 2½in (22.91m), (Inter) 74ft 6½in (22.72m)
Height: 12ft 5¼in (3.79m)   Engine: 1 x Perkins 2006 TWH of 350hp per vehicle
Width: 9ft 2½in (2.81m)   Horsepower: 700hp (522kW)
Seats (total/car): 183S, 89S/94S

Number	Formation DMSL+DMS	Depot	Livery	Owner	Operator
165001	58801+58834	AL	CRW	ANG	CRW
165002	58802+58835	AL	CRW	ANG	CRW
165003	58803+58836	AL	CRW	ANG	CRW
165004	58804+58837	AL	CRW	ANG	CRW
165005	58805+58838	AL	CRW	ANG	CRW
165006	58806+58839	AL	CRW	ANG	CRW
165007	58807+58840	AL	CRW	ANG	CRW
165008	58808+58841	AL	CRW	ANG	CRW
165009	58809+58842	AL	CRW	ANG	CRW
165010	58810+58843	AL	CRW	ANG	CRW
165011	58811+58844	AL	CRW	ANG	CRW
165012	58812+58845	AL	CRW	ANG	CRW
165013	58813+58846	AL	CRW	ANG	CRW
165014	58814+58847	AL	CRW	ANG	CRW
165015	58815+58848	AL	CRW	ANG	CRW
165016	58816+58849	AL	CRW	ANG	CRW
165017	58817+58850	AL	CRW	ANG	CRW
165018	58818+58851	AL	CRW	ANG	CRW
165019	58819+58852	AL	CRW	ANG	CRW
165020	58820+58853	AL	CRW	ANG	CRW
165021	58821+58854	AL	CRW	ANG	CRW
165022	58822+58855	AL	CRW	ANG	CRW
165023	58873+58867	AL	CRW	ANG	CRW
165024	58874+58868	AL	CRW	ANG	CRW
165025	58874+58869	AL	CRW	ANG	CRW
165026	58876+58870	AL	CRW	ANG	CRW
165027	58877+58871	AL	CRW	ANG	CRW
165028	58878+58872	AL	CRW	ANG	CRW

Class 165/0 (3-car)
Networker Turbo

Vehicle Length: (driving) 75ft 2½in (22.91m), (Inter) 74ft 6½in (22.72m)
Height: 12ft 5¼in (3.79m)   Engine: 1 x Perkins 2006 TWH of 350hp per vehicle
Width: 9ft 2½in (2.81m)   Horsepower: 1,050hp (783kW)
Seats (total/car): 289S, 89S/106S/94S

Number	Formation DMSL+MS+DMS	Depot	Livery	Owner	Operator
165029	58823+55404+58856	AL	CRW	ANG	CRW
165030	58824+55405+58857	AL	CRW	ANG	CRW
165031	58825+55406+58858	AL	CRW	ANG	CRW
165032	58826+55407+58859	AL	CRW	ANG	CRW
165033	58827+55408+58860	AL	CRW	ANG	CRW
165034	58828+55409+58861	AL	CRW	ANG	CRW
165035	58829+55410+58862	AL	CRW	ANG	CRW
165036	58830+55411+58863	AL	CRW	ANG	CRW
165037	58831+55412+58864	AL	CRW	ANG	CRW
165038	58832+55413+58865	AL	CRW	ANG	CRW
165039	58833+55414+58866	AL	CRW	ANG	CRW

Left: *Introduced in the days of Network SouthEast to modernise the Chiltern and Thames Valley routes, Chiltern currently operates a fleet of 39 Class 165 'Networker Turbo' sets; 28 are formed as two-cars and 11 as three-car sets. All have been refurbished and now sport more smooth front end body profiles. All are currently painted in Chiltern suburban white and blue colours. Three-car set No. 165036 departs from Banbury on 29 May 2014 with an all-stations service to London Marylebone.* **CJM**

Class 168/0
Turbostar

Vehicle Length: 77ft 6in (23.62m)
Height: 12ft 4½in (3.77m)
Width: 8ft 10in (2.69m)

Engine: 1 x MTU 6R 183TD13H pf 422hp per vehicle
Horsepower: 1,688hp (1,259kW)
Seats (total/car): 278S, 60S/73S/77S/68S

Number	Formation DMSL(A)+MSL+MS+DMSL(B)	Depot	Livery	Owner	Operator
168001	58151+58651+58451+58251	AL	CRG	PTR	CRW
168002	58152+58652+58452+58252	AL	CRG	PTR	CRW
168003	58153+58653+58453+58253	AL	CRG	PTR	CRW
168004	58154+58654+58454+58254	AL	CRG	PTR	CRW
168005	58155+58655+58455+58255	AL	CRG	PTR	CRW

Right: *Chiltern Railways' core fleet of longer-distance stock is a fleet of Class 168s of which 19 sets of three sub-classes are in use, all allocated to Aylesbury. Sets now sport the new Chiltern silver, grey and white livery. The five sets of Class 168/0 sport the early 'Turbostar' body style, while later sets use the standard design. Four-car set No. 168005 is seen departing from Banbury.* **CJM**

Class 168/1
Turbostar

Vehicle Length: 77ft 6in (23.62m)
Height: 12ft 4½in (3.77m)
Width: 8ft 10in (2.69m)

Engine: 1 x MTU 6R 183TD13H of 422hp per vehicle
Horsepower: 3/4-car 1,266hp (944kW)/1,688hp (1,259kW)
Seats (total/car): 3-car - 208S, 59S/73S/76S, 4-car - 284S, 59S/73S/76S/76S

Number	Formation DMSL(A)+MS+MS+DMSL(B)	Depot	Livery	Owner	Operator	Notes
168106	58156+58756§+58456+58256	AL	CRG	PTR	CRW	§ is a MSL vehicle
168107	58157+58457+58757§+58257	AL	CRG	PTR	CRW	§ is a MSL vehicle
168108	58158+58458+58258	AL	CRG	PTR	CRW	
168109	58159+58459+58259	AL	CRG	PTR	CRW	
168110	58160+58460+58260	AL	CRG	PTR	CRW	
168111	58161+58461+58261	AL	CRW	EVL	CRW	58461 was originally 58661
168112	58162+58462+58262	AL	CRG	EVL	CRW	58462 was originally 58662
168113	58163+58463+58263	AL	CRW	EVL	CRW	58463 was originally 58663

Class 168/2
Turbostar

Vehicle Length: 77ft 6in (23.62m)
Height: 12ft 4½in (3.77m)
Width: 8ft 10in (2.69m)

Engine: 1 x MTU 6R 183TD13H of 422hp per vehicle
Horsepower: 3/4-car 1,266hp (944kW)/1,688hp (1,259kW)
Seats (total/car): 3-car - 204S, 59S/76S/69S, 4-car - 277S, 59S/73S/76S/69S

Number	Formation DMSL(A)+MS+MS+DMSL(B)	Depot	Livery	Owner	Operator
168214	58164+58464+58264	AL	CRG	PTR	CRW
168215	58165+58465+58365+58265	AL	CRG	PTR	CRW
168216	58166+58466+58366+58266	AL	CRG	PTR	CRW
168217	58167+58467+58367+58267	AL	CRG	PTR	CRW
168218	58168+58468+58268	AL	CRG	PTR	CRW
168219	58169+58469+58269	AL	CRG	PTR	CRW

Right: *Examples of both Class 168/1 and 168/2 come in either three- or four-car form and all are on the traditional 'Turbostar' body style. These 'Clubman'-style sets with all one class seat between 204 and 284 depending on configuration. Seating is in the 2+2 style. Sets are painted in the latest silver, grey and white Chiltern colours and are allocated to Aylesbury depot. Set No. 168216 leads a four-car formation into Banbury with a Birmingham Snow Hill-bound service.* **CJM**

Passenger Train Operating Companies - Chiltern Railways

Chiltern Railways

Class 172/1

Vehicle Length: 73ft 4in (22.37m)
Height: 12ft 4½in (3.77m)
Width: 8ft 8in (2.69m)

Engine: MTU 6H1800 of 360kW
Horsepower: 965hp (720kW)
Seats (total/car): 121S, 53S/68S

Number	Formation DMS+DMS	Depot	Livery	Owner	Operator		Number	Formation	Depot	Livery	Owner	Operator
172101	59111+59211	AL	CRW	ANG	CRW		172103	59113+59213	AL	CRW	ANG	CRW
172102	59112+59212	AL	CRW	ANG	CRW		172104	59114+59214	AL	CRW	ANG	CRW

Left: *The most modern multiple unit stock operated by Chiltern Railways are four Class 172/1 sets, these are the final development of the 'Turbostar' product range. East set seats 121 and the fleet is painted in Chiltern blue and white. No. 172104 is unusually seen paired with a Class 168, passing West Ruislip with the 10.40 Birmingham Snow Hill to Marylebone on 25 August 2013.* **Antony Guppy**

Class 68 'UK Light'

Vehicle Length: 67ft 3in (20.5m)
Height: 12ft 6½in (3.82m)
Speed: 100mph (161km/h)

Engine: Caterpillar C175-16
Horsepower: 3,750hp (2,800kW)
Electrical Equipment: ABB

Number	Depot	Pool	Livery	Owner	Operator
68011	CG	XHVE	CRG	BEA	DRS/CRW
68012	CG	XHVE	CRG	BEA	DRS/CRW
68013	CG	XHVE	CRG	BEA	DRS/CRW
68014	CG	XHVE	CRG	BEA	DRS/CRW
68015	CG	XHVE	CRG	BEA	DRS/CRW

Left: *Until 2015, the Chiltern loco-hauled Mk3 trains were powered by Class 67s hired in from DB Schenker. However, a new motive power deal was struck in 2015 seeing five of the brand new Direct Rail Services Class 68s dedicated to the service, with locos 68011-015 painted in the two-tone Chiltern grey livery. The locos are based at Crewe Gresty Bridge, but operate for extended periods and receive daily maintenance at Wembley. Loco No. 68011 is illustrated during its shakedown period in late 2014 working DRS freight traffic.* **Stuart Hillis**

Mk3 Hauled Stock (Passenger)

Vehicle Length: 75ft 0in (22.86m)
Height: 12ft 9in (3.88m)   Width: 8ft 11in (2.71m)
Bogie Type: BT10

AJ1F - GFW *Seating 30F*

Number		Depot	Livery	Owner
10271	(10236/10018)	AL	CRG	DBR
10272	(10208/40517)	AL	CRG	DBR
10273	(10230/10021)	AL	CRG	DBR
10274	(10255/11010)	AL	CRG	DBR

AC2G - TSO/TSOL* *Seating 72S*

Number		Depot	Livery	Owner
12602	(12072)	AL	CRG	DBR

12603*	(12053)	AL	CRG	DBR
12604	(12131)	AL	CRG	DBR
12605*	(11040)	AL	CRG	DBR
12606	(12048)	AL	CRG	DBR
12607*	(12038)	AL	CRG	DBR
12608	(12069)	AL	CRG	DBR
12609*	(12014)	AL	CRG	DBR
12612	(12117)	AL	CRG	DBR
12613*	(12173/11042)	AL	CRG	DBR
12614	(12145)	AL	CRG	DBR

12615*	(12059)	AL	CRG	DBR
12616	(12127)	AL	CRG	DBR
12617*	(12174/11050)	AL	CRG	DBR
12618	(12169)	AL	CRG	DBR
12619*	(12175/11052)	AL	CRG	DBR

12620	(12124)	AL	CRG	DBR
12621	(11046)	AL	CRG	DBR
12623	(11019)	AL	CRG	DBR
12625	(11030)	AL	CRG	DBR
12627	(11054)	AL	CRG	DBR

Right: *The Chiltern Railways loco-hauled services between London and Birmingham have seen huge investment in terms of refurbishment and the fitting of sliding plug passenger doors. The passenger interiors are some of the best in the UK using a Mk3 body profile. Painted in full Chiltern livery, GFW No. 10272 is shown from the first or business class seating end which can accommodate 30 in the 2+1 style.* **CJM**

Mk3 Hauled Stock (NPCCS)

Vehicle Length: 75ft 0in (22.86m)
Height: 12ft 9in (3.88m)
Width: 8ft 11in (2.71m)
Bogie Type: BT7

NZAG - DVT

Number	Depot	Livery	Owner
82301 (82117)	AL	CRG	DBR
82302 (82151)	AL	CRG	DBR
82303 (82135)	AL	CRG	DBR

82304 (82130)	AL	CRG	DBR
82305 (82134)	AL	CRG	DBR
82309 (82104)	AL	CRG	DBR

Right: *To provide remote driving facilities for the Chiltern loco-hauled services, six Mk3 Driving Van Trailers are in use, heavily rebuilt from their previous duties with Virgin Trains. Each now sports a Penta TAD1352GE auxiliary diesel engine and generator to provide hotel power to the train when the hauling loco is shut down. This generator is housed in the former luggage van directly to the rear of the cab and has a ventilation grille built into the original door position and an underframe-mounted fuel tank. Chiltern DVT No. 82301 is illustrated.* **CJM**

Class 960 – Service Units

Class 121	
Length: 64ft 6in (19.66m)	Engine: 2 x Leyland 150hp
Height: 12ft 8½in (3.87m)	Horsepower: 300hp (224kW)
Width: 9ft 3in (2.81m)	Seats (total/car): None

Class 117	
Length: 64ft 0in (19.50m)	Engine: 2 x Leyland 150hp
Height: 12ft 8½in (3.87m)	Horsepower: 300hp (224kW)
Width: 9ft 3in (2.81m)	Seats (total/car): None

Number	Formation	Depot	Livery	Owner	Operator	Notes
960014	977873	AL	BLG	CRW	CRW	Ex-Class 121 55022, Route Learning/Sandite
960301	977987+977992+977988	AL	GRN	CRW	CRW	Ex-Class 117, 51371/51375/51413 - used for water jetting

Class 01.5 (0-6-0)

Number	Depot	Pool	Livery	Owner	Operator	Name
01509 (433) RH468043	AL	MBDL	BLU	CRW	CRW	*Lesley*

CrossCountry Trains

Address: ✉ Cannon House, 18 The Priory, Queensway, Birmingham, B4 6BS
📠 info@crosscountrytrains.co.uk
📞 0870 0100084
ⓘ www.crosscountrytrains.co.uk

Managing Director: Andy Cooper
Franchise Dates: 11 November 2007 - 31 March 2016*
Principal Routes: Penzance/Paignton -
Manchester/Edinburgh/Aberdeen
Bournemouth - Manchester/
Edinburgh/Aberdeen
Birmingham - Stansted
Nottingham - Cardiff
Depots: Central Rivers (CZ),
Tyseley (TS),
Craigentinny (EC)
Parent Company: Deutsche Bahn AG
(DB Regio) / Arriva

* Proposed extension to
November 2019

Aberdeen
Stonehaven
Arbroath
Dundee
Leuchars
Cupar
Markinch
Kirkcaldy
Motherwell
Glasgow Central
Haymarket
Edinburgh
Dunbar
Berwick-upon-Tweed
Alnmouth
Morpeth
Newcastle
Manchester Piccadilly
Chester-le-Street
Durham
Darlington
York
Leeds
Stockport
Doncaster
Wakefield Westgate
Macclesfield
Congleton
Wilmslow
Crewe
Sheffield
Chesterfield
Stoke-on-Trent
Nottingham
Stafford
Wolverhampton
Birmingham New Street
Water Orton
Tamworth
Derby
Burton-on-Trent
Cheltenham Spa
Coleshill Parkway
Gloucester
Chepstow
Lydney
Bristol Parkway
Nuneaton
Narborough
Caldicot
Bristol Temple Meads
Weston-super-Mare
Birmingham International
Leicester
Melton Mowbray
Oakham
Stamford
Newport
Taunton
Coventry
Peterborough
Ely
Tiverton Parkway
Cardiff
Exeter St Davids
Dawlish
Teignmouth
Newton Abbot
Leamington Spa
Banbury
Oxford
Cambridge
Audley End
Stansted Airport
Totnes
Torquay
Reading
Paignton
Guildford
Plymouth
Liskeard
Bodmin Parkway
Par
St Austell
Basingstoke
Winchester
Newquay
Truro
Redruth
Camborne
St Erth
Southampton Airport Parkway
Southampton Central
Brockenhurst
Penzance
Bournemouth

Class 43 – HST

Vehicle Length: 58ft 5in (18.80m)
Height: 12ft 10in (3.90m)
Width: 8ft 11in (2.73m)

Engine: MTU 16V4000 R41R
Horsepower: 2,250hp (1,680kW)
Electrical Equipment: Brush

Number	Depot	Pool	Livery	Owner	Operator
43207 (43007)	EC	EHPC	AXC	ANG	AXC
43285 (43085)	EC	EHPC	AXC	PTR	AXC
43301 (43101)	EC	EHPC	AXC	PTR	AXC
43303 (43103)	EC	EHPC	AXC	PTR	AXC
43304 (43104)	EC	EHPC	AXC	ANG	AXC
43321 (43121)	EC	EHPC	AXC	PTR	AXC
43357 (43157)	EC	EHPC	AXC	PTR	AXC
43366 (43166)	EC	EHPC	AXC	ANG	AXC
43378 (43178)	EC	EHPC	AXC	ANG	AXC
43384 (43184)	EC	EHPC	AXC	ANG	AXC

Right: *CrossCountry Trains has a fleet of 10 Class 43 power cars on its books, allocated to Edinburgh Craigentinny depot. Usually three or a maximum of four HST rosters are operated each day on the main and most heavily used services from the North/Scotland to the West Country. All power cars and stock are painted in CrossCountry livery. All Class 43s are refurbished with MTU power units. On 25 May 2014 No. 43285 brings up the rear of the 06.40 service from York arriving at Plymouth.* **CJM**

HST passenger fleet

Vehicle Length: 75ft 0in (22.86m)
Height: 12ft 9in (3.88m)

Width: 8ft 11in (2.71m)
Bogie Type: BT10

GH1G - TF *Seating 40F*

Number	Depot	Livery	Owner	
41026	EC	AXC	ANG	
41035	EC	AXC	ANG	
41193 (11060)	EC	AXC	PTR	
41194 (11016)	EC	AXC	PTR	
41195¤ (11020)	EC	AXC	PTR	¤ = TFD

GH2G - TS *Seating 82S*

Number	Depot	Livery	Owner	
42036	EC	AXC	ANG	
42037	EC	AXC	ANG	
42038	EC	AXC	ANG	
42051	EC	AXC	ANG	
42052	EC	AXC	ANG	
42053	EC	AXC	ANG	
42097	EC	AXC	ANG	
42234	EC	AXC	PTR	
42290	EC	AXC	PTR	
42342 (44082)	EC	AXC	ANG	
42366 (12007)	EC	AXC	PTR	
42367 (12025)	EC	AXC	PTR	
42368 (12028)	EC	AXC	PTR	
42369 (12050)	EC	AXC	PTR	
42370 (12086)	EC	AXC	PTR	
42371 (12052)	EC	AXC	PTR	
42372 (12055)	EC	AXC	PTR	
42373 (12071)	EC	AXC	PTR	
42374 (12075)	EC	AXC	PTR	
42375 (12113)	EC	AXC	PTR	
42376 (12085)	EC	AXC	PTR	
42377 (12102)	EC	AXC	PTR	
42378 (12123)	EC	AXC	PTR	
42379* (41036)	EC	AXC	ANG	*=TSD
42380* (41025)	EC	AXC	ANG	*=TSD

GJ2G - TGS *Seating 67S*

Number	Depot	Livery	Owner
44012	EC	AXC	ANG
44017	EC	AXC	ANG
44021	EC	AXC	ANG
44052	EC	AXC	PTR
44072	EC	AXC	PTR

GH3G - TCC *Seating 30F/10S*

Number	Depot	Livery	Owner
45001 (12004)	EC	AXC	PTR
45002 (12106)	EC	AXC	PTR
45003 (12076)	EC	AXC	PTR
45004 (12077)	EC	AXC	PTR
45005 (12080)	EC	AXC	PTR

Passenger Train Operating Companies - CrossCountry Trains

CrossCountry Trains

Above: *Forty intermediate HST passenger vehicles are on the books of CrossCountry of four types; all are refurbished and carry CrossCountry XC livery and branding. Five Trailer Composite Catering (TCC) coaches are in the fleet numbered in the series 45001-005 and are converted from Mk3 loco-hauled TS stock. These vehicles seat 30 first and 10 standard class passengers and house the catering area. Vehicle No. 45004 is illustrated, showing the first class area on the left, which is usually marshalled adjacent to the TF vehicle.* **Antony Christie**

Class 170/1
Turbostar

Vehicle Length: 77ft 6in (23.62m)			Engine: 1 x MTU 6R 183TD13H of 422hp per vehicle		
Height: 12ft 4½in (3.77m)			Horsepower: 1,266hp (944kW)		
Width: 8ft 10in (2.69m)			Seats (total/car): 9F/191S 52S/80S/9F-59S		

Number	Formation DMS+MS+DMCL	Depot	Livery	Owner	Operator
170101	50101+55101+79101	TS	AXC	PTR	AXC
170102	50102+55102+79102	TS	AXC	PTR	AXC
170103	50103+55103+79103	TS	AXC	PTR	AXC
170104	50104+55104+79104	TS	AXC	PTR	AXC
170105	50105+55105+79105	TS	AXC	PTR	AXC
170106	50106+55106+79106	TS	AXC	PTR	AXC
170107	50107+55107+79107	TS	AXC	PTR	AXC
170108*	50108+55108+79108	TS	AXC	PTR	AXC
170109*	50109+55109+79109	TS	AXC	PTR	AXC
170110	50110+55110+79110	TS	AXC	PTR	AXC

Left: *CrossCountry Trains operates 'Turbostar' DMU stock on most of its secondary cross-country routes, such as those from Nottingham to Cardiff and services from Stansted Airport. A fleet of 10 three-car Class 170/1 sets is allocated to Tyseley, together with seven two-car sets. Two-car set No. 170114 passes Stenson Junction near Burton-on-Trent on 15 May 2014 forming service 1G16, the 09.41 Nottingham to Birmingham New Street.* **CJM**

Vehicle Length: 77ft 6in (23.62m)			Engine: 1 x MTU 6R 183TD13H of 422hp per vehicle		
Height: 12ft 4½in (3.77m)			Horsepower: 844hp (629kW)		
Width: 8ft 10in (2.69m)			Seats (total/car): 9F-111S 59S/9F-52S		

Number	Formation DMS+DMCL	Depot	Livery	Owner	Operator	Number	Formation	Depot	Livery	Owner	Operator
						170114	50114+79114	TS	AXC	PTR	AXC
						170115	50115+79115	TS	AXC	PTR	AXC
170111*	50111+79111	TS	AXC	PTR	AXC	170116	50116+79116	TS	AXC	PTR	AXC
170112	50112+79112	TS	AXC	PTR	AXC	170117	50117+79117	TS	AXC	PTR	AXC
170113	50113+79113	TS	AXC	PTR	AXC						

* Fitted with passenger counters

Class 170/3
Turbostar

		Vehicle Length: 77ft 6in (23.62m)		Engine: 1 x MTU 6R 183TD13H of 422hp per vehicle
		Height: 12ft 4½in (3.77m)		Horsepower: 1,266hp (944kW)
		Width: 8ft 10in (2.69m)		Seats (total/car): 9F-191S 59S/80S/9F-52S

Number	Formation DMSL+MS+DMCL	Depot	Livery	Owner	Operator
170397	50397+56397+79397	TS	AXC	PTR	AXC
170398	50398+56398+79398	TS	AXC	PTR	AXC

Right: *Two of the original five Class 170/3 development sets are now in the hands of CrossCountry Trains. All of the Class 170s with XC are operated in a common pool and all have been refurbished to the same standard with a common interior design. Carrying standard CrossCountry advertising livery, set No. 170398 is seen at Tamworth High Level bound for Nottingham on 10 July 2014.*
Antony Christie

Class 170/5
Turbostar

		Vehicle Length: 77ft 6in (23.62m)		Engine: 1 x MTU 6R 183TD13H of 422hp per vehicle
		Height: 12ft 4½in (3.77m)		Horsepower: 844hp (629kW)
		Width: 8ft 10in (2.69m)		Seats (total/car): 9F-111S 59S/9F-52S

Number	Formation DMSL+DMCL	Depot	Livery	Owner	Operator
170518	50518+79518	TS	AXC	PTR	AXC
170519	50519+79519	TS	AXC	PTR	AXC
170520	50520+79520	TS	AXC	PTR	AXC
170521	50521+79521	TS	AXC	PTR	AXC
170522	50522+79522	TS	AXC	PTR	AXC
170523	50523+79523	TS	AXC	PTR	AXC

Class 170/6
Turbostar

		Vehicle Length: 77ft 6in (23.62m)		Engine: 1 x MTU 6R 183TD13H of 422hp per vehicle
		Height: 12ft 4½in (3.77m)		Horsepower: 1,266hp (944kW)
		Width: 8ft 10in (2.69m)		Seats (total/car): 9F-191S 59S/80S/9F-52S

Number	Formation DMSL+MS+DMCL	Depot	Livery	Owner	Operator
170636	50636+56636+79636	TS	AXC	PTR	AXC
170637	50637+56637+79637	TS	AXC	PTR	AXC
170638	50638+56638+79638	TS	AXC	PTR	AXC
170639	50639+56639+79639	TS	AXC	PTR	AXC

Right: *Four three-car Class 170/6 sets are in the XC fleet, again sharing duties with other three-car members of the global '170' fleet. With its DMSL vehicle leading, set No. 170639 passes Stenson Junction on 15 May 2014 forming the 09.19 Birmingham New Street to Nottingham service.* **CJM**

Passenger Train Operating Companies - CrossCountry Trains

CrossCountry Trains

Class 220
Voyager

Vehicle Length: 77ft 6in (23.62m)		Engine: 1 x Cummins of 750hp per vehicle
Height: 12ft 4in (3.75m)		Horsepower: 3,000hp (2,237kW)
Width: 8ft 11in (2.73m)		Seats (total/car): 26F/174S 42S/66S/66S/26F

Number	Formation DMS+MS+MS+DMF	Depot	Livery	Owner	Operator
220001	60301+60701+60201+60401	CZ	AXC	HBS	AXC
220002	60302+60702+60202+60402	CZ	AXC	HBS	AXC
220003	60303+60703+60203+60403	CZ	AXC	HBS	AXC
220004	60304+60704+60204+60404	CZ	AXC	HBS	AXC
220005	60305+60705+60205+60405	CZ	AXC	HBS	AXC
220006	60306+60706+60206+60406	CZ	AXC	HBS	AXC
220007	60307+60707+60207+60407	CZ	AXC	HBS	AXC
220008	60308+60708+60208+60408	CZ	AXC	HBS	AXC
220009	60309+60709+60209+60409	CZ	AXC	HBS	AXC
220010	60310+60710+60210+60410	CZ	AXC	HBS	AXC
220011	60311+60711+60211+60411	CZ	AXC	HBS	AXC
220012	60312+60712+60212+60412	CZ	AXC	HBS	AXC
220013	60313+60713+60213+60413	CZ	AXC	HBS	AXC
220014	60314+60714+60214+60414	CZ	AXC	HBS	AXC
220015	60315+60715+60215+60415	CZ	AXC	HBS	AXC
220016	60316+60716+60216+60416	CZ	AXC	HBS	AXC
220017	60317+60717+60217+60417	CZ	AXC	HBS	AXC
220018	60318+60718+60218+60418	CZ	AXC	HBS	AXC
220019	60319+60719+60219+60419	CZ	AXC	HBS	AXC
220020	60320+60720+60220+60420	CZ	AXC	HBS	AXC
220021	60321+60721+60221+60421	CZ	AXC	HBS	AXC
220022	60322+60722+60222+60422	CZ	AXC	HBS	AXC
220023	60323+60723+60223+60423	CZ	AXC	HBS	AXC
220024	60324+60724+60224+60424	CZ	AXC	HBS	AXC
220025	60325+60725+60225+60425	CZ	AXC	HBS	AXC
220026	60326+60726+60226+60426	CZ	AXC	HBS	AXC
220027	60327+60727+60227+60427	CZ	AXC	HBS	AXC
220028	60328+60728+60228+60428	CZ	AXC	HBS	AXC
220029	60329+60729+60229+60429	CZ	AXC	HBS	AXC
220030	60330+60730+60230+60430	CZ	AXC	HBS	AXC
220031	60331+60731+60231+60431	CZ	AXC	HBS	AXC
220032	60332+60732+60232+60432	CZ	AXC	HBS	AXC
220033	60333+60733+60233+60433	CZ	AXC	HBS	AXC
220034	60334+60734+60234+60434	CZ	AXC	HBS	AXC

Below: The core long-distance CrossCountry operation is operated by two fleets of 'Voyager' stock, originally introduced under the Virgin Trains banner. A fleet of 34 non-tilt four-car sets is allocated to Central Rivers and operates alongside the Class 221 fleet. All are painted in standard silver, brown and pink XC colours. Set No. 220009 departs from Doncaster on 23 April 2014 forming the 07.00 Edinburgh to Reading service. **CJM**

Class 221
Super Voyager

Vehicle Length: 77ft 6in (23.62m)	Engine: 1 x Cummins of 750hp per vehicle
Height: 12ft 4in (3.75m)	Horsepower: 3,750hp (2,796kW)
Width: 8ft 11in (2.73m)	Seats (total/car): 26F/236S 42S/66S/66S/62S/26F

Originally fitted with tilt system to allow higher speeds over curves. Equipment now isolated.

Number	Formation DMS+MS+MS+MS+DMF	Depot	Livery	Owner	Operator
221119	60369+60769+60969+60869+60469	CZ	AXC	HBS	AXC
221120	60370+60770+60970+60870+60470	CZ	AXC	HBS	AXC
221121	60371+60771+60971+60871+60471	CZ	AXC	HBS	AXC
221122	60372+60772+60972+60872+60472	CZ	AXC	HBS	AXC
221123	60373+60773+60973+60873+60473	CZ	AXC	HBS	AXC
221124	60374+60774+60974+60874+60474	CZ	AXC	HBS	AXC
221125	60375+60775+60975+60875+60475	CZ	AXC	HBS	AXC
221126	60376+60776+60976+60876+60476	CZ	AXC	HBS	AXC
221127	60377+60777+60977+60877+60477	CZ	AXC	HBS	AXC
221128	60378+60778+60978+60878+60478	CZ	AXC	HBS	AXC
221129	60379+60779+60979+60879+60479	CZ	AXC	HBS	AXC
221130	60380+60780+60980+60880+60480	CZ	AXC	HBS	AXC
221131	60381+60781+60981+60881+60481	CZ	AXC	HBS	AXC
221132	60382+60782+60982+60882+60482	CZ	AXC	HBS	AXC
221133	60383+60783+60983+60883+60483	CZ	AXC	HBS	AXC
221134	60384+60784+60984+60884+60484	CZ	AXC	HBS	AXC
221135	60385+60785+60985+60885+60485	CZ	AXC	HBS	AXC
221136	60386+60786+60986+60886+60486	CZ	AXC	HBS	AXC
221137	60387+60787+60987+60887+60487	CZ	AXC	HBS	AXC
221138	60388+60788+60988+60888+60488	CZ	AXC	HBS	AXC
221139	60389+60789+60989+60889+60489	CZ	AXC	HBS	AXC
221140	60390+60790+60990+60890+60490	CZ	AXC	HBS	AXC
221141	60391+60791+60991+–+60491	CZ	AXC	HBS	AXC (Four-car set)

Below: *Operating alongside the Class 220 fleet are 23 'Super Voyager' sets originally fitted with a tilting system; 22 of these sets are five-car formation and one is a four-car set. The interior and deployment of the sets is the same as for a Class 220 and sets operate together in a common pool. The '221' sets are immediately recognisable against the Class 220s in having a much heavier bogie design. On 9 April 2014 No. 221123 passes Eastleigh with the 09.45 Bournemouth to Manchester Piccadilly.* **CJM**

East Midlands Trains

Address: ✉ 1 Prospect Place, Millennium Way, Pride Park, Derby, DE24 8HG
📠 getintouch@eastmidlandstrains.co.uk
✆ 08457 125678
ⓘ www.eastmidlandstrains.co.uk

Managing Director: Jake Kelly
Franchise Dates: 11 November 2007 - October 2017
Principal Routes: St Pancras - Sheffield/York/Leeds/Nottingham
Norwich/Skegness/Cleethorpes - Nottingham/Crewe/
Liverpool and Matlock
Depots: Derby (DY), Nottingham (NM), Neville Hill (NL)
Parent Company: Stagecoach Group

Passenger Train Operating Companies - East Midlands Trains

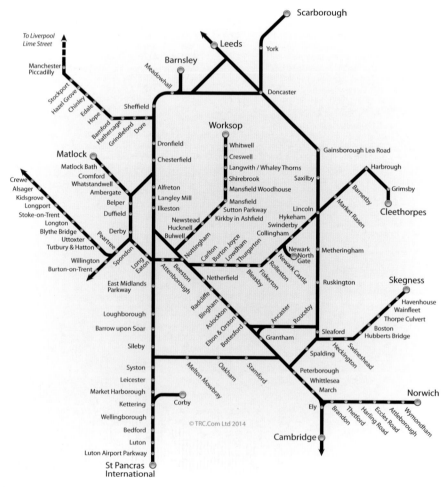

Class 08

Vehicle Length: 29ft 3in (8.91m)			Engine: English Electric 6K		
Height: 12ft 8⅝in (3.87m)			Horsepower: 400hp (298kW)		
Width: 8ft 6in (2.59m)			Electrical Equipment: English Electric		

Number	Depot	Pool	Livery	Owner	Operator	Name
08525	NL	EMSL	EMT	EMT	EMT	Duncan Bedford
08690	NL	EMSL	EMT	EMT	EMT	David Thirkill
08899	DY	EMSL	MAR	EMT	EMT	Midland Counties Railway 175 1839-2014
08908	DY	EMSL	EMT	EMT	EMT	Ivan Stephenson
08950	NL	EMSL	EMT	EMT	EMT	David Lightfoot

Right: *Five Class 08 locomotives are operated by East Midlands Trains, and are based at either Leeds Neville Hill or Derby Etches Park. With the exception of No. 08899, which carries Midland Counties maroon colours, all are painted in a version of Stagecoach blue and red livery, as depicted on No. 08525.* **Paul Bigland**

Class 43 – HST

Vehicle Length: 58ft 5in (18.80m)			Engine: Paxman VP185		
Height: 12ft 10in (3.90m)			Horsepower: 2,100hp (1,565kW)		
Width: 8ft 11in (2.73m)			Electrical Equipment: Brush		

Number	Depot	Pool	Livery	Owner	Operator		Number	Depot	Pool	Livery	Owner	Operator
43043	NL	EMPC	SCE	PTR	EMT		43066	NL	EMPC	SCE	PTR	EMT
43044	NL	EMPC	SCE	PTR	EMT		43073	NL	EMPC	SCE	PTR	EMT
43045	NL	EMPC	SCE	PTR	EMT		43075	NL	EMPC	SCE	PTR	EMT
43046	NL	EMPC	SCE	PTR	EMT		43076	NL	EMPC	SCE	PTR	EMT
43047	NL	EMPC	SCE	PTR	EMT		43081	NL	EMPC	SCE	PTR	EMT
43048	NL	EMPC	SCE	PTR	EMT		43082	NL	EMPC	SCE	PTR	EMT
43049	NL	EMPC	SCE	PTR	EMT		43083	NL	EMPC	SCE	PTR	EMT
43050	NL	EMPC	SCE	PTR	EMT		43089	NL	EMPC	SCE	PTR	EMT
43052	NL	EMPC	SCE	PTR	EMT							
43054	NL	EMPC	SCE	PTR	EMT		*Names applied*					
43055	NL	EMPC	SCE	PTR	EMT		43048	*T. C. B Miller MBE*				
43058	NL	EMPC	SCE	PTR	EMT		43049	*Neville Hill*				
43059	NL	EMPC	SCE	PTR	EMT		43055	*The Sheffield Star 125 Years*				
43060	NL	EMPC	SCE	PTR	EMT		43076	*In Support of Help for Heroes*				
43061	NL	EMPC	SCE	PTR	EMT		43082	*Railway Children The Voice for Street*				
43064	NL	EMPC	SCE	PTR	EMT			*Children Worldwide*				

Right: *Stagecoach-owned East Midlands Trains operates a fleet of 24 Class 43 HST power cars, allocated to Leeds Neville Hill. These are the only Class 43s still to retain Paxman power units. The EMT HSTs operate alongside the Class 222s on main-line duties and are usually concentrated on the London St Pancras to Nottingham corridor. All carry standard Stagecoach-style blue swirl livery with East Midlands Trains branding. No. 43064 is illustrated at Leicester on 18 July 2014.* **Antony Christie**

East Midlands Trains

Class 153

		Vehicle Length: 76ft 5in (23.29m)		Engine: 1 x NT855R5 of 285hp
		Height: 12ft 3½in (3.75m)		Horsepower: 285hp (213kW)
		Width: 8ft 10in (2.70m)		Seats (total/car): 66S

Number	Formation DMSL	Depot	Livery	Owner	Operator
153302	52302	NM	EMT	ANG	EMT
153308	52308	NM	EMT	ANG	EMT
153310	52310	NM	EMT	PTR	EMT
153311	52311	NM	EMT	PTR	EMT
153313	52313	NM	EMT	PTR	EMT
153319	52319	NM	EMT	ANG	EMT
153321	52321	NM	EMT	PTR	EMT
153326	52326	NM	EMT	PTR	EMT
153355	57355	NM	EMT	ANG	EMT
153357	57357	NM	EMT	ANG	EMT
153374	57374	NM	EMT	ANG	EMT
153376	57376	NM	EMT	PTR	EMT
153379	57379	NM	EMT	PTR	EMT
153381	57381	NM	EMT	PTR	EMT
153383	57383	NM	EMT	PTR	EMT
153384	57384	NM	EMT	PTR	EMT
153385	57385	NM	EMT	PTR	EMT

Name applied
153376 X-24 Expeditious

Left: *Rural branch-line services feature largely in the East Midlands Trains portfolio and the operator has a fleet of 17 single-car Class 153s for use on low-patronage routes. All vehicles are painted in the Stagecoach blue outer-suburban colours and are based at Nottingham Eastcroft depot. Ownership is with Angel Trains (6 sets) and Porterbrook (11 sets). No. 153384 is viewed at Doncaster from its original cab end.* **CJM**

Class 156

		Vehicle Length: 75ft 6in (23.03m)		Engine: 1 x Cummins NT855R5 of 285hp
		Height: 12ft 6in (3.81m)		Horsepower: 570hp (425kW)
		Width: 8ft 11in (2.73m)		Seats (total/car): 148S, 72S/76S

Number	Formation DMSL+DMS	Depot	Livery	Owner	Operator
156401	52401+57401	NM	EMT	PTR	EMT
156403	52403+57403	NM	EMT	PTR	EMT
156404	52404+57404	NM	EMT	PTR	EMT
156405	52405+57405	NM	EMT	PTR	EMT
156406	52406+57406	NM	EMT	PTR	EMT
156408	52408+57408	NM	EMT	PTR	EMT
156410	52410+57410	NM	EMT	PTR	EMT
156411	52411+57411	NM	EMT	PTR	EMT
156413	52413+57413	NM	EMT	PTR	EMT
156414	52414+57414	NM	EMT	PTR	EMT
156415	52415+57415	NM	EMT	PTR	EMT
156470	52470+57470	NM	EMT	PTR	EMT
156473	52473+57473	NM	EMT	PTR	EMT
156497	52497+57497	NM	EMT	PTR	EMT
156498	52498+57498	NM	EMT	PTR	EMT

Left: *For longer-distance domestic services, East Midlands Trains operates a fleet of 15 two-car Class 156s, allocated to Nottingham Eastcroft and painted in Stagecoach outer-suburban blue swirl livery. These sets each seat 148 standard class passengers in the low-density 2+2 style. On 15 May 2014 set No. 156497 is seen near Stenson Junction forming the 09.07 Crewe to Derby .* **CJM**

Class 158

Vehicle Length: 76ft 1¾in (23.21m)
Height: 12ft 6in (3.81m)
Width: 9ft 3¼in (2.82m)

Engine: 158770-813 - 1 x Cummins NT855R5 of 350hp
Horsepower: 700hp (522kW)
Engine: 158846-862 - 1 x Perkins 2006TWH of 350hp
Horsepower: 700hp (522kW)
Engine: 158863-866 - 1 x Cummins NT855R5 of 400hp
Horsepower: 800hp (597kW)
Seats (total/car): 146S - 74S, 72S

Number	Formation DMSL+DMSL	Depot	Livery	Owner	Operator
158770	52770+57770	NM	SCE	PTR	EMT
158773	52773+57773	NM	SCE	PTR	EMT
158774	52774+57774	NM	SCE	PTR	EMT
158777	52777+57777	NM	SCE	PTR	EMT
158780	52780+57780	NM	SCE	ANG	EMT
158783	52783+57783	NM	SCE	ANG	EMT
158785	52785+57785	NM	SCE	ANG	EMT
158788	52788+57788	NM	SCE	ANG	EMT
158799	52799+57799	NM	SCE	PTR	EMT
158806	52806+57806	NM	SCE	PTR	EMT
158810	52810+57810	NM	SCE	PTR	EMT
158812	52812+57812	NM	SCE	PTR	EMT
158813	52813+57813	NM	SCE	PTR	EMT
158846	52846+57846	NM	SCE	ANG	EMT
158847	52847+57847	NM	SCE	ANG	EMT
158852	52852+57852	NM	SCE	ANG	EMT
158854	52854+57854	NM	SCE	ANG	EMT
158856	52856+57856	NM	SCE	ANG	EMT
158857	52857+57857	NM	SCE	ANG	EMT
158858	52858+57858	NM	SCE	ANG	EMT
158862	52862+57862	NM	SCE	ANG	EMT
158863	52863+57863	NM	SCE	ANG	EMT
158864	52864+57864	NM	SCE	ANG	EMT
158865	52865+57865	NM	SCE	ANG	EMT
158866	52866+57866	NM	SCE	ANG	EMT

Right: *The 25 East Midlands Trains longer-distance Class 158 sets are finished in Stagecoach white main-line colours. The livery on these sets is slightly different from that applied to the Class 158s operated by sister Stagecoach company South West Trains, with these sets having a blip in the base blue band behind the cab doors. Set No. 158858 is seen near Marholm on the East Coast Main Line on 24 April 2014 forming the 11.52 Liverpool Lime Street to Norwich.* **CJM**

Class 222

Vehicle Length: 77ft 6in (23.62m)
Height: 12ft 4in (3.75m)
Width: 8ft 11in (2.73m)
Engine: 1 x Cummins OSK9R of 750hp per vehicle

Horsepower: 5,250hp (3,914kW)
Seats (total/car): 106F/236S
38S/68S/68S/62S/42F/42F/22F

Number	Formation DMS+MS+MS+MSRMB+MF+MF+DMRFO	Depot	Livery	Owner	Op'r	Name
222001	60161+60551+60561+60621+60341+60445+60241	DY	SCE	EVL	EMT	The Entrepreneur Express
222002	60162+60544+60562+60622+60342+60346+60242	DY	SCE	EVL	EMT	The Cutlers' Company
222003	60163+60553+60563+60623+60343+60446+60243	DY	SCE	EVL	EMT	Tornado
222004	60164+60554+60564+60624+60344+60345+60244	DY	SCE	EVL	EMT	Childrens Hospital Sheffield
222005	60165+60555+60565+60625+60443+60347+60245	DY	SCE	EVL	EMT	
222006	60166+60556+60566+60626+60441+60447+60246	DY	SCE	EVL	EMT	The Carbon Cutter

Vehicle Length: 77ft 6in (23.62m)
Height: 12ft 4in (3.75m)
Width: 8ft 11in (2.73m)
Engine: 1 x Cummins OSK9R of 750hp per vehicle

Horsepower: 3,750hp (2,796kW)
Seats (total/car): 50F/190S
38S/68S/62S/28F-22S/22F

Number	Formation DMS+MS+MSRMB+MC+DMRFO	Depot	Livery	Owner	Operator	Name
222007	60167+60567+60627+60442+60247	DY	SCE	EVL	EMT	
222008	60168+60545+60628+60918+60248	DY	SCE	EVL	EMT	Derby Etches Park
222009	60169+60557+60629+60919+60249	DY	SCE	EVL	EMT	
222010	60170+60546+60630+60920+60250	DY	SCE	EVL	EMT	
222011	60171+60531+60631+60921+60251	DY	SCE	EVL	EMT	Sheffield City Battalion 1914 - 1918
222012	60172+60532+60632+60922+60252	DY	SCE	EVL	EMT	

East Midlands Trains

Number	Formation	Depot	Livery	Owner	Operator	
222013	60173+60536+60633+60923+60253	DY	SCE	EVL	EMT	
222014	60174+60534+60634+60924+60254	DY	SCE	EVL	EMT	
222015	60175+60535+60635+60925+60255	DY	SCE	EVL	EMT	*175 Years of Derby's Railways 1839-2014*
222016	60176+60533+60636+60926+60256	DY	SCE	EVL	EMT	
222017	60177+60537+60637+60927+60257	DY	SCE	EVL	EMT	
222018	60178+60444+60638+60928+60258	DY	SCE	EVL	EMT	
222019	60179+60547+60639+60929+60259	DY	SCE	EVL	EMT	
222020	60180+60543+60640+60930+60260	DY	SCE	EVL	EMT	
222021	60181+60552+60641+60931+60261	DY	SCE	EVL	EMT	
222022	60182+60542+60642+60932+60262	DY	SCE	EVL	EMT	*Invest in Nottingham*
222023	60183+60541+60643+60933+60263	DY	SCE	EVL	EMT	

Left: *East Midlands Trains long-distance services not operated by HST stock are formed of Class 222 fixed- formation sets marshalled as either four, five or seven car sets. Six seven-car formations can be found on busy peak trains, while the 17 five-car sets operate most services. Five-car set No. 222008 is seen from its DMS end at Leicester. A five-car Class 222 can accommodate 50 first and 190 standard class passengers.* **Antony Christie**

Class 222/1

Vehicle Length: 77ft 6in (23.62m)	Horsepower: 3,000hp (2,237kW)
Height: 12ft 4in (3.75m)	Seats (total/car): 33F/148S
Width: 8ft 11in (2.73m)	22F/11F-46S/62S/40S
Engine: 1 x Cummins QSK9R of 750hp per vehicle	

Number	Formation DMF+MC+MSRMB+DMS	Depot	Livery	Owner	Operator	
222101	60271+60571+60681+60191	DY	SCE	EVL	EMT	**Below:** *The four members of Class 222/1 were originally used by Hull Trains, but are now part of the core EMT fleet allocated to Derby. Set No. 222104 is seen passing Harpenden.* **Tim Easter**
222102	60272+60572+60682+60192	DY	SCE	EVL	EMT	
222103	60273+60573+60683+60193	DY	SCE	EVL	EMT	
222104	60274+60574+60684+60194	DY	SCE	EVL	EMT	

HST Passenger Fleet

Vehicle Length: 75ft 0in (22.86m)
Height: 12ft 9in (3.88m)
Width: 8ft 11in (2.71m)
Bogie Type: BT10

GK1G - TRFB *Seating 17F*

Number	Depot	Livery	Owner
40700	NL	SCE	PTR
40728	NL	SCE	PTR
40730	NL	SCE	PTR
40741	NL	SCE	PTR
40746	NL	SCE	PTR
40749	NL	SCE	PTR
40751	NL	SCE	PTR
40753	NL	SCE	PTR
40754	NL	SCE	PTR
40756	NL	SCE	PTR

GH1G - TF *Seating 46F*

Number	Depot	Livery	Owner
41041	NL	SCE	PTR
41046	NL	SCE	PTR
41057	NL	SCE	PTR
41061	NL	SCE	PTR
41063	NL	SCE	PTR
41064	NL	SCE	PTR
41067	NL	SCE	PTR
41068	NL	SCE	PTR
41069	NL	SCE	PTR
41070	NL	SCE	PTR
41071	NL	SCE	PTR
41072	NL	SCE	PTR
41075	NL	SCE	PTR
41076	NL	SCE	PTR
41077	NL	SCE	PTR
41079	NL	SCE	PTR
41084	NL	SCE	PTR

41111	NL	SCE	PTR
41112	NL	SCE	PTR
41113	NL	SCE	PTR
41117	NL	SCE	PTR
41156	NL	SCE	PTR

GH2G - TS *Seating 74S*

Number	Depot	Livery	Owner
42100	NL	SCE	PTR
42111	NL	SCE	PTR
42112	NL	SCE	PTR
42113	NL	SCE	PTR
42119	NL	SCE	PTR
42120	NL	SCE	PTR
42121	NL	SCE	PTR
42124	NL	SCE	PTR
42131	NL	SCE	PTR
42132	NL	SCE	PTR
42133	NL	SCE	PTR
42135	NL	SCE	PTR
42136	NL	SCE	PTR
42137	NL	SCE	PTR
42139	NL	SCE	PTR
42140	NL	SCE	PTR
42141	NL	SCE	PTR
42148	NL	SCE	PTR
42149	NL	SCE	PTR
42151	NL	SCE	PTR
42152	NL	SCE	PTR
42153	NL	SCE	PTR
42155	NL	SCE	PTR
42156	NL	SCE	PTR

42157	NL	SCE	PTR
42164	NL	SCE	PTR
42165	NL	SCE	PTR
42194	NL	SCE	PTR
42220	NL	SCE	PTR
42225	NL	SCE	PTR
42227	NL	SCE	PTR
42229	NL	SCE	PTR
42230	NL	SCE	PTR
42327	NL	SCE	PTR
42328	NL	SCE	PTR
42329	NL	SCE	PTR
42331	NL	SCE	PTR
42337	NL	SCE	PTR
42339	NL	SCE	PTR
42341	NL	SCE	PTR
42384¤	NL	SCE	PTR

¤ Modified from 41078

GJ2G - TGS *Seating 63S*

Number	Depot	Livery	Owner
44027	NL	SCE	PTR
44041	NL	SCE	PTR
44044	NL	SCE	PTR
44046	NL	SCE	PTR
44047	NL	SCE	PTR
44048	NL	SCE	PTR
44051	NL	SCE	PTR
44054	NL	SCE	PTR
44070	NL	SCE	PTR
44071	NL	SCE	PTR
44085	NL	SCE	PTR

Service Stock

HST Barrier Vehicles

Number	Depot	Livery	Owner	Former Identity
6398	NL	MAI	EMT	BG - 81471/92126
6399	NL	MAI	EMT	BG - 81367/92994

Above: *A total of 84 HST Mk3 passenger vehicles are operated by East Midlands Trains allocated to Leeds Neville Hill depot. All carry full EMT white livery with red passenger doors. A Trailer Standard (TS) is illustrated.* **Antony Christie**

Eurostar

Address: ✉ Eurostar, Times House, Bravingtons Walk, Regent Quarter,
London, N1 9AW
✆ new.comments@eurostar.com
✆ 08701 606 600
ⓘ www.eurostar.com

Managing Director: Nicolas Petrovic

Principal Routes: St Pancras International - Brussels and Paris, also serving
Disneyland Paris, Avignon and winter sport service
to Bourg St Maurice

Owned Stations: St Pancras International, Stratford International, Ebbsfleet

Depots: Temple Mills [UK] (TI), Forest [Belgium] (FF), Le Landy [France] (LY)

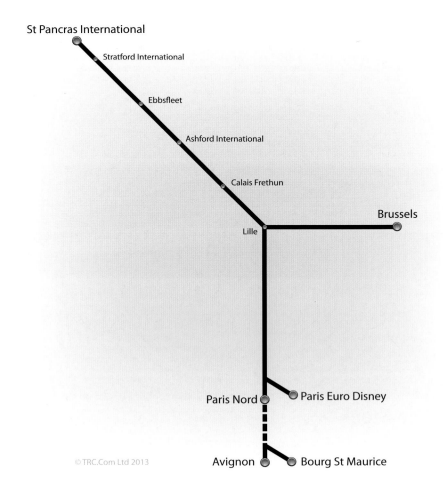

Class 373

Vehicle Length: (DM) 72ft 8in (22.15m), (MS) 71ft 8in (21.84m)
(TS, RB, TF, TBF) 61ft 4in (18.70m)
Height: 12ft 4½in (3.77m)
Width: 9ft 3in (2.81m)
Horsepower: 16,400hp (12,249kW)
Seats (total/car): 102F/272S, 0/48S/56S/56S/56S/0/39F/39F/24F

Formation: DM+MSO+TSO+TSO+TSO+RB+TFO+TFO+TBFO

Number	Formation	Depot	Livery	Owner	Operator	Name
UK sets (Class 373/0)						
373001	3730010+3730011+3730012+3730013+3730014+3730015+3730016+3730017+3730018+3730019	TI	EUS	EUS	EUS	Tread Lightly
373002	3730020+3730021+3730022+3730023+3730024+3730025+3730026+3730027+3730028+3730029	TI	EUS	EUS	EUS	Voyage Vert
373003	3730030+3730031+3730032+3730033+3730034+3730035+3730036+3730037+3730038+3730039	TI	EUS	EUS	EUS	Tri City Athlon 2010
373004	3730040+3730041+3730042+3730043+3730044+3730045+3730046+3730047+3730048+3730049	TI	EUS	EUS	EUS	Tri City Athlon 2010
373005	3730050+3730051+3730052+3730053+3730054+3730055+3730056+3730057+3730058+3730059	TI	EUS	EUS	EUS	
373006	3730060+3730061+3730062+3730063+3730064+3730065+3730066+3730067+3730068+3730069	TI	EUS	EUS	EUS	
373007	3730070+3730071+3730072+3730073+3730074+3730075+3730076+3730077+3730078+3730079	TI	EUS	EUS	EUS	Waterloo Sunset
373008	3730080+3730081+3730082+3730083+3730084+3730085+3730086+3730087+3730088+3730089	TI	EUS	EUS	EUS	Waterloo Sunset
373009	3730090+3730091+3730092+3730093+3730094+3730095+3730096+3730097+3730098+3730099	TI	EUS	EUS	EUS	Remembering Fromelles
373010	3730100+3730101+3730102+3730103+3730104+3730105+3730106+3730107+3730108+3730109	TI	EUS	EUS	EUS	Remembering Fromelles
373011	3730110+3730111+3730112+3730113+3730114+3730115+3730116+3730117+3730118+3730119	TI	EUS	EUS	EUS	
373012	3730120+3730121+3730122+3730123+3730124+3730125+3730126+3730127+3730128+3730129	TI	EUS	EUS	EUS	
373013	3730130+3730131+3730132+3730133+3730134+3730135+3730136+3730137+3730138+3730139	TI	EUS	EUS	EUS	
373014	3730140+3730141+3730142+3730143+3730144+3730145+3730146+3730147+3730148+3730149	TI	EUS	EUS	EUS	
373015	3730150+3730151+3730152+3730153+3730154+3730155+3730156+3730157+3730158+3730159	TI	EUS	EUS	EUS	
373016	3730160+3730161+3730162+3730163+3730164+3730165+3730166+3730167+3730168+3730169	TI	EUB	EUS	EUS	London 2012
373017	3730170+3730171+3730172+3730173+3730174+3730175+3730176+3730177+3730178+3730179	TI	EUB	EUS	EUS	London 2012
373018	3730180+3730181+3730182+3730183+3730184+3730185+3730186+3730187+3730188+3730189	TI	EUS	EUS	EUS	
373019	3730190+3730191+3730192+3730193+3730194+3730195+3730196+3730197+3730198+3730199	TI	EUS	EUS	EUS	
373020	3730200+3730201+3730202+3730203+3730204+3730205+3730206+3730207+3730208+3730209	TI	EUS	EUS	EUS	
373021	3730210+3730211+3730212+3730213+3730214+3730215+3730216+3730217+3730218+3730219	TI	EUS	EUS	EUS	
373022	3730220+3730221+3730222+3730223+3730224+3730225+3730226+3730227+3730228+3730229	TI	EUS	EUS	EUS	
Belgian sets (Class 373/1)						
373101	3731010+3731011+3731012+3731013+3731014+3731015+3731016+3731017+3731018+3731019	FF[S]	EUS	SNB	EUS	
373102	3731020+3731021+3731022+3731023+3731024+3731025+3731026+3731027+3731028+3731029	FF[S]	EUS	SNB	EUS	
373103	3731030+3731031+3731032+3731033+3731034+3731035+3731036+3731037+3731038+3731039	FF	EUS	SNB	EUS	
373104	3731040+3731041+3731042+3731043+3731044+3731045+3731046+3731047+3731048+3731049	FF	EUS	SNB	EUS	
373105	3731050+3731051+3731052+3731053+3731054+3731055+3731056+3731057+3731058+3731059	FF	EUS	SNB	EUS	
373106	3731060+3731061+3731062+3731063+3731064+3731065+3731066+3731067+3731068+3731069	FF	EUS	SNB	EUS	
373107	3731070+3731071+3731072+3731073+3731074+3731075+3731076+3731077+3731078+3731079	FF	EUS	SNB	EUS	
373108	3731080+3731081+3731082+3731083+3731084+3731085+3731086+3731087+3731088+3731089	FF	EUS	SNB	EUS	
French sets (Class 373/2)						
373201	3732010+3732011+3732012+3732013+3732014+3732015+3732016+3732017+3732018+3732019	LY	EUS	SNF	EUS	
373202	3732020+3732021+3732022+3732023+3732024+3732025+3732026+3732027+3732028+3732029	LY	EUS	SNF	EUS	
373203(S)	3732030+3732031+3732032+3732033+3732034+3732035+3732036+3732037+3732038+3732039	LY	SNT	SNF	EUS	
373204(S)	3732040+3732041+3732042+3732043+3732044+3732045+3732046+3732047+3732048+3732049	LY	SNT	SNF	EUS	
373205	3732050+3732051+3732052+3732053+3732054+3732055+3732056+3732057+3732058+3732059	LY	EUS	SNF	EUS	
373206	3732060+3732061+3732062+3732063+3732064+3732065+3732066+3732067+3732068+3732069	LY	EUS	SNF	EUS	

Train Operating Companies

Eurostar

Number	Formation	Depot	Livery	Owner	Operator	Name
373207	3732070+3732071+3732072+3732073+3732074+3732075+3732076+3732077+3732078+3732079	LY	EUS	SNF	EUS	*Michel Hollard*
373208	3732080+3732081+3732082+3732083+3732084+3732085+3732086+3732087+3732088+3732089	LY	EUS	SNF	EUS	*Michel Hollard*
373209	3732090+3732091+3732092+3732093+3732094+3732095+3732096+3732097+3732098+3732099	LY	EUS	SNF	EUS	*The Da Vinci Code*
373210	3732100+3732101+3732102+3732103+3732104+3732105+3732106+3732107+3732108+3732109	LY	EUS	SNF	EUS	*The Da Vinci Code*
373211	3732110+3732111+3732112+3732113+3732114+3732115+3732116+3732117+3732118+3732119	LY	EUS	SNF	EUS	
373212	3732120+3732121+3732122+3732123+3732124+3732125+3732126+3732127+3732128+3732129	LY	EUS	SNF	EUS	
373213	3732130+3732131+3732132+3732133+3732134+3732135+3732136+3732137+3732138+3732139	LY	EUS	SNF	EUS	
373214	3732140+3732141+3732142+3732143+3732144+3732145+3732146+3732147+3732148+3732149	LY	EUS	SNF	EUS	
373215	3732150+3732151+3732152+3732153+3732154+3732155+3732156+3732157+3732158+3732159	LY	EUS	SNF	EUS	
373216	3732160+3732161+3732162+3732163+3732164+3732165+3732166+3732167+3732168+3732169	LY	EUS	SNF	EUS	
373217	3732170+3732171+3732172+3732173+3732174+3732175+3732176+3732177+3732178+3732179	LY	EUS	SNF	EUS	
373218	3732180+3732181+3732182+3732183+3732184+3732185+3732186+3732187+3732188+3732189	LY	EUS	SNF	EUS	
373219	3732190+3732191+3732192+3732193+3732194+3732195+3732196+3732197+3732198+3732199	LY	EUS	SNF	EUS	
373220	3732200+3732201+3732202+3732203+3732204+3732205+3732206+3732207+3732208+3732209	LY	EUS	SNF	EUS	
373221	3732210+3732211+3732212+3732213+3732214+3732215+3732216+3732217+3732218+3732219	LY	EUS	SNF	EUS	
373222	3732220+3732221+3732222+3732223+3732224+3732225+3732226+3732227+3732228+3732229	LY	EUS	SNF	EUS	
373223	3732230+3732231+3732232+3732233+3732234+3732235+3732236+3732237+3732238+3732239	LY	EUS	SNF	EUS	
373224	3732240+3732241+3732242+3732243+3732244+3732245+3732246+3732247+3732248+3732249	LY	EUS	SNF	EUS	
373225(S)	3732250+3732251+3732252+3732253+3732254+3732255+3732256+3732257+3732258+3732259	LY	EUS	SNF	SNT	
373226(S)	3732260+3732261+3732262+3732263+3732264+3732265+3732266+3732267+3732268+3732269	LY	EUS	SNF	SNT	
373227(S)	3732270+3732271+3732272+3732273+3732274+3732275+3732276+3732277+3732278+3732279	LY	EUS	SNF	SNT	
373228(S)	3732280+3732281+3732282+3732283+3732284+3732285+3732286+3732287+3732288+3732289	LY	EUS	SNF	EUS	
373229	3732290+3732291+3732292+3732293+3732294+3732295+3732296+3732297+3732298+3732299	LY	EUS	SNF	EUS	
373230	3732300+3732301+3732302+3732303+3732304+3732305+3732306+3732307+3732308+3732309	LY	EUS	SNF	EUS	
373231	3732310+3732311+3732312+3732313+3732314+3732315+3732316+3732317+3732318+3732319	LY	EUS	SNF	EUS	
373232	3732320+3732321+3732322+3732323+3732324+3732325+3732326+3732327+3732328+3732329	LY	EUS	SNF	EUS	

(S) Were operated in France on domestic services, now stored.

Number   Formation   Depot   Livery   Owner   Operator

DM+MSO+TSO+TSO+TSO+RB+TFO+TBFO

Regional sets (373/3)

Number	Formation	Depot	Livery	Owner	Operator
373301	3733010+3733011+3733012+3733013+3733015+3733016+3733017+3733019	LY	EUS	EUS	SNF
373302	3733020+3733021+3733022+3733023+3733025+3733026+3733027+3733029	LY	EUS	EUS	SNF
373303(S)	3733030+3733031+3733032+3733033+3733035+3733036+3733037+3733039	LY	EUS	EUS	SNF
373304(S)	3733040+3733041+3733042+3733043+3733045+3733046+3733047+3733049	LY	EUS	EUS	SNF
373305	3733050+3733051+3733052+3733053+3733055+3733056+3733057+3733059	LY	EUS	EUS	SNF
373306	3733060+3733061+3733062+3733063+3733065+3733066+3733067+3733069	LY	EUS	EUS	SNF
373307(S)	3733070+3733071+3733072+3733073+3733075+3733076+3733077+3733079	LY	EUS	EUS	SNF
373308(S)	3733080+3733081+3733082+3733083+3733085+3733086+3733087+3733089	LY	EUS	EUS	SNF
373309	3733090+3733091+3733092+3733093+3733095+3733096+3733097+3733099	LY	EUS	EUS	SNF
373310	3733100+3733101+3733102+3733103+3733105+3733106+3733107+3733109	LY	EUS	EUS	SNF
373311	3733110+3733111+3733112+3733113+3733115+3733116+3733117+3733119	LY	EUS	EUS	SNF
373312	3733120+3733121+3733122+3733123+3733125+3733126+3733127+3733129	LY	EUS	EUS	SNF
373313	3733130+3733131+3733132+3733133+3733135+3733136+3733137+3733139	LY	EUS	EUS	SNF
373314	3733140+3733141+3733142+3733143+3733145+3733146+3733147+3733149	LY	EUS	EUS	SNF

Vehicle Length: (DM) 72ft 8in (22.15m), (MS) 71ft 8in (21.84m) (TS, RB, TF, TBF) 61ft 4in (18.70m)
Height: 12ft 4½in (3.77m)
Width: 9ft 3in (2.81m)
Horsepower: 16,400hp (12,249kW)
Seats (total/car): 102F/272S, 0/48S/56S/56S/56S/56S/0/39F/39F/24F

■ These 14 short half-sets are loaned to SNCF for domestic duties until early 2015.

Spare DM

Number		Depot	Livery	Owner	Operator
3999	(Spare vehicle used as required to cover for maintenance)	TI	EUS	EUS	EUS

Right: *In 2014 a start was made on repainting the Eurostar fleet into a new corporate livery, in keeping with the new Class 374 stock now on delivery. The entire appearance of the train is changed by the colour change and looks very impressive. The new colours are shown on set No. 373212, one of the French-owned trains at Paris Gare du Nord. Set No. 373211 was on the rear of the train.* **Chris Horner**

Below: *Two of the Forest-allocated sets, Nos. 373107 and 373108, cross the Medway Viaduct in Kent on HS1 bound for London St Pancras.* **Antony Christie**

Class 374 (e320)

Vehicle Length: Car 1 - 26.075m, Car 2-8 - 24.775m. Train length (8-car) 199.46m
Height: Details awaited   Width: Details awaited
Horsepower: 25kV ac operation - 21,000hp (16,000kW) 3,000V dc, 1,500V dc tba
Seats (total/car): 107F/336S. 40F/36F/31F/76S/76S/76S/76S/32S (half train)
Electrical Equipment: Siemens

● Thirtyfour new Eurostar e320 eight-car Class 374 sets are on order from Siemens for delivery in 2015-16; these have a 200mph (320km/h) top speed capability and two half-sets will seat 214F/672S passengers. Train length is 398m with an all-in weight of 910 tonnes.

The 374 sets have the ability to operate throughout Europe, but on delivery will not be fitted with universal signalling, only for operation in the UK, France and Belgium.

Set Number	Formation eight vehicles [half-set] DM, T, M, T, T, M, T, M		Depot	Livery	Owner	Operator
374001	93-70-3740-011 GB-EIL – 93-70-3740-018 GB-EIL	*(under test)*	TI	EUN	EUS	EUS
374002	93-70-3740-021 GB-EIL – 93-70-3740-028 GB-EIL	*(under test)*	TI	EUN	EUS	EUS
374003	93-70-3740-031 GB-EIL – 93-70-3740-038 GB-EIL	*(under test)*	TI	EUN	EUS	EUS
374004	93-70-3740-041 GB-EIL – 93-70-3740-048 GB-EIL	*(under test)*	TI	EUN	EUS	EUS
374005	93-70-3740-051 GB-EIL – 93-70-3740-058 GB-EIL	*(under test)*	TI	EUN	EUS	EUS
374006	93-70-3740-061 GB-EIL – 93-70-3740-068 GB-EIL	*(under test)*	TI	EUN	EUS	EUS
374007	93-70-3740-071 GB-EIL – 93-70-3740-078 GB-EIL	*(under test)*	TI	EUN	EUS	EUS

Eurostar

374008	93-70-3740-081 GB-EIL – 93-70-3740-088 GB-EIL *(under test)*	TI	EUN	EUS	EUS
374009	93-70-3740-091 GB-EIL – 93-70-3740-098 GB-EIL *(under test)*	TI	EUN	EUS	EUS
374010	93-70-3740-101 GB-EIL – 93-70-3740-108 GB-EIL *(under test)*	TI	EUN	EUS	EUS
374011	93-70-3740-111 GB-EIL – 93-70-3740-118 GB-EIL *(under test)*	TI	EUN	EUS	EUS
374012	93-70-3740-121 GB-EIL – 93-70-3740-128 GB-EIL *(under test)*	TI	EUN	EUS	EUS
374013	93-70-3740-131 GB-EIL – 93-70-3740-138 GB-EIL *(under test)*	TI	EUN	EUS	EUS
374014	93-70-3740-141 GB-EIL – 93-70-3740-148 GB-EIL *(under test)*	TI	EUN	EUS	EUS
374015	93-70-3740-151 GB-EIL – 93-70-3740-158 GB-EIL *(under test)*	TI	EUN	EUS	EUS
374016	93-70-3740-161 GB-EIL – 93-70-3740-168 GB-EIL *(under test)*	TI	EUN	EUS	EUS
374017	93-70-3740-171 GB-EIL – 93-70-3740-178 GB-EIL *(under test)*	TI	EUN	EUS	EUS
374018	93-70-3740-181 GB-EIL – 93-70-3740-188 GB-EIL *(under test)*	TI	EUN	EUS	EUS
374019	93-70-3740-191 GB-EIL – 93-70-3740-198 GB-EIL *(under test)*	TI	EUN	EUS	EUS
374020	93-70-3740-201 GB-EIL – 93-70-3740-208 GB-EIL *(under test)*	TI	EUN	EUS	EUS
374021	93-70-3740-211 GB-EIL – 93-70-3740-218 GB-EIL *(under assembly)*	TI	EUN	EUS	EUS
374022	93-70-3740-221 GB-EIL – 93-70-3740-228 GB-EIL *(under assembly)*	TI	EUN	EUS	EUS
374023	93-70-3740-231 GB-EIL – 93-70-3740-238 GB-EIL *(under assembly)*	TI	EUN	EUS	EUS
374024	93-70-3740-241 GB-EIL – 93-70-3740-248 GB-EIL *(under assembly)*	TI	EUN	EUS	EUS
374025	93-70-3740-251 GB-EIL – 93-70-3740-258 GB-EIL *(under assembly)*	TI	EUN	EUS	EUS
374026	93-70-3740-261 GB-EIL – 93-70-3740-268 GB-EIL *(under assembly)*	TI	EUN	EUS	EUS
374027	93-70-3740-271 GB-EIL – 93-70-3740-278 GB-EIL *(under assembly)*	TI	EUN	EUS	EUS
374028	93-70-3740-281 GB-EIL – 93-70-3740-288 GB-EIL *(under assembly)*	TI	EUN	EUS	EUS
374029	93-70-3740-291 GB-EIL – 93-70-3740-298 GB-EIL *(under assembly)*	TI	EUN	EUS	EUS
374030	93-70-3740-301 GB-EIL – 93-70-3740-308 GB-EIL *(under assembly)*	TI	EUN	EUS	EUS
374031	93-70-3740-311 GB-EIL – 93-70-3740-318 GB-EIL *(under assembly)*	TI	EUN	EUS	EUS
374032	93-70-3740-321 GB-EIL – 93-70-3740-328 GB-EIL *(under assembly)*	TI	EUN	EUS	EUS
374033	93-70-3740-331 GB-EIL – 93-70-3740-338 GB-EIL *(under assembly)*	TI	EUN	EUS	EUS
374034	93-70-3740-341 GB-EIL – 93-70-3740-348 GB-EIL *(under assembly)*	TI	EUN	EUS	EUS

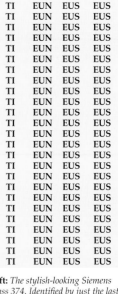

Left: *The stylish-looking Siemens Class 374. Identified by just the last four digits of its number, half-set No. 4012 is seen under the great Barlow roof at London St Pancras.* **Antony Christie**

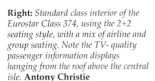

Right: *Standard class interior of the Eurostar Class 374, using the 2+2 seating style, with a mix of airline and group seating. Note the TV- quality passenger information displays hanging from the roof above the central isle.* **Antony Christie**

Right: *The Class 374 uses the 2+1 seating style for the first and premier class seating areas, again with a mix of group and airline style seats. The airline seating has high-quality fold-down tables, allowing an at-seat meal service to be provided.*
Antony Christie

Left: *The Class 374 driving cab layout is a lot more streamlined and less cluttered than the previous Class 373 Eurostar sets.* **Antony Christie**

Class 08

Vehicle Length: 29ft 3in (8.91m)			Engine: English Electric 6K		
Height: 12ft 8⅝in (3.87m)			Horsepower: 400hp (298kW)		
Width: 8ft 6in (2.59m)			Electrical Equipment: English Electric		

Number	Depot	Pool	Livery	Owner	Operator
08948	TI	GPSS	TTG	EUS	EUS

Right: *Eurostar has one Class 08 on its books, No. 08948, which is based at the Temple Mills depot in East London. The loco is fitted with hinged Scharfenberg couplings for attachment to Class 373 and 374 stock. It is painted in Channel Tunnel grey livery.*
Antony Christie

First Great Western

Address: ✉ Milford House, 1 Milford Street, Swindon, SN1 1HL
📠 fgwfeedback@firstgroup.com
✆ 08457 000125 ⓘ www.firstgreatwestern.co.uk

Managing Director: Mark Hopwood
Franchise Dates: 1 April 2006 - Extension to July 2016
Principal Routes: Paddington - Penzance/Paignton, Bristol, Swansea
Thames Valley local lines, to Worcester, Hereford and Gloucester
Local lines in Bristol, Exeter, Plymouth and Cornwall
Bristol - Weymouth, Portsmouth/Brighton/Great Malvern
Depots: Exeter (EX), Old Oak Common (OO), Laira (LA), Landore (LE),
St Philip's Marsh (PM), Penzance (PZ), Reading (RG)
Parent Company: First Group PLC

Class 08

Vehicle Length: 29ft 3in (8.91m)
Height: 12ft 8⅝in (3.87m)
Width: 8ft 6in (2.59m)
Engine: English Electric 6K
Horsepower: 400hp (298kW)
Electrical Equipment: English Electric

Number	Depot	Pool	Livery	Owner	Operator
08410	LA	EFSH	FGB	FGP	FGW
08483	OO	EFSH	GWG	FGP	FGW
08641	LA	EFSH	BLU	FGP	FGW
08644	PZ	EFSH	BLU	FGP	FGW
08645	LA	EFSH	GRY	FGP	FGW
08663	PM	EFSH	FGB	FGP	FGW
08795	LE	EFSH	BLK	FGP	FGW
08822	LE	EFSH	FGB	FGP	FGW
08836	OC	EFSH	GWG	FGP	FGW

Names applied

08644	*Laira Diesel Depot 50 Years 1962-2012*
08645	*Mike Baggott*
08663	*Jack*
08822	*John*

Below: *First Great Western operates a fleet of nine standard Class 08 0-6-0 diesel-electric shunting locomotives for depot pilotage operations and the limited movement of stock between main depots and terminal stations. To allow main-line operation, some locomotives are fitted with main-line safety equipment, such as TPWS and OTMR. Some examples are also fitted with headlights and others have drophead or hinged knuckle couplers to enable attachment to HST trailer stock. No. 08836 illustrated is one loco authorised for main-line operation and can haul sleeper stock between Old Oak Common depot and Paddington station when no main-line loco is available. Painted in FGW blue, No. 08836 is seen at Paddington station.* **Antony Christie**

Class 43 – HST

Vehicle Length: 58ft 5in (18.80m)
Height: 12ft 10in (3.90m)
Width: 8ft 11in (2.73m)

Engine: MTU 16V4000 R41R
Horsepower: 2,250hp (1,680kW)
Electrical Equipment: Brush

Number	Depot	Pool	Livery	Owner	Operator
43002	LA	EFPC	FGB	ANG	FGW
43003	LA	EFPC	FGB	ANG	FGW
43004	LA	EFPC	FGB	ANG	FGW
43005	LA	EFPC	FGB	ANG	FGW
43009	LA	EFPC	FGB	ANG	FGW
43010	LA	EFPC	FGB	ANG	FGW
43012	LA	EFPC	FGB	ANG	FGW
43015	LA	EFPC	FGB	ANG	FGW
43016	LA	EFPC	FGB	ANG	FGW
43017	LA	EFPC	FGB	ANG	FGW
43018	LA	EFPC	FGB	ANG	FGW
43020	LA	EFPC	FGB	ANG	FGW
43021	LA	EFPC	FGB	ANG	FGW
43022	LA	EFPC	FGB	ANG	FGW
43023	LA	EFPC	FGB	ANG	FGW
43024	LA	EFPC	FGB	ANG	FGW
43025	LA	EFPC	FGB	ANG	FGW
43026	LA	EFPC	FGB	ANG	FGW
43027	LA	EFPC	FGB	ANG	FGW
43028	LA	EFPC	FGB	ANG	FGW
43029	LA	EFPC	FGB	ANG	FGW
43030	LA	EFPC	FGB	ANG	FGW
43031	LA	EFPC	FGB	ANG	FGW
43032	LA	EFPC	FGB	ANG	FGW
43033	LA	EFPC	FGB	ANG	FGW
43034	LA	EFPC	FGB	ANG	FGW
43035	LA	EFPC	FGB	ANG	FGW
43036	LA	EFPC	FGB	ANG	FGW
43037	LA	EFPC	FGB	ANG	FGW
43040	LA	EFPC	FGB	ANG	FGW
43041	LE	EFPC	FGB	ANG	FGW
43042	LE	EFPC	FGB	ANG	FGW
43053	LE	EFPC	FGB	PTR	FGW
43056	LE	EFPC	FGB	PTR	FGW
43063	LE	EFPC	FGB	PTR	FGW
43069	LE	EFPC	FGB	PTR	FGW
43070	LE	EFPC	FGB	PTR	FGW
43071	LE	EFPC	FGB	PTR	FGW
43078	LE	EFPC	FGB	PTR	FGW
43079	LE	EFPC	FGB	PTR	FGW
43086	OO	EFPC	FGB	PTR	FGW
43087	OO	EFPC	FGB	PTR	FGW
43088	OO	EFPC	FGB	PTR	FGW
43091	OO	EFPC	FGB	PTR	FGW
43092	OO	EFPC	FGB	PTR	FGW
43093	OO	EFPC	FGB	PTR	FGW
43094	OO	EFPC	FGB	PTR	FGW
43097	OO	EFPC	FGB	PTR	FGW
43098	OO	EFPC	FGB	PTR	FGW
43122	OO	EFPC	FGB	FGP	FGW
43124	LE	EFPC	FGB	ANG	FGW
43125	LE	EFPC	FGB	ANG	FGW
43126	LE	EFPC	FGB	ANG	FGW
43127	LE	EFPC	FGB	ANG	FGW
43128	LE	EFPC	FGB	ANG	FGW
43129	LE	EFPC	FGB	ANG	FGW
43130	LE	EFPC	FGB	ANG	FGW
43131	LE	EFPC	FGB	ANG	FGW
43132	LE	EFPC	FGB	ANG	FGW
43133	LE	EFPC	FGB	ANG	FGW
43134	LE	EFPC	FGB	ANG	FGW
43135	LE	EFPC	FGB	ANG	FGW
43136	LE	EFPC	FGB	ANG	FGW

Below: *In 2015 the largest user of Class 43 HST power cars is First Great Western, with almost all main-line services formed of HST stock. All power cars are refurbished with MTU engines and all but one carry standard FGW blue livery. Power cars are allocated to Laira, Old Oak Common and Landore depots. No. 43004 is illustrated at Swindon on 9 September 2014.* **CJM**

Passenger Train Operating Companies - First Great Western

Train Operating Companies

First Great Western

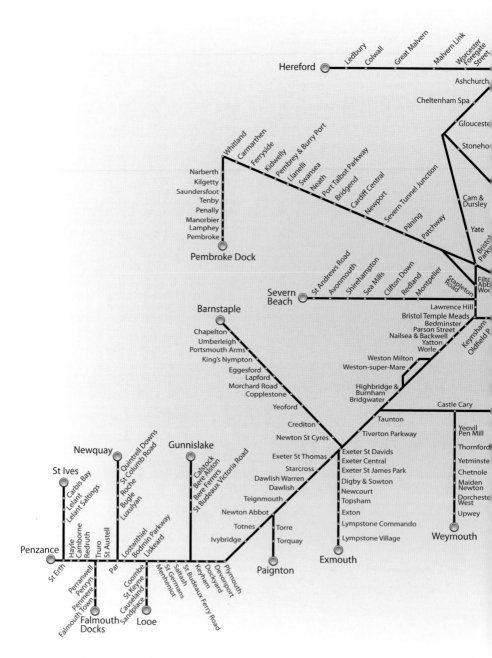

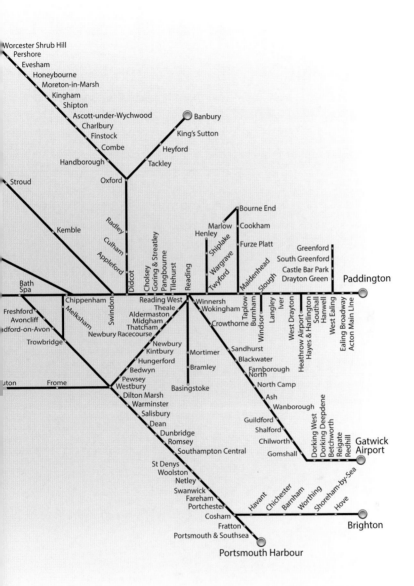

First Great Western

43137	LE	EFPC	FGB	ANG	FGW	43168	OO	EFPC	FGB	ANG	FGW
43138	LE	EFPC	FGB	ANG	FGW	43169	OO	EFPC	FGB	ANG	FGW
43139	LE	EFPC	FGB	ANG	FGW	43170	OO	EFPC	FGB	ANG	FGW
43140	LE	EFPC	FGB	ANG	FGW	43171	OO	EFPC	FGB	ANG	FGW
43141	LE	EFPC	FGB	ANG	FGW	43172	OO	EFPC	FGB	ANG	FGW
43142	LE	EFPC	FGB	ANG	FGW	43174	OO	EFPC	FGB	ANG	FGW
43143	LE	EFPC	FGB	ANG	FGW	43175	OO	EFPC	FGB	ANG	FGW
43144	LE	EFPC	FGB	ANG	FGW	43176	OO	EFPC	FGB	ANG	FGW
43145	LE	EFPC	FGB	ANG	FGW	43177	OO	EFPC	FGB	ANG	FGW
43146	LE	EFPC	FGB	ANG	FGW	43179	OO	EFPC	FGB	ANG	FGW
43147	LE	EFPC	FGB	ANG	FGW	43180	OO	EFPC	FGB	PTR	FGW
43148	LE	EFPC	FGB	ANG	FGW	43181	OO	EFPC	FGB	ANG	FGW
43149	LE	EFPC	FGB	ANG	FGW	43182	OO	EFPC	FGB	ANG	FGW
43150	LE	EFPC	FGB	ANG	FGW	43183	OO	EFPC	FGB	ANG	FGW
43151	LE	EFPC	FGB	ANG	FGW	43185	OO	EFPC	FGB	ANG	FGW
43152	LE	EFPC	FGB	ANG	FGW	43186	OO	EFPC	FGB	ANG	FGW
43153	OO	EFPC	FGB	FGP	FGW	43187	OO	EFPC	FGB	ANG	FGW
43154	OO	EFPC	FGB	FGP	FGW	43188	OO	EFPC	FGB	ANG	FGW
43155	OO	EFPC	FGB	FGP	FGW	43189	OO	EFPC	FGB	ANG	FGW
43156	OO	EFPC	FGB	PTR	FGW	43190	OO	EFPC	FGB	ANG	FGW
43158	OO	EFPC	FGB	FGP	FGW	43191	OO	EFPC	FGB	ANG	FGW
43159	OO	EFPC	FGB	PTR	FGW	43192	OO	EFPC	FGB	ANG	FGW
43160	OO	EFPC	FGB	PTR	FGW	43193	OO	EFPC	FGB	PTR	FGW
43161	OO	EFPC	FGB	PTR	FGW	43194	OO	EFPC	FGB	FGP	FGW
43162	OO	EFPC	FGB	ANG	FGW	43195	OO	EFPC	FGB	PTR	FGW
43163	OO	EFPC	FGA§	ANG	FGW	43196	OO	EFPC	FGB	PTR	FGW
43164	OO	EFPC	FGB	ANG	FGW	43197	OO	EFPC	FGB	PTR	FGW
43165	OO	EFPC	FGB	ANG	FGW	43198	OO	EFPC	FGB	FGP	FGW

FGA§ - Visit Plymouth branding

Names applied

43003	*Isambard Kingdom Brunel*
43004	*First for the Future / First ar gyfer y dyfodol*
43017	*Hannahs discoverhannahs.org*
43020	*MTU Power Passion Partnership*
43021	*David Austin – Cartoonist*
43024	*Great Western Society 1961-2011*
	Didcot Railway Centre
43025	*The Institution of Railway Operators*
43027	*Glorious Devon*
43030	*Christian Lewis Trust*
43033	*Driver Brian Cooper 15 June 1947 – 5 October 1999*
43037	*Penydarren*
43040	*Bristol St Philip's Marsh*
43041	*Meningitis Trust Support for Life*
43053	*University of Worcester*
43056	*The Royal British Legion*
43070	*The Corps of Royal Electrical and Mechanical Engineers*
43087	*11 Explosive Ordnance Disposal Regiment Royal Logistic Corps*
43097	*Environment Agency*
43127	*Sir Peter Parker 1924-2002 – Cotswold Line 150*
43132	*We Save the Children - Will You?*
43137	*Newton Abbot 150*
43139	*Driver Stan Martin 25 June 1960 – 6 November 2004*
43140	*Depo Diesel Glandŵr 1963 Dathlu 50 Mlynedd 2013 Landore Diesel Depot 1963 Celebrating 50 Years 2013*
43142	*Reading Panel Signal Box 1965 - 2010*
43143	*Stroud 700*
43147	*Royal Marines Celebrating 300 Years*
43149	*University of Plymouth*
43155	*The Red Arrows 50 Seasons of Excellence*
43156	*Dartington International Summer School*
43160	*Sir Moir Lockhead OBE*
43165	*Prince Michael of Kent*
43169	*The National Trust*
43175	*GWR 175th Anniversary*
43179	*Pride of Laira*
43185	*Great Western*
43189	*Railway Heritage Trust*
43198	*Oxfordshire 2007*

Left: *Thirty-seven of the FGW power car fleet carry cast nameplates. These reflect people, locations or organisations, with the number of named vehicles greatly reduced in recent years. No. 43143* Stroud 700 *is seen at Paddington on 4 June 2014.*
CJM

Class 57/6

Vehicle Length: 63ft 6in (19.38m)		*Engine: EMD 645-12E3*				
Height: 12ft 10⅛in (3.91m)		*Horsepower: 2,500hp (1,860kW)*				
Width: 9ft 2in (2.79m)		*Electrical Equipment: Brush*				

Number	Depot	Pool	Livery	Owner	Operator	Name
57602 (47337)	OO	EFOO	FGB	PTR	FGW	*Restormel Castle*
57603 (47349)	OO	EFOO	FGB	PTR	FGW	*Tintagel Castle*
57604 (47209)	OO	EFOO	GWR	PTR	FGW	*Pendennis Castle*
57605 (47206)	OO	EFOO	FGB	PTR	FGW	*Totnes Castle*

Right: *To operate the franchise-required overnight sleeper service from London to Penzance, First Great Western has a fleet of four Class 57/6 locos based at Old Oak Common to operate the one westbound and one eastbound train each day. The other two locos provide a spare and a London-based empty stock loco. Three of the four locos are painted in FGW blue, the odd man out being No. 57604 painted in Great Western green. Blue-liveried No. 57602 is illustrated. All four locos are named after West Country castles.* **CJM**

HST Passenger Fleet

Vehicle Length: 75ft 0in (22.86m)		*Width: 8ft 11in (2.71m)*	
Height: 12ft 9in (3.88m)		*Bogie Type: BT10*	

GN2G - TSRMB *Seating 70S*

Number	Depot	Livery	Owner
40101 (42170)	LA	FGW	PTR
40102 (42223)	LA	FGW	PTR
40103 (42316)	LA	FGW	PTR
40104 (42254)	LA	FGW	PTR
40105 (42084)	LA	FGW	PTR
40106 (42162)	LA	FGW	PTR
40107 (42334)	LA	FGW	PTR
40108 (42314)	LA	FGW	PTR
40109 (42262)	LA	FGW	PTR
40110 (42187)	LA	FGW	PTR
40111 (42248)	LA	FGW	PTR
40112 (42336)	LA	FGW	PTR
40113 (42309)	LA	FGW	PTR
40114 (42086)	LA	FGW	PTR
40115 (42320)	LA	FGW	PTR
40116 (42147)	LA	FGW	PTR
40117 (42249)	LA	FGW	PTR
40118 (42338)	LA	FGW	PTR
40119 (42090)	LA	FGW	PTR

GN1G - TRFB *Seating 23F*

Number	Depot	Livery	Owner
40204	LA	FGW	ANG
40205	LA	FGW	ANG
40207	LA	FGW	ANG
40210	LA	FGW	ANG
40221	LA	FGW	ANG
40231	LA	FGW	ANG

GK1G - TRFB *Seating 17F*

Number	Depot	Livery	Owner
40703	LA	FGW	ANG
40707	LA	FGW	ANG
40710	LA	FGW	ANG
40713	LA	FGW	ANG
40715	LA	FGW	ANG
40716	LA	FGW	ANG
40718	OO	FGW	ANG
40721	LA	FGW	ANG
40722	LA	FGW	ANG
40727	LA	FGW	ANG

Number	Depot	Livery	Owner
40733	LA	FGW	ANG
40734	LA	FGW	ANG
40739	LA	FGW	ANG
40743	LA	FGW	ANG
40752	LA	FGW	ANG
40755	LA	FGW	ANG
40757	LA	FGW	ANG

GL1G - TRFB *Seating 17F*

Number	Depot	Livery	Owner
40801	OO	FGW	PTR
40802	OO	FGW	PTR
40803	OO	FGW	PTR
40806	OO	FGW	PTR
40807	OO	FGW	PTR
40808	OO	FGW	PTR
40809	OO	FGW	PTR
40810	OO	FGW	PTR
40811	OO	FGW	PTR

Right: *A total of 51 catering vehicles of four different types operate for First Great Western. Of these 32 can provide a full sit-down catering service for 17-23 passengers. TRFB No. 40808 is shown at Newport, viewed from its catering end, equipment side. This is one of nine vehicles of this type owned by Porterbrook and operated from Old Oak Common depot.* **CJM**

First Great Western

GN1G - TRB *Seating 23F*

Number	Depot	Livery	Owner
40900	LA	FGW	FGP
40901	LA	FGW	FGP
40902	LA	FGW	FGP
40903	LA	FGW	FGP
40904	LA	FGW	FGP

GH1G - TF *Seating 48F*

Number	Depot	Livery	Owner
41004	OO	FGW	ANG
41006	OO	FGW	ANG
41008	OO	FGW	ANG
41010	LA	FGW	ANG
41012	LA	FGW	ANG
41016	LA	FGW	ANG
41018	OO	FGW	ANG
41020	LA	FGW	ANG
41022	LA	FGW	ANG
41024	LA	FGW	ANG
41028	OO	FGW	ANG
41030	OO	FGW	ANG
41032	OO	FGW	ANG
41034	OO	FGW	ANG
41038	LA	FGW	ANG
41052	LA	FGW	ANG
41056	OO	FGW	ANG
41059	LA	FGW	FGP
41089	OO	FGW	ANG
41094	LA	FGW	ANG
41102	OO	FGW	ANG
41103	LA	FGW	ANG
41104	LA	FGW	ANG
41106	OO	FGW	ANG
41108	OO	FGW	PTR
41110	OO	FGW	ANG
41116	LA	FGW	ANG
41122	LA	FGW	ANG
41124	LA	FGW	ANG
41126	OO	FGW	ANG
41128	OO	FGW	ANG
41130	LA	FGW	ANG
41132	OO	FGW	ANG
41134	LA	FGW	ANG
41135	LA	FGW	ANG
41136	OO	FGW	ANG
41137	OO	FGW	ANG
41138	OO	FGW	ANG
41140	OO	FGW	ANG
41142	LA	FGW	ANG
41144	LA	FGW	ANG
41146	LA	FGW	ANG
41149	OO	FGW	PTR
41158	LA	FGW	ANG
41160	LA	FGW	FGP
41161	OO	FGW	PTR
41162	LA	FGW	FGP
41166	LA	FGW	FGP
41167	LA	FGW	FGP
41169	OO	FGW	PTR
41176	OO	FGW	PTR
41180	OO	FGW	ANG
41182	OO	FGW	PTR
41183	OO	FGW	PTR
41186	OO	FGW	PTR
41187	OO	FGW	PTR
41189	OO	FGW	PTR
41192	OO	FGW	PTR

GH2G - TS *Seating 68-84S*

Number	Depot	Livery	Owner
42003	OO	FGW	ANG
42004	LA	FGW	ANG
42005 ●	LA	FGW	ANG
42006	LA	FGW	ANG
42007	LA	FGW	ANG
42008	OO	FGW	ANG
42009	LA	FGW	ANG
42010 ●	LA	FGW	ANG
42012	LA	FGW	ANG
42013	LA	FGW	ANG
42014	LA	FGW	ANG
42015	LA	FGW	ANG
42016	LA	FGW	ANG
42019 ●	LA	FGW	ANG
42021	LA	FGW	ANG
42023	LA	FGW	ANG
42024	OO	FGW	ANG
42025	OO	FGW	ANG
42026	OO	FGW	ANG
42027	OO	FGW	ANG
42028	LA	FGW	ANG
42029	LA	FGW	ANG
42030	LA	FGW	ANG
42031	LA	FGW	ANG
42032	LA	FGW	ANG
42033 ●	LA	FGW	ANG
42034	LA	FGW	ANG
42035	LA	FGW	ANG
42039 ●	OO	FGW	ANG
42040	OO	FGW	ANG
42041	OO	FGW	ANG
42042 ●	OO	FGW	ANG
42043	OO	FGW	ANG
42044	OO	FGW	ANG
42045 ●	LA	FGW	ANG
42046	LA	FGW	ANG
42047	LA	FGW	ANG
42048 ●	OO	FGW	ANG
42049	OO	FGW	ANG
42050	OO	FGW	ANG
42054 ●	LA	FGW	ANG
42055	LA	FGW	ANG
42056	LA	FGW	ANG
42060	OO	FGW	ANG
42061	OO	FGW	ANG
42066	OO	FGW	ANG
42067	OO	FGW	ANG
42068	OO	FGW	ANG
42069	OO	FGW	ANG
42070 ●	OO	FGW	ANG
42071	OO	FGW	ANG
42072	LA	FGW	ANG
42073 ●	OO	FGW	ANG
42074 ●	OO	FGW	ANG
42075 ●	LA	FGW	ANG
42076 ●	LA	FGW	ANG
42077	LA	FGW	ANG
42078	LA	FGW	ANG
42079	OO	FGW	ANG
42080	OO	FGW	ANG
42081	OO	FGW	ANG
42083	OO	FGW	ANG
42085 ●	OO	FGW	ANG
42087	OO	FGW	ANG
42089	OO	FGW	ANG
42092	LA	FGW	FGP
42093	LA	FGW	FGP
42094	LA	FGW	FGP
42095	LA	FGW	FGP
42096 ●	LA	FGW	ANG
42098 ●	OO	FGW	ANG
42099	OO	FGW	ANG
42101	OO	FGW	PTR
42102	OO	FGW	PTR
42103	LA	FGW	FGP
42105	LA	FGW	FGP
42107	LA	FGW	ANG
42108	LA	FGW	FGP
42115 ●	OO	FGW	PTR
42118	OO	FGW	ANG
42126	OO	FGW	ANG
42129 ●	LA	FGW	ANG
42138	OO	FGW	ANG
42143	LA	FGW	ANG
42144	LA	FGW	ANG
42145	LA	FGW	ANG
42166 ●	OO	FGW	PTR
42167	LA	FGW	FGP
42168 ●	LA	FGW	FGP
42169	LA	FGW	FGP
42173	OO	FGW	PTR
42174	OO	FGW	PTR
42175	LA	FGW	FGP

Left: *The largest fleet of First Great Western catering vehicles consists of a fleet of 19 Trailer Standard Restaurant Micro Buffet (TSRMB). These were converted from standard TS vehicles with one seating bay and the toilet compartment removed and a small buffet counter and food preparation area installed. These vehicles operate in sets where a trolley service is provided. No. 40116, rebuilt from TS No. 42147, is illustrated from its catering end.* **CJM**

42176 ●	LA	FGW	FGP	42279	LA	FGW	ANG	42508 (40725)	OO	FGW	ANG
42177	LA	FGW	FGP	42280	LA	FGW	ANG	42509 (40736)	OO	FGW	ANG
42178 ●	OO	FGW	PTR	42281	LA	FGW	ANG	42510 (40717)	OO	FGW	ANG
42183	LA	FGW	ANG	42283	OO	FGW	ANG	42511 (40709)	OO	FGW	ANG
42184 ●	LA	FGW	ANG	42284	OO	FGW	ANG	42512 (40208)	OO	FGW	ANG
42185	LA	FGW	ANG	42285	OO	FGW	ANG	42513 (40738)	OO	FGW	ANG
42195	OO	FGW	PTR	42287	OO	FGW	ANG	42514 (40726)	OO	FGW	ANG
42196	OO	FGW	ANG	42288	OO	FGW	ANG	42515 (40747)	LA	FGW	ANG
42197 ●	OO	FGW	ANG	42289	OO	FGW	ANG	42516 (40723)	LA	FGW	ANG
42200	LA	FGW	ANG	42291	LA	FGW	ANG	42517 (40745)	LA	FGW	ANG
42201	OO	FGW	ANG	42292	LA	FGW	ANG	42518 (40403)	LA	FGW	ANG
42202	OO	FGW	ANG	42293	LA	FGW	ANG	42519 (40416)	LA	FGW	ANG
42203	OO	FGW	ANG	42294	OO	FGW	PTR	42520 (40434)	LA	FGW	ANG
42204	OO	FGW	ANG	42295	LA	FGW	ANG	42551 (41003)	LA	FGW	ANG
42206	LA	FGW	ANG	42296	LA	FGW	ANG	42552 (41007)	LA	FGW	ANG
42207	LA	FGW	ANG	42297	LA	FGW	ANG	42553 (41009)	LA	FGW	ANG
42208	LA	FGW	ANG	42299	LA	FGW	ANG	42554 (41011)	LA	FGW	ANG
42209	LA	FGW	ANG	42300	LA	FGW	ANG	42555 (41015)	LA	FGW	ANG
42211	OO	FGW	ANG	42301	LA	FGW	ANG	42556 (41017)	LA	FGW	ANG
42212 ●	OO	FGW	ANG	42302	LA	FGW	FGP	42557 (41019)	LA	FGW	ANG
42213	OO	FGW	ANG	42303 ●	LA	FGW	FGP	42558 (41021)	LA	FGW	ANG
42214	OO	FGW	ANG	42304	LA	FGW	FGP	42559 (41023)	LA	FGW	ANG
42216 ●	OO	FGW	ANG	42305	LA	FGW	FGP	42560 (41027)	LA	FGW	ANG
42217	OO	FGW	PTR	42308 ●	OO	FGW	PTR	42561 (41031)	LA	FGW	ANG
42218	OO	FGW	PTR	42310	OO	FGW	PTR	42562 (41037)	LA	FGW	ANG
42221 ●	OO	FGW	ANG	42315 ●	OO	FGW	PTR	42563 (41045)	LA	FGW	FGP
42222 ●	OO	FGW	PTR	42317	OO	FGW	PTR	42564 (41051)	LA	FGW	ANG
42224	OO	FGW	PTR	42319 ●	OO	FGW	PTR	42565 (41085)	LA	FGW	FGP
42231	LA	FGW	FGP	42321	OO	FGW	PTR	42566 (41086)	LA	FGW	FGP
42232 ●	LA	FGW	FGP	42325 ●	LA	FGW	ANG	42567 (41093)	LA	FGW	ANG
42233	LA	FGW	FGP	42332 ●	LA	FGW	ANG	42568 (41101)	LA	FGW	ANG
42236 ●	OO	FGW	ANG	42333	LA	FGW	ANG	42569 (41105)	LA	FGW	ANG
42245	LA	FGW	ANG	42343 ●	LA	FGW	ANG	42570 (41114)	LA	FGW	FGP
42247 ●	OO	FGW	PTR	42344	OO	FGW	ANG	42571 (41121)	LA	FGW	ANG
42250	LA	FGW	ANG	42345	LA	FGW	ANG	42572 (41123)	LA	FGW	ANG
42251	LA	FGW	ANG	42346	OO	FGW	ANG	42573 (41127)	LA	FGW	ANG
42252	LA	FGW	ANG	42347	OO	FGW	ANG	42574 (41129)	LA	FGW	ANG
42253	LA	FGW	ANG	42348	OO	FGW	ANG	42575 (41131)	LA	FGW	ANG
42255	LA	FGW	ANG	42349 ●	OO	FGW	ANG	42576 (41133)	LA	FGW	ANG
42256	LA	FGW	ANG	42350 ●	LA	FGW	ANG	42577 (41141)	LA	FGW	ANG
42257	LA	FGW	ANG	42351 ●	LA	FGW	ANG	42578 (41143)	LA	FGW	ANG
42258 ●	OO	FGW	PTR	42353	LA	FGW	FGP	42579 (41145)	LA	FGW	ANG
42259	LA	FGW	ANG	42356	OO	FGW	ANG	42580 (41155)	LA	FGW	PTR
42260	OO	FGW	ANG	42360 ●	LA	FGW	ANG	42581 (41157)	LA	FGW	ANG
42261	OO	FGW	ANG	42361	LA	FGW	ANG	42582 (41163)	LA	FGW	FGP
42263 ●	LA	FGW	ANG	42362 ●	OO	FGW	ANG	42583 (42385)	LA	FGW	PTR
42264	OO	FGW	ANG	42364	OO	FGW	PTR	● Volo Television fitted			
42265 ●	LA	FGW	ANG	42365	OO	FGW	PTR				
42266	OO	FGW	PTR	42381 (41058)	OO	FGW	PTR	GJ2?? - TC *Seating 24F/39S*			
42267	LA	FGW	ANG	42382 (12128)	OO	FGW	PTR	*Number*	*Depot*	*Livery*	*Owner*
42268	LA	FGW	ANG	42383 (12172)	OO	FGW	PTR	46001 (41005)	LA	FGW	ANG
42269	LA	FGW	ANG	42501 (40744)	OO	FGW	ANG	46002 (41029)	LA	FGW	ANG
42271	OO	FGW	ANG	42502 (40731)	OO	FGW	ANG	46003 (41033)	LA	FGW	ANG
42272	OO	FGW	ANG	42503 (40712)	OO	FGW	ANG	46004 (41055)	LA	FGW	ANG
42273	OO	FGW	ANG	42504 (40714)	OO	FGW	ANG	46005 (41065)	LA	FGW	ANG
42275	LA	FGW	ANG	42505 (40228)	OO	FGW	ANG	46006 (41081)	LA	FGW	PTR
42276	LA	FGW	ANG	42506 (40724)	OO	FGW	ANG	46007 (41096)	LA	FGW	PTR
42277	LA	FGW	ANG	42507 (40209)	OO	FGW	ANG	46008 (41109)	LA	FGW	PTR

Right: *Standard class seating on the FGW HST fleet is provided by a fleet of TS and TGS vehicles. Seating on the TS vehicles varies between 68 and 84 depending on the internal layout, whether it is high or low density and how many tables are fitted. TS No. 42056 is illustrated.* **CJM**

First Great Western

46009 (41119)	LA	FGW	PTR	44013	OO	FGW	ANG	44043	OO	FGW	ANG
46010 (41125)	LA	FGW	ANG	44014	OO	FGW	ANG	44049	LA	FGW	ANG
46011 (41139)	LA	FGW	ANG	44015	LA	FGW	ANG	44055	LA	FGW	FGP
46012 (41147)	LA	FGW	PTR	44016	OO	FGW	ANG	44059	LA	FGW	ANG
46013 (41148)	LA	FGW	PTR	44018	LA	FGW	ANG	44060	OO	FGW	PTR
46014 (41168)	LA	FGW	PTR	44020	OO	FGW	ANG	44064	OO	FGW	ANG
46015 (41179)	LA	FGW	ANG	44022	OO	FGW	ANG	44066	LA	FGW	ANG
46016 (41181)	LA	FGW	PTR	44023	OO	FGW	ANG	44067	OO	FGW	ANG
46017 (41184)	LA	FGW	PTR	44024	OO	FGW	ANG	44068	LA	FGW	FGP
46018 (41191)	LA	FGW	PTR	44025	LA	FGW	ANG	44069	OO	FGW	PTR
				44026	OO	FGW	ANG	44074	LA	FGW	FGP

GJ2G - TGS *Seating 67-71S*

Number	Depot	Livery	Owner								
44000	OO	FGW	PTR	44028	LA	FGW	ANG	44076	LA	FGW	FGP
44001	LA	FGW	ANG	44029	LA	FGW	ANG	44078	OO	FGW	PTR
44002	OO	FGW	ANG	44030	OO	FGW	ANG	44079	OO	FGW	PTR
44003	OO	FGW	ANG	44032	LA	FGW	ANG	44081	LA	FGW	FGP
44004	LA	FGW	ANG	44033	OO	FGW	ANG	44083	OO	FGW	PTR
44005	LA	FGW	ANG	44034	LA	FGW	ANG	44086	LA	FGW	ANG
44007	LA	FGW	ANG	44035	LA	FGW	ANG	44090	OO	FGW	PTR
44008	OO	FGW	ANG	44036	OO	FGW	ANG	44091	OO	FGW	PTR
44009	LA	FGW	ANG	44037	OO	FGW	ANG	44093	OO	FGW	ANG
44010	LA	FGW	ANG	44038	LA	FGW	ANG	44097	OO	FGW	PTR
44011	LA	FGW	ANG	44039	LA	FGW	ANG	44100	LA	FGW	FGP
				44040	LA	FGW	ANG	44101	OO	FGW	PTR
				44042	OO	FGW	PTR				

Left: *A fleet of 58 Trailer Guards Standard (TGS) vehicles is operated by FGW; one is marshalled in each passenger set between the standard class vehicles and the power car, providing a conductor's office and luggage stowage area. TGS No. 44000, the first of the build, is illustrated at Oxford.* **CJM**

Class 143
Pacer

Vehicle Length: 51ft 0½in (15.55m)
Height: 12ft 2¼in (3.73m)
Width: 8ft 10½in (2.70m)

Engine: 1 x Cummins LTA10-R per vehicle
Horsepower: 460hp (343kW)
Seats (total/car): 92S, 48S/44S

Number	Formation	Depot	Livery	Owner	Operator						
	DMS+DMSL					143617	55644+55683	EX	FGL	PTR	FGW
						143618	55659+55684	EX	FGL	PTR	FGW
143603	55658+55689	EX	FGL	PTR	FGW	143619	55660+55685	EX	FGL	PTR	FGW
143611	55652+55677	EX	FGL	PTR	FGW	143620	55661+55686	EX	FGL	PTR	FGW
143612	55653+55678	EX	FGL	PTR	FGW	143621	55662+55687	EX	FGL	PTR	FGW

Left: *Eight Class 143 'Pacer' sets are allocated to Exeter and operate on the Exeter to Barnstaple, Exmouth and Paignton branch lines, making rare visits to Plymouth and Bristol. All are painted in FGW Local Lines location livery. Due to passenger numbers these sets often operate in pairs, especially at peak and holiday periods. Set No. 143620 is seen at Exeter St David's forming a Barnstaple service.* **CJM**

Class 150/0
Sprinter

Vehicle Length: (Driving) 65ft 9¾in (20.05m), (Inter) 66ft 2½in (20.18m)
Height: 12ft 4½in (3.77m)
Width: 9ft 3⅛in (2.82m)

Engine: 1 x Cummins NT855R4 of 285hp per car
Horsepower: 855hp (638kW)
Seats (total/car): 240S, 72S/92S/76S

Number	Formation	Depot	Livery	Owner	Op'r						
	DMSL+MS+DMS										
150001	55200+55400+55300	RG	FGB	ANG	FGW	150002	55201+55401+55301	RG	FGB	ANG	FGW

Class 150/1
Sprinter

Vehicle Length: 64ft 9¾in (19.74m)			Engine: 1 x NT855R5 of 285hp per vehicle		
Height: 12ft 4½in (3.77m)			Horsepower: 570hp (425kW)		
Width: 9ft 3⅛in (2.82m)			Seats (total/car): 141S, 71S/70S		

Two-car sets

Number	Formation DMSL+DMS	Depot	Livery	Owner	Operator
150101	52101+57101	PM	FGB	PTR	FGW
150102	52102+57102	PM	FGB	PTR	FGW
150104	52104+57104	PM	FGB	PTR	FGW
150106	52106+57106	PM	FGB	PTR	FGW
150108	52108+57108	PM	FGB	PTR	FGW
150120	52120+57120	EX	FGB	PTR	FGW
150121	52121+57121	EX	FGB	PTR	FGW
150122	52122+57122	EX	FGB	PTR	FGW
150123	52123+57123	EX	FGB	PTR	FGW
150124	52124+57124	EX	FGB	PTR	FGW
150127	52127+57127	EX	FGB	PTR	FGW
150128	52128+57128	EX	FGB	PTR	FGW
150129	52129+57129	EX	FGB	PTR	FGW
150130	52130+57130	EX	FGB	PTR	FGW
150131	52130+57130	EX	FGB	PTR	FGW

Three-car sets

Number	Formation DMSL+DMS+DMS	Depot	Livery	Owner	Op'r
150925	52125+57209+57125	EX	FGB	PTR	FGW
150926	52126+57212+57126	EX	FGB	PTR	FGW

Names applied
150925 *The Heart of Wessex Line*
150129 *Devon & Cornwall Rail Partnership*
150130 *Severnside Community Rail Partnership*

Right: *The Class 150/1 two-car fleet is allocated to Exeter and Bristol depots and operates in the Bristol, Exeter and West of England area. The sets still retain the 2+3 seating. All sets sport blue livery, with three sets carrying stick-on nameplates in support of route and railway partnerships. Set No. 150130 poses 'on shed' at Exeter depot on 22 June 2014.* **CJM**

Class 150/2
Sprinter

Vehicle Length: 64ft 9¾in (19.74m)			Engine: 1 x NT855R5 of 285hp per vehicle		
Height: 12ft 4½in (3.77m)			Horsepower: 570hp (425kW)		
Width: 9ft 3⅛in (2.82m)			Seats (total/car): 116S, 60S/56S		

Number	Formation DMSL+DMS	Depot	Livery	Owner	Operator
150202	52202+57202	PM	FGB	ANG	FGW
150216	52216+57216	PM	FGB	ANG	FGW
150219	52219+57219	PM	FGL	PTR	FGW
150221	52221+57221	PM	FGL	PTR	FGW
150232	52232+57232	PM	FGL	PTR	FGW
150233	52233+57233	PM	FGL	PTR	FGW
150234	52234+57234	PM	FGL	PTR	FGW
150238	52238+57238	PM	FGL	PTR	FGW
150239	52239+57239	PM	FGL	PTR	FGW
150243	52243+57243	PM	FGL	PTR	FGW
150244	52244+57244	PM	FGL	PTR	FGW
150246	52246+57246	PM	FGL	PTR	FGW
150247	52247+57247	PM	FGL	PTR	FGW
150248	52248+57248	PM	FGL	PTR	FGW
150249	52249+57249	PM	FGL	PTR	FGW
150261	52261+57261	PM	FGB	PTR	FGW
150263	52263+57263	PM	FGL	PTR	FGW
150265	52265+57265	PM	FGL	PTR	FGW
150266	52266+57266	PM	FGL	PTR	FGW

Name applied
150261 *The Tarka Line The First 25 Years 1989-2014*

Right: *Bristol depot has an allocation of 19 Class 150/2 corridor sets, which operate in the Bristol, Wiltshire, Gloucestershire, Avon, Somerset and Cornwall areas alongside the Class 150/1 sets. With the exception of Nos. 150202/216, all were until late 2014 painted in FGW Local Lines colours, but a start has now been made on repainting into FGW blue. All sets have the refurbished 2+2 interior layout. Set No. 150233 is illustrated.* **CJM**

First Great Western

Class 153

Vehicle Length: 76ft 5in (23.29m)		Engine: 1 x NT855R5 of 285hp
Height: 12ft 3⅛in (3.75m)		Horsepower: 285hp (213kW)
Width: 8ft 10in (2.70m)		Seats (total/car): 72S

Number	Formation DMSL	Depot	Livery	Owner	Operator		Number	Formation	Depot	Livery	Owner	Operator
153305	52305	EX	FGL	ANG	FGW		153368	57368	EX	FGL	ANG	FGW
153318	52318	EX	FGL	ANG	FGW		153369	57369	EX	FGB	ANG	FGW
153325	52325	EX	LMI	PTR	FGW		153370	57370	EX	FGL	ANG	FGW
153329	52329	EX	FGB	ANG	FGW		153372	57372	EX	FGL	ANG	FGW
153333	52333	EX	LMI	PTR	FGW		153373	57373	EX	FGB	ANG	FGW
153361	57361	EX	FGB	ANG	FGW		153377	57377	EX	FGL	ANG	FGW
							153380	57380	EX	FGB	ANG	FGW
							153382	57382	EX	FGL	ANG	FGW

Left: Fourteen single-car Class 153s are allocated to Exeter depot and operate on all branch lines radiating from Exeter as well as on lines in Cornwall, Avon, Wiltshire and Gloucestershire. The single cars can be used on their own, or to supplement two-car sets to provide extra seating at busy times. Sets are either painted in Local Lines or all-blue livery. Set No. 153377 is viewed at Westbury on 9 September 2014 on a Swindon shuttle service. It is viewed from its small cab end. **CJM**

Class 158/0 (2-car)

Vehicle Length: 76ft 1¾in (23.21m)		Engine: 1 x Cummins NTA855R of 350hp per vehicle
Height: 12ft 6in (3.81m)		Horsepower: 700hp (522kW)
Width: 9ft 3¾in (2.82m)		Seats (total/car): 134S, 66S/68S

Number	Formation DMSL+DMSL	Depot	Livery	Owner	Operator		Number	Formation	Depot	Livery	Owner	Operator
158763	52763+57763	PM	FGL	PTR	FGW		158766	52766+57766	PM	FGL	PTR	FGW

Class 158/0 (3-car)

158798

Vehicle Length: 76ft 1¾in (23.21m)		Engine: 1 x Cummins NTA855R of 350hp per vehicle
Height: 12ft 6in (3.81m)		Horsepower: 1,050hp (783kW)
Width: 9ft 3¼in (2.82m)		Seats (total/car): 200S, 66S/66S/68S

158950 - 158961

Vehicle Length: 76ft 1¾in (23.21m)		Engine: 1 x Cummins NTA855R of 350hp per vehicle
Height: 12ft 6in (3.81m)		Horsepower: 1,050hp (783kW)
Width: 9ft 3¼in (2.82m)		Seats (total/car): 204S, 66S/70S/68S

Number	Formation DMSL+MSL+DMSL		Depot	Livery	Owner	Operator
158798	52798+58715+57798		PM	ADV	PTR	FGW

Number	Formation DMSL+DMSL+DMSL		Depot	Livery	Owner	Operator
158950	(158751/761)	52751+52761+57761	PM	FGL	PTR	FGW
158951	(158751/764)	52751+52764+57764	PM	FGL	PTR	FGW
158952	(158745/762)	52745+52762+57762	PM	FGL	PTR	FGW
158953	(158745/750)	52745+52750+57750	PM	FGL	PTR	FGW
158954	(158747/760)	52747+52760+57760	PM	FGL	PTR	FGW
158955	(158747/765)	52747+52765+57765	PM	FGL	PTR	FGW
158956	(158748/768)	52748+52768+57768	PM	FGL	PTR	FGW
158957	(158748/771)	52748+52771+57771	PM	FGL	PTR	FGW
158958	(158746/776)	52746+52776+57776	PM	FGL	PTR	FGW
158959	(158746/778)	52746+52778+57778	PM	FGL	PTR	FGW
158960	(158769/749)	57769+52769+57749	PM	FGL	PTR	FGW
158961	(158767/749)	57767+52767+52749	PM	FGL	PTR	FGW

Right: *Deployed on longer-distance services mainly in the Bristol and Cardiff area is a fleet of 15 Class 158s. Two are formed as two-car and 13 as three-car. Class 158s are used on such routes as the Cardiff-Portsmouth. Twelve of the three-car sets are formed of three driving cars, and can be split to operate as two-car sets if needed. Most sets are formed of ex-Scottish Region sets and thus have modified obstacle deflector plates. Purpose-built three-car No. 158798 is seen at Gloucester on 17 December 2014 displaying a Portsmouth advertising livery.* **CJM**

Class 165/1 (3-car)
Networker Turbo

Vehicle Length: (Driving) 75ft 2½in (22.91m), (Inter) 74ft 6½in (22.72m)
Height: 12ft 5¼in (3.79m)
Width: 9ft 5½in (2.81m)
Engine: 1 x Perkins 2006TWH of 350hp per car
Horsepower: 1,050hp (783kW)
Seats (total/car): 16F/270S, 16F-66S/106S/98S

Number	Formation DMCL+MS+DMS	Depot	Livery	Owner	Operator
165101	58953+55415+58916	RG	FGT	ANG	FGW
165102	58954+55416+58917	RG	FGT	ANG	FGW
165103	58955+55417+58918	RG	FGT	ANG	FGW
165104	58956+55418+58919	RG	FGT	ANG	FGW
165105	58957+55419+58920	RG	FGT	ANG	FGW
165106	58958+55420+58921	RG	FGT	ANG	FGW
165107	58959+55421+58922	RG	FGT	ANG	FGW
165108	58960+55422+58923	RG	FGT	ANG	FGW
165109	58961+55423+58924	RG	FGT	ANG	FGW
165110	58962+55424+58925	RG	FGT	ANG	FGW
165111	58963+55425+58926	RG	FGT	ANG	FGW
165112	58964+55426+58927	RG	FGT	ANG	FGW
165113	58965+55427+58928	RG	FGT	ANG	FGW
165114	58966+55428+58929	RG	FGT	ANG	FGW
165116	58968+55430+58931	RG	FGT	ANG	FGW
165117	58969+55431+58932	RG	FGT	ANG	FGW

Class 165/1 (2-car)
Networker Turbo

Vehicle Length: 75ft 2½in (22.91m)
Height: 12ft 5¼in (3.79m)
Width: 9ft 5½in (2.81m)
Engine: 1 x Perkins 2006TWH of 350hp per car
Horsepower: 700hp (522kW)
Seats (total/car): 16F/170S, 16F-72S/98S

Number	Formation DMCL+DMS	Depot	Livery	Owner	Operator	Number	Formation	Depot	Livery	Owner	Operator
						165122	58883+58937	RG	FGT	ANG	FGW
						165123	58884+58938	RG	FGT	ANG	FGW
165118	58879+58933	RG	FGT	ANG	FGW	165124	58885+58939	RG	FGT	ANG	FGW
165119	58880+58934	RG	FGT	ANG	FGW	165125	58886+58940	RG	FGT	ANG	FGW
165120	58881+58935	RG	FGT	ANG	FGW	165126	58887+58941	RG	FGT	ANG	FGW
165121	58882+58936	RG	FGT	ANG	FGW	165127	58888+58942	RG	FGT	ANG	FGW

Right: *Introduced under the Network SouthEast modernisation plan for the Thames Valley and Chiltern lines, the Class 165 'Networker Turbo' sets still form the backbone of local services out of Paddington. In the near future this will largely change following the opening of Crossrail and the electrification of the FGW lines. '165s' are formed in either two-or three-car formations. All are allocated to Reading. Sets are painted in FGW Dynamic Lines colours. Unit No. 165128 is viewed at Oxford, with its DMS vehicle nearest the camera.* **CJM**

First Great Western

165128	58889+58943	RG	FGT	ANG	FGW	165133	58894+58948	RG	FGT	ANG	FGW
165129	58890+58944	RG	FGT	ANG	FGW	165134	58895+58949	RG	FGT	ANG	FGW
165130	58891+58945	RG	FGT	ANG	FGW	165135	58896+58950	RG	FGT	ANG	FGW
165131	58892+58946	RG	FGT	ANG	FGW	165136	58897+58951	RG	FGT	ANG	FGW
165132	58893+58947	RG	FGT	ANG	FGW	165137	58898+58952	RG	FGT	ANG	FGW

Passenger Train Operating Companies - First Great Western

Class 166
Networker Turbo Express

Vehicle Length: (Driving) 75ft 2½in (22.91m), (Inter) 74ft 6½in (22.72m)
Height: 12ft 5¼in (3.79m)   Engine: 1 x Perkins 2006TWH of 350hp per car
Width: 9ft 5½in (2.81m)   Horsepower: 1,050hp (783kW)
Seats (total/car): 16F/258S, 90S/96S/16F-72S

Number	Formation DMSL+MS+DMCL	Depot	Livery	Owner	Operator	Name
166201	58101+58601+58122	RG	FGB	ANG	FGW	
166202	58102+58602+58123	RG	FGT	ANG	FGW	
166203	58103+58603+58124	RG	FGT	ANG	FGW	
166204	58104+58604+58125	RG	FGT	ANG	FGW	
166205	58105+58605+58126	RG	FGT	ANG	FGW	
166206	58106+58606+58127	RG	FGT	ANG	FGW	
166207	58107+58607+58128	RG	FGT	ANG	FGW	
166208	58108+58608+58129	RG	FGT	ANG	FGW	
166209	58109+58609+58130	RG	FGT	ANG	FGW	
166210	58110+58610+58131	RG	FGT	ANG	FGW	
166211	58111+58611+58132	RG	FGT	ANG	FGW	
166212	58112+58612+58133	RG	FGT	ANG	FGW	
166213	58113+58613+58134	RG	FGT	ANG	FGW	
166214	58114+58614+58135	RG	FGT	ANG	FGW	
166215	58115+58615+58136	RG	FGT	ANG	FGW	
166216	58116+58616+58137	RG	FGT	ANG	FGW	
166217	58117+58617+58138	RG	FGT	ANG	FGW	
166218	58118+58618+58139	RG	FGT	ANG	FGW	
166219	58119+58619+58140	RG	FGT	ANG	FGW	
166220	58120+58620+58141	RG	FGT	ANG	FGW	
166221	58121+58621+58142	RG	FGB	ANG	FGW	*Reading Train Care Depot*

Left: *When the 'Networker Turbo' stock was introduced, a fleet of 21 outer-suburban or main-line three-car sets were introduced for the express services on the Paddington-Oxford corridor. Until 2013 sets had first class seating in both outer vehicles, but this has now been reduced to one coach to provide extra standard class accommodation. In 2014 a start was made on fleet refurbishment and the fitting of disabled access toilets. The refurbished sets have emerged painted in all blue rather than Dynamic Lines colours. Set No. 166216 is seen at Oxford on 29 May 2014 with a service from Paddington. CJM*

Class 180
Adelante

Vehicle Length: (Driving) 75ft 7in (23.71m), (Inter) 75ft 5in (23.03m)
Height: 12ft 4in (3.75m)   Engine: 1 x Cummins QSK19 of 750hp per car
Width: 9ft 2in (2.80m)   Horsepower: 3,750hp (2,796kW)
Seats (total/car): 42F/226S, 46S/42F/68S/56S/56S

Number	Formation DMSL(A)+MFL+MSL+MSLRB+DMSL(B)	Depot	Livery	Owner	Operator
180102	50902+54902+55902+56902+59902	OO	FGW	ANG	FGW
180103	50903+54903+55903+56903+59903	OO	FGW	ANG	FGW
180104	50904+54904+55904+56904+59904	OO	FGW	ANG	FGW
180106	50906+54906+55906+56906+59906	OO	FGW	ANG	FGW
180108	50908+54908+55908+56908+59908	OO	FGW	ANG	FGW

Right: *Today, First Great Western operates a fleet of five Class 180 'Adelante' sets. These main-line sets were introduced post-privatisation to supplement the HST fleet, but eventually fell from favour and were transferred away from the FGW area. The current allocation returned a few years ago to assist with fleet shortages. All are refurbished and sport Dynamic Lines colours and are based at Old Oak Common; they are mainly used on the Paddington-Oxford-Worcester corridor. Set No. 180106 is viewed at Oxford.* **CJM**

Mk3 Hauled Stock

Vehicle Length: 75ft 0in (22.86m)	Width: 8ft 11in (2.71m)
Height: 12ft 9in (3.88m)	Bogie Type: BT10

AJ1G - RFB *Seating 18F*

Number	Depot	Livery	Owner
10219	PZ	FGW	PTR
10225	PZ	FGW	PTR
10232	PZ	FGW	PTR

AU4G - SLEP *Comps 12*

Number	Depot	Livery	Owner
10532	PZ	FGW	PTR
10534	PZ	FGW	PTR
10563	PZ	FGW	PTR
10584	PZ	FGW	PTR

10589	PZ	FGW	PTR
10590	PZ	FGW	PTR
10594	PZ	FGW	PTR
10596	PZ	FGW	PTR
10601	PZ	FGW	PTR
10612	PZ	FGW	PTR
10616	PZ	FGW	PTR

AC2G - TSO *Seating 45S*

Number	Depot	Livery	Owner
12100	PZ	FGW	PTR
12142	PZ	FGW	PTE

12161	PZ	FGW	PTR

AE1H - BFO *Seating 36F*

Number	Depot	Livery	Owner
17173	PZ	FGW	PTR
17174	PZ	FGW	PTR
17175	PZ	FGW	PTR

Right: *The only loco-hauled stock operated by First Great Western are the Mk3 vehicles used on the 'Night Riviera' sleeping car train on the Paddington-Penzance corridor. This fleet consists of 11 sleeping cars and nine saloon vehicles. RFB No. 10232 is shown; these three vehicles provide refreshment services and also seat 18 in first-class-style seats. All saloon seating on the sleeper services is of the first class design.* **CJM**

Class 800 and 801 'Super Express'

In summer 2012 Agility Trains signed a contract with the Department for Transport (DfT) to design, build, finance and maintain 596 state-of-the-art carriages for the Great Western Main Line and East Coast Main Line as part of the Intercity Express Programme to replace HST and IC225 trains.

Hitachi Rail Europe and John Laing are the main shareholders of Agility Trains and in summer 2013 the Secretary of State for Transport announced that an additional contract for the provision of an extra 270 carriages for the East Coast Main Line was to be placed, bringing the total number of vehicles ordered to 866.

Great Western will have between 2016 and 2019 46 five-car Class 800 dual mode and 12 nine-car electric Class 801 trains sets delivered. The first 12 trains are to be built by Hitachi in Kasado, Japan, with the remainder built at a new Hitachi plant at Newton Aycliffe.

Service Stock

HST Barrier Vehicles

Number	Depot	Livery	Owner	Former Identity					
6330	PM	FGB	ANG	BFK - 14084	6338	LA	FGB	ANG	BG - 81581/92180
6336	LA	FGB	ANG	BG - 81591/92185	6348	PM	FGB	ANG	BG - 81233/92963

First Hull Trains

Address: ⊠ Europa House, 184 Ferensway, Kingston-upon-Hull, HU1 3UT
　　　　　　 ✆ customer.services@hulltrains.co.uk
　　　　　　 ✆ 0845 676 9905
　　　　　　 ⓘ www.hulltrains.co.uk

Managing Director:　　Will Dunnett　**General Manager:**　　Cath Bellamy
Franchise Dates:　　Private Open Access Operator, agreement to December 2016
Principal Route:　　London King's Cross - Hull
Depots:　　Old Oak Common (OO) [Operated by FGW], Crofton (XW)
Parent Company:　　First Group PLC

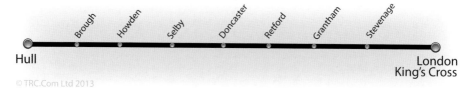

© TRC.Com Ltd 2013

Hull — Brough — Howden — Selby — Doncaster — Retford — Grantham — Stevenage — London King's Cross

Class 180
Adelante

Vehicle Length: (Driving) 75ft 7in (23.71m), (Inter) 75ft 5in (23.03m)
Height: 12ft 4in (3.75m)　　*Engine: 1 x Cummins QSK19 of 750hp per vehicle*
Width: 9ft 2in (2.80m)　　*Horsepower: 3,750hp (2,796kW)*
　　　　　　　　　　　　Seats (total/car): 42F/226S, 46S/42F/68S/56S/56S

Number	Formation	Depot	Livery	Owner	Operator
	DMSL(A)+MFL+MSF+MSLRB+DMSL(B)				
180109	50909+54909+55909+56909+59909	OO/XW	FHT	ANG	FHT
180110	50910+54910+55910+56910+59910	OO/XW	FHT	ANG	FHT
180111	50911+54911+55911+56911+59911	OO/XW	FHT	ANG	FHT
180113	50913+54913+55913+56913+59913	OO/XW	FHT	ANG	FHT

Below: *Open access operator First Hull Trains uses four Class 180 sets on its London King's Cross to Hull services. These five-car trains replaced Class 222 stock which in turn had replaced Class 170 stock, the operator continually requiring longer trains to meet demand. The refurbished sets, painted in First Dynamic Lines livery, are maintained at Old Oak Common and Crofton. All sets have lost their original cowling around the Dellner coupling. Set No. 180111 is seen at Selby on 22 April 2014.* **CJM**

Abellio ScotRail

Address: ✉ Atrium Court, 50 Waterloo Street, Glasgow, G2 6HQ

✆ scotrail.enquiries@firstgroup.com, ✆ 08700 005151

ⓘ www.firstscotrail.com

Managing Director: Steve Montgomery

Franchise Dates: 17 October 2004 - March 2015

From 1 April 2015 Scottish Railways will be operated by Abellio Scotland, with a new 7 to 10 year franchise

Principal Routes: All Scottish services

Depots: Corkerhill (CK), Glasgow Shields Road (GW), Haymarket (HA), Inverness (IS)

Class 156

Vehicle Length: 75ft 6in (23.03m)	Engine: 1 x Cummins NT855R5 of 285hp per car
Height: 12ft 6in (3.81m)	Horsepower: 570hp (425kW)
Width: 8ft 11in (2.73m)	Seats (total/car): 142S, 70 or 72S

Number	Formation DMSL+DMS	Depot	Livery	Owner	Operator
156430	52430+57430	CK	FSS	ANG	FSR
156431	52431+57431	CK	FSS	ANG	FSR
156432	52432+57432	CK	FSS	ANG	FSR
156433	52433+57433	CK	FSS	ANG	FSR
156434	52434+57434	CK	FSS	ANG	FSR
156435	52435+57435	CK	FSS	ANG	FSR
156436	52436+57436	CK	FSS	ANG	FSR
156437	52437+57437	CK	FSS	ANG	FSR
156439	52439+57439	CK	FSS	ANG	FSR
156442	52442+57442	CK	FSS	ANG	FSR
156445	52445+57445	CK	FSS	ANG	FSR
156446	52446+57446	CK	FSR	ANG	FSR
156447	52447+57447	CK	FSR	ANG	FSR
156449	52449+57449	CK	FSR	ANG	FSR
156450	52450+57450	CK	FSR	ANG	FSR
156453	52453+57453	CK	FSR	ANG	FSR
156456	52456+57456	CK	FSR	ANG	FSR
156457	52457+57457	CK	FSR	ANG	FSR
156458	52458+57458	CK	FSR	ANG	FSR
156462	52462+57462	CK	FSR	ANG	FSR
156465	52465+57465	CK	FSR	ANG	FSR
156467	52467+57467	CK	FSR	ANG	FSR
156474	52474+57474	CK	FSR	ANG	FSR
156476	52476+57476	CK	FSR	ANG	FSR
156477	52477+57477	CK	FSR	ANG	FSR
156478	52478+57478	CK	FSR	ANG	FSR
156485	52485+57485	CK	FSR	ANG	FSR
156492	52492+57492	CK	FSS	ANG	FSR
156493	52493+57493	CK	FSS	ANG	FSR
156494	52494+57494	CK	FSS	ANG	FSR
156495	52495+57495	CK	FSS	ANG	FSR
156496	52496+57496	CK	FSR	ANG	FSR
156499	52499+57499	CK	FSR	ANG	FSR
156500	52500+57500	CK	FSS	ANG	FSR
156501	52501+57501	CK	FSS	ANG	FSR
156502	52502+57502	CK	FSS	ANG	FSR
156503	52503+57503	CK	FSR	ANG	FSR
156504	52504+57504	CK	FSR	ANG	FSR
156505	52505+57505	CK	FSR	ANG	FSR
156506	52506+57506	CK	FSR	ANG	FSR
156507	52507+57507	CK	FSR	ANG	FSR
156508	52508+57508	CK	FSR	ANG	FSR
156509	52509+57509	CK	FSR	ANG	FSR
156510	52510+57510	CK	FSS	ANG	FSR
156511	52511+57511	CK	FSS	ANG	FSR
156512	52512+57512	CK	FSS	ANG	FSR
156513	52513+57513	CK	FSS	ANG	FSR
156514	52514+57514	CK	FSS	ANG	FSR

Right: *Currently the largest operator of Class 156s in the UK is First ScotRail, which in 2015 has an allocation of 48 sets maintained at Corkerhill depot in Glasgow. The sets are used on medium-distance passenger services mainly in the Scottish Lowland area. All sets have 2+2 seating and repainting into the latest First ScotRail Saltire livery is progressing. Set No. 156514 is seen under the roof at Glasgow Central station.* **CJM**

Train Operating Companies

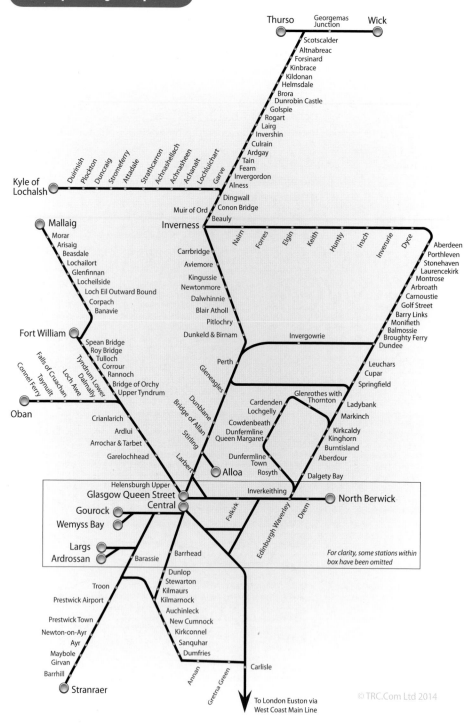

For clarity, some stations within box have been omitted

© TRC.Com Ltd 2014

To London Euston via West Coast Main Line

Class 158

Vehicle Length: 76ft 1¾in (23.21m)
Height: 12ft 6in (3.81m)
Width: 9ft 3¼in (2.82m)

Engine: 1 x Cummins NTA855R of 350hp per vehicle
Horsepower: 700hp (522kW)
Seats (total/car): 14F/116S, 14F-46S/70S, * 138S, 68S/70S

Number	Formation DMCL/DMSL *+DMS	Depot	Livery	Owner	Operator
158701	52701+57701	IS	FSR	PTR	FSR
158702	52702+57702	IS	FSR	PTR	FSR
158703	52703+57703	IS	FSR	PTR	FSR
158704	52704+57704	IS	FSR	PTR	FSR
158705	52705+57705	IS	FSR	PTR	FSR
158706	52706+57706	IS	FSR	PTR	FSR
158707	52707+57707	IS	FSR	PTR	FSR
158708	52708+57708	IS	FSR	PTR	FSR
158709	52709+57709	IS	FSR	PTR	FSR
158710	52710+57710	IS	FSR	PTR	FSR
158711	52711+57711	IS	FSR	PTR	FSR
158712	52712+57712	IS	FSR	PTR	FSR
158713	52713+57713	IS	FSR	PTR	FSR
158714	52714+57714	IS	FSR	PTR	FSR
158715	52715+57715	IS	FSR	PTR	FSR
158716	52716+57716	IS	FSR	PTR	FSR
158717	52717+57717	IS	FSR	PTR	FSR
158718	52718+57718	IS	FSR	PTR	FSR
158719	52719+57719	IS	FSR	PTR	FSR
158720	52720+57720	IS	FSR	PTR	FSR
158721	52721+57721	IS	FSR	PTR	FSR
158722	52722+57722	IS	FSR	PTR	FSR
158723	52723+57723	IS	FSR	PTR	FSR
158724	52724+57724	IS	FSR	PTR	FSR
158725	52725+57725	IS	FSR	PTR	FSR
158726	52726+57726	HA	FSR	PTR	FSR
158727	52727+57727	IS	FSR	PTR	FSR
158728	52728+57728	IS	FSR	PTR	FSR
158729	52729+57729	HA	FSR	PTR	FSR
158730	52730+57730	HA	FSR	PTR	FSR
158731	52731+57731	HA	FSR	PTR	FSR
158732	52732+57732	HA	FSR	PTR	FSR
158733	52733+57733	HA	FSR	PTR	FSR
158734	52734+57734	HA	FSR	PTR	FSR
158735	52735+57735	HA	FSR	PTR	FSR
158736	52736+57736	HA	FSR	PTR	FSR
158737	52737+57737	HA	FSR	PTR	FSR
158738	52738+57738	HA	FSR	PTR	FSR
158739	52739+57739	HA	FSR	PTR	FSR
158740	52740+57740	HA	FSR	PTR	FSR
158741	52741+57741	HA	FSR	PTR	FSR
158782	52782*+57782	HA	FSS	ANG	FSR
158786	52786*+57786	HA	FSS	ANG	FSR
158789	52789*+57789	HA	FSS	ANG	FSR
158867	52867*+57867	HA	FSS	ANG	FSR
158868	52868*+57868	HA	FSS	ANG	FSR
158869	52869*+57869	HA	FSS	ANG	FSR
158870	52870*+57870	HA	FSS	ANG	FSR
158871	52871*+57871	HA	FSS	ANG	FSR

Name applied
158707 *Far North Line*

Right: *Inverness and Haymarket depots have an allocation of 49 two-car Class 158s which share longer-distance work with the Class 170 fleet. In 2015 the fleet is painted in a mix of First Group 'swirl' and blue/white Saltire liveries. Several different styles of front-end lamp cluster and obstacle deflector plate can be found on this fleet. Set No. 158730 is seen at Edinburgh Waverley.* **CJM**

Class 170/3
Turbostar

Vehicle Length: 77ft 6in (23.62m)
Height: 12ft 4½in (3.77m)
Width: 8ft 10in (2.69m)

Engine: 1 x MTU 6R 183TD13H of 422hp per vehicle
Horsepower: 1,266hp (944kW)
Seats (total/car): 164S, 57S/43S/64S

Number	Formation DMSL+MS+DMSL	Depot	Livery	Owner	Operator	
170393	50393+56393+79393	HA	FSS	PTR	FSR	
170394+	50394+56394+79394	HA	FSS	PTR	FSR	
170395+	50395+56395+79395	HA	FSS	PTR	FSR	
170396	50396+56396+79396	HA	FSR	PTR	FSR	+ Standard class only

Class 170/4
Turbostar

Vehicle Length: 77ft 6in (23.62m)
Height: 12ft 4½in (3.77m)
Width: 8ft 10in (2.69m)

Engine: 1 x MTU 6R 183TD13H of 422hp per vehicle
Horsepower: 1,266hp (944kW)
(170431/432 have 3 x 483hp engines giving 1,449hp)
Seats (total/car): 18F/168S 9F-43S/76S/9F-49S

Number	Formation DMCL+MS+DMCL	Depot	Livery	Owner	Operator	Name
170401	50401+56401+79401	HA	FSR	PTR	FSR	*Sir Moir Lockhead OBE*
170402	50402+56402+79402	HA	FSS	PTR	FSR	
170403	50403+56403+79403	HA	FSR	PTR	FSR	
170404	50404+56404+79404	HA	FSR	PTR	FSR	

Abellio ScotRail

170405	50405+56405+79405	HA	FSR	PTR	FSR	*Riverside Museum*
170406	50406+56406+79406	HA	FSR	PTR	FSR	
170407	50407+56407+79407	HA	FSR	PTR	FSR	*University of Aberdeen*
170408	50408+56408+79408	HA	FSR	PTR	FSR	
170409	50409+56409+79409	HA	FSR	PTR	FSR	
170410	50410+56410+79410	HA	FSR	PTR	FSR	
170411	50411+56411+79411	HA	FSR	PTR	FSR	
170412	50412+56412+79412	HA	FSS	PTR	FSR	
170413	50413+56413+79413	HA	FSR	PTR	FSR	
170414	50414+56414+79414	HA	FSR	PTR	FSR	
170415	50415+56415+79415	HA	FSS	PTR	FSR	
170416	50416+56416+79416	HA	FSR	EVL	FSR	
170417	50417+56417+79417	HA	FSR	EVL	FSR	
170418	50418+56418+79418	HA	FSS	EVL	FSR	
170419	50419+56419+79419	HA	FSR	EVL	FSR	
170420	50420+56420+79420	HA	FSR	EVL	FSR	
170421	50421+56421+79421	HA	FSR	EVL	FSR	
170422	50422+56422+79422	HA	FSR	EVL	FSR	
170423	50423+56423+79423	HA	FSR	EVL	FSR	
170424	50424+56424+79424	HA	FSR	EVL	FSR	
170425	50425+56425+79425	HA	FSS	PTR	FSR	
170426	50426+56426+79426	HA	FSS	PTR	FSR	
170427	50427+56427+79427	HA	FSS	PTR	FSR	
170428	50428+56428+79428	HA	FSS	PTR	FSR	
170429	50429+56429+79429	HA	FSS	PTR	FSR	
170430	50430+56430+79430	HA	FSS	PTR	FSR	
170431	50431+56431+79431	HA	FSS	PTR	FSR	
170432	50432+56432+79432	HA	FSS	PTR	FSR	
170433	50433+56433+79433	HA	FSS	PTR	FSR	
170434	50434+56434+79434	HA	FSS	PTR	FSR	

Class 170/4
Turbostar

Vehicle Length: 77ft 6in (23.62m)
Height: 12ft 4½in (3.77m)
Width: 8ft 10in (2.69m)

Engine: 1 x MTU 6R 183TD13H of 422hp per vehicle
Horsepower: 1,266hp (944kW)
Seats: 170450-170457 (total/car) 9F/180S, 55S/76S/9F,49S
170458-170478 (total/car) 200S, 57S/76S/67S

Number	Formation	Depot	Livery	Owner	Op'r
	DMSL+MS+DMSL/DMCL§				
170450	50450+56450+79450§	HA	FSS	PTR	FSR
170451	50451+56451+79451§	HA	FSS	PTR	FSR
170452	50452+56452+79452§	HA	FSS	PTR	FSR
170453	50453+56453+79453§	HA	FSS	PTR	FSR
170454	50454+56454+79454§	HA	FSS	PTR	FSR
170455	50455+56455+79455§	HA	FSS	PTR	FSR
170456	50456+56456+79456§	HA	FSS	PTR	FSR
170457	50457+56457+79457§	HA	FSS	PTR	FSR
170458	50458+56458+79458	HA	FSS	PTR	FSR
170459	50459+56459+79459	HA	FSS	PTR	FSR
170460	50460+56460+79460	HA	FSS	PTR	FSR
170461	50461+56461+79461	HA	FSS	PTR	FSR
170470	50470+56470+79470	HA	FSS	PTR	FSR
170471	50471+56471+79471	HA	FSS	PTR	FSR
170472	50472+56472+79472	HA	FSS	PTR	FSR
170473	50473+56473+79473	HA	FSS	PTR	FSR
170474	50474+56474+79474	HA	FSS	PTR	FSR
170475	50475+56475+79475	HA	FSS	PTR	FSR
170476	50476+56476+79476	HA	FSS	PTR	FSR
170477	50477+56477+79477	HA	FSS	PTR	FSR
170478	50478+56478+79478	HA	FSS	PTR	FSR

Left: *First ScotRail has a fleet of 59 Class 170 'Turbostar' DMUs on its books allocated to Haymarket. The sets come with different internal configurations with some including first class accommodation and set out for main-line operations, while others are configured for more outer-suburban duties with all-standard-class seating. Livery is a mix of First Group and blue/white Saltire colours. Showing the latest livery, set No. 170451, one of the sets which now sports first class seating in one driving car, is seen departing from Edinburgh Waverley.*
CJM

Passenger Train Operating Companies - Abellio ScotRail

Class 314

Vehicle Length: (Driving) 64ft 11½in (19.80m)
(Inter) 65ft 4¼in (19.92m)
Height: 11ft 6½in (3.58m)
Width: 9ft 3in (2.82m)
Horsepower: 880hp (656kW)
Seats (total/car): 212S, 68S/76S/68S

Number	Formation DMSO(A)+PTSO+DMSO(B)	Depot	Livery	Owner	Operator
314201	64583+71450+64584	GW	FSP	ANG	FSR
314202	64585+71451+64586	GW	FSP	ANG	FSR
314203	64587+71452+64588*	GW	FSS	ANG	FSR
314204	64589+71453+64590	GW	FSS	ANG	FSR
314205	64591+71454+64592	GW	FSS	ANG	FSR
314206	64593+71455+64594	GW	FSP	ANG	FSR
314207	64595+71456+64596	GW	FSP	ANG	FSR
314208	64597+71457+64598	GW	FSS	ANG	FSR
314209	64599+71458+64600	GW	FSP	ANG	FSR
314210	64601+71459+64602	GW	FSP	ANG	FSR
314211	64603+71460+64604	GW	FSS	ANG	FSR
314212	64604+71461+64606	GW	FSS	ANG	FSR
314213	64607+71462+64608	GW	FSP	ANG	FSR
314214	64609+71463+64610	GW	FSS	ANG	FSR
314215	64611+71464+64612	GW	FSP	ANG	FSR
314216	64613+71465+64614	GW	FSP	ANG	FSR

* 64588 was rebuilt from Class 507 car No. 64426 and seats 74S

Right: _Some of the Glasgow area suburban services are operated by a fleet of 16 1972-design BREL-built three-car sets. These units have been largely refurbished and many now sport the latest ScotRail blue/white livery, as shown on set No. 314208 under the great roof at Glasgow Central on 2 July 2014. These sets seat 212 standard class passengers in a mix of 2+2 and 2+3 seating._ **CJM**

Class 318

Vehicle Length: (Driving) 65ft 0¾in (19.83m)
(Inter) 65ft 4¼in (19.92m)
Height: 12ft 1½in (3.70m)
Width: 9ft 3in (2.82m)
Horsepower: 1,328hp (996kW)
Seats (total/car): 216S, 66S/79S/71S

Number	Formation DTSO(A)+MSO+DTSO(B)	Depot	Livery	Owner	Operator	Name
318250	77240+62866+77260	GW	FSP	EVL	FSR	
318251	77241+62867+77261	GW	FSS	EVL	FSR	
318252	77242+62868+77262	GW	FSS	EVL	FSR	
318253	77243+62869+77263	GW	FSP	EVL	FSR	
318254	77244+62870+77264	GW	FSS	EVL	FSR	
318255	77245+62871+77265	GW	FSP	EVL	FSR	
318256	77246+62872+77266	GW	FSP	EVL	FSR	
318257	77247+62873+77267	GW	FSS	EVL	FSR	
318258	77248+62874+77268	GW	FSP	EVL	FSR	
318259	77249+62875+77269	GW	FSS	EVL	FSR	
318260	77250+62876+77270	GW	FSP	EVL	FSR	
318261	77251+62877+77271	GW	FSP	EVL	FSR	
318262	77252+62878+77272	GW	FSP	EVL	FSR	
318263	77253+62879+77273	GW	FSP	EVL	FSR	
318264	77254+62880+77274	GW	FSS	EVL	FSR	
318265	77255+62881+77275	GW	FSP	EVL	FSR	
318266	77256+62882+77276	GW	FSP	EVL	FSR	_Strathclyder_
318267	77257+62883+77277	GW	FSP	EVL	FSR	
318268	77258+62884+77278	GW	FSP	EVL	FSR	
318269	77259+62885+77279	GW	FSP	EVL	FSR	
318270	77288+62890+77289	GW	FSP	EVL	FSR	

Left: *Glasgow Shields Road depot has a fleet of 21 three-car Class 318 outer-suburban EMUs, which usually operate on the Argyle line. These sets originally had front-end gangway doors, but several years ago these were removed to provide a full-width driving cab and improve visibility. Sets can be found in both Glasgow-based carmine and cream and the latest ScotRail blue/white Saltire colours. Set No. 318251 is shown.* **Robin Ralston**

Class 320

Vehicle Length: (Driving) 65ft 0¾in (19.83m)		Width: 9ft 3in (2.82m)	
(Inter) 65ft 4¼in (19.92m)		Horsepower: 1,328hp (996kW)	
Height: 12ft 4¾in (3.78m)		Seats (total/car): 227S, 76S/76S/75S	

Number	Formation DTSO(A)+MSO+DTSO(B)	Depot	Livery	Owner	Operator
320301	77899+63021+77921	GW	FSS	EVL	FSR
320302	77900+63022+77922	GW	FSS	EVL	FSR
320303	77901+63023+77923	GW	FSS	EVL	FSR
320304	77902+63024+77924	GW	FSS	EVL	FSR
320305	77903+63025+77925	GW	FSS	EVL	FSR
320306	77904+63026+77926	GW	FSS	EVL	FSR
320307	77905+63027+77927	GW	FSS	EVL	FSR
320308	77906+63028+77928	GW	FSS	EVL	FSR
320309	77907+63029+77929	GW	FSS	EVL	FSR
320310	77908+63030+77930	GW	FSS	EVL	FSR
320311	77909+63031+77931	GW	FSS	EVL	FSR
320312	77910+63032+77932	GW	FSS	EVL	FSR
320313	77911+63033+77933	GW	FSS	EVL	FSR
320314	77912+63034+77934	GW	FSS	EVL	FSR
320315	77913+63035+77935	GW	FSS	EVL	FSR
320316	77914+63036+77936	GW	FSS	EVL	FSR
320317	77915+63037+77937	GW	FSS	EVL	FSR
320318	77916+63038+77938	GW	FSS	EVL	FSR
320319	77917+63039+77939	GW	FSS	EVL	FSR
320320	77918+63040+77940	GW	FSS	EVL	FSR
320321	77919+63041+77941	GW	FSS	EVL	FSR
320322	77920+63042+77942	GW	FSS	EVL	FSR

Left: *A fleet of 22 Class 320 three-car sets is based at Glasgow Shields Road and operates on the Glasgow outer-suburban routes. These sets were based on the Class 321 stock and in their present form can seat 227 standard class passengers. Set No. 320303 is illustrated.* **Robin Ralston**

Class 334
Juniper

Vehicle Length: (Driving) 69ft 0¾in (21.04m)	Width: 9ft 2¾in (2.80m)	
(Inter) 65ft 4½in (19.93m)	Horsepower: 1,448hp (1,080kW)	
Height: 12ft 3in (3.77m)	Seats (total/car): 183S, 64S/55S/64S	

Number	Formation DMSO(A)+PTSO+DMSO(B)	Depot	Livery	Owner	Operator
334001	64101+74301+65101	GW	FSS	EVL	FSR
334002	64102+74302+65102	GW	FSS	EVL	FSR
334003	64103+74303+65103	GW	FSS	EVL	FSR
334004	64104+74304+65104	GW	FSS	EVL	FSR
334005	64105+74305+65105	GW	FSS	EVL	FSR
334006	64106+74306+65106	GW	FSS	EVL	FSR
334007	64107+74307+65107	GW	FSS	EVL	FSR
334008	64108+74308+65108	GW	FSS	EVL	FSR
334009	64109+74309+65109	GW	FSS	EVL	FSR
334010	64110+74310+65110	GW	FSS	EVL	FSR
334011	64111+74311+65111	GW	FSS	EVL	FSR
334012	64112+74312+65112	GW	FSS	EVL	FSR
334013	64113+74313+65113	GW	FSS	EVL	FSR
334014	64114+74314+65114	GW	FSS	EVL	FSR
334015	64115+74315+65115	GW	FSS	EVL	FSR
334016	64116+74316+65116	GW	FSS	EVL	FSR
334017	64117+74317+65117	GW	FSS	EVL	FSR
334018	64118+74318+65118	GW	FSS	EVL	FSR
334019	64119+74319+65119	GW	FSS	EVL	FSR
334020	64120+74320+65120	GW	FSS	EVL	FSR
334021	64121+74321+65121	GW	FSS	EVL	FSR
334022	64122+74322+65122	GW	FSS	EVL	FSR
334023	64123+74323+65123	GW	FSS	EVL	FSR
334024	64124+74324+65124	GW	FSS	EVL	FSR
334025	64125+74325+65125	GW	FSS	EVL	FSR
334026	64126+74326+65126	GW	FSS	EVL	FSR
334027	64127+74327+65127	GW	FSS	EVL	FSR
334028	64128+74328+65128	GW	FSS	EVL	FSR
334029	64129+74329+65129	GW	FSS	EVL	FSR
334030	64130+74330+65130	GW	FSS	EVL	FSR
334031	64131+74331+65131	GW	FSS	EVL	FSR
334032	64132+74332+65132	GW	FSS	EVL	FSR
334033	64133+74333+65133	GW	FSS	EVL	FSR
334034	64134+74334+65134	GW	FSS	EVL	FSR
334035	64135+74335+65135	GW	FSS	EVL	FSR
334036	64136+74336+65136	GW	FSS	EVL	FSR
334037	64137+74337+65137	GW	FSS	EVL	FSR
334038	64138+74338+65138	GW	FSS	EVL	FSR
334039	64139+74339+65139	GW	FSS	EVL	FSR
334040	64140+74340+65140	GW	FSS	EVL	FSR

Right: *In the immediate post-privatisation period, Alstom supplied 40 three-car sets to Scotland based on its 'Juniper' platform, of similar technical design to the Class 458 and 460 stock used in the south. These non-gangway sets are based at Glasgow Shields and operate in the Glasgow and Edinburgh areas especially on the North Clyde route. All sets carry the latest ScotRail blue/white livery and in 2015-2016 a major refurbishment package is to be effected. Set No. 334031 is shown at Edinburgh Haymarket.* **CJM**

Abellio ScotRail

Class 380/0
Desiro

Vehicle Length: 77ft 3in (23.57m)		Horsepower: 1,341hp (1,000kW)		
Height: 12ft 1½in (3.7m)		Seats (total/car): 191S, 70S/57S/64S		
Width: 9ft 2in (2.7m)				

Number	Formation DMSO(A)+PTSO+DMSO(B)	Depot	Livery	Owner	Operator
380001	38501+38601+38701	GW	FSS	EVL	FSR
380002	38502+38602+38702	GW	FSS	EVL	FSR
380003	38503+38603+38703	GW	FSS	EVL	FSR
380004	38504+38604+38704	GW	FSS	EVL	FSR
380005	38505+38605+38705	GW	FSS	EVL	FSR
380006	38506+38606+38706	GW	FSS	EVL	FSR
380007	38507+38607+38707	GW	FSS	EVL	FSR
380008	38508+38608+38708	GW	FSS	EVL	FSR
380009	38509+38609+38709	GW	FSS	EVL	FSR
380010	38510+38610+38710	GW	FSS	EVL	FSR
380011	38511+38611+38711	GW	FSS	EVL	FSR
380012	38512+38612+38712	GW	FSS	EVL	FSR
380013	38513+38613+38713	GW	FSS	EVL	FSR
380014	38514+38614+38714	GW	FSS	EVL	FSR
380015	38515+38615+38715	GW	FSS	EVL	FSR
380016	38516+38616+38716	GW	FSS	EVL	FSR
380017	38517+38617+38717	GW	FSS	EVL	FSR
380018	38518+38618+38718	GW	FSS	EVL	FSR
380019	38519+38619+38719	GW	FSS	EVL	FSR
380020	38520+38620+38720	GW	FSS	EVL	FSR
380021	38521+38621+38721	GW	FSS	EVL	FSR
380022	38522+38622+38722	GW	FSS	EVL	FSR

Class 380/1
Desiro

Vehicle Length: 77ft 3in (23.57m)		Horsepower: 1,341hp (1,000kW)		
Height: 12ft 1½in (3.7m)		Seats (total/car): 265S, 70S/57S/74S/64S		
Width: 9ft 2in (2.7m)				

Number	Formation DMSO(A)+PTSO+MSO+DMSO(B)	Depot	Livery	Owner	Operator
380101	38551+38651+38851+38751	GW	FSS	EVL	FSR
380102	38552+38652+38852+38752	GW	FSS	EVL	FSR
380103	38553+38653+38853+38753	GW	FSS	EVL	FSR
380104	38554+38654+38854+38754	GW	FSS	EVL	FSR
380105	38555+38655+38855+38755	GW	FSS	EVL	FSR
380106	38556+38656+38856+38756	GW	FSS	EVL	FSR
380107	38557+38657+38857+38757	GW	FSS	EVL	FSR
380108	38558+38658+38858+38758	GW	FSS	EVL	FSR
380109	38559+38659+38859+38759	GW	FSS	EVL	FSR
380110	38560+38660+38860+38760	GW	FSS	EVL	FSR
380111	38561+38661+38861+38761	GW	FSS	EVL	FSR
380112	38562+38662+38862+38762	GW	FSS	EVL	FSR
380113	38563+38663+38863+38763	GW	FSS	EVL	FSR
380114	38564+38664+38864+38764	GW	FSS	EVL	FSR
380115	38565+38665+38865+38765	GW	FSS	EVL	FSR
380116	38566+38666+38866+38766	GW	FSS	EVL	FSR

Left: *The most modern EMUs to operate in Scotland are the Class 380 design, built by Siemens in Germany to its 'Desiro' product line. Sets in both three-and four-car form are in operation and allocated to Glasgow Shields, they mainly operate on Ayrshire and Inverclyde services. All are painted in blue/white Saltire livery. These sets were built with a retractable front end gangway, but observation shows these are never now pushed back into the bodywork as the original design intended. Three-car set No. 380012 is viewed at Glasgow Central.* **CJM**

Mk2 and Mk3 Hauled Stock

Mk2
Vehicle Length: 66ft 0in (20.11m)   Width: 9ft 3in (2.81m)
Height: 12ft 9½in (3.89m)   Seats (total/car): 60S

Mk3
Vehicle Length: 75ft 0in (22.86m)   Width: 8ft 11in (2.71m)
Height: 12ft 9in (3.88m)   Bogie Type: BT10

AN1F (Mk2) - RLO *Seating 28-30F*

Number	Depot	Livery	Owner
6700 (3347)	IS	FSS	EVL
6701 (3346)	IS	FSR	EVL
6702 (3421)	IS	FSR	EVL
6703 (3308)	IS	FSR	EVL
6704 (3341)	IS	FSR	EVL
6705 (3310)	IS	FSR	EVL
6706 (3283)	IS	FSR	EVL
6707 (3276)	IS	FSR	EVL
6708 (3370)	IS	FSR	EVL

AN1F (Mk2) - BUO *Seating 31U*

Number	Depot	Livery	Owner
9800 (5751)	IS	FSR	EVL
9801 (5760)	IS	FSR	EVL
9802 (5772)	IS	FSR	EVL
9803 (5799)	IS	FSR	EVL
9804 (5826)	IS	FSR	EVL
9805 (5833)	IS	FSR	EVL
9806 (5840)	IS	FSR	EVL
9807 (5851)	IS	FSS	EVL
9808 (5871)	IS	FSS	EVL
9809 (5890)	IS	FSR	EVL
9810 (5892)	IS	FSR	EVL

AU4G (Mk3) - SLEP *Comps 12*

Number	Depot	Livery	Owner
10501	IS	FSR	PTR
10502	IS	FSR	PTR
10504	IS	FSR	PTR
10506	IS	FSR	PTR
10507	IS	FSR	PTR
10508	IS	FSR	PTR
10513	IS	FSR	PTR
10516	IS	FSS	PTR
10519	IS	FSR	PTR
10520	IS	FSR	PTR
10522	IS	FSR	PTR
10523	IS	FSR	PTR
10526	IS	FSR	PTR
10527	IS	FSR	PTR
10529	IS	FSR	PTR
10531	IS	FSR	PTR
10542	IS	FSR	PTR
10543	IS	FSR	PTR
10544	IS	FSR	PTR
10548	IS	FSR	PTR
10551	IS	FSR	PTR
10553	IS	FSR	PTR
10561	IS	FSR	PTR
10562	IS	FSS	PTR
10565	IS	FSR	PTR
10580	IS	FSR	PTR
10597	IS	FSR	PTR
10598	IS	FSR	PTR
10600	IS	FSR	PTR
10605	IS	FSR	PTR
10607	IS	FSR	PTR
10610	IS	FSR	PTR

10613	IS	FSR	PTR
10614	IS	FSR	PTR
10617	IS	FSR	PTR

AS4G (MK3) - SLE *Comps 13*

Number	Depot	Livery	Owner
10675	IS	FSR	PTR
10683	IS	FSR	PTR
10688	IS	FSR	PTR
10690	IS	FSR	PTR
10693	IS	FSR	PTR
10703	IS	FSR	PTR

AQ4G (Mk3) - SLED *Comps 11*

Number	Depot	Livery	Owner
10648	IS	FSR	PTR
10650	IS	FSR	PTR
10666	IS	FSR	PTR
10680	IS	FSR	PTR
10689	IS	FSR	PTR
10699	IS	FSR	PTR
10706	IS	FSR	PTR
10714	IS	FSR	PTR
10718	IS	FSR	PTR
10719	IS	FSR	PTR
10722	IS	FSR	PTR
10723	IS	FSR	PTR

Above: *Until April 2015 First ScotRail was responsible for the operation of the London to Scotland overnight sleeper services, for which 73 Mk2 and Mk3 vehicles are allocated to Inverness. Most vehicles are painted in First blue livery with pink and white body stripes and branded as 'Caledonian Sleeper'. Here we see Mk2 RLO No. 6703, a vehicle which seats 30 first class passengers in a lounge setting.* **Antony Christie**

■ From April 2015 the Scottish Sleeper operation becomes a new separate franchise operated by Caledonian Sleepers owned by Serco Group plc, which will manage the new 15-year franchise under the leadership of Managing Director Peter Strachan.

New franchise and train orders for Scotland

A new 10-year Scottish Railway franchise commences on 1 April 2015, which has been awarded to Abellio, the Dutch operator that currently operates the Greater Anglia franchise.

As part of the franchise deal, Abellio has placed an order for 234 new electric multiple unit vehicles, consisting of 46 three-car sets and 24 four-car sets for delivery from 2017. The new build order has been placed with Hitachi Rail Europe for its yet to be tested AT200 series train. The first trains will be constructed entirely in Japan with the remaining 66 built at the new Hitachi plant in Newton Aycliffe, County Durham.

The sets will be fitted with end corridors and have 2+2 seating, and at least the four-car sets will have first class accommodation.

The new Scottish franchise has also announced that it is to introduce a fleet of 27 2+5 refurbished High Speed Trains (Class 43s and Mk3 stock fitted with plug doors) on main inter-city routes by December 2018, and make a significant investment in refurbishing Class 158s for Scottish scenic routes. It is also understood that around seven Class 321s will move to Scotland to operate alongside the Class 320s in the Glasgow area.

First TransPennine Express

Address: ✉ Floor 7, Bridgewater House, 60 Whitworth Street, Manchester, M1 6LT
✆ tpecustomer.relations@firstgroup.com
✆ 0845 600 1671
ⓘ www.tpexpress.co.uk

Managing Director: Nick Donovan
Franchise Dates: 1 February 2004 - Extension proposed to February 2016
Principal Routes: Newcastle, Middlesbrough, Scarborough, Hull, Cleethorpes
to Manchester, Liverpool, Barrow, Carlisle, Edinburgh and
Glasgow
Depots: Ardwick (AK) - Siemens-operated, York (YK), Crofton (XW)
Parent Company: First Group, Keolis

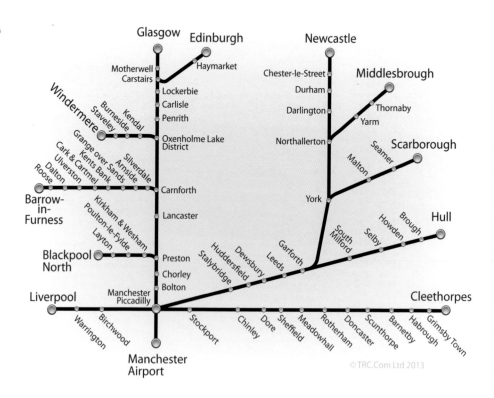

©TRC.Com Ltd 2013

Class 170/3
Turbostar

Vehicle Length: 77ft 6in (23.62m)			Engine: 1 x MTU 6R 183TD13H of 422hp per vehicle		
Height: 12ft 4½in (3.77m)			Horsepower: 844hp (629kW)		
Width: 8ft 10in (2.69m)			Seats (total/car): 8F/108S 8F-43S/65S		

Number	Formation DMCL+DMS	Depot	Livery	Owner	Operator
170301	50301+79301	XW	FTP	PTR	FTP
170302	50302+79302	XW	FTP	PTR	FTP
170303	50303+79303	XW	FTP	PTR	FTP
170304	50304+79304	XW	FTP	PTR	FTP
170305	50305+79305	XW	FTP	PTR	FTP
170306	50306+79306	XW	FTP	PTR	FTP
170307	50307+79307	XW	FTP	PTR	FTP
170308	50308+79308	XW	FTP	PTR	FTP
170309	50399+79399	XW	FTP	PTR	FTP

For transfer to Chiltern Railways in spring 2015, to be renumbered 168301 - 168309

Above: *The 'Turbostar' Class 170/3 sets have had a very mixed life since they were first introduced in 2000. Originally the sets went to South West Trains, where they were replaced by extra Class 159 conversions. The sets then transferred to First TransPennine Express to operate mainly on the Manchester to Hull and East Coast route. Now, in 2015, the sets are due to move again, transferring to Chiltern Railways. In this view recorded at Selby, we see set No. 170304 forming a Hull to Manchester service with the DMCL vehicle nearest the camera. At present the sets carry First Dynamic Lines colours.* **CJM**

Class 185
Desiro

Vehicle Length: (Driving) 77ft 11in (23.76m), (Inter) 77ft 10in (23.75m)			
Height: 12ft 4in (3.75m)		Engine: 1 x Cummins OSK19 of 750hp per vehicle	
Width: 9ft 3in (2.81m)		Horsepower: 2,250hp (1,680kW)	
		Seats (total/car): 15F/154S, 15F-18S/72S/64S	

Number	Formation DMCL+MSL+DMS	Depot	Livery	Owner	Operator
185101	51101+53101+54101	AK	FTP	EVL	FTP
185102	51102+53102+54102	AK	FTP	EVL	FTP
185103	51103+53103+54103	AK	FTP	EVL	FTP
185104	51104+53104+54104	AK	FTP	EVL	FTP
185105	51105+53105+54105	AK	FTP	EVL	FTP
185106	51106+53106+54106	AK	FTP	EVL	FTP
185107	51107+53107+54107	AK	FTP	EVL	FTP
185108	51108+53108+54108	AK	FTP	EVL	FTP
185109	51109+53109+54109	AK	FTP	EVL	FTP
185110	51110+53110+54110	AK	FTP	EVL	FTP
185111	51111+53111+54111	AK	FTP	EVL	FTP
185112	51112+53112+54112	AK	FTP	EVL	FTP
185113	51113+53113+54113	AK	FTP	EVL	FTP
185114	51114+53114+54114	AK	FTP	EVL	FTP
185115	51115+53115+54115	AK	FTP	EVL	FTP
185116	51116+53116+54116	AK	FTP	EVL	FTP
185117	51117+53117+54117	AK	FTP	EVL	FTP
185118	51118+53118+54118	AK	FTP	EVL	FTP
185119	51119+53119+54119	AK	FTP	EVL	FTP

First TransPennine Express

185120	51120+53120+54120	AK	FTP	EVL	FTP
185121	51121+53121+54121	AK	FTP	EVL	FTP
185122	51122+53122+54122	AK	FTP	EVL	FTP
185123	51123+53123+54123	AK	FTP	EVL	FTP
185124	51124+53124+54124	AK	FTP	EVL	FTP
185125	51125+53125+54125	AK	FTP	EVL	FTP
185126	51126+53126+54126	AK	FTP	EVL	FTP
185127	51127+53127+54127	AK	FTP	EVL	FTP
185128	51128+53128+54128	AK	FTP	EVL	FTP
185129	51129+53129+54129	AK	FTP	EVL	FTP
185130	51130+53130+54130	AK	FTP	EVL	FTP
185131	51131+53131+54131	AK	FTP	EVL	FTP
185132	51132+53132+54132	AK	FTP	EVL	FTP
185133	51133+53133+54133	AK	FTP	EVL	FTP
185134	51134+53134+54134	AK	FTP	EVL	FTP
185135	51135+53135+54135	AK	FTP	EVL	FTP
185136	51136+53136+54136	AK	FTP	EVL	FTP
185137	51137+53137+54137	AK	FTP	EVL	FTP
185138	51138+53138+54138	AK	FTP	EVL	FTP
185139	51139+53139+54139	AK	FTP	EVL	FTP
185140	51140+53140+54140	AK	FTP	EVL	FTP
185141	51141+53141+54141	AK	FTP	EVL	FTP
185142	51142+53142+54142	AK	FTP	EVL	FTP
185143	51143+53143+54143	AK	FTP	EVL	FTP
185144	51144+53144+54144	AK	FTP	EVL	FTP
185145	51145+53145+54145	AK	FTP	EVL	FTP
185146	51146+53146+54146	AK	FTP	EVL	FTP
185147	51147+53147+54147	AK	FTP	EVL	FTP
185148	51148+53148+54148	AK	FTP	EVL	FTP
185149	51149+53149+54149	AK	FTP	EVL	FTP
185150	51150+53150+54150	AK	FTP	EVL	FTP
185151	51151+53151+54151	AK	FTP	EVL	FTP

Below: *The core First TransPennine operation is operated by a fleet of 51 high-quality Siemens-built 'Desiro' DMUs, based in depot facilities at Ardwick, Manchester. These three-car sets operate the long-distance trans-Pennine operations from Manchester to Cleethorpes, Hull, Scarborough, Middlesbrough and Newcastle in the east and Liverpool, Blackpool, Barrow and Windermere in the west. All sets are finished in First Dynamic Lines livery and have seating for 15 first and 154 standard class passengers. The final example of the fleet, No. 185151, is seen at Doncaster from its DMCL vehicle.* **CJM**

Right: *The intermediate vehicles of the Class 185s seat 72 standard class passengers in the low-density 2+2 style. Passenger access is by two pairs of bi-parting sliding plug doors on each side. Underslung equipment consists of the power unit - a Cummins OSK19 - transmission equipment, fuel tank and control systems. Vehicle No. 53147 from set No. 185147 is illustrated.* **CJM**

Class 350/4
Desiro

Vehicle Length: 66ft 9in (20.4m)	Horsepower: 1,341hp (1,000kW)
Height: 12ft 1½in (3.78m)	Seats (total/car): 19F/178S
Width: 9ft 2in (2.7m)	

Number	Formation DMSO(A)+TCO+PTSO+DMSO(B)	Depot	Livery	Owner	Operator
350401	60691+60901+60941+60671	AK	FTP	ANG	FTP
350402	60692+60902+60942+60672	AK	FTP	ANG	FTP
350403	60693+60903+60943+60673	AK	FTP	ANG	FTP
350404	60694+60904+60944+60674	AK	FTP	ANG	FTP
350405	60695+60905+60945+60675	AK	FTP	ANG	FTP
350406	60696+60906+60946+60676	AK	FTP	ANG	FTP
350407	60697+60907+60947+60677	AK	FTP	ANG	FTP
350408	60698+60908+60948+60678	AK	FTP	ANG	FTP
350409	60699+60909+60949+60679	AK	FTP	ANG	FTP
350410	60700+60910+60950+60680	AK	FTP	ANG	FTP

Below: *In 2014 the 10 Class 350/4 'Desiro' sets, built in Germany by Siemens, entered traffic for First TransPennine Express on its Manchester to Edinburgh/Glasgow corridor via the West Coast Main Line. Delivered in base grey, the sets now sport a variation of the First Dynamic Lines colours. Set No. 350410 is seen arriving at Edinburgh Waverley on 2 July with the 07.25 from Manchester Airport.* **CJM**

Grand Central

Address: ✉ River House, 17 Museum Street, York, YO1 7DJ

✆ info@grandcentral.com

© 0845 603 4852

ⓘ www.grandcentral.co.uk

Managing Director: Richard McLean

Franchise Dates: Private Open Access Operator, to December 2026

Principal Routes: London King's Cross - Sunderland/Bradford

Depots: Heaton (HT)

Parent Company: Arriva PLC

Below: *Grand Central operates six Class 43 power cars; all are buffer-fitted examples based at Heaton depot, Newcastle. Usually two HST sets are in operation daily. A northbound London to Sunderland service passes through Doncaster with car No. 43423 on the rear.* **CJM**

Sunderland ○
Hartlepool ○
Eaglescliffe ○
Northallerton ○
Thirsk ○
Bradford ○ Halifax Wakefield York ○
Interchange Kirkgate
Brighouse
Pontefract
Monkhill
Doncaster ○

London ○
King's Cross

© TRC.Com Ltd 2013

Class 43 – HST

Vehicle Length: 58ft 5in (18.80m)			Engine: MTU 16V4000 R41R			
Height: 12ft 10in (3.90m)			Horsepower: 2,250hp (1,680kW)			
Width: 8ft 11in (2.73m)			Electrical Equipment: Brush			

Number	Depot	Pool	Livery	Owner	Operator
43423 (43123)	HT	GCHP	GTO	ANG	GTL
43465 (43065)	HT	GCHP	GTO	ANG	GTL
43467 (43067)	HT	GCHP	GTO	ANG	GTL
43468 (43068)	HT	GCHP	GTO	ANG	GTL
43480 (43080)	HT	GCHP	GTO	ANG	GTL
43484 (43084)	HT	GCHP	GTO	ANG	GTL

Names applied
43423 *'Valenta' 1972 - 2010*
43484 *Peter Fox 1942 - 2011*

Class 180
Zephyr

Vehicle Length: (Driving) 75ft 7in (23.71m), (Inter) 75ft 5in (23.03m)		
Height: 12ft 4in (3.75m)		Engine: 1 x Cummins OSK19 of 750hp per vehicle
Width: 9ft 2in (2.80m)		Horsepower: 3,750hp (2,796kW)
		Seats (total/car): 42F/226S, 46S/42F/68S/56S/56S

Number	Formation DMSL(A)+MFL+MSL+MSLRB+DMSL(B)	Depot	Livery	Owner	Operator	Name
180101	50901+54901+55901+56901+59901	HT	GTO	ANG	GTL	
180105	50905+54905+55905+56905+59905	HT	GTO	ANG	GTL	*The Yorkshire Artist Ashley Jackson*
180107	50907+54907+55907+56907+59907	HT	GTO	ANG	GTL	*Hart of the North*
180112	50912+54912+55912+56912+59912	HT	GTO	ANG	GTL	*James Herriot*
180114	50914+54914+55914+56914+59914	HT	GTO	ANG	GTL	

Above: *Grand Central now operates five of the original First Great Western Class 180 sets on its London to Bradford corridor. All have been refurbished and sport the black and orange GC livery, standard class carriages have silver doors and first class vehicles have gold doors. The GC logo and branding is applied to both ends of each vehicle. Set No. 180105* The Yorkshire Artist - Ashley Jackson *passes Knottingley on 22 April 2014 bound for Bradford.* **CJM**

■ Grand Central announced in late 2014, that it had received agreement to take over the five Class 180s currently operating with First Great Western from 2017, allowing Grand Central to cease using its present fleet of HSTs which would be taken off lease and returned to Angel Trains. A major refurbishing project for all 10 Class 180s would be undertaken. ■

Mk3 HST Stock

				Vehicle Length: 75ft 0in (22.86m)		*Width: 8ft 11in (2.71m)*
				Height: 12ft 9in (3.88m)		*Bogie Type: BT10*

GK2G - TRSB *Seating 33S*

Number		Depot	Livery	Owner
40424	(40024)	HT	GTO	ANG
40426	(40026)	HT	GTO	ANG
40433	(40033)	HT	GTO	ANG

GH1G - TF *Seating 48F*

Number		Depot	Livery	Owner
41201	(11045)	HT	GTO	ANG
41202	(11017)	HT	GTO	ANG
41203	(11038)	HT	GTO	ANG
41204	(11023)	HT	GTO	ANG
41205	(11036)	HT	GTO	ANG
41206	(11055)	HT	GTO	ANG

GH2G - TS *Seating 64S *TSD Seating 60S*

Number		Depot	Livery	Owner
42401	(12149)	HT	GTO	ANG

42402	(12155)	HT	GTO	ANG
42403*	(12033)	HT	GTO	ANG
42404	(12152)	HT	GTO	ANG
42405	(12136)	HT	GTO	ANG
42406*	(12112)	HT	GTO	ANG
42407	(12044)	HT	GTO	ANG
42408	(12121)	HT	GTO	ANG
42409*	(12088)	HT	GTO	ANG

GJ2G - TGS *Seating 67S*

Number	Depot	Livery	Owner
44065 (S)	HT/LM	GTO	GTL
44088 (S)	HT/LM	GTO	GTL
44089 (S)	HT/LM	GTO	GTL

Right: *A fleet of 21 Mk3 vehicles operates within the Grand Central HST fleet. The buffet and TGS vehicles are from the original HST build, while the TF and TS coaches are rebuilds from loco-hauled Mk3 stock to HST standards. Vehicles are based at Heaton depot, Newcastle and all are painted in GC black and orange livery with silver doors for standard class and gold doors for first class. First class vehicles also have a yellow cantrail-height band. TF No. 41203 is illustrated.* **CJM**

Greater Anglia

Address: ✉ 2nd Floor, East Anglia House, 12-34 Great Eastern Street, London, EC2A 3EH

☏ contactcentre@greateranglia.co.uk

☎ 0845 600 7245

ⓘ www.greateranglia.co.uk

Managing Director: Jamie Burles

Franchise Dates: 1 February 2012 - October 2016

Principal Routes: London Liverpool Street to Norwich, Cambridge, Enfield Town, Hertford East, Upminster, Southend Victoria, Southminster, Braintree, Sudbury, Clacton, Walton, Harwich Town, Felixstowe, Lowestoft, Great Yarmouth, Sheringham, Stansted Airport and Peterborough

Depots: Ilford (IL), Norwich (NC), Clacton (CC)

Parent Company: Abellio

Class 90/0

Vehicle Length: 61ft 6in (18.74m) Power Collection: 25kV ac overhead
Height: 13ft 0¼in (3.96m) Horsepower: 7,860hp (5,860kW)
Width: 9ft 0in (2.74m) Electrical Equipment: GEC

Number	Depot	Pool	Livery	Owner	Operator	Name
90001	NC	IANA	AWT	PTR	GAR	*Crown Point*
90002	NC	IANA	ORA	PTR	GAR	*Eastern Daily Press 1870-2010 Serving Norfolk for 140 years*
90003	NC	IANA	GAR	PTR	GAR	*Raedwald of East Anglia*
90004	NC	IANA	ORA	PTR	GAR	*City of Chelmsford*
90005	NC	IANA	AWT	PTR	GAR	*Vice-Admiral Lord Nelson*
90006	NC	IANA	ORA	PTR	GAR	*Roger Ford / Modern Railways Magazine*
90007	NC	IANA	ORA	PTR	GAR	*Sir John Betjeman*
90008	NC	IANA	GAR	PTR	GAR	*The East Anglian*
90009	NC	IANA	ORA	PTR	GAR	*Diamond Jubilee*
90010	NC	IANA	AWT	PTR	GAR	*Bressingham Steam and Gardens*
90011	NC	IANA	AWT	PTR	GAR	*East Anglian Daily Times Suffolk & Proud*
90012	NC	IANA	ORA	PTR	GAR	*Royal Anglian Regiment*
90013	NC	IANA	AWT	PTR	GAR	*The Evening Star*
90014	NC	IANA	AWT	PTR	GAR	*Norfolk and Norwich Festival*
90015	NC	IANA	GAR	PTR	GAR	*Colchester Castle*

Left: *The present operator of the Greater Anglia franchise is Abellio, which in 2014-15 has been overhauling and repainting its 15-strong Class 90 fleet, which now displays the white base livery with a dark grey upper panel, onto which the cast nameplate is attached. No. 90005* Vice-Admiral Lord Nelson *is seen at Norwich. The AGA Class 90s are used exclusively on the London Liverpool Street to Norwich services.* **Antony Christie**

■ From 31 May 2015 Transport for London will take over the Liverpool Street suburban services to Cheshunt, Chingford and Enfield Town. This will see the Class 315s pass to TfL control.

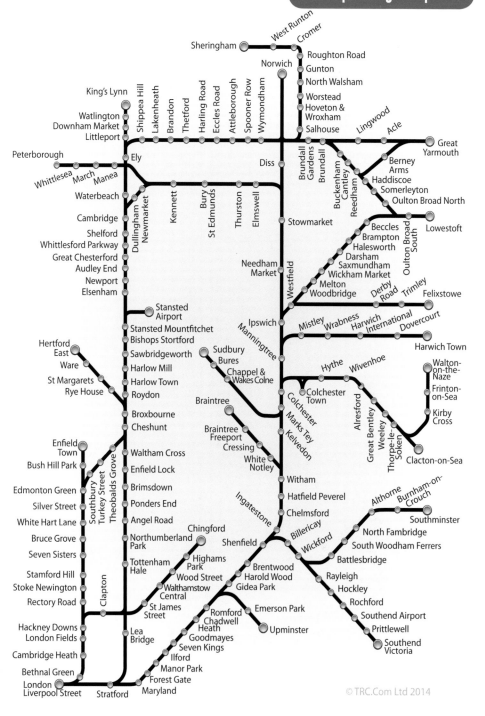

Passenger Train Operating Companies - Greater Anglia

© TRC.Com Ltd 2014

Greater Anglia

Mk3 Hauled Stock

	Vehicle Length: 75ft 0in (22.86m)	Width: 8ft 11in (2.71m)
	Height: 12ft 9in (3.88m)	Bogie Type: BT10

Passenger Train Operating Companies - Greater Anglia

AJ1G - RFM *Seating 24F*

Number	Depot	Livery	Owner
10200 (40519)	NC	AWT	PTR
10203 (40506)	NC	AWT	PTR
10214 (11034)	NC	AWT	PTR
10216 (11041)	NC	AWT	PTR
10223 (11043)	NC	AWT	PTR
10228 (11035)	NC	AWT	PTR
10229 (11059)	NC	AWT	PTR
10247 (10011)	NC	ORA	PTR

AN2G - TSOB *Seating 52S*

10401 (12168)	NC	AWT	PTR
10402 (12010)	NC	ORA	PTR
10403 (12135)	NC	ORA	PTR
10404 (12068)	NC	ORA	PTR
10405 (12137)	NC	ORA	PTR
10406 (12020)	NC	ORA	PTR

AD1G - FO, *FOD *Seating 48F/34F*

11066	NC	ORA	PTR
11067	NC	AWT	PTR
11068	NC	AWT	PTR
11069	NC	AWT	PTR
11070	NC	ORA	PTR
11072*	NC	ORA	PTR
11073*	NC	AWT	PTR
11075	NC	AWT	PTR
11076	NC	ORA	PTR
11077	NC	ORA	PTR
11078*	NC	ORA	PTR
11080	NC	ORA	PTR
11081	NC	ORA	PTR
11082	NC	AWT	PTR
11085*	NC	ORA	PTR
11087*	NC	AWT	PTR
11088*	NC	AWT	PTR
11090*	NC	ORA	PTR
11091*	NC	AWT	PTR
11092	NC	AWT	PTR
11093*	NC	AWT	PTR
11094*	NC	ORA	PTR
11095*	NC	ORA	PTR
11096*	NC	AWT	PTR
11098*	NC	ORA	PTR
11099*	NC	ORA	PTR
11100*	NC	AWT	PTR
11101*	NC	ORA	PTR

AC2G - TSO *Seating 80S*

12005	NC	ORA	PTR
12009	NC	AWT	PTR
12012	NC	AWT	PTR
12013	NC	AWT	PTR
12015	NC	AWT	PTR
12016	NC	ORA	PTR
12019	NC	AWT	PTR
12021	NC	AWT	PTR
12024	NC	ORA	PTR
12026	NC	AWT	PTR
12027	NC	AWT	PTR
12030	NC	AWT	PTR
12031	NC	ORA	PTR
12032	NC	ORA	PTR
12034	NC	ORA	PTR
12035	NC	AWT	PTR
12037	NC	ORA	PTR
12040	NC	AWT	PTR
12041	NC	ORA	PTR
12042	NC	ORA	PTR
12046	NC	ORA	PTR
12049	NC	ORA	PTR
12051	NC	AWT	PTR
12056	NC	ORA	PTR
12057	NC	ORA	PTR
12060	NC	ORA	PTR
12061	NC	ORA	PTR
12062	NC	ORA	PTR
12064	NC	ORA	PTR
12066	NC	ORA	PTR
12067	NC	ORA	PTR
12073	NC	ORA	PTR
12079	NC	ORA	PTR
12081	NC	ORA	PTR
12082	NC	AWT	PTR
12084	NC	GAR	PTR
12089	NC	ORA	PTR
12090	NC	AWT	PTR
12091	NC	AWT	PTR
12093	NC	ORA	PTR
12097	NC	AWT	PTR
12098	NC	ORA	PTR
12099	NC	ORA	PTR
12103	NC	ORA	PTR
12105	NC	ORA	PTR
12107	NC	ORA	PTR
12108	NC	AWT	PTR

12109	NC	ORA	PTR
12110	NC	ORA	PTR
12111	NC	AWT	PTR
12114	NC	AWT	PTR
12115	NC	ORA	PTR
12116	NC	AWT	PTR
12118	NC	AWT	PTR
12120	NC	AWT	PTR
12125	NC	ORA	PTR
12126	NC	ORA	PTR
12129	NC	AWT	PTR
12130	NC	ORA	PTR
12132	NC	AWT	PTR
12137	NC	ORA	PTR
12139	NC	ORA	PTR
12141	NC	ORA	PTR
12143	NC	AWT	PTR
12146	NC	AWT	PTR
12147	NC	AWT	PTR
12148	NC	AWT	PTR
12150	NC	AWT	PTR
12151	NC	ORA	PTR
12153	NC	AWT	PTR
12154	NC	AWT	PTR
12159	NC	ORA	PTR
12164	NC	ORA	PTR
12166	NC	ORA	PTR
12167	NC	ORA	PTR
12170	NC	AWT	PTR
12171	NC	AWT	PTR

NZAH - DVT

82102	NC	ORA	PTR
82103§	NC	AWT	PTR
82105	NC	AWT	PTR
82107	NC	AWT	PTR
82112	NC	ORA	PTR
82114	NC	ORA	PTR
82118	NC	AWT	PTR
82121	NC	AWT	PTR
82127	NC	AWT	PTR
82132	NC	ORA	PTR
82133	NC	ORA	PTR
82136	NC	AWT	PTR
82139	NC	ORA	PTR
82143	NC	AWT	PTR
82152	NC	AWT	PTR

§ Fitted with de-icing equipment

Left: *As with the Class 90 locomotives, an ongoing project continues to refurbish and repaint the Abellio Greater Anglia Mk3 passenger stock into white AGA livery, supported by red passenger doors. First class areas are identified by a yellow cantrail band and refreshment vehicles by a red band. RFM No. 10229, shown from its first class seating end, is able to accommodate 24 passengers in the 2+1 style.* **Antony Christie**

The following vehicles are on loan to Abellio Greater Anglia and were previously used by Virgin Trains West Coast. The vehicles allocated to Norwich will supply cover for the duration of the Mk3 refurbishment project until October 2016.

| 10217 (S) | NC | VAB | PTE |
| | | | |

AD1G - FO *Seating 48F*

Number	Depot	Livery	Owner
11007	NC	VAB	PTR
11018	NC	VAB	PTR
11048	NC	VAB	PTR

AC2G - TS0 (*TSOD) *Seating 76/70*S*

Number	Depot	Livery	Owner
12011	NC	VAB	PTR

12078	NC	VAB	PTR
12122*	NC	VAB	PTR
12133	NC	VAB	PTR
12138	NC	VAB	PTR

NL - DVT

Number	Depot	Livery	Owner
82126	NC	VAB	PTR

AJ1G - RFB *Seating 18F*

Number	Depot	Livery	Owner
10212	NC	VAB	PTR

Class 153

Vehicle Length: 76ft 5in (23.29m)
Height: 12ft 3⅛in (3.75m)
Width: 8ft 10in (2.70m)

Engine: 1 x NT855R5 of 285hp
Horsepower: 285hp (213kW)
Seats (total/car): 72S

Number	Formation DMSL	Depot	Livery	Owner	Operator	Name
153306	52306	NC	AWT	PTR	GAR	
153309	52309	NC	AWT	PTR	GAR	*Gerard Fiennes*
153314	52314	NC	AWT	PTR	GAR	
153322	52322	NC	AWT	PTR	GAR	*Benjamin Britten*
153335	52335	NC	AWT	PTR	GAR	*Michael Palin*

Right: *For use on the East Anglia rural branch lines, a fleet of five Class 153 'Bubble cars' is based at Norwich Crown point. These are all painted in the Abellio Greater Anglia white livery with orange doors, and three of the five retain names applied in the late BR days twinning local famous people with the rail industry. No. 153309 Gerard Fiennes is seen departing from Norwich with the small cab nearest the camera.* **CJM**

Class 156

Vehicle Length: 75ft 6in (23.03m)
Height: 12ft 6in (3.81m)
Width: 8ft 11in (2.73m)

Engine: 1 x Cummins NT855R5 of 285hp per car
Horsepower: 570hp (425kW)
Seats (total/car): 146S, 70/76S

Number	Formation DMSL+DMS	Depot	Livery	Owner	Operator
156402	52402+57402	NC	AWT	PTR	GAR
156407	52407+57407	NC	AWT	PTR	GAR
156409	52409+57409	NC	AWT	PTR	GAR
156412	52412+57412	NC	AWT	PTR	GAR
156416	52416+57416	NC	AWT	PTR	GAR
156417	52417+57417	NC	AWT	PTR	GAR
156418	52418+57418	NC	AWT	PTR	GAR
156419	52419+57419	NC	AWT	PTR	GAR
156422	52422+57422	NC	AWT	PTR	GAR

Name applied
156416 Saint Edmund

Right: *For longer-distance secondary routes in East Anglia, nine Class 156s are allocated to Norwich Crown Point. These carry the Abellio white livery and a start was made in 2014 to install the latest disabled access toilets, which has seen some changes to the bodyside windows in the DMSL vehicle. Set No. 156416 is illustrated at Norwich with its DMS vehicle nearest the camera.* **CJM**

Greater Anglia

Class 170/2
Turbostar

Vehicle Length: 77ft 6in (23.62m)
Height: 12ft 4½in (3.77m)
Width: 8ft 10in (2.69m)

Engine: 1 x MTU 6R 183TD13H of 422hp per vehicle
Horsepower: 1,266hp (944kW)
Seats (total/car): 7F-173S 7F-39S/68S/66S

Number	Formation	Depot	Livery	Owner	Operator
	DMCL+MSL+DMSL				
170201	50201+56201+79201	NC	ORA	PTR	GAR
170202	50202+56202+79202	NC	ORA	PTR	GAR
170203	50203+56203+79203	NC	ORA	PTR	GAR
170204	50204+56204+79204	NC	ORA	PTR	GAR
170205	50205+56205+79205	NC	ORA	PTR	GAR
170206	50206+56206+79206	NC	ORA	PTR	GAR
170207	50207+56207+79207	NC	ORA	PTR	GAR
170208	50208+56208+79208	NC	ADV	PTR	GAR

Vehicle Length: 77ft 6in (23.62m)
Height: 12ft 4½in (3.77m)
Width: 8ft 10in (2.69m)

Engine: 1 x MTU 6R 183TD13H of 422hp per vehicle
Horsepower: 844hp (629kW)
Seats (total/car): 9F-110S 57S/9F-53S

Number	Formation	Depot	Livery	Owner	Operator						
	DMSL+DMCL					170271	50271+79271	NC	ANN	PTR	GAR
170270	50270+79270	NC	ORA	PTR	GAR	170272	50272+79272	NC	ANN	PTR	GAR
						170273	50273+79273	NC	ANN	PTR	GAR

Left: *Abellio Greater Anglia has two fleets of modern Class 170 'Turbostar' units based at Norwich, eight three-car and four two-car sets. These units operate the longer-distance services and have a better interior environment than earlier DMUs. Most sets still retain the old One Railway blue livery with Abellio Greater Anglia branding, while one set, No. 170208, illustrated, carries 'The Brecks' route advertising livery.*
Antony Christie

Class 315

Vehicle Length: (Driving) 64ft 11½in (19.80m)
(Inter) 65ft 4½in (19.92m)
Height: 11ft 6½in (3.58m)

Width: 9ft 3in (2.82m)
Horsepower: 880hp (656kW)
Seats (total/car): 318S, 74S/86S/84S/74S

Number	Formation	Depot	Livery	Owner	Operator	Name
	DMSO(A)+TSO+PTSO+DMSO(B)					
315801	64461+71281+71389+64462	IL	AWT	EVL	GAR	
315802	64463+71282+71390+64464	IL	AWT	EVL	GAR	
315803	64465+71283+71391+64466	IL	AWT	EVL	GAR	
315804	64467+71284+71392+64468	IL	AWT	EVL	GAR	
315805	64469+71285+71393+64470	IL	AWT	EVL	GAR	
315806	64471+71286+71394+64472	IL	AWT	EVL	GAR	
315807	64473+71287+71395+64474	IL	AWT	EVL	GAR	
315808	64475+71288+71396+64476	IL	AWT	EVL	GAR	
315809	64477+71289+71397+64478	IL	AWT	EVL	GAR	
315810	64479+71290+71398+64480	IL	AWT	EVL	GAR	
315811	64481+71291+71399+64482	IL	AWT	EVL	GAR	
315812	64483+71292+71400+64484	IL	AWT	EVL	GAR	
315813	64485+71293+71401+64486	IL	AWT	EVL	GAR	
315814	64487+71294+71402+64488	IL	AWT	EVL	GAR	
315815	64489+71295+71403+64490	IL	AWT	EVL	GAR	
315816	64491+71296+71404+64492	IL	AWT	EVL	GAR	
315817	64493+71297+71405+64494	IL	AWT	EVL	GAR	*Transport for London*
315818	64495+71298+71406+64496	IL	AWT	EVL	GAR	

315819	64497+71299+71407+64498	IL	AWT	EVL	GAR	
315820	64499+71300+71408+64500	IL	AWT	EVL	GAR	
315821	64501+71301+71409+64502	IL	AWT	EVL	GAR	
315822	64503+71302+71410+64504	IL	AWT	EVL	GAR	
315823	64505+71303+71411+64506	IL	AWT	EVL	GAR	
315824	64507+71304+71412+64508	IL	AWT	EVL	GAR	
315825	64509+71305+71413+64510	IL	AWT	EVL	GAR	
315826	64511+71306+71414+64512	IL	AWT	EVL	GAR	
315827	64513+71307+71415+64514	IL	AWT	EVL	GAR	
315828	64515+71308+71416+64516	IL	AWT	EVL	GAR	
315829	64517+71309+71417+64518	IL	AWT	EVL	GAR	*London Borough of Havering Celebrating 40 Years*
315830	64519+71310+71418+64520	IL	AWT	EVL	GAR	
315831	64521+71311+71419+64522	IL	AWT	EVL	GAR	
315832	64523+71312+71420+64524	IL	AWT	EVL	GAR	
315833	64525+71313+71421+64526	IL	AWT	EVL	GAR	
315834	64527+71314+71422+64528	IL	AWT	EVL	GAR	
315835	64529+71315+71423+64530	IL	AWT	EVL	GAR	
315836	64531+71316+71424+64532	IL	ORA	EVL	GAR	
315837	64533+71317+71425+64534	IL	ORA	EVL	GAR	
315838	64535+71318+71426+64536	IL	ORA	EVL	GAR	
315839	64537+71319+71427+64538	IL	AWT	EVL	GAR	
315840	64539+71320+71428+64540	IL	AWT	EVL	GAR	
315841	64541+71321+71429+64542	IL	AWT	EVL	GAR	
315842	64543+71322+71430+64544	IL	ORA	EVL	GAR	
315843	64545+71323+71431+64546	IL	ORA	EVL	GAR	
315844	64547+71324+71432+64548	IL	AWT	EVL	GAR	
315845	64549+71325+71433+64550	IL	AWT	EVL	GAR	*Herbie Woodward*
315846	64551+71326+71434+64552	IL	AWT	EVL	GAR	
315847	64553+71327+71435+64554	IL	ORA	EVL	GAR	
315848	64555+71328+71436+64556	IL	ORA	EVL	GAR	
315849	64557+71329+71437+64558	IL	ORA	EVL	GAR	
315850	64559+71330+71438+64560	IL	NXU	EVL	GAR	
315851	64561+71331+71439+64562	IL	AWT	EVL	GAR	
315852	64563+71332+71440+64564	IL	AWT	EVL	GAR	
315853	64565+71333+71441+64566	IL	ORA	EVL	GAR	
315854	64567+71334+71442+64568	IL	AWT	EVL	GAR	
315855	64569+71335+71443+64570	IL	AWT	EVL	GAR	
315856	64571+71336+71444+64572	IL	ORA	EVL	GAR	
315857	64573+71337+71445+64574	IL	ORA	EVL	GAR	
315858	64575+71338+71446+64576	IL	AWT	EVL	GAR	
315859	64577+71339+71447+64578	IL	ORA	EVL	GAR	
315860	64579+71340+71448+64580	IL	ORA	EVL	GAR	
315861	64581+71341+71449+64582	IL	ORA	EVL	GAR	

Right: *At present a fleet of 61 four-car 1972-design Class 315s operates local services from London Liverpool Street to Shenfield. However, major changes to this route will be seen in the near future with the opening of London CrossRail and the taking over of some local services on the Great Eastern route by Transport for London. With a revised front end and painted in the base Abellio Greater Anglia white and orange livery, set No. 315809 arrives at Theobalds Grove on 8 August 2014, with the 14.15 Liverpool Street to Cheshunt (Southbury loop) service.*
John Binch

Greater Anglia

Class 317/5

Vehicle Length: (Driving) 65ft 0¾in (19.83m) Width: 9ft 3in (2.82m)
(Inter) 65ft 4¼in (19.92m) Horsepower: 1,000hp (746kW)
Height: 12ft 1½in (3.58m) Seats (total/car): 291S, 74S/79S/68S/70S

Number	Former Number	Formation DTSO(A)+MSO+TCO+DTSO(B)	Depot	Livery	Owner	Operator	Name
317501	(317301)	77024+62661+71577+77048	IL	GAR	ANG	GAR	
317502	(317302)	77001+62662+71578+77049	IL	GAR	ANG	GAR	
317503	(317303)	77002+62663+71579+77050	IL	GAR	ANG	GAR	
317504	(317304)	77003+62664+71580+77051	IL	GAR	ANG	GAR	
317505	(317305)	77004+62665+71581+77052	IL	GAR	ANG	GAR	
317506	(317306)	77005+62666+71582+77053	IL	GAR	ANG	GAR	
317507	(317307)	77006+62667+71583+77054	IL	GAR	ANG	GAR	*University of Cambridge 800 years 1209-2009*
317508	(317311)	77010+62697+71587+77058	IL	GAR	ANG	GAR	
317509	(317312)	77011+62672+71588+77059	IL	GAR	ANG	GAR	
317510	(317313)	77012+62673+71589+77060	IL	GAR	ANG	GAR	
317511	(317315)	77014+62675+71591+77062	IL	NXU	ANG	GAR	
317512	(317316)	77015+62676+71592+77063	IL	NXU	ANG	GAR	
317513	(317317)	77016+62677+71593+77064	IL	GAR	ANG	GAR	
317514	(317318)	77017+62678+71594+77065	IL	GAR	ANG	GAR	
317515	(317320)	77019+62680+71596+77067	IL	GAR	ANG	GAR	

Class 317/6

Vehicle Length: (Driving) 65ft 0¾in (19.83m) Width: 9ft 3in (2.82m)
(Inter) 65ft 4¼in (19.92m) Horsepower: 1,000hp (746kW)
Height: 12ft 1½in (3.58m) Seats (total/car): 24F/244S, 64S/70S/62S/24F-48S

Number	Former Number	Formation DTSO+MSO+TSO+DTCO	Depot	Livery	Owner	Operator	Name
317649	(317349)	77200+62846+71734+77220	IL	NXU	ANG	GAR	
317650	(317350)	77201+62847+71735+77221	IL	NXU	ANG	GAR	
317651	(317351)	77202+62848+71736+77222	IL	NXU	ANG	GAR	
317652	(317352)	77203+62849+71739+77223	IL	NXU	ANG	GAR	
317653	(317353)	77204+62850+71738+77224	IL	NXU	ANG	GAR	
317654	(317354)	77205+62851+71737+77225	IL	NXU	ANG	GAR	*Richard Wells*
317655	(317355)	77206+62852+71740+77226	IL	AWT	ANG	GAR	
317656	(317356)	77207+62853+71742+77227	IL	AWT	ANG	GAR	
317657	(317357)	77208+62854+71741+77228	IL	NXU	ANG	GAR	
317658	(317358)	77209+62855+71743+77229	IL	AWT	ANG	GAR	
317659	(317359)	77210+62856+71744+77230	IL	AWT	ANG	GAR	
317660	(317360)	77211+62857+71745+77231	IL	AWT	ANG	GAR	
317661	(317361)	77212+62858+71746+77232	IL	AWT	ANG	GAR	
317662	(317362)	77213+62859+71747+77233	IL	AWT	ANG	GAR	
317663	(317363)	77214+62860+71748+77234	IL	AWT	ANG	GAR	
317664	(317364)	77215+62861+71749+77235	IL	AWT	ANG	GAR	
317665	(317365)	77216+62862+71750+77236	IL	AWT	ANG	GAR	
317666	(317366)	77217+62863+71752+77237	IL	NXU	ANG	GAR	
317667	(317367)	77218+62864+71751+77238	IL	AWT	ANG	GAR	
317668	(317368)	77219+62865+71753+77239	IL	AWT	ANG	GAR	
317669	(317369)	77280+62886+71762+77284	IL	NXU	ANG	GAR	
317670	(317370)	77281+62887+71763+77285	IL	AWT	ANG	GAR	
317671	(317371)	77282+62888+71764+77286	IL	AWT	ANG	GAR	
317672	(317372)	77283+62889+71765+77287	IL	AWT	ANG	GAR	

Class 317/7

Vehicle Length: (Driving) 65ft 0¾in (19.83m) Width: 9ft 3in (2.82m)
(Inter) 65ft 4¼in (19.92m) Horsepower: 1,000hp (746kW)
Height: 12ft 1½in (3.58m) Seats (total/car): 22F/172S, 52S/62S/42S/22F-16S

Number	Former Number	Formation DTSO+MSO+TSO+DTCO	Depot	Livery	Owner	Operator
317708(S)	(317308)	77007+62668+71584+77055	IL	AWT	ANG	GAR
317729(S)	(317329)	77028+62689+71605+77076	IL	AWT	ANG	GAR

Class 317/8

Vehicle Length: (Driving) 65ft 0¾in (19.83m) Width: 9ft 3in (2.82m)
(Inter) 65ft 4¼in (19.92m) Horsepower: 1,000hp (746kW)
Height: 12ft 1½in (3.58m) Seats (total/car): 20F/265S, 74S/79S/20F-42S/70S

Number	Former Number	Formation DTSO(A)+MSO+TCO+DTSO(B)	Depot	Livery	Owner	Operator	Name
317881	(317321)	77020+62681+71597+77068	IL	GAR	ANG	GAR	
317882	(317324)	77023+62684+71600+77071	IL	NXU	ANG	GAR	

317883	(317325)	77000+62685+71601+77072	IL	NXU	ANG	GAR		
317884	(317326)	77025+62686+71602+77073	IL	NXU	ANG	GAR		
317885	(317327)	77026+62687+71603+77074	IL	NXU	ANG	GAR		
317886	(317328)	77027+62688+71604+77075	IL	NXU	ANG	GAR		
317887	(317330)	77043+62704+71606+77077	IL	NXU	ANG	GAR		
317888	(317331)	77030+62691+71607+77078	IL	GAR	ANG	GAR		
317889	(317333)	77032+62693+71609+77080	IL	GAR	ANG	GAR		
317890	(317334)	77033+62694+71610+77081	IL	GAR	ANG	GAR		
317891	(317335)	77034+62695+71611+77082	IL	GAR	ANG	GAR		
317892	(317336)	77035+62696+71612+77083	IL	GAR	ANG	GAR	*Ilford Depot*	

Below: *A fleet of Class 317s, incorporating two distinct body designs, operates the Abellio Greater Anglia outer-suburban network. Sets are painted in a mix of One Railway blue, National Express white and grey and Abellio white. Set No. 317502, a phase one set, is seen at Hertford East on 1 August 2014.* **John Binch**

Class 317/7 No. 317722 is in traffic based at Ilford as a traction and rolling stock development train, fitted with different interior layouts. The set is formed of vehicles 77021+62682+71598+77069.

Class 321/3

Vehicle Length: (Driving) 65ft 0¾in (19.83m) Width: 9ft 3in (2.82m)
(Inter) 65ft 4¼in (19.92m) Horsepower: 1,328hp (996kW)
Height: 12ft 4¾in (3.78m) Seats (total/car): 16F/292S, 16F-57S/82S/75S/78S

Number	Formation	Depot	Livery	Owner	Operator	Name
	DTCO+MSO+TSO+DTSO					
321301	78049+62975+71880+77853	IL	GAR	EVL	GAR	
321302	78050+62976+71881+77854	IL	GAR	EVL	GAR	
321303	78051+62977+71882+77855	IL	GAR	EVL	GAR	
321304	78052+62978+71883+77856	IL	GAR	EVL	GAR	
321305	78053+62979+71884+77857	IL	GAR	EVL	GAR	
321306	78054+62980+71885+77858	IL	GAR	EVL	GAR	
321307	78055+62981+71886+77859	IL	GAR	EVL	GAR	
321308	78056+62982+71887+77860	IL	GAR	EVL	GAR	
321309	78057+62983+71888+77861	IL	GAR	EVL	GAR	
321310	78058+62984+71889+77862	IL	NGE	EVL	GAR	
321311	78059+62985+71890+77863	IL	GAR	EVL	GAR	
321312	78060+62986+71891+77864	IL	GAR	EVL	GAR	*Southend-on-Sea*
321313	78061+62987+71892+77865	IL	GAR	EVL	GAR	*University of Essex*
321314	78062+62988+71893+77866	IL	NGE	EVL	GAR	
321315	78063+62989+71894+77867	IL	GAR	EVL	GAR	
321316	78064+62990+71895+77868	IL	GAR	EVL	GAR	
321317	78065+62991+71896+77869	IL	GAR	EVL	GAR	
321318	78066+62992+71897+77870	IL	GAR	EVL	GAR	
321319	78067+62993+71898+77871	IL	GAR	EVL	GAR	
321320	78068+62994+71899+77872	IL	GAR	EVL	GAR	
321321	78069+62995+71900+77873	IL	GAR	EVL	GAR	*NSPCC Essex Full Stop*
321322	78070+62996+71901+77874	IL	GAR	EVL	GAR	
321323	78071+62997+71902+77875	IL	GAR	EVL	GAR	
321324	78072+62998+71903+77876	IL	GAR	EVL	GAR	
321325	78073+62999+71904+77877	IL	GAR	EVL	GAR	
321326	78074+63000+71905+77878	IL	GAR	EVL	GAR	

Greater Anglia

321327	78075+63001+71906+77879	IL	NXU	EVL	GAR		
321328	78076+63002+71907+77880	IL	GAR	EVL	GAR		
321329	78077+63003+71908+77881	IL	GAR	EVL	GAR		
321330	78078+63004+71909+77882	IL	NXU	EVL	GAR		
321331	78079+63005+71910+77883	IL	NXU	EVL	GAR		
321332	78080+63006+71911+77884	IL	NXU	EVL	GAR		
321333	78081+63007+71912+77885	IL	NXU	EVL	GAR	*Amsterdam*	
321334	78082+63008+71913+77886	IL	NXU	EVL	GAR		
321335	78083+63009+71914+77887	IL	NXU	EVL	GAR	*Geoffrey Freeman Allen*	
321336	78084+63010+71915+77888	IL	NXU	EVL	GAR		
321337	78085+63011+71916+77889	IL	NXU	EVL	GAR		
321338	78086+63012+71917+77890	IL	NXU	EVL	GAR		
321339	78087+63013+71918+77891	IL	NXU	EVL	GAR		
321340	78088+63014+71919+77892	IL	NXU	EVL	GAR		
321341	78089+63015+71920+77893	IL	NXU	EVL	GAR		
321342	78090+63016+71921+77894	IL	NXU	EVL	GAR	*R Barnes*	
321343	78091+63017+71922+77895	IL	NXU	EVL	GAR		
321344	78092+63018+71923+77896	IL	NXU	EVL	GAR		
321345	78093+63019+71924+77897	IL	NXU	EVL	GAR		
321346	78094+63020+71925+77898	IL	NGU	EVL	GAR		
321347	78131+63105+71991+78280	IL	NXU	EVL	GAR		
321348	78132+63106+71992+78281	IL	NXU	EVL	GAR		
321349	78133+63107+71993+78282	IL	NGE	EVL	GAR		
321350	78134+63108+71994+78283	IL	NXU	EVL	GAR	*Gurkha*	
321351	78135+63109+71995+78284	IL	NXU	EVL	GAR	*London Southend Airport*	
321352	78136+63110+71996+78285	IL	NXU	EVL	GAR		
321353	78137+63111+71997+78286	IL	NXU	EVL	GAR		
321354	78138+63112+71998+78287	IL	NXU	EVL	GAR		
321355	78139+63113+71999+78288	IL	NXU	EVL	GAR		
321356	78140+63114+72000+78289	IL	NGU	EVL	GAR		
321357	78141+63115+72001+78290	IL	NGE	EVL	GAR		
321358	78142+63116+72002+78291	IL	NXU	EVL	GAR		
321359	78143+63117+72003+78292	IL	AWT	EVL	GAR		
321360	78144+63118+72004+78293	IL	NXU	EVL	GAR	*Phoenix*	
321361	78145+63119+72005+78294	IL	AWT	EVL	GAR		
321362	78146+63120+72006+78295	IL	AWT	EVL	GAR		
321363	78147+63121+72007+78296	IL	AWT	EVL	GAR		
321364	78148+63122+72008+78297	IL	AWT	EVL	GAR		
321365	78149+63123+72009+78298	IL	AWT	EVL	GAR		
321366	78150+63124+72010+78299	IL	AWT	EVL	GAR		

Below: *The majority of Abellio Greater Anglia outer-suburban trains are formed of Class 321 four-car EMUs, with 66 Class 321/3s (introduced for Great Eastern use) and 28 Class 321/4s (introduced originally for Midland use) based at Ilford depot. These sets have both first and standard class seating and many have been refurbished. A mix of National Express and Abellio white liveries can be found, with doors either finished in blue or red. Set No. 321344 is illustrated at Ipswich from its DTCO end.* **Nathan Williamson**

Class 321/4

Vehicle Length: (Driving) 65ft 0¾in (19.83m) Width: 9ft 3in (2.82m)
(Inter) 65ft 4¼in (19.92m) Horsepower: 1,328hp (996kW)
Height: 12ft 4¾in (3.78m) Seats (total/car): 16F/283S, 16F-52S/79S/74S/78S

Number	Formation DTCO+MSO+TSO+DTSO	Depot	Livery	Owner	Operator	Name
321421	78115+63083+71969+77963	IL	NXU	EVL	GAR	
321422	78116+63084+71970+77964	IL	NXU	EVL	GAR	
321423	78117+63085+71971+77965	IL	NXU	EVL	GAR	
321424	78118+63086+71972+77966	IL	GAR	EVL	GAR	
321425	78119+63087+71973+77967	IL	AWT	EVL	GAR	
321426	78120+63088+71974+77968	IL	GAR	EVL	GAR	
321427	78121+63089+71975+77969	IL	GAR	EVL	GAR	
321428	78122+63090+71976+77970	IL	AWT	EVL	GAR	*The Essex Commuter*
321429	78123+69031+71977+77971	IL	GAR	EVL	GAR	
321430	78124+63092+71978+77972	IL	GAR	EVL	GAR	
321431	78151+63125+72011+78300	IL	GAR	EVL	GAR	
321432	78152+63126+72012+78301	IL	NXU	EVL	GAR	
321433	78153+63127+72013+78302	IL	NXU	EVL	GAR	
321434	78154+63128+72014+78303	IL	NXU	EVL	GAR	
321435	78155+63129+72015+78304	IL	NXU	EVL	GAR	
321436	78156+63130+72016+78305	IL	NXU	EVL	GAR	
321437	78157+63131+72017+78306	IL	NXU	EVL	GAR	
321438	78158+63132+72018+78307	IL	AWT	EVL	GAR	
321439	78159+63133+72019+78308	IL	AWT	EVL	GAR	
321440	78160+63134+72020+78309	IL	AWT	EVL	GAR	
321441	78161+63135+72021+78310	IL	AWT	EVL	GAR	
321442	78162+63136+72022+78311	IL	AWT	EVL	GAR	*Crouch Valley 1889-2014*
321443	78125+63099+71985+78274	IL	AWT	EVL	GAR	
321444	78126+63100+71986+78275	IL	AWT	EVL	GAR	*Essex Lifeboats*
321445	78127+63101+71987+78276	IL	AWT	EVL	GAR	
321446	78128+63102+71988+78277	IL	AWT	EVL	GAR	*George Mullings*
321447	78129+63103+71989+78278	IL	AWT	EVL	GAR	
321448	78130+63104+71990+78279	IL	ADV	EVL	§	

§ Eversholt development train consisting of two vehicles with Metro interior and two with suburban, seating 246 passengers and allocated to Ilford for demonstration running on Abellio Greater Anglia services.

Below: After being replaced by more modern stock on the Midland Region, the majority of Class 321/4 sets found their way to the Anglia route to be based alongside the Class 321/3 fleet at Ilford. Today the fleets are operated as one pool, even though some minor seating differences exist on the 321/4 fleet. Set No. 321442 is shown from its DTCO coach. **Antony Christie**

Passenger Train Operating Companies - Greater Anglia

Greater Anglia

Class 360/1
Desiro

Vehicle Length: 66ft 9in (20.4m)
Height: 12ft 1½in (3.7m)
Width: 9ft 2in (2.79m)

Horsepower: 1,341hp (1,000kW)
Seats (total/car): 16F/265S, 8F-59S/69S/78S/8F-59S

Number	Formation	Depot	Livery	Owner	Operator
	DMCO(A)+PTSO+TSO+DMCO(B)				
360101	65551+72551+74551+68551	IL	FNA	ANG	GAR
360102	65552+72552+74552+68552	IL	FNA	ANG	GAR
360103	65553+72553+74553+68553	IL	FNA	ANG	GAR
360104	65554+72554+74554+68554	IL	FNA	ANG	GAR
360105	65555+72555+74555+68555	IL	FNA	ANG	GAR
360106	65556+72556+74556+68556	IL	FNA	ANG	GAR
360107	65557+72557+74557+68557	IL	FNA	ANG	GAR
360108	65558+72558+74558+68558	IL	FNA	ANG	GAR
360109	65559+72559+74559+68559	IL	FNA	ANG	GAR
360110	65560+72560+74560+68560	IL	FNA	ANG	GAR
360111	65561+72561+74561+68561	IL	FNA	ANG	GAR
360112	65562+72562+74562+68562	IL	FNA	ANG	GAR
360113	65563+72563+74563+68563	IL	FNA	ANG	GAR
360114	65564+72564+74564+68564	IL	FNA	ANG	GAR
360115	65565+72565+74565+68565	IL	ENA	ANG	GAR
360116	65566+72566+74566+68566	IL	FNA	ANG	GAR
360117	65567+72567+74567+68567	IL	FNA	ANG	GAR
360118	65568+72568+74568+68568	IL	FNA	ANG	GAR
360119	65569+72569+74569+68569	IL	FNA	ANG	GAR
360120	65570+72570+74570+68570	IL	FNA	ANG	GAR
360121	65571+72571+74571+68571	IL	FNA	ANG	GAR

Left: *When First Group held the Great Eastern franchise, modernisation saw a fleet of 21 Class 360/1 Siemens 'Desiro' sets introduced for outer-suburban and long-distance service. Originally finished in Great Eastern blue, one set sports Abellio branded National Express colours. By early 2015 no sets had been repainted in Abellio white. The '360s' are allocated to Ilford. Set No. 360110 passes Pudding Mill Lane, east London, with a Colchester service.* **Antony Christie**

Class 379
Electrostar

Vehicle Length: (Driving) 66ft 9in (20.40m)
(Inter) 65ft 6in (19.99m)
Height: 12ft 4in (3.77m)

Width: 9ft 2in (2.80m)
Horsepower: 2,010hp (1,500kW)
Seats (total/car): 20F/189S, 60S/62S/43S/20F-24S

Number	Formation	Depot	Livery	Owner	Operator	Name
	DMSO(A)+MSO+TSO+DMCO					
379001	61201+61701+61901+62101	IL	NXU	MAG	GAR	
379002	61202+61702+61902+62102	IL	NXU	MAG	GAR	
379003	61203+61703+61903+62103	IL	NXU	MAG	GAR	
379004	61204+61704+61904+62104	IL	NXU	MAG	GAR	
379005	61205+61705+61905+62105	IL	NXU	MAG	GAR	*Stansted Express*
379006	61206+61706+61906+62106	IL	NXU	MAG	GAR	
379007	61207+61707+61907+62107	IL	NXU	MAG	GAR	
379008	61208+61708+61908+62108	IL	NXU	MAG	GAR	
379009	61209+61709+61909+62109	IL	NXU	MAG	GAR	
379010	61210+61710+61910+62110	IL	NXU	MAG	GAR	
379011	61211+61711+61911+62111	IL	NXU	MAG	GAR	*Ely Cathedral*
379012	61212+61712+61912+62112	IL	NXU	MAG	GAR	*The West Anglian*
379013§	61213+61713+61913+62113	IL	NXU	MAG	GAR	
379014	61214+61714+61914+62114	IL	NXU	MAG	GAR	

379015	61215+61715+61915+62115	IL	NXU	MAG	GAR	*City of Cambridge*
379016	61216+61716+61916+62116	IL	NXU	MAG	GAR	
379017	61217+61717+61917+62117	IL	NXU	MAG	GAR	
379018	61218+61718+61918+62118	IL	NXU	MAG	GAR	
379019	61219+61719+61919+62119	IL	NXU	MAG	GAR	
379020	61220+61720+61920+62120	IL	NXU	MAG	GAR	
379021	61221+61721+61921+62121	IL	NXU	MAG	GAR	
379022	61222+61722+61922+62122	IL	NXU	MAG	GAR	
379023	61223+61723+61923+62123	IL	NXU	MAG	GAR	
379024	61224+61724+61924+62124	IL	NXU	MAG	GAR	
379025	61225+61725+61925+62125	IL	NXU	MAG	GAR	*Go Discover*
379026	61226+61726+61926+62126	IL	NXU	MAG	GAR	
379027	61227+61727+61927+62127	IL	NXU	MAG	GAR	
379028	61228+61728+61928+62128	IL	NXU	MAG	GAR	
379029	61229+61729+61929+62129	IL	NXU	MAG	GAR	
379030	61230+61730+61930+62130	IL	NXU	MAG	GAR	

IPEMU: § *379013 modified as Independently Powered Electric Multiple Unit (IPEMU) for battery electric operation, fitted at Bombardier Derby in 5-7 2014. Battery Trailer from Motor Open, power bogie now unpowered, six battery rafts, toilet tank out for use on Marks Tey - Sudbury and Sudbury - Colchester.*

Above: *The most modern EMUS operated by Abellio Greater Anglia are 30 Class 379 'Electrostar' sets introduced for Cambridge and Stansted Airport services. Painted in Abellio white with blue doors, set No. 379010 is illustrated at Cheshunt on 8 August 2014.* **John Binch**

Heathrow Express / Heathrow Connect

Address: ✉ 6th Floor, 50 Eastbourne Terrace, Paddington, London, W2 6LX
🖥 Queries@heathrowexpress.com or queries@heathrowconnect.com
✆ 020 8750 6600
ⓘ www.heathrowexpress.com or www.heathrowconnect.com

Managing Director: Keith Greenfield
Franchise Dates: Private Open Access Operator
Principal Routes: London Paddington - Heathrow Airport
Owned Stations: Heathrow Central, Heathrow Terminal 4, Heathrow Terminal 5
Depots: Old Oak Common HEX (OH)
Parent Company: Heathrow Express - Heathrow Airport Ltd
Heathrow Connect - Heathrow Airport Ltd / First Group

Heathrow Express

© TRC.Com Ltd 2013

Heathrow Airport Terminal 5 — Heathrow Airport Terminals 1-3 — London Paddington

Heathrow Connect

Heathrow Airport Terminal 4 — Heathrow Airport Terminals 1-3 — Hayes — Southall — Hanwell — West Ealing — Ealing Broadway — London Paddington

Shuttle

Below: *The Heathrow Express service linking central London with Heathrow Airport is operated by a fleet of 14 Class 332 EMUS either formed as four- or five-car sets. Trains operate every 15 minutes and the journey between Paddington and the Airport takes just 15 minutes. The Heathrow Express or HEX service is operated by Heathrow Airport Ltd under an Open Access agreement. Trains carry a sponsorship livery; in 2015 this was Vodafone. Set No. 332011 is viewed at Paddington from its DMFO vehicle.* **CJM**

Class 332

Vehicle Length: (Driving) 77ft 10¾in (23.74m)
         (Inter) 75ft 11in (23.143m)
Height: 12ft 1½in (3.70m)
Width: 9ft 1in (2.75m)
Horsepower: 1,876hp (1,400kW)
Seats 4-car (total/car): 26F-148S, 26F/56S/44S/48S
    5-car (total/car): 26F-204S, 26F/56S/44S/56S/48S

Number	Formation	Depot	Livery	Owner	Operator
	DMFO+TSO+PTSO+(TSO)+DMSO				
332001	78400+72412+63400+ - +78401	OH	HEX	BAA	HEX
332002	78402+72409+63406+ - +78403	OH	HEX‡	BAA	HEX
332003	78404+72407+63402+ - +78405	OH	HEX	BAA	HEX
332004	78406+72406+63403+ - +78407	OH	HEX‡	BAA	HEX
332005	78408+72411+63404+72417+78409	OH	HEX‡	BAA	HEX
332006	78410+72410+63405+72415+78411	OH	HEX‡	BAA	HEX
332007	78412+72401+63401+72414+78413	OH	HEX‡	BAA	HEX

Vehicle Length: (Driving) 77ft 10¾in (23.74m)
         (Inter) 75ft 11in (23.143m)
Height: 12ft 1½in (3.70m)
Width: 9ft 1in (2.75m)
Horsepower: 1,876hp (1,400kW)
Seats 4-car (total/car): 14F-148S, 48S/56S/44S/14F
    5-car (total/car): 14F-204S, 48S/56S/44S/56S/14F

	DMSO+TSO+PTSO+(TSO)+DMFLO				
332008	78414+72413+63407+72418+78415	OH	HEX‡	BAA	HEX
332009	78416+72400+63408+72416+78417	OH	HEX‡	BAA	HEX
332010	78418+72402+63409+ - +78419	OH	HEX	BAA	HEX
332011	78420+72403+63410+ - +78421	OH	HEX‡	BAA	HEX
332012	78422+72404+63411+ - +78423	OH	HEX	BAA	HEX
332013	78424+72408+63412+ - +78425	OH	HEX	BAA	HEX
332014	78426+72406+63413+ - +78427	OH	HEX‡	BAA	HEX

‡ First class vehicles carry Vodafone advertising livery

Class 360/2
Desiro

Vehicle Length: 66ft 9in (20.4m)
Height: 12ft 1½in (3.7m)
Width: 9ft 2in (2.79m)
Horsepower: 1,341hp (1,000kW)
Seats (total/car): 340S, 63S/66S/74S/74S/63S
    (360205 - 280S using 2+2 seats)

Number	Formation	Depot	Livery	Owner	Operator
	DMSO(A)+PTSO+TSO+TSO+DMSO(B)				
360201	78431+63421+72431+72421+78441	OH	HEC	BAA	HEC
360202	78432+63422+72432+72422+78442	OH	HEC	BAA	HEC
360203	78433+63423+72433+72423+78443	OH	HEC	BAA	HEC
360204	78434+63424+72434+72424+78444	OH	HEC	BAA	HEC
360205	78435+63425+72435+72425+78445	OH	HEL	BAA	HEC

Below: Heathrow Airport Ltd and First Great Western operate the stopping service between Paddington and Heathrow Airport. These trains are formed of five-car Class 360 stock. Sets Nos. 360202 and 360204 are shown at West Ealing. **CJM**

Passenger Train Operating Companies - Island Line

Island Line

Address: ✉ Ryde St Johns Road Station, Ryde, Isle of Wight, PO33 2BA
📠 info@island-line.co.uk ✆ 01983 812591 ⓘ www.island-line.co.uk
Managing Director: Tim Shoveller (South West Trains) **General Manager:** Andy Naylor
Franchise Dates: Part of SWT franchise 2 February 2007 - 3 February 2017
Principal Route: Ryde Pier Head - Shanklin
Owned Stations: All
Depots: Ryde St Johns Road (RY)
Parent Company: Stagecoach

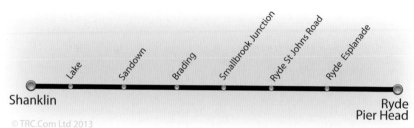

© TRC.Com Ltd 2013

Class 483

Vehicle Length: 52ft 4in (15.95m)	Horsepower: 670hp (500kW)
Height: 9ft 5¹⁄₂in (2.88m)	Seats (total/car): 82S, 40S/42S
Width: 8ft 8¹⁄₂in (2.65m)	

Number	Formation DMSO+DMSO	Depot	Livery	Owner	Operator
483002	122+224	RY	LUL	SWT	SIL
483004	124+224	RY	LUL	SWT	SIL
483006	126+226	RY	LUL	SWT	SIL
483007	127+227	RY	LUL	SWT	SIL
483008	128+228	RY	LUL	SWT	SIL
483009	129+229	RY	LUL	SWT	SIL

Below: *The self-contained Isle of Wight railway is operated by a fleet of rebuilt 1938-design two-car EMUs, maintained at Ryde St Johns Road depot and currently painted in mock London Transport red livery. The sets are in need of replacement, but continue to provide an important service. Set No. 006 is seen traversing Ryde Pier in summer 2014.* **CJM**

London Midland

Address: ✉ 102 New Street, Birmingham, B2 4JB

✎ comments@londonmidland.com

✆ 0844 811 0133

ⓘ www.londonmidland.com

Managing Director: Patrick Verwer

Franchise Dates: 11 November 2007 - March 2016

Principal Routes: London Euston - Liverpool Lime Street, West Midlands routes to Stratford-upon-Avon, Worcester, Hereford, Shrewsbury, plus Bedford and St Albans Abbey branches

Depots: Northampton (NN)§, Soho (SI), Tyseley (TS), Stourbridge Junction (SJ) § Operated by Siemens

Parent Company: Govia

Class 08

						Vehicle Length: 29ft 3in (8.91m)	Engine: English Electric 6K
						Height: 12ft 8⅝in (3.87m)	Horsepower: 400hp (298kW)
						Width: 8ft 6in (2.59m)	Electrical Equipment: English Electric

Number	Depot	Pool	Livery	Owner	Operator	Name
08616 (3783)	TS	EJLO	LMI	LMI	LMI	*Tyseley 100*
08805	SI	EJLO	BLU	LMI	LMI	*Concorde*

Class 139

| | | | | | Vehicle Length: 28ft 6in (8.7m) | Engine: 1 x MVH420 2.0ltr LPG, flywheel hybrid |
| | | | | | Width: 7ft 8in (2.4m) | Seats (total/car): 18S |

Number	Formation	Depot	Livery	Owner	Operator
	DMS				
139001	39001	SJ	LMI	LMI	LMI
139002	39002	SJ	LMI	LMI	LMI

Below: *The two London Midland 'Parry People Mover' Class 139s Nos. 139001 and 139002 are now in sole charge of services on the Stourbridge Junction to Stourbridge Town branch. The branch operates seven days a week and on Sunday 3 August 2014 No. 139002 rounds the curve into Stourbridge Junction with the 12.50 shuttle service from Stourbridge Town.* **John Binch**

Train Operating Companies

London Midland

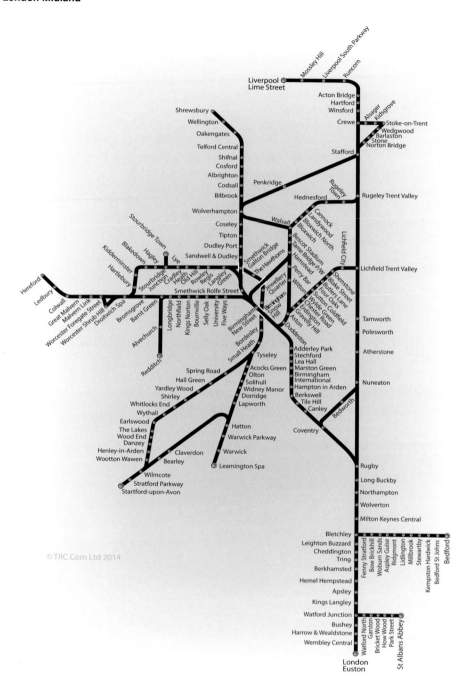

Passenger Train Operating Companies - London Midland

© TRC.Com Ltd 2014

Class 150/1
Sprinter

	Vehicle Length: 64ft 9¾in (19.74m)	Engine: 1 x NT855R5 of 285hp per vehicle
	Height: 12ft 4½in (3.77m)	Horsepower: 570hp (425kW)
	Width: 9ft 3⅛in (2.82m)	Seats (total/car): 148S, 76S/72S

Number	Formation	Depot	Livery	Owner	Operator
	DMSL+DMS				
150105	52105+57105	TS	CTL	ANG	LMI
150107	52107+57107	TS	LMI	ANG	LMI
150109	52109+57109	TS	CTL	ANG	LMI

Right: *Surprisingly, after the introduction of Class 172s to London Midland, three Class 150/1 sets were retained at Tyseley depot for deployment on the Bedford to Bletchley line as well as a handful of 'fill-in' duties mainly on the Birmingham to Hereford corridor. The three sets have received a full facelift overhaul and sport the full London Midland livery. Set No. 150105 is illustrated from its 52xxx end.* **CJM**

Class 153

	Vehicle Length: 76ft 5in (23.29m)	Engine: 1 x NT855R5 of 285hp
	Height: 12ft 3⅛in (3.75m)	Horsepower: 285hp (213kW)
	Width: 8ft 10in (2.70m)	Seats (total/car): 72S

Number	Formation	Depot	Livery	Owner	Operator		Number	Formation	Depot	Livery	Owner	Operator
	DMSL						153364	57364	TS	LMI	PTR	LMI
153334	52334	TS	LMI	PTR	LMI		153365	57365	TS	LMI	PTR	LMI
153354	57354	TS	LMI	PTR	LMI		153366	57366	TS	LMI	PTR	LMI
153356	57356	TS	LMI	PTR	LMI		153371	57371	TS	LMI	PTR	LMI
							153375	57375	TS	LMI	PTR	LMI

Right: *In 2015, London Midland still retained a fleet of eight Class 153 single-car or 'bubble cars' for branch line or lightly used services. Allocated to Tyseley, the vehicles all sport London Midland livery. Set No. 153366 (57366) is shown from its large (original) cab end at Bedworth.* **John Binch**

Class 170/5
Turbostar

	Vehicle Length: 77ft 6in (23.62m)	Engine: 1 x MTU 6R 183TD13H of 422hp per vehicle
	Height: 12ft 4½in (3.77m)	Horsepower: 844hp (629kW)
	Width: 8ft 10in (2.69m)	Seats (total/car): 122S 55S/67S

Number	Formation	Depot	Livery	Owner	Operator		Number	Formation	Depot	Livery	Owner	Operator
	DMSL+DMSL						170504	50504+79504	TS	LMI	PTR	LMI
							170505	50505+79505	TS	LMI	PTR	LMI
170501	50501+79501	TS	LMI	PTR	LMI		170506	50506+79506	TS	LMI	PTR	LMI
170502	50502+79502	TS	LMI	PTR	LMI		170507	50507+79507	TS	LMI	PTR	LMI
170503	50503+79503	TS	LMI	PTR	LMI		170508	50508+79508	TS	LMI	PTR	LMI

London Midland

170509	50509+79509	TS	LMI	PTR	LMI		170514	50514+79514	TS	LMI	PTR	LMI
170510	50510+79510	TS	LMI	PTR	LMI		170515	50515+79515	TS	LMI	PTR	LMI
170511	50511+79511	TS	LMI	PTR	LMI		170516	50516+79516	TS	LMI	PTR	LMI
170512	50512+79512	TS	LMI	PTR	LMI		170517	50517+79517	TS	LMI	PTR	LMI
170513	50513+79513	TS	LMI	PTR	LMI							

Above: *Two sub-classes of Class 170 'Turbostar' DMU stock are operated by London Midland, with 17 two-car and six three-car sets of Class 170/5 and 170/6 allocated to Tyseley depot. These refurbished sets are deployed on longer-distance outer-suburban routes and carry the London Midland City livery. Set No. 170512 is illustrated.* **CJM**

Class 170/6
Turbostar

Vehicle Length: 77ft 6in (23.62m)	*Engine: 1 x MTU 6R 183TD13H of 422hp per vehicle*
Height: 12ft 4½in (3.77m)	*Horsepower: 1,266hp (944kW)*
Width: 8ft 10in (2.69m)	*Seats (total/car): 196S 55S/74S/67S*

Number	Formation DMSL+MS+DMSL	Depot	Livery	Owner	Operator
170630	50630+56630+79630	TS	LMI	PTR	LMI
170631	50631+56631+79631	TS	LMI	PTR	LMI
170632	50632+56632+79632	TS	LMI	PTR	LMI
170633	50633+56633+79633	TS	LMI	PTR	LMI
170634	50634+56634+79634	TS	LMI	PTR	LMI
170635	50635+56635+79635	TS	LMI	PTR	LMI

Class 172/2
Turbostar

Vehicle Length: 73ft 4in (22.37m)	*Engine: MTU 6H1800 of of 482hp (360kW) per vehicle*
Height: 12ft 4½in (3.77m)	*Horsepower: 965hp (720kW)*
Width: 8ft 8in (2.69m)	*Seats (total/car): 121S, 53S/68S*

Number	Formation DMS+DMS	Depot	Livery	Owner	Operator		Number	Formation	Depot	Livery	Owner	Operator
							172216	50216+79216	TS	LMI	PTR	LMI
							172217	50217+79217	TS	LMI	PTR	LMI
172211	50211+79211	TS	LMI	PTR	LMI		172218	50218+79218	TS	LMI	PTR	LMI
172212	50212+79212	TS	LMI	PTR	LMI		172219	50219+59219	TS	LMI	PTR	LMI
172213	50213+79213	TS	LMI	PTR	LMI		172220	50220+79220	TS	LMI	PTR	LMI
172214	50214+79214	TS	LMI	PTR	LMI		172221	50221+79221	TS	LMI	PTR	LMI
172215	50215+79215	TS	LMI	PTR	LMI		172222	50222+79222	TS	LMI	PTR	LMI

Right: *Introduced in 2011-2012, 12 two-car and 15 three-car Bombardier Class 172 sets were introduced by London Midland to replace aging Class 150 stock on Birmingham area services. These are the only gangway-fitted example of the Class 172 design, with their front-end structure closely following that of the Bombardier 'Electrostar'-build. Seating 121 standard class passengers, two-car set No. 172218 is seen at Kidderminster on 31 May 2014.* **CJM**

Class 172/3
Turbostar

Vehicle Length: (Driving) 73ft 4in (22.37m)	Engine: MTU 6H1800 of 482hp (360kW) per vehicle
(Inter): 76ft 7in (23.36m)	Horsepower: 1,446hp (1,080kW)
Height: 12ft 4½in (3.77m)	Seats (total/car): 193S, 53S/72S/68S
Width: 8ft 8in (2.69m)	

Number	Formation DMSO+MS+DMSO	Depot	Livery	Owner	Operator
172331	50331+56331+79331	TS	LMI	PTR	LMI
172332	50332+56332+79332	TS	LMI	PTR	LMI
172333	50333+56333+79333	TS	LMI	PTR	LMI
172334	50334+56334+79334	TS	LMI	PTR	LMI
172335	50335+56335+79335	TS	LMI	PTR	LMI
172336	50336+56336+79336	TS	LMI	PTR	LMI
172337	50337+56337+79337	TS	LMI	PTR	LMI
172338	50338+56338+79338	TS	LMI	PTR	LMI
172339	50339+56339+79339	TS	LMI	PTR	LMI
172340	50340+56340+79340	TS	LMI	PTR	LMI
172341	50341+56341+79341	TS	LMI	PTR	LMI
172342	50342+56342+79342	TS	LMI	PTR	LMI
172343	50343+56343+79343	TS	LMI	PTR	LMI
172344	50344+56344+79344	TS	LMI	PTR	LMI
172345	50345+56345+79345	TS	LMI	PTR	LMI

Below: *Due to the high number of passengers travelling over the Birmingham area non-electrified network, 15 Class 172s were built as three-car sets, increasing seats by 72 per train to 193. The three-car sets form sub-class 172/3 and are allocated to Tyseley depot. Set No. 172332 is illustrated.* **CJM**

Left: *Class 172/3 intermediate vehicle, seating 72 in the low-density 2+2 style. These air-conditioned vehicles have two pairs of bi-parting sliding-plug doors on each side, feeding directly into the main passenger compartment. Vehicle No. 56332 from set 172332 is illustrated.* **CJM**

Class 321/4

Vehicle Length: (Driving) 65ft 0¾in (19.83m) *Width: 9ft 3in (2.82m)*
(Inter) 65ft 4¼in (19.92m) *Horsepower: 1,328hp (996kW)*
Height: 12ft 4¾in (3.78m) *Seats (total/car): 28F/271S, 28F-40S/79S/74S/78S*

Number	Formation DMCO+MSO+TSO+DMSO	Depot	Livery	Owner	Operator
321411	78105+63073+71959+77953	NN	LMI	EVL	LMI
321412	78106+63074+71960+77954	NN	LMI	EVL	LMI
321413	78107+63075+71961+77955	NN	LMI	EVL	LMI
321414	78108+63076+71962+77956	NN	LMI	EVL	LMI
321415	78109+63077+71963+77957	NN	LMI	EVL	LMI
321416	78110+63078+71964+77958	NN	LMI	EVL	LMI
321417	78111+63079+71965+77959	NN	LMI	EVL	LMI

Left: *The London Midland service requirement dictated that even after the introduction of Class 350 'Desiro' stock, London Midland was required to retain seven of the Class 321 four-car sets mainly for peak-hour operation. The sets are allocated to Northampton depot and usually operate the shorter-distance services. Set No. 321417 is illustrated from its first class end, identifiable by the black triangle on the left side of the front end.* **CJM**

Class 323

Vehicle Length: (Driving) 76ft 8¼in (23.37m) *Width: 9ft 2¼in (2.80m)*
(Inter) 76ft 10¾in (23.44m) *Horsepower: 1,565hp (1,168kW)*
Height: 12ft 4¾in (3.78m) *Seats (total/car): 284S, 98S/88S/98S*

Number	Formation DMSO(A)+PTSO+DMSO(B)	Depot	Livery	Owner	Op'r
323201	64001+72201+65001	SI	LMI	PTR	LMI
323202	64002+72202+65002	SI	LMI	PTR	LMI
323203	64003+72203+65003	SI	LMI	PTR	LMI
323204	64004+72204+65004	SI	LMI	PTR	LMI
323205	64005+72205+65005	SI	LMI	PTR	LMI
323206	64006+72206+65006	SI	LMI	PTR	LMI
323207	64007+72207+65007	SI	LMI	PTR	LMI
323208	64008+72208+65008	SI	LMI	PTR	LMI
323209	64009+72209+65009	SI	LMI	PTR	LMI
323210	64010+72210+65010	SI	LMI	PTR	LMI
323211	64011+72211+65011	SI	LMI	PTR	LMI
323212	64012+72212+65012	SI	LMI	PTR	LMI
323213	64013+72213+65013	SI	LMI	PTR	LMI

323214	64014+72214+65014 SI	LMI	PTR	LMI		323221	64021+72221+65021 SI	LMI	PTR	LMI
323215	64015+72215+65015 SI	LMI	PTR	LMI		323222	64022+72222+65022 SI	LMI	PTR	LMI
323216	64016+72216+65016 SI	LMI	PTR	LMI		323240	64040+72340+65040 SI	LMI	PTR	LMI
323217	64017+72217+65017 SI	LMI	PTR	LMI		323241	64041+72341+65041 SI	LMI	PTR	LMI
323218	64018+72218+65018 SI	LMI	PTR	LMI		323242	64042+72342+65042 SI	LMI	PTR	LMI
323219	64019+72219+65019 SI	LMI	PTR	LMI		323243	64043+72343+65043 SI	LMI	PTR	LMI
323220	64020+72220+65020 SI	LMI	PTR	LMI						

Right: *The Birmingham 'CrossCity' line, the Walsall-Wolverhampton and the Birmingham-Coventry routes are operated by a fleet of 26 three-car Class 323 units allocated to Birmingham Soho depot. Owned by Porterbrook Leasing, the sets seat 284 standard class passengers. All LM sets are painted in standard London Midland City livery, as displayed on set No. 323215 at Four Oaks.*
Antony Christie

Class 350/1
Desiro

Vehicle Length: 66ft 9in (20.4m)	Horsepower: 1,341hp (1,000kW)
Height: 12ft 1½in (3.78m)	Seats (total/car): 24F-209S, 60S/24F-32S/57S/60S
Width: 9ft 2in (2.7m)	

Number	Formation DMSO(A)+TCO+PTSO+DMSO(B)	Depot	Livery	Owner	Operator
350101	63761+66811+66861+63711	NN	LMI	ANG	LMI
350102	63762+66812+66862+63712	NN	LMI	ANG	LMI
350103	63765+66813+66863+63713	NN	LMI	ANG	LMI
350104	63764+66814+66864+63714	NN	LMI	ANG	LMI
350105	63763+66815+66868+63715	NN	LMI	ANG	LMI
350106	63766+66816+66866+63716	NN	LMI	ANG	LMI
350107	63767+66817+66867+63717	NN	LMI	ANG	LMI
350108	63768+66818+66865+63718	NN	LMI	ANG	LMI
350109	63769+66819+66869+63719	NN	LMI	ANG	LMI
350110	63770+66820+66870+63720	NN	LMA	ANG	LMI
350111	63771+66821+66871+63721	NN	LMI	ANG	LMI
350112	63772+66822+66872+63722	NN	LMI	ANG	LMI
350113	63773+66823+66873+63723	NN	LMI	ANG	LMI
350114	63774+66824+66874+63724	NN	LMI	ANG	LMI
350115	63775+66825+66875+63725	NN	LMI	ANG	LMI
350116	63776+66826+66876+63726	NN	LMI	ANG	LMI
350117	63777+66827+66877+63727	NN	LMI	ANG	LMI
350118	63778+66828+66878+63728	NN	LMI	ANG	LMI
350119	63779+66829+66879+63729	NN	LMI	ANG	LMI
350120	63780+66830+66880+63730	NN	LMI	ANG	LMI
350121	63781+66831+66881+63731	NN	LMI	ANG	LMI
350122	63782+66832+66882+63732	NN	LMI	ANG	LMI
350123	63783+66833+66883+63733	NN	LMI	ANG	LMI
350124	63784+66834+66884+63734	NN	LMI	ANG	LMI
350125	63785+66835+66885+63735	NN	LMI	ANG	LMI
350126	63786+66836+66886+63736	NN	LMI	ANG	LMI
350127	63787+66837+66887+63737	NN	LMI	ANG	LMI
350128	63788+66838+66888+63738	NN	LMI	ANG	LMI
350129	63789+66839+66889+63739	NN	LMI	ANG	LMI
350130	63790+66840+66890+63740	NN	LMI	ANG	LMI

Train Operating Companies

London Midland

Left: *Three batches of Class 350 'Desiro' stock are operated by London Midland on its longer-distance passenger services from London Euston to the Midlands and North West. Thirty Class 350/1 sets are allocated to Northampton, these were the original build and were first destined for South West Trains, but changing franchise commitments saw them moved to the then Central Trains operation. These sets seat 24 first and 209 standard class passengers. The Class 350/1 sets have a full-height yellow gangway door. Set No. 350108 is illustrated.* **Antony Christie**

Class 350/2
Desiro

Vehicle Length: 66ft 9in (20.4m)	Horsepower: 1,341hp (1,000kW)	
Height: 12ft 1½in (3.78m)	Seats (total/car): 24F-243S, 70S/24F-42S/61S/70S	
Width: 9ft 2in (2.7m)		

Number	Formation DMSO(A)+TCO+PTSO+DMSO(B)	Depot	Livery	Owner	Operator	Name
350231	61431+65231+67531+61531	NN	LMI	PTR	LMI	
350232	61432+65232+67532+61532	NN	LMI	PTR	LMI	*Chad Varah*
350233	61433+65233+67533+61533	NN	LMI	PTR	LMI	
350234	61434+65234+67534+61534	NN	LMI	PTR	LMI	
350235	61435+65235+67535+61535	NN	LMI	PTR	LMI	
350236	61436+65236+67536+61536	NN	LMI	PTR	LMI	
350237	61437+65237+67537+61537	NN	LMI	PTR	LMI	
350238	61438+65238+67538+61538	NN	LMI	PTR	LMI	
350239	61439+65239+67539+61539	NN	LMI	PTR	LMI	
350240	61440+65240+67540+61540	NN	LMI	PTR	LMI	
350241	61441+65241+67541+61541	NN	LMI	PTR	LMI	
350242	61442+65242+67542+61542	NN	LMI	PTR	LMI	
350243	61443+65243+67543+61543	NN	LMI	PTR	LMI	
350244	61444+65244+67544+61544	NN	LMI	PTR	LMI	
350245	61445+65245+67545+61545	NN	LMI	PTR	LMI	
350246	61446+65246+67546+61546	NN	LMI	PTR	LMI	
350247	61447+65247+67547+61547	NN	LMI	PTR	LMI	
350248	61448+65248+67548+61548	NN	LMI	PTR	LMI	
350249	61449+65249+67549+61549	NN	LMI	PTR	LMI	
350250	61450+65250+67550+61550	NN	LMI	PTR	LMI	
350251	61451+65251+67551+61551	NN	LMI	PTR	LMI	
350252	61452+65252+67552+61552	NN	LMI	PTR	LMI	
350253	61453+65253+67553+61553	NN	LMI	PTR	LMI	
350254	61454+65254+67554+61554	NN	LMI	PTR	LMI	
350255	61455+65255+67555+61555	NN	LMI	PTR	LMI	
350256	61456+65256+67556+61556	NN	LMI	PTR	LMI	
350257	61457+65257+67557+61557	NN	LMI	PTR	LMI	
350258	61458+65258+67558+61558	NN	LMI	PTR	LMI	
350259	61459+65259+67559+61559	NN	LMI	PTR	LMI	
350260	61460+65260+67560+61560	NN	LMI	PTR	LMI	
350261	61461+65261+67561+61561	NN	LMI	PTR	LMI	
350262	61462+65262+67562+61562	NN	LMI	PTR	LMI	
350263	61463+65263+67563+61563	NN	LMI	PTR	LMI	
350264	61464+65264+67564+61564	NN	LMI	PTR	LMI	
350265	61465+65265+67565+61565	NN	LMI	PTR	LMI	

350266	61466+65266+67566+61566	NN	LMI	PTR	LMI
350267	61467+65267+67567+61567	NN	LMI	PTR	LMI

Above: *The second delivery of Class 350s to London Midland consisted of 37 Class 350/2 sets with increased seating for 24 first and 243 standard by introducing 2+3 seating. The Class 350/2 sets sport a black top section of the front gangway door, as demonstrated on set No. 350245 recorded from its DMSO(B) vehicle at Cheddington.* **Tim Easter**

Class 350/3
Desiro

Vehicle Length: 66ft 9in (20.4m)
Height: 12ft 1½in (3.78m)
Width: 9ft 2in (2.7m)

Horsepower: 1,341hp (1,000kW)
Seats (total/car): 24F-209S, 60S/24F-32S/57S/60S

Number	Formation DMSO(A)+TCO+PTSO+DMSO(B)	Depot	Livery	Owner	Operator
350368	60141+60511+60651+60151	NN	LMI	ANG	LMI
350369	60142+60512+60652+60152	NN	LMI	ANG	LMI
350370	60143+60513+60653+60153	NN	LMI	ANG	LMI
350371	60144+60514+60654+60154	NN	LMI	ANG	LMI
350372	60145+60515+60655+60155	NN	LMI	ANG	LMI
350373	60146+60516+60656+60156	NN	LMI	ANG	LMI
350374	60147+60517+60657+60157	NN	LMI	ANG	LMI
350375	60148+60518+60658+60158	NN	LMI	ANG	LMI
350376	60149+60519+60659+60159	NN	LMI	ANG	LMI
350377	60150+60520+60660+60160	NN	LMI	ANG	LMI

Below: *In 2014, a further fleet of 10 Class 350/3 'Desiro' sets was delivered to London Midland at Northampton from Siemens in Germany. These sets are identical to the Class 350/2s and also have the half black painted front gangway door. Set No. 350373 is illustrated at Crewe from its DMSO(B) vehicle.* **Jim Wade**

London Overground

Address: ✉ 125 Finchley Road, London, NW3 6HY
📱 overgroundinfo@tfl.gov.uk
📞 0845 601 4867
ⓘ www.tfl.gov.uk/overground

Managing Director: Steve Murphy
Principal Routes: Clapham Junction - Willesden, Richmond - Stratford
Gospel Oak - Barking, Euston - Watford
East London Line – Dalston - West Croydon
Depots: Willesden (WN), New Cross Gate (NX), Silwood Sidings
Parent Company: Transport for London

Passenger Train Operating Companies - London Overground

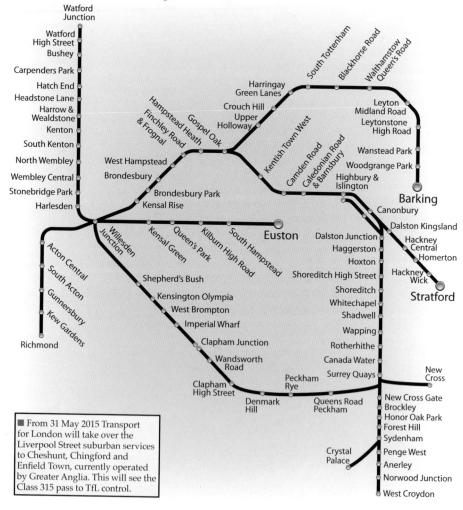

■ From 31 May 2015 Transport
for London will take over the
Liverpool Street suburban services
to Cheshunt, Chingford and
Enfield Town, currently operated
by Greater Anglia. This will see the
Class 315 pass to TfL control.

Class 09/0

Vehicle Length: 29ft 3in (8.91m)		Engine: English Electric 6K			
Height: 12ft 8⅝in (3.87m)		Horsepower: 400hp (298kW)			
Width: 8ft 6in (2.59m)		Electrical Equipment: English Electric			

Number	Depot	Pool	Livery	Owner	Operator
09007 (D3671)	WN	-	GRN	LOG	LOG

Right: *Transport for London's, London Overground operation has just one loco on its books, Class 09 400hp diesel-electric shunting loco No. 09007, or D3671 as it is currently numbered. The loco is based at Willesden depot in North London is not Network Rail certified for main-line operation and is technically in industrial use, but is included in this book for completeness. The loco is painted in 1950s BR green with yellow/black 'wasp' ends, a red buffer beam and carries the 1950s BR 'Lion-on-Wheel' logo on its battery boxes. The air-brake-only loco is used as required to shunt TfL stock at Willesden depot.* **Antony Christie**

Class 172/0
Turbostar

Vehicle Length: 73ft 4in (22.37m)		Engine: MTU 6H1800R83 of 360kW (483hp) per car			
Height: 12ft 4½in (3.77m)		Horsepower: 965hp (720kW)			
Width: 8ft 8in (2.69m)		Seats (total/car): 124S, 60S/64S			

Number	Formation DMS+DMS	Depot	Livery	Owner	Operator
172001	59311+59411	WN	LOG	ANG	LOG
172002	59312+59412	WN	LOG	ANG	LOG
172003	59313+59413	WN	LOG	ANG	LOG
172004	59314+59414	WN	LOG	ANG	LOG
172005	59315+59415	WN	LOG	ANG	LOG
172006	59316+59416	WN	LOG	ANG	LOG
172007	59317+59417	WN	LOG	ANG	LOG
172008	59318+59418	WN	LOG	ANG	LOG

Right: *At present, a fleet of eight two-car Class 172/0 sets is operated by London Overground on the short non-electrified branch between Gospel Oak and Barking. The sets are allocated to Willesden and do not operate on any other route. Each set seats 124 standard class passengers in the 2+2 style with a sizeable amount of standing space. The Gospel Oak to Barking line is currently being electrified and when this is complete the Class 172/0 sets will be transferred to another operator; at this stage this is likely to be Chiltern Railways which also operates like units. Set No. 172001 is illustrated.* **CJM**

London Overground

Class 378/1
Capitalstar

Vehicle Length: (Driving) 20.46m, (Inter) 20.14m
Height: 11ft 9in (3.58m)
750V dc sets

Width: 9ft 2in (2.80m)
Horsepower: 2,010hp (1,500kW)
Seats (total/car): 146S, 36S/40S/34S/36S

Number	Formation DMSO+MSO+TSO+(MSO)+DMSO	Depot	Livery	Owner	Operator
378135	38035+38235+38335+38435+38135	NG	LOG	QWR	LOG
378136	38036+38236+38336+(38436)+38136	NG	LOG	QWR	LOG
378137	38037+38237+38337+38437+38137	NG	LOG	QWR	LOG
378138	38038+38238+38338+38438+38138	NG	LOG	QWR	LOG
378139	38039+38239+38339+(38439)+38139	NG	LOG	QWR	LOG
378140	38040+38240+38340+38440+38140	NG	LOG	QWR	LOG
378141	38041+38241+38341+(38441)+38141	NG	LOG	QWR	LOG
378142	38042+38242+38342+(38442)+38142	NG	LOG	QWR	LOG
378143	38043+38243+38343+38443+38143	NG	LOG	QWR	LOG
378144	38044+38244+38344+38444+38144	NG	LOG	QWR	LOG
378145	38045+38245+38345+38445+38145	NG	LOG	QWR	LOG
378146	38046+38246+38346+38446+38146	NG	LOG	QWR	LOG
378147	38047+38247+38347+(38447)+38147	NG	LOG	QWR	LOG
378148	38048+38248+38348+(38448)+38148	NG	LOG	QWR	LOG
378149	38049+38249+38349+(38449)+38149	NG	LOG	QWR	LOG
378150	38050+38250+38350+(38450)+38150	NG	LOG	QWR	LOG
378151	38051+38251+38351+(38451)+38151	NG	LOG	QWR	LOG
378152	38052+38252+38352+(38452)+38152	NG	LOG	QWR	LOG
378153	38053+38253+38353+(38453)+38153	NG	LOG	QWR	LOG
378154	38054+38254+38354+(38454)+38154	NG	LOG	QWR	LOG

Sets 378150-378154 fitted with de-icing equipment

Left and Below: *London Overground operations as detailed on the map on page 94, with the exception of the Gospel Oak-Barking line, are operated by a fleet of Class 378 units. The Class 378/1 sets are only fitted for third rail dc power operation and operate on the Highbury & Islington to Croydon, New Cross and Clapham Junction route. These sets could be ac-fitted with a pantograph in the future if required. A TSO vehicle is shown left and set No. 378138 is seen below. Both:* **CJM**

Class 378/2
Capitalstar

Vehicle Length: (Driving) 20.46m, (Inter) 20.14m	Width: 9ft 2in (2.80m)	
Height: 11ft 9in (3.58m)	Horsepower: 2,010hp (1,500kW)	
Dual voltage - 750V dc third rail and 25kV ac overhead	Seats (total/car): 146S, 36S/40S/34S/36S	

Sets built as 3-car units as Class 378/0, MSO added and reclassified as 378/2

Number	Formation DMSO+MSO+PTSO+(MSO)+DMSO	Depot	Livery	Owner	Operator
378201 (378001)	38001+38201+38301+38401+38101	NG	LOG	QWR	LOG
378202 (378002)	38002+38202+38302+(38402)+38102	NG	LOG	QWR	LOG
378203 (378003)	38003+38203+38303+(38403)+38103	NG	LOG	QWR	LOG
378204 (378004)	38004+38204+38304+(38404)+38104	NG	LOG	QWR	LOG
378205 (378005)	38005+38205+38305+(38405)+38105	NG	LOG	QWR	LOG
378206 (378006)	38006+38206+38306+(38406)+38106	NG	LOG	QWR	LOG
378207 (378007)	38007+38207+38307+(38407)+38107	NG	LOG	QWR	LOG
378208 (378008)	38008+38208+38308+(38408)+38108	NG	LOG	QWR	LOG
378209 (378009)	38009+38209+38309+(38409)+38109	NG	LOG	QWR	LOG
378210 (378010)	38010+38210+38310+(38410)+38110	NG	LOG	QWR	LOG
378211 (378011)	38011+38211+38311+(38411)+38111	NG	LOG	QWR	LOG
378212 (378012)	38012+38212+38312+(38412)+38112	NG	LOG	QWR	LOG
378213 (378013)	38013+38213+38313+(38413)+38113	NG	LOG	QWR	LOG
378214 (378014)	38014+38214+38314+(38414)+38114	NG	LOG	QWR	LOG
378215 (378015)	38015+38215+38315+(38415)+38115	NG	LOG	QWR	LOG
378216 (378016)	38016+38216+38316+(38416)+38116	NG	LOG	QWR	LOG
378217 (378017)	38017+38217+38317+(38417)+38117	NG	LOG	QWR	LOG
378218 (378018)	38018+38218+38318+(38418)+38118	NG	LOG	QWR	LOG
378219 (378019)	38019+38219+38319+(38419)+38119	NG	LOG	QWR	LOG
378220 (378020)	38020+38220+38320+(38420)+38120	NG	LOG	QWR	LOG
378221 (378021)	38021+38221+38321+(38421)+38121	NG	LOG	QWR	LOG
378222 (378022)	38022+38222+38322+(38422)+38122	NG	LOG	QWR	LOG
378223 (378023)	38023+38223+38323+(38423)+38123	NG	LOG	QWR	LOG
378224 (378024)	38024+38224+38324+(38424)+38124	NG	LOG	QWR	LOG

Sets 378216-378220 fitted with de-icing equipment

Number	Formation DMSO+MSO+TSO+(MSO)+DMSO	Depot	Livery	Owner	Operator	Name
378225	38025+38225+38325+(38425)+38125	NG	LOG	QWR	LOG	
378226	38026+38226+38326+(38426)+38126	NG	LOG	QWR	LOG	
378227	38027+38227+38327+(38427)+38127	NG	LOG	QWR	LOG	
378228	38028+38228+38328+(38428)+38128	NG	LOG	QWR	LOG	
378229	38029+38229+38329+(38429)+38129	NG	LOG	QWR	LOG	
378230	38030+38230+38330+(38430)+38130	NG	LOG	QWR	LOG	
378231	38031+38231+38331+(38431)+38131	NG	LOG	QWR	LOG	
378232	38032+38232+38332+(38432)+38132	NG	LOG	QWR	LOG	
378233	38033+38233+38333+(38433)+38133	NG	LOG	QWR	LOG	Ian Brown CBE
378234	38034+38234+38334+(38434)+38134	NG	LOG	QWR	LOG	
378255	38055+38255+38355+(38455)+38155	NG	LOG	QWR	LOG	
378256	38056+38256+38356+(38456)+38156	NG	LOG	QWR	LOG	
378257	38057+38257+38357+(38457)+38157	NG	LOG	QWR	LOG	

Right: The Class 378/2 sets are equipped for ac/dc operation and used on the Euston-Watford and Richmond-Stratford routes. The sets are identical to the Class 378/1s in terms of design and interior layout. Set No. 378233 is illustrated from its DMSO(A) end.
CJM

■ All sets are currently being strengthened to five car by inserting an additional MSO; this project will be completed in 2015.

Merseyrail

Address: ✉ Rail House, Lord Nelson Street, Liverpool, L1 1JF
✍ comment@merseyrail.org
✆ 0151 702 2534
ⓘ www.merseyrail.org
Managing Director: Alan Chaplin (interim)
Franchise Dates: 20 July 2003 - 19 July 2028
Principal Routes: All non-main-line services in Liverpool area
Depots: Birkenhead North (BD)
Parent Company: Serco / Abellio

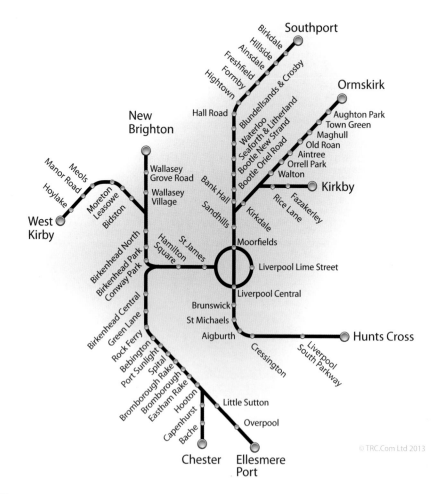

Passenger Train Operating Companies - Merseyrail

Class 507

Vehicle Length: (Driving) 64ft 11½in (19.80m) Width: 9ft 3in (2.82m)
(Inter) 65ft 4¼in (19.92m) Horsepower: 880hp (656kW)
Height: 11ft 6½in (3.58m) Seats (total/car): 186S, 56S/74S/56S

Number	Formation DMSO+TSO+DMSO	Depot	Livery	Owner	Operator	Name
507001	64367+71342+64405	BD	MEY	ANG	MER	
507002	64368+71343+64406	BD	ADV	ANG	MER	
507003	64369+71344+64407	BD	MEY	ANG	MER	
507004	64388+71345+64408	BD	MER	ANG	MER	Bob Paisley
507005	64371+71346+64409	BD	MEY	ANG	MER	
507006	64372+71347+64410	BD	MEY	ANG	MER	
507007	64373+71348+64411	BD	MER	ANG	MER	
507008	64374+71349+64412	BD	MER	ANG	MER	Harold Wilson
507009	64375+71350+64413	BD	MER	ANG	MER	Dixie Dean
507010	64376+71351+64414	BD	MEY	ANG	MER	
507011	64377+71352+64415	BD	MEY	ANG	MER	
507012	64378+71353+64416	BD	MEY	ANG	MER	
507013	64379+71354+64417	BD	MER	ANG	MER	
507014	64380+71355+64418	BD	MEY	ANG	MER	
507015	64381+71356+64419	BD	MEY	ANG	MER	
507016	64382+71357+64420	BD	MEY	ANG	MER	
507017	64383+71358+64421	BD	MEY	ANG	MER	
507018	64384+71359+64422	BD	MEY	ANG	MER	
507019	64385+71360+64423	BD	MEY	ANG	MER	
507020	64386+71361+64424	BD	MEY	ANG	MER	
507021	64387+71362+64425	BD	MEY	ANG	MER	
507023	64389+71364+64427	BD	MEY	ANG	MER	Operating Inspector Stuart Mason
507024	64390+71365+64428	BD	MER	ANG	MER	
507025	64391+71366+64429	BD	MEY	ANG	MER	
507026	64392+71367+64430	BD	MEY	ANG	MER	
507027	64393+71368+64431	BD	MEY	ANG	MER	
507028	64394+71369+64432	BD	MEY	ANG	MER	
507029	64395+71370+64433	BD	MER	ANG	MER	
507030	64396+71371+64434	BD	MEY	ANG	MER	
507031	64397+71372+64435	BD	MEY	ANG	MER	
507032	64398+71373+64436	BD	MEY	ANG	MER	
507033	64399+71374+64437	BD	MER	ANG	MER	Councillor Jack Spriggs

Above: *The Liverpool Merseyrail system operates a fleet of 32 Class 507 three-car sets, based on the original 1972-design PEP units. The sets are allocated to Birkenhead North depot and owned by Angel Trains. All sets are now refurbished with high-back 2+2 seats and a much improved passenger interior including information systems. Livery is a mix of Merseyrail silver, yellow and advertising branding. Set No. 507002 is seen at Blundellsands & Crosby with a Southport to Hunts Cross service and displays a vinyl advertisement in support of Liverpool Hope University.* **Peter Marsh**

Passenger Train Operating Companies - Merseyrail

Class 508/1

Vehicle Length: (Driving) 64ft 11½in (19.80m)		Width: 9ft 3in (2.82m)		
(Inter) 65ft 4¼in (19.92m)		Horsepower: 880hp (656kW)		
Height: 11ft 6½in (3.58m)		Seats (total/car): 186S, 56S/74S/56S		

Number	Formation DMSO+TSO+DMSO	Depot	Livery	Owner	Operator	Name
508103	64651+71485+64694	BD	MER	ANG	MER	
508104	64652+71486+64964	BD	MER	ANG	MER	
508108	64656+71490+64699	BD	MEY	ANG	MER	
508110	64658+71492+64701	BD	MEY	ANG	MER	
508111	64659+71493+64702	BD	SPL	ANG	MER	*The Beatles*
508112	64660+71494+64703	BD	MER	ANG	MER	
508114	64662+71496+64705	BD	MEY	ANG	MER	
508115	64663+71497+64708	BD	MEY	ANG	MER	
508117	64665+71499+64908	BD	MEY	ANG	MER	
508120	64668+71502+64711	BD	MEY	ANG	MER	
508122	64670+71504+64713	BD	MEY	ANG	MER	
508123	64671+71505+64714	BD	MEY	ANG	MER	*William Roscoe*
508124	64672+71506+64715	BD	MEY	ANG	MER	
508125	64673+71507+64716	BD	MER	ANG	MER	
508126	64674+71508+64717	BD	MEY	ANG	MER	
508127	64675+71509+64718	BD	MER	ANG	MER	
508128	64676+71510+64719	BD	MEY	ANG	MER	
508130	64678+71512+64721	BD	MEY	ANG	MER	
508131	64679+71513+64722	BD	MER	ANG	MER	
508134	64682+71516+64725	BD	MER	ANG	MER	
508136	64684+71518+64727	BD	MEY	ANG	MER	*Wilfred Owen MC*
508137	64685+71519+64728	BD	MEY	ANG	MER	
508138	64686+71520+64729	BD	MEY	ANG	MER	
508139	64687+71521+64730	BD	MEY	ANG	MER	
508140	64688+71522+64731	BD	MEY	ANG	MER	
508141	64689+71523+64732	BD	MEY	ANG	MER	
508143	64691+71525+64734	BD	MEY	ANG	MER	

Above: *Operating alongside the Class 507 fleet are 27 Class 508s which were originally introduced on the Southern Region and transferred to Merseyside upon introduction of Class 455s. The sets are identical to the Class 507s and again sport a mix of grey and yellow livery. Showing the grey colours and the revised front end received at a past refurbishment, set No. 508140 is illustrated at Meols.* **John Binch**

Northern Rail

Address:	✉ Northern House, 9 Rougier Street, York, YO1 6HZ
	✎ customer.relations@northernrail.org
	ℂ 0845 000125
	ⓘ www.northernrail.org
Managing Director:	Alex Hynes
Franchise Dates:	12 December 2004 - 1 February 2016
Principal Routes:	Regional services in Merseyside, Greater Manchester, South/ North Yorkshire, Lancashire, Cumbria and the North East
Depots:	Newton Heath (NH), Heaton (HT), Longsight (LG), Neville Hill (NL), Allerton (AN)
Parent Company:	Serco/Abellio

Class 142
Pacer

Vehicle Length: 51ft 0½in (15.55m)
Height: 12ft 8in (3.86m)
Width: 9ft 2¼in (2.80m)
Engine: 1 x Cummins LTA10-R per vehicle
Horsepower: 460hp (343kW)
Seats (total/car): 106S, 56S/50S

Number	Formation DMS+DMSL	Depot	Livery	Owner	Operator		Number	Formation	Depot	Livery	Owner	Operator
142001	55542+55592	NH	NOU	ANG	NOR		142044	55585+55635	NH	NOR	ANG	NOR
142003	55544+55594	NH	NOR	ANG	NOR		142045	55586+55636	NH	NOR	ANG	NOR
142004	55545+55595	NH	NOR	ANG	NOR		142046	55587+55637	NH	NOR	ANG	NOR
142005	55546+55596	NH	NOR	ANG	NOR		142047	55588+55638	NH	NOR	ANG	NOR
142007	55548+55598	NH	NOR	ANG	NOR		142048	55589+55639	NH	NOR	ANG	NOR
142009	55550+55600	NH	NOU	ANG	NOR		142049	55590+55640	NH	NOR	ANG	NOR
142011	55552+55602	NH	NOR	ANG	NOR		142050	55591+55641	HT	NOR	ANG	NOR
142012	55553+55603	NH	NOR	ANG	NOR		142051	55701+55747	NH	NOR	ANG	NOR
142013	55554+55604	NH	NOR	ANG	NOR		142052	55702+55748	NH	NOR	ANG	NOR
142014	55555+55605	NH	NOR	ANG	NOR		142053	55703+55749	NH	NOR	ANG	NOR
142015	55556+55606	HT	NOR	ANG	NOR		142054	55704+55750	NH	NOR	ANG	NOR
142016	55557+55607	HT	NOR	ANG	NOR		142055	55705+55751	NH	NOR	ANG	NOR
142017	55558+55608	HT	NOR	ANG	NOR		142056	55706+55752	NH	NOR	ANG	NOR
142018	55559+55609	HT	NOR	ANG	NOR		142057	55707+55753	NH	NOR	ANG	NOR
142019	55560+55610	HT	NOR	ANG	NOR		142058	55708+55754	NH	NOR	ANG	NOR
142020	55561+55611	HT	NOR	ANG	NOR		142060	55710+55756	NH	NOR	ANG	NOR
142021	55562+55612	HT	NOR	ANG	NOR		142061	55711+55757	NH	NOR	ANG	NOR
142022	55563+55613	HT	NOR	ANG	NOR		142062	55712+55758	NH	NOR	ANG	NOR
142023	55564+55614	NH	NOR	ANG	NOR		142063	55713+55759	NH	NOU	ANG	NOR
142024	55565+55615	HT	NOR	ANG	NOR		142064	55714+55760	NH	NOU	ANG	NOR
142025	55566+55616	HT	NOR	ANG	NOR		142065	55715+55761	HT	NOR	ANG	NOR
142026	55567+55617	HT	NOR	ANG	NOR		142066	55716+55762	HT	NOR	ANG	NOR
142027	55568+55618	NH	NOR	ANG	NOR		142067	55717+55763	NH	NOR	ANG	NOR
142028	55569+55619	NH	NOR	ANG	NOR		142068	55718+55764	NH	NOU	ANG	NOR
142029	55570+55620	NH	NOU	ANG	NOR		142070	55720+55766	HT	NOR	ANG	NOR
142030	55571+55621	NH	NOU	ANG	NOR		142071	55721+55767	HT	NOR	ANG	NOR
142031	55572+55622	NH	NOR	ANG	NOR		142078	55728+55768	HT	NOR	ANG	NOR
142032	55573+55623	NH	NOR	ANG	NOR		142079	55729+55769	HT	NOR	ANG	NOR
142033	55574+55624	NH	NOR	ANG	NOR		142084	55764+55780	NH	NOR	ANG	NOR
142034	55575+55625	HT	NOR	ANG	NOR		142086	55736+55782	HT	NOR	ANG	NOR
142035	55576+55626	NH	NOR	ANG	NOR		142087	55737+55783	HT	NOR	ANG	NOR
142036	55577+55627	NH	NOR	ANG	NOR		142088	55738+55784	HT	NOR	ANG	NOR
142037	55578+55628	NH	NOR	ANG	NOR		142089	55739+55785	HT	NOR	ANG	NOR
142038	55579+55629	NH	NOR	ANG	NOR		142090	55740+55786	HT	NOR	ANG	NOR
142039	55580+55630	NH	NOR	ANG	NOR		142091	55741+55787	HT	NOR	ANG	NOR
142040	55581+55631	NH	NOR	ANG	NOR		142092	55742+55788	HT	NOR	ANG	NOR
142041	55582+55632	NH	NOR	ANG	NOR		142093	55743+55789	HT	NOR	ANG	NOR
142042(S)	55583+55633	NH	NOR	ANG	NOR		142094	55744+55790	HT	NOR	ANG	NOR
142043	55584+55634	NH	NOR	ANG	NOR		142095	55745+55791	HT	NOR	ANG	NOR
							142096	55746+55792	HT	NOR	ANG	NOR

Passenger Train Operating Companies – Northern Rail

© TRC.Com Ltd 2013

Due to size of network only principal stations shown

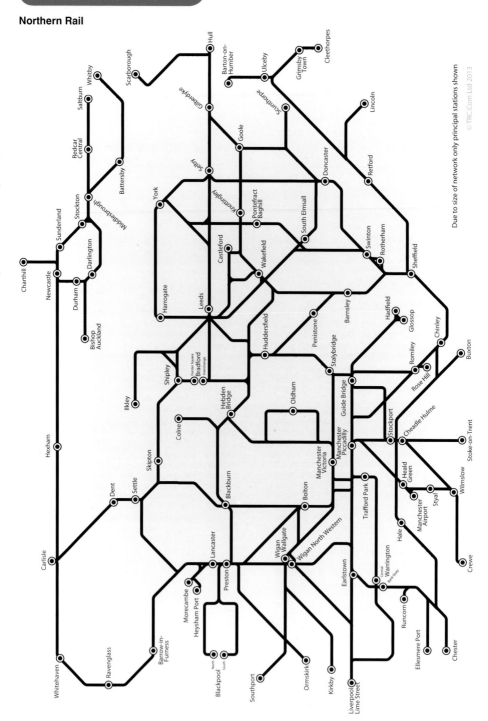

Right: *The largest operator of Class 142 'Pacer' stock is Northern Rail with in 2015 79 sets.in 2015 allocated to either Newton Heath or Heaton depots. All sets sport the Northern Rail livery of blue, mauve and white and operate over the entire Northern network. Seating is for 106 standard class passengers per set. Set No. 142070 is seen from its DMSL vehicle end at Doncaster.* **CJM**

Class 144
Pacer

Vehicle Length: 50ft 2in (15.25m)			Engine: 1 x Cummins LTA10-R per vehicle		
Height: 12ft 2½in (3.73m)			Horsepower: 460hp (343kW)		
Width: 8ft 10½in (2.70m)			Seats (total/car): 87S, 45S/42S		

Number	Formation DMS+DMSL	Depot	Livery	Owner	Operator
144001	55801+55824	NL	NOR	PTR	NOR
144002	55802+55825	NL	NOR	PTR	NOR
144003	55803+55826	NL	NOR	PTR	NOR
144004	55804+55827	NL	NOR	PTR	NOR
144005	55805+55828	NL	NOR	PTR	NOR
144006	55806+55829	NL	NOR	PTR	NOR
144007	55807+55830	NL	NOR	PTR	NOR
144008	55808+55831	NL	NOR	PTR	NOR
144009	55809+55832	NL	NOR	PTR	NOR
144010	55810+55833	NL	NOR	PTR	NOR
144011	55811+55834	NL	NOR	PTR	NOR
144012	55812+55835	NL	NOR	PTR	NOR
144013	55813+55836	NL	NOR	PTR	NOR

Name applied
144001   *The Penistone Line Partnership*

Vehicle Length: 50ft 2in (15.25m)			Engine: 1 x Cummins LTA10-R per vehicle		
Height: 12ft 2½in (3.73m)			Horsepower: 690hp (515kW)		
Width: 8ft 10½in (2.70m)			Seats (total/car): 145S, 45S/58S/42S		

Number	Formation DMS+MS+DMSL	Depot	Livery	Owner	Operator
144014	55814+55850+55837	NL	NOR	PTR	NOR
144015	55815+55851+55838	NL	NOR	PTR	NOR
144016	55816+55852+55839	NL	NOR	PTR	NOR
144017	55817+55853+55840	NL	NOR	PTR	NOR
144018	55818+55854+55841	NL	NOR	PTR	NOR
144019	55819+55855+55842	NL	NOR	PTR	NOR
144020	55820+55856+55843	NL	NOR	PTR	NOR
144021	55821+55857+55844	NL	NOR	PTR	NOR
144022	55822+55858+55845	NL	NOR	PTR	NOR
144023	55823+(55859)+55846	NL	NOR	PTR	NOR

Right: *The BREL/Walter Alexander-built Class 144s operate in both two-car sets (13) and three-car sets (10). All are allocated to Leeds Neville Hill depot and are painted in standard Northern colours. These sets usually operate within the Yorkshire area. All sets have 2+2 seating with a two-car set accommodating 87 and a three-car set 145 passengers. Set No. 144005 is seen from its DMS vehicle at Knottingley.* **CJM**

Northern Rail

Class 150/1
Sprinter

Vehicle Length: 64ft 9¾in (19.74m)
Height: 12ft 4½in (3.77m)
Width: 9ft 3⅛in (2.82m)

Engine: 1 x NT855R5 of 285hp per vehicle
Horsepower: 570hp (425kW)
Seats (total/car): 124S, 59S/65S

Number	Formation DMSL+DMS	Depot	Livery	Owner	Operator
150103	52103+57103	NH	NOR	ANG	NOR
150110	52110+57110	NH	NOR	ANG	NOR
150111	52111+57111	NH	NOR	ANG	NOR
150112	52112+57112	NH	NOR	ANG	NOR
150113	52113+57113	NH	NOR	ANG	NOR
150114	52114+57114	NH	NOR	ANG	NOR
150115	52115+57115	NH	NOR	ANG	NOR
150116	52116+57116	NH	NOR	ANG	NOR
150117	52117+57117	NH	NOR	ANG	NOR
150118	52118+57118	NH	NOR	ANG	NOR
150119	52119+57119	NH	NOR	ANG	NOR
150132	52132+57132	NH	NOR	ANG	NOR
150133	52133+57133	NH	NOR	ANG	NOR
150134	52134+57134	NH	NOR	ANG	NOR
150135	52135+57135	NH	NOR	ANG	NOR
150136	52136+57136	NH	NOR	ANG	NOR
150137	52137+57137	NH	NOR	ANG	NOR
150138	52138+57138	NH	NOR	ANG	NOR
150139	52139+57139	NH	NOR	ANG	NOR
150140	52140+57140	NH	NOR	ANG	NOR
150141	52141+57141	NH	NOR	ANG	NOR
150142	52142+57142	NH	NOR	ANG	NOR
150143	52143+57143	NH	NOR	ANG	NOR
150144	52144+57144	NH	NOR	ANG	NOR
150145	52145+57145	NH	NOR	ANG	NOR
150146	52146+57146	NH	NOR	ANG	NOR
150147	52147+57147	NH	NOR	ANG	NOR
150148	52148+57148	NH	NOR	ANG	NOR
150149	52149+57149	NH	NOR	ANG	NOR
150150	52150+57150	NH	NOR	ANG	NOR

Left: A fleet of 30 Class 150/1 non-gangwayed 'Sprinter' sets is operated by Northern from Newton Heath depot in Manchester, and are owned by Angel Trains. The sets are all painted in standard Northern Rail livery. Set No. 150111 is seen at Chinley.
John Binch

Class 150/2
Sprinter

Vehicle Length: 64ft 9¾in (19.74m)
Height: 12ft 4½in (3.77m)
Width: 9ft 3⅛in (2.82m)

Engine: 1 x NT855R5 of 285hp per vehicle
Horsepower: 570hp (425kW)
Seats (total/car): 132S, 62S/70S

Number	Formation DMSL+DMS	Depot	Livery		Owner	Operator
150201	52201+57201	NH	NOR		ANG	NOR
150203	52203+57203	NH	NOR	¤	ANG	NOR
150204	52204+57204	NH	NOR		ANG	NOR
150205	52205+57205	NH	NOR	¤	ANG	NOR
150206	52206+57206	NH	NOR		ANG	NOR
150207	52207+57207	NH	NOR	¤	ANG	NOR
150210	52210+57210	NH	NOR		ANG	NOR
150211	52211+57211	NH	NOR	¤	ANG	NOR
150214	52214+57214	NH	NOR		ANG	NOR
150215	52215+57215	NH	NOR	¤	ANG	NOR
150218	52218+57218	NH	NOR	¤	ANG	NOR
150220	52220+57220	NH	NOR		ANG	NOR
150222	52222+57222	NH	NOR	¤	ANG	NOR
150223	52223+57223	NH	NOR		ANG	NOR
150224	52224+57224	NH	NOR		ANG	NOR
150225	52225+57225	NH	NOR	¤	ANG	NOR
150226	52226+57226	NH	NOR		ANG	NOR
150228	52228+57228	NH	NOR	¤	PTR	NOR
150268	52268+57268	NH	NOR	¤	PTR	NOR
150269	52269+57269	NH	NOR	¤	PTR	NOR
150270	52270+57270	NH	NOR	¤	PTR	NOR
150271	52271+57271	NH	NOR	¤	PTR	NOR
150272	52272+57272	NH	NOR	¤	PTR	NOR
150273	52273+57273	NH	NOR	¤	PTR	NOR
150274	52274+57274	NH	NOR	¤	PTR	NOR
150275	52275+57275	NH	NOR	¤	PTR	NOR
150276	52276+57276	NH	NOR	¤	PTR	NOR
150277	52277+57277	NH	NOR	¤	PTR	NOR

¤ **Advertising liveries**
150203 - Yorkshire
150205 - Yorkshire
150207 - Yorkshire
150211 - Yorkshire
150215 - Yorkshire
150218 - Yorkshire
150222 - Yorkshire
150225 - Yorkshire
150228 - Yorkshire
150268 - Heritage
150269 - Yorkshire
150270 - City Life
150271 - Arts
150272 - Colne Festival
150273 - Yorkshire
150274 - Events
150275 - Yorkshire
150276 - Sport
150277 - Yorkshire

Above: *Northern Rail operates a fleet of 28 gangway-fitted Class 150/2s for medium-distance local services, allocated to Newton Heath depot in Manchester. A large number of these sets carry route advertising branding, as shown on set No. 150228 at Knottingley, advertising Yorkshire.* **CJM**

Class 153

Vehicle Length: 76ft 5in (23.29m)
Height: 12ft 3⅛in (3.75m)
Width: 8ft 10in (2.70m)

Engine: 1 x NT855R5 of 285hp
Horsepower: 285hp (213kW)
Seats (total/car): 70S

Number	Formation DMSL	Depot	Livery	Owner	Operator
153301	52301	NL	NOR	ANG	NOR
153304	52304	NL	NOR	ANG	NOR
153307	52307	NL	NOR	ANG	NOR
153315	52315	NL	NOR	ANG	NOR
153316	52316	NL	NOR	PTR	NOR
153317	52317	NL	NOR	ANG	NOR
153324	52324	NL	NOR	PTR	NOR
153328	52328	NL	NOR	ANG	NOR
153330	52330	NL	NOR	PTR	NOR
153331	52331	NL	NOR	ANG	NOR
153332	52332	NL	NOR	ANG	NOR
153351	57351	NL	NOR	ANG	NOR
153352	57352	NL	NOR	ANG	NOR
153358	57358	NL	NOR	PTR	NOR
153359	57359	NL	NOR	PTR	NOR
153360	57360	NL	NOR	PTR	NOR
153363	57363	NL	NOR	PTR	NOR
153378	57378	NL	NOR	ANG	NOR

Name applied
153316 *John 'Longitude' Harrison*
Inventor of the Marine Chronometer

Right: *Both Angel Trains and Porterbrook Leasing supply single-car Class 153s to Northern Rail, with a fleet of 18 vehicles based at Leeds Neville Hill depot for use on lightly used branch-line services or to augment two-car sets to three to provide required accommodation on some routes. Sporting standard Northern Rail blue, mauve and white livery, set No. 153301 (vehicle 52301) is illustrated from its small cab end.* **CJM**

Class 155

Vehicle Length: 76ft 5in (23.29m)
Height: 12ft 3⅛in (3.75m)
Width: 8ft 10in (2.70m)

Engine: 1 x NT855R5 of 285hp per vehicle
Horsepower: 570hp (425kW)
Seats (total/car): 156S, 76S/80S

Number	Formation DMSL+DMS	Depot	Livery	Owner	Operator
155341	52341+57341	NL	NOR	PTR	NOR
155342	52342+57342	NL	NOR	PTR	NOR
155343	52343+57343	NL	NOR	PTR	NOR
155344	52344+57344	NL	NOR	PTR	NOR
155345	52345+57345	NL	NOR	PTR	NOR
155346	52346+57346	NL	NOR	PTR	NOR
155347	52347+57347	NL	NOR	PTR	NOR

Train Operating Companies

Northern Rail

Left: *A small fleet of seven Class 155/3 sets is operated by Northern from Leeds Neville Hill depot on mainly Calder Valley services. All sets sport high-quality pictogram branding promoting the Leeds - Bradford - Manchester corridor. Sets have 2+2 seating and are the last of the once large fleet of Class 155s introduced for longer-distance services in the Provincial Railways days. The remainder of the sets were rebuilt as single-car Class 153s. Set No. 155346 is seen at Selby.* **CJM**

Class 156
Super Sprinter

Vehicle Length: 75ft 6in (23.03m)
Height: 12ft 6in (3.81m)
Width: 8ft 11in (2.73m)

Engine: 1 x Cummins NT855R5 of 285hp per car
Horsepower: 570hp (425kW)
Seats (total/car): 146S, 70/76S

Number	Formation DMSL+DMS	Depot	Livery	Owner	Operator
156420	52420+57420	AN	NOR	PTR	NOR
156421	52421+57421	AN	NOR	PTR	NOR
156423	52423+57423	AN	NOR	PTR	NOR
156424	52424+57424	AN	NOR	PTR	NOR
156425	52425+57425	AN	NOR	PTR	NOR
156426	52426+57426	AN	NOR	PTR	NOR
156427	52427+57427	AN	NOR	PTR	NOR
156428	52428+57428	AN	NOR	PTR	NOR
156429	52429+57429	AN	NOR	PTR	NOR
156438	52438+57438	HT	NOR	ANG	NOR
156440	52440+57440	AN	NOR	PTR	NOR
156441	52441+57441	AN	§	PTR	NOR
156443	52443+57443	HT	NOR	ANG	NOR
156444	52444+57444	HT	NOR	ANG	NOR
156448	52448+57448	HT	NOR	ANG	NOR
156451	52451+57451	HT	NOR	ANG	NOR
156452	52452+57452	AN	NOR	PTR	NOR
156454	52454+57454	HT	NOR	ANG	NOR
156455	52455+57455	AN	NOR	PTR	NOR
156459	52459+57459	AN	NOR	PTR	NOR
156460	52460+57460	AN	NOR	PTR	NOR
156461	52461+57461	AN	NOR	PTR	NOR
156463	52463+57463	HT	NOR	ANG	NOR
156464	52464+57464	AN	SPL	PTR	NOR
156466	52466+57466	AN	NOR	PTR	NOR
156468	52468+57468	AN	NOR	ANG	NOR
156469	52469+57469	HT	NOR	ANG	NOR
156471	52471+57471	AN	NOR	ANG	NOR
156472	52472+57472	AN	NOR	ANG	NOR
156475	52475+57475	HT	NOR	ANG	NOR
156479	52479+57479	AN	NOR	ANG	NOR
156480	52480+57480	HT	NOR	ANG	NOR
156481	52481+57481	AN	NOR	ANG	NOR
156482	52482+57482	AN	NOR	ANG	NOR
156483	52483+57483	AN	NOR	ANG	NOR
156484	52484+57484	HT	NOR	ANG	NOR
156486	52486+57486	AN	NOR	ANG	NOR
156487	52487+57487	AN	NOR	ANG	NOR
156488	52488+57488	AN	NOR	ANG	NOR
156489	52489+57489	AN	NOR	ANG	NOR
156490	52490+57490	HT	NOR	ANG	NOR
156491	52491+57491	AN	NOR	ANG	NOR

§ - Liverpool & Manchester Railway livery

Names applied
156438 *Timothy Hackworth*
156440 *George Bradshaw*
156441 *William Huskisson MP*
156444 *Councillor Bill Cameron*

156448 *Bram Stoker*
    Creator of Dracula
156459 *Benny Rothman -*
    The Manchester Rambler
156460 *Driver John Axon GC*

156466 *Gracie Fields*
156464 *Lancashire DalesRail*
156482 *Elizabeth Gaskell*
156490 *Captain James Cook*

Left: *Northern Rail operates a fleet of 42 Class 156s allocated to Heaton or Allerton depots. The high-quality 'Super Sprinter' sets operate longer-distance services. Some sets carry stick-on names while some carry advertising or promotional liveries, all based on the Northern Rail livery style. Set No. 156441* William Huskisson MP, *with Liverpool and Manchester Railway branding, is seen at Preston.* **CJM**

Class 158/0

Vehicle Length: 76ft 1¾in (23.21m)   Engine: 1 x Cummins NTA855R of 350hp per vehicle
Height: 12ft 6in (3.81m)   Horsepower: 1,050hp (783kW)
Width: 9ft 3¼in (2.82m)   Seats (total/car): 208S, 68S/70S/70S

Number	Formation DMSL+MSL+DMSL	Depot	Livery	Owner	Operator
158752	52752+58716+57752	NL	NOR	PTR	NOR
158753	52753+58710+57753	NL	NOR	PTR	NOR
158754	52754+58708+57754	NL	NOR	PTR	NOR
158755	52755+58702+57755	NL	NOR	PTR	NOR
158756	52756+58712+57756	NL	NOR	PTR	NOR
158757	52757+58706+57757	NL	NOR	PTR	NOR
158758	52758+58714+57758	NL	NOR	PTR	NOR
158759	52759+58713+57759	NL	NOR	PTR	NOR

Below: *Northern Rail operates a fleet of eight three-car Class 158s, formed with some of the original non-driving MSL vehicles. Allocated to Leeds Neville Hill, the sets are deployed on longer-distance services over the Pennines. The sets sport standard NR livery, with the intermediate MSL carrying all blue. Set No. 158756 is illustrated at Preston.* **CJM**

Names applied
158784 *Barbara Castle*
158791 *County of Nottinghamshire*
158796 *Fred Trueman - Cricketing Legend*
158797 *Jane Tomlinson*
158860 *Ian Dewhirst*
158910 *William Wilberforce*

Vehicle Length: 76ft 1¾in (23.21m)   Engine: 1 x Cummins NTA855R of 350hp per vehicle
Height: 12ft 6in (3.81m)   Horsepower: 700hp (522kW)
Width: 9ft 3¼in (2.82m)   Seats (total/car): 138S, 68S/70S

Number	Formation DMSL+DMSL	Depot	Livery	Owner	Operator
158784	52784+57784	NH	NOR	ANG	NOR
158787	52787+57787	NH	NOR	ANG	NOR
158790	52790+57790	NH	NOR	ANG	NOR
158791	52791+57791	NH	NOR	ANG	NOR
158792	52792+57792	NH	NOR	ANG	NOR
158793	52793+57793	NH	NOR	ANG	NOR
158794	52794+57794	NH	NOR	ANG	NOR
158795	52795+57795	NH	NOR	ANG	NOR
158796	52796+57796	NH	NOR	ANG	NOR
158797	52797+57797	NH	NOR	ANG	NOR
158815	52815+57815	NL	NOR	ANG	NOR
158816	52816+57816	NL	NOR	ANG	NOR
158817	52817+57817	NL	NOR	ANG	NOR
158842	52842+57842	NL	NOR	ANG	NOR
158843	52843+57843	NL	NOR	ANG	NOR
158844	52844+57844	NL	NOR	ANG	NOR
158845	52845+57845	NL	NOR	ANG	NOR
158848	52848+57848	NL	NOR	ANG	NOR
158849	52849+57849	NL	§	ANG	NOR
158850	52850+57850	NL	NOR	ANG	NOR
158851	52851+57851	NL	NOR	ANG	NOR
158853	52853+57853	NL	NOR	ANG	NOR
158855	52855+57855	NL	NOR	ANG	NOR
158859	52859+57859	NL	NOR	ANG	NOR
158860	52860+57860	NL	NOR	ANG	NOR
158861	52861+57861	NL	NOR	ANG	NOR
158872	52872+57872	NL	NOR	ANG	NOR

§ Carries Welcome to Yorkshire livery

Right: *A fleet of 27 standard Class 158 two-car sets is allocated to Neville Hill and Newton Heath depots. Along with the three-car sets above, these operate longer-distance services. The majority of sets carry standard Northern Rail livery as displayed on set No. 158872 at Selby on a Hull-bound service.* **CJM**

Class 158/9

Vehicle Length: 76ft 1¾in (23.21m)   Engine: 1 x Cummins NTA855R of 350hp per vehicle
Height: 12ft 6in (3.81m)   Horsepower: 700hp (522kW)
Width: 9ft 3¼in (2.82m)   Seats (total/car): 142S, 70S/72S

Number	Formation DMSL+DMS	Depot	Livery	Owner	Operator
158901	52901+57901	NL	NOR	EVL	NOR
158902	52902+57902	NL	NOR	EVL	NOR
158903	52903+57903	NL	NOR	EVL	NOR
158904	52904+57904	NL	NOR	EVL	NOR
158905	52905+57905	NL	NOR	EVL	NOR
158906	52906+57906	NL	NOR	EVL	NOR
158907	52907+57907	NL	NOR	EVL	NOR
158908	52908+57908	NL	NOR	EVL	NOR
158909	52909+57909	NL	NOR	EVL	NOR
158910	52910+57910	NL	NOR	EVL	NOR

Northern Rail

Class 319/3

Vehicle Length: (Driving) 65ft 0¾in (19.83m) Width: 9ft 3in (2.82m)
(Inter) 65ft 4¼in (19.92m) Horsepower: 1,326hp (990kW)
Height: 11ft 9in (3.58m) Seats (total/car): 300S, 70S/78S/74S/78S

Number	Formation	Depot	Livery	Owner	Operator
	DTCO+MSO+TSO+DTSO				
319361	77459+63043+71929+77458	AN	NOR	PTR	NOR
319362	77461+63044+71930+77460	AN	NOR	PTR	NOR
319363	77463+63045+71931+77462	AN	NOR	PTR	NOR
319364	77465+63046+71932+77464	AN	NOR	PTR	NOR
319365	77467+63047+71933+77466	AN	NOR	PTR	NOR
319380	77497+63062+71948+77496	AN	NOR	PTR	NOR

Set Nos. 319368/372/379/382 scheduled to transfer from Thameslink in early 2015

Class 321/9

Vehicle Length: (Driving) 65ft 0¾in (19.83m) Width: 9ft 3in (2.82m)
(Inter) 65ft 4¼in (19.92m) Horsepower: 1,328hp (996kW)
Height: 12ft 4¾in (3.78m) Seats (total/car): 293S, 70S/79S/74S/70S

Number	Formation	Depot	Livery	Owner	Operator
	DTCO+MSO+TSO+DTSO				
321901	77990+63153+72128+77993	NL	NOM	EVL	NOR
321902	77991+63154+72129+77994	NL	NOM	EVL	NOR
321903	77992+63155+72130+77995	NL	NOM	EVL	NOR

Left: Northern Rail operates a fleet of three Class 321 four-car sets, based at Neville Hill for use on the Leeds-Doncaster route. The sets are painted in Northern red and mauve livery with grey passenger doors. Set No. 321903 is illustrated. **Antony Christie**

Class 322

Vehicle Length: (Driving) 65ft 0¾in (19.83m) Width: 9ft 3in (2.82m)
(Inter) 65ft 4¼in (19.92m) Horsepower: 1,328hp (996kW)
Height: 12ft 4¾in (3.78m) Seats (total/car): 291S, 74S/83S/76S/58S

Number	Formation	Depot	Livery	Owner	Operator
	DTSO(A)+MSO+TSO+DTSO(B)				
322481	78163+63137+72023+77985	NL	NOR	EVL	NOR
322482	78164+63138+72024+77986	NL	NOR	EVL	NOR
322483	78165+63139+72025+77987	NL	NOR	EVL	NOR
322484	78166+63140+72026+77988	NL	NOR	EVL	NOR
322485	78167+63141+72027+77989	NL	NOR	EVL	NOR

Left: In 2011 Northern Rail was allocated the five members of Class 322, which started life working on the Stansted Express services and later worked in the North West and Scotland. Now allocated to Neville Hill, the sets operate on the Doncaster-Leeds and Aire Valley routes. In 2014-15 the sets were undergoing a major refurbishment programme. Set No. 322482 is seen in the bay platform at Doncaster. **Nathan Williamson**

Class 323

Vehicle Length: (Driving) 76ft 8¼in (23.37m)
(Inter) 76ft 10¾in (23.44m)
Height: 12ft 4¾in (3.78m)

Width: 9ft 2¼in (2.80m)
Horsepower: 1,565hp (1,168kW)
Seats (total/car) 323223-225: 244S, 82S/80S/82S
323226-239: 284S, 98S/88S/98S

Number	Formation	Depot	Livery	Owner	Opt'r
	DMSO(A)+PTSO+DMSO(B)				
323223	64023+72223+65023	LG	NOR	PTR	NOR
323224	64024+72224+65024	LG	NOR	PTR	NOR
323225	64025+72225+65025	LG	FSN	PTR	NOR
323226	64026+72226+65026	LG	FSN	PTR	NOR
323227	64027+72227+65027	LG	FSN	PTR	NOR
323228	64028+72228+65028	LG	NOR	PTR	NOR
323229	64029+72229+65029	LG	NOR	PTR	NOR
323230	64030+72230+65030	LG	FSN	PTR	NOR
323231	64031+72231+65031	LG	NOR	PTR	NOR
323232	64032+72232+65032	LG	NOR	PTR	NOR
323233	64033+72233+65033	LG	NOR	PTR	NOR
323234	64034+72234+65034	LG	NOR	PTR	NOR
323235	64035+72235+65035	LG	NOR	PTR	NOR
323236	64036+72236+65036	LG	NOR	PTR	NOR
323237	64037+72237+65037	LG	NOR	PTR	NOR
323238	64038+72238+65038	LG	FSN	PTR	NOR
323239	64039+72239+65039	LG	FSN	PTR	NOR

Right: *Electrified local services in the Manchester area are operated by a fleet of 17 three-car Class 323 units allocated to Longsight. Painted in standard Northern Rail livery, the sets come with two internal configurations, with sets 323223-225 having a lower density and extra luggage space for Manchester Airport services. Set No. 323230 is illustrated arriving at Kidsgrove.* **Antony Christie**

Class 333

Vehicle Length: (Driving) 77ft 10¾in (23.74m)
(Inter) 75ft 11in (23.14m)
Height: 12ft 1½in (3.79m)

Width: 9ft 0¼in (2.75m)
Horsepower: 1,877hp (1,400kW)
Seats (total/car): 353S, 90S/73S/100S/90S

Number	Formation	Depot	Livery	Owner	Opt'r
	DMSO(A)+PTSO+TSO+DMSO(B)				
333001	78451+74461+74477+78452	NL	NOM	ANG	NOR
333002	78453+74462+74478+78454	NL	NOM	ANG	NOR
333003	78455+74463+74479+78456	NL	NOM	ANG	NOR
333004	78457+74464+74480+78458	NL	NOM	ANG	NOR
333005	78459+74465+74481+78460	NL	NOM	ANG	NOR
333006	78461+74466+74482+78462	NL	NOM	ANG	NOR
333007	78463+74467+74483+78464	NL	NOM	ANG	NOR
333008	78465+74468+74484+78466	NL	NOM	ANG	NOR
333009	78467+74469+74485+78468	NL	NOM	ANG	NOR
333010	78469+74470+74486+78470	NL	NOM	ANG	NOR
333011	78471+74471+74487+78472	NL	NOM	ANG	NOR
333012	78473+74472+74488+78474	NL	NOM	ANG	NOR
333013	78475+74473+74489+78476	NL	NOM	ANG	NOR
333014	78477+74474+74490+78478	NL	NOM	ANG	NOR
333015	78479+74475+74491+78480	NL	NOM	ANG	NOR
333016	78481+74476+74492+78482	NL	NOM	ANG	NOR

Name applied
333007 *Alderman J Arthur Godwin - First Lord Mayor of Bradford 1907*

The Aire Valley electrified route radiating from Leeds uses a fleet of 16 CAF-built Class 333 sets allocated to Leeds Neville Hill depot. Set No. 333007 is seen at Leeds station from its DMSO(A) vehicle. **Antony Christie**

South West Trains

Address: Friars Bridge Court, 41-45 Blackfriars Road, London, SE1 8NZ
✉ customerrelations@swtrains.co.uk
℡ 08700 00 5151   ⓘ www.southwesttrains.co.uk

Managing Director: Tim Shoveller
Franchise Dates: 4 December 1996 - April 2019
Principal Routes: London Waterloo - Weymouth, Exeter, Portsmouth and suburban services in Surrey, Berkshire, Hampshire
Depots: Wimbledon Park (WD), Bournemouth (BM), Clapham Junction (CJ) [Stabling point], Salisbury (SA), Northam (Siemens Transportation) (NT)
Parent Company: Stagecoach Group

Class 158

Vehicle Length: 76ft 1¾in (23.21m)   Engine: 1 x Cummins NTA855R of 350hp per vehicle
Height: 12ft 6in (3.81m)   Horsepower: 700hp (522kW)
Width: 9ft 3¼in (2.82m)   Seats (total/car): 13F-114S, 13F-44S/70S

Number	Formation DMCL+DMSL	Depot	Livery	Owner	Operator
158880 (158737)	52737+57737	SA	SWM	PTR	SWT
158881 (158742)	52742+57742	SA	SWM	PTR	SWT
158882 (158743)	52743+57743	SA	SWM	PTR	SWT
158883 (158744)	52744+57744	SA	SWM	PTR	SWT
158884 (158772)	52772+57772	SA	SWM	PTR	SWT
158885 (158775)	52775+57775	SA	SWM	PTR	SWT
158886 (158779)	52779+57779	SA	SWM	PTR	SWT
158887 (158781)	52781+57781	SA	SWM	PTR	SWT
158888 (158802)	52802+57802	SA	SWM	PTR	SWT
158889 (158808)	52808+57808	SA	SWM	PTR	SWT
158890 (158814)	52814+57814	SA	SWM	PTR	SWT

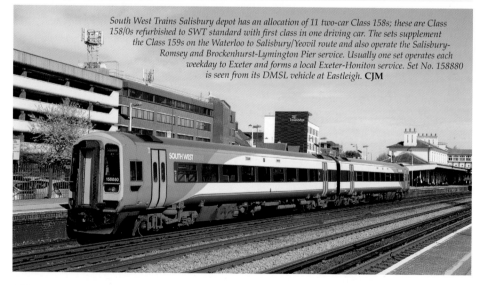

South West Trains Salisbury depot has an allocation of 11 two-car Class 158s; these are Class 158/0s refurbished to SWT standard with first class in one driving car. The sets supplement the Class 159s on the Waterloo to Salisbury/Yeovil route and also operate the Salisbury-Romsey and Brockenhurst-Lymington Pier service. Usually one set operates each weekday to Exeter and forms a local Exeter-Honiton service. Set No. 158880 is seen from its DMSL vehicle at Eastleigh. CJM

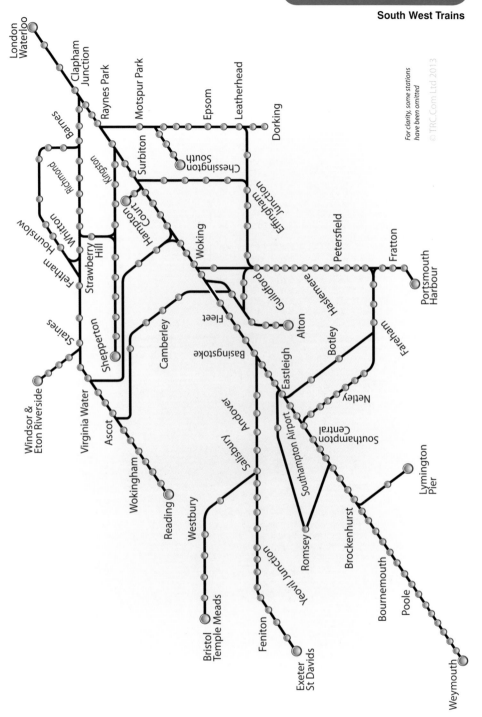

Passenger Train Operating Companies - South West Trains

For clarity, some stations have been omitted

© TRC.Com Ltd 2013

South West Trains

Class 159/0

Vehicle Length: 76ft 1¾in (23.21m) Engine: 1 x Cummins NTA855R of 400hp per vehicle
Height: 12ft 6in (3.81m) Horsepower: 1,200hp (895kW)
Width: 9ft 3¼in (2.82m) Seats (total/car): 24F-172S, 24F-28S/72S/72S

Number	Formation DMCL+MSL+DMS	Depot	Livery	Owner	Operator	Name
159001	52873+58718+57873	SA	SWM	PTR	SWT	City of Exeter
159002	52874+58719+57874	SA	SWM	PTR	SWT	City of Salisbury
159003	52875+58720+57875	SA	SWM	PTR	SWT	Templecombe
159004	52876+58721+57876	SA	SWM	PTR	SWT	Basingstoke and Deane
159005	52877+58722+57877	SA	SWM	PTR	SWT	West of England Line
159006	52878+58723+57878	SA	SWM	PTR	SWT	Seaton Tramway, Seaton-Colyford-Colyton
159007	52879+58724+57879	SA	SWM	PTR	SWT	
159008	52880+58725+57880	SA	SWM	PTR	SWT	
159009	52881+58726+57881	SA	SWM	PTR	SWT	
159010	52882+58727+57882	SA	SWM	PTR	SWT	
159011	52883+58728+57883	SA	SWM	PTR	SWT	
159012	52884+58729+57884	SA	SWM	PTR	SWT	
159013	52885+58730+57885	SA	SWM	PTR	SWT	
159014	52886+58731+57886	SA	SWM	PTR	SWT	
159015	52887+58732+57887	SA	SWM	PTR	SWT	
159016	52888+58733+57888	SA	SWM	PTR	SWT	
159017	52889+58734+57889	SA	SWM	PTR	SWT	
159018	52890+58735+57890	SA	SWM	PTR	SWT	
159019	52891+58736+57891	SA	SWM	PTR	SWT	
159020	52892+58737+57892	SA	SWM	PTR	SWT	
159021	52893+58738+57893	SA	SWM	PTR	SWT	
159022	52894+58739+57894	SA	SWM	PTR	SWT	

Above: On modernisation of the Waterloo to Exeter line under Network SouthEast, a fleet of 22 three-car Class 159s was ordered. These were built as part of the Class 158 project and then converted to high standards and reclassified as '159'. The sets were allocated to a new depot at Salisbury. Displaying standard Stagecoach/SWT white main-line colours, set No. 159011 leads a six-car formation at Exeter St David's; the DMS vehicle is nearest the camera. **CJM**

Class 159/1

Vehicle Length: 76ft 1¾in (23.21m) Engine: 1 x Cummins NTA855R of 350hp per vehicle
Height: 12ft 6in (3.81m) Horsepower: 1,050hp (782kW)
Width: 9ft 3¼in (2.82m) Seats (total/car): 24F-170S, 24F-28S/70S/72S

Number	Formation DMCL+MSL+DMSL	Depot	Livery	Owner	Operator
159101 (158800)	52800+58717+57800	SA	SWM	PTR	SWT
159102 (158803)	52803+58703+57803	SA	SWM	PTR	SWT
159103 (158804)	52804+58704+57804	SA	SWM	PTR	SWT
159104 (158805)	52805+58705+57805	SA	SWM	PTR	SWT
159105 (158807)	52807+58707+57807	SA	SWM	PTR	SWT
159106 (158809)	52809+58709+57809	SA	SWM	PTR	SWT
159107 (158811)	52811+58711+57811	SA	SWM	PTR	SWT
159108 (158801)	52801+58701+57801	SA	SWM	PTR	SWT

Right: *It was soon discovered that the Class 159/0 fleet was inadequate to cope with passenger demand, and a further batch of Class 159s was sought. These were delivered in 2006-07 when eight three-car Class 158s were upgraded to Class 159 and SWT standards at Doncaster Works. Classified as 159/1, the sets are almost identical to the 158/0s, except for slight revision to opening hopper windows (two per coach side) and minor differences to seating positions. Set No. 159104 is seen departing west from Andover.* **Mark V. Pike**

Class 444
Desiro

Vehicle Length: 77ft 3in (23.57m)
Height: 12ft 1½in (3.7m)
Width: 9ft 2in (2.7m)
Horsepower: 2,682hp (2,000kW)
Seats (total/car): 35F-299S, 35F-24S/47S/76S/76S/76S

Number	Formation DMCO+TSO+TSO+TSRMB+DMSO	Depot	Livery	Owner	Operator	Name
444001	63801+67101+67151+67201+63851	NT	SWM	ANG	SWT	Naomi House
444002	63802+67102+67152+67202+63852	NT	SWM	ANG	SWT	
444003	63803+67103+67153+67203+63853	NT	SWM	ANG	SWT	
444004	63804+67104+67154+67204+63854	NT	SWM	ANG	SWT	
444005	63805+67105+67155+67205+63855	NT	SWM	ANG	SWT	
444006	63806+67106+67156+67206+63856	NT	SWM	ANG	SWT	
444007	63807+67107+67157+67207+63857	NT	SWM	ANG	SWT	
444008	63808+67108+67158+67208+63858	NT	SWM	ANG	SWT	
444009	63809+67109+67159+67209+63859	NT	SWM	ANG	SWT	
444010	63810+67110+67160+67210+63860	NT	SWM	ANG	SWT	
444011	63811+67111+67161+67211+63861	NT	SWM	ANG	SWT	
444012	63812+67112+67162+67212+63862	NT	SWM	ANG	SWT	Destination Weymouth
444013	63813+67113+67163+67213+63863	NT	SWM	ANG	SWT	
444014	63814+67114+67164+67214+63864	NT	SWM	ANG	SWT	
444015	63815+67115+67165+67215+63865	NT	SWM	ANG	SWT	
444016	63816+67116+67166+67216+63866	NT	SWM	ANG	SWT	
444017	63817+67117+67167+67217+63867	NT	SWM	ANG	SWT	
444018	63818+67118+67168+67218+63868	NT	SWM	ANG	SWT	The FAB 444
444019	63819+67119+67169+67219+63869	NT	SWM	ANG	SWT	
444020	63820+67120+67170+67220+63870	NT	SWM	ANG	SWT	
444021	63821+67121+67171+67221+63871	NT	SWM	ANG	SWT	
444022	63822+67122+67172+67222+63872	NT	SWM	ANG	SWT	
444023	63823+67123+67173+67223+63873	NT	SWM	ANG	SWT	
444024	63824+67124+67174+67224+63874	NT	SWM	ANG	SWT	
444025	63825+67125+67175+67225+63875	NT	SWM	ANG	SWT	
444026	63826+67126+67176+67226+63876	NT	SWM	ANG	SWT	
444027	63827+67127+67177+67227+63877	NT	SWM	ANG	SWT	
444028	63828+67128+67178+67228+63878	NT	SWM	ANG	SWT	
444029	63829+67129+67179+67229+63879	NT	SWM	ANG	SWT	
444030	63830+67130+67180+67230+63880	NT	SWM	ANG	SWT	
444031	63831+67131+67181+67231+63881	NT	SWM	ANG	SWT	
444032	63832+67132+67182+67232+63882	NT	SWM	ANG	SWT	
444033	63833+67133+67183+67233+63883	NT	SWM	ANG	SWT	
444034	63834+67134+67184+67234+63884	NT	SWM	ANG	SWT	
444035	63835+67135+67185+67235+63885	NT	SWM	ANG	SWT	
444036	63836+67136+67186+67236+63886	NT	SWM	ANG	SWT	
444037	63837+67137+67187+67237+63887	NT	SWM	ANG	SWT	
444038	63838+67138+67188+67238+63888	NT	SWM	ANG	SWT	South Western Railway
444039	63839+67139+67189+67239+63889	NT	SWM	ANG	SWT	
444040	63840+67140+67190+67240+63890	NT	SWM	ANG	SWT	

South West Trains

444041	63841+67141+67191+67241+63891	NT	SWM	ANG	SWT
444042	63842+67142+67192+67242+63892	NT	SWM	ANG	SWT
444043	63843+67143+67193+67243+63893	NT	SWM	ANG	SWT
444044	63844+67144+67194+67244+63894	NT	SWM	ANG	SWT
444045	63845+67145+67195+67245+63895	NT	SWM	ANG	SWT

Left: *The mass replacement of slam-door stock on the South West lines from Waterloo saw the privatised operator South West Trains order German-built Siemens 'Desiro' stock for main-line use. As part of this order, 44 five-car express sets of Class 444 were ordered; these sets are the 'Rolls Royce' of the 'Desiro' build, offering high-quality first and standard class accommodation. Sets are based at Northam depot near Southampton and deployed on main line services from London to Bournemouth, Weymouth and Portsmouth. Set No. 444016 passes Eastleigh bound for Weymouth.* **CJM**

Class 450/0
Desiro

Vehicle Length: 66ft 9in (20.4m)
Height: 12ft 1½in (3.7m)
Width: 9ft 2in (2.7m)
Horsepower: 2,682hp (2,000kW)
Seats (total/car): 24F-237S, 70S/24F-36S/61S/70S

Number	Formation	Depot	Livery	Owner	Operator	Name
	DMSO+TCO+TSO+DMSO					
450001	63201+64201+68101+63601	NT	SWO	ANG	SWT	
450002	63202+64202+68102+63602	NT	SWO	ANG	SWT	
450003	63203+64203+68103+63603	NT	SWO	ANG	SWT	
450004	63204+64204+68104+63604	NT	SWO	ANG	SWT	
450005	63205+64205+68205+63605	NT	SWO	ANG	SWT	
450006	63206+64206+68206+63606	NT	SWO	ANG	SWT	
450007	63207+64207+68207+63607	NT	SWO	ANG	SWT	
450008	63208+64208+68108+63608	NT	SWO	ANG	SWT	
450009	63209+64209+68109+63609	NT	SWO	ANG	SWT	
450010	63210+64210+68110+63610	NT	SWO	ANG	SWT	
450011	63211+64211+68111+63611	NT	SWO	ANG	SWT	
450012	63212+64212+68112+63612	NT	SWO	ANG	SWT	
450013	63213+64213+68113+63613	NT	SWO	ANG	SWT	
450014	63214+64214+68114+63614	NT	SWO	ANG	SWT	
450015	63215+64215+68115+63615	NT	SWO	ANG	SWT	Desiro
450016	63216+64216+68116+63616	NT	SWO	ANG	SWT	
450017	63217+64217+68117+63617	NT	SWO	ANG	SWT	
450018	63218+64218+68118+63618	NT	SWO	ANG	SWT	
450019	63219+64219+68119+63619	NT	SWO	ANG	SWT	
450020	63220+64220+68120+63620	NT	SWO	ANG	SWT	
450021	63221+64221+68121+63621	NT	SWO	ANG	SWT	
450022	63222+64222+68122+63622	NT	SWO	ANG	SWT	
450023	63223+64223+68123+63623	NT	SWO	ANG	SWT	
450024	63224+64224+68124+63624	NT	SWO	ANG	SWT	
450025	63225+64225+68125+63625	NT	SWO	ANG	SWT	
450026	63226+64226+68126+63626	NT	SWO	ANG	SWT	
450027	63227+64227+68127+63627	NT	SWO	ANG	SWT	
450028	63228+64228+68128+63628	NT	SWO	ANG	SWT	
450029	63229+64229+68129+63629	NT	SWO	ANG	SWT	
450030	63230+64230+68130+63630	NT	SWO	ANG	SWT	
450031	63231+64231+68131+63631	NT	SWO	ANG	SWT	
450032	63232+64232+68132+63632	NT	SWO	ANG	SWT	
450033	63233+64233+68133+63633	NT	SWO	ANG	SWT	
450034	63234+64234+68134+63634	NT	SWO	ANG	SWT	
450035	63235+64235+68135+63635	NT	SWO	ANG	SWT	
450036	63236+64236+68136+63636	NT	SWO	ANG	SWT	

450037	63237+64237+68137+63637	NT	SWO	ANG	SWT	
450038	63238+64238+68138+63638	NT	SWO	ANG	SWT	
450039	63239+64239+68139+63639	NT	SWO	ANG	SWT	
450040	63240+64240+68140+63640	NT	SWO	ANG	SWT	
450041	63241+64241+68141+63641	NT	SWO	ANG	SWT	
450042	63242+64242+68142+63642	NT	SWO	ANG	SWT	*Treloar College*
450071	63271+64271+68171+63671	NT	SWO	ANG	SWT	
450072	63272+64272+68172+63672	NT	SWO	ANG	SWT	
450073	63273+64273+68173+63673	NT	SWO	ANG	SWT	
450074	63274+64274+68174+63674	NT	SWO	ANG	SWT	
450075	63275+64275+68175+63675	NT	SWO	ANG	SWT	
450076	63276+64276+68176+63676	NT	SWO	ANG	SWT	
450077	63277+64277+68177+63677	NT	SWO	ANG	SWT	
450078	63278+64278+68178+63678	NT	SWO	ANG	SWT	
450079	63279+64279+68179+63679	NT	SWO	ANG	SWT	
450080	63280+64280+68180+63680	NT	SWO	ANG	SWT	
450081	63281+64281+68181+63681	NT	SWO	ANG	SWT	
450082	63282+64282+68182+63682	NT	SWO	ANG	SWT	
450083	63283+64283+68183+63683	NT	SWO	ANG	SWT	
450084	63284+64284+68184+63684	NT	SWO	ANG	SWT	
450085	63285+64285+68185+63685	NT	SWO	ANG	SWT	
450086	63286+64286+68186+63686	NT	SWO	ANG	SWT	
450087	63287+64287+68187+63687	NT	SWO	ANG	SWT	
450088	63288+64288+68188+63688	NT	SWO	ANG	SWT	
450089	63289+64289+68189+63689	NT	SWO	ANG	SWT	
450090	63290+64290+68190+63690	NT	SWO	ANG	SWT	
450091	63291+64291+68191+63691	NT	SWO	ANG	SWT	
450092	63292+64292+68192+63692	NT	SWO	ANG	SWT	
450093	63293+64293+68193+63693	NT	SWO	ANG	SWT	
450094	63294+64294+68194+63694	NT	SWO	ANG	SWT	
450095	63295+64295+68195+63695	NT	SWO	ANG	SWT	
450096	63296+64296+68196+63696	NT	SWO	ANG	SWT	
450097	63297+64297+68197+63697	NT	SWO	ANG	SWT	
450098	63298+64298+68198+63698	NT	SWO	ANG	SWT	
450099	63299+64299+68199+63699	NT	SWO	ANG	SWT	
450100	63300+64300+68200+63700	NT	SWO	ANG	SWT	
450101	63701+66851+66801+63751	NT	SWO	ANG	SWT	
450102	63702+66852+66802+63752	NT	SWO	ANG	SWT	
450103	63703+66853+66803+63753	NT	SWO	ANG	SWT	
450104	63704+66854+66804+63754	NT	SWO	ANG	SWT	
450105	63705+66855+66805+63755	NT	SWO	ANG	SWT	
450106	63706+66856+66806+63756	NT	SWO	ANG	SWT	
450107	63707+66857+66807+63757	NT	SWO	ANG	SWT	
450108	63708+66858+66808+63758	NT	SWO	ANG	SWT	
450109	63709+66859+66809+63759	NT	SWO	ANG	SWT	
450110	63710+66860+66810+63750	NT	SWO	ANG	SWT	
450111	63901+66921+66901+63921	NT	SWO	ANG	SWT	
450112	63902+66922+66902+63922	NT	SWO	ANG	SWT	
450113	63903+66923+66903+63923	NT	SWO	ANG	SWT	
450114	63904+66924+66904+63924	NT	SWO	ANG	SWT	*Fairbridge - investing in the Future*
450115	63905+66925+66905+63925	NT	SWO	ANG	SWT	
450116	63906+66926+66906+63926	NT	SWO	ANG	SWT	
450117	63907+66927+66907+63927	NT	SWO	ANG	SWT	
450118	63908+66928+66908+63928	NT	SWO	ANG	SWT	
450119	63909+66929+66909+63929	NT	SWO	ANG	SWT	
450120	63910+66930+66910+63930	NT	SWO	ANG	SWT	
450121	63911+66931+66911+63931	NT	SWO	ANG	SWT	
450122	63912+66932+66912+63932	NT	SWO	ANG	SWT	
450123	63913+66933+66913+63933	NT	SWO	ANG	SWT	
450124	63914+66934+66914+63934	NT	SWO	ANG	SWT	
450125	63915+66935+66915+63935	NT	SWO	ANG	SWT	
450126	63916+66936+66916+63936	NT	SWO	ANG	SWT	
450127	63917+66937+66917+63937	NT	SWO	ANG	SWT	

Above: *The main outer-suburban SWT units are the 'Desiro' Class 450 four-car sets. Of the 127 sets built, 99 retain their 'as built' interior and seat 24 first and 237 standard class passengers and are classified as 450/0. Set No. 450076 is seen at Eastleigh with a London Waterloo-bound service.* **CJM**

Passenger Train Operating Companies - South West Trains

Class 450/5
Desiro

Vehicle Length: 66ft 9in (20.4m)	Horsepower: 2,682hp (2,000kW)	
Height: 12ft 1½in (3.7m)	Seats (total/car):	
Width: 9ft 2in (2.7m)	24F/206S, 64S-24F/32S/56S/54S	

Number	Formation DMSO+TCO+TSO+DMSO	Depot	Livery	Owner	Operator
450543 (450043)	63243+64243+68143+63643	NT	SWO	ANG	SWT
450544 (450044)	63244+64244+68144+63644	NT	SWO	ANG	SWT
450545 (450045)	63245+64245+68145+63645	NT	SWO	ANG	SWT
450546 (450046)	63246+64246+68146+63646	NT	SWO	ANG	SWT
450547 (450047)	63247+64247+68147+63647	NT	SWO	ANG	SWT
450548 (450048)	63248+64248+68148+63648	NT	SWO	ANG	SWT
450549 (450049)	63249+64249+68149+63649	NT	SWO	ANG	SWT
450550 (450050)	63250+64250+68150+63650	NT	SWO	ANG	SWT
450551 (450051)	63251+64251+68151+63651	NT	SWO	ANG	SWT
450552 (450052)	63252+64252+68152+63652	NT	SWO	ANG	SWT
450553 (450053)	63253+64253+68153+63653	NT	SWO	ANG	SWT
450554 (450054)	63254+64254+68154+63654	NT	SWO	ANG	SWT
450555 (450055)	63255+64255+68155+63655	NT	SWO	ANG	SWT
450556 (450056)	63256+64256+68156+63656	NT	SWO	ANG	SWT
450557 (450057)	63257+64257+68157+63657	NT	SWO	ANG	SWT
450558 (450058)	63258+64258+68158+63658	NT	SWO	ANG	SWT
450559 (450059)	63259+64259+68159+63659	NT	SWO	ANG	SWT
450560 (450060)	63260+64260+68160+63660	NT	SWO	ANG	SWT
450561 (450061)	63261+64261+68161+63661	NT	SWO	ANG	SWT
450562 (450062)	63262+64262+68162+63662	NT	SWO	ANG	SWT
450563 (450063)	63263+64263+68163+63663	NT	SWO	ANG	SWT
450564 (450064)	63264+64264+68164+63664	NT	SWO	ANG	SWT
450565 (450065)	63265+64265+68165+63665	NT	SWO	ANG	SWT
450566 (450066)	63266+64266+68166+63666	NT	SWO	ANG	SWT
450567 (450067)	63267+64267+68167+63667	NT	SWO	ANG	SWT
450568 (450068)	63268+64268+68168+63668	NT	SWO	ANG	SWT
450569 (450069)	63269+64269+68169+63669	NT	SWO	ANG	SWT
450570 (450070)	63270+64270+68170+63670	NT	SWO	ANG	SWT

Soon after introduction, standard class accommodation became at a premium on the Waterloo Windsor lines and extra capacity was needed; this was addressed by modifying 28 Class 450/0s as 'High Capacity' sets, with revised seating to allow more standees, while removing the first class area. In more recent times the first class seating has been returned, while the high-capacity standard class areas have been retained. These sets are classified as 450/5. St No. 450561 is illustrated. **Antony Christie**

Class 455/7

Vehicle Length: (Driving) 65ft 0½in (19.83m)
(Inter) 65ft 4½in (19.92m)
Height: 12ft 1½in (3.79m) [TSO- 11ft 6½in (3.58m)]
Width: 9ft 3¼in (2.82m)
Horsepower: 1,000hp (746kW)
Seats (total/car): 244S, 54S/68S/68S/54S

Number	Formation DMSO(A)+MSO+TSO+DTSO(B)	Depot	Livery	Owner	Operator	Notes
(45)5701	77727+62783+71545+77728	WD	SWS	PTR	SWT	
(45)5702	77729+62784+71547+77730	WD	SWS	PTR	SWT	
(45)5703	77731+62785+71540+77732	WD	SWS	PTR	SWT	
(45)5704	77733+62786+71548+77734	WD	SWS	PTR	SWT	
(45)5705	77735+62787+71565+77736	WD	SWS	PTR	SWT	
(45)5706	77737+62788+71534+77738	WD	SWS	PTR	SWT	
(45)5707	77739+62789+71536+77740	WD	SWS	PTR	SWT	
(45)5708	77741+62790+71560+77742	WD	SWS	PTR	SWT	
(45)5709	77743+62791+71532+77744	WD	SWS	PTR	SWT	
(45)5710	77745+62792+71566+77746	WD	SWS	PTR	SWT	
(45)5711	77747+62793+71542+77748	WD	SWS	PTR	SWT	
(45)5712	77749+62794+71546+77750	WD	SWS	PTR	SWT	
(45)5713	77751+62795+71567+77752	WD	SWS	PTR	SWT	
(45)5714	77753+62796+71539+77754	WD	SWS	PTR	SWT	
(45)5715	77755+62796+71535+77756	WD	SWS	PTR	SWT	
(45)5716	77757+62798+71564+77758	WD	SWS	PTR	SWT	
(45)5717	77759+62799+71528+77760	WD	SWS	PTR	SWT	
(45)5718	77761+62800+71557+77762	WD	SWS	PTR	SWT	
(45)5719	77763+62801+71558+77764	WD	SWS	PTR	SWT	
(45)5720	77765+62802+71568+77766	WD	SWS	PTR	SWT	
(45)5721	77767+62803+71553+77768	WD	SWS	PTR	SWT	
(45)5722	77769+62804+71533+77770	WD	SWS	PTR	SWT	
(45)5723	77771+62805+71526+77772	WD	SWS	PTR	SWT	
(45)5724	77773+62806+71561+77774	WD	SWS	PTR	SWT	
(45)5725	77775+62807+71541+77776	WD	SWS	PTR	SWT	
(45)5726	77777+62608+71556+77778	WD	SWS	PTR	SWT	
(45)5727	77779+62809+71562+77780	WD	SWS	PTR	SWT	
(45)5728	77781+62810+71527+77782	WD	SWS	PTR	SWT	
(45)5729	77783+62811+71550+77784	WD	SWS	PTR	SWT	
(45)5730	77785+62812+71551+77786	WD	SWS	PTR	SWT	
(45)5731	77787+62813+71555+77788	WD	SWS	PTR	SWT	
(45)5732	77789+62814+71552+77790	WD	SWS	PTR	SWT	
(45)5733	77791+62815+71549+77792	WD	SWS	PTR	SWT	
(45)5734	77793+62816+71531+77794	WD	SWS	PTR	SWT	
(45)5735	77795+62817+71563+77796	WD	SWS	PTR	SWT	
(45)5736	77797+62818+71554+77798	WD	SWS	PTR	SWT	
(45)5737	77799+62819+71544+77800	WD	SWS	PTR	SWT	
(45)5738	77801+62820+71529+77802	WD	SWS	PTR	SWT	
(45)5739	77803+62821+71537+77804	WD	SWS	PTR	SWT	
(45)5740	77805+62822+71530+77806	WD	SWS	PTR	SWT	
(45)5741	77807+62823+71559+77808	WD	SWS	PTR	SWT	
(45)5742	77809+62824+71543+77810	WD	SWS	PTR	SWT	
(45)5750*	77811+62825+71538+77812	WD	SWS	PTR	SWT	* Originally numbered (45)5743

Left: *Suburban South West Trains services are operated by three sub-classes of Class 455, originally introduced in 1982-85. All sets are now refurbished with high-back seats and large 'stand-back' areas to increase capacity. All sets are painted in Stagecoach/SWT suburban red swirl livery. The Class 455/7 sub-class includes one ex-Class 508 TSO vehicle. Set No. (45)5721 is seen at Clapham Junction.* **CJM**

Class 455/8

Vehicle Length: (Driving) 65ft 0½in (19.83m)		Width: 9ft 3¼in (2.82m)		
(Inter) 65ft 4½in (19.92m)		Horsepower: 1,000hp (746kW)		
Height: 12ft 1½in (3.79m)		Seats (total/car): 268S, 50S/84S/84S/50S		

Number	Formation DMSO(A)+MSO+TSO+DTSO(B)	Depot	Livery	Owner	Operator
(45)5847	77671+62755+71683+77672	WD	SWS	PTR	SWT
(45)5848	77673+62756+71684+77674	WD	SWS	PTR	SWT
(45)5849	77675+62757+71685+77676	WD	SWS	PTR	SWT
(45)5850	77677+62758+71686+77678	WD	SWS	PTR	SWT
(45)5851	77679+62759+71687+77680	WD	SWS	PTR	SWT
(45)5852	77681+62760+71688+77682	WD	SWS	PTR	SWT
(45)5853	77683+62761+71689+77684	WD	SWS	PTR	SWT
(45)5854	77685+62762+71690+77686	WD	SWS	PTR	SWT
(45)5855	77687+62763+71691+77688	WD	SWS	PTR	SWT
(45)5856	77689+62764+71692+77690	WD	SWS	PTR	SWT
(45)5857	77691+62765+71693+77692	WD	SWS	PTR	SWT
(45)5858	77693+62766+71694+77694	WD	SWS	PTR	SWT
(45)5859	77695+62767+71695+77696	WD	SWS	PTR	SWT
(45)5860	77697+62768+71696+77698	WD	SWS	PTR	SWT
(45)5861	77699+62769+71697+77700	WD	SWS	PTR	SWT
(45)5862	77701+62770+71698+77702	WD	SWS	PTR	SWT
(45)5863	77703+62771+71699+77704	WD	SWS	PTR	SWT
(45)5864	77705+62772+71700+77706	WD	SWS	PTR	SWT
(45)5865	77707+62773+71701+77708	WD	SWS	PTR	SWT
(45)5866	77709+62774+71702+77710	WD	SWS	PTR	SWT
(45)5867	77711+62775+71703+77712	WD	SWS	PTR	SWT
(45)5868	77713+62776+71704+77714	WD	SWS	PTR	SWT
(45)5869	77715+62777+71705+77716	WD	SWS	PTR	SWT
(45)5870	77717+62778+71706+77718	WD	SWS	PTR	SWT
(45)5871	77719+62779+71707+77720	WD	SWS	PTR	SWT
(45)5872	77721+62780+71708+77722	WD	SWS	PTR	SWT
(45)5873	77723+62781+71709+77724	WD	SWS	PTR	SWT
(45)5874	77725+62782+71710+77726	WD	SWS	PTR	SWT

Left: *The original batch of Class 455s, classified as 455/8s, have a different cab end design, with a more cluttered roof line and two roof-mounted warning horns. All three sub-classes of the Class 455 fleet operate as one pool based at Wimbledon depot. Class 455/8 No. (45)5853 is illustrated. Over the coming months the Class 455 fleet will be the backbone of the new 10-car SWT suburban railway following commissioning of Class 456 sets now under refurbishment.* **Antony Christie**

Class 455/9

Vehicle Length: (Driving) 65ft 0½in (19.83m)
(Inter) 65ft 4½in (19.92m)
Height: 12ft 1½in (3.79m)

Width: 9ft 3¼in (2.82m)
Horsepower: 1,000hp (746kW)
Seats (total/car): 236S, 50S/68S/68S/50S

Number	Formation DMSO(A)+MSO+TSO+DTSO(B)	Depot	Livery	Owner	Operator
(45)5901	77813+62826+71714+77814	WD	SWS	PTR	SWT
(45)5902	77815+62827+71715+77816	WD	SWS	PTR	SWT
(45)5903	77817+62828+71716+77818	WD	SWS	PTR	SWT
(45)5904	77819+62829+71717+77820	WD	SWS	PTR	SWT
(45)5905	77821+62830+71725+77822	WD	SWS	PTR	SWT
(45)5906	77823+62831+71719+77824	WD	SWS	PTR	SWT
(45)5907	77825+62832+71720+77826	WD	SWS	PTR	SWT
(45)5908	77827+62833+71721+77828	WD	SWS	PTR	SWT
(45)5909	77829+62834+71722+77830	WD	SWS	PTR	SWT
(45)5910	77831+62835+71723+77832	WD	SWS	PTR	SWT
(45)5911	77833+62836+71724+77834	WD	SWS	PTR	SWT
(45)5912	77835+62837+67400+77836	WD	SWS	PTR	SWT
(45)5913	77837+62838+71726+77838	WD	SWS	PTR	SWT
(45)5914	77839+62839+71727+77840	WD	SWS	PTR	SWT
(45)5915	77841+62840+71728+77842	WD	SWS	PTR	SWT
(45)5916	77843+62841+71729+77844	WD	SWS	PTR	SWT
(45)5917	77845+62842+71730+77846	WD	SWS	PTR	SWT
(45)5918	77847+62843+71732+77848	WD	SWS	PTR	SWT
(45)5919	77849+62844+71718+77850	WD	SWS	PTR	SWT
(45)5920	77851+62845+71733+77852	WD	SWS	PTR	SWT

Above: The final batch of Class 455s to be built were 20 Class 455/9s; these were slightly different again with the by then standard rounded-roof cab end design, but housed revised ventilation having larger roof-mounted vent grilles. Set No. (45)5911 is illustrated. In common with the entire fleet, modified light clusters are now fitted with a joint LED marker/tail light. **Antony Christie**

Class 456

Vehicle Length: (Driving) 65ft 3¼in (19.89m)
Height: 12ft 4½in (3.77m)
Width: 9ft 3in (2.81m)

Horsepower: 500hp (370kW)
Seats (total/car): 152S, 79S/73S

Number	Formation DMSO+DTSO	Depot	Livery	Owner	Operator
456001	64735+78250	WD	§	PTR	SWT
456002	64736+78251	WD	§	PTR	SWT
456003	64737+78252	WD	SWS	PTR	SWT
456004	64738+78253	WD	§	PTR	SWT
456005	64739+78254	WD	§	PTR	SWT
456006	64740+78255	WD	SWS	PTR	SWT
456007	64741+78256	WD	§	PTR	SWT
456008	64742+78257	WD	§	PTR	SWT
456009	64743+78258	WD	§	PTR	SWT
456010	64744+78259	WD	§	PTR	SWT
456011	64745+78260	WD	§	PTR	SWT
456012	64746+78261	WD	SWS	PTR	SWT
456013	64747+78262	WD	§	PTR	SWT
456014	64748+78263	WD	SWS	PTR	SWT

South West Trains

456015	64749+78264	WD	SWS	PTR	SWT		456020	64754+78269	WD	§	PTR	SWT
456016	64750+78265	WD	§	PTR	SWT		456021	64755+78270	WD	§	PTR	SWT
456017	64751+78266	WD	§	PTR	SWT		456022	64756+78271	WD	§	PTR	SWT
456018	64752+78267	WD	§	PTR	SWT		456023	64757+78272	WD	§	PTR	SWT
456019	64753+78268	WD	§	PTR	SWT		456024	64758+78273	WD	§	PTR	SWT

Left: *In 2014 the 24 Class 456 two-car sets were transferred to SWT from Southern. Sets will be rebuilt to SWT Class 455 standards by Wolverton Works and together with the Class 455s will form the SWT 10-car suburban railway. To cover stock shortages some Class 456s in Southern green entered service on SWT in 2014 mainly working on the Guildford-Ascot route. Sets Nos. 456001 and 456007 are seen at Aldershot.*
Antony Christie

§ SWT branded Southern

Class 458
Juniper

Vehicle Length: (Driving) 69ft 6in (21.16m) Width: 9ft 2in (2.79m)
(Inter) 65ft 4in (19.91m) Horsepower: 2,172hp (1,620kW)
Height: 12ft 3in (3.73m) Seats 4-car sets (total/car): 24F-250S, 12F-63S/49S/75S/12F-63S
5-car sets (total/car): 266S, 60S/52S/42S/52S/60S

4-JOP / 5-JUP

Number	New Number	Formation DMCO(A)+TSO+MSO+(TSO)+DTCO(B)	Depot	Livery	Owner	Operator
458501	(x458001)	67601+74431+74001+74101+67701	WD	SWM	PTR	SWT
458502	(x458002)	67602+74421+74002+74102+67702	WD	SWM	PTR	SWT
458503	(x458003)	67603+74441+74003+74103+67703	WD	SWM	PTR	SWT
458504	(x458004)	67604+74451+74004+74104+67704	WD	SWM	PTR	SWT
(45)8005	(458505)	67605+74005+74105+(74451)+67705	WD	SWM	PTR	SWT
(45)8006	(458506)	67606+74006+74106+(74426)+67706	WD	SWM	PTR	SWT
(45)8007	(458507)	67607+74007+74107+(74406)+67707	WD	SWM	PTR	SWT
(45)8008	(458508)	67608+74008+74108+(74442)+67708	WD	SWM	PTR	SWT
(45)8009	(458509)	67609+74009+74109+(74432)+67709	WD	SWM	PTR	SWT
(45)8010	(458510)	67610+74010+74110+(74434)+67710	WD	SWM	PTR	SWT
(45)8011	(458511)	67611+74011+74111+(74451)+67711	WD	SWM	PTR	SWT
(45)8012	(458512)	67612+74012+74112+(74436)+67712	WD	SWM	PTR	SWT
(45)8013	(458513)	67613+74013+74113+(74427)+67713	WD	SWM	PTR	SWT
(45)8014	(458514)	67614+74014+74114+(74407)+67714	WD	SWM	PTR	SWT
(45)8015	(458515)	67615+74015+74115+(74424)+67715	WD	SWM	PTR	SWT
(45)8016	(458516)	67616+74016+74116+(74428)+67716	WD	SWM	PTR	SWT
(45)8017	(458517)	67617+74017+74117+(74433)+67717	WD	SWM	PTR	SWT
(45)8018	(458518)	67618+74018+74118+(74412)+67718	WD	SWM	PTR	SWT
(45)8019	(458519)	67619+74019+74119+(74403)+67719	WD	SWM	PTR	SWT
(45)8020	(458520)	67620+74020+74120+(74441)+67720	WD	SWM	PTR	SWT
(45)8021	(458521)	67621+74021+74121+(74408)+67721	WD	SWM	PTR	SWT
(45)8022	(458522)	67622+74022+74122+(74404)+67722	WD	SWM	PTR	SWT
(45)8023	(458523)	67623+74023+74123+(74437)+67723	WD	SWM	PTR	SWT
(45)8024	(458524)	67624+74024+74124+(74422)+67724	WD	SWM	PTR	SWT
(45)8025	(458525)	67625+74025+74125+(74435)+67725	WD	SWM	PTR	SWT
(45)8026	(458526)	67626+74026+74126+(74452)+67726	WD	SWM	PTR	SWT
(45)8027	(458527)	67627+74027+74127+(74402)+67727	WD	SWM	PTR	SWT
(45)8028	(458528)	67628+74028+74128+(74438)+67728	WD	SWM	PTR	SWT
(45)8029	(458529)	67629+74029+74129+(74423)+67729	WD	SWM	PTR	SWT
458030	(458530)	67630+74411+74030+74130+67730	WD	SWM	PTR	SWT

5-JUP

		DMSO(A)+TSO+MST+TSO+DMSO(B)				
458531		67913+74418+74446+74458+67912	WD	SWO	PTR	SWT
458532		67904+74417+74447+74457+67905	WD	SWO	PTR	SWT
458533		67917+74413+74443+74453+67916	WD	SWO	PTR	SWT
458534		67914+74414+74444+74454+67918	WD	SWO	PTR	SWT

■ A total of 36 five-car Class 458/5s are currently under conversion from the 30 original Class 458/0 sets, each with one additional TS vehicle, plus six additional sets rebuilt totally from Class 460 stock. All but four of the Class 460 vehicles will be converted. Each 'new' set will be formed of five vehicles, allowing SWT to operate 10-car trains on the outer-suburban routes. The sets have new front ends with modern gangways and sport 2+2 seating. The sets are numbered in the 458501- 458536 series. Sets 8001-30 will be converted in 2014-15.

458535	67915+74415+74445+74455+67911	WD	SWO	PTR	SWT
458536	67906+74416+74448+74456+67902	WD	SWO	PTR	SWT

Above: *The new Class 458/5 five-car suburban sets are in the process of delivery, being converted from Class 458/0 and 460 stock at Wabtec Doncaster and Loughborough. Rebuilt entirely from Class 460 stock with a new front-end design, set No. 458531 is seen at East Wimbledon depot.* **CJM**

Class 707

New rolling stock: In summer 2014 South West Trains announced that it had placed an order through Angel Trains for 30 five-car Siemens 'Desiro City' EMUs for delivery in 2017-18. These sets of like profile to the Class 700 sets used on Thameslink will initially operate on the Waterloo to Windsor and Reading corridor. The sets will be constructed in Germany and based at Wimbledon Park depot. Full details are awaited.

Class 73/2

Vehicle Length: 53ft 8in (16.35m)	*Power:* 750V dc third rail or English Electric 6K	
Height: 12ft 5⅜in (3.79m)	*Horsepower: electric* - 1,600hp (1,193kW)	
Width: 8ft 8in (2.64m)	*Horsepower: diesel* - 600hp (447kW)	
	Electrical Equipment: English Electric	

Number	Depot	Pool	Livery	Owner	Operator
73235 (73125)	WD	HYWD	SWO	SWT	SWT

Right: *Officially South West Trains still retains the use of one Class 73 electro-diesel, based at East Wimbledon, but frequently found stabled at Bournemouth. The loco is used for rescue of failed trains, driver's route training or the transfer of sets between depots. Painted in full SWT outer-suburban blue livery to match the 'Desiro' Class 450s, No. 73235 sees little work and might well be sold to another operator in the future.* **Mark V. Pike**

South Eastern

Address: ✉ Friars Bridge Court, 41-45 Blackfriars Road, London, SE1 8NZ
🖰 info@southeasternrailway.co.uk
✆ 08700 000 2222
ⓘ www.southeasternrailway.co.uk

Managing Director:	Charles Horton
Franchise Dates:	1 April 2006 - 24 June 2018
Principal Routes:	London to Kent and parts of East Sussex, domestic services on HS1
Depots:	Slade Green (SG), Ramsgate (RM), Ashford* (AD)
Parent Company:	Govia
	* Operated by Hitachi

Class 375/3
Electrostar

Vehicle Length: (Driving) 66ft 9in (20.3m)
(Inter) 65ft 6in (19.96m)
Height: 12ft 4in (3.75m)
Width: 9ft 2in (2.79m)
Horsepower: 1,341hp (1,000kW)
Seats (total/car): 24F-152S, 12F-48S/56S/12F-48S

Number	Formation DMCO(A)+TSO+DMCO(B)	Depot	Livery	Owner	Operator	Name
375301	67921+74351+67931	RM	SET	EVL	SET	
375302	67922+74352+67932	RM	SET	EVL	SET	
375303	67923+74353+67933	RM	SET	EVL	SET	
375304	67924+74354+67934	RM	SET	EVL	SET	*Medway Valley Line 1856-2006*
375305	67925+74355+67935	RM	SET	EVL	SET	
375306	67926+74356+67936	RM	SET	EVL	SET	
375307	67927+74357+67937	RM	SET	EVL	SET	
375308	67928+74358+67938	RM	SET	EVL	SET	
375309	67929+74359+67939	RM	SET	EVL	SET	
375310	67930+74360+67940	RM	SET	EVL	SET	

Class 375/6
Electrostar

Vehicle Length: (Driving) 66ft 9in (20.3m)
(Inter) 65ft 6in (19.96m)
Height: 12ft 4in (3.75m)
Width: 9ft 2in (2.79m)
Horsepower: 2,012hp (1,500kW)
Seats (total/car): 24F-218S, 12F-48S/66S/56S/12F-48S

Number	Formation DMCO(A)+MSO+TSO+DMCO(B)	Depot	Livery	Owner	Operator	Name
375601	67801+74251+74201+67851	RM	SET	EVL	SET	
375602	67802+74252+74202+67852	RM	SET	EVL	SET	
375603	67803+74253+74203+67853	RM	SET	EVL	SET	
375604	67804+74254+74204+67854	RM	SET	EVL	SET	
375605	67805+74255+74205+67855	RM	SET	EVL	SET	
375606	67806+74256+74206+67856	RM	SET	EVL	SET	
375607	67807+74257+74207+67857	RM	SET	EVL	SET	
375608	67808+74258+74208+67858	RM	SET	EVL	SET	*Bromley Travelwise*
375609	67809+74259+74209+67859	RM	SET	EVL	SET	
375610	67810+74260+74210+67860	RM	SET	EVL	SET	*Royal Tunbridge Wells*
375611	67811+74261+74211+67861	RM	SET	EVL	SET	*Dr William Harvey*
375612	67812+74262+74212+67862	RM	SET	EVL	SET	
375613	67813+74263+74213+67863	RM	SET	EVL	SET	
375614	67814+74264+74214+67864	RM	SET	EVL	SET	
375615	67815+74265+74215+67865	RM	SET	EVL	SET	
375616	67816+74266+74216+67866	RM	SET	EVL	SET	
375617	67817+74267+74217+67867	RM	SET	EVL	SET	
375618	67818+74268+74218+67868	RM	SET	EVL	SET	
375619	67819+74269+74219+67869	RM	SET	EVL	SET	*Driver John Neve*

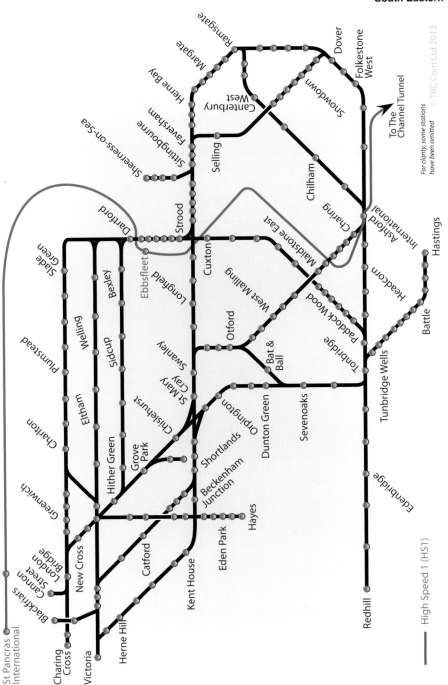

Passenger Train Operating Companies - South Eastern

© TRC.Com Ltd 2013

For clarity, some stations
have been omitted

To The
Channel Tunnel

Ramsgate
Margate
Herne Bay
Sheerness-on-Sea
Sittingbourne
Faversham
Canterbury West
Dover
Folkestone West
Snowdown
Selling
Chilham
Charing
Ashford International
Hastings
Strood
Dartford
Cuxton
Maidstone East
Headcorn
Slade Green
Bexley
Ebbsfleet
Longfield
West Malling
Paddock Wood
Battle
Welling
Sidcup
Swanley
Otford
Tonbridge
Plumstead
Eltham
Chislehurst
St Mary Cray
Bat & Ball
Tunbridge Wells
Charlton
Hither Green
Grove Park
Shortlands
Orpington
Dunton Green
Sevenoaks
Greenwich
Beckenham Junction
Hayes
New Cross
Catford
Eden Park
Kent House
Edenbridge
Stratford International
Cannon Street
London Bridge
Charing Cross
Victoria
Herne Hill
Blackfriars
St Pancras International
Redhill

High Speed 1 (HS1)

Passenger Train Operating Companies - South Eastern

South Eastern

375620	67820+74270+74220+67870	RM	SET	EVL	SET	
375621	67821+74271+74221+67871	RM	SET	EVL	SET	
375622	67822+74272+74222+67872	RM	SET	EVL	SET	
375623	67823+74273+74223+67873	RM	SET	EVL	SET	*Hospice in the Weald*
375624	67824+74274+74224+67874	RM	SET	EVL	SET	
375625	67825+74275+74225+67875	RM	SET	EVL	SET	
375626	67826+74276+74226+67876	RM	SET	EVL	SET	
375627	67827+74277+74227+67877	RM	SET	EVL	SET	
375628	67828+74278+74228+67878	RM	SET	EVL	SET	
375629	67829+74279+74229+67879	RM	SET	EVL	SET	
375630	67830+74280+74230+67880	RM	SET	EVL	SET	

Class 375/7
Electrostar

Vehicle Length: (Driving) 66ft 9in (20.3m)   *Width: 9ft 2in (2.79m)*
(Inter) 65ft 6in (19.96m)   *Horsepower: 2,012hp (1,500kW)*
Height: 12ft 4in (3.75m)   *Seats (total/car): 24F-218S, 12F-48S/66S/56S/12F-48S*

Number	Formation	Depot	Livery	Owner	Operator	Name
	DMCO(A)+MSO+TSO+DMCO(B)					
375701	67831+74281+74231+67881	RM	SET	EVL	SET	*Kent Air Ambulance Explorer*
375702	67832+74282+74232+67882	RM	SET	EVL	SET	
375703	67833+74283+74233+67883	RM	SET	EVL	SET	
375704	67834+74284+74234+67884	RM	SET	EVL	SET	
375705	67835+74285+74235+67885	RM	SET	EVL	SET	
375706	67836+74286+74236+67886	RM	SET	EVL	SET	
375707	67837+74287+74237+67887	RM	SET	EVL	SET	
375708	67838+74288+74238+67888	RM	SET	EVL	SET	
375709	67839+74289+74239+67889	RM	SET	EVL	SET	
375710	67840+74290+74240+67890	RM	SET	EVL	SET	
375711	67841+74291+74241+67891	RM	SET	EVL	SET	
375712	67842+74292+74242+67892	RM	SET	EVL	SET	
375713	67843+74293+74243+67893	RM	SET	EVL	SET	
375714	67844+74294+74244+67894	RM	SET	EVL	SET	
375715	67845+74295+74245+67895	RM	SET	EVL	SET	

Class 375/8
Electrostar

Vehicle Length: (Driving) 66ft 9in (20.3m)   *Width: 9ft 2in (2.79m)*
(Inter) 65ft 6in (19.96m)   *Horsepower: 2,012hp (1,500kW)*
Height: 12ft 4in (3.75m)   *Seats (total/car): 24F-218S, 12F-48S/66S/56S/12F-48S*

Number	Formation	Depot	Livery	Owner	Operator	Name
	DMCO(A)+MSO+TSO+DMCO(B)					
375801	73301+79001+78201+73701	RM	SET	EVL	SET	
375802	73302+79002+78202+73702	RM	SET	EVL	SET	
375803	73303+79003+78203+73703	RM	SET	EVL	SET	
375804	73304+79004+78204+73704	RM	SET	EVL	SET	
375805	73305+79005+78205+73705	RM	SET	EVL	SET	
375806	73306+79006+78206+73706	RM	SET	EVL	SET	
375807	73307+79007+78207+73707	RM	SET	EVL	SET	
375808	73308+79008+78208+73708	RM	SET	EVL	SET	
375809	73309+79009+78209+73709	RM	SET	EVL	SET	
375810	73310+79010+78210+73710	RM	SET	EVL	SET	
375811	73311+79011+78211+73711	RM	SET	EVL	SET	
375812	73312+79012+78212+73712	RM	SET	EVL	SET	
375813	73313+79013+78213+73713	RM	SET	EVL	SET	
375814	73314+79014+78214+73714	RM	SET	EVL	SET	
375815	73315+79015+78215+73715	RM	SET	EVL	SET	
375816	73316+79016+78216+73716	RM	SET	EVL	SET	
375817	73317+79017+78217+73717	RM	SET	EVL	SET	
375818	73318+79018+78218+73718	RM	SET	EVL	SET	
375819	73319+79019+78219+73719	RM	SET	EVL	SET	
375820	73320+79020+78220+73720	RM	SET	EVL	SET	
375821	73321+79021+78221+73721	RM	SET	EVL	SET	
375822	73322+79022+78222+73722	RM	SET	EVL	SET	
375823	73323+79023+78223+73723	RM	SET	EVL	SET	
375824	73324+79024+78224+73724	RM	SET	EVL	SET	
375825	73325+79025+78225+73725	RM	SET	EVL	SET	

375826	73326+79026+78226+73726	RM	SET	EVL	SET	
375827	73327+79027+78227+73727	RM	SET	EVL	SET	
375828	73328+79028+78228+73728	RM	SET	EVL	SET	
375829	73329+79029+78229+73729	RM	SET	EVL	SET	
375830	73330+79030+78230+73730	RM	SET	EVL	SET	*City of London*

Set 375812 fitted with de-icing equipment

Class 375/9
Electrostar

Vehicle Length: (Driving) 66ft 9in (20.3m)
(Inter) 65ft 6in (19.96m)
Height: 12ft 4in (3.75m)
Width: 9ft 2in (2.79m)
Horsepower: 2,012hp (1,500kW)
Seats (total/car): 24F-250S, 12F-59S/73S/59S/12F-59S

Number	Formation	Depot	Livery	Owner	Operator
	DMCO(A)+MSO+TSO+DMCO(B)				
375901	73331+79031+79061+73731	RM	SET	EVL	SET
375902	73332+79032+79062+73732	RM	SET	EVL	SET
375903	73333+79033+79063+73733	RM	SET	EVL	SET
375904	73334+79034+79064+73734	RM	SET	EVL	SET
375905	73335+79035+79065+73735	RM	SET	EVL	SET
375906	73336+79036+79066+73736	RM	SET	EVL	SET
375907	73337+79037+79067+73737	RM	SET	EVL	SET
375908	73338+79038+79068+73738	RM	SET	EVL	SET
375909	73339+79039+79069+73739	RM	SET	EVL	SET
375910	73340+79040+79070+73740	RM	SET	EVL	SET
375911	73341+79041+79071+73741	RM	SET	EVL	SET
375912	73342+79042+79072+73742	RM	SET	EVL	SET
375913	73343+79043+79073+73743	RM	SET	EVL	SET
375914	73344+79044+79074+73744	RM	SET	EVL	SET
375915	73345+79045+79075+73745	RM	SET	EVL	SET
375916	73346+79046+79076+73746	RM	SET	EVL	SET
375917	73347+79047+79077+73747	RM	SET	EVL	SET
375918	73348+79048+79078+73748	RM	SET	EVL	SET
375919	73349+79049+79079+73749	RM	SET	EVL	SET
375920	73350+79050+79080+73750	RM	SET	EVL	SET
375921	73351+79051+79081+73751	RM	SET	EVL	SET
375922	73352+79052+79082+73752	RM	SET	EVL	SET
375923	73353+79053+79083+73753	RM	SET	EVL	SET
375924	73354+79054+79084+73754	RM	SET	EVL	SET
375925	73355+79055+79085+73755	RM	SET	EVL	SET
375926	73356+79056+79086+73756	RM	SET	EVL	SET
375927	73357+79057+79087+73757	RM	SET	EVL	SET

Below: *The backbone of the modern SouthEastern operation is a large fleet of Class 375 'Electrostar' units, formed into five sub-classes. The entire fleet of 112 units is owned by Eversholt Leasing and based at Ramsgate depot. Painted in SouthEastern white and beige livery offset with yellow passenger doors, Class 375/8 No. 375824 is illustrated. On all Class 375s, the first class area is located directly behind the driving cab in both driving cars.* **Antony Christie**

South Eastern

Class 376
Electrostar

Vehicle Length: (Driving) 66ft 9in (20.3m)
(Inter) 65ft 6in (19.96m)
Height: 12ft 4in (3.75m)
Width: 9ft 2in (2.79m)
Horsepower: 2,682hp (2,000kW)
Seats (total/car): 216S, 36S/48S/48S/48S/36S + 116 perch

Passenger Train Operating Companies - South Eastern

Number	Formation DMSO(A)+MSO+TSO+MSO+DMSO(B)	Depot	Livery	Owner	Operator
376001	61101+63301+64301+63501+61601	SG	SET	EVL	SET
376002	61102+63302+64302+63502+61602	SG	SET	EVL	SET
376003	61103+63303+64303+63503+61603	SG	SET	EVL	SET
376004	61104+63304+64304+63504+61604	SG	SET	EVL	SET
376005	61105+63305+64305+63505+61605	SG	SET	EVL	SET
376006	61106+63306+64306+63506+61606	SG	SET	EVL	SET
376007	61107+63307+64307+63507+61607	SG	SET	EVL	SET
376008	61108+63308+64308+63508+61608	SG	SET	EVL	SET
376009	61109+63309+64309+63509+61609	SG	SET	EVL	SET
376010	61110+63310+64310+63510+61610	SG	SET	EVL	SET
376011	61111+63311+64311+63511+61611	SG	SET	EVL	SET
376012	61112+63312+64312+63512+61612	SG	SET	EVL	SET
376013	61113+63313+64313+63513+61613	SG	SET	EVL	SET
376014	61114+63314+64314+63514+61614	SG	SET	EVL	SET
376015	61115+63315+64315+63515+61615	SG	SET	EVL	SET
376016	61116+63316+64316+63516+61616	SG	SET	EVL	SET
376017	61117+63317+64317+63517+61617	SG	SET	EVL	SET
376018	61118+63318+64318+63518+61618	SG	SET	EVL	SET
376019	61119+63319+64319+63519+61619	SG	SET	EVL	SET
376020	61120+63320+64320+63520+61620	SG	SET	EVL	SET
376021	61121+63321+64321+63521+61621	SG	SET	EVL	SET
376022	61122+63322+64322+63522+61622	SG	SET	EVL	SET
376023	61123+63323+64323+63523+61623	SG	SET	EVL	SET
376024	61124+63324+64324+63524+61624	SG	SET	EVL	SET
376025	61125+63325+64325+63525+61625	SG	SET	EVL	SET
376026	61126+63326+64326+63526+61626	SG	SET	EVL	SET
376027	61127+63327+64327+63527+61627	SG	SET	EVL	SET
376028	61128+63328+64328+63528+61628	SG	SET	EVL	SET
376029	61129+63329+64329+63529+61629	SG	SET	EVL	SET
376030	61130+63330+64330+63530+61630	SG	SET	EVL	SET
376031	61131+63331+64331+63531+61631	SG	SET	EVL	SET
376032	61132+63332+64332+63532+61632	SG	SET	EVL	SET
376033	61133+63333+64333+63533+61633	SG	SET	EVL	SET
376034	61134+63334+64334+63534+61634	SG	SET	EVL	SET
376035	61135+63335+64335+63535+61635	SG	SET	EVL	SET
376036	61136+63336+64336+63536+61636	SG	SET	EVL	SET

Below: *To answer a huge demand for train travel, especially in the two peak periods on the routes from the Kent towns to London, a fleet of 36 high-capacity five-car Class 376 'Electrostar' sets was built. These are very basic 'Metro'-style trains with reduced seating but with large standing areas. The sets have bi-parting sliding doors and each five-car train has just 216 seats and 116 perch positions, but a crush capacity figure of over 900 people. Painted in SouthEastern white and beige livery with yellow doors, set No. 376009 is seen on the approach to London Bridge. These sets are based at Slade Green.* **Antony Christie**

Class 395
Javelin

Vehicle Length: (Driving) 67ft 7in (20.6m)	Width: 9ft 2in (2.79m)
(Inter) 67ft 6in (20.5m)	Horsepower: 2,252hp (1,680kW)
Height: 12ft 6in (3.81m)	Seats (total/car): 340S, 28S/66S/66S/66S/66S/48S

Passenger Train Operating Companies - South Eastern

Number	Formation DMSO(A)+MSO(A)+MSO(B)+ MSO(C)+MSO(D)+DMSO(B)	Depot	Livery	Owner	Operator	Name
395001	39011+39012+39013+39014+39015+39016	AD	HS1	EVL	SET	Dame Kelly Holmes
395002	39021+39022+39023+39024+39025+39026	AD	HS1	EVL	SET	Sebastian Coe
395003	39031+39032+39033+39034+39035+39036	AD	HS1	EVL	SET	Sir Steve Redgrave
395004	39041+39042+39043+39044+39045+39046	AD	HS1	EVL	SET	Sir Chris Hoy
395005	39051+39052+39053+39054+39055+39056	AD	HS1	EVL	SET	Dame Tanni Grey-Thompson
395006	39061+39062+39063+39064+39065+39066	AD	HS1	EVL	SET	Daley Thompson
395007	39071+39072+39073+39074+39075+39076	AD	HS1	EVL	SET	Steve Backley
395008	39081+39082+39083+39084+39085+39086	AD	HS1	EVL	SET	Ben Ainslie
395009	39091+39092+39093+39094+39095+39096	AD	HS1	EVL	SET	Rebecca Adlington
395010	39101+39102+39103+39104+39105+39106	AD	HS1	EVL	SET	Duncan Goodhew
395011	39111+39112+39113+39114+39115+39116	AD	HS1	EVL	SET	Katherine Grainger
395012	39121+39122+39123+39124+39125+39126	AD	HS1	EVL	SET	
395013	39131+39132+39133+39134+39135+39136	AD	HS1	EVL	SET	
395014	39141+39142+39143+39144+39145+39146	AD	HS1	EVL	SET	The Victoria Cross
395015	39151+39152+39153+39154+39155+39156	AD	HS1	EVL	SET	
395016	39161+39162+39163+39164+39165+39166	AD	HS1	EVL	SET	Jamie Staff
395017	39171+39172+39173+39174+39175+39176	AD	HS1	EVL	SET	Dame Sarah Storey
395018	39181+39182+39183+39184+39185+39186	AD	HS1	EVL	SET	Mo Farah
395019	39191+39192+39193+39194+39195+39196	AD	HS1	EVL	SET	Jessica Ennis
395020	39201+39202+39203+39204+39205+39206	AD	HS1	EVL	SET	Jason Kenny
395021	39211+39212+39213+39214+39215+39216	AD	HS1	EVL	SET	Ed Clancy MBE
395022	39221+39222+39223+39224+39225+39226	AD	HS1	EVL	SET	Alistair Brownlee
395023	39231+39232+39233+39234+39235+39236	AD	HS1	EVL	SET	Ellie Simmonds
395024	39241+39242+39243+39244+39245+39246	AD	HS1	EVL	SET	Jonnie Peacock
395025	39251+39252+39253+39254+39255+39256	AD	HS1	EVL	SET	Victoria Pendleton
395026	39261+39262+39263+39264+39265+39266	AD	HS1	EVL	SET	Marc Woods
395027	39271+39272+39273+39274+39275+39276	AD	HS1	EVL	SET	Hannah Cockcroft
395028	39281+39282+39283+39284+39285+39286	AD	HS1	EVL	SET	Laura Trott
395029	39291+39292+39293+39294+39295+39296	AD	HS1	EVL	SET	David Weir

Below: *One of the conditions on building HS1 between London St Pancras and the Channel Tunnel was the ability to operate domestic services over its tracks, enabling much reduced journey times from the mid and far Kent towns into London. To operate the service a fleet of 29 six-car Hitachi-built Class 395 'Javelin' sets was introduced. Based at Ashford, Kent, these sets can operate at up to 140mph (225km/h) over HS1. All sets are painted in a dark blue and black livery with light blue single-leaf passenger doors. Set No. 395002 is seen on HS1 near Rainham, Kent.* **Michael J. Collins**

Passenger Train Operating Companies - South Eastern

South Eastern

Class 465/0
Networker

Vehicle Length: (Driving) 68ft 6½in (20.89m) Width: 9ft 3in (2.81m)
(Inter) 65ft 9¾in (20.05m) Horsepower: 2,252hp (1,680kW)
Height: 12ft 4½in (3.77m) Seats (total/car): 348S, 86S/90S/86S/86S

Number	Formation	Depot	Livery	Owner	Operator
	DMSO(A)+TSO+TSO+DMSO(B)				
465001	64759+72028+72029+64809	SG	SET	EVL	SET
465002	64760+72030+72031+64810	SG	SET	EVL	SET
465003	64761+72032+72033+64811	SG	SET	EVL	SET
465004	64762+72034+72035+64812	SG	SET	EVL	SET
465005	64763+72036+72037+64813	SG	SET	EVL	SET
465006	64764+72038+72039+64814	SG	SET	EVL	SET
465007	64765+72040+72041+64815	SG	SET	EVL	SET
465008	64766+72042+72043+64816	SG	SET	EVL	SET
465009	64767+72044+72045+64817	SG	SET	EVL	SET
465010	64768+72046+72047+64818	SG	SET	EVL	SET
465011	64769+72048+72049+64819	SG	SET	EVL	SET
465012	64770+72050+72051+64820	SG	SET	EVL	SET
465013	64771+72052+72053+64821	SG	SET	EVL	SET
465014	64772+72054+72055+64822	SG	SET	EVL	SET
465015	64773+72056+72057+64823	SG	SET	EVL	SET
465016	64774+72058+72059+64824	SG	SET	EVL	SET
465017	64775+72060+72061+64825	SG	SET	EVL	SET
465018	64776+72062+72063+64826	SG	SET	EVL	SET
465019	64777+72064+72065+64827	SG	SET	EVL	SET
465020	64778+72066+72067+64828	SG	SET	EVL	SET
465021	64779+72068+72069+64829	SG	SET	EVL	SET
465022	64780+72070+72071+64830	SG	SET	EVL	SET
465023	64781+72072+72073+64831	SG	SET	EVL	SET
465024	64782+72074+72075+64832	SG	SET	EVL	SET
465025	64783+72076+72077+64833	SG	SET	EVL	SET
465026	64784+72078+72079+64834	SG	SET	EVL	SET
465027	64785+72080+72081+64835	SG	SET	EVL	SET
465028	64786+72082+72083+64836	SG	SET	EVL	SET
465029	64787+72084+72085+64837	SG	SET	EVL	SET
465030	64788+72086+72087+64838	SG	SET	EVL	SET
465031	64789+72088+72089+64839	SG	SET	EVL	SET
465032	64790+72090+72091+64840	SG	SET	EVL	SET
465033	64791+72092+72093+64841	SG	SET	EVL	SET
465034	64792+72094+72095+64842	SG	SET	EVL	SET
465035	64793+72096+72097+64843	SG	SET	EVL	SET
465036	64794+72098+72099+64844	SG	SET	EVL	SET
465037	64795+72100+72101+64845	SG	SET	EVL	SET
465038	64796+72102+72103+64846	SG	SET	EVL	SET
465039	64797+72104+72105+64847	SG	SET	EVL	SET
465040	64798+72106+72107+64848	SG	SET	EVL	SET
465041	64799+72108+72109+64849	SG	SET	EVL	SET
465042	64800+72110+72111+64850	SG	SET	EVL	SET
465043	64801+72112+72113+64851	SG	SET	EVL	SET
465044	64802+72114+72115+64852	SG	SET	EVL	SET
465045	64803+72116+72117+64853	SG	SET	EVL	SET
465046	64804+72118+72119+64854	SG	SET	EVL	SET
465047	64805+72120+72121+64855	SG	SET	EVL	SET
465048	64806+72122+72123+64856	SG	SET	EVL	SET
465049	64807+72124+72125+64857	SG	SET	EVL	SET
465050	64808+72126+72127+64858	SG	SET	EVL	SET

Class 465/1
Networker

Vehicle Length: (Driving) 68ft 6½in (20.89m) Width: 9ft 3in (2.81m)
(Inter) 65ft 9¾in (20.05m) Horsepower: 2,252hp (1,680kW)
Height: 12ft 4½in (3.77m) Seats (total/car): 348S, 86S/90S/86S/86S

Number	Formation	Depot	Livery	Owner	Operator
	DMSO(A)+TSO+TSO+DMSO(B)				
465151	65800+72900+72901+65847	SG	SET	EVL	SET
465152	65801+72902+72903+65848	SG	SET	EVL	SET
465153	65802+72904+72905+65849	SG	SET	EVL	SET

465154	65803+72906+72907+65850	SG	SET	EVL	SET
465155	65804+72908+72909+65851	SG	SET	EVL	SET
465156	65805+72910+72911+65852	SG	SET	EVL	SET
465157	65806+72912+72913+65853	SG	SET	EVL	SET
465158	65807+72914+72915+65854	SG	SET	EVL	SET
465159	65808+72916+72917+65855	SG	SET	EVL	SET
465160	65809+72918+72919+65856	SG	SET	EVL	SET
465161	65810+72920+72921+65857	SG	SET	EVL	SET
465162	65811+72922+72923+65858	SG	SET	EVL	SET
465163	65812+72924+72925+65859	SG	SET	EVL	SET
465164	65813+72926+72927+65860	SG	SET	EVL	SET
465165	65814+72928+72929+65861	SG	SET	EVL	SET
465166	65815+72930+72931+65862	SG	SET	EVL	SET
465167	65816+72932+72933+65863	SG	SET	EVL	SET
465168	65817+72934+72935+65864	SG	SET	EVL	SET
465169	65818+72936+72937+65865	SG	SET	EVL	SET
465170	65819+72938+72939+65866	SG	SET	EVL	SET
465171	65820+72940+72941+65867	SG	SET	EVL	SET
465172	65821+72942+72943+65868	SG	SET	EVL	SET
465173	65822+72944+72945+65869	SG	SET	EVL	SET
465174	65823+72946+72947+65870	SG	SET	EVL	SET
465175	65824+72948+72949+65871	SG	SET	EVL	SET
465176	65825+72950+72951+65872	SG	SET	EVL	SET
465177	65826+72952+72952+65873	SG	SET	EVL	SET
465178	65827+72954+72955+65874	SG	SET	EVL	SET
465179	65828+72956+72957+65875	SG	SET	EVL	SET
465180	65829+72958+72959+65876	SG	SET	EVL	SET
465181	65830+72960+72961+65877	SG	SET	EVL	SET
465182	65831+72962+72963+65878	SG	SET	EVL	SET
465183	65832+72964+72965+65879	SG	SET	EVL	SET
465184	65833+72966+72967+65880	SG	SET	EVL	SET
465185	65834+72968+72969+65881	SG	SET	EVL	SET
465186	65835+72970+72971+65882	SG	SET	EVL	SET
465187	65836+72972+72973+65883	SG	SET	EVL	SET
465188	65837+72974+72975+65884	SG	SET	EVL	SET
465189	65838+72976+72977+65885	SG	SET	EVL	SET
465190	65839+72978+72979+65886	SG	SET	EVL	SET
465191	65840+72980+72981+65887	SG	SET	EVL	SET
465192	65841+72982+72983+65888	SG	SET	EVL	SET
465193	65842+72984+72985+65889	SG	SET	EVL	SET
465194	65843+72986+72987+65890	SG	SET	EVL	SET
465195	65844+72988+72989+65891	SG	SET	EVL	SET
465196	65845+72990+72991+65892	SG	SET	EVL	SET
465197	65846+72992+72993+65893	SG	SET	EVL	SET

Below: *Introduced by Network SouthEast to modernise the Kent commuter network, the Class 465 units were known as 'Networkers', being built by BREL/ABB and Metro-Cammell. Today four different sub-classes exist; Class 465/0 and 465/1 were built by BREL/ABB at York, while the Class 465/2 fleet was built by Metro-Cammell. Today a large number of Class 465/2s have been rebuilt as Class 465/9 and fitted with limited first class seating for longer-distance commuter services. All sets carry the South Eastern white livery offset by dark blue and blue passenger doors. Class 465/1 No. 465187 is illustrated at Lewisham.* **CJM**

South Eastern

Class 465/2
Networker

Vehicle Length: (Driving) 68ft 6½in (20.89m)	Width: 9ft 3in (2.81m)
(Inter) 65ft 9¾in (20.05m)	Horsepower: 2,252hp (1,680kW)
Height: 12ft 4½in (3.77m)	Seats (total/car): 348S, 86S/90S/86S/86S

Number	Formation DMSO(A)+TSO+TSO+DMSO(B)	Depot	Livery	Owner	Operator
465235	65734+72787+72788+65784	SG	SET	ANG	SET
465236	65735+72789+72790+65785	SG	SET	ANG	SET
465237	65736+72791+72792+65786	SG	SET	ANG	SET
465238	65737+72793+72794+65787	SG	SET	ANG	SET
465239	65738+72795+72796+65788	SG	SET	ANG	SET
465240	65739+72797+72798+65789	SG	SET	ANG	SET
465241	65740+72799+72800+65790	SG	SET	ANG	SET
465242	65741+72801+72802+65791	SG	SET	ANG	SET
465243	65742+72803+72804+65792	SG	SET	ANG	SET
465244	65743+72805+72806+65793	SG	SET	ANG	SET
465245	65744+72807+72808+65794	SG	SET	ANG	SET
465246	65745+72809+72810+65795	SG	SET	ANG	SET
465247	65746+72811+72812+65796	SG	SET	ANG	SET
465248	65747+72813+72814+65797	SG	SET	ANG	SET
465249	65748+72815+72816+65798	SG	SET	ANG	SET
465250	65749+72817+72818+65799	SG	SET	ANG	SET

Class 465/9
Networker

Vehicle Length: (Driving) 68ft 6½in (20.89m)	Width: 9ft 3in (2.81m)
(Inter) 65ft 9¾in (20.05m)	Horsepower: 2,252hp (1,680kW)
Height: 12ft 4½in (3.77m)	Seats (total/car): 24F-302S, 12F-68S/76S/90S/12F-68S

Number	Formation DMCO(A)+TSO+TSO+DMCO(B)	Depot	Livery	Owner	Operator
465901 (465201)	65700+72719+72720+65750	SG	SET	ANG	SET
465902 (465202)	65701+72721+72722+65751	SG	SET	ANG	SET
465903 (465203)	65702+72723+72724+65752	SG	SET	ANG	SET
465904 (465204)	65703+72725+72726+65753	SG	SET	ANG	SET
465905 (465205)	65704+72727+72728+65754	SG	SET	ANG	SET
465906 (465206)	65705+72729+72730+65755	SG	SET	ANG	SET
465907 (465207)	65706+72731+72732+65756	SG	SET	ANG	SET
465908 (465208)	65707+72733+72734+65757	SG	SET	ANG	SET
465909 (465209)	65708+72735+72736+65758	SG	SET	ANG	SET
465910 (465210)	65709+72737+72738+65759	SG	SET	ANG	SET
465911 (465211)	65710+72739+72740+65760	SG	SET	ANG	SET
465912 (465212)	65711+72741+72742+65761	SG	SET	ANG	SET
465913 (465213)	65712+72743+72744+65762	SG	SET	ANG	SET
465914 (465214)	65713+72745+72746+65763	SG	SET	ANG	SET
465915 (465215)	65714+72747+72748+65764	SG	SET	ANG	SET
465916 (465216)	65715+72749+72750+65765	SG	SET	ANG	SET
465917 (465217)	65716+72751+72752+65766	SG	SET	ANG	SET
465918 (465218)	65717+72753+72754+65767	SG	SET	ANG	SET
465919 (465219)	65718+72755+72756+65768	SG	SET	ANG	SET
465920 (465220)	65719+72757+72758+65769	SG	SET	ANG	SET
465921 (465221)	65720+72759+72760+65770	SG	SET	ANG	SET
465922 (465222)	65721+72761+72762+65771	SG	SET	ANG	SET
465923 (465223)	65722+72763+72764+65772	SG	SET	ANG	SET
465924 (465224)	65723+72765+72766+65773	SG	SET	ANG	SET
465925 (465225)	65724+72767+72768+65774	SG	SET	ANG	SET
465926 (465226)	65725+72769+72770+65775	SG	SET	ANG	SET
465927 (465227)	65726+72771+72772+65776	SG	SET	ANG	SET
465928 (465228)	65727+72773+72774+65777	SG	SET	ANG	SET
465929 (465229)	65728+72775+72776+65778	SG	SET	ANG	SET
465930 (465230)	65729+72777+72778+65779	SG	SET	ANG	SET
465931 (465231)	65730+72779+72780+65780	SG	SET	ANG	SET
465932 (465232)	65731+72781+72782+65781	SG	SET	ANG	SET
465933 (465233)	65732+72783+72784+65782	SG	SET	ANG	SET
465934 (465234)	65733+72785+72786+65783	SG	SET	ANG	SET

Right: *The Class 465 fleet took over from the 1950s-built EPB stock on the South Eastern lines radiating from London and is based at Slade Green depot. Since original introduction, some minor modifications have been made to the front ends to remove flat surfaces on which train surfers could stand. One of the Metro-Cammell-built Class 465/2 sets, No. 465238, is illustrated at London Bridge.*
Antony Christie

Class 466
Networker

Vehicle Length: (Driving) 68ft 6½in (20.89m) Horsepower: 1,126hp (840kW)
Height: 12ft 4½in (3.77m)   Seats (total/car): 168S, 86S/82S
Width: 9ft 3in (2.81m)

Number	Formation DMSO+DTSO	Depot	Livery	Owner	Operator
466001	64860+78312	SG	SET	ANG	SET
466002	64861+78313	SG	SET	ANG	SET
466003	64862+78314	SG	SET	ANG	SET
466004	64863+78315	SG	SET	ANG	SET
466005	64864+78316	SG	SET	ANG	SET
466006	64865+78317	SG	SET	ANG	SET
466007	64866+78318	SG	SET	ANG	SET
466008	64867+78319	SG	SET	ANG	SET
466009	64868+78320	SG	SET	ANG	SET
466010	64869+78321	SG	SET	ANG	SET
466011	64870+78322	SG	SET	ANG	SET
466012	64871+78323	SG	SET	ANG	SET
466013	64872+78324	SG	SET	ANG	SET
466014	64873+78325	SG	SET	ANG	SET
466015	64874+78326	SG	SET	ANG	SET
466016	64875+78327	SG	SET	ANG	SET
466017	64876+78328	SG	SET	ANG	SET
466018	64877+78329	SG	SET	ANG	SET
466019	64878+78330	SG	SET	ANG	SET
466020	64879+78331	SG	SET	ANG	SET
466021	64880+78332	SG	SET	ANG	SET
466022	64881+78333	SG	SET	ANG	SET
466023	64882+78334	SG	SET	ANG	SET
466024	64883+78335	SG	SET	ANG	SET
466025	64884+78336	SG	SET	ANG	SET
466026	64885+78337	SG	SET	ANG	SET
466027	64886+78338	SG	SET	ANG	SET
466028	64887+78339	SG	SET	ANG	SET
466029	64888+78340	SG	SET	ANG	SET
466030	64889+78341	SG	SET	ANG	SET
466031	64890+78342	SG	SET	ANG	SET
466032	64891+78343	SG	SET	ANG	SET
466033	64892+78344	SG	SET	ANG	SET
466034	64893+78345	SG	SET	ANG	SET
466035	64894+78346	SG	SET	ANG	SET
466036	64895+78347	SG	SET	ANG	SET
466037	64896+78348	SG	SET	ANG	SET
466038	64897+78349	SG	SET	ANG	SET
466039	64898+78350	SG	SET	ANG	SET
466040	64899+78351	SG	SET	ANG	SET
466041	64900+78352	SG	SET	ANG	SET
466042	64901+78353	SG	SET	ANG	SET
466043	64902+78354	SG	SET	ANG	SET

Right: *When the Network SouthEast 'Networker' order was placed it included 43 two-car sets, formed with one powered and one trailer vehicle to enable the operation of six- or ten-car formations, or to operate on their own on branch lines. The sets, classified as 466, were built by Metro-Cammell and are almost identical to the Class 465/2s. These sets contain the only non-powered 'Networker' driving vehicles. Sets are painted in standard SouthEastern colours and are based at Slade Green. Set No. 466009 leads a ten-car formation of 'Networker' stock near Brixton.* **Antony Guppy**

Thameslink, Southern & Great Northern

Address: Thameslink, Hertford House, 1 Cranwood Street, London, EC1V 9QS
✉ icustomer service@thameslinkrailway.com ✆ 0345 0264700
ⓘ www.thameslinkrailway.com

Managing Director: Charles Horton
Franchise Dates: September 2014 - September 2021
Principal Routes: London Victoria/London Bridge to Brighton, 'Coastway' route, Uckfield/East Grinstead. Services to Surrey/ Sussex, London King's Cross - King's Lynn, Peterborough/Cambridge, Moorgate - Hertford Loop/Letchworth, Bedford - Brighton/Sutton/Wimbledon
Depots: Bedford Cauldwell Walk (BF), Brighton (BI), Hornsey (HE), Selhurst (SU), Stewarts Lane (SL)
Parent Company: Govia

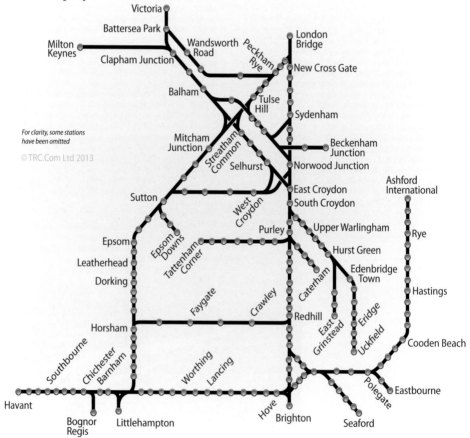

For clarity, some stations have been omitted

© TRC.Com Ltd 2013

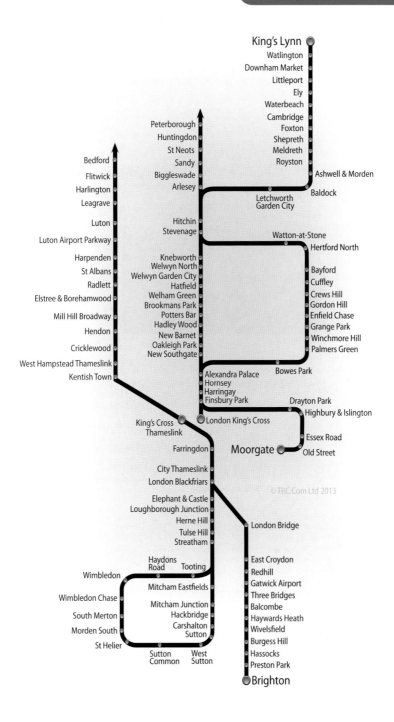

Passenger Train Operating Companies - Thameslink, Southern, Great Northern

King's Lynn
Watlington
Downham Market
Littleport
Ely
Waterbeach
Cambridge
Peterborough   Foxton
Huntingdon   Shepreth
St Neots   Meldreth
Bedford   Sandy   Royston
Flitwick   Biggleswade   Ashwell & Morden
Harlington   Arlesey   Baldock
Leagrave   Letterworth
                      Garden City
Luton   Hitchin
Luton Airport Parkway Stevenage   Watton-at-Stone
                                    Hertford North
Harpenden   Knebworth
St Albans   Welwyn North   Bayford
Radlett   Welwyn Garden City   Cuffley
Elstree & Borehamwood Hatfield   Crews Hill
             Welham Green   Gordon Hill
Mill Hill Broadway Brookmans Park   Enfield Chase
Hendon   Potters Bar   Grange Park
             Hadley Wood   Winchmore Hill
Cricklewood New Barnet   Palmers Green
             Oakleigh Park
West Hampstead Thameslink New Southgate
Kentish Town   Bowes Park
             Alexandra Palace
             Hornsey
             Harringay
             Finsbury Park   Drayton Park
                                   Highbury & Islington
King's Cross   London King's Cross
Thameslink   Essex Road
Farringdon   Moorgate   Old Street
City Thameslink
London Blackfriars
Elephant & Castle
Loughborough Junction
Herne Hill   London Bridge
Tulse Hill
Streatham
Haydons   East Croydon
Road   Tooting   Redhill
Wimbledon   Gatwick Airport
             Mitcham Eastfields   Three Bridges
Wimbledon Chase   Balcombe
             Mitcham Junction   Haywards Heath
South Merton Hackbridge   Wivelsfield
             Carshalton   Burgess Hill
Morden South   Sutton   Hassocks
St Helier   Preston Park
             Sutton   West
             Common   Sutton
             Brighton

© TRC.Com Ltd 2013

Class 09

Vehicle Length: 29ft 3in (8.91m)
Height: 12ft 8⅝in (3.87m)
Width: 8ft 6in (2.59m)

Engine: English Electric 6K
Horsepower: 400hp (298kW)
Electrical Equipment: English Electric

Number	Depot	Pool	Livery	Owner	Operator	Name
09026	BI	HWSU	GRN	SOU	TSG	*Cedric Wares*

Class 73/2

Vehicle Length: 53ft 8in (16.35m)
Height: 12ft 5⅜in (3.79m)
Width: 8ft 8in (2.64m)

Power: 750V dc third rail or English Electric 6K
Horsepower: E/D - 1,600hp (1,193kW) / 600hp (447kW)
Electrical Equipment: English Electric

Number	Depot	Pool	Livery	Owner	Operator
73202 (73137)	SL	MBED	SOU	PTR	TSG

Left: *The new Thameslink, Southern & Great Northern franchise formed in 2014-15 is one of the biggest in the country in terms of route and rolling stock. One Class 73/2 No. 73202 is maintained at Stewarts Lane and was previously the responsibility of Gatwick Express. It is used for 'Thunderbird' rescue and driver route training duties. The loco currently carries the Southern green and white livery with both Southern and Gatwick Express branding.* **Mark V. Pike**

Class 171/7
Turbostar

Vehicle Length: 77ft 6in (23.62m)
Height: 12ft 4½in (3.77m)
Width: 8ft 10in (2.69m)

Engine: 1 x MTU 6R 183TD13H of 422hp per vehicle
Horsepower: 844hp (629kW)
Seats (total/car): 9F-107S 9F-43S/64S

Number	Formation DMCL+DMSL	Depot	Livery	Owner	Operator					
171721	50721+79721	SU	SOU	PTR	TSG	171726	50726+79726	SU	SOU	PTR TSG
171722	50722+79722	SU	SOU	PTR	TSG	171727	50727+79727	SU	SOU	PTR TSG
171723	50723+79723	SU	SOU	PTR	TSG	171728	50728+79728	SU	SOU	PTR TSG
171724	50724+79724	SU	SOU	PTR	TSG	171729	50729+79729	SU	SOU	PTR TSG
171725	50725+79725	SU	SOU	PTR	TSG	171730	50392+79392	SU	SOU	PTR TSG

171730 previously numbered 170392

Class 171/8
Turbostar

Vehicle Length: 77ft 6in (23.62m)
Height: 12ft 4½in (3.77m)
Width: 8ft 10in (2.69m)

Engine: 1 x MTU 6R 183TD13H of 422hp per vehicle
Horsepower: 1,688hp (1,259kW)
Seats (total/car): 18F-241S 9F-43S/74S/74S/9F-50S

Number	Formation DMCL(A)+MS+MS+DMCL(B)	Depot	Livery	Owner	Operator
171801	50801+54801+56801+79801	SU	SOU	PTR	TSG
171802	50802+54802+56802+79802	SU	SOU	PTR	TSG
171803	50803+54803+56803+79803	SU	SOU	PTR	TSG
171804	50804+54804+56804+79804	SU	SOU	PTR	TSG
171805	50805+54805+56805+79805	SU	SOU	PTR	TSG
171806	50806+54806+56806+79806	SU	SOU	PTR	TSG

Left: *A fleet of 10 two-car and six four-car Class 171 'Turbostar' sets is on the books of TSGN, operating non-electrified routes of the former Southern franchise. The sets are allocated to Selhurst. In the near future some changes are likely to take place with some ex-Scottish Class 170s joining the fleet and the four-car '171s' being re-allocated to other parts of the country. Set No. 171801 is illustrated.* **CJM**

Class 313/0 and 313/1

	Vehicle Length: (Driving) 64ft 11½in (20.75m)	Width: 9ft 3in (2.82m)
	(Inter) 65ft 4¼in (19.92m)	Horsepower: 880hp (656kW)
	Height: 11ft 9in (3.58m)	Seats (total/car): 231S, 74S/83S/74S

Number	Formation DMSO+PTSO+BDMSO	Depot	Livery	Owner	Operator	Name
313018	62546+71230+62160	HE	FCC	EVL	TSG	
313024	62552+71236+62616	HE	FCC	EVL	TSG	
313025	62553+71237+62617	HE	FCC	EVL	TSG	
313026	62554+71238+62618	HE	FCC	EVL	TSG	
313027	62555+71239+62619	HE	FCC	EVL	TSG	
313028	62556+71240+62620	HE	FCC	EVL	TSG	
313029	62557+71241+62621	HE	FCC	EVL	TSG	
313030	62558+71242+62622	HE	FCC	EVL	TSG	
313031	62559+71243+62623	HE	FCC	EVL	TSG	
313032	62560+71244+62643	HE	FCC	EVL	TSG	
313033	62561+71245+62625	HE	FCC	EVL	TSG	
313035	62563+71247+62627	HE	FCC	EVL	TSG	
313036	62564+71248+62628	HE	FCC	EVL	TSG	
313037	62565+71249+62629	HE	FCC	EVL	TSG	
313038	62566+71250+62630	HE	FCC	EVL	TSG	
313039	62567+71251+62631	HE	FCC	EVL	TSG	
313040	62568+71252+62632	HE	FCC	EVL	TSG	
313041	62569+71253+62633	HE	FCC	EVL	TSG	
313042	62570+71254+62634	HE	FCC	EVL	TSG	
313043	62571+71255+62635	HE	FCC	EVL	TSG	
313044	62572+71256+62636	HE	FCC	EVL	TSG	
313045	62573+71257+62637	HE	FCC	EVL	TSG	
313046	62574+71258+62638	HE	FCC	EVL	TSG	
313047	62575+71259+62639	HE	FCC	EVL	TSG	
313048	62576+71260+62640	HE	FCC	EVL	TSG	
313049	62577+71261+62641	HE	FCC	EVL	TSG	
313050	62578+71262+62649	HE	FCC	EVL	TSG	
313051	62579+71263+62624	HE	FCC	EVL	TSG	
313052	62580+71264+62644	HE	FCC	EVL	TSG	
313053	62581+71265+62645	HE	FCC	EVL	TSG	
313054	62582+71266+62646	HE	FCC	EVL	TSG	Captain William Leefe Robinson VC
313055	62583+71267+62647	HE	FCC	EVL	TSG	
313056	62584+71268+62648	HE	FCC	EVL	TSG	
313057	62585+71269+62642	HE	FCC	EVL	TSG	
313058	62586+71270+62650	HE	FCC	EVL	TSG	
313059	62587+71271+62651	HE	FCC	EVL	TSG	
313060	62588+71272+62652	HE	FCC	EVL	TSG	
313061	62589+71273+62653	HE	FCC	EVL	TSG	
313062	62590+71274+62654	HE	FCC	EVL	TSG	
313063	62591+71275+62655	HE	FCC	EVL	TSG	
313064	62592+71276+62656	HE	FCC	EVL	TSG	
313122	62550+71234+62614	HE	FCC	EVL	TSG	Eric Roberts 1946-2012 'The Flying Nottsman'
313123	62551+71235+62615	HE	FCC	EVL	TSG	
313134	62562+71246+62626	HE	FCC	EVL	TSG	City of London

Right: The Great Northern local services operated by TSGN use a fleet of 44 Class 313/0 and 313/1 units allocated to Hornsey. The new franchise calls for these sets to be replaced. The '313s' were the first production trains to emerge from the 1972-design PEP development train. Sets are currently painted in the First Capital Connect colour scheme of the previous franchise holder with Great Northern branding. Set No. 313046 is illustrated. **Antony Christie**

Thameslink, Southern, Great Northern

Class 313/2

Vehicle Length: (Driving) 64ft 11½in (20.75m) Width: 9ft 3in (2.82m)
(Inter) 65ft 4½in (19.92m) Horsepower: 880hp (656kW)
Height: 11ft 9in (3.58m) Seats (total/car): 202S, 66S/70S/66S

Number	Formation DMSO+PTSO+BDMSO	Depot	Livery	Owner	Operator
313201 (313101)	62529+71213+62593	BI	SOU	BEA	TSG
313202 (313102)	62530+71214+62594	BI	SOU	BEA	TSG
313203 (313103)	62531+71215+62595	BI	SOU	BEA	TSG
313204 (313104)	62532+71216+62596	BI	SOU	BEA	TSG
313205 (313105)	62533+71217+62597	BI	SOU	BEA	TSG
313206 (313106)	62534+71218+62598	BI	SOU	BEA	TSG
313207 (313107)	62535+71219+62599	BI	SOU	BEA	TSG
313208 (313108)	62536+71220+62600	BI	SOU	BEA	TSG
313209 (313109)	62537+71221+62601	BI	SOU	BEA	TSG
313210 (313110)	62538+71222+62602	BI	SOU	BEA	TSG
313211 (313111)	62539+71223+62603	BI	SOU	BEA	TSG
313212 (313112)	62540+71224+62604	BI	SOU	BEA	TSG
313213 (313113)	62541+71225+62605	BI	SOU	BEA	TSG
313214 (313114)	62542+71226+62606	BI	SOU	BEA	TSG
313215 (313115)	62543+71227+62607	BI	SOU	BEA	TSG
313216 (313116)	62544+71228+62608	BI	SOU	BEA	TSG
313217 (313117)	62545+71229+61609	BI	SOU	BEA	TSG
313219 (313119)	62547+71231+61611	BI	SOU	BEA	TSG
313220 (313120)	62548+71232+61612	BI	SOU	BEA	TSG

The Southern 'Coastway' service radiating along the south coast from Brighton is operated by a fleet of 19 three-car Class 313/2 sets; these were modified from 313/1 units by the removal of their ac power system. All sets are painted in Southern green and white livery, offset by route specific pictogram branding. Set No. 313202 is illustrated departing from Fratton. **CJM**

Class 317/3

Vehicle Length: (Driving) 65ft 0¾in (19.83m) Width: 9ft 3in (2.82m)
(Inter) 65ft 4¼in (19.92m) Horsepower: 1,000hp (746kW)
Height: 12ft 1½in (3.58m) Seats (total/car): 22F/269S, 74S/79S/22F-46S/70S

Number	Formation DTSO+MSO+TCO+DTSO	Depot	Livery	Owner	Operator	Name
317337	77036+62671+71613+77084	HE	FCC	ANG	TSG	
317338	77037+62698+71614+77085	HE	FCC	ANG	TSG	
317339	77038+62699+71615+77086	HE	FCC	ANG	TSG	
317340	77039+62700+71616+77087	HE	FCC	ANG	TSG	
317341	77040+62701+71617+77088	HE	FCC	ANG	TSG	
317342	77041+62702+71618+77089	HE	FCC	ANG	TSG	
317343	77042+62703+71619+77090	HE	FCC	ANG	TSG	
317344	77029+62690+71620+77091	HE	FCC	ANG	TSG	
317345	77044+62705+71621+77092	HE	FCC	ANG	TSG	Driver John Webb
317346	77045+62706+71622+77093	HE	FCC	ANG	TSG	
317347	77046+62707+71623+77094	HE	FCC	ANG	TSG	
317348	77047+62708+71624+77095	HE	FCC	ANG	TSG	Richard A. Jenner

Right: *A fleet of 12 Class 317s is on the books of Hornsey depot to operate on the Great Northern route outer-suburban network. Painted in the former operator First Capital Connect's livery with Great Northern branding, these sets are due to be phased out as new stock enters service and major rolling stock changes are implemented by the new TSGN franchise. Set No. 317343 is shown at King's Cross.*
Antony Christie

Class 319/0

Vehicle Length: (Driving) 65ft 0¾in (19.83m) Width: 9ft 3in (2.82m)
(Inter) 65ft 4¼in (19.92m) Horsepower: 1,326hp (990kW)
Height: 11ft 9in (3.58m) Seats (total/car): 319S, 82S/82S/77S/78S

Number	Formation	Depot	Livery	Owner	Operator	Name
	DTSO(A)+MSO+TSO+DTSO(B)					
319001	77291+62891+71772+77290	SU	TLK	PTR	TSG	*Driver Mick Winnett*
319002	77293+62892+71773+77292	SU	FCC	PTR	TSG	
319003	77295+62893+71774+77294	SU	FCC	PTR	TSG	
319004	77297+62894+71775+77296	SU	TLK	PTR	TSG	
319005	77299+62895+71776+77298	SU	TLK	PTR	TSG	
319006	77301+62896+71777+77300	SU	TLK	PTR	TSG	
319007	77303+62897+71778+77302	SU	FCC	PTR	TSG	
319008	77305+62898+71779+77304	SU	SOU	PTR	TSG	*Cheriton*
319009	77307+62899+71780+77306	SU	TLK	PTR	TSG	*Coquelles*
319010	77309+62900+71781+77308	SU	TLK	PTR	TSG	
319011	77311+62901+71782+77310	SU	TLK	PTR	TSG	*John Ruskin College*
319012	77313+62902+71783+77312	SU	SOU	PTR	TSG	
319013	77315+62903+71784+77314	SU	SOU	PTR	TSG	*The Surrey Hills*

Class 319/2

Vehicle Length: (Driving) 65ft 0¾in (19.83m) Width: 9ft 3in (2.82m)
(Inter) 65ft 4¼in (19.92m) Horsepower: 1,326hp (990kW)
Height: 11ft 9in (3.58m) Seats (total/car): 18F/212S, 64S/60S/52S/18F-36S

Number	Formation	Depot	Livery	Owner	Operator	Name/Notes
	DTSO+MSO+TSO+DTCO					
319214	77317+62904+71785+77316	SU	SOU	PTR	TSG	
319215	77319+62905+71786+77318	SU	ADV	PTR	TSG	
319216	77321+62906+71787+77320	SU	SOU	PTR	TSG	
319217	77323+62907+71788+77322	BF	SOU	PTR	TSG	*Brighton*
319218	77325+62908+71789+77324	BF	ADV	PTR	TSG	*Croydon*
319219	77327+62909+71790+77326	BF	SOU	PTR	TSG	
319220	77329+62910+71791+77328	BF	SOU	PTR	TSG	

Class 319/3

Vehicle Length: (Driving) 65ft 0¾in (19.83m) Width: 9ft 3in (2.82m)
(Inter) 65ft 4¼in (19.92m) Horsepower: 1,326hp (990kW)
Height: 11ft 9in (3.58m) Seats (total/car): 300S, 70S/78S/74S/78S

Number	Formation	Depot	Livery	Owner	Operator	Name
	DTSO(A)+MSO+TSO+DTSO(B)					
319366	77469+63048+71934+77468	BF	FCC	PTR	TSG	
319367	77471+63049+71935+77470	BF	FCC	PTR	TSG	
319368	77473+63050+71936+77472	BF	FCC	PTR	TSG	
319369	77475+63051+71937+77474	BF	FCC	PTR	TSG	
319370	77477+63052+71938+77476	BF	FCC	PTR	TSG	
319371	77479+63053+71939+77478	BF	FCC	PTR	TSG	
319372	77481+63054+71940+77480	BF	FCC	PTR	TSG	
319373	77483+63055+71941+77482	BF	TLK	PTR	TSG	*Bedford Cauldwell Walk TMD*
319374	77485+63056+71942+77484	BF	FCC	PTR	TSG	
319375	77487+63057+71943+77486	BF	FCC	PTR	TSG	

Thameslink, Southern, Great Northern

319376	77489+63058+71944+77488	BF	FCC	PTR	TSG
319377	77491+63059+71945+77490	BF	FCC	PTR	TSG
319378	77493+63060+71946+77492	BF	FCC	PTR	TSG
319379	77495+63061+71947+77494	BF	FCC	PTR	TSG
319381	77973+63093+71979+77974	BF	FCC	PTR	TSG
319382	77975+63094+71980+77976	BF	FCC	PTR	TSG
319383	77977+63096+71981+77978	BF	FCC	PTR	TSG
319384	77979+63096+71982+77980	BF	FCC	PTR	TSG
319385	77981+63097+71983+77982	BF	FCC	PTR	TSG
319386	77983+63098+71984+77984	BF	FCC	PTR	TSG

Above: *Until the completion of the modernisation of the Thameslink services and introduction of new trains, the north-south cross-London service is operated by Class 319 stock of various sub-classes. Painted in the all light grey colours of the new TSGN franchise, set No. 319010 is seen at Blackfriars station with Thameslink branding.* **Antony Christie**

Class 319/4

Vehicle Length: (Driving) 65ft 0¾in (19.83m) *Width: 9ft 3in (2.82m)*
(Inter) 65ft 4¼in (19.92m) *Horsepower: 1,326hp (990kW)*
Height: 11ft 9in (3.58m) *Seats (total/car): 12F/277S, 12F-54S/77S/72S/74S*

Number	Formation DTCO+MSO+TSO+DTSO	Depot	Livery	Owner	Operator	Name
319421	77331+62911+71792+77330	BF	FCC	PTR	TSG	
319422	77333+62912+71793+77332	BF	FCC	PTR	TSG	
319423	77335+62913+71794+77334	BF	FCC	PTR	TSG	
319424	77337+62914+71795+77336	BF	FCC	PTR	TSG	
319425	77339+62915+71796+77338	BF	FCC	PTR	TSG	*Transforming Travel*
319426	77341+62916+71797+77340	BF	TLK	PTR	TSG	
319427	77343+62917+71798+77342	BF	FCC	PTR	TSG	
319428	77345+62918+71799+77344	BF	FCC	PTR	TSG	
319429	77347+62919+71800+77346	BF	FCC	PTR	TSG	
319430	77349+62920+71801+77348	BF	FCC	PTR	TSG	
319431	77351+62921+71802+77350	BF	FCC	PTR	TSG	
319432	77353+62922+71803+77352	BF	FCC	PTR	TSG	
319433	77355+62923+71804+77354	BF	FCC	PTR	TSG	
319434	77357+62924+71805+77356	BF	FCC	PTR	TSG	
319435	77359+62925+71806+77358	BF	FCC	PTR	TSG	*Adrian Jackson-Robbins Chairman 1987-2007 Association of Public Transport Users*
319436	77361+62926+71807+77360	BF	FCC	PTR	TSG	
319437	77363+62927+71808+77362	BF	TLK	PTR	TSG	
319438	77365+62928+71809+77364	BF	TLK	PTR	TSG	
319439	77367+62929+71810+77366	BF	FCC	PTR	TSG	
319440	77369+62930+71811+77368	BF	FCC	PTR	TSG	
319441	77371+62931+71812+77370	BF	FCC	PTR	TSG	

319442	77373+62932+71813+77372	BF	FCC	PTR	TSG	
319443	77375+62933+71814+77374	BF	TLK	PTR	TSG	
319444	77377+62934+71815+77376	BF	FCC	PTR	TSG	*City of St Albans*
319445	77379+62935+71816+77378	BF	FCC	PTR	TSG	
319446	77381+62936+71817+77380	BF	FCC	PTR	TSG	
319447	77431+62961+71866+77430	BF	FCC	PTR	TSG	
319448	77433+62962+71867+77432	BF	FCC	PTR	TSG	
319449	77435+62963+71868+77434	BF	FCC	PTR	TSG	
319450	77437+62964+71869+77436	BF	FCC	PTR	TSG	
319451	77439+62965+71870+77438	BF	FCC	PTR	TSG	
319452	77441+62966+71871+77440	BF	FCC	PTR	TSG	
319453	77443+62967+71872+77442	BF	FCC	PTR	TSG	
319454	77445+62968+71873+77444	BF	FCC	PTR	TSG	
319455	77447+62969+71874+77446	BF	FCC	PTR	TSG	
319456	77449+62970+71875+77448	BF	FCC	PTR	TSG	
319457	77451+62971+71876+77450	BF	FCC	PTR	TSG	
319458	77453+62972+71877+77452	BF	FCC	PTR	TSG	
319459	77455+62973+71878+77454	BF	FCC	PTR	TSG	
319460	77457+62974+71879+77456	BF	FCC	PTR	TSG	

Class 321/4

Vehicle Length: (Driving) 65ft 0¾in (19.83m)
(Inter) 65ft 4¼in (19.92m)
Height: 12ft 4¾in (3.78m)
Width: 9ft 3in (2.82m)
Horsepower: 1,328hp (996kW)
Seats (total/car): 28F/271S, 28F-40S/79S/74S/78S

Number	Formation	Depot	Livery	Owner	Operator	Name
	DMCO+MSO+TSO+DMSO					
321401	78095+63063+71949+77943	HE	FCC	EVL	TSG	
321402	78096+63064+71950+77944	HE	FCC	EVL	TSG	
321403	78097+63065+71951+77945	HE	FCC	EVL	TSG	*Stewart Fleming Signalman King's Cross*
321404	78098+63066+71952+77946	HE	FCC	EVL	TSG	
321405	78099+63067+71953+77947	HE	FCC	EVL	TSG	
321406	78100+63068+71954+77948	HE	FCC	EVL	TSG	
321407	78101+63069+71955+77949	HE	FCC	EVL	TSG	
321408	78102+63070+71956+77959	HE	FCC	EVL	TSG	
321409	78103+63071+71957+77960	HE	FCC	EVL	TSG	*Dame Alice Owen's School 400 years of Learning*
321410	78104+63072+71958+77961	HE	FCC	EVL	TSG	
321418	78112+63080+71968+77962	HE	FCC	EVL	TSG	
321419	78113+63081+71969+77963	HE	FCC	EVL	TSG	
321420	78114+63082+71970+77964	HE	FCC	EVL	TSG	*We are proud supporters of Movember*

Left: Another small fleet operating for TSGN is 13 Class 321/4s, retained to ease overcrowding on GN line services. Sets are painted in the former FCC livery and now carry Thameslink branding. They will come off lease when new stock is delivered. The sets are destined to supplement the Class 320 fleet in Scotland. Set No. 321421 is illustrated. **Antony Christie**

Class 365
Networker Express

Vehicle Length: (Driving) 68ft 6½in (20.89m)
(Inter) 65ft 9¼in (20.89m)
Height: 12ft 4⅓in (3.77m)
Width: 9ft 2½in (2.81m)
Horsepower: 1,684hp (1,256kW)
Seats (total/car): 24F/239S, 12F-56S/59S/68S/12F-56S

Number	Formation	Depot	Livery	Owner	Operator	Name
	DMCO(A)+TSO+PTSO+DMCO(B)					
365501	65894+72241+72240+65935	HE	FCC	EVL	TSG	
365502	65895+72243+72242+65936	HE	FCC	EVL	TSG	
365503	65896+72245+72244+65937	HE	FCC	EVL	TSG	

Thameslink, Southern, Great Northern

365504	65897+72247+72246+65938	HE	FCC	EVL	TSG	
365505	65898+72249+72248+65939	HE	FCC	EVL	TSG	
365506	65899+72251+72250+65940	HE	FCC	EVL	TSG	*The Royston Express*
365507	65900+72253+72252+65941	HE	FCC	EVL	TSG	
365508	65901+72255+72254+65942	HE	FCC	EVL	TSG	
365509	65902+72257+72256+65943	HE	FCC	EVL	TSG	
365510	65903+72259+72258+65944	HE	FCC	EVL	TSG	
365511	65904+72261+72260+65945	HE	FCC	EVL	TSG	
365512	65905+72263+72262+65946	HE	FCC	EVL	TSG	
365513	65906+72265+72264+65947	HE	FCC	EVL	TSG	*Hornsey Depot*
365514	65907+72267+72266+65948	HE	FCC	EVL	TSG	*Captain George Vancouver*
365515	65908+72269+72268+65949	HE	FCC	EVL	TSG	
365516	65909+72271+72270+65950	HE	FCC	EVL	TSG	
365517	65910+72273+72272+65951	HE	TLK	EVL	TSG	*Supporting Red Balloon*
365518	65911+72275+72274+65952	HE	FCC	EVL	TSG	*The Fenman*
365519	65912+72277+72276+65953	HE	TLK	EVL	TSG	
365520	65913+72279+72278+65954	HE	TLK	EVL	TSG	
365521	65914+72281+72280+65955	HE	TLK	EVL	TSG	
365522	65915+72283+72282+65956	HE	TLK	EVL	TSG	
365523	65916+72285+72284+65957	HE	TLK	EVL	TSG	
365524	65917+72287+72286+65958	HE	TLK	EVL	TSG	
365525	65918+72289+72288+65959	HE	TLK	EVL	TSG	
365527	65920+72293+72292+65961	HE	FCC	EVL	TSG	*Robert Stripe Passengers' Champion*
365528	65921+72296+72294+65962	HE	TLK	EVL	TSG	
365529	65922+72297+72296+65963	HE	TLK	EVL	TSG	
365530	65923+72299+72298+65964	HE	FCC	EVL	TSG	*The Interlink Partnership Promoting Integrated Transport Since 1999*
365531	65924+72301+72300+65965	HE	FCC	EVL	TSG	
365532	65925+72303+72302+65966	HE	FCC	EVL	TSG	
365533	65926+72305+72304+65967	HE	TLK	EVL	TSG	*Max Appeal*
365534	65927+72307+72306+65968	HE	FCC	EVL	TSG	
365535	65928+72309+72308+65969	HE	FCC	EVL	TSG	
365536	65929+72311+72310+65970	HE	FCC	EVL	TSG	
365537	65930+72313+72312+65971	HE	TLK	EVL	TSG	*Daniel Edwards (1974-2010) Cambridge Driver*
365538	65931+72315+72314+65972	HE	TLK	EVL	TSG	
365539	65932+72317+72316+65973	HE	FCC	EVL	TSG	
365540	65933+72319+72318+65974	HE	TLK	EVL	TSG	
365541	65934+72321+72320+65975	HE	FCC	EVL	TSG	

Left: *A fleet of 40 'Networker Express' Class 365 sets operates from Hornsey on Great Northern main-line and longer-distance services. A start has been made to paint these in the new TSGN white livery offset by light blue passenger doors. Sets have also recently been refurbished internally. Set No. 365520 is shown.* **Antony Christie**

■ The Class 365 fleet will be returned to Eversholt Leasing upon introduction of Class 700 stock.

Class 377/1
Electrostar

Vehicle Length: (Driving) 66ft 9in (20.3m) Width: 9ft 2in (2.79m)
(Inter) 65ft 6in (19.96m) Horsepower: 2,012hp (1,500kW)
Height: 12ft 4in (3.75m) Seats (total/car): 24F-210S or 244S 12F-48S(56S)/62S(70S)/52S(62S)/12F-48S(56S)

Number	Formation DMCO(A)+MSO+TSO+DMCO(B)	Depot	Livery	Owner	Operator
377101	78501+77101+78901+78701	BI	SOU	PTR	TSG
377102	78502+77102+78902+78702	BI	SOU	PTR	TSG

377103	78503+77103+78903+78703	BI	SOU	PTR	TSG
377104	78504+77104+78904+78704	BI	SOU	PTR	TSG
377105	78505+77105+78905+78705	BI	SOU	PTR	TSG
377106	78506+77106+78906+78706	BI	SOU	PTR	TSG
377107	78507+77107+78907+78707	BI	SOU	PTR	TSG
377108	78508+77108+78908+78708	BI	SOU	PTR	TSG
377109	78509+77109+78909+78709	BI	SOU	PTR	TSG
377110	78510+77110+78910+78710	BI	SOU	PTR	TSG
377111	78511+77111+78911+78711	BI	SOU	PTR	TSG
377112	78512+77112+78912+78712	BI	SOU	PTR	TSG
377113	78513+77113+78913+78713	BI	SOU	PTR	TSG
377114	78514+77114+78914+78714	BI	SOU	PTR	TSG
377115	78515+77115+78915+78715	BI	SOU	PTR	TSG
377116	78516+77116+78916+78716	BI	SOU	PTR	TSG
377117	78517+77117+78917+78717	BI	SOU	PTR	TSG
377118	78518+77118+78918+78718	BI	SOU	PTR	TSG
377119	78519+77119+78919+78719	BI	SOU	PTR	TSG
377120	78520+77120+78920+78720	BI	SOU	PTR	TSG
377121	78521+77121+78921+78721	BI	SOU	PTR	TSG
377122	78522+77122+78922+78722	BI	SOU	PTR	TSG
377123	78523+77123+78923+78723	BI	SOU	PTR	TSG
377124	78524+77124+78924+78724	BI	SOU	PTR	TSG
377125	78525+77125+78925+78725	BI	SOU	PTR	TSG
377126	78526+77126+78926+78726	BI	SOU	PTR	TSG
377127	78527+77127+78927+78727	BI	SOU	PTR	TSG
377128	78528+77128+78928+78728	BI	SOU	PTR	TSG
377129	78529+77129+78929+78729	BI	SOU	PTR	TSG
377130	78530+77130+78930+78730	BI	SOU	PTR	TSG
377131	78531+77131+78931+78731	BI	SOU	PTR	TSG
377132	78532+77132+78932+78732	BI	SOU	PTR	TSG
377133	78533+77133+78933+78733	BI	SOU	PTR	TSG
377134	78534+77134+78934+78734	BI	SOU	PTR	TSG
377135	78535+77135+78935+78735	BI	SOU	PTR	TSG
377136	78536+77136+78936+78736	BI	SOU	PTR	TSG
377137	78537+77137+78937+78737	BI	SOU	PTR	TSG
377138	78538+77138+78938+78738	BI	SOU	PTR	TSG
377139	78539+77139+78939+78739	BI	SOU	PTR	TSG
377140	78540+77140+78940+78740	BI	SOU	PTR	TSG
377141	78541+77141+78941+78741	BI	SOU	PTR	TSG
377142	78542+77142+78942+78742	BI	SOU	PTR	TSG
377143	78543+77143+78943+78743	BI	SOU	PTR	TSG
377144	78544+77144+78944+78744	BI	SOU	PTR	TSG
377145	78545+77145+78945+78745	BI	SOU	PTR	TSG
377146	78546+77146+78946+78746	BI	SOU	PTR	TSG
377147	78547+77147+78947+78747	BI	SOU	PTR	TSG

Right: *The previous Southern section of the present TSGN franchise concentrated on Bombardier-built 'Electrostar' stock for its outer-suburban and main-line services, with several sub-classes in operation. A fleet of 64 Class 377/1 sets is in operation allocated to Brighton and operated in a common pool with other Class 377s. Set No. 377101 is illustrated at Redhill.* **CJM**

Thameslink, Southern, Great Northern

Passenger Train Operating Companies - Thameslink, Southern, Great Northern

377148	78548+77148+78948+78748	BI	SOU	PTR	TSG
377149	78549+77149+78949+78749	BI	SOU	PTR	TSG
377150	78550+77150+78950+78750	BI	SOU	PTR	TSG
377151	78551+77151+78951+78751	BI	SOU	PTR	TSG
377152	78552+77152+78952+78752	BI	SOU	PTR	TSG
377153	78553+77153+78953+78753	BI	SOU	PTR	TSG
377154	78554+77154+78954+78754	BI	SOU	PTR	TSG
377155	78555+77155+78955+78755	BI	SOU	PTR	TSG
377156	78556+77156+78956+78756	BI	SOU	PTR	TSG
377157	78557+77157+78957+78757	BI	SOU	PTR	TSG
377158	78558+77158+78958+78758	BI	SOU	PTR	TSG
377159	78559+77159+78959+78759	BI	SOU	PTR	TSG
377160	78560+77160+78960+78760	BI	SOU	PTR	TSG
377161	78561+77161+78961+78761	BI	SOU	PTR	TSG
377162	78562+77162+78962+78762	SU	SOU	PTR	TSG
377163	78563+77163+78963+78763	SU	SOU	PTR	TSG
377164	78564+77164+78964+78764	SU	SOU	PTR	TSG

Class 377/2
Electrostar

Vehicle Length: (Driving) 66ft 9in (20.3m)   *Width: 9ft 2in (2.79m)*
(Inter) 65ft 6in (19.96m)   *Horsepower: 2,012hp (1,500kW)*
Height: 12ft 4in (3.75m)   *Seats (total/car): 24F-222S, 12F-48S/69S/57S/12F-48S*

Number	Formation	Depot	Livery	Owner	Operator
	DMCO(A)+MSO+PTSO+DMCO(B)				
377201	78571+77171+78971+78771	BI	SOU	PTR	TSG
377202	78572+77172+78972+78772	BI	SOU	PTR	TSG
377203	78573+77173+78973+78773	BI	SOU	PTR	TSG
377204	78574+77174+78974+78774	BI	SOU	PTR	TSG
377205	78575+77175+78975+78775	SU	SOU	PTR	TSG
377206	78576+77176+78976+78776	SU	SOU	PTR	TSG
377207	78577+77177+78977+78777	BF	SOU	PTR	TSG
377208	78578+77178+78978+78778	BF	SOU	PTR	TSG
377209	78579+77179+78979+78779	BI	SOU	PTR	TSG
377210	78580+77180+78980+78780	SU	SOU	PTR	TSG
377211	78581+77181+78981+78781	BF	SOU	PTR	TSG
377212	78582+77182+78982+78782	BF	SOU	PTR	TSG
377213	78583+77183+78983+78783	BF	SOU	PTR	TSG
377214	78584+77184+78984+78784	BF	SOU	PTR	TSG
377215	78585+77185+78985+78785	BF	SOU	PTR	TSG

Left: The 15 members of Class 377/2 are set up for dual ac/dc operation and until 2015 were deployed on the Croydon-Milton Keynes route where dual-voltage equipment was required. Following replacement by Class 377/7s, these sets are now being used on the Thameslink route to bolster stock availability until new trains are delivered. Set No. 377214 is shown working in ac mode. **CJM**

Class 377/3
Electrostar

Vehicle Length: (Driving) 66ft 9in (20.3m)   *Width: 9ft 2in (2.79m)*
(Inter) 65ft 6in (19.96m)   *Horsepower: 2,012hp (1,500kW)*
Height: 12ft 4in (3.75m)   *Seats (total/car): 24F-152S, 12F-48S/56S/12F-48S*

Number		Formation	Depot	Livery	Owner	Operator
		DMCO(A)+TSO+DMCO(B)				
377301	(375311)	68201+74801+68401	SU	SOU	PTR	TSG
377302	(375312)	68202+74802+68402	SU	SOU	PTR	TSG
377303	(375313)	68203+74803+68403	SU	SOU	PTR	TSG
377304	(375314)	68204+74804+68404	SU	SOU	PTR	TSG

377305	(375315)	68205+74805+68405	SU	SOU	PTR	TSG
377306	(375316)	68206+74806+68406	SU	SOU	PTR	TSG
377307	(375317)	68207+74807+68407	SU	SOU	PTR	TSG
377308	(375318)	68208+74808+68408	SU	SOU	PTR	TSG
377309	(375319)	68209+74809+68409	SU	SOU	PTR	TSG
377310	(375320)	68210+74810+68410	SU	SOU	PTR	TSG
377311	(375321)	68211+74811+68411	SU	SOU	PTR	TSG
377312	(375322)	68212+74812+68412	SU	SOU	PTR	TSG
377313	(375323)	68213+74813+68413	SU	SOU	PTR	TSG
377314	(375324)	68214+74814+68414	SU	SOU	PTR	TSG
377315	(375325)	68215+74815+68415	SU	SOU	PTR	TSG
377316	(375326)	68216+74816+68416	SU	SOU	PTR	TSG
377317	(375327)	68217+74817+68417	SU	SOU	PTR	TSG
377318	(375328)	68218+74818+68418	SU	SOU	PTR	TSG
377319	(375329)	68219+74819+68419	SU	SOU	PTR	TSG
377320	(375330)	68220+74820+68420	SU	SOU	PTR	TSG
377321	(375331)	68221+74821+68421	SU	SOU	PTR	TSG
377322	(375332)	68222+74822+68422	SU	SOU	PTR	TSG
377323	(375333)	68223+74823+68423	SU	SOU	PTR	TSG
377324	(375334)	68224+74824+68424	SU	SOU	PTR	TSG
377325	(375335)	68225+74825+68425	SU	SOU	PTR	TSG
377326	(375336)	68226+74826+68426	SU	SOU	PTR	TSG
377327	(375337)	68227+74827+68427	SU	SOU	PTR	TSG
377328	(375338)	68228+74828+68428	SU	SOU	PTR	TSG

Right: *The Class 377/3 fleet comprises 28 three-car sets deployed on more lighter used services and routes. These sets were originally introduced as Class 375s and modified as Class 377s upon installation of Dellner couplings. The sets are allocated to Selhurst, and No. 377312 is illustrated at Clapham Junction.* **Antony Christie**

Class 377/4
Electrostar

Vehicle Length: (Driving) 66ft 9in (20.3m) Width: 9ft 2in (2.79m)
(Inter) 65ft 6in (19.96m) Horsepower: 2,012hp (1,500kW)
Height: 12ft 4in (3.75m) Seats (total/car): 20F-221S, 10F-48S/69S/56S/10F-48S

Number	Formation	Depot	Livery	Owner	Operator
	DMCO(A)+MSO+TSO+DMCO(B)				
377401	73401+78801+78601+73801	BI	SOU	PTR	TSG
377402	73402+78802+78602+73802	BI	SOU	PTR	TSG
377403	73403+78803+78603+73803	BI	SOU	PTR	TSG
377404	73404+78804+78604+73804	BI	SOU	PTR	TSG
377405	73405+78805+78605+73805	BI	SOU	PTR	TSG
377406	73406+78806+78606+73806	BI	SOU	PTR	TSG
377407	73407+78807+78607+73807	BI	SOU	PTR	TSG
377408	73408+78808+78608+73808	BI	SOU	PTR	TSG
377409	73409+78809+78609+73809	BI	SOU	PTR	TSG
377410	73410+78810+78610+73810	BI	SOU	PTR	TSG
377411	73411+78811+78611+73811	BI	SOU	PTR	TSG
377412	73412+78812+78612+73812	BI	SOU	PTR	TSG
377413	73413+78813+78613+73813	BI	SOU	PTR	TSG

Thameslink, Southern, Great Northern

377414	73414+78814+78614+73814	BI	SOU	PTR	TSG
377415	73415+78815+78615+73815	BI	SOU	PTR	TSG
377416	73416+78816+78616+73816	SU	SOU	PTR	TSG
377417	73417+78817+78617+73817	BI	SOU	PTR	TSG
377418	73418+78818+78618+73818	BI	SOU	PTR	TSG
377419	73419+78819+78619+73819	BI	SOU	PTR	TSG
377420	73420+78820+78620+73820	BI	SOU	PTR	TSG
377421	73421+78821+78621+73821	BI	SOU	PTR	TSG
377422	73422+78822+78622+73822	BI	SOU	PTR	TSG
377423	73423+78823+78623+73823	BI	SOU	PTR	TSG
377424	73424+78824+78624+73824	BI	SOU	PTR	TSG
377425	73425+78825+78625+73825	BI	SOU	PTR	TSG
377426	73426+78826+78626+73826	BI	SOU	PTR	TSG
377427	73427+78827+78627+73827	BI	SOU	PTR	TSG
377428	73428+78828+78628+73828	BI	SOU	PTR	TSG
377429	73429+78829+78629+73829	SU	SOU	PTR	TSG
377430	73430+78830+78630+73830	BI	SOU	PTR	TSG
377431	73431+78831+78631+73831	BI	SOU	PTR	TSG
377432	73432+78832+78632+73832	BI	SOU	PTR	TSG
377433	73433+78833+78633+73833	BI	SOU	PTR	TSG
377434	73434+78834+78634+73834	BI	SOU	PTR	TSG
377435	73435+78835+78635+73835	BI	SOU	PTR	TSG
377436	73436+78836+78636+73836	BI	SOU	PTR	TSG
377437	73437+78837+78637+73837	BI	SOU	PTR	TSG
377438	73438+78838+78638+73838	BI	SOU	PTR	TSG
377439	73439+78839+78639+73839	BI	SOU	PTR	TSG
377440	73440+78840+78640+73840	BI	SOU	PTR	TSG
377441	73441+78841+78641+73841	BI	SOU	PTR	TSG
377442	73442+78842+78642+73842	BI	SOU	PTR	TSG
377443	73443+78843+78643+73843	BI	SOU	PTR	TSG
377444	73444+78844+78644+73844	BI	SOU	PTR	TSG
377445	73445+78845+78645+73845	BI	SOU	PTR	TSG
377446	73446+78846+78646+73846	BI	SOU	PTR	TSG
377447	73447+78847+78647+73847	SU	SOU	PTR	TSG
377448	73448+78848+78648+73848	BI	SOU	PTR	TSG
377449	73449+78849+78649+73849	BI	SOU	PTR	TSG
377450	73450+78850+78650+73850	BI	SOU	PTR	TSG
377451	73451+78851+78651+73851	BI	SOU	PTR	TSG
377452	73452+78852+78652+73852	SU	SOU	PTR	TSG
377453	73453+78853+78653+73853	BI	SOU	PTR	TSG
377454	73454+78854+78654+73854	BI	SOU	PTR	TSG
377455	73455+78855+78655+73855	BI	SOU	PTR	TSG
377456	73456+78856+78656+73856	BI	SOU	PTR	TSG
377457	73457+78857+78657+73857	BI	SOU	PTR	TSG
377458	73458+78858+78658+73858	BI	SOU	PTR	TSG

Left: *A fleet of 75 sets forms the Class 377/4 sub-class. Seating in this design is for 20 first and 221 standard class passengers. First class seating (in the 2+2 style) is provided in both driving cars in the area directly behind the driving cab. All sets are painted in the Southern TOC livery of white and green. Set No. 377463 is seen passing through Transport for London-operated Honor Oak Park station.* **CJM**

377459	73459+78859+78659+73859	BI	SOU	PTR	SOU	
377460	73460+78860+78660+73860	SU	SOU	PTR	SOU	
377461	73461+78861+78661+73861	BI	SOU	PTR	SOU	
377462	73462+78862+78662+73862	BI	SOU	PTR	SOU	
377463	73463+78863+78663+73863	BI	SOU	PTR	SOU	
377464	73464+78864+78664+73864	BI	SOU	PTR	SOU	
377465	73465+78865+78665+73865	BI	SOU	PTR	SOU	
377466	73466+78866+78666+73866	BI	SOU	PTR	SOU	
377467	73467+78867+78667+73867	BI	SOU	PTR	SOU	
377468	73468+78868+78668+73868	BI	SOU	PTR	SOU	
377469	73469+78869+78669+73869	BI	SOU	PTR	SOU	
377470	73470+78870+78670+73870	BI	SOU	PTR	SOU	
377471	73471+78871+78671+73871	BI	SOU	PTR	SOU	
377472	73472+78872+78672+73872	BI	SOU	PTR	SOU	
377473	73473+78873+78673+73873	BI	SOU	PTR	SOU	
377474	73474+78874+78674+73874	BI	SOU	PTR	SOU	
377475	73475+78875+78675+73875	BI	SOU	PTR	SOU	

Class 377/5
Electrostar

Vehicle Length: (Driving) 66ft 9in (20.40m)
(Inter) 65ft 6in (19.99m)
Height: 12ft 4in (3.77m)

Width: 9ft 2in (2.80m)
Horsepower: 2,012hp (1,500kW) (ac), dual-voltage sets
Seats (total/car): 20F-221S, 10F-48S/69S/56S/10F-48S

Number	Formation	Depot	Livery	Owner	Operator
	DMCO(A)+MSO+PTSO+DMCO(B)				
377501	73501+75901+74901+73601	BF	FCC	PTR	TSG
377502	73502+75902+74902+73602	BF	FCC	PTR	TSG
377503	73503+75903+74903+73603	BF	FCC	PTR	TSG
377504	73504+75904+74904+73604	BF	FCC	PTR	TSG
377505	73505+75905+74905+73605	BF	FCC	PTR	TSG
377506	73506+75906+74906+73606	BF	FCC	PTR	TSG
377507	73507+75907+74907+73607	BF	FCC	PTR	TSG
377508	73508+75908+74908+73608	BF	FCC	PTR	TSG
377509	73509+75909+74909+73609	BF	FCC	PTR	TSG
377510	73510+75910+74910+73610	BF	FCC	PTR	TSG
377511	73511+75911+74911+73611	BF	FCC	PTR	TSG
377512	73512+75912+74912+73612	BF	FCC	PTR	TSG
377513	73513+75913+74913+73613	BF	FCC	PTR	TSG
377514	73514+75914+74914+73614	BF	FCC	PTR	TSG
377515	73515+75915+74915+73615	BF	FCC	PTR	TSG
377516	73516+75916+74916+73616	BF	FCC	PTR	TSG
377517	73517+75917+74917+73617	BF	FCC	PTR	TSG
377518	73518+75918+74918+73618	BF	FCC	PTR	TSG
377519	73519+75919+74919+73619	BF	FCC	PTR	TSG
377520	73520+75920+74920+73620	BF	FCC	PTR	TSG
377521	73521+75921+74921+73621	BF	FCC	PTR	TSG
377522	73522+75922+74922+73622	BF	FCC	PTR	TSG
377523	73523+75923+74923+73623	BF	FCC	PTR	TSG

Right: *The 23 members of Class 377/5 are dual-voltage sets which were originally ordered for the Southern franchise then sub-leased to the prior First Capital Connect operation for Thameslink use and were thus painted in FCC livery. These sets are allocated to Bedford depot and are used on the longer-distance Thameslink services. Two sets with No. 366506 nearest the camera are illustrated at King's Cross International, now carrying Thameslink branding.*
Antony Christie

Thameslink, Southern, Great Northern

Passenger Train Operating Companies - Thameslink, Southern, Great Northern

Class 377/6
Electrostar

Vehicle Length: (Driving) 66ft 9in (20.3m) Width: 9ft 2in (2.79m)
(Inter) 65ft 6in (19.96m) Horsepower: 2,012hp (1,500kW)
Height: 12ft 4in (3.75m) Seats (total/car): 298S-60S/64S/46S/66S/62S

Number	Formation DMSO(A)+MSO+TSO+MSO+DMSO(B)	Depot	Livery	Owner	Operator
377601	70101+70201+70301+70401+70501	BI	SOU	PTR	TSG
377602	70102+70202+70302+70402+70502	BI	SOU	PTR	TSG
377603	70103+70203+70303+70403+70503	BI	SOU	PTR	TSG
377604	70104+70204+70304+70404+70504	BI	SOU	PTR	TSG
377605	70105+70205+70305+70405+70505	BI	SOU	PTR	TSG
377606	70106+70206+70306+70406+70506	BI	SOU	PTR	TSG
377607	70107+70207+70307+70407+70507	BI	SOU	PTR	TSG
377608	70108+70208+70308+70408+70508	BI	SOU	PTR	TSG
377609	70109+70209+70309+70409+70509	BI	SOU	PTR	TSG
377610	70110+70210+70310+70410+70510	BI	SOU	PTR	TSG
377611	70111+70211+70311+70411+70511	BI	SOU	PTR	TSG
377612	70112+70212+70312+70412+70512	BI	SOU	PTR	TSG
377613	70113+70213+70313+70413+70513	BI	SOU	PTR	TSG
377614	70114+70214+70314+70414+70514	BI	SOU	PTR	TSG
377615	70115+70215+70315+70415+70515	BI	SOU	PTR	TSG
377616	70116+70216+70316+70416+70516	BI	SOU	PTR	TSG
377617	70117+70217+70317+70417+70517	BI	SOU	PTR	TSG
377618	70118+70218+70318+70418+70518	BI	SOU	PTR	TSG
377619	70119+70219+70319+70419+70519	BI	SOU	PTR	TSG
377620	70120+70220+70320+70420+70520	BI	SOU	PTR	TSG
377621	70121+70221+70321+70421+70521	BI	SOU	PTR	TSG
377622	70122+70222+70322+70422+70522	BI	SOU	PTR	TSG
377623	70123+70223+70323+70423+70523	BI	SOU	PTR	TSG
377624	70124+70224+70324+70424+70524	BI	SOU	PTR	TSG
377625	70125+70225+70325+70425+70525	BI	SOU	PTR	TSG
377626	70126+70226+70326+70426+70526	BI	SOU	PTR	TSG

Left: The 'Electrostar' structural design changed with the building of the Class 377/6 sub-class with the replacement of the ribbon glazing with separate window frames to reduce costs. These sets were also fitted with a front skirt-mounted track light. These five-car sets with seating for 298 standard class passengers are used on the busy South London Metro-type services on lines radiating from Victoria/London Bridge. Set No. 377618 is shown at Clapham Junction. **Antony Christie**

Class 377/7
Electrostar

Vehicle Length: (Driving) 66ft 9in (20.3m) Width: 9ft 2in (2.79m)
(Inter) 65ft 6in (19.96m) Horsepower: 2,012hp (1,500kW)
Height: 12ft 4in (3.75m) Seats (total/car): 298S-60S/64S/46S/66S/62S
Dual voltage sets

Number	Formation DMSO(A)+MSO+TSO+MSO+DMSO(B)	Depot	Livery	Owner	Operator
377701	65201+70601+65601+70701+65401	BI	SOU	PTR	TSG
377702	65202+70602+65602+70702+65402	BI	SOU	PTR	TSG
377703	65203+70603+65603+70703+65403	BI	SOU	PTR	TSG
377704	65204+70604+65604+70704+65404	BI	SOU	PTR	TSG
377705	65205+70605+65605+70705+65405	BI	SOU	PTR	TSG
377706	65206+70606+65606+70706+65406	BI	SOU	PTR	TSG
377707	65207+70607+65607+70707+65407	BI	SOU	PTR	TSG
377708	65208+70608+65608+70708+65408	BI	SOU	PTR	TSG

Right: *In 2014 a small fleet of eight 298-seat five-car Class 377/7 sets was introduced by then operator Southern for use on cross-London services from Croydon to the West Coast Main Line at Milton Keynes. Set No. 377707 is seen inside the test hall at the Bombardier plant at Litchurch Lane, Derby. These sets sport the revised window frame body structure and skirt-mounted track light.* **CJM**

Class 387/1
Electrostar

Vehicle Length: (Driving) 66ft 9in (20.3m) *Width: 9ft 2in (2.79m)*
(Inter) 65ft 6in (19.96m) *Horsepower: 2,012hp (1,500kW)*
Height: 12ft 4in (3.75m) *Seats (total/car): To be advised*

Number	Formation	Depot	Livery	Owner	Operator
	DMSO(A)+MSO+TSO+DMSO(B)				
387101	421101+422101+423101+424101	BI	TMK	PTR	TSG
387102	421102+422102+423102+424102	BI	TMK	PTR	TSG
387103	421103+422103+423103+424103	BI	TMK	PTR	TSG
387104	421104+422104+423104+424104	BI	TMK	PTR	TSG
387105	421105+422105+423105+424105	BI	TMK	PTR	TSG
387106	421106+422106+423106+424106	BI	TMK	PTR	TSG
387107	421107+422107+423107+424107	BI	TMK	PTR	TSG
387108	421108+422108+423108+424108	BI	TMK	PTR	TSG
387109	421109+422109+423109+424109	BI	TMK	PTR	TSG
387110	421110+422110+423110+424110	BI	TMK	PTR	TSG
387111	421111+422111+423111+424111	BI	TMK	PTR	TSG
387112	421112+422112+423112+424112	BI	TMK	PTR	TSG
387113	421113+422113+423113+424113	BI	TMK	PTR	TSG
387114	421114+422114+423114+424114	BI	TMK	PTR	TSG
387115	421115+422115+423115+424115	BI	TMK	PTR	TSG
387116	421116+422116+423116+424116	BI	TMK	PTR	TSG
387117	421117+422117+423117+424117	BI	TMK	PTR	TSG
387118	421118+422118+423118+424118	BI	TMK	PTR	TSG
387119	421119+422119+423119+424119	BI	TMK	PTR	TSG
387120	421120+422120+423120+424120	BI	TMK	PTR	TSG
387121	421121+422121+423121+424121	BI	TMK	PTR	TSG
387122	421122+422122+423122+424122	BI	TMK	PTR	TSG
387123	421123+422123+423123+424123	BI	TMK	PTR	TSG
387124	421124+422124+423124+424124	BI	TMK	PTR	TSG
387125	421125+422125+423125+424125	BI	TMK	PTR	TSG
387126	421126+422126+423126+424126	BI	TMK	PTR	TSG
387127	421127+422127+423127+424127	BI	TMK	PTR	TSG
387128	421128+422128+423128+424128	BI	TMK	PTR	TSG
387129	421129+422129+423129+424129	BI	TMK	PTR	TSG

■ As part of the new TSGN franchise a fleet of 27 Class 387/2 'Electrostar' sets has been ordered from Bombardier for use on the Gatwick Express route to replace Class 442s. The new sets are due for delivery in 2015-16 and will be numbered 387201-387227.

Right: *A fleet of 29 four-car Class 387 'Electrostar' dual voltage sets were introduced from late 2014 for initial use on the Thameslink route, allowing the cascade of Class 319s to Northern Rail. In the future after the full introduction of Class 700s on Thameslink, these sets are likely to find work on either the Greater Western or Midland Mainline franchises. Sets Nos. 387109/108/110 pass Daventry on 20 November 2014 with a test run.* **Nathan Williamson**

Passenger Train Operating Companies - Thameslink, Southern, Great Northern

Class 442

Vehicle Length: (Driving) 75ft 11½in (23.15m)   Width: 8ft 11½in (2.73m)
(Inter) 75ft 5½in (22.99m)   Horsepower: 1,608hp (1,200kW)
Height: 12ft 4in (3.81m)   Seats (total/car): 24F-318S, 74S/76S/24F-28S/66S/74S

Number	Formation DTSO(A)+TSO+MBC+TSO+DTSO(B)	Depot	Livery	Owner	Operator
442401	77382+71818+62937+71841+77414	SL	SGX	ANG	TSG
442402	77383+71819+62938+71842+77407	SL	SGX	ANG	TSG
442403	77384+71820+62941+71843+77408	SL	SGX	ANG	TSG
442404	77385+71821+62939+71844+77409	SL	SGX	ANG	TSG
442405	77386+71822+62944+71845+77410	SL	SGX	ANG	TSG
442406	77389+71823+62942+71846+77411	SL	SGX	ANG	TSG
442407	77388+71824+62943+71847+77412	SL	SGX	ANG	TSG
442408	77387+71825+62945+71848+77413	SL	SGX	ANG	TSG
442409	77390+71826+62946+71849+77406	SL	SGX	ANG	TSG
442410	77391+71827+62948+71850+77415	SL	SGX	ANG	TSG
442411	77392+71828+62940+71851+77422	SL	SGX	ANG	TSG
442412	77393+71829+62947+71858+77417	SL	SGX	ANG	TSG
442413	77394+71830+62949+71853+77418	SL	SGX	ANG	TSG
442414	77395+71831+62950+71854+77419	SL	SGX	ANG	TSG
442415	77396+71832+62951+71855+77420	SL	SGX	ANG	TSG
442416	77397+71833+62952+71856+77421	SL	SGX	ANG	TSG
442417	77398+71834+62953+71857+77416	SL	SGX	ANG	TSG
442418	77399+71835+62954+71852+77423	SL	SGX	ANG	TSG
442419	77400+71836+62955+71859+77424	SL	SGX	ANG	TSG
442420	77401+71837+62956+71860+77425	SL	SGX	ANG	TSG
442421	77402+71838+62957+71861+77426	SL	SGX	ANG	TSG
442422	77403+71839+62958+71862+77427	SL	SGX	ANG	TSG
442423	77404+71840+62959+71863+77428	SL	SGX	ANG	TSG
442424	77405+71841+62960+71864+77429	SL	SGX	ANG	TSG

Left: *The 24 five-car Class 442 sets, originally built for use on the Waterloo to Weymouth line, are currently in use by the TSGN franchise on the Gatwick Express route. However, new 'Electrostar' based stock has now been ordered for this service and the '442s' will be phased out in the coming years. A further use for these quality vehicles is likely to be found. Set No. 442416 is seen at Gatwick Airport, with its DTSO(B) driving car nearest the camera.* **CJM**

Class 455/8

Vehicle Length: (Driving) 65ft 0½in (19.83m)   Width: 9ft 3¼in (2.82m)
(Inter) 65ft 4½in (19.92m)   Horsepower: 1,000hp (746kW)
Height: 12ft 1½in (3.79m)   Seats (total/car): 310S, 74S/78S/84S/74S

Number	Formation DTSO(A)+MSO+TSO+DTSO(B)	Depot	Livery	Owner	Operator
455801	77627+62709+71657+77580	SL	SOU	EVL	TSG
455802	77581+62710+71664+77582	SL	SOU	EVL	TSG
455803	77583+62711+71639+77584	SL	SOU	EVL	TSG
455804	77585+62712+71640+77586	SL	SOU	EVL	TSG
455805	77587+62713+71641+77588	SL	SOU	EVL	TSG
455806	77589+62714+71642+77590	SL	SOU	EVL	TSG
455807	77591+62715+71643+77592	SL	SOU	EVL	TSG
455808	77637+62716+71644+77594	SL	SOU	EVL	TSG
455809	77623+62717+71648+77602	SL	SOU	EVL	TSG
455810	77597+62718+71646+77598	SL	SOU	EVL	TSG
455811	77599+62719+71647+77600	SL	SOU	EVL	TSG
455812	77595+62720+71645+77626	SL	SOU	EVL	TSG
455813	77603+62721+71649+77604	SL	SOU	EVL	TSG
455814	77605+62722+71650+77606	SL	SOU	EVL	TSG
455815	77607+62723+71651+77608	SL	SOU	EVL	TSG

455816	77609+62724+71652+77633	SL	SOU	EVL	TSG
455817	77611+62725+71653+77612	SL	SOU	EVL	TSG
455818	77613+62726+71654+77632	SL	SOU	EVL	TSG
455819	77615+62727+71637+77616	SL	SOU	EVL	TSG
455820	77617+62728+71656+77618	SL	SOU	EVL	TSG
455821	77619+62729+71655+77620	SL	SOU	EVL	TSG
455822	77621+62730+71658+77622	SL	SOU	EVL	TSG
455823	77601+62731+71659+77596	SL	SOU	EVL	TSG
455824	77593+62732+71660+77624	SL	SOU	EVL	TSG
455825	77579+62733+71661+77628	SL	SOU	EVL	TSG
455826	77630+62734+71662+77629	SL	SOU	EVL	TSG
455827	77610+62735+71663+77614	SL	SOU	EVL	TSG
455828	77631+62736+71638+77634	SL	SOU	EVL	TSG
455829	77635+62737+71665+77636	SL	SOU	EVL	TSG
455830	77625+62743+71666+77638	SL	SOU	EVL	TSG
455831	77639+62739+71667+77640	SL	SOU	EVL	TSG
455832	77641+62740+71668+77642	SL	SOU	EVL	TSG
455833	77643+62741+71669+77644	SL	SOU	EVL	TSG
455834	77645+62742+71670+77646	SL	SOU	EVL	TSG
455835	77647+62738+71671+77648	SL	SOU	EVL	TSG
455836	77649+62744+71672+77650	SL	SOU	EVL	TSG
455837	77651+62745+71673+77652	SL	SOU	EVL	TSG
455838	77653+62746+71674+77654	SL	SOU	EVL	TSG
455839	77655+62747+71675+77656	SL	SOU	EVL	TSG
455840	77657+62748+71676+77658	SL	SOU	EVL	TSG
455841	77659+62749+71677+77660	SL	SOU	EVL	TSG
455842	77661+62750+71678+77662	SL	SOU	EVL	TSG
455843	77663+62751+71679+77664	SL	SOU	EVL	TSG
455844	77665+62752+71680+77666	SL	SOU	EVL	TSG
455845	77667+62753+71681+77668	SL	SOU	EVL	TSG
455846	77669+62754+71682+77670	SL	SOU	EVL	TSG

Right: *Southern-route Metro services are operated by a fleet of 46 four-car Class 455s dating from the early 1980s. These sets have been rebuilt and now sport cab air conditioning at the expense of a between-set gangway door. The 455s are allocated to Stewarts Lane and are currently painted in the Southern white and green livery. If compared with a South West Trains Class 455/8 the front-end changes are easily seen. Set No. 455818 is illustrated.* **CJM**

Class 700

Vehicle Length: (Driving) 20m	Weight: 278tonne / 410 tonne
(Inter) 20m	Power output: 3.3 / 5.0MW
Height: tba	Seats (total/car): 8-car - 427 52F/375S,
	12-car 666 52F/614S

Number	Formation	Depot	Livery	Owner	Operator
	DMCO+PTSO+MSO+TSO+TSO+MSO+PTSO+DMCO				
700001	401001+402001+403001+406001+407001+410001+411001+412001	HE	TMK		TSG
700002	401002+402002+403002+406002+407002+410002+411002+412002	HE	TMK		TSG
700003	401003+402003+403003+406003+407003+410003+411003+412003	HE	TMK		TSG
700004	401004+402004+403004+406004+407004+410004+411004+412004	HE	TMK		TSG
700005	401005+402005+403005+406005+407005+410005+411005+412005	HE	TMK		TSG
700006	401006+402006+403006+406006+407006+410006+411006+412006	HE	TMK		TSG
700007	401007+402007+403007+406007+407007+410007+411007+412007	HE	TMK		TSG
700008	401008+402008+403008+406008+407008+410008+411008+412008	HE	TMK		TSG
700009	401009+402009+403009+406009+407009+410009+411009+412009	HE	TMK		TSG
700010	401010+402010+403010+406010+407010+410010+411010+412010	HE	TMK		TSG

Train Operating Companies

Thameslink, Southern, Great Northern

Number	Formation	Depot	Livery	Owner	Operator
700011	401011+402011+403011+406011+407011+410011+411011+412011	HE	TMK		TSG
700012	401012+402012+403012+406012+407012+410012+411012+412012	HE	TMK		TSG
700013	401013+402013+403013+406013+407013+410013+411013+412013	HE	TMK		TSG
700014	401014+402014+403014+406014+407014+410014+411014+412014	HE	TMK		TSG
700015	401015+402015+403015+406015+407015+410015+411015+412015	HE	TMK		TSG
700016	401016+402016+403016+406016+407016+410016+411016+412016	HE	TMK		TSG
700017	401017+402017+403017+406017+407017+410017+411017+412016	HE	TMK		TSG
700018	401018+402018+403018+406018+407018+410018+411018+412018	HE	TMK		TSG
700019	401019+402019+403019+406019+407019+410019+411019+412019	HE	TMK		TSG
700020	401020+402020+403020+406020+407020+410020+411020+412020	HE	TMK		TSG
700021	401021+402021+403021+406021+407021+410021+411021+412021	HE	TMK		TSG
700022	401022+402022+403022+406022+407022+410022+411022+412022	HE	TMK		TSG
700023	401023+402023+403023+406023+407023+410023+411023+412023	HE	TMK		TSG
700024	401024+402024+403024+406024+407024+410024+411024+412024	HE	TMK		TSG
700025	401025+402025+403025+406025+407025+410025+411025+412025	HE	TMK		TSG
700026	401026+402026+403026+406026+407026+410026+411026+412026	HE	TMK		TSG
700027	401027+402027+403027+406027+407027+410027+411027+412027	HE	TMK		TSG
700028	401028+402028+403028+406028+407028+410028+411028+412028	HE	TMK		TSG
700029	401029+402029+403029+406029+407029+410029+411029+412029	HE	TMK		TSG
700030	410030+402030+403030+406030+407030+410030+411030+412030	HE	TMK		TSG
700031	401031+402031+403031+406031+407031+410031+411031+412031	HE	TMK		TSG
700032	401032+402032+403032+406032+407032+410032+411032+412032	HE	TMK		TSG
700033	401033+402033+403033+406033+407033+410033+411033+412033	HE	TMK		TSG
700034	401034+402034+403034+406034+407034+410034+411034+412034	HE	TMK		TSG
700035	401035+402035+403035+406035+407035+410035+411035+412035	HE	TMK		TSG
700036	401036+402036+403036+406036+407036+410036+411036+412036	HE	TMK		TSG
700037	401037+402037+403037+406037+407037+410037+411037+412037	HE	TMK		TSG
700038	401038+402038+403038+406038+407038+410038+411038+412038	HE	TMK		TSG
700039	401039+402039+403039+406039+407039+410039+411039+412039	HE	TMK		TSG
700040	401040+402040+403040+406040+407040+410040+411040+412040	HE	TMK		TSG
700041	401041+402041+403041+406041+407041+410041+411041+412041	HE	TMK		TSG
700042	401042+402042+403042+406042+407042+410042+411042+412042	HE	TMK		TSG
700043	401043+402043+403043+406043+407043+410043+411043+412043	HE	TMK		TSG
700044	401044+402044+403044+406044+407044+410044+411044+412044	HE	TMK		TSG
700045	401045+402045+403045+406045+407045+410045+411045+412045	HE	TMK		TSG
700046	401046+402046+403046+406046+407046+410046+411046+412046	HE	TMK		TSG
700047	401047+402047+403047+406047+407047+410047+411047+412047	HE	TMK		TSG
700048	401048+402048+403048+406048+407048+410048+411048+412048	HE	TMK		TSG
700049	401049+402049+403049+406049+407049+410049+411049+412049	HE	TMK		TSG
700050	401050+402050+403050+406050+407050+410050+411050+412050	HE	TMK		TSG
700051	401051+402051+403051+406051+407051+410051+411051+412051	HE	TMK		TSG
700052	401052+402052+403052+406052+407052+410052+411052+412052	HE	TMK		TSG
700053	401053+402053+403053+406053+407053+410053+411053+412053	HE	TMK		TSG
700054	401054+402054+403054+406054+407054+410054+411054+412054	HE	TMK		TSG
700055	401055+402055+403055+406055+407055+410055+411055+412055	HE	TMK		TSG
700056	401056+402056+403056e+406056+407056+410056+411056+412056	HE	TMK		TSG
700057	401057+402057+403057+406057+407057+410057+411057+412057	HE	TMK		TSG
700058	401058+402058+403058+406058+407058+410058+411058+412058	HE	TMK		TSG
700059	401059+402059+403059+406059+407059+410059+411059+412059	HE	TMK		TSG
700060	410060+402060+406030+406060+407060+410060+411060+412060	HE	TMK		TSG

Number	Formation DMCO+PTSO+MSO+MSO+TSO+TSO+ TSO+TSO+MSO+MSO+PTSO+DMCO	Depot	Livery	Owner	Operator
700101	401101+402101+403101+404101+405101+406101+ 407101+408101+409101+410101+411101+412101	HE	TMK		TSG
700102	401102+402102+403102+404102+405102+406102+ 407102+408102+409102+410102+411102+412102	HE	TMK		TSG
700103	401103+402103+403103+404103+405103+406103+ 407103+408103+409103+410103+411103+412103	HE	TMK		TSG
700104	401104+402104+403104+404104+405104+406104+ 407104+408104+409104+410104+411104+412104	HE	TMK		TSG
700105	401105+402105+403105+404105+405105+406105+ 407105+408105+409105+410105+411105+412105	HE	TMK		TSG
700106	401106+402106+403106+404106+405106+406106+ 407106+408106+409106+410106+411106+412106	HE	TMK		TSG

700107	401107+402107+403107+404107+405107+406107+ 407107+408107+409107+410107+411107+412107	HE	TMK	TSG
700108	401108+402108+403108+404108+405108+406108+ 407108+408108+409108+410108+411108+412108	HE	TMK	TSG
700109	401109+402109+403109+404109+405109+406109+ 407109+408109+409109+410109+411109+412109	HE	TMK	TSG
700110	401110+402110+403110+404110+405110+406110+ 407110+408110+409110+410110+411110+412110	HE	TMK	TSG
700111	401111+402111+403111+404111+405111+406111+ 407111+408111+409111+411101+411111+412111	HE	TMK	TSG
700112	401112+402112+403112+404112+405112+406112+ 407112+408112+409112+410112+411112+412102	HE	TMK	TSG
700113	401113+402113+403113+404113+405113+406113+ 407113+408113+409113 410113+411113+412113	HE	TMK	TSG
700114	401114+402114+403114+404114+405114+406114+ 407114+408114+409114+410114+411114+412114	HE	TMK	TSG
700115	401115+402115+403115+404115+405115+406115+ 407115+408115+409115+410115+411105+412115	HE	TMK	TSG
700116	401116+402116+403116+404116+405116+406116+ 407116+408116+409116+410116+411116+412116	HE	TMK	TSG
700117	401117+402117+403117+404117+405117+406117+ 407117+408117+409117+410117+411107+412117	HE	TMK	TSG
700118	401118+402118+403118+404118+405118+406118+ 407118+408118+409118+410118+411108+412118	HE	TMK	TSG
700119	401119+402119+403119+404119+405119+406119+ 407119+408119+409119+410119+411109+412119	HE	TMK	TSG
700120	401120+402120+403120+404120+405120+406120+ 407120+408120+409120+410120+411120+412120	HE	TMK	TSG
700121	401121+402121+403121+404121+405121+406121+ 407121+408121+409121+410121+411121+412121	HE	TMK	TSG
700122	401122+402122+403122+404122+405122+406122+ 407122+408122+409122+410122+411122+412122	HE	TMK	TSG
700123	401123+402123+403123+404123+405123+406123+ 407123+408123+409123+410123+411123+412123	HE	TMK	TSG
700124	401124+402124+403124+404124+405124+406124+ 407124+408124+409124+410124+411124+412124	HE	TMK	TSG
700125	401125+402125+403125+404125+405125+406125+ 407125+408125+409125+410125+411125+412125	HE	TMK	TSG
700126	401126+402126+403126+404126+405126+406126+ 407126+408126+409126+410126+411126+412126	HE	TMK	TSG
700127	401127+402127+403127+404127+405127+406127+ 407127+408127+409127+410127+411127+412127	HE	TMK	TSG
700128	401128+402128+403128+404128+405128+406128+ 407128+408128+409128+410128+411128+412128	HE	TMK	TSG
700129	401129+402129+403129+404129+405129+406129+ 407129+408129+409129+410129+411129+412129	HE	TMK	TSG
700130	401130+402130+403130+404130+405130+406130+ 40713+408130+409130+410130+411130+412130	HE	TMK	TSG
700131	401131+402131+403131+404131+405131+406131+ 407131+408131+409131+410131+411131+412131	HE	TMK	TSG
700132	400132+402132+403132+404132+405132+406132+ 407132+408132+409132+410132+411132+412132	HE	TMK	TSG
700133	400133+402133+403133+404133+405133+406133+ 407133+408133+409133+410133+411133+412133	HE	TMK	TSG
700134	400134+402134+403134+404134+405134+406134+ 407134+408134+409134+410134+411134+412134	HE	TMK	TSG
700135	400135+402135+403135+404135+405135+406135+ 407135+408135+409135+410135+411135+412135	HE	TMK	TSG
700136	400136+402136+403136+404136+405136+406136+ 407136+408136+409136+410136+411136+412136	HE	TMK	TSG
700137	400137+402137+403137+404137+405137+406137+ 407137+408137+409137+410137+411137+412137	HE	TMK	TSG
700138	400138+402138+403138+404138+405138+406138+ 407138+408138+409138+410138+411138+412138	HE	TMK	TSG
700139	400139+402139+403139+404139+405139+406139+ 407139+408139+409139+410139+411139+412139	HE	TMK	TSG

Thameslink, Southern, Great Northern

700140	400140+402140+403140+404140+405140+406140+ 407140+408140+409140+410140+411140+412140	HE	TMK	TSG
700141	400141+402141+403141+404141+405141+406141+ 407141+408141+409141+410141+411141+412141	HE	TMK	TSG
700142	400142+402142+403142+404142+405142+406142+ 407142+408142+409142+410142+411142+412142	HE	TMK	TSG
700143	400143+402143+403143+404143+405143+406143+ 407143+408143+409143+410143+411143+412143	HE	TMK	TSG
700144	400144+402144+403144+404144+405144+406144+ 407144+408144+409144+410144+411144+412144	HE	TMK	TSG
700145	400145+402145+403145+404145+405145+406145+ 407145+408145+409145+410145+411145+412145	HE	TMK	TSG
700146	400146+402146+403146+404146+405146+406146+ 407146+408146+409146+410146+411146+412146	HE	TMK	TSG
700147	400147+402147+403147+404147+405147+406147+ 407147+408147+409147+410147+411147+412147	HE	TMK	TSG
700148	400148+402148+403148+404148+405148+406148+ 407148+408148+409148+410148+411148+412148	HE	TMK	TSG
700149	400149+402149+403149+404149+405149+406149+ 407149+408149+409149+410149+411149+412149	HE	TMK	TSG
700150	400150+402150+403150+404150+405150+406150+ 407150+408150+409150+410150+411150+412150	HE	TMK	TSG
700151	400151+402151+403151+404151+405151+406151+ 407151+408151+409151+410151+411151+412151	HE	TMK	TSG
700152	400152+402152+403152+404152+405152+406152+ 407152+408152+409152+410152+411152+412152	HE	TMK	TSG
700153	400153+402153+403153+404153+405153+406153+ 407153+408153+409153+410153+411153+412153	HE	TMK	TSG
700154	400154+402154+403154+404154+405154+406154+ 407154+408154+409154+410154+411154+412154	HE	TMK	TSG
700155	400155+402155+403155+404155+405155+406155+ 407155+408155+409155+410155+411155+412155	HE	TMK	TSG

The 'Desiro City' Class 700 stock currently under construction and testing will be used for the new Thameslink operation. Three vehicles of the first of the fleet, forming set No. 700001 were displayed at the 2014 Innotrans event, where this image was captured. **CJM**

Above: *Class 700 driving cab design, with a combined power and brake controller on the left side, screens for train management and doors, and switch gear for automatic train operation through the Thameslink tunnels.* **CJM**

Below: *Class 700 standard class interior, which is very spartan when compared with any other modern state-of-the-art multiple unit and might not go down well with the travelling public.* **CJM**

Passenger Train Operating Companies - Thameslink, Southern, Great Northern

Virgin Trains East Coast

Passenger Train Operating Companies - East Coast

Address: ✉ East Coast House, 25 Skeldergate, York, YO1 6DH
📠 customers@eastcoast.co.uk
✆ 08457 225225
ⓘ www.eastcoast.co.uk

Managing Director: David Horne

Franchise Dates: 1 March 2015 - 31 March 2023

Principal Routes: London King's Cross - Aberdeen / Inverness, Edinburgh, Glasgow Hull, Leeds, Bradford, Skipton and Harrogate

Depots: Bounds Green (BN), Craigentinny (EC)

Parent Company: Stagecoach / Virgin Trains

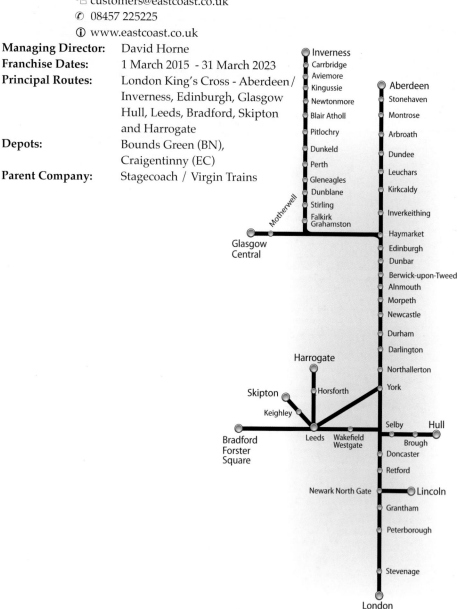

© TRC.Com Ltd 2013

Class 43 – HST

Vehicle Length: 58ft 5in (18.80m)		Engine: MTU 16V4000 R41R				
Height: 12ft 10in (3.90m)		Horsepower: 2,250hp (1,680kW)				
Width: 8ft 11in (2.73m)		Electrical Equipment: Brush				

Number		Depot	Pool	Livery	Owner	Operator	Name
43206	(43006)	EC	IECP	ECG	ANG	ICE	*Kingdom of Fife*
43208	(43008)	EC	IECP	NXE	ANG	ICE	*Lincolnshire Echo*
43238	(43038)	EC	IECP	ECG	ANG	ICE	
43239	(43039)	EC	IECP	ECG	ANG	ICE	
43251	(43051)	EC	IECP	ECG	PTR	ICE	
43257	(43057)	EC	IECP	ECG	PTR	ICE	
43272	(43072)	EC	IECP	ECG	PTR	ICE	
43274	(43074)	EC	IECP	ECG	PTR	ICE	
43277	(43077)	EC	IECP	ECG	PTR	ICE	
43290	(43090)	EC	IECP	NXE	PTR	ICE	*MTU Fascination of Power*
43295	(43095)	EC	IECP	ECG	ANG	ICE	
43296	(43096)	EC	IECP	ECG	PTR	ICE	
43299	(43099)	EC	IECP	ECG	PTR	ICE	
43300	(43100)	EC	IECP	ECG	PTR	ICE	*Craigentinny*
43302	(43102)	EC	IECP	ECG	PTR	ICE	
43305	(43105)	EC	IECP	ECG	ANG	ICE	
43306	(43106)	EC	IECP	NXE	ANG	ICE	
43307	(43107)	EC	IECP	ECG	ANG	ICE	
43308	(43108)	EC	IECP	ECG	ANG	ICE	*Highland Chieftain*
43309	(43109)	EC	IECP	ECG	ANG	ICE	
43310	(43110)	EC	IECP	ECG	ANG	ICE	
43311	(43111)	EC	IECP	ECG	ANG	ICE	
43312	(43112)	EC	IECP	ECG	ANG	ICE	
43313	(43113)	EC	IECP	ECG	ANG	ICE	
43314	(43114)	EC	IECP	ECG	ANG	ICE	
43315	(43115)	EC	IECP	ECG	ANG	ICE	
43316	(43116)	EC	IECP	ECG	ANG	ICE	
43317	(43117)	EC	IECP	ECG	ANG	ICE	
43318	(43118)	EC	IECP	ECT		ICE	
43319	(43119)	EC	IECP	ECG	ANG	ICE	
43320	(43120)	EC	IECP	NXE	ANG	ICE	
43367	(43167)	EC	IECP	ECG	ANG	ICE	*Deltic 50 1955 - 2005 v*

Right: *In addition to its core electric fleet, East Coast operates 32 Class 43 HST power cars. All are refurbished with MTU engines. The fleet is allocated to Edinburgh Craigentinny depot. The HST fleet operates services over the longer-distance routes to Aberdeen and Inverness which are not electrified, as well as assisting with providing a more frequent service over the London-Leeds, York and Edinburgh corridor. Class 43 No. 43277 is seen in East Coast grey livery at Doncaster on 23 April 2014.* **CJM**

Class 91

Vehicle Length: 63ft 8in (19.40m)		Power Collection: 25kV ac overhead	
Height: 12ft 4in (3.75m)		Horsepower: 6,300hp (4,700kW)	
Width: 9ft 0in (2.74m)		Electrical Equipment: GEC	

Number		Depot	Pool	Livery	Owner	Operator	Name
91101	(91001)	BN	IECA	ADV	EVL	ICE	*Flying Scotsman* (branding)
91102	(91002)	BN	IECA	ECG	EVL	ICE	*City of York*
91103	(91003)	BN	IECA	ECW	EVL	ICE	
91104	(91004)	BN	IECA	ECG	EVL	ICE	
91105	(91005)	BN	IECA	ECW	EVL	ICE	
91106	(91006)	BN	IECA	ECS	EVL	ICE	
91107	(91007)	BN	IECA	ECS	EVL	ICE	*Skyfall*

East Coast

91108	(91008)	BN	IECA	ECG	EVL	ICE
91109	(91009)	BN	IECA	ECG	EVL	ICE	Sir Bobby Robson
91110	(91010)	BN	IECA	ADV	EVL	ICE	Battle of Britain Memorial Flight - Spitfire Hurricane Lancaster Dakota
91111	(91011)	BN	IECA	SPL	EVL	ICE	For the Fallen
91112	(91012)	BN	IECA	ECG	EVL	ICE
91113	(91013)	BN	IECA	ECG	EVL	ICE
91114	(91014)	BN	IECA	ECG	EVL	ICE	Durham Cathedral
91115	(91015)	BN	IECA	ECG	EVL	ICE	Blaydon Races
91116	(91016)	BN	IECA	ECG	EVL	ICE
91117	(91017)	BN	IECA	ECG	EVL	ICE	West Riding Limited
91118	(91018)	BN	IECA	ECG	EVL	ICE
91119	(91019)	BN	IECA	ECG	EVL	ICE
91120	(91020)	BN	IECA	ECG	EVL	ICE
91121	(91021)	BN	IECA	ECG	EVL	ICE
91122	(91022)	BN	IECA	ECG	EVL	ICE
91124	(91024)	BN	IECA	ECG	EVL	ICE
91125	(91025)	BN	IECA	ECG	EVL	ICE
91126	(91026)	BN	IECA	ECG	EVL	ICE
91127	(91027)	BN	IECA	ECS	EVL	ICE
91128	(91028)	BN	IECA	ECG	EVL	ICE
91129	(91029)	BN	IECA	ECG	EVL	ICE
91130	(91030)	BN	IECA	ECW	EVL	ICE
91131	(91031)	BN	IECA	ECG	EVL	ICE
91132	(91023)	BN	IECA	ECG	EVL	ICE

Below: *The 31 Class 91 high-output electric locos and Mk4 stock allocated to Bounds Green form the backbone of the East Coast operation. The semi-fixed formations operate with a Class 91 on the north end, standard, buffet and first class intermediate vehicles and a Mk4 Driving Van Trailer (DVT) coupled at the London end. No. 91105 approaches Doncaster on 23 April 2014 with the 08.30 London King's Cross to Newcastle service.* **CJM**

Class 800 and 801 'Super Express'

In summer 2012 Agility Trains signed a contract with the Department for Transport (DfT) to design, build, finance and maintain 596 state-of-the-art carriages for the East Coast Main Line and Great Western Main Line as part of the Intercity Express Programme to replace HST and IC225 trains.

Hitachi Rail Europe and John Laing are the main shareholders of Agility Trains and in summer 2013 the Secretary of State for Transport announced that an additional contract for the provision of an extra 270 carriages for the East Coast Main Line was to be placed, bringing the total number of vehicles ordered to 866.

East Coast will have between 2017 and 2019 13 nine-car Class 800 dual mode and 51 nine-car electric Class 801 train sets delivered. The first 12 trains are to be built by Hitachi in Kasado, Japan, with the remainder built at a new Hitachi plant at Newton Aycliffe.

Mk3 HST Stock

Vehicle Length: 75ft 0in (22.86m)   Width: 8ft 11in (2.71m)
Height: 12ft 9in (3.88m)   Bogie Type: BT10

GK1G - TRFB *Seating 17F*

Number	Depot	Livery	Owner
40701	EC	NXE	PTR
40702	EC	NXE	PTR
40704	EC	NXE	ANG
40705	EC	NXE	ANG
40706	EC	NXE	ANG
40708	EC	ECT	PTR
40711	EC	NXE	ANG
40720	EC	NXE	ANG
40732	EC	ECG	PTR
40735	EC	NXE	ANG
40737	EC	NXE	ANG
40740	EC	NXE	ANG
40742	EC	NXE	ANG
40748	EC	NXE	ANG
40750	EC	NXE	ANG
40805	EC	NXG	ANG

GH1G - TF *Seating 48F*

Number	Depot	Livery	Owner
41039	EC	NXE	ANG
41040	EC	NXE	ANG
41043	EC	ECS	ANG
41044	EC	NXE	ANG
41058	EC	NXE	PTR
41062	EC	ECG	PTR
41066	EC	NXE	ANG
41083	EC	NXE	PTR
41087	EC	NXE	ANG
41088	EC	NXE	ANG
41090	EC	NXE	ANG
41091	EC	NXE	ANG
41092	EC	NXE	ANG
41095	EC	NXE	ANG
41097	EC	NXE	ANG
41098	EC	NXE	ANG
41099	EC	NXE	ANG
41100	EC	NXE	ANG
41115	EC	NXE	PTR
41118	EC	NXE	ANG
41120	EC	ECT	ANG
41150	EC	ECT	ANG
41151	EC	NXE	ANG
41152	EC	NXE	ANG
41154	EC	ECG	PTR
41159	EC	NXE	PTR
41164	EC	NXE	ANG
41165	EC	NXE	PTR
41170(41001)	EC	NXE	ANG
41185(42313	EC	NXE	PTR
41190(42088)	EC	NXG	PTR

GH2G - TS (*TSD) *Seating 76/62*S*

Number	Depot	Livery	Owner
42057	EC	NXE	ANG
42058	EC	NXE	ANG
42059	EC	NXE	ANG
42063	EC	NXE	ANG
42064	EC	NXE	ANG
42065	EC	NXE	ANG

42091*	EC	ECT	ANG
42106	EC	NXE	ANG
42109	EC	NXE	PTR
42110	EC	NXE	PTR
42116*	EC	NXE	ANG
42117	EC	NXE	PTR
42123	EC	ECG	ANG
42125	EC	ECG	PTR
42127*	EC	NXE	ANG
42128*	EC	NXE	ANG
42130	EC	NXE	PTR
42134	EC	NXE	ANG
42146	EC	ECT	ANG
42147	EC	NXE	PTR
42150	EC	ECT	ANG
42154	EC	ECT	ANG
42158	EC	NXE	ANG
42159*	EC	NXE	PTR
42160	EC	NXE	PTR
42161*	EC	NXE	PTR
42163	EC	NXE	PTR
42171	EC	NXE	ANG
42172	EC	NXE	ANG
42179	EC	NXE	ANG
42180	EC	NXE	ANG
42181	EC	NXE	ANG
42182	EC	NXE	ANG
42186	EC	ECT	ANG
42188*	EC	NXE	ANG
42189*	EC	NXE	ANG
42190	EC	NXE	ANG
42191	EC	NXE	ANG
42192	EC	NXE	ANG
42193	EC	NXE	ANG
42198	EC	NXE	ANG
42199	EC	NXE	ANG
42205	EC	ECG	PTR
42210	EC	ECG	PTR
42215	EC	ECT	ANG
42219	EC	NXE	ANG
42226	EC	NXE	ANG
42228	EC	ECT	PTR

42235	EC	NXE	ANG
42237	EC	NXE	PTR
42238*	EC	NXE	ANG
42239*	EC	NXE	ANG
42240	EC	NXE	ANG
42241	EC	NXE	ANG
42242	EC	NXE	ANG
42243	EC	NXE	ANG
42244	EC	NXE	ANG
42286	EC	ECT	PTR
42306	EC	NXE	PTR
42307	EC	NXE	PTR
42322	EC	ECT	PTR
42323	EC	NXE	ANG
42326	EC	NXE	PTR
42330	EC	NXE	PTR
42335	EC	ECG	PTR
42340	EC	NXE	ANG
42352(41176)	EC	NXE	PTR
42354(41175)	EC	ECT	ANG
42355(41172)	EC	NXE	ANG
42357(41174)	EC	NXE	ANG
42363(41082)	EC	NXE	ANG

GJ2G - TGS *Seating 65S*

Number	Depot	Livery	Owner
44019	EC	NXE	ANG
44031	EC	NXE	ANG
44045	EC	NXE	ANG
44050	EC	ECT	PTR
44056	EC	NXE	ANG
44057	EC	NXE	PTR
44058	EC	NXE	ANG
44061	EC	NXE	ANG
44063	EC	NXE	ANG
44073	EC	ECG	PTR
44075	EC	NXE	PTR
44077	EC	NXE	ANG
44080	EC	NXE	ANG
44094	EC	ECT	ANG
44098	EC	NXE	ANG

Below: *Up to 15 East Coast HST sets can be formed at any one time, but usually fewer than this are in daily service. The stock carries a number of livery variations; some carry East Coast branded National Express-style colours, while one set is not in full East Coast grey. TRFB No. 40704 is illustrated.* **CJM**

East Coast

Mk4 Stock

Vehicle Length: 75ft 5in (23m) Width: 8ft 11in (2.73m)
Height: 12ft 5in (3.79m) Bogie Type: BT41

Passenger Train Operating Companies - East Coast

AJ2J - RSB *Seating 30S*

Number	Depot	Livery	Owner
10300	BN	ECS	EVL
10301	BN	ECG	EVL
10302	BN	ECS	EVL
10303	BN	ECS	EVL
10304	BN	ECG	EVL
10305	BN	ECG	EVL
10306	BN	ECG	EVL
10307	BN	ECS	EVL
10308	BN	ECS	EVL
10309	BN	ECG	EVL
10310	BN	ECG	EVL
10311	BN	ECG	EVL
10312	BN	ECG	EVL
10313	BN	ECG	EVL
10315	BN	ECG	EVL
10317	BN	ECG	EVL
10318	BN	ECG	EVL
10319	BN	ECG	EVL
10320	BN	ECS	EVL
10321	BN	ECG	EVL
10323	BN	ECS	EVL
10324	BN	ECG	EVL
10325	BN	ECG	EVL
10326	BN	ECS	EVL
10328	BN	ECG	EVL
10329	BN	ECG	EVL
10330	BN	ECG	EVL
10331	BN	ECS	EVL
10332	BN	ECG	EVL
10333	BN	ECG	EVL

AD1J - FO *Seating 46F*

Number	Depot	Livery	Owner
11201	BN	ECG	EVL
11219	BN	ECS	EVL
11229	BN	ECG	EVL
11237	BN	ECG	EVL
11241	BN	ECG	EVL
11244	BN	ECG	EVL
11273	BN	ECG	EVL
11277(12408)	BN	ECS	EVL
11278(12479)	BN	ECS	EVL
11279(12521)	BN	ECG	EVL
11280(12523)	BN	ECS	EVL
11281(12418)	BN	ECG	EVL
11282(12524)	BN	ECS	EVL
11283(12435)	BN	ECS	EVL
11284(12487)	BN	ECG	EVL
11285(12537)	BN	ECG	EVL
11286(12482)	BN	ECG	EVL
11287(12527)	BN	ECG	EVL
11288(12517)	BN	ECG	EVL
11289(12528)	BN	ECG	EVL
11290(12530)	BN	ECG	EVL
11291(12535)	BN	ECG	EVL
11292(12451)	BN	ECG	EVL
11293(12536)	BN	ECG	EVL
11294(12529)	BN	ECG	EVL
11295(12475)	BN	ECG	EVL
11298(12416)	BN	ECS	EVL
11299(12532)	BN	ECS	EVL

AL1J - FOD *Seating 42F*

Number	Depot	Livery	Owner
11301(11215)	BN	ECS	EVL
11302(11203)	BN	ECS	EVL
11303(11211)	BN	ECS	EVL
11304(11257)	BN	ECS	EVL
11305(11261)	BN	ECS	EVL
11306(11276)	BN	ECG	EVL
11307(11217)	BN	ECS	EVL
11308(11263)	BN	ECG	EVL
11309(11262)	BN	ECG	EVL
11310(11272)	BN	ECS	EVL
11311(11221)	BN	ECS	EVL
11312(11225)	BN	ECG	EVL
11313(11210)	BN	ECG	EVL
11314(11207)	BN	ECG	EVL
11315(11238)	BN	ECG	EVL
11316(11227)	BN	ECG	EVL
11317(11223)	BN	ECG	EVL
11318(11251)	BN	ECG	EVL
11319(11247)	BN	ECG	EVL
11320(11255)	BN	ECG	EVL
11321(11245)	BN	ECG	EVL
11322(11228)	BN	ECG	EVL
11323(11235)	BN	ECG	EVL
11324(11253)	BN	ECG	EVL
11325(11231)	BN	ECG	EVL
11326(11206)	BN	ECG	EVL
11327(11236)	BN	ECG	EVL
11328(11274)	BN	ECG	EVL
11329(11243)	BN	ECG	EVL
11330(11249)	BN	ECG	EVL

AD1J - FO *Seating 46F*

Number	Depot	Livery	Owner
11401(11214)	BN	ECS	EVL
11402(11216)	BN	ECS	EVL
11403(11258)	BN	ECS	EVL
11404(11202)	BN	ECS	EVL
11405(11204)	BN	ECS	EVL
11406(11205)	BN	ECG	EVL
11407(11256)	BN	ECS	EVL
11408(11218)	BN	ECG	EVL
11409(11259)	BN	ECG	EVL
11410(11260)	BN	ECG	EVL
11411(11240)	BN	ECS	EVL
11412(11209)	BN	ECG	EVL
11413(11212)	BN	ECG	EVL
11414(11246)	BN	ECG	EVL
11415(11208)	BN	ECG	EVL
11416(11254)	BN	ECG	EVL
11417(11226)	BN	ECG	EVL
11418(11222)	BN	ECG	EVL
11419(11250)	BN	ECG	EVL
11420(11242)	BN	ECG	EVL
11421(11220)	BN	ECG	EVL
11422(11232)	BN	ECG	EVL
11423(11230)	BN	ECG	EVL
11424(11239)	BN	ECG	EVL
11425(11234)	BN	ECG	EVL
11426(11252)	BN	ECG	EVL
11427(11200)	BN	ECG	EVL
11428(11233)	BN	ECG	EVL

Number	Depot	Livery	Owner
11429(11275)	BN	ECG	EVL
11430(11248)	BN	ECG	EVL
11998(10314)	BN	ECG	EVL
11999(10316)	BN	ECG	EVL

AI2J - TSOE *Seating 76S*

Number	Depot	Livery	Owner
12200	BN	ECG	EVL
12201	BN	ECS	EVL
12202	BN	ECS	EVL
12203	BN	ECS	EVL
12204	BN	ECG	EVL
12205	BN	ECG	EVL
12207	BN	ECS	EVL
12208	BN	ECG	EVL
12209	BN	ECS	EVL
12210	BN	ECG	EVL
12211	BN	ECG	EVL
12212	BN	ECG	EVL
12213	BN	ECG	EVL
12214	BN	ECS	EVL
12215	BN	ECG	EVL
12216	BN	ECG	EVL
12217	BN	ECG	EVL
12218	BN	ECG	EVL
12219	BN	ECG	EVL
12220	BN	ECG	EVL
12222	BN	ECG	EVL
12223	BN	ECG	EVL
12224	BN	ECG	EVL
12225	BN	ECG	EVL
12226	BN	ECG	EVL
12227	BN	ECG	EVL
12228	BN	ECG	EVL
12229	BN	ECG	EVL
12230	BN	ECG	EVL
12231	BN	ECS	EVL
12232	BN	ECS	EVL

AL2J - TSOD *Seating 68S*

Number	Depot	Livery	Owner
12300	BN	ECS	EVL
12301	BN	ECS	EVL
12302	BN	ECS	EVL
12303	BN	ECG	EVL
12304	BN	ECG	EVL
12305	BN	ECS	EVL
12307	BN	ECS	EVL
12308	BN	ECG	EVL
12309	BN	ECG	EVL
12310	BN	ECG	EVL
12311	BN	ECG	EVL
12312	BN	ECG	EVL
12313	BN	ECG	EVL
12315	BN	ECG	EVL
12316	BN	ECG	EVL
12317	BN	ECG	EVL
12318	BN	ECG	EVL
12319	BN	ECG	EVL
12320	BN	ECG	EVL
12321	BN	ECG	EVL
12322	BN	ECG	EVL
12323	BN	ECG	EVL

12324	BN	ECG	EVL
12325	BN	ECG	EVL
12326	BN	ECG	EVL
12327	BN	ECS	EVL
12328	BN	ECG	EVL
12329	BN	ECS	EVL
12330	BN	ECG	EVL
12331(12531)	BN	ECG	EVL

AC2J - TSO *Seating 76S*

Number	Depot	Livery	Owner
12400	BN	ECG	EVL
12401	BN	ECS	EVL
12402	BN	ECS	EVL
12403	BN	ECG	EVL
12404	BN	ECG	EVL
12405	BN	ECS	EVL
12406	BN	ECG	EVL
12407	BN	ECG	EVL
12409	BN	ECG	EVL
12410	BN	ECG	EVL
12411	BN	ECS	EVL
12414	BN	ECS	EVL
12415	BN	ECS	EVL
12417	BN	ECS	EVL
12419	BN	ECS	EVL
12420	BN	ECG	EVL
12421	BN	ECS	EVL
12422	BN	ECG	EVL
12423	BN	ECG	EVL
12424	BN	ECG	EVL
12425	BN	ECG	EVL
12426	BN	ECG	EVL
12427	BN	ECG	EVL
12428	BN	ECG	EVL
12429	BN	ECG	EVL
12430	BN	ECG	EVL
12431	BN	ECG	EVL
12432	BN	ECG	EVL
12433	BN	ECG	EVL
12434	BN	ECG	EVL
12436	BN	ECS	EVL
12437	BN	ECS	EVL
12438	BN	ECG	EVL
12439	BN	ECG	EVL
12440	BN	ECG	EVL
12441	BN	ECG	EVL
12442	BN	ECG	EVL
12443	BN	ECS	EVL
12444	BN	ECG	EVL
12445	BN	ECG	EVL
12446	BN	ECG	EVL
12447	BN	ECG	EVL
12448	BN	ECS	EVL
12449	BN	ECG	EVL
12450	BN	ECS	EVL
12452	BN	ECG	EVL
12453	BN	ECG	EVL
12454	BN	ECG	EVL
12455	BN	ECG	EVL
12456	BN	ECG	EVL
12457	BN	ECG	EVL
12458	BN	ECG	EVL
12459	BN	ECS	EVL
12460	BN	ECG	EVL
12461	BN	ECG	EVL
12462	BN	ECG	EVL
12463	BN	ECG	EVL
12464	BN	ECG	EVL
12465	BN	ECG	EVL
12466	BN	ECG	EVL
12467	BN	ECG	EVL
12468	BN	ECG	EVL
12469	BN	ECG	EVL
12470	BN	ECG	EVL
12471	BN	ECG	EVL
12472	BN	ECG	EVL
12473	BN	ECG	EVL
12474	BN	ECG	EVL
12476	BN	ECG	EVL
12477	BN	ECG	EVL
12478	BN	ECS	EVL
12480	BN	ECS	EVL
12481	BN	ECG	EVL
12483	BN	ECG	EVL
12484	BN	ECS	EVL
12485	BN	ECG	EVL
12486	BN	ECS	EVL
12488	BN	ECS	EVL
12489	BN	ECS	EVL
12513	BN	ECG	EVL
12514	BN	ECG	EVL
12515	BN	ECG	EVL
12518	BN	ECS	EVL
12519	BN	ECG	EVL
12520	BN	ECS	EVL
12522	BN	ECS	EVL
12526	BN	ECG	EVL
12533	BN	ECG	EVL
12534	BN	ECG	EVL
12538	BN	ECG	EVL

NZAJ - DVT

Number	Depot	Livery	Owner
82200	BN	ECG	EVL
82201	BN	ECG	EVL
82202	BN	ECS	EVL
82203	BN	ECG	EVL
82204	BN	ECW	EVL
82205	BN	ADV	EVL
82206	BN	ECG	EVL
82207	BN	ECS	EVL
82208	BN	ECG	EVL
82209	BN	ECG	EVL
82210	BN	ECS	EVL
82211	BN	ECS	EVL
82212	BN	ECG	EVL
82213	BN	ECG	EVL
82214	BN	ECG	EVL
82215	BN	ECG	EVL
82216	BN	EDG	EVL
82217	BN	ECG	EVL
82218	BN	ECS	EVL
82219	BN	ECW	EVL
82220	BN	ECG	EVL
82222	BN	ECG	EVL
82223	BN	ECG	EVL
82224	BN	ECG	EVL
82225	BN	ECG	EVL
82226	BN	ECG	EVL
82227	BN	ECG	EVL
82228	BN	ECG	EVL
82229	BN	ECG	EVL
82230	BN	ECG	EVL
82231	BN	ECG	EVL

82205 Flying Scotsman livery

Below: *The Mk4 fleet, based at Bounds Green, is in a mix of grey/white ex-National Express colours and all-over grey East Coast livery. TSO No. 12410 is illustrated. These vehicles seat 76 in the 2+2 style.* **CJM**

Service Stock

HST and Mk4 Barrier Vehicles

Number	Depot	Livery	Owner	Former Identity
6340	EC	NEG	ANG	BCK - 21251
6344	EC	NEG	ANG	BG - 92080
6346	EC	NEG	ANG	BSO - 9422
6352	BN	NEG	ANG	SK - 19465
6353	BN	NEG	ANG	SK - 19478
6354	BN	NEG	ANG	BSO - 9459
6355	BN	NEG	ANG	BSO - 9477
6358	BN	NEG	EVL	BSO - 9432
6359	BN	NEG	EVL	BSO - 9429
9393	EC	PTR	PTR	BG - 92196
9394	EC	PTR	PTR	BG - 92906

Virgin West Coast

Address: 85 Smallbrook Queensway,
Birmingham, B5 4HA
✍ info@virgintrains.co.uk
✆ 0845 000 8000
ⓘ www.virgintrains.co.uk

Lead Executive: Phil Whittingham

Franchise Dates: 12 December 2006 - April 2017

Principal Routes: London Euston - Birmingham,
Holyhead, Manchester
Liverpool, Glasgow and
Edinburgh

Depots: Edge Hill** (LL), Longsight**
(MA), Oxley** (OY),
Wembley** (WB), Central
Rivers (CZ)
** Operated by Alstom

Parent Company: Virgin Group

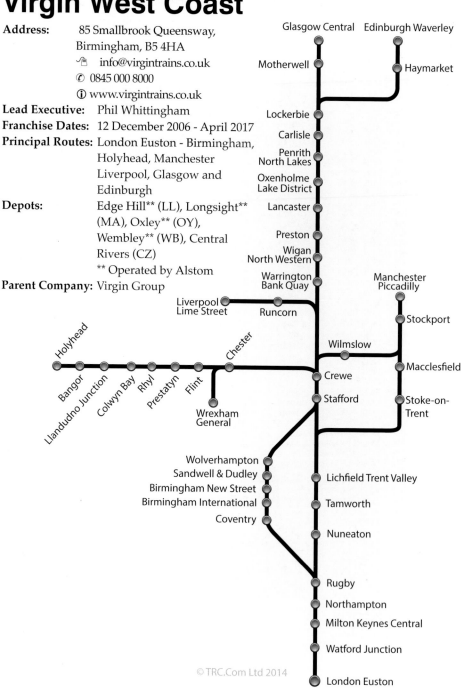

Glasgow Central   Edinburgh Waverley
Motherwell   Haymarket
Lockerbie
Carlisle
Penrith
North Lakes
Oxenholme
Lake District
Lancaster
Preston
Wigan
North Western
Warrington
Bank Quay   Manchester
Piccadilly
Liverpool
Lime Street   Runcorn   Stockport
Holyhead   Wilmslow
Chester   Macclesfield
Bangor   Crewe
Llandudno Junction   Colwyn Bay   Rhyl   Prestatyn   Flint   Stafford   Stoke-on-Trent
Wrexham
General
Wolverhampton
Sandwell & Dudley   Lichfield Trent Valley
Birmingham New Street
Birmingham International   Tamworth
Coventry
Nuneaton
Rugby
Northampton
Milton Keynes Central
Watford Junction
© TRC.Com Ltd 2014   London Euston

Passenger Train Operating Companies - Virgin West Coast

Class 221
Super Voyager

Vehicle Length: 77ft 6in (23.62m)
Height: 12ft 4in (3.75m)
Width: 8ft 11in (2.73m)
Engine: 1 x Cummins 750hp per vehicle
Horsepower: 5-car - 3,750hp (2,796kW). 4-car - 3,000hp (2,237kW)
Seats (total/car): 26F/214S 42S/60S/60S/52S*/26F (*not in 4-car set)

Passenger Train Operating Companies - Virgin West Coast

Number	Formation DMS+MS+MS+MSRMB+DMF	Depot	Livery	Owner	Operator	Name
221101	60351+60951+60851+60751+60451	CZ	VWC	HBS	VWC	Louis Bleriot
221102	60352+60952+60852+60752+60452	CZ	VWC	HBS	VWC	John Cabot
221103	60353+60953+60853+60753+60453	CZ	VWC	HBS	VWC	Christopher Columbus
221104	60354+60954+60854+60754+60454	CZ	VWC	HBS	VWC	Sir John Franklin
221105	60355+60955+60855+60755+60455	CZ	VWC	HBS	VWC	William Baffin
221106	60356+60956+60856+60756+60456	CZ	VWC	HBS	VWC	Willem Barents
221107	60357+60957+60857+60757+60457	CZ	VWC	HBS	VWC	Sir Martin Frobisher
221108	60358+60958+60858+60758+60458	CZ	VWC	HBS	VWC	Sir Ernest Shackleton
221109	60359+60959+60859+60759+60459	CZ	VWC	HBS	VWC	Marco Polo
221110	60360+60960+60860+60760+60460	CZ	VWC	HBS	VWC	James Cook
221111	60361+60961+60861+60761+60461	CZ	VWC	HBS	VWC	Roald Amundsen
221112	60362+60962+60862+60762+60462	CZ	VWC	HBS	VWC	Ferdinand Magellan
221113	60363+60963+60863+60763+60463	CZ	VWC	HBS	VWC	Sir Walter Raleigh
221114	60364+60964+60864+60764+60464	CZ	VWC	HBS	VWC	
221115	60365+60965+60865+60765+60465	CZ	VWC¤	HBS	VWC	Polmadie Depot
221116	60366+60966+60866+60766+60466	CZ	VWC	HBS	VWC	
221117	60367+60967+60867+60767+60467	CZ	VWC	HBS	VWC	The Wrekin Giant
221118	60368+60968+60868+60768+60468	CZ	VWC	HBS	VWC	
221142	60392+60992+60994ø+60792+60492	CZ	VWC	HBS	VWC	Bombardier Voyager
221143	60393+60993+60794+60793+60493	CZ	VWC	HBS	VWC	Auguste Picard
221144§	60394+-+-+-+60494	CZ	VWC	HBS	(spare)	

¤ One driving car carries Bombardier branding. ø MRSMB vehicle

§ The two spare driving cars from set No. 221144 are stored at Central Rivers.

Below: *The present Virgin West Coast operation has a fleet of 21 five-car Class 221 'Super Voyager' sets on its books. Allocated to Central Rivers Bombardier depot near Burton, these sets operate mainly on the non-electrified route over the North Wales Coast, but also supplement the electric fleet forming some Birmingham to London services. With its first class vehicle leading, identifiable by the yellow cover to the coupling drum box, set No. 221106* **Willem Barents** *passes South Kenton on 21 May 2014 forming the 13.10 Euston to Chester service.* **CJM**

Virgin West Coast

Class 390
Pendolino

Vehicle Length Driving: 75ft 6in (23.01m)	Horsepower: 6,840hp (5,100kW)
Height: 11ft 6in (3.50m)	Seats (total/car): 147F/300S, 18F/39F/44F/46F/74S/76S/76S/66S/48S/64S/46S
Width: 8ft 11in (2.71m)	31 sets are now formed of 11 vehicles 147F/450S

Formation: DMRFO+MFO+PTFO+MFO+PTSO+MSO+PTSRMB+MSO+DMSO

Number	Formation	Name	Owner	Operator	Livery	Depot
390001	69101+69401+69501+69601+68801+69701+69801+69901+69201	Virgin Pioneer	ANG	VWC	VWC	MA
390002	69102+69402+69502+69602+68802+69702+69802+69902+69202	Virgin Angel	ANG	VWC	VWC	MA
390103	69103+69403+69503+69603+65303+68803+68903+69703+69803+69903+69203	Virgin Hero	ANG	VWC	VWC	MA
390104	69104+69404+69504+69604+65304+68804+68904+69704+69804+69904+69204	Alstom Pendolino	ANG	VWC	VWC	MA
390005	69105+69405+69505+69605+68805+69705+69805+69905+69205	City of Wolverhampton	ANG	VWC	VWC	MA
390006	69106+69406+69506+69606+68806+69706+69806+69906+69206	Tate Liverpool	ANG	VWC	VWC	MA
390107	69107+69407+69507+69607+68807+69707+69807+69907+69207	Virgin Lady (branded Abigail Irozuru)	ANG	VWC	VWC	MA
390008	69108+69408+69508+69608+68808+69708+69808+69908+69208	Virgin King	ANG	VWC	VWC	MA
390009	69109+69409+69509+69609+68809+69709+69809+69909+69209	Treaty of Union	ANG	VWC	VWC	MA
390010	69110+69410+69510+69610+68810+69710+69810+69910+69210	A Decade of Progress	ANG	VWC	VWC	MA
390011	69111+69411+69511+69611+68811+69711+69811+69911+69211	City of Lichfield	ANG	VWC	VWC	MA
390112	69112+69412+69512+69612+65312+68812+68912+69712+69812+69912+69212	Virgin Star	ANG	VWC	VWC	MA
390013	69113+69413+69513+69613+68813+69713+69813+69913+69213	Virgin Spirit	ANG	VWC	VWC	MA
390114	69114+69414+69514+69614+65314+68814+68914+69714+69814+69914+69214	City of Manchester	ANG	VWC	VWC	MA
390115	69115+69415+69515+69615+68815+69715+69815+69915+69215	Virgin Crusader	ANG	VWC	VWC	MA
390016	69116+69416+69516+69616+68816+69716+69816+69916+69216	Virgin Champion	ANG	VWC	VWC	MA
390117§	69117+69417+69517+69617+65317+68817+68917+69717+69817+69917+69217	Virgin Prince	ANG	VWC	VWC	MA
390118	69118+69418+69518+69618+68818+69718+69818+69918+69218	Virgin Princess	ANG	VWC	VWC	MA
390119	69119+69419+69519+69619+68819+69719+69819+69919+69219	Virgin Warrior	ANG	VWC	VWC	MA
390020	69120+69420+69520+69620+68820+69720+69820+69920+69220	Virgin Cavalier	ANG	VWC	VWC	MA
390121	69121+69421+69521+69621+68821+69721+69821+69921+69221	Virgin Dream	ANG	VWC	VWC	MA
390122	69122+69422+69522+69622+65322+68822+68922+69722+69822+69922+69222	Penny the Pendolino	ANG	VWC	VWC	MA
390123	69123+69423+69523+69623+65323+68823+68923+69723+69823+69923+69223	Virgin Glory	ANG	VWC	VWC	MA
390124	69124+69424+69524+69624+65324+68824+68924+69724+69824+69924+69224	Virgin Venturer	ANG	VWC	VWC	MA
390125	69125+69425+69525+69625+68825+69725+69825+69925+69225	Virgin Stagecoach	ANG	VWC	VWC	MA
390126	69126+69426+69526+69626+68826+69726+69826+69926+69226	Virgin Enterprise	ANG	VWC	VWC	MA
390127§	69127+69427+69527+69627+68827+69727+69827+69927+69227	Virgin Buccaneer	ANG	VWC	VWC	MA
390128	69128+69428+69528+69628+68828+69728+69828+69928+69228	City of Preston	ANG	VWC	VWC	MA
390129	69129+69429+69529+69629+68829+69729+69829+69929+69229	City of Stoke-on-Trent	ANG	VWC	VWC	MA
390130	69130+69430+69530+69630+68830+69730+69830+69930+69230	City of Edinburgh	ANG	VWC	VWC	MA
390131§	69131+69431+69531+69631+68831+69731+69831+69931+69231	City of Liverpool	ANG	VWC	VWC	MA
390132	69132+69432+69532+69632+68832+69732+69832+69932+69232	City of Birmingham	ANG	VWC	VWC	MA
390134	69134+69434+69534+69634+68834+69734+69834+69934+69234	City of Carlisle	ANG	VWC	VWC	MA
390135	69135+69435+69535+69635+68835+69735+69835+69935+69235	City of Lancaster	ANG	VWC	VWC	MA
390136	69136+69436+69536+69636+68836+69736+69836+69936+69236	City of Coventry	ANG	VWC	VWC	MA
390137	69137+69437+69537+69637+68837+69737+69837+69937+69237	Virgin Difference	ANG	VWC	VWC	MA
390138	69138+69438+69538+69638+68838+69738+69838+69938+69238	City of London	ANG	VWC	VWC	MA
390039	69139+69439+69539+69639+68839+69739+69839+69939+69239	Virgin Quest	ANG	VWC	VWC	MA
390040	69140+69440+69540+69640+68840+69740+69840+69940+69240	Virgin Pathfinder	ANG	VWC	VWC	MA

Set	Formation					Name
390141	69141+69441+69541+65541+69841+68841+69741+69841+69941+69241	MA	VWC	ANG	VWC	*City of Chester*
390042	69142+69442+69542+69642+68842+69742+69842+69942+69242	MA	VWC	ANG	VWC	*City of Bangor / Dinas Bangor*
390043	69143+69443+69543+69643+68843+69743+69843+69943+69243	MA	VWC	ANG	VWC	*Virgin Explorer*
390044	69144+69444+69544+69644+68844+69744+69844+69944+69244	MA	VWC	ANG	VWC	*Virgin Lionheart*
390045	69145+69445+69545+69645+68845+69745+69845+69945+69245	MA	VWC	ANG	VWC	*101 Squadron*
390046	69146+69446+69546+69646+68846+69746+69846+69946+69246	MA	VWC	ANG	VWC	*Virgin Soldiers*
390047	69147+69447+69547+69647+68847+69747+69847+69947+69247	MA	VWC	ANG	VWC	*Clic Sargent*
390148	69148+69448+69548+68648+69848+68848+69748+69848+69948+69248	MA	VWC	ANG	VWC	*Virgin Harrier*
390149	69149+69449+69549+69649+68849+69749+69849+69949+69249	MA	VWC	ANG	VWC	*Virgin Express*
390050	69150+69450+69550+69650+68850+69750+69850+69950+69250	MA	VWC	ANG	VWC	*Virgin Invader*
390151	69151+69451+69551+65351+69851+68851+69751+69851+69951+69251	MA	VWC	ANG	VWC	*Virgin Ambassador*
390152	69152+69452+69552+65352+69852+68852+69752+69852+69952+69252	MA	VWC	ANG	VWC	*Alison Waters*
390153	69153+69453+69553+65353+69853+68853+69753+69853+69953+69253	MA	VWC	ANG	VWC	*Mission Accomplished*
390154	69154+69454+69554+65354+69854+68854+69754+69854+69954+69254	MA	VWC	ANG	VWC	*Matthew Flinders*
390155	69155+69455+69555+69655+68855+69755+69855+69955+69255	MA	VWC	ANG	VWC	*X-Men Days of Future Past*
390156	69156+69456+69556+69656+68856+69756+69856+69956+69256	MA	VWC	ANG	VWC	*Stockport 170*
390157	69157+69457+69557+69657+68857+69757+69857+69957+69257	MA	VWC	ANG	VWC	*Chad Varah*

■ Pendolino set No. 390033 *City of Glasgow*, which was involved in the Grayrigg derailment on 23 February 2007, was withdrawn from service. After spending a period stored at Long Marston, some of the vehicles have now seen further use.

Cars 69133 and 69833 have been rebuilt as static training vehicles for use at the Virgin Trains training school in Crewe.

Nos. 69933 and 69733 are in use at the fire training school in Moreton-in-Marsh.

Vehicle No. 69233 has been broken up.

§ 'Fly the Flag' branding.

Above: *Eleven-car Class 390/1 No. 390135 City of Lancaster, showing the standard Virgin Pendolino livery, passes South Kenton travelling north over the slow lines on 21 May 2014. These sets are usually operated with the standard class accommodation at the north end of formations.* CJM

Colas Rail Freight

Address: ✉ Dacre House, 19 Dacre Street, London, SW1H 0DJ

📠 enquiries@colasrail.co.uk, ✆ 0207 593 5353, ① www.colasrail.co.uk

Chairman: Charles-Albert Giral

Depots: Washwood Heath (AW), Rugby (RU), Eastleigh Works (ZG)

Class 37

Vehicle Length: 61ft 6in (18.74m)
Height: 13ft 0¼in (3.96m)
Width: 8ft 11⅝in (2.73m)
Class 37/4 - Electric Train Heat fitted

Engine: English Electric 12CSVT
Horsepower: 1,750hp (1,304kW)
Electrical Equipment: English Electric

Number	Depot	Pool	Livery	Owner	Operator	Name
37116(S)	RU	COTS	-	COL	COL	
37175	RU	COTS	COL	COL	COL	
37219	RU	COTS	COL	COL	COL	
37421 (37267)(S)	RU	COTS	COL	COL	COL	

Left: *Colas Rail Freight currently has four Class 37s on its books, two of which are operational and two are under restoration to operational condition. For the leaf fall RHTT season in late 2014 the two operational locos were used on this duty based in the Birmingham area. Class 37/0 No. 37219 is illustrated from its No. 2 end.* **Tom Dumelow**

Class 47/7

Vehicle Length: 63ft 6in (19.35m)
Height: 12ft 10⅜in (3.91m)
Width: 9ft 2in (2.79m)
Electric Train Heat fitted

Engine: Sulzer 12LDA28C
Horsepower: 2,580hp (1,922kW)
Electrical Equipment: Brush

Number	Depot	Pool	Livery	Owner	Operator	Name
47727 (47569)	ZE	COLO	COL	COL	COL	Rebecca
47739 (47594)	ZE	COLO	COL	COL	COL	Robin of Templecombe 1938-2013
47749 (47625)	ZE	COLO	COL	COL	COL	Demelza

Three ETS-fitted Class 47/7s are operated by Colas and are deployed on both freight and multiple unit transfer moves where their ETS is required to operate with translator vehicles. No. 47727 is shown. **Mark V. Pike**

Class 56

			Vehicle Length: 63ft 6in (19.35m)		Engine: Ruston Paxman 16RK3CT	
			Height: 13ft 0in (3.96m)		Horsepower: 3,250hp (2,420kW)	
			Width: 9ft 2in (2.79m)		Electrical Equipment: Brush	

Number	Depot	Pool	Livery	Owner	Operator	Notes
56049(S)	RU	COLS	?	COL	-	Awaiting overhaul
56051(S)	RU	COLS	?	COL	-	Awaiting overhaul
56078	RU	COFS	COL	COL	COL	
56087	RU	COFS	COL	COL	COL	
56090(S)	RU	COLS	?	COL	-	Awaiting overhaul
56094	RU	COFS	COL	COL	COL	
56096	RU	COFS	?	COL	-	Awaiting overhaul
56105	RU	COFS	COL	COL	COL	
56113	RU	COFS	COL	COL	COL	
56302 (56124)	RU	COFS	COL	COL	COL	

Right: *At the start of 2015, six Class 56 locomotives were in operation, powering the heavier long-distance freight flows worked by the company; this frequently involved log traffic transporting long heavy trains of felled timber to the Kronospan plant at Chirk in North Wales. Painted in full Colas Rail Freight livery, No. 56078 is seen from its cooler group end in the bay at Newton Abbot while engaged in a Teigngrace to Chirk duty.* **CJM**

Class 60

			Vehicle Length: 70ft 0½in (21.34m)		Engine: Mirrlees MB275T	
			Height: 12ft 10⅝in (3.92m)		Horsepower: 3,100hp (2,240kW)	
			Width: 8ft 8in (2.64m)		Electrical Equipment: Brush	

Number	Depot	Pool	Livery	Owner	Operator	Name
60002	RU	COLS	COL	COL	COL	
60021	RU	COLO	COL	COL	COL	
60026	RU	COLS		COL	-	
60047	RU	COLS		COL	-	
60056	RU	COLS		COL	-	
60076	RU	COLO	COL	COL	COL	
60085	RU	COLS	COL	COL	COL	
60087	RU	COLO	COL	COL	COL	CLIC Sargent
60095	RU	COLS		COL	-	
60096	RU	COLS		COL	-	

Right: *In a surprising move in 2014, DB Schenker sold 10 Class 60s to Colas Rail Freight and then carried out a full 'Super 60' refurbishment programme on the locos at Toton depot. By the start of 2015 four locos were in use. These locos are likely to power the heavier train consists as well as infrastructure flows. The first Colas '60' to enter traffic, No. 60087, is illustrated passing Wimbledon piloting a 'top and tailed' Class 70-powered engineers train.* **Mark V. Pike**

Colas Rail Freight

Class 66/8

Vehicle Length: 70ft 0½in (21.34m)
Height: 12ft 10in (3.91m)
Width: 8ft 8¼in (2.65m)

Engine: EMD 12N-710G3B-EC
Horsepower: 3,300hp (2,462kW)
Electrical Equipment: EMD

Number		Depot	Pool	Livery	Owner	Operator	Name
66846	(66573)	RU	COLO	COL	COL	COL	
66847	(66574)	RU	COLO	COL	COL	COL	
66848	(66575)	RU	COLO	COL	COL	COL	
66849	(66576)	RU	COLO	COL	COL	COL	*Wylam Dilly*
66850	(66577)	RU	COLO	COL	COL	COL	*David Maidment OBE*
							www.railwaychildren.org.uk

Above: *Five former Freightliner Class 66s are operated by Colas Rail Freight, classified as 66/8 and officially allocated to Rugby. These locos are frequently used on Colas coal trains. No. 66848, the original No. 66575, is shown.* **CJM**

Class 70 - PH37ACmi

Vehicle Length: 71ft 2½in (21.71m)
Height: 12ft 10in (3.91m)
Width: 8ft 8in (2.64m)

Engine: GE V16-cylinder PowerHaul 616
Horsepower: 3,700hp (2,750kW)
Electrical Equipment: General Electric

Number		Depot	Pool	Livery	Owner	Operator	Notes
70801	(70099)	RU	COLO	COL	COL	COL	
70802		RU	COLO	COL	COL	COL	
70803		RU	COLO	COL	COL	COL	
70804		RU	COLO	COL	COL	COL	
70805		RU	COLO	COL	COL	COL	
70806		RU	COLO	COL	COL	COL	
70807		RU	COLO	COL	COL	COL	
70808		RU	COLO	COL	COL	COL	
70809		RU	COLO	COL	COL	COL	
70810		RU	COLO	COL	COL	COL	

70099 constructed as a demonstrator loco at the GE plant in Turkey, tested in Mainland Europe and then the UK, sold to Colas.

Above: *The most modern locos in the Colas Rail Freight portfolio are ten Class 70s, which were introduced in 2014. Loco 70801 was built as a demonstrator in Turkey and then sold to Colas, while nine new locos were built at the GE plant in Erie, Pennsylvania, USA. These locos are almost identical to the Freightliner fleet but have a number of upgrade modifications which are now being retrofitted to the Freightliner fleet. No. 70808 is viewed at Westbury which, together with Eastleigh and Hinksey, are strongholds for seeing the fleet.* **CJM**

Hauled Stock (NPCCS)

Mk1	Height: 12ft 9½in (3.89m)
Vehicle Length: 64ft 6in (19.65m)	Width: 9ft 3in (2.81m)

Barrier Vans

AW51

Number	Depot	Livery	Owner
6376 (ADB975973, 1021)	RU	BLU	PTR
6377 (ADB975975, 1042)	RU	BLU	PTR
6378 (ADB975971, 1054)	RU	BLU	PTR
6379 (ADB975972, 1039)	RU	BLU	PTR

Motorail Vans

96602 (96150)	NV	COL	RU	96604 (96156)	NV	COL	OO	96607 (96215) NV	COL RU
96603 (96155)	NV	COL	OO	96605 (96157)	NV	COL	RU	96608 (96216) NV	COL ZK
				96606 (96213)	NV	COL	RU	96609 (96217) NV	COL ZK

Right: *Eight of the former First Great Western Motorail vans are now operated by Colas Rail Freight, offering a low-cost freight handling operation using station platforms to load semi-containerised goods. The vehicles retain their FGW green and gold livery which is adorned with customer stickers, in the case illustrated that of parcels carrier TNT. Vehicle No. 96608 is illustrated at the Colas base at Rugby.* **Antony Christie**

DB Schenker - EWS

Address (UK):	✉ Lakeside Business Park, Caroline Way, Doncaster, DN4 5PN
	🖶 info@rail.dbschenker.co.uk
	✆ 0870 140 5000 ⓘ www.rail.dbschenker.co.uk
Chief Executive:	Geoff Spencer

Class 08

Vehicle Length: 29ft 3in (8.91m)
Height: 12ft 8⅝in (3.87m)
Width: 8ft 6in (2.59m)
Engine: English Electric 6K
Horsepower: 400hp (298kW)
Electrical Equipment: English Electric

Number	Depot	Pool	Livery	Owner	Operator
08480(S)*	TO	WNYX	EWS	DBS	-
08495¤(S)	EH	WSSK	EWS	DBS	-
08499	WQ	WSXX	BLU	DBS	PUL
08500(S)	WQ	WNYX	EWS	DBS	-
08567(S)	TO	WNYX	EWS	DBS	-
08578¤(S)	TO	WNXX	EWS	DBS	-
08580(S)	BS	WNXX	EWS	DBS	-
08593(S)	CE	WNXX	EWS	DBS	-
08605¤(S)	TO	WQAA	EWS	DBS	-
08623(S)	TO	WSSC	DBS	DBS	DBS
08630(S)	TO	WNXX	EWS	DBS	-
08632(S)	TO	WSRC	EWS	DBS	DBS
08653(S)	TO	WNXX	EWS	DBS	-
08676(S)	TO	WQAA	EWS	DBS	
08701¤(S)	TO	WNXX	PCL	DBS	-
08706¤(S)	TO	WNYX	EWS	DBS	-
08709(S)	BS	WNXX	EWS	DBS	-
08711(S)	TE	WNXX	PCL	DBS	-
08714(S)	CE	WQAA	DBS	DBS	-
08735¤(S)	EH	WNYX	EWS	DBS	-
08737(S)	TO	WSSI	EWS	DBS	-
08738(S)	TO	WNTS	ECR	DBS	-
08757¤(S)	TO	WNYX	RES	DBS	-
08784¤(S)	TO	WNTS	EWS	DBS	-
08804¤(S)	TO	WNYX	EWS	DBS	-
08824(S)	WQ	WQAA	BLK	DBS	-
08865(S)	CE	WSSK	EWS	DBS	-
08877(S)	WQ	WSXX	BRD	DBS	-
08886(S)	BS	WNXX	EWS	DBS	-
08922(S)	TO	WNTS	BRD	DBS	-
08939(S)	TO	WNTS	ECR	DBS	-
08993+	TO	WNTS	EWS	DBS	Axiom
08994+(S)	DR	WNTS	EWS	DBS	-
08995+(S)	TO	WSSK	EWS	DBS	-

Names applied
08495 *Noel Kirton OBE*
08630 *Bob Brown*
08701 *Type 100*
08799 *Andy Bower / Fred*

+ Named - Toton No. 1, 08993, was previously No. 08592, 08994 was previously No. 08562, 08995 was previously No. 08687.
¤ Remote control fitted.

The vast majority of DB Schenker 350hp 0-6-0 diesel-electric shunting locos were taken out of service in late 2014, with shunting and train marshalling being undertaken by train locos. In this view No. 08907, painted in full DB Schenker red livery, is seen at Bescot. **Antony Christie**

Class 09/0

Vehicle Length: 29ft 3in (8.91m)
Height: 12ft 8⅝in (3.87m)
Width: 8ft 6in (2.59m)

Engine: English Electric 6K
Horsepower: 400hp (298kW)
Electrical Equipment: English Electric

Number	Depot	Pool	Livery	Owner	Operator
09006(S)	TO	WNXX	EWS	DBS	-

Class 09/1

Vehicle Length: 29ft 3in (8.91m)
Height: 12ft 8⅝in (3.87m)
Width: 8ft 6in (2.59m)

Engine: English Electric 6K
Horsepower: 400hp (298kW)
Electrical Equipment: English Electric

Number		Depot	Pool	Livery	Owner	Operator
09106	(08759)	TO	WSSC	DBS	DBS	DBS

Class 09/2

Vehicle Length: 29ft 3in (8.91m)
Height: 12ft 8⅝in (3.87m)
Width: 8ft 6in (2.59m)

Engine: English Electric 6K
Horsepower: 400hp (298kW)
Electrical Equipment: English Electric

Number		Depot	Pool	Livery	Owner	Operator
09201(S)	(08421)	KY	WQAA	BRD	DBS	-

Class 58

Vehicle Length: 62ft 9½in (19.13m)
Height: 12ft 10in (3.91m)
Width: 9ft 1in (2.72m)

Engine: Ruston Paxman 12RK3ACT
Horsepower: 3,300hp (2,460kW)
Electrical Equipment: Brush

Number	Hire No.	Depot	Pool	Livery	Owner	Location	Operator	Name
58001	-		WNTS	ETF	DBS	France	ETF	
58004§	-		WNTS	TSO	DBS	France	TSO	
58005	-		WNTS	ETF	DBS	France	ETF	
58006§	-		WNTS	ETF	DBS	France	ETF	
58007	-		WNTS	TSO	DBS	France	TSO	
58008(S)	EH		WNTS	MLF	DBS	UK	-	
58009	-		WNTS	TSO	DBS	France	TSO	
58010	-		WNTS	FER	DBS	France	TSO	
58011§	-		WNTS	TSO	DBS	France	TSO	
58012(S)	TO		WNTS	MLG	DBS	UK	-	
58013	-		WNTS	ETF	DBS	France	ETF	
58015	L54	CON/SS	-	CON	DBS/T	Spain	TRN	
58017(S)	EH		WNTS	MLG	DBS	UK	-	
58018	EH		WNTS	TSO	DBS	France	TSO	
58020	L43	CON/SS	-	CON	DBS/T	Spain	TRN	
58021	-		WNTS	TSO	DBS	France	TSO	
58022(S)	CD		WNTS	MLG	DBS	UK	-	
58023(S)	TO		WNTS	MLF	DBS	UK	-	
58024	L42	CON/SS	-	CON	DBS/T	Spain	TRN	
58025	L41	CON/SS	-	CON	DBS	Spain	CON	
58026§	-		WNTS	TSO	DBS	France	TSO	
58027	L52	CON/SS	-	CON	DBS	Spain	CON	
58029	L44	CON/SS	-	CON	DBS/T	Spain	TRN	
58030	L46	CON/SS	-	CON	DBS/T	Spain	TRN	
58031	L45	CON/SS	-	CON	DBS/T	Spain	TRN	Cabellero Ferroviaro
58032	-		WNTS	ETF	DBS	France	ETF	
58033	-		WNTS	TSO	DBS	France	TSO	
58034	-		WNTS	TSO	DBS	France	TSO	
58035	-		WNTS	TSO	DBS	France	TSO	
58036	-		WNTS	ETF	DBS	France	ETF	
58038	58-038		WNTS	ETF	DBS	France	ETF	
58039	58-039		WNTS	ETF	DBS	France	ETF	
58040§	-		WNTS	TSO	DBS	France	TSO	
58041	L36	CON/SS	-	CON	DBS/T	Spain	TRN	
58042	-		WNTS	TSO	DBS	France	TSO	
58043	L37	CON/SS	-	CON	DBS/T	Spain	TRN	
58044	58-044	-	WZFF	ETF	DBS	France	ETF	
58046	-		WNTS	TSO	DBS	France	TSO	
58047	L51	CON/SS	-	CON	DBS/T	Spain	TRN	
58048(S)	CE		WNTS	EWS	DBS	UK	-	
50049§	-		WNTS	TSO	DBS	France	ETF	

DB Schenker

58050	L53	CON/SS	-	CON	DBS	Spain	CON	

§ Stored at Alizay (Rouen)

Class 59/2

Vehicle Length: 70ft 0½in (21.34m)
Height: 12ft 10in (3.91m)
Width: 8ft 8¼in (2.65m)
Engine: EMD 16-645 E3C
Horsepower: 3,000hp (2,462kW)
Electrical Equipment: EMD

Number	Depot	Pool	Livery	Owner	Operator	Name
59201	TO	WDAM	DBS	DBS	DBS	
59202	TO	WDAM	DBS	DBS	DBS	*Alan Meddows Taylor MD, Mendip Rail Limited*
59203	TO	WDAM	DBS	DBS	DBS	
59204	TO	WDAM	DBS	DBS	DBS	
59205	TO	WDAM	DBS	DBS	DBS	
59206	TO	WDAM	DBS	DBS	DBS	*John F. Yeoman Rail Pioneer*

Above: *DB Schenker operates a fleet of six Class 59/2 locos, which were previously operated by National Power. The six locos, all sporting DBS red and grey livery and operated from Westbury, alongside the Mendip Rail Class 59/0 and 59/1 locos, usually receive maintenance at either Merehead or Whatley depots. No. 59205 is illustrated at Acton.* **Antony Christie**

Class 60

Vehicle Length: 70ft 0½in (21.34m)
Height: 12ft 10⅝in (3.92m)
Width: 8ft 8in (2.64m)
Engine: Mirrlees MB275T
Horsepower: 3,100hp (2,240kW)
Electrical Equipment: Brush

Number	Depot	Pool	Livery	Owner	Operator	Name
60001‡	TO	WCAT	DBS	DBS	DBS	
60003(S)	TO	WNWX	EWS	DBS	-	*Freight Transport Association*
60004(S)	TO	WNTS	EWS	DBS	-	
60005(S)	TO	WNTS	EWS	DBS	-	
60007‡	TO	WFMU	DBS	DBS	-	*The Spirit of Tom Kendell*
60009(S)	TO	WNTS	EWS	DBS	-	
60010‡	TO	WCBT	DBS	DBS	DBS	
60011	TO	WCAT	DBS	DBS	DBS	
60012(S)	TO	WNWX	EWS	DBS	-	
60015‡	TO	WCBT	DBS	DBS	DBS	
60017‡	TO	WCBT	DBS	DBS	DBS	
60018(S)	TO	WNTS	EWS	DBS	-	
60019‡	TO	WCAT	DBS	DBS	DBS	*Port of Grimsby & Immingham*
60020‡	TO	WCBT	DBS	DBS	DBS	
60022(S)	TO	WNTS	EWS	DBS	-	
60024‡	TO	WCAT	DBS	DBS	DBS	*Clitheroe Castle*
60025(S)	TO	WNTS	EWS	DBS	-	
60027(S)	TO	WNTS	EWS	DBS	-	
60030(S)	TO	WNTS	EWS	DBS	-	
60032(S)	TO	WNWX	EWS	DBS	-	
60034(S)	TO	WNTS	RFE	DBS	-	*Carnedd Llewelyn*

Freight Operating Companies - DB Schenker

60035(S)	TO	WQBA	EWS	DBS	-
60036(S)	TO	WNTS	EWS	DBS	-	GEFCO
60037(S)	TO	WNWX	EWS	DBS	-
60039‡	TO	WCAT	DBS	DBS	DBS
60040‡	TO	WCAT	DBS	DBS	DBS	The Territorial Army Centenary
60043(S)	TO	WNWX	EWS	DBS	-
60044‡	TO	WCAT	DBS	DBS	-
60045(S)	TO	WCAT	EWS	DBS	-	The Permanent Way Institution
60049	TO	WCAT	EWS	DBS	DBS
60051(S)	TO	WNTS	EWS	DBS	-
60052(S)	TO	WNTS	EWS	DBS	-	Glofa Twr - The last deep mine in Wales - Tower Colliery
60053(S)	TO	WNTS	EWS	DBS	-
60054‡	TO	WCBT	DBS	DBS	DBS
60057(S)	TO	WNWX	RFE	DBS	-	Adam Smith
60059‡	TO	WCBT	DBS	DBS	DBS	Swinden Dalesman
60060(S)	TO	WNWX	RFE	DBS	-
60062‡	TO	WNTS	DBS	DBS	DBS	Stainless Pioneer
60063‡	TO	WCAT	DBS	DBS	DBS
60064(S)	TO	WNWX	RFE	DBS	-	Back Tor
60065	TO	WCAT	EWS	DBS	DBS	Spirit of Jaguar
60066‡	TO	WQAA	ADV	DBS	-
60067(S)	TO	WNWX	RFE	DBS	-
60069(S)	TO	WNWX	EWS	DBS	-	Slioch
60071(S)	TO	WQBA	DBS	DBS	-	Ribblehead Viaduct
60072(S)	TO	WNWX	RFE	DBS	-	Cairn Toul
60073(S)	TO	WNTS	RFE	DBS	-	Cairn Gorm
60074‡	TO	WCAT	DBS	DBS	DBS
60077(S)	TO	WNWX	RFE	DBS	-
60079‡	TO	WCAT	DBS	DBS	DBS
60083(S)	TO	WNTS	EWS	DBS	-
60084(S)	TO	WNTS	RFE	DBS	-	Cross Fell
60086(S)	TO	WNWX	RFE	DBS	-
60088(S)	TO	WNWX	MLG	DBS	-
60090(S)	TO	WNTS	RFE	DBS	-	Quinag
60091‡	TO	WCBT	DBS	DBS	DBS	Barry Needham
60092‡	TO	WCBT	DBS	DBS	DBS
60093(S)	TO	WNTS	EWS	DBS	-
60094(S)	CD	WNTS	EWS	DBS	-	Rugby Flyer
60097(S)	TO	WNTS	EWS	DBS	-
60099	TO	WCAT	TAT	DBS	DBS
60100‡	TO	WCAT	DBS	DBS	DBS
60500(S)*	TO	WNTS	EWS	DBS	-

* Previously numbered 60016. ‡ Refurbished 'Super 60'. ADV = Drax biomass livery.

Below: *At the start of 2015, 25 Class 60s were operational with DB S, of which 21 were refurbished or 'Super 60s'. The refurbished locos were generally in full DB S red and grey livery while the operational non-refurbished locos were in a mix of older colours. 'Super 60' No. 60010 is seen passing Selby with an aggregate train.* **CJM**

DB Schenker

Class 66

Vehicle Length: 70ft 0½in (21.34m)
Height: 12ft 10in (3.91m)
Width: 8ft 8¼in (2.65m)

Engine: EMD 12N-710G3B-EC
Horsepower: 3,300hp (2,462kW)
Electrical Equipment: EMD

Freight Operating Companies - DB Schenker

Number	Depot	Pool	Livery	Owner	Operator
66001‡	TO	WBTT	DBS	DBS	DBS
66002‡	TO	WBAT	EWS	DBS	DBS
66003	TO	WBAT	EWS	DBS	DBS
66004	TO	WBAT	EWS	DBS	DBS
66005	TO	WBSN	EWS	DBS	DBS
66006	TO	WBRT	EWS	DBS	DBS
66007	TO	WBRT	EWS	DBS	DBS
66008	TO	WBAT	EWS	DBS	DBS
66009	TO	WBAT	EWS	DBS	DBS
66010 ●	AZ	WBEN	EWS	DBS	DBS
66011	TO	WBAT	EWS	DBS	DBS
66012	TO	WBAT	EWS	DBS	DBS
66013 ●	TO	WBAT	EWS	DBS	DBS
66014	TO	WBAT	EWS	DBS	DBS
66015	TO	WBRT	EWS	DBS	DBS
66016	TO	WBAT	EWS	DBS	DBS
66017	TO	WBTT	EWS	DBS	DBS
66018	TO	WBAT	EWS	DBS	DBS
66019	TO	WBTT	EWS	DBS	DBS
66020	TO	WBAT	EWS	DBS	DBS
66021	TO	WBAT	EWS	DBS	DBS
66022 ●	AZ	WBEN	EWS	DBS	DBS
66023	TO	WBAT	EWS	DBS	DBS
66024	TO	WBAT	EWS	DBS	DBS
66025	TO	WBAT	EWS	DBS	DBS
66026 ●	TO	WBEN	EWS	DBS	ECR
66027	TO	WBAT	EWS	DBS	DBS
66028 ●	AZ	WBEN	EWS	DBS	ECR
66029 ●	AZ	WBEN	EWS	DBS	DBS
66030	TO	WBAT	EWS	DBS	DBS
66031 ●	AZ	WBAT	EWS	DBS	DBS
66032 ●	AZ	WBES	EWS	DBS	ECR
66033 ●	AZ	WBEN	EWS	DBS	DBS
66034	TO	WBAT	EWS	DBS	DBS
66035	TO	WBAT	EWS	DBS	DBS
66036 ●	AZ	WBEN	EWS	DBS	ECR
66037	TO	WBAT	EWS	DBS	DBS
66038 ●	AZ	WBEN	EWS	DBS	ECR
66039	TO	WBAT	EWS	DBS	DBS
66040	TO	WBAT	EWS	DBS	DBS
66041	TO	WBAT	EWS	DBS	DBS
66042 ●	AZ	WFMS	EWS	DBS	ECR
66043	TO	WBAT	EWS	DBS	DBS
66044	TO	WBAT	EWS	DBS	DBS
66045 ●	AZ	WBEN	EWS	DBS	ECR
66046	TO	WBRT	EWS	DBS	DBS
66047	TO	WBRT	EWS	DBS	DBS
66048(S)	TO	WNTS	STO	DBS	-
66049 ●	AZ	WBEN	EWS	DBS	ECR
66050	TO	WBAT	EWS	DBS	DBS
66051	TO	WBAT	EWS	DBS	DBS
66052 ●	AZ	WFMS	EWS	DBS	ECR
66053	TO	WBRT	EWS	DBS	DBS
66054	TO	WBAT	EWS	DBS	DBS
66055	TO	WBLT	EWS	DBS	DBS
66056	TO	WBLT	EWS	DBS	DBS
66057	TO	WBLT	EWS	DBS	DBS
66058	TO	WBLT	EWS	DBS	DBS
66059	TO	WBLT	EWS	DBS	DBS
66060	TO	WBAT	EWS	DBS	DBS
66061	TO	WBAT	EWS	DBS	DBS
66062 ●	AZ	WBEN	EWS	DBS	DBS
66063	TO	WBAT	EWS	DBS	DBS
66064 ●	AZ	WBEN	EWS	DBS	DBS
66065	TO	WBAT	EWS	DBS	DBS
66066	TO	WBAT	EWS	DBS	DBS
66067	TO	WBAT	EWS	DBS	DBS
66068	TO	WBAT	EWS	DBS	DBS
66069	TO	WBAT	EWS	DBS	DBS
66070	TO	WBAT	EWS	DBS	DBS
66071 ●	AZ	WBEN	EWS	DBS	DBS
66072 ●	AZ	WBEN	EWS	DBS	DBS
66073 ●	AZ	WBEN	EWS	DBS	ECR
66074	TO	WBAT	EWS	DBS	DBS
66075	TO	WBAT	EWS	DBS	DBS
66076	TO	WBAT	EWS	DBS	DBS
66077	TO	WBAT	EWS	DBS	DBS
66078	TO	WBAT	EWS	DBS	DBS
66079	TO	WBAT	EWS	DBS	DBS
66080	TO	WBAT	EWS	DBS	DBS
66081	TO	WBRT	EWS	DBS	DBS
66082	TO	WBAT	EWS	DBS	DBS
66083	TO	WBAT	EWS	DBS	DBS
66084	TO	WBAT	EWS	DBS	DBS
66085	TO	WBAT	EWS	DBS	DBS
66086	TO	WBAT	EWS	DBS	DBS
66087	TO	WBRT	EWS	DBS	DBS
66088	TO	WBAT	EWS	DBS	DBS
66089	TO	WBAT	EWS	DBS	DBS
66090	TO	WBAT	EWS	DBS	DBS
66091	TO	WBAT	EWS	DBS	DBS
66092	TO	WBAT	EWS	DBS	DBS
66093	TO	WBAT	EWS	DBS	DBS
66094	TO	WBAT	EWS	DBS	DBS
66095	TO	WBAT	EWS	DBS	DBS
66096	TO	WBAT	EWS	DBS	DBS
66097	TO	WBAT	DBS	DBS	DBS
66098	TO	WBAT	EWS	DBS	DBS
66099	TO	WBBT	EWS	DBS	DBS
66100	TO	WBBT	EWS	DBS	DBS
66101	TO	WBBT	DBS	DBS	DBS
66102	TO	WBBT	EWS	DBS	DBS
66103	TO	WBBT	EWS	DBS	DBS
66104	TO	WBBT	EWS	DBS	DBS
66105	TO	WBBT	EWS	DBS	DBS
66106	TO	WBBT	EWS	DBS	DBS
66107	TO	WBBT	EWS	DBS	DBS
66108	TO	WBBT	EWS	DBS	DBS
66109	TO	WBBT	EWS	DBS	DBS
66110	TO	WBRT	EWS	DBS	DBS
66111	TO	WBBT	EWS	DBS	DBS
66112	TO	WBBT	EWS	DBS	DBS
66113	TO	WBBT	EWS	DBS	DBS
66114	TO	WBBT	DBS	DBS	DBS
66115	TO	WBAT	EWS	DBS	DBS
66116	TO	WBAT	EWS	DBS	DBS
66117	TO	WBAT	EWS	DBS	DBS
66118	TO	WBAT	DBS	DBS	DBS
66119	TO	WBAT	EWS	DBS	DBS
66120	TO	WBAT	EWS	DBS	DBS
66121	TO	WBAT	EWS	DBS	DBS
66122	TO	WBES	EWS	DBS	DBS
66123 ●	AZ	WBES	EWS	DBS	DBS

66124	TO	WBAT	EWS	DBS	DBS
66125	TO	WBAT	EWS	DBS	DBS
66126	TO	WBAT	EWS	DBS	DBS
66127	TO	WBAT	EWS	DBS	DBS
66128	TO	WBAT	EWS	DBS	DBS
66129	TO	WBAT	EWS	DBS	DBS
66130	TO	WBAT	EWS	DBS	DBS
66131	TO	WBAT	EWS	DBS	DBS
66132	TO	WBAT	EWS	DBS	DBS
66133	TO	WBAT	EWS	DBS	DBS
66134	TO	WBAT	EWS	DBS	DBS
66135	TO	WBAT	EWS	DBS	DBS
66136	TO	WBAT	EWS	DBS	DBS
66137	TO	WBAT	EWS	DBS	DBS
66138	TO	WBAT	EWS	DBS	DBS
66139	TO	WBAT	EWS	DBS	DBS
66140	TO	WBRT	EWS	DBS	DBS
66141	TO	WQAA	EWS	DBS	DBS
66142	TO	WBAK	EWS	DBS	DBS
66143	TO	WBRT	EWS	DBS	DBS
66144	TO	WBAT	EWS	DBS	DBS
66145	TO	WBAT	EWS	DBS	DBS
66146 P	PN	WBEP	EWS	DBS	DBS
66147	TO	WBAT	EWS	DBS	DBS
66148	TO	WBAT	EWS	DBS	DBS
66149	TO	WBAT	EWS	DBS	DBS
66150	TO	WBAT	EWS	DBS	DBS
66151	TO	WBAT	EWS	DBS	DBS
66152	TO	WBAT	DBS	DBS	DBS
66153 P	PN	WBEP	EWS	DBS	DBS
66154	TO	WBAT	EWS	DBS	DBS
66155	TO	WBAT	EWS	DBS	DBS
66156	TO	WBAT	EWS	DBS	DBS
66157 P	PN	WBEP	EWS	DBS	DBS
66158	TO	WBAT	EWS	DBS	DBS
66159 P	PN	WBEP	EWS	DBS	DBS
66160	TO	WBAT	EWS	DBS	DBS
66161	TO	WBAK	EWS	DBS	DBS
66162	TO	WBAT	EWS	DBS	DBS
66163 P	PN	WBEP	DBS	DBS	DBS
66164	TO	WBRT	EWS	DBS	DBS
66165	TO	WBAT	EWS	DBS	DBS
66166 P	PN	WBEP	EWS	DBS	DBS
66167	TO	WBAT	EWS	DBS	DBS
66168	TO	WBAT	EWS	DBS	DBS
66169	TO	WBAT	EWS	DBS	DBS
66170	TO	WBAT	EWS	DBS	DBS
66171	TO	WBAT	EWS	DBS	DBS
66172	TO	WBAT	EWS	DBS	DBS
66173 P	PN	WBEP	EWS	DBS	DBS
66174	TO	WBAT	EWS	DBS	DBS
66175	TO	WBAT	EWS	DBS	DBS
66176	TO	WBAT	EWS	DBS	DBS
66177	TO	WBAT	EWS	DBS	DBS
66178 P	PN	WBEP	EWS	DBS	DBS
66179 ●	TO	WBAK	EWS	DBS	ECR
66180 P	PN	WBEP	EWS	DBS	DBS
66181	TO	WBAT	EWS	DBS	DBS
66182	TO	WBAT	EWS	DBS	DBS
66183	TO	WBRT	EWS	DBS	DBS
66184	TO	WQAA	EWS	DBS	DBS
66185	TO	WBAT	DBS	DBS	DBS
66186	TO	WBAT	EWS	DBS	DBS
66187	TO	WBAT	EWS	DBS	DBS
66188	TO	WBAT	EWS	DBS	DBS
66189 P	PN	WBEP	EWS	DBS	DBS
66190 ●	AZ	WBEN	EWS	DBS	ECR
66191 ●	AZ	WBEN	EWS	DBS	DBS
66192	TO	WBAT	EWS	DBS	DBS
66193	TO	WBAT	EWS	DBS	DBS
66194	TO	WBRT	EWS	DBS	DBS
66195 ●	TO	WBEN	EWS	DBS	ECR
66196 P	PN	WBEP	EWS	DBS	DBS
66197	TO	WBAT	EWS	DBS	DBS
66198	TO	WBRT	EWS	DBS	DBS
66199	TO	WBRT	EWS	DBS	DBS
66200	TO	WBAT	EWS	DBS	DBS
66201	TO	WBAT	EWS	DBS	DBS
66202 ●	AZ	WBEN	EWS	DBS	ECR
66203 ●	AZ	WBEN	EWS	DBS	ECR
66204	TO	WBAT	EWS	DBS	DBS
66205 ●	AZ	WBEN	EWS	DBS	ECR
66206	TO	WBAT	EWS	DBS	DBS
66207	TO	WBAT	EWS	DBS	DBS
66208 ●	AZ	WBEN	EWS	DBS	ECR
66209 ●	AZ	WBEN	EWS	DBS	ECR
66210 ●	AZ	WBEN	EWS	DBS	ECR
66211 ●	TO	WBEN	EWS	DBS	ECR
66212 ●	AZ	WBEN	EWS	DBS	ECR
66213	TO	WBAT	EWS	DBS	DBS
66214 ●	AZ	WBEN	EWS	DBS	ECR
66215 ●	AZ	WBEN	EWS	DBS	ECR
66216 ●	AZ	WBEN	EWS	DBS	ECR
66217 ●	AZ	WBEN	EWS	DBS	ECR
66218 ●	AZ	WGEA	EWS	DBS	ECR
66219 ●	AZ	WGEA	EWS	DBS	ECR
66220 P	TO	WBEP	DBS	DBS	DBS
66221	TO	WBAT	EWS	DBS	DBS
66222 ●	AZ	WBEN	EWS	DBS	ECR
66223 ●	AZ	WBEN	EWS	DBS	DBS
66224 ●	AZ	WBEN	EWS	DBS	ECR
66225 ●	AZ	WBEN	EWS	DBS	ECR
66226 ●	AZ	WBEN	EWS	DBS	ECR
66227 P	PN	WBEP	EWS	DBS	DBS
66228 ●	AZ	WBEN	EWS	DBS	ECR
66229 ●	AZ	WBEN	EWS	DBS	ECR
66230	TO	WBAT	EWS	DBS	DBS
66231 ●	AZ	WBEN	EWS	DBS	ECR
66232	TO	WBAT	EWS	DBS	DBS
66233 ●	AZ	WBEN	EWS	DBS	ECR
66234 ●	AZ	WBEN	EWS	DBS	ECR
66235 ●	AZ	WBEN	EWS	DBS	ECR
66236 ●	AZ	WBEN	EWS	DBS	ECR
66237 P	PN	WBEP	EWS	DBS	DBS
66238	TO	WBAT	EWS	DBS	DBS
66239 ●	AZ	WBEN	EWS	DBS	ECR
66240 ●	AZ	WBEN	EWS	DBS	ECR
66241 ●	AZ	WBEN	EWS	DBS	ECR
66242 ●	AZ	WGEA	EWS	DBS	ECR
66243 ●	TO	WBEN	EWS	DBS	ECR
66244 ●	AZ	WBEN	EWS	DBS	ECR
66245 ●	AZ	WBEN	EWS	DBS	DBS
66246 ●	AZ	WBEN	EWS	DBS	ECR
66247 ●	AZ	WBEN	EWS	DBS	ECR
66248 P	PN	WBEP	DBS	DBS	DBS
66249 ●	AZ	WBES	EWS	DBS	DBS
66250	TO	WBAT	EWS	DBS	DBS

‡ Not fitted with combination couplers

Freight Operating Companies

DB Schenker

Names applied

66002	*Lafarge Quorn*
66048	*James the Engine*
66050	*EWS Energy*
66077	*Benjamin Gimbert GC*
66079	*James Nightall GC*
66152	*Derek Holmes Railway Operator*
66172	*Paul Melleney*
66185	*DP World London Gateway*
66200	*Railway Heritage Committee*
66250	*Robert K. Romak (not standard nameplate)*

● Class 66/0s marked with this symbol are modified and can operate with Euro Cargo Rail in France. Usually around 60 locos are in France at one time, but this figure is reduced in the autumn when a number return to the UK for RHTT operations. Locos working in France operate in the pool WBEN.

P Locomotives marked with a 'P' are operated by DB Schenker in Poland. Only locos from the series 66146-250 can be modified for this contract.

Below: *Of the fleet of 250 Class 66/0s operated by DB-S only around 170 operate in the UK, 76 are modified for use in France and Poland, and several are long-term out of use. Most locos still sport the EWS maroon livery, with a gradual application of DB stickers starting to appear in 2014. A handful are painted in DB-S red and grey. No. 66007 in EWS maroon is illustrated at Doncaster.* **CJM**

Class 67

Vehicle Length: 64ft 7in (19.68m)
Height: 12ft 9in (3.88m)
Width: 8ft 9in (2.66m)

Engine: EMD 12N-710G3B-EC
Horsepower: 2,980hp (2,223kW)
Electrical Equipment: EMD

Number	Depot	Pool	Livery	Owner	Operator	Name
67001	CE	WAWC	ATW	DBS	DBS/ATW	
67002	CE	WAWC	ATW	DBS	DBS/ATW	
67003	CE	WAAC	ATW	DBS	DBS/ATW	
67004	CE	WABC	EWS	DBS	DBS	
67005	CE	WAAC	ROY	DBS	DBS	*Queen's Messenger*
67006	CE	WAAC	ROY	DBS	DBS	*Royal Sovereign*
67007	CE	WABC	EWS	DBS	DBS	
67008	CE	WACC	EWS	DBS	DBS	
67009	CE	WABC	EWS	DBS	DBS	
67010	CE	WACC	WSR	DBS	DBS	
67011	CE	WABC	EWS	DBS	DBS	
67012	CE	WACC	WSR	DBS	DBS	*A Shropshire Lad*
67013	CE	WAWC	WSR	DBS	DBS	
67014	CE	WACC	WSR	DBS	DBS	*Thomas Telford*
67015	CE	WAAC	WSR	DBS	DBS	*David J. Lloyd*
67016	CE	WAAC	EWS	DBS	DBS	
67017	CE	WACC	EWS	DBS	DBS	*Arrow*
67018	CE	WACC	DBS	DBS	DBS	*Keith Heller*
67019	CE	WAAC	EWS	DBS	DBS	
67020	CE	WAAC	EWS	DBS	DBS	
67021	CE	WAAC	EWS	DBS	DBS	
67022	CE	WAAC	EWS	DBS	DBS	
67023	CE	WACC	EWS	DBS	DBS	
67024	CE	WAAC	EWS	DBS	DBS	
67025	CE	WAAC	EWS	DBS	DBS	*Western Star*
67026	CE	WAAC	ROJ	DBS	DBS	*Diamond Jubilee*
67027	CE	WAAC	DBS	DBS	DBS	
67028	CE	WAAC	EWS	DBS	DBS	
67029	CE	WAAC	EWE	DBS	DBS	*Royal Diamond*
67030	CE	WABC	EWS	DBS	DBS	

Right: *In early 2015, the small fleet of Class 67s was kept busy powering the Scottish portions of the ScotRail sleeper service (to end in March 2015), the Arriva Trains Wales loco-hauled service, powering Chiltern Railways duties (which will end in 2015) and performing 'Thunderbird' duties on the East Coast. In addition the fleet powers charter and Network Rail trains. No. 67028 is illustrated stabled at Doncaster West Yard while performing 'Thunderbird' duties for East Coast.*
CJM

Class 90

	Vehicle Length: 61ft 6in (18.74m)	Power Collection: 25kV ac overhead
	Height: 13ft 0¼in (3.96m)	Horsepower: 7,860hp (5,860kW)
	Width: 9ft 0in (2.74m)	Electrical Equipment: GEC

Number		Depot	Pool	Livery	Owner	Operator	Name/Notes
90017		CE	WQBA	EWS	DBS	-	
90018		CE	WEAC	DBS	DBS	DBS	
90019		CE	WEAC	FGS	DBS	DBS	
90020		CE	WEAC	EWS	DBS	DBS	Collingwood
90021	(90221)	CE	WEAC	FGS	DBS	DBS	
90022(S)	(90222)	CE	WQBA	RFE	DBS	-	Freightconnection
90023(S)	(90223)	CE	WQBA	EWS	DBS	-	
90024	(90224)	CE	WEAC	FGS	DBS	-	
90025(S)	(90225)	CE	WQBA	RFD	DBS	-	
90026		CE	WEAC	EWS	DBS	DBS	
90027(S)	(90227)	CE	WQBA	RFD	DBS	-	Allerton T&RS Depot Quality Approved
90028		CE	WEAC	EWS	DBS	DBS	
90029		CE	WEAC	DBS	DBS	DBS	
90030(S)	(90130)	CE	WQBA	EWS	DBS	-	
90031(S)	(90131)	CE	WQBA	EWS	DBS	-	The Railway Children Partnership - Working for Street Children Worldwide
90032(S)	(90132)	CE	WQBA	EWS	DBS	-	
90033(S)	(90233)	CE	WQBA	RFI	DBS	DBS	
90034	(90134)	CE	WEDC	DRS	DBS	DBS	
90035	(90135)	CE	WEAC	EWS	DBS	DBS	
90036	(90136)	CE	WEAC	DBS	DBS	DBS	Driver Jack Mills
90037(S)	(90137)	CE	WQBA	EWS	DBS	-	Spirit of Dagenham
90038(S)	(90238)	CE	WQBA	RFI	DBS	-	
90039	(90239)	CE	WEAC	EWS	DBS	DBS	
90040(S)	(90140)	CE	WQAA	EWS	DBS	-	The Railway Mission
90050(S)	(90050)	BA	WNTS	FLG	DBS	-	(Stored at Crewe Basford Hall, for scrap

Right: *DB-S has a fleet of 24 Class 90s on its roster, but several are long-term stored at Crewe and some could be made available for sale to an overseas operator. Little booked work exists for the fleet, with some operating the London-Edinburgh/Glasgow legs of the ScotRail sleeper service (a contract which will end in 2015) together with a handful of freight services. Locos sport a variety of liveries, from trainload colours through EWS maroon to DB-S red and grey, with No. 90034 painted in full DRS colours. No. 90018, in full DB-S red and grey livery, is seen at London Euston.* **Antony Christie**

DB Schenker

Class 92

					Vehicle Length: 70ft 1in (21.34m)	Power Collection: 25kV ac overhead / 750V dc third rail
					Height: 13ft 0in (3.95m)	Horsepower: ac - 6,700hp (5,000kW) / dc 5,360hp (4,000kW)
					Width: 8ft 8in (2.66m)	Electrical Equipment: Brush

Number	Depot	Pool	Livery	Owner	Operator	Name
92001■	CE	WGEE	DBS	HBS	*Exported Romania*	Mircea Eliade
92002(S)	CE	WGEE	RFE	DBS	*(for Eastern Europe)*	H G Wells
92003	CE	WFBC	RFE	DBS	DBS	Beethoven
92004(S)	CE	WGEE	RFE	DBS	*(for Eastern Europe)*	Jane Austen
92005	CE	WFBC	RFE	DBS	DBS	Mozart
92007(S)	CE	WQAA	RFE	DBS	-	Schubert
92008(S)	CE	WQAB	RFE	DBS	-	Jules Verne
92009§(S)	CE	WQBA	DBS	DBS	-	Marco Polo
92011	CE	WFAC	RFE	DBS	DBS	Handel
92012■	CE	WGEE	DBS	HBS	*Exported Romania*	Mihai Eminescu
92013(S)	CE	WQBA	RFE	DBS	-	Puccini
92015§	CE	WFBC	DBS	DBS	DBS	
92016§	CE	WFBC	DBS	DBS	DBS	
92017(S)	CE	WQAA	STO	DBS	-	Bart the Engine
92019	CE	WFBC	RFE	DBS	DBS	Wagner
92022(S)	CE	WQAB	RFE	DBS	-	Charles Dickens
92024	CE	WFAC	RFE	DBS	DBS	J S Bach
92025±	-	WGEE	RFE	DBS	*Exported Bulgaria*	Oscar Wilde
92026(S)	CE	WGEE	RFE	DBS	*(for Eastern Europe)*	Britten
92027±	-	WGEE	RFE	DBS	*Exported Bulgaria*	George Eliot
92029	CE	WFCC	RFE	DBS	DBS	Dante
92030(S)	CE	WGEE	RFE	DBS	*(for Eastern Europe)*	Ashford
92031§	CE	WFBC	DBS	DBS	-	
92034±	-	WGEE	RFE	DBS	*Exported Bulgaria*	Kipling
92035(S)	CE	WQBA	RFE	DBS	-	Mendelssohn
92036§	CE	WFDC	RFE	DBS	DBS	Bertolt Brecht
92037	CE	WFAC	RFE	DBS	DBS	Sullivan
92039	CE	WFAC	RFE	DBS	DBS	Johann Strauss
92041	CE	WFBC	RFE	DBS	DBS	Vaughan Williams
92042§	CE	WFBC	DBS	DBS	DBS	

§ Fitted with equipment to allow operation over HS1
±   Exported to Bulgaria
■   Exported to Romania As
     92001 = 91 53 0472 002
     92012 = 91 53 0472 001

Left: *A significant number of Class 92s are still in long-term store as insufficient work exists for the fleet, even though some now power high-speed freight over HS1 between the Channel Tunnel and London. Painted in DB-S red and grey livery, No. 92015 is seen passing Kensington Olympia.* **Tim Easter**

Hauled Stock (Passenger)

Mk1	Height: 12ft 9½in (3.89m)
Vehicle Length: 64ft 6in (19.65m)	Width: 9ft 3in (2.81m)

Mk2	Height: 12ft 9½in (3.89m)
Vehicle Length: 66ft 0in (20.11m)	Width: 9ft 3in (2.81m)

Mk 3	Height: 12ft 9in (3.88m)
Vehicle Length: 75ft 0in (22.86m)	Width: 8ft 11in (2.71m)

AD1F - FO ‡ For sale

Number	Depot	Livery	Owner
3279	MH	MAR	DBR
3292	CE	MAR	DBR
3318	MH	MAR	DBR/FSR
3331	MH	MAR	DBR/FSR
3358	MH	MAR	DBR
3375(S) ‡	EH	MAR	DBR
3388(S)	FY	MAR	DBR

Number	Depot	Livery	Owner
3399(S)	FY	MAR	DBR
3400	MH	MAR	DBR/FSR
3424	MH	MAR	DBR/FSR

AC2B - TSO

Number	Depot	Livery	Owner
5482	TO	BLG	DBR

AC2D - TSO

Number	Depot	Livery	Owner
5631	TO	DBS	DBR
5632	TO	DBS	DBR
5657	TO	DBS	DBR

AC2F - TSO ‡ For sale

Number	Depot	Livery	Owner
5922 ‡	BS	MAR	DBR
5924 ‡	BS	MAR	DBR
5954	TO	DBS	DBR
5959 ‡	BS	MAR	DBR
6036 ‡	BS	MAR	DBR
6110	TO	DBS	DBR
6139(S)	MH	MAR	DBR
6152 ‡	BS	MAR	DBR

AX51 - GEN ‡ For sale

Number	Depot	Livery	Owner
6311(S) (92911) ‡	TO	BLU	DBR

AE2D - BSO

Number	Depot	Livery	Owner
9494	MH	MAR	DBR/FSR

AE2E - BSO

Number	Depot	Livery	Owner
9506	MH	MAR	DBR/FSR

AE2F - BSO

Number	Depot	Livery	Owner
9522	TO	DBS	DBR/FSR
9529(S)	BS	MAR	DBR
9531(S)	BS	MAR	DBR

AJ1G - RFM

Number		Depot	Livery	Owner
10201(S)	(40520)	LM	VIR	DBR
10202	(40504)	LM	BLG	DBR/CRW
10211	(40510)	TO	EWE	DBS
10215	(11032)	LM	BLG	DBR/CRW
10222(S)	(11063)	BY	BLG	DBR
10226(S)	(11015)	LM	VIR	DBR
10233(S)	(10013)	LM	VIR	DBR
10235	(10015)	LM	BLG	DBR/CRW
10237(S)	(10022)	BY	DRU	DBR
10242(S)	(10002)	LM	BLG	DBR
10246	(10114)	CF	BLG	DBR/ATW
10250(S)	(10020)	LM	VIR	DBR
10257(S)	(10007)	BY	BLG	DBR

AU4G - SLEP

Number	Depot	Livery	Owner
10540(S)	LM	FGW	DBR
10546	TO	EWE	DBS
10554(S)	LM	ICS	DBR (scrap)

AS4G - SLE

Number	Depot	Livery	Owner
10681(S)	LM	-	DBR
10682(S)	LM	ICS	DBR (scrap)
10710(S)	LM	CWR	DBR/CRW
10731(S)	LM	ICS	DBR (scrap)

AD1G - FO

Number	Depot	Livery	Owner
11005(S)	LM	VIR	DBR

11019(S)	ZB	DRU	DBR
11028(S)	ZB	VIR	DBR
11029	AL	CWR	DBR/CRW
11030(S)	ZB	DRU	DBR
11031	AL	BLG	DBR/CRW
11033(S)	LM	DRU	DBR
11039	TO	EWE	DBS
11046(S)	ZB	DRU	DBR
11054(S)	ZB	DRU	DBR
11079(S)	LM	BLG	DBR/CRW
11097(S)	LM	BLG	DBR

AB21 - BSK

Number	Depot	Livery	Owner
35290(S)	CP	CAR	DBR

GK2G - TRSB

Number		Depot	Livery	Owner
40402(S)	(40002)	LM	VIR	DBR
40403(S)	(40003)	LM	VIR	DBR
40416(S)	(40016)	LM	VIR	DBR
40419(S)	(40019)	LM	VIR	DBR
40434(S)	(40234)	LM	VIR	DBR

Saloon

Number	Depot	Livery	Owner
45020(S)	TO	MAR	DBR

Hauled Stock (NPCCS)

Mk 3 (DVT)	Height: 12ft 9in (3.88m)
Vehicle Length: 61ft 9in (18.83m)	Width: 8ft 11in (2.71m)

NZAG - DVT

Number	Depot	Livery	Owner
82106(S)	BRUSH	VIR	DBR
82110(S)	LM	VIR	DBR
82113(S)	LM	VIR	DBR
82116(S)	LM	VIR	DBR
82120(S)	LM	VIR	DBR
82122(S)	LM	VIR	DBR
82123(S)	LM	VIR	DBR
82137(S)	LM	VIR	DBR
82138(S)	LM	VIR	DBR
82141(S)	LM	VIR	DBR
82146	TO	DBE	DBS
82148(S)	LM	VIR	DBR
82150(S)	LM	VIR	DBR

Below: *DB-S has one operational Mk3 DVT , No. 82146, which is used at the non-powered end of the DB-S Management train. A number of other DVTs are stored at Long Marston and Brush Traction.* **Antony Christie**

DB Schenker

NOA1 - H-GUV

Number	Depot	Livery	Owner
95727 (95127)	WE	RES	DBS

95761 (95161)	WE	RES	DBS
95763 (95163)	BS	RES	DBS

Euro Cargo Rail A part of DB Schenker

Address: ✉ Immeuble la Palacio, 25-29 Place de la Madeleine, Paris, 75008
🖶 info@eurocargorail.com, ✆ +33 977 400000, ⓘ www.eurocargorail.com

Class 21

Vehicle Length: (21/5) 48ft 2in (14.70m), (21/6) 46ft 3in (14.13m)
Height: (21/5) 13ft 8in (4.16m), (21/6) 13ft 9in (4.19m)
Width: 8ft 8¼in (2.65m)
Engine: (21/5) Caterpillar 3512B DITA of 2,011hp
Engine: (21/6) MTU 8V 4000 R41L of 1,475hp
Hydraulic Equipment: Voith

Number	Depot	Pool	Livery	Owner	Operator
21544 (FB1544)	DM	WLAN	MAR	ANG	ECR
21545 (FB1545)	DM	WLAN	MAR	ANG	ECR
21546 (FB1546)	DM	WLAN	MAR	ANG	ECR

21547 (FB1547)	DM	WLAN	MAR	ANG	ECR
21610 (FB1610)	DM	WLAN	MAR	ANG	ECR
21611 (FB1611)	DM	WLAN	MAR	ANG	ECR

Left: *Euro Cargo Rail, a part of the DB Schenker company, operates a fleet of Class 21 and 77 locomotives. The Class 21s are permitted to pass through the Channel Tunnel as far as Dollands Moor and are thus given UK numbers. The Class 77s have to remain in mainland Europe. Loco No. FB1544 (21544) is seen light loco in the yard at Amberieu, France.* **CJM**

Class 77
(JT42CWRM)

Vehicle Length: 70ft 0½in (21.34m)
Height: 12ft 10in (3.91m)
Width: 8ft 8¼in (2.65m)
Engine: EMD 12N-710G3B-EC
Horsepower: 3,300hp (2,462kW)
Electrical Equipment: EMD

Number	Depot	Livery	Owner	Opt'r		Number	Depot	Livery	Owner	Opt'r		Number	Depot	Livery	Owner	Opt'r
77001	ND	ELR	DBS	ECR		77021	ND	ELR	DBS	ECR		77042‡	ND	ELR	DBS	ECR
77002	ND	ELR	DBS	ECR		77022	ND	ELR	DBS	ECR		77043‡	ND	ELR	DBS	ECR
77003	ND	ELR	DBS	ECR		77023	ND	ELR	DBS	ECR		77044‡	ND	ELR	DBS	ECR
77004	ND	ELR	DBS	ECR		77024	ND	ELR	DBS	ECR		77045	ND	ELR	DBS	ECR
77005	ND	ELR	DBS	ECR		77025	ND	ELR	DBS	ECR		77046‡	ND	ELR	DBS	ECR
77006	ND	ELR	DBS	ECR		77026‡	ND	ELR	DBS	ECR		77047	ND	ELR	DBS	ECR
77007‡	ND	ELR	DBS	ECR		77027	ND	ELR	DBS	ECR		77048	ND	ELR	DBS	ECR
77008	ND	ELR	DBS	ECR		77028	ND	ELR	DBS	ECR		77049‡	ND	ELR	DBS	ECR
77009	ND	ELR	DBS	ECR		77029‡	ND	ELR	DBS	ECR		77050‡	ND	ELR	DBS	ECR
77010	ND	ELR	DBS	ECR		77030	ND	ELR	DBS	ECR		77051‡	ND	ELR	DBS	ECR
77011	ND	ELR	DBS	ECR		77031‡	ND	ELR	DBS	ECR		77052‡	ND	ELR	DBS	ECR
77012	ND	ELR	DBS	ECR		77032	ND	ELR	DBS	ECR		77053‡	ND	ELR	DBS	ECR
77013	ND	ELR	DBS	ECR		77033	ND	ELR	DBS	ECR		77054‡	ND	ELR	DBS	ECR
77014	ND	ELR	DBS	ECR		77034‡	ND	ELR	DBS	ECR		77055‡	ND	ELR	DBS	ECR
77015	ND	ELR	DBS	RES		77035	ND	ELR	DBS	ECR		77056‡	ND	ELR	DBS	ECR
77016	ND	ELR	DBS	ECR		77036	ND	ELR	DBS	ECR		77057‡	ND	ELR	DBS	ECR
77017	ND	ELR	DBS	ECR		77037†	ND	ELR	DBS	ECR		77058	ND	ELR	DBS	ECR
77018	ND	ELR	DBS	ECR		77038‡	ND	ELR	DBS	ECR		77059	ND	ELR	DBS	ECR
77019	ND	ELR	DBS	ECR		77039‡	ND	ELR	DBS	ECR		77060	ND	ELR	DBS	ECR
77020‡	ND	ELR	DBS	ECR		77040	ND	ELR	DBS	ECR						
						77041‡	ND	ELR	DBS	ECR						

‡ Working for DBS in Germany, re-classified as Class 247, running in number range 247 007 onwards; final three digits remain the same.
† Working for MEG in Germany as 247-037.

Direct Rail Services

Address (UK): ✉ Kingmoor Depot, Etterby Road, Carlisle, Cumbria, CA3 9NZ

　　　　　　 ✈ info@directrailservices.com

　　　　　　 ℭ 01228 406600

　　　　　　 ⓘ www.directrailservices.com

Managing Director: Neil McNicholas

Depots: Carlisle Kingmoor (KM), Crewe Gresty Bridge (CG)

Class 20/3

						Vehicle Length: 46ft 9¼in (14.26m)	Engine: English Electric 8SVT Mk2
Height: 12ft 7⅝in (3.84m)	Horsepower: 1,000hp (745kW)
Width: 8ft 9in (2.66m)	Electrical Equipment: English Electric

Number		Depot	Pool	Livery	Owner	Operator	Name
20301(S)	(20047)	BH	XHSS	DRC	DRS	-	*Max Joule 1958 - 1999*
20302	(20084)	KM	XHNC	DRC	DRS	DRS	
20303	(20127)	KM	XHNC	DRC	DRS	DRS	
20304	(20120)	KM	XHNC	DRC	DRS	DRS	
20305	(20095)	KM	XHNC	DRC	DRS	DRS	*Gresty Bridge*
20308	(20187)	KM	XHNC	DRC	DRS	DRS	
20309	(20075)	KM	XHNC	DRC	DRS	DRS	
20312	(20042)	KM	XHNC	DRC	DRS	DRS	

Right: 1950s technology in the form of eight Class 20s is still on the books of Direct Rail Services (DRS) and in 2015 can still be found powering main line freight services. Allocated to Carlisle Kingmoor depot, the locos can also be found stabled at the DRS depot at Crewe Gresty Bridge, where this view of No. 20312 was recorded. In 2015 these locos are likely to receive overhauls to secure their operation up to 2020. **CJM**

Class 37/0

			Vehicle Length: 61ft 6in (18.74m)	Engine: English Electric 12CSVT
Height: 13ft 0¼in (3.96m)	Horsepower: 1,750hp (1,304kW)
Width: 8ft 11⅝in (2.73m)	Electrical Equipment: English Electric
Class 37/4 - Electric Train Heat fitted	

Number	Depot	Pool	Livery	Owner	Operator	Note
37038	KM	XHSS	DRS	DRS	-	
37059	KM	XHNC	DRR	DRS	DRS	
37069	KM	XHSS	DRC	DRS	-	
37194	KM	XHNC	DRC	DRS	DRS	
37218	KM	XHNC	DRR	DRS	DBS	
37259	KM	XHNC	DRU	DRS	DRS	
37261	-	XHNC	DRC	DRS	-	Restoration at Bo'ness by Scottish 37 Group

Class 37/4

Number		Depot	Pool	Livery	Owner	Operator	Name
37401(S)	(37268)	-	XHHP	BLL	DRS	-	*Mary Queen of Scots*
37402	(37274)	BH	XHAC	DRC	DBS	DRS	*Stephen Middlemore 23.12.1954 - 8.6.2013*
37405	(37282)	BH	XHAC	DRC	DRS	DRS	
37406(S)	(37295)	KM	XHHP	EWS	DRS	-	*The Saltire Society*
37409	(37270)	KM	XHAC	DRC	DRS	DRS	*Lord Hinton*
37419	(37291)	KM	XHAC	DRC	DRS	DRS	*Carl Haviland 1954-2012*

Direct Rail Services

37422(S)	(37266)	KM	XHHP	DRC	DRS	-	
37423	(37296)	KM	XHAC	DRR	DRS	DRS	Spirit of the Lakes
37425	(37292)	BH	XHAC	DRC	DRS	DRS	Sir Robert McAlpine / Concrete Bob

Left: Direct Rail Services operates a large number of Class 37s from various sub-classes. The majority have been refurbished and sport new-style light clusters and the DRS multiple control system. The locos carry several different designs of the DRS livery, with all repaints from mid 2014 seeing the latest stylised DRS Compass livery applied, as shown on Class 37/4 No. 37423 from its No. 1 end at Dawlish. All Class 37s are officially based at Carlisle Kingmoor, but can also be found at Crewe Gresty Bridge. Heavy maintenance is also carried out at Barrow Hill. **CJM**

Class 37/5

Number		Depot	Pool	Livery	Owner	Operator	Name
37503	(37021)	KM	XHHP	EWS	DRS	-	
37510(S)		KM/BH	XHHP	DRC	DRS	-	
37521	(37117)	KM	XHHP	EWS	DRS	-	
37667	(37151)	KM	XHNC	DRC	DRS	DRS	Kingmoor TMD
37670(S)	(37182)	KM	XHSS	EWS	DRS	-	
37682(S)	(37236)	KM	XHSS	DRC	DRS	-	
37688	(37205)	KM	XHNC	DRC	DRS	DRS	

Class 37/6

Number		Depot	Pool	Livery	Owner	Operator	Name
37601	(37501)	KM	XHNC	DRC	DRS	DRS	Class 37 – 'Fifty'
37602	(37502)	KM	XHNC	DRC	DRS	DRS	
37603	(37504)	KM	XHNC	DRC	DRS	DRS	
37604	(37506)	KM	XHNC	DRC	DRS	DRS	
37605	(37507)	KM	XHNC	DRC	DRS	DRS	
37606	(37508)	KM	XHNC	DRS	DRS	DRS	
37607	(37511)	KM	XHNC	DRC	DRS	DRS	
37608	(37512)	KM	XHNC	DRC	DRS	DRS	
37609	(37514)	KM	XHNC	DRC	DRS	DRS	
37610	(37687)	KM	XHNC	DRC	DRS	DRS	T.S. (Ted) Cassady 14.5.61-6.4.08
37611	(37690)	KM	XHNC	DRC	DRS	DRS	
37612	(37691)	KM	XHNC	DRS	DRS	DRS	

Left: All 12 of the Class 37/6 sub-class, originally rebuilt at Doncaster to power the non-electrified legs of Nightstar services from the UK to Mainland Europe, are now on the books of DRS and form the backbone of Class 37 operations, powering flask, freight and Network Rail trains. Nos. 37610 T.S. (Ted) Cassady 14.5.61-6.4.08 and 37609 pose outside Crewe Gresty Bridge depot. **CJM**

Class 37/7

Number		Hire No.	Depot	Pool	Livery	Owner	Operator	Notes
37703(S)	(37067)	L25	BH	XHHP	DRR	DRS	Bo'ness	
37714(S)	(37024)	L26	BH	XHHP	DRC	DRS	DRS	Used at Daventry as 'super shunter'
37716(S)	(37094)	L23	RTC	XHHP	DRC	DRS	DRS	Under renovation
37718(S)	(37084)	L22	RTC	XHHP	DRC	DRS	DRS	Under renovation

Class 47/4 and 47/7

Vehicle Length: 63ft 6in (19.35m)
Height: 12ft 10½in (3.91m)
Width: 9ft 2in (2.79m)
Electric Train Heat fitted

Engine: Sulzer 12LDA28C
Horsepower: 2,580hp (1,922kW)
Electrical Equipment: Brush

Number		Depot	Pool	Livery	Owner	Operator	Name
47501(S)		KM	XHSS	DRC	DRS	-	Craftsman
47790	(47673)	KM	XHNB	NBP	DRS	DRS	Galloway Princess
47805	(47650)	KM	XHAC	DRC	DRS	DRS	John Scott 12.5.45 - 22.5.12
47810	(47247/655)	KM	XHAC	DRR	DRS	DRS	Peter Bath MBE 1927-2006
47813	(47129/658)	KM	XHNB	DRC	DRS	DRS	Solent
47818	(47240/663)	BH	XHAC	DRC	DRS	DRS	
47828	(47266/629)	BH	XHAC	DRC	DRS	DRS	
47841(S)	(47622)	KM	XHSS	DRC	DRS	-	
47853	(47614)	KM	XHAC	DRC	DRS	DRS	Rail Express

Class 57/0

Vehicle Length: 63ft 6in (19.38m)
Height: 12ft 10½in (3.91m)
Width: 9ft 2in (2.79m)

Engine: EMD 645-12E3
Horsepower: 2,500hp (1,864kW)
Electrical Equipment: Brush

Number		Depot	Pool	Livery	Owner	Operator
57002	(47322)	KM	XHCK	DRC	PTR	DRS
57003(S)	(47317)	KM	XHSS	DRC	PTR	-
57004	(47347)	KM	XHCK	DRC	DRS	DRS
57007(S)	(47332)	KM	XHSS	DRC	PTR	-
57008	(47060)	KM	XHCK	DRC	PTR	DRS
57009	(47079)	KM	XHCK	DRC	PTR	DRS
57010	(47231)	KM	XHCK	DRC	PTR	DRS
57011	(47329)	KM	XHCK	DRC	PTR	DRS
57012	(47204)	KM	XHCK	DRC	PTR	DRS

Class 57/3

Vehicle Length: 63ft 6in (19.38m)
Height: 12ft 10½in (3.91m)
Width: 9ft 2in (2.79m)

Engine: EMD 645-12F3B
Horsepower: 2,750hp (2,051kW)
Electrical Equipment: Brush

Number		Depot	Pool	Livery	Owner	Operator	Name
57301	(47845)	KM	XHAC	DRC	DRS	DRS	Goliath
57302	(47827)	KM	XHAC	DRC	PTR	DRS	Chad Varah
57303	(47705)	KM	XHAC	DRC	DRS	DRS	Pride of Carlisle
57304	(47807)	KM	XHVT	DRC	PTR	DRS	Pride of Cheshire
57305	(47822)	KM	XHAC	NBP	DRS	DRS	Northern Princess
57306	(47814)	KM	XHAC	DRC	DRS	DRS	
57307	(47225)	KM	XHVT	DRA	PTR	DRB	Lady Penelope
57308	(47846)	KM	XHVT	DRC	PTR	DRS	County of Staffordshire
57309	(47806)	KM	XHVT	DRC	PTR	DRS	Pride of Crewe
57310	(47831)	KM	XHAC	DRS	DRS	DRS	Pride of Cumbria
57311	(47817)	KM	XHVT	DRC	PTR	DRS	Thunderbird
57312	(47330)	KM	XHAC	NBP	PTR	DRS	Solway Princess

57301, 57303 and 57306 fitted with Tightlock couplings, 57310 and 57312 fitted with modified Dellner couplings.

Right: *Cast nameplate* Chad Varah, *as applied to Class 57/3 No. 57302 at Crewe Gresty Bridge.* **CJM**

Direct Rail Services

Class 66/3, 66/4

Vehicle Length: 70ft 0½in (21.34m)
Height: 12ft 10in (3.91m)
Width: 8ft 8¼in (2.65m)

Engine: EMD 12N-710G3B-EC
Horsepower: 3,300hp (2,462kW)
Electrical Equipment: EMD

Number	Depot	Pool	Livery	Owner	Operator
66301	KM	XHIM	DRC	BEA	DRS
66302	KM	XHIM	DRC	BEA	DRS
66303	KM	XHIM	DRC	BEA	DRS
66304	KM	XHIM	DRC	BEA	DRS
66305	KM	XHIM	DRC	BEA	DRS
66421	KM	XHIM	DRC	HAL	DRS
66422	KM	XHIM	DRC	HAL	DRS
66423	KM	XHIM	DRC	HAL	DRS
66424	KM	XHIM	DRC	HAL	DRS
66425	KM	XHIM	DRC	HAL	DRS
66426	KM	XHIM	DRC	HAL	DRS
66427	KM	XHIM	DRC	HAL	DRS
66428	KM	XHIM	DRC	HAL	DRS
66429	KM	XHIM	DRC	HAL	DRS
66430	KM	XHIM	DRC	HAL	DRS
66431	KM	XHIM	DRC	HAL	DRS
66432	KM	XHIM	DRC	HAL	DRS
66433	KM	XHIM	DRC	HAL	DRS
66434	KM	XHIM	DRC	HAL	DRS

Left: *Two different sub-classes of Class 66 are operated by Direct Rail Services; all five members of Class 66/3, which were originally delivered to Fastline Freight, and 14 members of Class 66/4, from an original fleet of 34 locos. All locos are painted in Direct Rail Services early Compass livery. The Class 66s are based at Carlisle Kingmoor depot but are also to be found operating from Crewe Gresty Bridge. In the upper illustration No. 66303 is seen parked outside Crewe Gresty Bridge, while the lower picture shows No. 66423 inside Crewe Gresty Bridge depot. Both:* **CJM**

Class 68 'UK Light'

Vehicle Length: 67ft 3in (20.5m)
Height: 12ft 6½in (3.82m)
Speed: 100mph (161km/h)

Engine: Caterpillar C175-16
Horsepower: 3,750hp (2,800kW)
Electrical Equipment: ABB

Number	Depot	Pool	Livery	Owner	Operator	Name
68001	CR	XHVE	DRS	BEA	DRS	Evolution
68002	CR	XHVE	DRS	BEA	DRS	Intrepid
68003	CR	XHVE	DRS	BEA	DRS	Astute
68004	CR	XHVE	DRS	BEA	DRS	Rapid
68005	CR	XHVE	DRS	BEA	DRS	Defiant
68006	CR	XHVE	DRS	BEA	DRS	Daring
68007	CR	XHVE	DRS	BEA	DRS	Valiant
68008§	CR	XHVE	DRS	BEA	DRS	Avenger
68009§	CR	XHVE	DRS	BEA	DRS	Titan
68010§	CR	XHCE	CRG	BEA	DRS/CRW	
68011§	CR	XHCE	CRG	BEA	DRS/CRW	

68012§	CR	XHCE	CRG	BEA	DRS/CRW
68013§	CR	XHCE	CRG	BEA	DRS/CRW
68014§	CR	XHCE	CRG	BEA	DRS/CRW
68015§	CR	XHCE	CRG	BEA	DRS/CRW
68016	CR	XHVE	DRS	BEA	DRS
68017	CR	XHVE	DRS	BEA	DRS
68018	CR	XHVE	DRS	BEA	DRS
68019	CR	XHVE	DRS	BEA	DRS
68020	CR	XHVE	DRS	BEA	DRS
68021	CR	XHVE	DRS	BEA	DRS
68022	CR	XHVE	DRS	BEA	DRS
68023	CR	XHVE	DRS	BEA	DRS
68024	CR	XHVE	DRS	BEA	DRS
68025	CR	XHVE	DRS	BEA	DRS

§ Modified for operation with push-pull passenger stock

Right: *The newest power on the DRS roster is 25 Class 68s, built in Spain by Vossloh. The first order for 15 locos was delivered by autumn 2014 and the follow-on order for 10 locos was delivered at the year end. Six locos, Nos. 68010-68015, are finished in Chiltern Railways grey livery to operate on the London-Birmingham corridor. All locos are based at Crewe Gresty Bridge, where No. 68002 was photographed when brand new.* **CJM**

Class 88 'Dual Mode'

Number	Depot	Pool	Livery	Owner	Operator
88001	KM	XH??	DRS	BEA	On order
88002	KM	XH??	DRS	BEA	On order
88003	KM	XH??	DRS	BEA	On order
88004	KM	XH??	DRS	BEA	On order
88005	KM	XH??	DRS	BEA	On order
88006	KM	XH??	DRS	BEA	On order

Vehicle Length: 67ft 3in (20.5m)	Engine: Caterpillar
Height: 12ft 6½in (3.82m)	Horsepower: Electro-diesel
Speed: 100mph (161km/h)	Diesel - 938hp (700kW)
	Electric - 5,364kW (4,000kW)
Electric train supply	Electrical Equipment: ABB

88007	KM	XH??	DRS	BEA	On order
88008	KM	XH??	DRS	BEA	On order
88009	KM	XH??	DRS	BEA	On order
88010	KM	XH??	DRS	BEA	On order

Class 90

Vehicle Length: 61ft 6in (18.74m)	Power Collection: 25kV ac overhead
Height: 13ft 0¼in (3.96m)	Horsepower: 7,860hp (5,860kW)
Width: 9ft 0in (2.74m)	Electrical Equipment: GEC

Number	Depot	Pool	Livery	Owner	Operator
90034	CG	WEDC	DRC	DBS	DRS

Right: *In mid-2014, Direct Rail Services entered into a contract to hire a Class 90 (No. 90034) from DB Schenker and deploy it on a contract to power the Virgin Trains loco-hauled passenger set. The loco was repainted in full DRS colours and was usually kept at Wembley with the Mk3 formation. However, in October 2014 the Virgin Mk3 train was stood down, but the Class 90 remains in full DRS colours. No. 90034 is seen 'on shed' at Crewe Gresty Bridge.* **CJM**

Direct Rail Services

Coaching Stock

	Mk2					Height: 12ft 9½in (3.89m)
	Vehicle Length: 66ft 0in (20.11m)					Width: 9ft 3in (2.81m)

	Mk 3					Height: 12ft 9in (3.88m)
	Vehicle Length: 75ft 0in (22.86m)					Width: 8ft 11in (2.71m)

Number	Type	Depot	Livery	Operator
1254 (3391)	AJ1F/RFO	KM	BLG	DRS
3366	AD1F/FO	KM	BLG	DRS
3374	AD1F/FO	KM	BLG	DRS
5810	AC2E/TSO	KM	DRC	DRS
5919	AC2F/TSO	KM	DBC	DRS
5971	AC2F/TSO	KM	DRC	DRS
5995	AC25/TSO	NR	DRC	DRS
6001	AC2F/TSO	NR	DRC	DRS
6008	AC2F/TSO	NR	DRC	DRS
6046	AC2F/TSO	KM	DRC	DRS
6064	AC2F/TSO	KM	DRC	DRS
6117	AC2F/TSO	KM	DRC	DRS
6122	AC2F/TSO	KM	DRC	DRS
6173	AC2F/TSO	KM	DRS	DRS
9419	AC2E/TSO	KM	DRC	DRS
9428	AE2E/BSO	KM	DRC	DRS
9488	AE2E/BSO	KM	-	-
9508	AE2E/BSO	KM	BLG	DRS
9525	AE2E/BSO	NR	DRC	DRS
9705 (9519)	AF2F/DBSO	ZA	DRC	DRS

Number	Type	Depot	Livery	Operator
9707 (9511)	AF2F/DBSO	ZA	DRC	DRS
11006	AD1G/FO	BH	-	DRS
11011	AD1G/FO	BH	-	DRS
12047	AC2G/TSO	BH	-	DRS
12063	AC2G/TSO	KM	-	DRS
12065	AC2G/TSO	KM	-	DRS
12087	AC2G/TSO	KM	-	DRS
12134	AC2G/TSO	KM	-	DRS
17159	AB1D/BFK	KM	DRO	DRS
82101(S)	NZAK/DVT	BH	VIR	DRS

NX5G - NGV (Nightstar generators)

Number		Depot	Livery	Owner
96371(S)	(10545)	WB	EPS	DRS
96372(S)	(10564)	LM	EPS	DRS
96373(S)	(10568)	LM	EPS	DRS
96375(S)	(10587)	LM	EPS	DRS

Left: Direct Rail Services operates a small number of loco-hauled coaches, which are deployed as either escort vehicles for flask trains or for spot-hire to TOCs or charter operators. The vehicles are refurbished and in excellent external and internal condition. Mk2F TSO No. 6001 is illustrated stabled at Norwich Crown Point.
Antony Christie

Royal Mail (operations contracted to DB S)

Address: ✉ 148 Old Street, London, EC1V 9HQ

✍ press.office@royalmail.com   ✆ 0207 250 2468   ⓘ www.royalmailgroup.com

Class 325

	Vehicle Length: (Driving) 65ft 0¾in (19.82m)	Width: 9ft 2in (2.82m)
	(Inter) 65ft 4¼in (19.92m)	Horsepower: 1,278hp (990kW)
	Height: 12ft 4½in (3.76m)	Seats (total/car): None - luggage space

Number	Formation DTPMV+MPMV+TPMV+DTPMV	Depot	Livery	Owner	Operator	Name
325001	68300+68340+68360+68301	CE	RML	RML	DBS	
325002	68302+68341+68361+68303	CE	RML	RML	DBS	Royal Mail North Wales & North West
325003	68304+68342+68362+68305	CE	RMR	RML	DBS	
325004	68306+68343+68363+68307	CE	RML	RML	DBS	
325005	68308+68344+68364+68309	CE	RML	RML	DBS	John Grierson
325006	68310+68345+68365+68311	CE	RML	RML	DBS	
325007	68312+68346+68366+68313	CE	RML	RML	DBS	Peter Howarth C.B.E
325008	68314+68347+68367+68315	CE	RML	RML	DBS	
325009	68316+68348+68368+68317	CE	RML	RML	DBS	
325011	68320+68350+68370+68321	CE	RML	RML	DBS	
325012	68322+68351+68371+68323	CE	RML	RML	DBS	
325013	68324+68352+68372+68325	CE	RML	RML	DBS	
325014	68326+68353+68373+68327	CE	RML	RML	DBS	
325015	68328+68354+68374+68329	CE	RML	RML	DBS	
325016	68330+68355+68375+68331	CE	RML	RML	DBS	

Europorte – GB Railfreight (GBRf)

Address: ✉15-25 Artillery Lane, London, E1 7HA

✍ gbrfinfo@gbrailfreight.com

✆ 0207 983 5177

ⓘ www.gbrailfreight.com

Managing Director: John Smith

Depots: Peterborough (PT), Wembley (SV), St Leonards (SE), Coquelles (CQ)

Class 08/0, 09

Vehicle Length: 29ft 3in (8.91m)				Engine: English Electric 6K		
Height: 12ft 8⅝in (3.87m)				Horsepower: 400hp (298kW)		
Width: 8ft 6in (2.59m)				Electrical Equipment: English Electric		

Number	Depot	Pool	Livery	Owner	Operator
08401	±	GBWW	GRN	HEC	GBR
08925	CF	GBWW	GRN	GBF	GBR
08934	CF	GBWW	GRN	GBF	GBR

09002	§	GBWW	GRN	GBF	GBR
09009	§	GBWW	GRN	GBF	GBR

± Working at Boulby Potash

§ Working at Barton Dock, Trafford Park

Class 20

Vehicle Length: 46ft 9¼in (14.26m)			Engine: English Electric 8SVT Mk2		
Height: 12ft 7⅝in (3.84m)			Horsepower: 1,000hp (745kW)		
Width: 8ft 9in (2.66m)			Electrical Equipment: English Electric		

Number		Depot	Pool	Livery	Owner	Operator
20901	(20101)	PG	GBEE	GBN	HNR	GBR
20905	(20225)	PG	GBEE	GBN	HNR	GBR

Below: *A number of Class 20s are operated under the GB Railfreight safety case, mainly to power London Underground 'S' stock from and to Bombardier Derby Litchurch Lane Works. Two locos, Nos. 20901/905, sport GBRf livery. In this view taken near Burton-on-Trent No. 20227, sporting London Underground colours, leads GBRf No. 20905.* **John Tuffs**

Class 59/0

Vehicle Length: 70ft 0½in (21.34m)			Engine: EMD 16-645 E3C		
Height: 12ft 10in (3.91m)			Horsepower: 3,000hp (2,462kW)		
Width: 8ft 8¼in (2.65m)			Electrical Equipment: EMD		

Number	Depot	Pool	Livery	Owner	Operator	Name
59003	PG	GBYH	GBN	GBR	GBR	*Yeoman Highlander*

Freight Operating Companies - Europorte – GBRf

Europorte – GBRf

Class 66/7

Vehicle Length: 70ft 0½in (21.34m)
Height: 12ft 10in (3.91m)
Width: 8ft 8¼in (2.65m)

Engine: EMD 12N-710G3B-EC
Horsepower: 3,300hp (2,462kW)
Electrical Equipment: EMD

Number	Depot	Pool	Livery	Owner	Operator	Name/Notes
66701	PG	GBCM	GBR	EVL	GBR	
66702	PG	GBCM	GBR	EVL	GBR	Blue Lightning
66703	PG	GBCM	GNB	EVL	GBR	Doncaster PSB 1981 - 2002
66704	PG	GBCM	GBR	EVL	GBR	Colchester Power Signalbox
66705	PG	GBCM	GBR	EVL	GBR	Golden Jubilee
66706	PG	GBCM	GBR	EVL	GBR	Nene Valley
66707	PG	GBCM	GBR	EVL	GBR	Sir Sam Fay / Great Central Railway
66708	PG	GBCM	GBR	EVL	GBR	Jayne
66709	PG	GBCM	MSC	EVL	GBR	Sorrento
66710	PG	GBCM	GBN	EVL	GBR	Phil Packer
66711	PG	GBCM	GBR	EVL	GBR	
66712	PG	GBCM	GBN	EVL	GBR	Peterborough Power Signalbox
66713	PG	GBCM	GBN	EVL	GBR	Forest City
66714	PG	GBCM	GBR	EVL	GBR	Cromer Lifeboat
66715	PG	GBCM	GBR	EVL	GBR	Valour
66716	PG	GBCM	GBN	EVL	GBR	Locomotive & Carriage Institution Centenary 1911-2011
66717	PG	GBCM	GBN	EVL	GBR	Good Old Boy
66718	PG	GBCM	SPL	EVL	GBR	Sir Peter Hendy CBE
66719	PG	GBCM	GBN	EVL	GBR	Metro-Land
66720	PG	GBCM	SPL	EVL	GBR	
66721	PG	GBCM	SPL	EVL	GBR	Harry Beck
66722	PG	GBCM	GBN	EVL	GBR	Sir Edward Watkin
66723	PG	GBSD	GBF	EVL	GBR	Chinook
66724	PG	GBSD	GBF	EVL	GBR	Drax Power Station
66725	PG	GBSD	GBF	EVL	GBR	Sunderland
66726	PG	GBSD	GBF	EVL	GBR	Sheffield Wednesday
66727	PG	GBSD	GBF	EVL	GBR	Andrew Scott CBE
66728	PG	GBCM	GBN	PTR	GBR	Institution of Railway Operators
66729	PG	GBCM	GBN	PTR	GBR	Derby County
66730	PG	GBCM	GBF	PTR	GBR	Whitemoor
66731	PG	GBCM	GBN	PTR	GBR	interhubGB
66732	PG	GBCM	GBN	PTR	GBR	GBRf The First Decade 1999-2009 John Smith - MD
66733 (66401)	PG	GBFM	BLU	PTR	GBR	Cambridge PSB
66735 (66403)	PG	GBFM	GBN	PTR	GBR	
66736 (66404)	PG	GBFM	GBN	PTR	GBR	Wolverhampton Wanderers
66737 (66405)	PG	GBFM	GBN	PTR	GBR	Lesia
66738 (66578)	PG	GBCM	GBN	GBR	GBR	Huddersfield Town
66739 (66579)	PG	GBFM	GBN	GBR	GBR	Bluebell Railway
66740 (66580)	PG	GBCM	GBN	GBR	GBR	Sarah
66741 (66581)	PG	GBCM	GBN	GBR	GBR	
66742 (66406, 66841)	PG	GBRT	GBN	GBR	GBR	Port of Immingham Centenary 1912 - 2012
66743 (66407, 66842)	PG	GBRT	GBN	GBR	GBR	
66744 (66408, 66843)	PG	GBRT	GBN	GBR	GBR	Crossrail
66745 (66409, 66844)	PG	GBRT	GBN	GBR	GBR	Modern Railways - The First 50 years
66746 (66410, 66845)	PG	GBRT	GBN	GBR	GBR	
66747	PG	GBNL	GRY	GBR	GBR	Former EMD 20078968-004
66748	PG	GBNL	GRY	GBR	GBR	Former EMD 20078968-006
66749	PG	GBNL	GRY	GBR	GBR	Former EMD 20078968-007
66750	PG	GBDR	GRY	BEA	GBR	Converted from EMD 20038513-001
66751	PG	GBDR	GBN	BEA	GBR	Converted from EMD 20038513-004
66752	PG	GBNB	GBN	GBR	GBR	The Hoosier State
66753	PG	GBNB	GBN	GBR	GBR	EMD Roberts Road
66754	PG	GBNB	GBN	GBR	GBR	
66755	PG	GBNB	GBN	GBR	GBR	
66756	PG	GBNB	GBN	GBR	GBR	
66757	PG	GBNB	GBN	GBR	GBR	
66758	PG	GBNB	GBN	GBR	GBR	
66759	PG	GBNB	GBN	GBR	GBR	
66760	PG	GBNB	GBN	GBR	GBR	

66761	PG	GBNB	GBN	GBR	GBR
66762	PG	GBNB	GBN	GBR	GBR
66763	PG	GBNB	GBN	GBR	GBR
66764	PG	GBNB	GBN	GBR	GBR
66765	PG	GBNB	GBN	GBR	GBR
66766	PG	GBNB	GBN	GBR	GBR
66767	PG	GBNB	GBN	GBR	GBR
66768	PG	GBNB	GBN	GBR	GBR
66769	PG	GBNB	GBN	GBR	GBR
66770	PG	GBNB	GBN	GBR	GBR
66771	PG	GBNB	GBN	GBR	GBR
66772	PG	GBNB	GBN	GBR	GBR

A further seven Class 66s will be assembled in 2015-16 utilising a 'loop-hole' in the new 2015 emissions limits; these would be numbered in the series 66773-66779, using pre-registered power units in new body shells.

Right and Below: *GB Railfreight operates a fleet of 71 Class 66s, which includes some purpose-built locos, others from DRS and Freightliner, and five imported from mainland Europe. At the end of 2014 the final 'new build' Class 66s were imported from the US, just in advance of new emissions deadlines. Locos carry a variety of different GBRf liveries, but all new repaints are to the GBRf/Europorte design. On the right No. 66742 Port of Immingham Centenary 1912-2012 is seen near Peterborough, while in the view below No. 66745 Modern Railways - The First 50 Years approaches Banbury with an aggregate train from Westbury. Both:* **CJM**

Freight Operating Companies - Europorte – GBRf

Freight Operating Companies

Europorte – GBRf

Class 73

Vehicle Length: 53ft 8in (16.35m)
Height: 12ft 5⅝in (3.79m)
Width: 8ft 8in (2.64m)

Power: 750V dc third rail or English Electric 6K
Horsepower: electric - 1,600hp (1,193kW)
Horsepower: diesel - 600hp (447kW)
Electrical Equipment: English Electric

Number		Depot	Pool	Livery	Owner	Operator	Name
73103		SE	GBED	-	GBR	GBR	
73105		SE	GBED	-	GBR	GBR	
73107		SE	GBED	GRY	GBR	GBR	
73109		SE	GBED	BLU	GBR	GBR	
73117		SE	GBED	-	GBR	GBR	
73119		SE	GBED	BLU	GBR	GBR	
73136		SE	GBED	GBU	GBR	GBR	
73141		SE	GBED	GBU	GBR	GBR	
73201	(73142)	SE	GBED	BLU	GBR	GBR	Charlotte
73212	(73102)	SE	GBED	GBU	GBR	GBR	Broadlands
73213	(73112)	SE	GBED	GBU	GBR	GBR	Fiona
							Rhodalyn

Refurbished with new electrical equipment and MTU diesel power unit - MTU 8V4000R43L - set to deliver 1,500hp. Also fitted with AAR multiple control system in addition to blue star/27 wire

Number		Depot	Pool	Livery	Owner	Operator	Name
73961	(73209/120)	SE	GBBR	GBB	GBR	GBR	Alison
73962	(73204/125)	SE	GBBR	GBB	GBR	GBR	Dick Mabbutt
73963	(73206/123)	SE	GBBR	GBB	GBR	GBR	Janice
73964	(73205/124)	SE	GBBR	GBB	GBR	GBR	
73965	(73208/121)	SE	GBBR	GBB	GBR	GBR	
73966(S)	(73005)	SE	GBBR	GBB	GBR	GBR	
73967(S)	(73006)	SE	GBBR	GBB	GBR	GBR	

Left: *The initial testing of the first GBRf Class 73/9 was carried out on the Great Central Railway in autumn 2014, where No. 73961 is recorded. As can be seen, some major structural changes have been made with revised front-end equipment, changes to the bodyside air louvres, new between-bogie equipment and installing new Group Standard marker lights. The original two-digit headcode box has also been removed.* **Lindsay Atkinson**

Class 92

Vehicle Length: 70ft 1in (21.34m)
Height: 13ft 0in (3.95m)
Width: 8ft 8in (2.66m)

Power Collection: 25kV ac overhead / 750V dc third rail
Horsepower: ac - 6,700hp (5,000kW) / dc 5,360hp (4,000kW)
Electrical Equipment: Brush

Number	Depot	Pool	Livery	Owner	Operator	Name
92006(S)	Brush	PTXX	SNF	GBR	-	Louis Armand
92010	CO	GBET	EU2	GBR	GBR	Moliere
92014	CO	GBET	SNF	GBR	GBR	Emile Zola
92018	CO	PTXX	SNF	GBR	GBR	Stendhal
92020(S)	DM	PTXX	EU2	GBR	-	Milton
92021(S)	CO	PTXX	EU2	GBR	-	Purcell
92023	CO	PTXX	EU2	GBR	GBR	Ravel
92028	CO	GBET	EU2	GBR	GBR	Saint Saens
92032	CO	GBET	GBN	GBR	GBR	I Mech E Railway Division
92033	Brush	PTXX	SCS	GBR	GBR	Berlioz
92038	CE	GBET	EU2	GBR	GBR	Voltaire
92040(S)	CO	PTXX	EU2	GBR	-	Goethe
92043	CO	GBET	EU2	GBR	GBR	Debussy
92044	CO	GBET	EU2	GBR	GBR	Couperin
92045(S+)	Brush	PTXX	EU2	GBR	-	Chaucer
92046(S+)	Brush	PTXX	EU2	GBR	-	Sweelinck

GBRf is planning to return to front-line traffic a number of presently stored Class 92s, as new traffic commitments require a sizeable fleet, including the powering of the new Serco sleeper operation between London and Scotland from mid-2015. In grey livery with Europorte 2 branding, No. 92038 is shown.
Mark V. Pike

Class Di 8

Vehicle Length: 57ft 1in (17.38m)	Engine: Caterpillar 3516 DITA
Height: 13ft 3in (4.01m)	Horsepower: 2,100hp (1,566kW)
Width: 9ft 8in (2.95m)	Electrical Equipment: Siemens

GBRf purchased 12 former Cargo-Net, Norway, Class Di 8 locos for use within the SSI Lackenby Steelworks in Redcar a few years ago. The 2,100hp (1,566kW) locos were built in 1996-97 by Mak in Kiel, Germany, as an order for 20 locos. In the UK the fleet, classified by the UIC as 308, will be painted in a joint GBRf/SSI livery.

8.701	8.704	8.712	8.718
8.702	8.708	8.716	8.719
8.703	8.711	8.717	8.720

Industrial 0-6-0DH

DH50-1 Works No. TH278V - 0-6-0DH 50-ton design, built 1978, fitted with a Cummins engine
DH50-2 Works No. TH246V - 0-6-0DH 50-ton design, built 1973

The above two industrial locos are operated by GBRf at the Celsa steel plant in Cardiff.

Right: *Two industrial 0-6-0 diesel-hydraulic locos are on the GBRf books, operating at the Celsa steel plant in Cardiff. No. DH50-1 sports full GBRf blue and orange livery.*
Antony Christie

Freightliner

Address: ✉ 3rd Floor, The Podium, 1 Eversholt Street, London, NW1 2FL

✒ pressoffice@freightliner.co.uk

✆ 0207 200 3900

ⓘ www.freightliner.com

Chief Executive: Peter Maybury

Managing Director Intermodal: Adam Cunliffe

Managing Director Heavy Haul: Paul Smart

Depots: Freightliner Diesels (FD), Freightliner Electrics (FE), Freightliner Shunters (FS), Ipswich* (IP), Leeds Midland Road (LD), Southampton Maritime (SZ)

* Stabling point

Parent Company: Arcapita

Class 08/0

Vehicle Length: 29ft 3in (8.91m)	Engine: English Electric 6K
Height: 12ft 8⅝in (3.87m)	Horsepower: 400hp (298kW)
Width: 8ft 6in (2.59m)	Electrical Equipment: English Electric

Number	Depot	Pool	Livery	Owner	Operator
08393**	LH				
08530(S)	LH	DFLS	FLR	PTR	FLR
08531	TL	DFLS	FLR	PTR	FLR
08575	LH	DHLT	FLR	PTR	FLR
08585	FS	DFLS	FLR	PTR	FLR
08624	LH	DFLS	BLU	PTR	FLR
08691 ¤	SZ	DHLT	FLR	FLR	FLR
08785	LH	DFLS	FLR	PTR	FLR
08891	FD	DFLS	FLR	PTR	FLR

**08393 sold to L H Group Services

¤ 08691 at L H Group Services

Names applied
08585   Vicky
08691   Terri

Left: *While most Freightliner terminal shunting is performed by train locos, a handful of Class 08s still operate. Painted in Freightliner green and yellow, No. 08691* Terri *is seen at Southampton Maritime Terminal in autumn 2014.* **Antony Christie**

Class 47/4

Vehicle Length: 63ft 6in (19.35m)	Engine: Sulzer 12LDA28C
Height: 12ft 10⅝in (3.91m)	Horsepower: 2,580hp (1,922kW)
Width: 9ft 2in (2.79m)	Electrical Equipment: Brush
Electric Train Heat fitted	

Number		Depot	Pool	Livery	Owner	Operator
47811	(47656)	FD	DFLH	GRN	FLR	FLR (pilot)
47816(S)	(47661)	FD	DFLH	GRN	FLR	-
47830(S)	(47649)	BH	DFLH	GRN	FLR	-

Class 56

Vehicle Length: 63ft 6in (19.35m)	Engine: Ruston Paxman 16RK3CT
Height: 13ft 0in (3.96m)	Horsepower: 3,250hp (2,420kW)
Width: 9ft 2in (2.79m)	Electrical Equipment: Brush

Number	Depot	Pool	Livery	Owner	Operator
56081	FD	DFLH	GRY	URL	FLT (Basford Hall pilot)

Class 66/4

			Vehicle Length: 70ft 0½in (21.34m)		Engine: EMD 12N-710G3B-EC	
			Height: 12ft 10in (3.91m)		Horsepower: 3,300hp (2,462kW)	
			Width: 8ft 8¼in (2.65m)		Electrical Equipment: EMD	

Number	Depot	Pool	Livery	Owner	Operator	Name
66411	Exported, working in Poland for Freightliner Poland as 66013FPL					
66412	Exported, working in Poland for Freightliner Poland as 66015FPL					
66413	LD	DFHG	BLU	CBR	FLR	
66414	LD	DFIN	TES	HAL	FLT	
66415	LD	DFHG	DRC	HAL	FLT	
66416	LD	DFIN	FLP	HAL	FLT	
66417	Exported, working in Poland for Freightliner Poland as 66014FPL					
66418	LD	DFIN	DRC	HAL	FLT	
66419	LD	DFHG	DRC	HAL	FLT	
66420	LD	DFIN	DRU	HAL	FLT	

Class 66/5

			Vehicle Length: 70ft 0½in (21.34m)		Engine: EMD 12N-710G3B-EC	
			Height: 12ft 10in (3.91m)		Horsepower: 3,300hp (2,462kW)	
			Width: 8ft 8¼in (2.65m)		Electrical Equipment: EMD	

Number	Depot	Pool	Livery	Owner	Operator	Name
66501	LD	DFIM	FLR	PTR	FLR	Japan 2001
66502	LD	DFIM	FLR	PTR	FLR	Basford Hall Centenary 2001
66503	LD	DFIM	FLR	PTR	FLR	The Railway Magazine
66504	LD	DFIM	FLP	PTR	FLR	
66505	LD	DFIM	FLR	PTR	FLR	
66506	LD	DFHH	FLR	EVL	FLR	Crewe Regeneration
66507	LD	DFHH	FLR	EVL	FLR	
66508	LD	DFHH	FLR	EVL	FLR	
66509	LD	DFHH	FLR	EVL	FLR	
66510	LD	DFHH	FLR	EVL	FLR	
66511	LD	DFHH	FLR	EVL	FLR	
66512	LD	DFHH	FLR	EVL	FLR	
66513	LD	DFHH	FLR	EVL	FLR	
66514	LD	DFHH	FLR	EVL	FLR	
66515	LD	DFHH	FLR	EVL	FLR	
66516	LD	DFIM	FLR	EVL	FLR	
66517	LD	DFIM	FLR	EVL	FLR	
66518	LD	DFHH	FLR	EVL	FLR	
66519	LD	DFHH	FLR	EVL	FLR	
66520	LD	DFHH	FLR	EVL	FLR	
66522	LD	DFHH	FLR	EVL	FLR	east london express
66523	LD	DFHH	FLR	EVL	FLR	
66524	LD	DFHH	FLR	EVL	FLR	
66525	LD	DFHH	FLR	EVL	FLR	
66526	LD	DFHH	FLR	PTR	FLR	Driver Steve Dunn (George)
66527	LD	DFHH	FLR	EVL	FLR	Don Raider
66528	LD	DFHH	FLR	PTR	FLR	
66529	LD	DFHH	FLR	PTR	FLR	
66530	LD	DFHH	FLR	PTR	FLR	
66531	LD	DFHH	FLR	PTR	FLR	
66532	LD	DFIM	FLR	PTR	FLR	P&O Nedlloyd Atlas
66533	LD	DFIM	FLR	PTR	FLR	Hanjin Express / Senator Express
66534	LD	DFIM	FLR	PTR	FLR	OOCL Express
66535	LD	DFHH	FLR	PTR	FLR	
66536	LD	DFHH	FLR	PTR	FLR	
66537	LD	DFIM	FLR	PTR	FLR	
66538	LD	DFIM	FLR	EVL	FLR	
66539	LD	DFHH	FLR	EVL	FLR	
66540	LD	DFIM	FLR	EVL	FLR	Ruby
66541	LD	DFIM	FLR	EVL	FLR	
66542	LD	DFIM	FLR	EVL	FLR	
66543	LD	DFIM	FLR	EVL	FLR	
66544	LD	DFHH	FLR	PTR	FLR	
66545	LD	DFHH	FLR	PTR	FLR	

Freightliner

66546	LD	DFHH	FLR	PTR	FLR	
66547	LD	DFHH	FLR	PTR	FLR	
66548	LD	DFHH	FLR	PTR	FLR	
66549	LD	DFHH	FLR	PTR	FLR	
66550	LD	DFHH	FLR	PTR	FLR	
66551	LD	DFHH	FLR	PTR	FLR	
66552	LD	DFHH	FLR	PTR	FLR	*Maltby Raider*
66553	LD	DFHH	FLR	PTR	FLR	
66554	LD	DFHH	FLR	EVL	FLR	
66555	LD	DFHH	FLR	EVL	FLR	
66556	LD	DFIM	FLR	EVL	FLR	
66557	LD	DFHH	FLR	EVL	FLR	
66558	LD	DFIM	FLR	EVL	FLR	
66559	LD	DFHH	FLR	EVL	FLR	
66560	LD	DFHH	FLR	EVL	FLR	
66561	LD	DFHH	FLR	EVL	FLR	
66562	LD	DFHH	FLR	EVL	FLR	
66563	LD	DFHH	FLR	EVL	FLR	
66564	LD	DFHH	FLR	EVL	FLR	
66565	LD	DFHH	FLR	EVL	FLR	
66566	LD	DFIM	FLR	EVL	FLR	
66567	LD	DFIM	FLR	EVL	FLR	
66568	LD	DFIM	FLR	EVL	FLR	
66569	LD	DFIM	FLR	EVL	FLR	
66570	LD	DFIM	FLR	EVL	FLR	
66571	LD	DFIM	FLR	EVL	FLR	
66572	LD	DFIM	FLR	EVL	FLR	

66582 *Exported, working in Poland for Freightliner Poland as 66009FPL*
66583 *Exported, working in Poland for Freightliner Poland as 66010FPL*
66584 *Exported, working in Poland for Freightliner Poland as 66011FPL*

66585	LD	DFHG	FLR	HAL	FLR	*The Drax Flyer*

66586 *Exported, working in Poland for Freightliner Poland as 66008FPL*

66587	LD	DFIN	FLR	HAL	FLR	
66588	LD	DFIN	FLR	HAL	FLR	
66589	LD	DFIN	FLR	HAL	FLR	
66590	LD	DFIN	FLR	HAL	FLR	
66591	LD	DFIN	FLR	MAG	FLR	
66592	LD	DFIN	FLR	MAG	FLR	*Johnson Stevens Agencies*
66593	LD	DFIN	FLR	MAG	FLR	*3MG Mersey Multimodal Gateway*
66594	LD	DFIN	FLR	MAG	FLR	*NYK Spirit of Kyoto*
66595	LD	DFHG	FLR	BEA	FLR	
66596	LD	DFHG	FLR	BEA	FLR	
66597	LD	DFHG	FLR	BEA	FLR	*Viridor*
66598	LD	DFHG	FLR	BEA	FLR	
66599	LD	DFHG	FLR	BEA	FLR	

Left: *The Freightliner Class 66/5 fleet is operated between the intermodal and Heavy Haul businesses. All locos are officially allocated to Leeds Midland Road depot, but in reality receive maintenance at any of the Freightliner depots or terminals. By late 2014 just two UK locos carried the new 'Powerhaul' livery, while the majority of the earlier delivered locos were starting to look very tatty. Intermodal No. 66538 is seen passing Oxford.* **CJM**

Class 66/6

Number	Depot	Pool	Livery	Owner	Operator	Name
66601	LD	DFHH	FLR	PTR	FLR	The Hope Valley
66602	LD	DFHH	FLR	PTR	FLR	
66603	LD	DFHH	FLR	PTR	FLR	
66604	LD	DFHH	FLR	PTR	FLR	
66605	LD	DFHH	FLR	PTR	FLR	
66606	LD	DFHH	FLR	PTR	FLR	
66607	LD	DFHH	FLR	PTR	FLR	
66608 Exported, working in Poland for Freightliner Poland as 66603FPL						
66609 Exported, working in Poland for Freightliner Poland as 66605FPL						
66610	LD	DFHH	FLR	PTR	FLR	
66611 Exported, working in Poland for Freightliner Poland as 66604FPL						
66612 Exported, working in Poland for Freightliner Poland as 66606FPL						
66613	LD	DFHH	FLR	PTR	FLR	
66614	LD	DFHH	FLR	PTR	FLR	
66615	LD	DFHH	FLR	PTR	FLR	
66616	LD	DFHH	FLR	PTR	FLR	
66617	LD	DFHH	FLR	PTR	FLR	
66618	LD	DFHH	FLR	PTR	FLR	Railways Illustrated Annual Photographic Awards - Alan Barnes
66619	LD	DFHH	FLR	PTR	FLR	Derek W. Johnson MBE
66620	LD	DFHH	FLR	PTR	FLR	
66621	LD	DFHH	FLR	PTR	FLR	
66622	LD	DFHH	FLR	PTR	FLR	
66623	LD	DFHG	AIN	EVL	FLR	Bill Bolsover
66624 Exported, working in Poland for Freightliner Poland as 66602FPL						
66625 Exported, working in Poland for Freightliner Poland as 66601FPL						

Class 66/9

Number	Depot	Pool	Livery	Owner	Operator	Name
66951	LD	DFHG	FLR	EVL	FLR	
66952	LD	DFHG	FLR	EVL	FLR	
66953	LD	DFHG	FLR	BEA	FLR	
66954	LD	DFIN	FLR	BEA	FLR	
66955	LD	DFIN	FLR	BEA	FLR	
66956	LD	DFHG	FLR	BEA	FLR	
66957	LD	DFHG	FLR	BEA	FLR	Stephenson Locomotive Society 1909-2009

Right: *The seven Freightliner Class 66/9 locos were the first to have a reduced emission power unit assembly and are thus 'five-door' locos as it is impossible to walk from cab to cab due to extra equipment. This sub-class is operated by both intermodal and Heavy Haul sectors. No. 66956 is seen powering a coal train through Knottingley.* **CJM**

Freightliner

Class 70 - PH37ACmi

Vehicle Length: 71ft 2½in (21.71m)
Height: 12ft 10in (3.91m)
Width: 8ft 8in (2.64m)

Engine: GE V16-cylinder PowerHaul 616
Horsepower: 3,700hp (2,750kW)
Electrical Equipment: General Electric

Number	Depot	Pool	Livery	Owner	Operator	Name
70001	LD	DFGI	FLP	MAG	FLR	*PowerHaul*
70002	LD	DFGH	FLP	MAG	FLR	
70003	LD	DFGH	FLP	MAG	FLR	
70004	LD	DFGH	FLP	MAG	FLR	*The Coal Industry Society*
70005	LD	DFGH	FLP	MAG	FLR	
70006	LD	DFGH	FLP	MAG	FLR	
70007	LD	DFGI	FLP	MAG	FLR	
70008	LD	DFGI	FLP	MAG	FLR	
70009	LD	DFGI	FLP	MAG	FLR	
70010	LD	DFGH	FLP	MAG	FLR	
70011	LD	DFGH	FLP	MAG	FLR	
70013	LD	DFGI	FLP	MAG	FLR	
70014	LD	DFGI	FLP	MAG	FLR	
70015	LD	DFGI	FLP	MAG	FLR	
70016	LD	DFGI	FLP	MAG	FLR	
70017	LD	DFGI	FLP	MAG	FLR	
70018	LD	DFGI	FLP	MAG	FLR	
70019	LD	DFGI	FLP	MAG	FLR	
70020	LD	DFGI	FLP	MAG	FLR	

Above: *Freightliner operates 19 General Electric Class 70 locos; the 20th loco (No. 70012) was destroyed on delivery when it was dropped by the unloading crane. The locos operate a mix of container and Heavy Haul traffic and have not been the most reliable of locos, with several serious fires and major problems. A major retro-fit programme has been undertaken by Wabtec (Brush) and the fleet is now performing better. No further Freightliner Class 70s will be built; No. 70020 is seen passing Banbury with a container train bound for Southampton.* CJM

Class 86/5 and 86/6

Vehicle Length: 58ft 6in (17.83m)
Height: 13ft 0⅝in (3.97m)
Width: 8ft 8¼in (2.64m)

Power Collection: 25kV ac overhead
Horsepower: 5,900hp (4,400kW)
Electrical Equipment: GEC

Number		Depot	Pool	Livery	Owner	Operator
86501	(86608/86408)	FE	DFMC	FLR	FLR	FLR
86604	(86404)	FE	DFNC	FLR	FLR	FLR
86605	(86405)	FE	DFNC	FLR	FLR	FLR
86607	(86407)	FE	DFNC	FLR	FLR	FLR
86609	(86409)	FE	DFNC	FLR	PTR	FLR

86610	(86410)	FE	DFNC	FLR	PTR	FLR	
86612	(86412)	FE	DFNC	FLR	PTR	FLR	
86613	(86413)	FE	DFNC	FLR	PTR	FLR	
86614	(86414)	FE	DHNC	FLR	PTR	FLR	
86622	(86422)	FE	DFNC	FLP	PTR	FLR	
86627	(86427)	FE	DFNC	FLR	PTR	FLR	
86628	(86428)	FE	DFNC	FLR	PTR	FLR	
86632	(86432)	FE	DFNC	FLR	PTR	FLR	
86637	(86437)	FE	DFNC	FLP	PTR	FLR	
86638	(86438)	FE	DFNC	FLR	PTR	FLR	
86639	(86439)	FE	DFNC	FLR	PTR	FLR	

86247 is at LNWR Crewe in pool DHLT, providing spares for Freightliner

A fleet of 16 Class 86/5 and 86/6 locos are based at Crewe and used by Freightliner on intermodal duties mainly linking the North West with the East Coast port at Felixstowe, the locos frequently operating in pairs. Nos. 86639 and 86613 are seen passing South Kenton. **Nathan Williamson**

Class 90

Vehicle Length: 61ft 6in (18.74m)   Power Collection: 25kV ac overhead
Height: 13ft 0¼in (3.96m)   Horsepower: 7,860hp (5,860kW)
Width: 9ft 0in (2.74m)   Electrical Equipment: GEC

Number	Depot	Pool	Livery	Owner	Operator							
90016	CP	DFLC	FLR	PTR	FLR	90046	CP	DFLC	FLR	PTR	FLR
90041	CP	DFLC	FLR	PTR	FLR	90047	CP	DFLC	FLY	PTR	FLR
90042	CP	DFLC	FLP	PTR	FLR	90048	CP	DFLC	FLR	PTR	FLR
90043	CP	DFLC	FLY	PTR	FLR	90049	CP	DFLC	FLP	PTR	FLR
90044	CP	DFLC	FLY	PTR	FLR						
90045	CP	DFLC	FLP	PTR	FLR						

Name applied

90043 *Freightliner Coatbridge*

Above: *The most modern electric locos operated by Freightliner are a batch of 10 Class 90s, allocated to Crewe, and like the Class 86s used mainly on the Manchester/Crewe to Felixstowe corridor. Three locos of the fleet carry the latest PowerHaul livery scheme, as illustrated on No. 90045.* **Antony Christie**

Mendip Rail

Address: ✉ Torr Works, East Cranmore, Shepton Mallet, Somerset, BA4 5SQ
📧 info@mendip-rail.co.uk ✆ 01749 880672 ⓘ www.mendip-rail.co.uk

Managing Director: Alan Taylor
Depots: Merehead (MD), Whatley (WH)
Parent Company: Aggregate Industries and Hanson

Class 08

Vehicle Length: 29ft 3in (8.91m)
Height: 12ft 8⅝in (3.87m)
Width: 8ft 6in (2.59m)

Engine: English Electric 6K
Horsepower: 400hp (298kW)
Electrical Equipment: English Electric

Number	Depot	Pool	Livery	Owner	Operator						
08643	MD	MBDL	GRN	FOS	MRL	08652	WH	MBDL	HAN	HAN	MRL
08650	MD	MBDL	MRL	FOS	MRL	08731	MD	MBDL	BLU	FOS	MRL
						08947	WH	MBDL	BLU	FOS	MRL

Class 59/0 and 59/1

Vehicle Length: 70ft 0½in (21.34m)
Height: 12ft 10in (3.91m)
Width: 8ft 8¼in (2.65m)

Engine: EMD 16-645 E3C
Horsepower: 3,000hp (2,462kW)
Electrical Equipment: EMD

Number	Depot	Pool	Livery	Owner	Operator	Name
59001	MD	XYPO	AGI	FOS	MRL	Yeoman Endeavour
59002	MD	XYPO	AGI	FOS	MRL	Alan J Day
59004	MD	XYPO	FOS	FOS	MRL	Paul A Hammond
59005	MD	XYPO	AGI	FOS	MRL	Kenneth J Painter
59101	MD	XYPA	HAN	HAN	MRL	Village of Whatley
59102	MD	XYPA	HAN	HAN	MRL	Village of Chantry
59103	MD	XYPA	HAN	HAN	MRL	Village of Mells
59104	MD	XYPA	HAN	HAN	MRL	Village of Great Elm

Below: *The combined fleet of eight Class 59/0 and 59/1s operated by Mendip Rail is the backbone of aggregate motive power from the Mendips. No. 59005 in Aggregate Industries livery is seen passing Dawlish with empty stone hoppers bound for Burngullow on 12 January 2014.* **CJM**

SW1001 'Switcher'

Vehicle Length: 40ft 6in (12.34m)
Height: 14ft 3in (4.34m)
Width: 10ft 0in (3.04m)

Engine: GM 8-645E
Horsepower: 1,000hp (746kW)
Electrical Equipment: EMD

Number	Depot	Pool	Livery	Owner	Operator	Name
44	MD	-	FOS	FOS	MRL	Western Yeoman II
120	WH	-	HAN	HAN	MRL	

Eurotunnel

Address (UK): ✉ The Channel Tunnel Group Ltd, Ashford Road, Folkestone, CT18 8XX
📠 info@eurotunnel.com ✆ 01303 282222 ① www.eurotunnel.com

Chairman & CEO: Jacques Gounon **Depot:** Coquelles, France (CO)

Shuttle

All locomotives are allocated to the Eurotunnel Maintenance Facility in Coquelles, France, but can be stabled and receive light repair at Cheriton terminal in the UK.

Class 9/0

Vehicle Length: 72ft 2in (22m)	Power Collection: 25kV ac overhead
Height: 13ft 9in (4.20m)	Horsepower: 7,720hp (5,760kW)
Width: 9ft 9in (3.01m)	Electrical Equipment: Brush

Original loco order, many now rebuilt and upgraded to Class 9/8.

9005	Jessye Norman	9018	Wilhelmena Fernandez	9033	Montserrat Caballé
9007	Dame Joan Sutherland	9022	Dame Janet Baker	9036	Alain Fondary
9011	José Van Dam	9024	Gotthard 1882	9037	Gabriel Bacquier
9013	Maria Callas	9026	Furkatunnel 1982		
9015	Lötschberg 1913	9029	Thomas Allen		

Class 9/7

Vehicle Length: 72ft 2in (22m)	Power Collection: 25kV ac overhead
Height: 13ft 9in (4.20m)	Horsepower: 9,387hp (7,000kW)
Width: 9ft 9in (3.01m)	Electrical Equipment: Brush

9701	9704	9707	9713 (9103)	9716 (9106)	9719 (9109)	9722 (9112)
9702	9705	9711 (9101)	9714 (9104)	9717 (9107)	9720 (9110)	9723 (9113)
9703	9706	9712 (9102)	9715 (9105)	9718 (9108)	9721 (9111)	

Class 9/8

Rebuilt from Class 9/0 locos; 800 added to original running number on conversion.

Vehicle Length: 72ft 2in (22m)	Power Collection: 25kV ac overhead
Height: 13ft 9in (4.20m)	Horsepower: 9,387hp (7,000kW)
Width: 9ft 9in (3.01m)	Electrical Equipment: Brush

9801	Lesley Garrett	9814	Lucia Popp	9827	Barbara Hendricks
9802	Stuart Burrows	9816	Willard White	9828	Dame Kiri Te Kanawa
9803	Benjamin Luxon	9817(S)	José Carreras	9831	
9804	Victoria de Los Angeles	9819	Maria Ewing	9832	Renata Tebaldi
9806	Régine Crespin	9820	Nicolai Ghiaurov	9834	Mirella Freni
9808	Elisabeth Soderstrom	9821	Teresa Berganza	9835	Nicolai Gedda
9809	François Pollet	9823	Dame Elisabeth Legge-	9838	Hildegard Behrens
9810	Jean-Philippe Courtis		Schwarzkopf	9840	
9812	Luciano Pavarotti	9825			

Right: *The fleet of 58 Tri-Bo 'shuttle' locos which power the passenger/car and truck services through the Channel Tunnel from Cheriton to Coquelles are all allocated to the EuroTunnel depot at Coquelles, France, but some are out-based at the UK terminal. All trains are 'top and tailed' and locos of three sub-classes can be found.* **CJM**

MaK DE1004

Vehicle Length: 54ft 2in (16.50m)	Diesel Engine: MTU 12V396tc
Horsepower: 1,260hp (939.5kW)	Electrical Equipment: BBC

0001 (21901)	0003 (21903)	0005 (21905)	0007 (21907) [6457]
0002 (21902)	0004 (21904)	0006 (21906) [6456]	

Hunslet/Schöma

Diesel Engine: Deutz	Mechanical Equipment: Hunslet
Horsepower: 200hp (270kW)	

0031	0032	0033	0034	0035	0036	0037	0038	0039	0040	0041	0042

Network Rail

Address: Kings Place, 90 York Way, London, N1 9AG
   ✉ enquiries@networkrail.co.uk   ⓘ www.networkrail.co.uk
   ✆ Helpline: 08457 114141, Switchboard: 0203 356 9595
Chief Executive: Mark Carne   **Director Operations:** Robin Gisby
Depots: Heaton (HT), Barrow Hill (BH), Derby (DF), Rugby (RU), Eastleigh (ZG)

Class 08

	Vehicle Length: 29ft 3in (8.91m)	*Engine: English Electric 6K*
	Height: 12ft 8⅜in (3.87m)	*Horsepower: 400hp (298kW)*
	Width: 8ft 6in (2.59m)	*Electrical Equipment: English Electric*

Number	Depot	Pool	Livery	Owner	Operator
08417	DF	QADD	NRL	NRL	NRL
08956§	DF	QADD	BLU	NRL	NRL

§ At Old Dalby

Class 31/1 and 31/4

	Vehicle Length: 56ft 9in (17.29m)	*Engine: English Electric 12SVT*
	Height: 12ft 7in (3.91m)	*Horsepower: 1,470hp (1,097kW)*
	Width: 8ft 9in (2.65m)	*Electrical Equipment: Brush*
	31/4 Electric Train Heat fitted	

Number	Depot	Pool	Livery	Owner	Operator
31105	DF	QADD	NRL	NRL	NRL
31233	DF	QADD	NRL	NRL	NRL
31285	DF	QADD	NRL	NRL	NRL
31465*	DF	QADD	NRL	NRL	NRL

* Previously numbered 31565, 31213

Left: *Network Rail operates a fleet of four Class 31s to power test trains. These are all painted in Network Rail yellow and based at the RTC Derby. Various modifications in terms of front lighting have been made for their NR role. These locos are likely to be phased out of traffic in 2015. No. 31105 and Class 73 No. 73138 are illustrated on the Midland Mainline.* **Tim Easter**

Class 43

	Vehicle Length: 58ft 5in (18.80m)	*Engine: MTU 16V4000 R31R*
	Height: 12ft 10in (3.90m)	*Horsepower: 2,250hp (1,680kW)*
	Width: 8ft 11in (2.73m)	*Electrical Equipment: Brush*

Number	Depot	Pool	Livery	Owner	Operator	Name
43013	HT	QCAR	NRL	PTR	NRL	
43014	HT	QCAR	NRL	PTR	NRL	*The Railway Observer*
43062	HT	QCAR	NRL	PTR	NRL	*John Armitt*

Left: *The most important train in the Network Rail fleet of inspection trains is the HST-based New Measurement Train (NMT), based at Derby, with the power cars allocated to Heaton. The NMT operates over all the main core NR routes on a timetabled basis. The train is usually formed of either four or five Mk3 test vehicles. Led by power car No. 43013, with No. 43014 on the rear, the NMT passes Stenson Junction on 15 May 2014 while travelling from Derby to Crewe via Holyhead.* **CJM**

Class 73/1

Vehicle Length: 53ft 8in (16.35m)	Power: 750V dc third rail or English Electric 6K
Height: 12ft 5⁹⁄₁₆in (3.79m)	Horsepower: E/D - 1,600hp (1,193kW) / 600hp (447kW)
Width: 8ft 8in (2.64m)	Electrical Equipment: English Electric

Number	Depot	Pool	Livery	Owner	Operator
73138	DF	QADD	NRL	NRL	NRL

Right: *At the end of 2014 Network Rail officially had the use of one Class 73, No. 73138, to operate test trains as required, frequently operating with other Class 73s from GBRf or the private sector. In the future, a small fleet of modified Class 73/9s under conversion at RVEL Derby will be introduced. With its non-standard end nearest the camera, No. 73138 is seen with a four-vehicle test train on the South West Main Line.* **Mark V. Pike**

Class 37 and 97/3

Vehicle Length: 61ft 6in (18.74m)	Engine: English Electric 12CSVT
Height: 13ft 0¼in (3.96m)	Horsepower: 1,750hp (1,304kW)
Width: 8ft 11⅝in (2.73m)	Electrical Equipment: English Electric

Number		Depot	Pool	Livery	Owner	Operator	Name
37198		BH	MBDL	NRL	NRL	NRL	Chief Engineer
97301	(37100)§	ZA	QETS	NRL	NRL	NRL	
97302	(37170)±	ZA	QETS	NRL	NRL	NRL	
97303	(37178)±	ZA	QETS	NRL	NRL	NRL	
97304	(37217)±	ZA	QETS	NRL	NRL	NRL	John Tiley

§ Fitted with Hitachi ERTMS, ± Fitted with Ansaldo ERTMS

Right: *Five Class 37s, one Class 37/0 and four Class 97/3s, are operated by Network Rail. Based at Derby, the '97/3s' are fitted with ERTMS for development work; when not required for this work, the locos can be used for other Network Rail duties as required. The fleet is painted in NR yellow. No. 97301 is illustrated, in 2014 this loco was fitted with a new design of Hitachi ERTMS system.* **Mark V. Pike**

Class 950

Vehicle Length: 64ft 9¾in (19.74m)	Engine: 1 x NT855R5 of 285hp per vehicle
Height: 12ft 4½in (3.77m)	Horsepower: 570hp (425kW)
Width: 9ft 3⅛in (2.82m)	Seats (total/car): 124S, 59S/65S

Number	Formation	Depot	Livery	Owner	Operator	Note
950001	999600+999601	ZA	NRL	NRL	NRL	Track assessment train (Class 150 outline)

Right: *Two specialist Class 150 outline vehicles were built to form a then BR track assessment train, now operated by Network Rail. The set is classified as Class 950 and allocated the number 950001. It is based at the RTC Derby and operates all over the NR system on a timetabled basis. The set is seen on the sea wall near Dawlish.* **CJM**

Network Rail

Class 313/1

Vehicle Length: (Driving) 64ft 11½in (19.80m) Width: 9ft 3in (2.82m)
(Inter) 65ft 4¼in (19.92m) Horsepower: 880hp (656kW)
Height: 11ft 9in (3.58m)

Great Northern Route - ERTMS development unit

Number	Formation DMSO+PTSO+BDMSO	Depot	Livery	Owner	Operator
313121	62549+71233+61613	HR	YEL	BEA	NRL

Left: *As part of the development of the European Rail Traffic Management System (ERTMS), Network Rail took over Class 313 EMU No. 313121 and rebuilt the set as a travelling test facility working over a section of the Great Northern suburban network on the down line between Molwood Tunnel (Hertford North) and Watton-at-Stone, where this view of the train was recorded.* **Antony Christie**

De-icing Cars

Vehicle Length: 66ft 4in (20.22m) Horsepower: 500hp (370kW)
Height: 12ft 4in (3.75m) Seats (total/car): None
Width: 9ft 2in (2.82m)

Number	Vehicle	Depot	Livery	Owner	Operator	Notes
489102	68501 (977975)	TN	NRL	NRL	NRL	De-icing vehicle modified from Class 489 DMBS
489105	68504	TN	NRL	NRL	GBR	De-icing vehicle modified from Class 489 DMBS
489106	68505	TN	NRL	NRL	GBR	De-icing vehicle modified from Class 489 DMBS

Hauled Stock

Mk2 Height: 12ft 9½in (3.89m)
Vehicle Length: 66ft 0in (20.11m) Width: 9ft 3in (2.81m)

Royal Train

Mk 3 Height: 12ft 9in (3.88m)
Vehicle Length: 75ft 0in (22.86m) Width: 8ft 11in (2.71m)

Number	Type	Depot	Livery	Operator	Use
2903 (11001)	AT5G	ZN	ROY	NRL/DBS	HM The Queen's Saloon
2904 (12001)	AT5G	ZN	ROY	NRL/DBS	HRH The Duke of Edinburgh's Saloon
2915 (10735)	AT5G	ZN	ROY	NRL/DBS	Royal Household Sleeping Coach
2916 (40512)	AT5G	ZN	ROY	NRL/DBS	HRH The Prince of Wales's Dining Coach
2917 (40514)	AT5G	ZN	ROY	NRL/DBS	Kitchen Car and Royal Household Dining Coach
2918 (40515)	AT5G	ZN	ROY	NRL/DBS	Royal Household Coach
2919 (40518)	AT5G	ZN	ROY	NRL/DBS	Royal Household Coach
2920 (17109)	AT5B	ZN	ROY	NRL/DBS	Generator Coach and Household Sleeping Coach
2921 (17107)	AT5B	ZN	ROY	NRL/DBS	Brake, Coffin Carrier and Household Accommodation
2922	AT5G	ZN	ROY	NRL/DBS	HRH The Prince of Wales's Sleeping Coach
2923	AT5G	ZN	ROY	NRL/DBS	Royal Passenger Saloon

Left: *Eleven Mk2 and Mk3 vehicles make up the Royal Train, which is based at Wolverton and powered and staffed by DB Schenker. This illustration shows former Mk3 sleeper car 10735 now used as a staff sleeper and mess coach numbered 2915. Note the revised window arrangement on the left.* **Antony Christie**

Hauled Stock

Number	Type	Depot	Livery	Operator	Use
1256 (3296)	AJIF/RFO	ZA	NRL	NRL	Special vehicle - PLPR3
5981	AC2F/TSO	ZA	NRL	NRL	Special vehicle
6260 (92116)	AX51/GEN	ZA	RTK	NRL/LUL	Generator (owned by DBS)
6261 (92988)	AX51/GEN	ZA	NRL	NRL	Generator (owned by DBS)
6262 (92928)	AX51/GEN	ZA	NRL	NRL	Generator (owned by DBS)
6263 (92961)	AX51/GEN	ZA	NRL	NRL	Generator (owned by DBS)
6264 (92923)	AX51/GEN	ZA	NRL	NRL	Generator (owned by DBS)
9481	AE2D/BSO	ZA	NRL	NRL	Radio Survey coach
9516	AE2D/BSO	ZA	NRL	NRL	Ultrasonic test car support
9523	AE2D/BSO	ZA	NRL	NRL	Ultrasonic test car support
9701 (9528)	AF2F/DBSO	ZA	NRL	NRL	Remote driving car (Mentor train)
9702 (9510)	AF2F/DBSO	ZA	NRL	NRL	Remote driving car
9703 (9517)	AF2F/DBSO	ZA	NRL	NRL	Remote driving car
9708 (9530)	AF2F/DBSO	ZA	NRL	NRL	Remote driving car (Structure Gauging)
9713	AF2F/DBSO	ZA	NRL	NRL	Remote driving car
9714 (9536)	AF2F/DBSO	ZA	NRL	NRL	Remote driving car
62384	MBS	ZA	NRL	NRL	Structure Gauging test car (SGT2)
72612 (6156)	Mk2f/TSO	ZA	NRL	NRL	Brake force runner
72616 (6007)	Mk2f/TSO	ZA	NRL	NRL	Brake force runner
72630 (6094)	Mk2f/TSO	ZA	NRL	NRL	Brake force runner
72631 (6096)	Mk2f/TSO	ZA	NRL	NRL	Brake force runner
72639 (6070)	Mk2f/TSO	ZA	NRL	NRL	Brake force runner
82111	MK3/DVT	ZA	NRL	NRL	Driving Van Trailer
82115	MK3/DVT	ZA	VIR	NRL	Driving Van Trailer
82124	MK3/DVT	ZA	NRL	NRL	Driving Van Trailer
82129	MK3/DVT	ZA	NRL	NRL	Driving Van Trailer
82145	MK3/DVT	ZA	NRL	NRL	Driving Van Trailer
92114 (81443)	Mk1/BG	ZA	NRL	NRL	Special vehicle
92939 (92039)	Mk1/BG	ZA	INT	NRL	Special vehicle
99666 (3250)	Mk2e/FO	ZA	NRL	NRL	Ultrasonic Test Train
971001 (94150)	Mk1/NKA	BS	NRL	NRL	Tool Van
971002 (94190)	Mk1/NKA	±	NRL	NRL	Tool Van (± at Worksop)
971003 (94191)	Mk1/NKA	BS	NRL	NRL	Tool Van
971004 (94168)	Mk1/NKA	KY	NRL	NRL	Tool Van
975025 (60755)	6B Buffet	ZA	GRN	NRL	Control Inspection Saloon *Caroline*
975081 (35313)	Mk1/BSK	ZA	NRL	NRL	Structure Gauging Train
975091 (34615)	Mk1/BSK	ZA	NRL	NRL	Overhead line test coach *Mentor*
975280 (21263)	Mk1/BCK	ZA	NRL	NRL	Staff coach
975464 (35171)	Mk1/BSK	SP	NRL	NRL	Snowblower coach *Ptarmigan*
975486 (34100)	Mk1/BSK	SP	NRL	NRL	Snowblower coach *Polar Bear*

Infrastructure Companies - Network Rail

Right: *As part of the modernisation of the Derby-based Network Rail coaching stock fleet used for dynamic track testing, five former West Coast Mk3 Driving Van Trailers (DVTs) are now operated by Network Rail. All have been heavily rebuilt and most now carry on-board engines and alternators to power test equipment. New frontal lights and infrared lights have also been installed. No. 82124 is seen at Derby. All are painted in Network Rail yellow.* **CJM**

Network Rail

975814	(41000)	HST/TF	EC	NRL	NRL	NMT Conference coach
975984	(40000)	HST/TRUB	EC	NRL	NRL	NMT Lecture coach
977868	(5846)	Mk2e/TSO	ZA	NRL	NRL	Radio Survey coach
977869	(5858)	Mk2e/TSO	ZA	NRL	NRL	Radio Survey coach
977969	(14112)	Mk2/BFK	ZA	NRL	NRL	Staff coach (former Royal Saloon 2906)
977974	(5854)	Mk2e/TSO	ZA	NRL	NRL	Laboratory coach (owned by Delta Rail)
977983	(3407)	Mk2f/FO	ZA	NRL	NRL	Hot Box Detection coach
977984	(40501)	HST/TRFK	EC	NRL	NRL	NMT Staff coach
977985	(6019)	Mk2f/TSO	ZA	NRL	NRL	Structure Gauging Train (SGT2)
977986	(3189)	Mk2d/FO	ZA	NRL	NRL	Track Recording coach
977993	(44053)	HST/TGS	EC	NRL	NRL	NMT Overhead Line Test coach
977994	(44087)	HST/TGS	EC	NRL	NRL	NMT Recording coach
977995	(40719)	HST/TRFM	EC	NRL	NRL	NMT Generator coach
977997	(72613)	Mk2f/TSO	ZA	NRL	NRL	Radio Survey Test Vehicle (originally TSO 6126)
999508		Saloon	ZA	NRL	NRL	Track Recording coach - UTU3
999550		Mk2	ZA	NRL	NRL	Track Recording coach (purpose-built) TRC
999602	(62483)	Mk1/CIG	ZA	NRL	SEC	Ultrasonic Test coach - UTU3
999605	(62482)	Mk1/CIG	ZA	NRL	NRL	Ultrasonic Test coach - UTU2
999606	(62356)	Mk1/CIG	ZA	NRL	NRL	Ultrasonic Test coach - UTU4

Left: *One of the oldest Mk1 test vehicles still in operation is 975091, rebuilt from 34615 back in 1972. The vehicle has been rebuilt at the RTC Derby a number of times for different research, development and now Network Rail uses. The vehicle has flat roof sections at each end onto which non-power-collecting pantographs can be fitted.* **Antony Christie**

Right: *Former Mk2e TSO No. 3250 is now Network Rail vehicle 99666 and used as part of the Ultrasonic Test Unit (UTU). For its present role all its original windows have been plated over, and its external doors have been removed.* **Antony Christie**

Left: *When the Mk2f Driving Brake Standard Open (DBSO) vehicles were withdrawn for Anglia use, Network Rail took over several vehicles to provide remote driving control facilities for test trains. Several were structurally rebuilt for their new role, with front ends and windows being altered. Viewed from its inner end No. 9703 is seen at Ipswich. All are painted in Network Rail yellow.*
Antony Christie

Right: *A number of generator cars are required to operate within the Network Rail test train fleet, to provide non-traction power for test equipment. One such generator vehicle is No. 6264, rebuilt from BG No. 92923. This vehicle has two generators, one mounted at each end. The central guard's compartment is retained and two pairs of hinged doors are retained on each side.* **Antony Christie**

Snowploughs
Independent Drift Ploughs – ZZA

Number	Allocation
ADB965203	Tees
ADB965206	Doncaster
ADB965208	Inverness
ADB965209	Bristol Barton H
ADB965210	Tonbridge
ADB965211	March
ADB965217	Slateford
ADB965219	Mossend
ADB965223	Margam
ADB965224	Carlisle KM
ADB965230	Carlisle KM
ADB965231	Bristol Barton H
ADB965232	Peterborough
ADB965233	Peterborough
ADB965234	Carlisle
ADB965235	Margam
ADB965236	Tonbridge
ADB965237	March
ADB965240	Inverness
ADB965243	Slateford

Above: *Ten pairs of heavy duty Independent Drift Ploughs, TOPS code ZZA, are on the books of Network Rail and are located around the network as required. Normally Direct Rail Services provides traction for plough trains. Plough No. ADB965206 is illustrated.* **Antony Christie**

Beilhack Patrol Ploughs (ex-Class 40 bogies) – ZZA

Number	Allocation
ADB965576	Doncaster
ADB965577	Doncaster
ADB965578	Carlisle
ADB965579	Carlisle
ADB965580	Wigan
ADB965581	Wigan
ADB966098	Doncaster
ADB966099	Doncaster

Right: *Eight snowploughs converted from former Class 40 bogies are operated by Network Rail; again traction and staff to operate the ploughs are usually provided by Direct Rail Services. Plough No. ADB965581 is shown at DRS Crewe Gresty Bridge depot.* **CJM**

Beilhack Snow Blowers – ZWA

Number	Allocation		
ADB968500	Rutherglen	ADB968501	Rutherglen

Track Machines (On-Track Plant)

Plasser & Theurer DTS-62-N – Dynamic Track Stabiliser – ZWA

DR72211	Balfour Beatty	DR72213	Balfour Beatty

Plasser & Theurer 09-16-CSM – Tamper/Liner – ZWA

DR73105(S)	Colas

Plasser & Theurer 09-32-RT – Tamper/Liner – ZWA

DR73108	*Tiger*	Colas

Plasser & Theurer 09-3X – Tamper/Liner – ZWA

DR73109		SB Rail	DR73110	*Peter White* SB Rail

Plasser & Theurer 09-3X-D-RT – Tamper/Liner ZWA

DR73111 *Reading Panel 1965 - 2005*	Network Rail	DR73116	Network Rail
DR73113 *Dai Evans*	Network Rail	DR73117	Network Rail
DR73114 *Ron Henderson*	Network Rail	DR73118	Network Rail
DR73115	Network Rail		

Left: *Plasser & Theurer 09-3X-D-RT tamper and liner No. DR73117 is seen stabled between work at Derby.* **Antony Christie**

Plasser & Theurer 07-32 – Duomatic Tamper/Liner – ZWA

DR73434(S)	Balfour Beatty

Plasser & Theurer 08-16/90 – Tamper/Liner – ZWA

DR73502	Trackwork	DR73503 (S)	Balfour Beatty

Left: *One of only two Plasser & Theurer 08-16/90 tamper and lining machines, No. DR73502 is operated by Trackwork, which tends to transport this machine around the country by road, just using it within worksites. This view shows the machine at Newton Abbot, just after being railed from the road truck behind.* **Antony Christie**

Plasser & Theurer 08-32U RT – Plain Line Tamper – ZWA

DR73803 *Alexander Graham Bell*	SBRail	

Plasser & Theurer 08-16U RT – Plain Line Tamper – ZWA

DR73804 *James Watt*	SBRail

Plasser & Theurer 08-16(32)U RT – Plain Line Tamper – ZWA

DR73805	Colas	DR73806 *Karine* Colas

Plasser & Theurer 08-4x4/4S - RT – Switch/Crossing Tamper – ZWA

DR73904	Thomas Telford	SBRail	DR73908		Colas
DR73905	Eddie King	Colas	DR73909	Saturn	Colas
DR73906	Panther	Colas	DR73910	Jupiter	Colas
DR73907		Colas			

Plasser & Theurer 08-16/4x4C - RT – Switch/Crossing Tamper – ZWA

DR73911	Puma	Colas	DR73913	Colas
DR73912	Lynx	Colas		

Plasser & Theurer 08-4x4S - RT – Switch/Crossing Tamper – ZWA

DR73914	Robert McAlpine	SBRail

Plasser & Theurer 08-16/4x4C - RT – Switch/Crossing Tamper – ZWA

DR73915	William Arrol	SBRail	DR73916	First Engineering	SBRail

Plasser & Theurer 08-4x4S - RT – Switch/Crossing Tamper – ZWA

DR73917		Balfour Beatty	DR93918	Balfour Beatty

Plasser & Theurer 08-16/4x4 C100 - RT – Tamper – ZWA

DR73919	Colas

Plasser & Theurer 08-16/4x4C80 - RT – Tamper – ZWA

DR73920	Colas	DR73921	Colas	DR73922	John Snowdon	Colas

Plasser & Theurer 08-4x4S - RT – Switch/Crossing Tamper – ZWA

DR73923	Mercury	Colas

Plasser & Theurer 08-16/4x4C100 - RT – Tamper – ZWA

DR73924	Atlas	Colas	DR73927	Balfour Beatty
DR73925	Europa	Colas	DR73928	Balfour Beatty
DR73926	Stephen Keith Blanchard	Balfour Beatty		

Right: Painted in the distinctive Balfour Beatty white and blue livery, Plasser & Theurer 08-16/4x4C100 RT machine No. DR73927 is seen at Weymouth. Five of these machines are in traffic, two operated by Colas and three by Balfour Beatty. **Mark V. Pike**

Plasser & Theurer 08-4x4S - RT – Switch/Crossing Tamper – ZWA

DR73929	Colas	DR73930	Colas

Plasser & Theurer 08-16/4x4C100 - RT – Tamper – ZWA

DR73931	Colas

Plasser & Theurer 08-4x4/4S - RT – Switch/Crossing Tamper

DR73932	SBRail

Plasser & Theurer 08-16/4x4C100 - RT – Tamper – ZWA

DR73933	SBRail	DR73934	SB Rail

Plasser & Theurer 08-4x4/4S - RT – Switch/Crossing Tamper – ZWA

DR73935	Colas	DR73936	Colas

Network Rail

Plasser & Theurer 08-16/4x4C100 - RT – Tamper – ZWA

DR73937	Balfour Beatty	DR73939 *Pat Best*	Balfour Beatty
DR73938	Balfour Beatty		

Plasser & Theurer 08-4x4/4S - RT – Switch/Crossing Tamper – ZWA

Above: *One of the larger machines, Plasser & Theurer 08-4x4/4S-RT switch and crossing tamper No. DR73942, is seen painted in Colas Rail colours at Tamworth.* **Antony Christie**

DR73940	SBRail	DR73941	SBRail	DR73942	Colas

Plasser & Theurer 08-16/4x4C100 - RT – Tamper – ZWA

DR73943	Balfour Beatty	DR73944	Balfour Beatty	DR73945	Balfour Beatty

Plasser & Theurer Euromat 08-4x4/4S – ZWA

DR73946	VolkerRail

Plasser & Theurer 08-4x4/4S - RT – Switch/Crossing Tamper ZWA

DR73947	Colas	DR73948	Colas

Plasser & Theurer 08-16/90 275 – Switch/Crossing Tamper – ZWA

DR75201 (S)	Balfour Beatty	DR75202 (S)	Balfour Beatty

Plasser & Theurer 08-16/90 SP-T – Switch/Crossing Tamper – ZWA

DR75203	MLP Maintenance

Plasser & Theurer 08-275ZW – Switch/Crossing Tamper – ZWY

DR75204	Trackwork

Matisa B45 Tamper – ZWA

DR75301	VolkerRail	DR75302	VolkerRail	DR75303	VolkerRail
		Gary Wright			

Matisa B41UE Tamper – ZWA

DR75401	VolkerRail	DR75405	VolkerRail	DR75408	Balfour Beatty
DR75402	VolkerRail	DR75406	Colas	DR75409	Balfour Beatty
DR75403	VolkerRail	*Eric Machell*		DR75410	Balfour Beatty
DR75404	VolkerRail	DR75407	Colas	DR75411	Balfour Beatty

Right: *As part of the two-month-long blockage of the Dawlish sea wall in February-March 2014 following serious storm damage, Matisa B41UE No. DR75406* Eric Machell *was deployed to operate over the reinstated section. The orange, black and yellow machine is seen at Dawlish.* **CJM**

Matisa B66UC Tamper – ZWA

DR75501	Balfour Beatty	DR75502	Balfour Beatty

Plasser & Theurer RM74 – Ballast Cleaner – ZWB

DR76304(S)	Plasser	DR76318(S)	Plasser

Plasser & Theurer RM95RT – Ballast Cleaner – ZWA

DR76323	Network Rail	DR76324	Network Rail

Plasser & Theurer RM900RT Ballast Cleaner – ZWA / ZWQ

DR76501 (HOBC-1)	Network Rail	DR76503 (HOBC-3)	Network Rail
DR76502 (HOBC-2)	Network Rail		

Plasser & Theurer VM80 NR – ZWA

DR76701	(HOBC-3)	Network Rail	DR76710(S) (HOTRT-2)	Network Rail
DR76702	(HOBC-2)	Network Rail	DR76711(S) (HOTRT-1)	Network Rail
DR76703	(HOBC-1)	Network Rail		

Matisa D75 Undercutter – ZWA

DR76750	(HRTRT-2)	Network Rail	DR76751	(HRTRT-1)	Network Rail

Plasser & Theurer 09-16 CM NR – ZWA

DR76801	(HOBC-3)	Network Rail

Plasser & Theurer AFM 2000 RT – Rail Finishing Machine – ZWA

DR77001	SBRail	DR77002	SBRail

Plasser & Theurer USP 5000C – Ballast Regulator – ZWA

DR77315(S)	Balfour Beatty	DR77322	Balfour Beatty	DR77336 (S)	Balfour Beatty
DR77316(S)	Balfour Beatty	DR77327	Colas		

Matisa R24S – Ballast Regulator – ZWA

DR77801	VolkerRail	DR77802	VolkerRail

Plasser & Theurer USP 5000RT – Ballast Regulator – ZWA

Right: *An increasing number of high-output track machines are now owned and operated by Network Rail, such as this Plasser & Theurer USP 5000RT Track Regulator No. DR 77903* Frank Jones. *NR own five of these machines, while Colas and SB Rail own one each.* **Nathan Williamson**

Infrastructure Companies

Network Rail

DR77901		Colas	DR77906			Network Rail
DR77903	*Frank Jones*	Network Rail	DR77907			Network Rail
DR77904		Network Rail	DR77908*			SBRail
DR77905		Network Rail	* Previously DR77902			

Plasser & Theurer Self-Propelled Heavy Duty Twin Jib Crane – YJB

DR78213	VolkerRail	DR78218	Balfour Beatty	DR78223	Balfour Beatty
DR78215	SB Rail	DR78219	SB Rail	DR78224	Balfour Beatty
DR78216	Balfour Beatty	DR78221	Balfour Beatty		
DR78217	SB Rail	DR78222	Balfour Beatty		

Cowans Sheldon Self-Propelled Heavy Duty Twin Jib Crane – YJB

DR78226	Colas	DR78231	Network Rail	DR78235	Colas
DR78229	Network Rail	DR78234	Network Rail	DR78237	Network Rail

Below: *Six Cowans Sheldon self-propelled twin jib cranes, used for track renewal work, are in traffic; two are owned by Colas and four by Network Rail. The two Colas vehicles, Nos. DR78226 and DR78235, are illustrated.* **Antony Christie**

Donelli PD350 Single Line Track Relayer

DR78416	Balfour Beatty	DR78417	Balfour Beatty	DR78490	VolkerRail

Harsco Track Technologies NTC Power Wagon – YJA

DR78701	Balfour Beatty	DR78702	Balfour Beatty

Matisa P95 Track Renewal Train – YJA

DR78801	Network Rail	DR78811	Network Rail	DR78821	Network Rail	DR78831	Network Rail
DR78802	Network Rail	DR78812	Network Rail	DR78822	Network Rail	DR78832	Network Rail

Schweebau SPML15 – Rail Grinder – ZWA

DR79200	Loram

Loram/Barclay SPML17 – Rail Grinder – ZWA

DR79201	Loram

Speno RPS 32-2 – Rail Grinder – ZWA

DR79221	Speno	DR79223	Speno	DR79225	Speno
DR79222	Speno	DR79224	Speno	DR79226	Speno

Loram C21 – Rail Grinder – ZWA

Set 01		Set 02		Set 03	
DR79231	Loram	DR79241	Loram	DR79251	Loram
DR79232	Loram	DR79242	Loram	DR79252	Loram
DR79233	Loram	DR79243	Loram	DR79253	Loram
DR79234	Loram	DR79244	Loram	DR79254	Loram
DR79235	Loram	DR79245	Loram	DR79255	Loram
DR79236	Loram	DR79246	Loram	DR79256	Loram
DR79237	Loram	DR79247 *Roger Smith*	Loram	DR79257	Loram

Harsco Track Technologies RGH-20C Switch/Crossing Rail Grinder – ZWA

DR79261 + DR79271	Network Rail	DR79265 + DR79275	Network Rail
DR79262 + DR79272	Network Rail	DR79266 + DR79276	Network Rail
DR79263 + DR79273	Network Rail	DR79267 + DR79277	Network Rail
DR79264 + DR79274	Network Rail		

Right: *Keeping the correct rail head profile on the rails is an important feature in maintaining a smooth and safe railway. For this purpose a fleet of rail grinders is in traffic. Several Harsco twin-vehicles are owned by Network Rail. Twin set No. DR79273 and DR79263 is seen receiving maintenance at Slough.*
Antony Christie

Pandrol Jackson – Stoneblower – YZA

DR80201	Network Rail	DR80206	Network Rail	DR80210	Network Rail
DR80202(S)	Network Rail	DR80207(S)	Network Rail	DR80211	Network Rail
DR80203(S)	Network Rail	DR80208	Network Rail	DR80212(S)	Network Rail
DR80205	Network Rail	DR80209	Network Rail		

Right: *A fleet of 11 Pandrol Jackson 'Stoneblowers' is operated by Network Rail, but in 2015 four were stored out of use. These twin-length machines inject ballast under high pressure below the track to ensure a stable base. Vehicle No. DR80206 is seen passing west through Totnes.*
Nathan Williamson

Harsco Track Technologies – Stoneblower – YZA

DR80213	Network Rail	DR80215	Network Rail	DR80217	Network Rail
DR80214	Network Rail	DR80216	Network Rail		

Harsco Track Technologies – General Purpose Stoneblower – YZA

DR80301	*Stephen Cornish*	Network Rail	DR80303	Network Rail
DR80302		Network Rail		

Plasser & Theurer Heavy Duty Diesel Hydraulic Crane – YOB

DR81505	Balfour Beatty	DR81513(S)	Balfour Beatty	DR81525	Balfour Beatty
DR81507	Balfour Beatty	DR51517	Balfour Beatty	DR81532	Balfour Beatty
DR81508(S)	Balfour Beatty	DR81519	Balfour Beatty		
DR81511(S)	Balfour Beatty	DR81522	Balfour Beatty		

Infrastructure Companies – Network Rail

Network Rail

Cowans Sheldon Heavy Duty Diesel Hydraulic Crane

DR81541	Corus	DR81545	Corus

Kirow KRC810UK 100 tonne Diesel Hydraulic Crane – ZOA

DR81601	*Nigel Chester*	VolkerRail	DR81602	Balfour Beatty

Kirow KRC1200UK 125 tonne Diesel Hydraulic Crane – ZOA

DR81611	*Malcolm L Pearce*	Balfour Beatty	DR81613	VolkerRail
DR81612		Colas		

Kirow KRC250UK Heavy Duty Diesel Hydraulic Crane – ZOA

DR81621	VolkerRail	DR81623	SBRail	DR81625	SBRail
DR81622	VolkerRail	DR81624	SBRail		

Plasser & Theurer Loading Station

DR88101	Network Rail

Starfer Single Line Spoil Handling System Train

DR92201	Network Rail	DR92205	Network Rail	DR92209	Network Rail
DR92202	Network Rail	DR92206	Network Rail	DR92210	Network Rail
DR92203	Network Rail	DR92207	Network Rail	DR92211	Network Rail
DR92204	Network Rail	DR92208	Network Rail	DR92212	Network Rail

Skako Ballast Distribution Train – YDA 'Octopus'

DR92213	Network Rail	DR92217	Network Rail	DR92221	Network Rail
DR92214	Network Rail	DR92218	Network Rail	DR92222	Network Rail
DR92215	Network Rail	DR92219	Network Rail		
DR92216	Network Rail	DR92220	Network Rail		

Plasser & Theurer NFS-D Ballast Distribution Train Hopper – YDA

DR92223	Network Rail	DR92229	Network Rail	DR92235	Network Rail
DR92224	Network Rail	DR92230	Network Rail	DR92236	Network Rail
DR92225	Network Rail	DR92231	Network Rail	DR92237	Network Rail
DR92226	Network Rail	DR92232	Network Rail	DR92238	Network Rail
DR92227	Network Rail	DR92233	Network Rail	DR92239	Network Rail
DR92228	Network Rail	DR92234	Network Rail	DR92240	Network Rail

Plasser & Theurer MFS-D Ballast Distribution Train Hopper – YDA

DR92241	Network Rail	DR92246	Network Rail	DR92251	Network Rail
DR92242	Network Rail	DR92247	Network Rail	DR92252	Network Rail
DR92243	Network Rail	DR92248	Network Rail	DR92253	Network Rail
DR92244	Network Rail	DR92249	Network Rail	DR92254	Network Rail
DR92245	Network Rail	DR92250	Network Rail		

Plasser & Theurer MFS-SB Swivel Conveyer Wagon – YDA

DR92259	Network Rail	DR92261	Network Rail
DR92260	Network Rail	DR92262	Network Rail

Plasser & Theurer MFS-PW Single Line Handling Train Power Wagon – YOA

DR92263	Network Rail

Plasser & Theurer NB-PW Ballast Distribution Train Power Wagon – YOA

DR92264	Network Rail

Plasser & Theurer MFS-D Ballast Distribution Train Hopper – YDA

DR92265	Network Rail	DR92270	Network Rail	DR92275	Network Rail
DR92266	Network Rail	DR92271	Network Rail	DR92276	Network Rail
DR92267	Network Rail	DR92272	Network Rail	DR92277	Network Rail
DR92268	Network Rail	DR92273	Network Rail	DR92278	Network Rail
DR92269	Network Rail	DR92274	Network Rail	DR92279	Network Rail

Plasser & Theurer MFS-SB Swivel Conveyer Wagon – YDA

DR92280	Network Rail	DR92281	Network Rail

Plasser & Theurer MFS-A Materials Handling Train Interface Wagon – YDA

DR92282	Network Rail	DR92283	Network Rail

Plasser & Theurer PW-RT Materials Handling Train Power Wagon – YOA

DR92285	Network Rail

Plasser & Theurer NPW-RT Materials Handling Train Power Wagon – YOA

DR92286	Network Rail

Plasser & Theurer MFS-SB Swivel Conveyer Wagon – YDA

DR92287	Network Rail	DR92290	Network Rail	DR92293	Network Rail
DR92288	Network Rail	DR92291	Network Rail	DR92294	Network Rail
DR92289	Network Rail	DR92292	Network Rail		

Plasser & Theurer MFS-D Ballast Distribution Train Hopper – YDA

DR92295	Network Rail	DR92307	Network Rail	DR92319	Network Rail
DR92296	Network Rail	DR92308	Network Rail	DR92320	Network Rail
DR92297	Network Rail	DR92309	Network Rail	DR92321	Network Rail
DR92298	Network Rail	DR92310	Network Rail	DR92322	Network Rail
DR92299	Network Rail	DR92311	Network Rail	DR92323	Network Rail
DR92300	Network Rail	DR92312	Network Rail	DR92324	Network Rail
DR92301	Network Rail	DR92313	Network Rail	DR92325	Network Rail
DR92302	Network Rail	DR92314	Network Rail	DR92326	Network Rail
DR92303	Network Rail	DR92315	Network Rail	DR92327	Network Rail
DR92304	Network Rail	DR92316	Network Rail	DR92328	Network Rail
DR92305	Network Rail	DR92317	Network Rail	DR92329	Network Rail
DR92306	Network Rail	DR92318	Network Rail	DR92330	Network Rail

Plasser & Theurer PW-RT Materials Handling Train Power Wagon – YOA

DR92331	Network Rail

Plasser & Theurer NPW-RT Materials Handling Train Power Wagon – YOA

DR92332	Network Rail

Plasser & Theurer MFS-SB Swivel Conveyer Wagon – YDA

DR92333	Network Rail	DR92336	Network Rail	DR92339	Network Rail
DR92334	Network Rail	DR92337	Network Rail	DR92340	Network Rail
DR92335	Network Rail	DR92338	Network Rail		

Plasser & Theurer MFS-D Ballast Distribution Train Hopper – YDA

DR92341	Network Rail	DR92354	Network Rail	DR92367	Network Rail
DR92342	Network Rail	DR92355	Network Rail	DR92368	Network Rail
DR92343	Network Rail	DR92356	Network Rail	DR92369	Network Rail
DR92344	Network Rail	DR92357	Network Rail	DR92370	Network Rail
DR92345	Network Rail	DR92358	Network Rail	DR92371	Network Rail
DR92346	Network Rail	DR92359	Network Rail	DR92372	Network Rail
DR92347	Network Rail	DR92360	Network Rail	DR92373	Network Rail
DR92348	Network Rail	DR92361	Network Rail	DR92374	Network Rail
DR92349	Network Rail	DR92362	Network Rail	DR92375	Network Rail
DR92350	Network Rail	DR92363	Network Rail	DR92376	Network Rail
DR92351	Network Rail	DR92364	Network Rail	DR92377	Colas
DR92352	Network Rail	DR92365	Network Rail		
DR92353	Network Rail	DR92366	Network Rail		

Plasser & Theurer MFS-A Materials Handling Train Interface Wagon – YDA

DR92400	Colas

Plasser & Theurer PW-RT Materials Handling Train Power Wagon

DR92431	Network Rail

Network Rail

Plasser & Theurer NPW-RT Materials Handling Train Power Wagon

DR92432	Network Rail

Plasser & Theurer MFS-SB Swivel Conveyer Wagon

DR92433	Network Rail	DR92436	Network Rail	DR92439	Network Rail
DR92434	Network Rail	DR92437	Network Rail	DR92440	Network Rail
DR92435	Network Rail	DR92438	Network Rail		

Plasser & Theurer MFS-D Ballast Distribution Train Hopper – YDA

DR92441	Network Rail	DR92453	Network Rail	DR92465	Network Rail
DR92442	Network Rail	DR92454	Network Rail	DR92466	Network Rail
DR92443	Network Rail	DR92455	Network Rail	DR92467	Network Rail
DR92444	Network Rail	DR92456	Network Rail	DR92468	Network Rail
DR92445	Network Rail	DR92457	Network Rail	DR92469	Network Rail
DR92446	Network Rail	DR92458	Network Rail	DR92470	Network Rail
DR92447	Network Rail	DR92459	Network Rail	DR92471	Network Rail
DR92448	Network Rail	DR92460	Network Rail	DR92472	Network Rail
DR92449	Network Rail	DR92461	Network Rail	DR92473	Network Rail
DR92450	Network Rail	DR92462	Network Rail	DR92474	Network Rail
DR92451	Network Rail	DR92463	Network Rail	DR92475	Network Rail
DR92452	Network Rail	DR92464	Network Rail	DR92476	Network Rail

Sleeper Delivery Train – Generator Wagon – YFA

DR92501	(Stored)	DR92502	(Stored)	DR92503	(Stored)

Twin Jib Rail Recovery Train 'Slinger' – YFA

DR92504	(Stored)	DR92507	(Stored)	DR92510	(Stored)
DR92505	(Stored)	DR92508	(Stored)	DR92511	(Stored)
DR92506	(Stored)	DR92509	(Stored)	DR92512	(Stored)

Single Jib Rail Recovery Train 'Slinger' – YFA

DR92513	(Stored)	DR92515	(Stored)	DR92517	(Stored)
DR92514	(Stored)	DR92516	(Stored)	DR92518	(Stored)

Sleeper Delivery Train – Twin Crane 'Slinger' – YFA

DR92519	(Stored)

Sleeper Delivery Train – Generator Wagon 'Slinger' – YFA

DR92520	(Stored)	DR92522	(Stored)	DR92524	(Stored)
DR92521	(Stored)	DR92523	(Stored)	DR92525	(Stored)

Sleeper Delivery Train – Twin Crane 'Slinger' – YFA

DR92526	(Stored)	DR92528	(Stored)	DR92530	(Stored)	DR92532	(Stored)
DR92527	(Stored)	DR92529	(Stored)	DR92531	(Stored)		

Sleeper Delivery Train – Generator Wagon 'Slinger' – YFA

DR92533	(Stored)	DR92534	(Stored)

Sleeper Delivery Train – Twin Crane 'Slinger' – YFA

DR92535	(Stored)	DR92538	(Stored)	DR92541	(Stored)	DR92544	(Stored)
DR92536	(Stored)	DR92539	(Stored)	DR92542	(Stored)	DR92545	(Stored)
DR92537	(Stored)	DR92540	(Stored)	DR92543	(Stored)	DR92546	(Stored)

Sleeper Delivery Train – Generator Wagon 'Slinger' – YFA

DR92547	(Stored)	DR92548	(Stored)	DR92549	(Stored)

Sleeper Delivery Train – Twin Crane 'Slinger' – YFA

DR92550	(Stored)	DR92553	(Stored)	DR92556	(Stored)	DR92559	(Stored)
DR92551	(Stored)	DR92554	(Stored)	DR92557	(Stored)	DR92560	(Stored)
DR92552	(Stored)	DR92555	(Stored)	DR92558	(Stored)	DR92561	(Stored)

DR92562	(Stored)	DR92566	(Stored)	DR92570	(Stored)
DR92563	(Stored)	DR92567	(Stored)	DR92571	(Stored)
DR92564	(Stored)	DR92568	(Stored)		
DR92565	(Stored)	DR92569	(Stored)		

W H Davis Sleeper Wagons – YXA

DR92601	Network Rail	DR92623	Network Rail	DR92645	Network Rail
DR92602	Network Rail	DR92624	Network Rail	DR92646	Network Rail
DR92603	Network Rail	DR92625	Network Rail	DR92647	Network Rail
DR92604	Network Rail	DR92626	Network Rail	DR92648	Network Rail
DR92605	Network Rail	DR92627	Network Rail	DR92649	Network Rail
DR92606	Network Rail	DR92628	Network Rail	DR92650	Network Rail
DR92607	Network Rail	DR92629	Network Rail	DR92651	Network Rail
DR92608	Network Rail	DR92630	Network Rail	DR92652	Network Rail
DR92609	Network Rail	DR92631	Network Rail	DR92653	Network Rail
DR92610	Network Rail	DR92632	Network Rail	DR92654	Network Rail
DR92611	Network Rail	DR92633	Network Rail	DR92655	Network Rail
DR92612	Network Rail	DR92634	Network Rail	DR92656	Network Rail
DR92613	Network Rail	DR92635	Network Rail	DR92657	Network Rail
DR92614	Network Rail	DR92636	Network Rail	DR92658	Network Rail
DR92615	Network Rail	DR92637	Network Rail	DR92659	Network Rail
DR92616	Network Rail	DR92638	Network Rail	DR92660	Network Rail
DR92617	Network Rail	DR92639	Network Rail	DR92661	Network Rail
DR92618	Network Rail	DR92640	Network Rail	DR92662	Network Rail
DR92619	Network Rail	DR92641	Network Rail	DR92663	Network Rail
DR92620	Network Rail	DR92642	Network Rail	DR92664	Network Rail
DR92621	Network Rail	DR92643	Network Rail	DR92665	Network Rail
DR92622	Network Rail	DR92644	Network Rail		

International Sleeper Wagons – YXA

3170 4629 001 9	*629001* Network Rail	3170 4629 018 3	*629018* Network Rail	3170 4629 035 7	*629035* Network Rail
3170 4629 002 7	*629002* Network Rail	3170 4629 019 1	*629019* Network Rail	3170 4629 036 5	*629036* Network Rail
3170 4629 003 5	*629003* Network Rail	3170 4629 020 9	*629020* Network Rail	3170 4629 037 3	*629037* Network Rail
3170 4629 004 3	*629004* Network Rail	3170 4629 021 7	*629021* Network Rail	3170 4629 038 1	*629038* Network Rail
3170 4629 005 0	*629005* Network Rail	3170 4629 022 5	*629022* Network Rail	3170 4629 039 9	*629039* Network Rail
3170 4629 006 8	*629006* Network Rail	3170 4629 023 3	*629023* Network Rail	3170 4629 040 7	*629040* Network Rail
3170 4629 007 6	*629007* Network Rail	3170 4629 024 1	*629024* Network Rail	3170 4629 041 5	*629041* Network Rail
3170 4629 008 4	*629008* Network Rail	3170 4629 025 8	*629025* Network Rail	3170 4629 042 3	*629042* Network Rail
3170 4629 009 2	*629009* Network Rail	3170 4629 026 6	*629026* Network Rail	3170 4629 043 1	*629043* Network Rail
3170 4629 010 0	*629010* Network Rail	3170 4629 027 4	*629027* Network Rail	3170 4629 044 9	*629044* Network Rail
3170 4629 011 8	*629011* Network Rail	3170 4629 028 2	*629028* Network Rail	3170 4629 045 6	*629045* Network Rail
3170 4629 012 6	*629012* Network Rail	3170 4629 029 0	*629029* Network Rail	3170 4629 046 4	*629046* Network Rail
3170 4629 013 4	*629013* Network Rail	3170 4629 030 8	*629030* Network Rail	3170 4629 047 2	*629047* Network Rail
3170 4629 014 2	*629014* Network Rail	3170 4629 031 6	*629031* Network Rail	3170 4629 048 0	*629048* Network Rail
3170 4629 015 9	*629015* Network Rail	3170 4629 032 4	*629032* Network Rail	3170 4629 049 8	*629049* Network Rail
3170 4629 016 7	*629016* Network Rail	3170 4629 033 2	*629033* Network Rail	3170 4629 050 6	*629050* Network Rail
3170 4629 017 5	*629017* Network Rail	3170 4629 034 0	*629034* Network Rail		

Sleeper Delivery Train – Manipulator, Clamp*, Chute§ – JZA

DR93325	Network Rail	DR93383	Network Rail	DR93601*	Network Rail
DR93327	Network Rail	DR93418	Network Rail	DR93603*	Network Rail
DR93334	Network Rail	DR93463	Network Rail	DR93608*	Network Rail
DR93339	Network Rail	DR93465	Network Rail	DR93609*	Network Rail
DR93346	Network Rail	DR93480	Network Rail	DR97501§	Network Rail

W H Davis Flat/Workshop/Barrier Wagons – YSA

DR92701	Network Rail	DR92703	Network Rail	DR92705	Network Rail
DR92702	Network Rail	DR92704	Network Rail	DR92706	Network Rail

Cowans Sheldon 75 tonne Diesel Hydraulic Recovery Crane – ZIA* ZIB¤

ARDC96710¤ Network Rail (BS)	ARDC96714* Network Rail (MG)	
ARDC96713¤ Network Rail (SP)	ARDC96715¤ Network Rail (TO)	

Infrastructure Companies - Network Rail

Network Rail

Eiv de Brieve DU94BA – TRAMM – ZWA

DR97001   High Speed 1 (HS1)

Windhoff Overhead Line – MPV – YXA

DR97011	High Speed 1 (HS1)	DR97013	High Speed 1 (HS1)
DR97012	High Speed 1 (HS1)	DR97014	High Speed 1 (HS1)

Windhoff Overhead Line – MPV – YXA

DR98001 Network Rail	DR98004 Network Rail	DR98007 Network Rail	DR98010 Network Rail
DR98002 Network Rail	DR98005 Network Rail	DR98008 Network Rail	DR98011 Network Rail
DR98003 Network Rail	DR98006 Network Rail	DR98009 Network Rail	DR98014 Network Rail

Names applied:
DR98003 *Anthony Wrighton*   DR98009 *Melvin Smith*   DR98010 *Benjamin Gautrey*

Above: *Windhoff built several multi-vehicle self-propelled overhead wiring trains for use in the Midlands and the North West. Painted white, the sets operate formed of a number of intermediate vehicles with a driving vehicle at the outer ends. A three-car formation led by driving car No. DR98009 is recorded at Preston.* **CJM**

Plasser & Theurer General Purpose Machine (GP-TRAMM) – ZWA

DR98215 Balfour Beatty	DR98217 Balfour Beatty	DR98219 Balfour Beatty
DR98216 Balfour Beatty	DR98218 Balfour Beatty	DR98220 Balfour Beatty

Geismar General Purpose Machine (GP-TRAMM)

DR98303   BAR

Geismar VMT860 PL/UM – ZWA

DR98305 Network Rail	DR98306 Network Rail	DR98307(S) Colas	DR98308(S) Colas

Rail Head Treatment Train (RHTT) FEA-F

642001	Network Rail	642014	Network Rail	642027	Network Rail	642040	Network Rail
642002	Network Rail	642015	Network Rail	642028	Network Rail	642041	Network Rail
642003	Network Rail	642016	Network Rail	642029	Network Rail	642042	Network Rail
642004	Network Rail	642017	Network Rail	642030	Network Rail	642043	Network Rail
642005	Network Rail	642018	Network Rail	642031	Network Rail	642044	Network Rail
642006	Network Rail	642019	Network Rail	642032	Network Rail	642045	Network Rail
642007	Network Rail	642020	Network Rail	642033	Network Rail	642046	Network Rail
642008	Network Rail	642021	Network Rail	642034	Network Rail	642047	Network Rail
642009	Network Rail	642022	Network Rail	642035	Network Rail	642048	Network Rail
642010	Network Rail	642023	Network Rail	642036	Network Rail	642049	Network Rail
642011	Network Rail	642024	Network Rail	642037	Network Rail	642050	Network Rail
642012	Network Rail	642025	Network Rail	642038	Network Rail		
642013	Network Rail	642026	Network Rail	642039	Network Rail		

Windhoff Multi Purpose Vehicle (MPV) – YXA

DR98901 + DR98951 Network Rail	DR98912 + DR98962 Network Rail	DR98923 + DR98973 Network Rail
DR98902 + DR98952 Network Rail	DR98913 + DR98963 Network Rail	DR98924 + DR98974 Network Rail
DR98903 + DR98953 Network Rail	DR98914 + DR98964 Network Rail	DR98925 + DR98975 Network Rail
DR98904 + DR98954 Network Rail	DR98915 + DR98965 Network Rail	DR98926 + DR98976 Network Rail
DR98905 + DR98955 Network Rail	DR98916 + DR98966 Network Rail	DR98927 + DR98977 Network Rail
DR98906 + DR98956 Network Rail	DR98917 + DR98967 Network Rail	DR98928 + DR98978 Network Rail
DR98907 + DR98957 Network Rail	DR98918 + DR98968 Network Rail	DR98929 + DR98979 Network Rail
DR98908 + DR98958 Network Rail	DR98919 + DR98969 Network Rail	DR98930 + DR98980 Network Rail
DR98909 + DR98959 Network Rail	DR98920 + DR98970 Network Rail	DR98931 + DR98981 Network Rail
DR98910 + DR98960 Network Rail	DR98921 + DR98971 Network Rail	DR98932 + DR98982 Network Rail
DR98911 + DR98961 Network Rail	DR98922 + DR98972 Network Rail	

Names applied:
DR98926+DR98976 John Denyer

Right: *Windhoff has a fleet of 32 two-section Multi-Purpose Vehicles (MPVs) operating throughout Network Rail. The vehicles carry various 'pods' for different applications, such as track maintenance, track cleaning, de-icing, weed control or rail head treatment. Fitted with weed control 'pods', set Nos. 98958 and 98908 emerges from Kennaway Tunnel, Dawlish.* **CJM**

Rail Wagon – YEA 'Perch'

DR979001 Network Rail	DR979035 Network Rail	DR979069 Network Rail	DR979103 Network Rail
DR979002 Network Rail	DR979036 Network Rail	DR979070 Network Rail	DR979104 Network Rail
DR979003 Network Rail	DR979037 Network Rail	DR979071 Network Rail	DR979105 Network Rail
DR979004 Network Rail	DR979038 Network Rail	DR979072 Network Rail	DR979106 Network Rail
DR979005 Network Rail	DR979039 Network Rail	DR979073 Network Rail	DR979107 Network Rail
DR979006 Network Rail	DR979040 Network Rail	DR979074 Network Rail	DR979108 Network Rail
DR979007 Network Rail	DR979041 Network Rail	DR979075 Network Rail	DR979109 Network Rail
DR979008 Network Rail	DR979042 Network Rail	DR979076 Network Rail	DR979110 Network Rail
DR979009 Network Rail	DR979043 Network Rail	DR979077 Network Rail	DR979111 Network Rail
DR979010 Network Rail	DR979044 Network Rail	DR979078 Network Rail	DR979112 Network Rail
DR979011 Network Rail	DR979045 Network Rail	DR979079 Network Rail	DR979113 Network Rail
DR979012 Network Rail	DR979046 Network Rail	DR979080 Network Rail	DR979114 Network Rail
DR979013 Network Rail	DR979047 Network Rail	DR979081 Network Rail	DR979115 Network Rail
DR979014 Network Rail	DR979048 Network Rail	DR979082 Network Rail	DR979116 Network Rail
DR979015 Network Rail	DR979049 Network Rail	DR979083 Network Rail	DR979117 Network Rail
DR979016 Network Rail	DR979050 Network Rail	DR979084 Network Rail	DR979118 Network Rail
DR979017 Network Rail	DR979051 Network Rail	DR979085 Network Rail	DR979119 Network Rail
DR979018 Network Rail	DR979052 Network Rail	DR979086 Network Rail	DR979120 Network Rail
DR979019 Network Rail	DR979053 Network Rail	DR979087 Network Rail	DR979121 Network Rail
DR979020 Network Rail	DR979054 Network Rail	DR979088 Network Rail	DR979122 Network Rail
DR979021 Network Rail	DR979055 Network Rail	DR979089 Network Rail	DR979123 Network Rail
DR979022 Network Rail	DR979056 Network Rail	DR979090 Network Rail	DR979124 Network Rail
DR979023 Network Rail	DR979057 Network Rail	DR979091 Network Rail	DR979125 Network Rail
DR979024 Network Rail	DR979058 Network Rail	DR979092 Network Rail	DR979126 Network Rail
DR979025 Network Rail	DR979059 Network Rail	DR979093 Network Rail	DR979127 Network Rail
DR979026 Network Rail	DR979060 Network Rail	DR979094 Network Rail	DR979128 Network Rail
DR979027 Network Rail	DR979061 Network Rail	DR979095 Network Rail	DR979129 Network Rail
DR979028 Network Rail	DR979062 Network Rail	DR979096 Network Rail	DR979130 Network Rail
DR979029 Network Rail	DR979063 Network Rail	DR979097 Network Rail	DR979131 Network Rail
DR979030 Network Rail	DR979064 Network Rail	DR979098 Network Rail	DR979132 Network Rail
DR979031 Network Rail	DR979065 Network Rail	DR979099 Network Rail	DR979133 Network Rail
DR979032 Network Rail	DR979066 Network Rail	DR979100 Network Rail	DR979134 Network Rail
DR979033 Network Rail	DR979067 Network Rail	DR979101 Network Rail	
DR979034 Network Rail	DR979068 Network Rail	DR979102 Network Rail	

Continuous Welded Rail Clamping Wagon – YEA 'Perch'

DR979409	Network Rail	DR979412	Network Rail	DR979415	Network Rail

Continuous Welded Rail End of Train Wagon – YEA 'Porpoise'

DR979505	Network Rail	DR979509	Network Rail	DR979513	Network Rail	DR979515	Network Rail
DR979506	Network Rail	DR979511	Network Rail	DR979514	Network Rail		

Continuous Welded Rail 'Chute' Wagon – YEA 'Porpoise'

DR979500	Network Rail	DR979502	Network Rail	DR979507	Network Rail	DR979510	Network Rail
DR979501	Network Rail	DR979503	Network Rail	DR979508	Network Rail	DR979512	Network Rail

Continuous Welded Rail Gantry Wagon – YEA 'Perch'

DR979604	Network Rail	DR979611	Network Rail	DR979614	Network Rail
DR979607	Network Rail	DR979612	Network Rail		
DR979609	Network Rail	DR979613	Network Rail		

Plasser & Theurer EM-SAT RT900 Survey Vehicle

DR999800(S)	*Richard Spoors*	Network Rail
DR999801(S)		Network Rail

Railvac Machine - Swedish Rail Vacuum KFA

99-70-9515-001-4 (99709)	Railcare, Sweden*	* Operated in the UK - based at Totton
99-70-9515-002-2	Railcare, Sweden*	* Operated in the UK - based at Bletchley
99-70-9515-003-0	Railcare, Sweden*	* Operated in the UK

Left: *The use of industrial vacuum cleaners to remove unwanted debris and rubbish from the rail track system has grown in recent years, with specialised vacuum machines now available. Owned by Railcare in Sweden, international numbered vehicle 90 70 9515 001-4 is seen powered by two Devon Cornwall Railway Class 31s. When not is use the Railvac wagons are frequently stabled at Totton near Southampton.* **Nathan Williamson**

Windhoff MPV - High Output Plant System (GW electrification train)

DR 99 70 9131 001	Network Rail	DR 99 70 9131 009	Network Rail	DR 99 70 9131 017	Network Rail
DR 99 70 9131 002	Network Rail	DR 99 70 9131 010	Network Rail	DR 99 70 9131 018	Network Rail
DR 99 70 9131 003	Network Rail	DR 99 70 9131 011	Network Rail	DR 99 70 9131 019	Network Rail
DR 99 70 9131 004	Network Rail	DR 99 70 9131 012	Network Rail	DR 99 70 9131 020	Network Rail
DR 99 70 9131 005	Network Rail	DR 99 70 9131 013	Network Rail	DR 99 70 9131 021	Network Rail
DR 99 70 9131 006	Network Rail	DR 99 70 9131 014	Network Rail	DR 99 70 9131 022	Network Rail
DR 99 70 9131 007	Network Rail	DR 99 70 9131 015	Network Rail	DR 99 70 9131 023	Network Rail
DR 99 70 9131 008	Network Rail	DR 99 70 9131 016	Network Rail		

The 23 Windhoff MPV-style vehicles are for the Great Western route electrification train based at Swindon. The 23-vehicle train can operate to worksites at 60mph and then be split to form several small work trains for the erection of overhead power equipment.
DR 99 70 9131 001 named *Brunel*

Winter Snow Patrol Train 'Perch'

99709594014-1 IS	977986 IS

Balfour Beatty Rail Services

Address: ✉ 130 Wilton Road, London, SW1V 4LQ
✎ info@bbrail.com
✆ 0207 216 6800
ⓘ www.bbrail.com

Managing Director: Peter Anderson   **Depot:** Ashford (AD)

Hauled Stock

	Mk1		Height: 12ft 9½in (3.89m)		
	Vehicle Length: 64ft 6in (19.65m)		Width: 9ft 3in (2.81m)		

Number		Type	Depot	Livery	Operator	Use
977163	(35487)	Mk1/BSK	AD	BBR	BBR	Staff & Generator coach
977165	(35408)	Mk1/BSK	AD	BBR	BBR	Staff & Generator coach
977166	(35419)	Mk1/BSK	AD	BBR	BBR	Staff & Generator coach
977167	(35400)	Mk1/BSK	AD	BBR	BBR	Staff & Generator coach
977168	(35289)	Mk1/BSK	AD	BBR	BBR	Staff & Generator coach

Class 20

Vehicle Length: 46ft 9¼in (14.26m)	Engine: English Electric 8SVT Mk2
Height: 12ft 7⅝in (3.84m)	Horsepower: 1,000hp (745kW)
Width: 8ft 9in (2.66m)	Electrical Equipment: English Electric

Number	Depot	Pool	Livery	Owner	Operator
20142	SK	GBEE	BBR	20189Ltd	BBR
20189	SK	GBEE	BBR	20189Ltd	BBR

Above and Right: *For use on engineering trains, especially those involved with the Great Western electrification project, Balfour Beatty hires a pair of Class 20s from 20189 Ltd. The locos, Nos. 20142 and 20189, sport Balfour Beatty white and blue livery. In the upper illustration No. 20142 is seen leading an engineers train, while in the image right, both locos are seen at Derby.*
Both: **Antony Christie**

Infrastructure Companies - Balfour Beatty

Alstom Transport

Address: ✉ PO Box 70, Newbold Road, Rugby, Warwickshire, CV21 2WR
⌨ info@transport.alstom.com ✆ 01788 577111 ⓘ www.transport.alstom.com
Managing Director: Paul Robinson
Facilities: Following the assembly of the Virgin Trains Class 390 'Pendolino' stock, Alstom closed down its UK production facility at Washwood Heath, Birmingham. However, the company still operates from many specialist sites in mainland Europe and if Alstom wins further new-build contracts in the UK, these will be assembled in Europe.
Depots: Chester (CH), Liverpool - Edge Hill (LL), Manchester - Longsight (MA), Wolverhampton - Oxley (OY), Wembley (WB)

Class 08

Vehicle Length: 29ft 3in (8.91m)
Height: 12ft 8⅝in (3.87m)
Width: 8ft 6in (2.59m)
Engine: English Electric 6K
Horsepower: 400hp (298kW)
Electrical Equipment: English Electric

Number	Depot	Pool	Livery	Owner	Operator
08451	AT	ATZZ	BLK	ALS	ALS
08454	WB	ATLO	BLK	ALS	ALS
08611	MA	ATLO	VT1	ALS	ALS
08617	WB	ATLO	BLK	ALS	ALS
08696	PO	ATLO	GRN	ALS	ALS
08721	AT	ATLO	BLU	ALS	ALS

Number	Depot	Pool	Livery	Owner	Operator
08790	AT	ATLO	BLU	ALS	ALS
08887	AT	ATZZ	BLK	ALS	ALS

Names applied
08451 *M A Smith*
08790 *Starlet*
08721 *Downside CS*

Bombardier Transportation

Address: ✉ Litchurch Lane, Derby, DE24 8AD
⌨ info@bombardier.com ✆ 01332 344666 ⓘ www.bombardier.com
Chief Country Representative: Paul Roberts
Works: Derby (ZD), Crewe (ZC)
Facilities: Bombardier Transportation is one of the largest transport builders in the world, with offices and building facilities in many countries. Its product range extends well beyond rail vehicles and includes aircraft, boats and leisure equipment. In terms of the UK, two main sites are located in Derby (Litchurch Lane) and Crewe. New-build work is undertaken at the Derby site, which mainly concentrates on electric and diesel multiple unit designs.

Class 08

Vehicle Length: 29ft 3in (8.91m)
Height: 12ft 8⅝in (3.87m)
Width: 8ft 6in (2.59m)
Engine: English Electric 6K
Horsepower: 400hp (298kW)
Electrical Equipment: English Electric

Number	Depot	Pool	Livery	Owner	Operator	Name
08602 (004)	ZD	KDSD	BLU	BOM	BOM	
08631	ZD	-	NSE	PRI	BOM	
08682 (D3849)	ZD	KDSD	SPL	BOM	BOM	*Lionheart*
08846 (003)	ZD	KDSD	BOM	BOM	BOM	

Left: *To shunt rolling stock within the confines of Derby Litchurch Lane Works, four ex-BR Class 08s can be found. However, it is unlikely that all would be found in an operational condition at the same time. Painted in a mid-blue colour with 'wasp' ends is No. 08602, which also carries Bombardier No. 004. Some of these shunting locos carry special adaptor couplings for attaching to bar couplings as well as Dellner and Tightlock couplings.* **CJM**

Electro-Motive Diesels (EMD)

Address: ✉ Electro-Motive Diesels Inc, 9301 West 55th Street, LaGrange, Illinois, USA, 60525
Electro-Motive Diesels Inc, Muncie, Indiana, USA
🖰 info@emdiesels.com ✆ +1 (800) 255 5355, ① www.emdiesels.com

Facilities: Formerly part of General Motors, Electro-Motive is one of the two largest loco builders in the world. Its main production facility is in Muncie, Indiana, USA. Production from this site took over from the London, Ontario, Canada, plant in 2012.

In terms of the UK, the JT42CWRM or Class 66 were all built at the Canadian facility; however, the latest and final order placed in 2013 by GBRf saw production move to Muncie, Indiana. EMD is now owned by Progress Rail, which is part of the Caterpillar Group. In the UK Electro-Motive Services International operates from premises at Stoke-on-Trent.

Right: *In October 2006, Electro-Motive purchased the main UK EMU after sales business of Turner Diesels and commenced trading as Electro-Motive Services International, using rail-connected workshops at Stoke-on-Trent. The site frequently sees Class 66s receiving extended overhaul and modification work. In this view one of the short-lived Advenza Rail freight locos No. 66842, stands in the Stoke-on-Trent yard.* **Cliff Beeton**

General Electric (GE)

Address: ✉ GE Transportation Rail, 2901 East Lake Road, Erie, Pennsylvania, USA, 16531
UK office: Inspira House, Martinfield, Welwyn Garden City, Herts, AL7 1GW
🖰 info@getransportation.com ✆ 01707 383700 ① www.getransportation.com

Chief Executive Officer: Lorenzo Simonelli

Facilities: General Electric entered the UK loco arena in recent years, and fulfilled an order for 'PowerHaul' locomotives for Freightliner. GE operates a huge construction facility in Erie, Pennsylvania, USA, where the UK locos were built alongside North American designs.

Hitachi Europe Ltd

Address: ✉ 16 Upper Woburn Place, London, WC1H 0AF
🖰 hirofumi.ojima@hitachi-eu.com ✆ 0207 970 2700, ① www.hitachi-rail.com

Facilities: Hitachi Rail, one of the newer names to the UK rail scene, won the contract to design, build, test and manage the fleet of Class 395 EMUs used for domestic services on HS1. In 2009 the company formed the construction arm of Agility Trains, awarded the IEP project to design, build and introduce the next generation of high-speed passenger trains in the UK.

Hitachi is now building construction facilities in the UK at Newton Aycliffe, County Durham.

In 2012 it was announced that the DfT required 596 IEP vehicles for the Great Western franchise and Phase 1 of the East Coast operation, equating to 92 trains. A further 498 vehicles would be needed for the second phase of East Coast, Great Western, West Coast and Cambridge line operations. For the core routes of Phase 1, Great Western will operate a mix of five-car bi-mode and eight-car electric sets on a daily basis plus spare sets, while East Coast will operate 10 five-car electric sets, eight bi-mode sets and 10 nine-car bi-mode sets on a daily basis. This equates to a total of 77 sets being in passenger service every day. 250 vehicles will incorporate one MTU 12V 1600R80L underfloor engine.

Arlington Fleet Services

Address: ✉ Eastleigh Rail Works, Campbell Road, Eastleigh, Hampshire, SO50 5AD
✉ info@Arlington-fleet.co.uk ✆ 02380 698789 ① www.arlington-fleet.com
Managing Director: Barry Stephens
Facilities: Arlington Fleet Group offers high-quality rail engineering services to all vehicle owners. The company is based in the former loco/carriage works at Eastleigh.
Depots: Eastleigh (ZG), Shoeburyness (SN)

Class 07

			Vehicle Length: 26ft 9½in (8.16m)		Engine: Paxman 6RPHL MkIII
			Height: 12ft 10in (3.91m)		Horsepower: 275hp (205kW)
			Width: 8ft 6in (2.59m)		Electrical Equipment: AEI

Number	Depot	Pool	Livery	Owner	Operator
07007 (D2991)	ZG	MBDL	BLU	AFG	AFG

Left: *Arlington Fleet Services, which occupies a major part of the old Eastleigh Works, is now a major player in the engineering field, and sees a significant amount of stock passing through its complex. To shunt stock, former BR Southampton Docks Class 07 No. 07007 is employed, which is painted in 1960s BR Rail Blue.* **Antony Christie**

Ex-DB (Germany) Class 323

Former German shunting locos, built by Gmeinder and now owned by Northumbria Rail and used at Eastleigh Works by Arlington Fleet Services for pilotage.

Number	Depot	Pool	Livery	Owner	Operator
323-539-7	ZG	-	GRN	NHR	AFG
323-674-2	ZG	-	GRN	NHR	AFG

Ex-Class 508 Barrier Vehicles

Former Class 508 driving cars now used as barrier vehicles, maintained and based at Eastleigh.

Number	Depot	Pool	Livery	Owner	Operator	Name
64664	ZG	-	GRN	ANG	AFG	*James D Rowlands*
64707	ZG	-	GRN	ANG	AFG	*Sir David Rowlands*

Left: *In 2014, two former off-lease Class 508 driving cars were modified at Arlington Fleet Services as multiple unit barrier vehicles, using their former driving cab ends to couple to modern EMU stock. The inner end of the vehicles were fitted with buffers and standard draw gear together with jumper cables and air pipes. A small generator was mounted inside the coach. All windows have been plated over, with access being by way of the former cab sliding doors. The pair of vehicles are seen being hauled coupled cab to cab.* **Chris Wilson**

London & North Western Railway Co

Address: ✉ LNWR Co Ltd, PO Box 111, Crewe, Cheshire, CW1 2FB
📠 allservicedeliverymanagers@lnwr.com ℂ 01270 508000 ⓘ www.lnwr.com
Managing Director: Mark Knowles
Facilities: LNWR is owned by Arriva and based at Crewe, with outbased facilities at Bristol, Eastleigh, Cambridge and Tyne.
Depot: Crewe (CO), Bristol Barton Hill (BK), Eastleigh (EH), Cambridge (CA), Tyne (TY)

Number	Depot	Pool	Livery	Owner	Operator	Name
08442	EH	MBDL	BRT	LNW	LNW	*Richard J Wenham Eastleigh Depot December 1989 - July 1999*
08516	BK	MBDL	LNW	LNW	LNW	*Rory*
08810	EH	MBDL	LNW	LNW	LNW	
08830	CO	MBDL	BLU	LNW	LNW	
09204	CC	MBDL	BRD	LNW	LNW	

Pullman Group (Colas Rail Freight)

Address: ✉ Train Maintenance Depot, Leckwith Road, Cardiff, CF11 8HP
📠 sales@pullmans.net ℂ 029 2036 8850 ⓘ www.pullmans.net
Managing Director: Colin Robinson
Facilities: Pullman Rail operates from part of the former Canton depot in Cardiff and provides a quality engineering service to all types of rail vehicles.
Depots: Cardiff Canton (CF)

Class 08

Vehicle Length: 29ft 3in (8.91m)	*Engine: English Electric 6K*	
Height: 12ft 8⅝in (3.87m)	*Horsepower: 400hp (298kW)*	
Width: 8ft 6in (2.59m)	*Electrical Equipment: English Electric*	

Number	Depot	Pool	Livery	Owner	Operator
08499	CF	WSXX	BLU	DBS	PUL

Knorr Bremse Rail Services

Address: ✉ Wolverton Works, Stratford Road, Wolverton, Milton Keynes, MK12 5NT
📠 info@railcare.co.uk ℂ 08000 741122 ⓘ www.railcare.co.uk
Managing Director: Colin Love **Depots:** Glasgow (ZH), Wolverton (ZN)
Owner: Knorr Bremse

Class 08

Vehicle Length: 29ft 3in (8.91m)	*Engine: English Electric 6K*	
Height: 12ft 8⅝in (3.87m)	*Horsepower: 400hp (298kW)*	
Width: 8ft 6in (2.59m)	*Electrical Equipment: English Electric*	

Number	Depot	Pool	Livery	Owner	Operator	Name
08568	ZH	RCZH	KBR	KBR	KBR	*St Rollox*
08629	ZN	RCZN	KBR	KBR	KBR	*Wolverton*
08649	ZN	RCZN	KBR	KBR	KBR	*Bradwell*
08730	ZH	RCZH	KBR	KBR	KBR	*The Caley*

Hauled stock
82140 (Mk3 DVT)

Rail Vehicle Engineering Ltd

Address: ✉ Vehicles Workshop, RTC Business Park, London Road, Derby, DE24 8UP
📠 enquiries@rvel.co.uk ℂ 01332 331210 ⓘ www.rvel.co.uk
Managing Director: Andy Lynch **Depot:** Derby (DF)
Parent Company: Loram

Class 08

Vehicle Length: 29ft 3in (8.91m)
Height: 12ft 8⅝in (3.87m)
Width: 8ft 6in (2.59m)

Engine: English Electric 6K
Horsepower: 400hp (298kW)
Electrical Equipment: English Electric

Number	Depot	Pool	Livery	Owner	Operator
08536	DF	RVLS	-	RVE	RVE

Class 31/1 and 31/4

Vehicle Length: 56ft 9in (17.29m)
Height: 12ft 7in (3.91m)
Width: 8ft 9in (2.65m)
Class 31/4 - Electric Train Heat fitted

Engine: English Electric 12SVT
Horsepower: 1,470hp (1,097kW)
Electrical Equipment: Brush

Number		Depot	Pool	Livery	Owner	Operator	Name
31106		DF	RVLO	BLU	HJA	RVE	
31459	(31256)	DF	RVLO	BLK	RVE	RVE	Hydra
31468(S)	(31568, 31321)	DF	RVLS	BLK	RVE	RVE	

Left: *Derby-based Rail Vehicle Engineering Ltd has three Class 31s on its books, one Class 31/1 and two Class 31/4s. These locos are used for spot hire contracts and sometimes hired to Network Rail. Rail Blue-liveried No. 31106 is illustrated, powering three Network Rail vehicles.* **Mark V. Pike**

Class 73/1 and 73/9

Vehicle Length: 53ft 8in (16.35m)
Height: 12ft 5⅛in (3.79m)
Width: 8ft 8in (2.64m)

Power: 750V dc third rail or English Electric 6K
Horsepower: electric - 1,600hp (1,193kW)
Horsepower: diesel - 600hp (447kW)
Electrical Equipment: English Electric

Number	Depot	Pool	Livery	Owner	Operator	Notes
73101(S)	DF	RVLO	PUL	RVE	-	
73951 (73104)	DF	RVLO	NRL	RVE	NRL	Ultra 73 project
73139(S)	DF	RVLO	PUL	RVE	-	
73952 (73211)	DF	RVLO	NRL	RVE	NRL	Ultra 73 project

73951 and 73952 rebuilt with 2 x Cummins CSK19 755hp engines to provide high-output electro-diesel loco.

Left: *For the last couple of years Rail Vehicle Engineering Ltd has been working closely with Network Rail on a redesign of the Class 73 electro-diesel, running concurrently with the GBRf/ Brush project. These are a totally different design, and the RVEL project incorporates a number of new and novel features. Dubbed as the Ultra 73 project, No. 73952 is seen at the RTC Derby. Note the new light clusters, the windscreen wipers attached at the bottom of the window and the new bodyside louvres.* **Paul Bigland**

Train Engineering Companies – RVEL

Siemens Transportation

Address: ✉ Kings Heath Facility, Heathfield Way, Kings Heath, Northampton, NN5 7QP
📧 enquiries@siemenstransportation.co.uk ℂ 01604 594500
ⓘ www.siemenstransportation.co.uk
✉ Ashby Park, Ashby de la Zouch, Leicestershire, LE65 1JD
📧 uk.mobility@siemens.com ℂ 01530 258000 ⓘ www.siemens.co.uk/mobility

Managing Director UK: Steve Scrimshaw

Depots: Ardwick, Manchester (AK), Kings Heath, Northampton (NN), Northam (NT)

Facilities: Siemens is a provider of UK EMU and DMU rolling stock with various derivatives of its 'Desiro' product line. While having maintenance facilities in the UK, Siemens performs all new-build work in mainland Europe at its Krefeld/Uerdingen factory in Germany. Testing of vehicles is performed in Germany before delivery at the world-famous test track at Wildenrath.

Class 01.5

Number	Depot	Pool	Livery	Owner	Operator	Name
01551 (H016)	AK	MBDL	WAB	WAB	SIE	*Lancelot*

Right: *Siemens Transportation run several depots to maintain their 'Desiro' electric and diesel multiple unit fleets. All are purpose-built facilities with state-of-the-art equipment. A Class 444 unit operated by South West Trains is seen inside the Northam facility near Southampton.* **CJM**

Wabtec
Brush Traction, Loughborough

Address: ✉ PO Box 17, Loughborough, Leicestershire, LE11 1HS
📧 sales@brushtraction.com ℂ 01509 617000 ⓘ www.brushtraction.com

Managing Director: John Bidewell

Facilities: The world-famous name of Brush Traction, based in Loughborough, is now part of the Wabtec Group. In recent years the site has been responsible for the majority of UK loco building. The company has been synonymous with loco building for the UK and overseas markets for many years. Although recent main-line loco builds have been awarded overseas, the facilities at the Loughborough plant from which the Class 31, 47, 57, 60 and Eurotunnel Shuttle locos emerged are still available for new-build work. Recently the site has concentrated on rebuild operations including the highly successful re-engining of the HST fleet with MTU power units for First Group, East Coast, Grand Central and Network Rail. In 2012-13 the site was undertaking work for General Electric/Freightliner, Arriva and First Group, as well as the re-engining of a Class 73 with an MTU power unit. The site is fully rail connected. In late 2012, Wabtec purchased L H Group Services.

Doncaster

Address: ✉ PO Box 400, Doncaster Works, Hexthorpe Road, Doncaster, DN1 1SL
📧 wabtecrail@wabtec.com ℂ 01302 340700 ⓘ www.wabtecrail.co.uk

Managing Director: John Meehan **Depot:** Doncaster (ZB)

Class 08

Vehicle Length: 29ft 3in (8.91m)	Engine: English Electric 6K
Height: 12ft 8⅝in (3.87m)	Horsepower: 400hp (298kW)
Width: 8ft 6in (2.59m)	Electrical Equipment: English Electric

Number	Depot	Pool	Livery	Owner	Operator	Name
08472	EC	HBSH	BLK	WAB	ICE	

08571	ZB	HBSH	WAB	WAB	ICE	
08596(S)	ZB	HBSH	WAB	WAB	NXE	
08615	ZB	HBSH	WAB	WAB	NXE	
08669	ZB	HBSH	WAB	WAB	WAB	*Bob Machin*
08724	ZB	HBSH	WAB	WAB	WAB	
08764	ZB	MBDL	BLU	WAB	ALS	*Old Tom*
08853	ZB	HBSH	BLU	WAB	WAB	
08871	ZB	MBDL	GRN	WAB	Weardale	

Above: *The sizeable Wabtec plant located adjacent to Doncaster station deals with a lot of multiple unit and stock overhauls and modifications. A number of shunting locos are available to pilot stock around the yard. Painted in black Wabtec livery, No. 08669 Bob Machin is seen at Doncaster West Yard.* **Antony Christie**

Coaching Stock

Vehicle Length: 75ft 0in (22.86m)		Width: 8ft 11in (2.71m)	
Height: 12ft 9in (3.88m)		Bogie Type: BT10	

NX5G - NGV

Number		Depot	Livery	Owner	
96374(S)	(10585)	ZB	EPS	WAB	Internal user (generator)

Left: *To provide static electric train supply for coach overhauls, Wabtec Doncaster obtained one of the former Nightstar generator vehicles No. 6374. Still painted in its original Eurostar Passenger Services livery, the former Mk3 sleeping coach can usually be seen either in Doncaster West Yard or the main workshop yards.* **Nathan Williamson**

Scotland (previously Brush Barclay)

Address: ✉ Caledonia Works, West Langlands Street, Kilmarnock, Ayrshire, KA1 2QD

📠 sales@brushtraction.com ✆ 01563 523573 ⓘ www.brushtraction.com

Managing Director: John Bidewell

Facilities: The Wabtec site in Scotland concentrates on vehicle overhaul and refurbishment, including EMU, DMU and loco-hauled vehicles as well as HST stock.

Europhoenix Ltd

Address: ✉ 58A High Street, Stony Stratford, Milton Keynes, MK11 1AX
📧 info@europhoenix.eu ✆ 01467 624366 ⓘ www.europhoenix.eu

Facilities: Europhoenix has purchased redundant Class 56, 86 and 87 locos; these are offered to Continental European operators fully refurbished and modified to suit customer needs.

Class 37/7

			Vehicle Length: 61ft 6in (18.74m)	*Engine: Ruston*	
			Height: 13ft 0¼in (3.96m)	*Horsepower: 1,750hp (1,304kW)*	
			Width: 8ft 11⅝in (2.73m)	*Electrical Equipment: English Electric*	

Number	Owner	Location	Livery	Owner	Operator/Notes
37800 (37143)	EPX	BH	EPX	EPX	Spot hire
37884 (37183)	EPX	BH	EPX	EPX	Spot hire

Right: *Spot hire company Europhoenix has had limited success in exporting Class 56, 86 and 87 locomotives to mainland Europe for extended hire, mainly involving operators in Hungary and Bulgaria. In 2014 a pair of Class 37s were overhauled at Washwood Heath for the operator and painted in a green and grey phoenix livery. The two heavyweight '37s' have yet to find an operator from either the UK or mainland Europe. No. 37884 is shown from its No. 2 end being hauled from Washwood Heath to Barrow Hill for testing.* **John Tuffs**

Class 56

				Vehicle Length: 63ft 6in (19.35m)	*Engine: Ruston Paxman 16RK3CT*
				Height: 13ft 0in (3.96m)	*Horsepower: 3,250hp (2,420kW)*
				Width: 9ft 2in (2.79m)	*Electrical Equipment: Brush*

Number	Owner	Location	Livery	Operator
56096	EPX	WH	COL	COL
56101 (92 55 0659 001-5)	EPX	-	BLK	Hire to Floyd (Hungary)
56115 (92 55 0659 002-3)	EPX	-	BLK	Hire to Floyd (Hungary)
56117 (92 55 0659 003-1)	EPX	-	BLK	Hire to Floyd (Hungary)
56301 (56045)	EPX	-	FLF	EPX

Class 86

			Vehicle Length: 58ft 6in (17.83m)	*Power Collection: 25kV ac overhead*
			Height: 13ft 0⅝in (3.97m)	*Horsepower: 5,900hp (4,400kW)*
			Width: 8ft 8¼in (2.64m)	*Electrical Equipment: GEC*

Number	Location	Hire to	Number	Location	Hire to	Number	Location	Hire to
86215	EXP	Floyd (Hungary)	86231	LM	-	86247	LNWR	(spares)±
86217	EXP	Floyd (Hungary)	86232	LM	-	86248	EXP	Floyd (Hungary)
86218	EXP	Floyd (Hungary)	86233	EXP	Floyd (Hungary)	86250	EXP	Floyd (Hungary)
86226	LM	-	86234	LM	-	86251	LM	-
86228	EXP	Floyd (Hungary)	86235	LM	-	86424	EXP	Floyd (Hungary)
86229	LM	-	86242	EXP	Floyd (Hungary)			(for spares)
			86246	LM	-	± DHLT pool		

Class 87

					Vehicle Length: 58ft 6in (17.83m)	*Power Collection: 25kV ac overhead*
					Height: 13ft 1¼in (3.99m)	*Horsepower: 7,860hp (5,680kW)*
					Width: 8ft 8¼in (2.64m)	*Electrical Equipment: GEC*

Number	Owner	Status	Location	Livery	Name
87009	EPX	Operational	EXP	BUL	
87017	EPX	Operational	EXP	EPX	*Iron Duke*
87023	EPX	Operational	EXP	EPX	*Velocity*
87025	EPX	Stored	EXP	VIR	

(Hire locomotives in Bulgaria working for short line operator Bulmarket)

Porterbrook

Address: ✉ Burdett House, Becket Street, Derby, DE1 1JP

✒ enquiries@porterbrook.co.uk ☎ 01332 262405 ⓘ www.porterbrook.co.uk

Managing Director: Paul Francis

Facilities: Porterbrook Leasing has made available the off-lease Class 87s to mainland European operators, with a significant number being exported to operate in Bulgaria.

Exported

Number	Present operator				
87003	BZK Bulgaria	87010	BZK Bulgaria	87026	BZK Bulgaria
87004	BZK Bulgaria	87012	BZK Bulgaria	87028	BZK Bulgaria
	Britannia	87013	BZK Bulgaria	87029	BZK Bulgaria
87006	BZK Bulgaria	87014	BZK Bulgaria	87033	BZK Bulgaria
87007	BZK Bulgaria	87019	BZK Bulgaria	87034	BZK Bulgaria
87008	BZK Bulgaria	87020	BZK Bulgaria		
		87022	BZK Bulgaria		

Above and Below: *A fleet of 17 Porterbrook Class 87s are currently on lease to BZK in Bulgaria powering freight and the occasional passenger duty. The locos are in a mix of liveries and have been modified for their present use with different head/marker lights, couplings and pantographs. In the above view we see Nos. 87007 and 87003, while the image below shows Nos. 87033 and 87020. Both:* **Keith Fender**

Angel Trains

Address: ✉ Portland House, Bressenden Place, London, SW1E 5BH

✆ reception@angeltrains.co.uk ✆ 0207 592 0500 ⓘ www.angeltrains.co.uk

Chief Executive: Malcolm Brown

Owned by: Babcock Brown, AMP Capital and Deutsche Bank

British American Railway Services

Incorporating: RMS Locotec, RT Rail, Dartmoor Railway, Devon & Cornwall Railways, Weardale Railway, Ealing Community Transport and Hanson Rail

Address: ✉ London Riverside, London, SE1 2AQ

President: Ed Ellis

Depots: RMS Wakefield (ZS), Washwood Heath (WH)

UK operation is part of Iowa Pacific Holdings. BARS is also a Train Operating Company.

Class 08

Vehicle Length: 29ft 3in (8.91m)				*Engine: English Electric 6K*						
Height: 12ft 8⅝in (3.87m)				*Horsepower: 400hp (298kW)*						
Width: 8ft 6in (2.59m)				*Electrical Equipment: English Electric*						

Number	Depot	Pool	Livery	Owner	Operator					
08308	‡	MRSO	RMS	ECT	IND	08750	‡	MRSO	BLK	ECT	IND
08423	W	INDL	RMS	RMS	IND	08754	NR	MRSO	BLU	ECT	IND
08523	IS	MRSO	RMS	RMS	FSR	08756	MR	MRSO	GRY	ECT	GBR
08573	ZB	MRSO	BLK	ECT	BOM	08762	ZB	MRSO	BLK	ECT	CEM
08588	WH	MRSO	BLK	ECT	IND	08870	ZS	MBDL	BLG	RMS	IND
08613	§	MOLO	BLU	RMS	IND	08873	ZB	MRSO	HUN	ECT	FLR
08622	K	INDL	BLU	RMS	IND	08874	ZB	MBDL	SIL	RMS	GAR
08648	HT	INDL	GTO	BAR	G Cent	08885	ZS	INDL	GBR	RMS	GBR
						08936	ZS	MBDL	BLU	RMS	IND

§ at Onllwyn, K - Ketton, ‡ - at Middlesbrough as No. 23, W - Weardale

Right: *One of the key suppliers of spot hire locos to the UK rail industry is British American Railway Services (BARS). The operator has a number of ex-BR Class 08s on its books, one of which is Silverlink-liveried No. 08874, which is currently on hire to Greater Anglia Railways at Norwich Crown Point depot.* **Antony Christie**

Class 31/1, 31/4 & 31/6

Vehicle Length: 56ft 9in (17.29m)			*Engine: English Electric 12SVT*			
Height: 12ft 7in (3.91m)			*Horsepower: 1,470hp (1,097kW)*			
Width: 8ft 9in (2.65m)			*Electrical Equipment: Brush*			
31/4 Electric Train Heat fitted, 31/6 through wired						

Number		Depot	Pool	Livery	Owner	Operator
31190		WH	HTLX	GRN	BAR	- (Spot hire)
31452	(31552/279)	WH	HTLX	DCG	ECT	ECT
31454	(31554, 31228)	WH	HTLX	ICS	BAR	Weardale
31601	(31186)	WH	HTLX	DCG	BAR	RVE
31602	(31191)	WH	HTLX	NRL	BAR	RVE

Rolling Stock Hire Companies – Angel, British American Railway

Class 56

Vehicle Length: 63ft 6in (19.35m)
Height: 13ft 0in (3.96m)
Width: 9ft 2in (2.79m)

Engine: Ruston Paxman 16RK3CT
Horsepower: 3,250hp (2,420kW)
Electrical Equipment: Brush

Number		Depot	Pool	Livery	Owner	Operator	Name
56091		WH	HTLX	GRY	BAR	BAR	
56103		WH	HTLX	GRY	BAR	BAR	
56303	(56125)	WH	HTLX	GRN	BAR	BAR	
56311	(56057)	WH	HTLX	GRY	BAR	BAR	
56312	(56003)	WH	HTLX	DCN	BAR	BAR	Jeremiah Dixon Son of County Durham Surveyor of the Mason-Dixon Line U.S.A
(56313) (S) 56128		WH	HTLX	FRB	BAR	-	

Coaching Stock

Mk2
Vehicle Length: 66ft 0in (20.11m)

Height: 12ft 9½in (3.89m)
Width: 9ft 3in (2.81m)

AF2F - DBSO

Number	Depot	Livery	Owner					
9704	EH	-	BAR		9710	EH	-	BAR
9709	EH	-	BAR					

UK Rail Leasing

Address: ✉ Leicester Depot, Leicester.
CEO: Mark Winter **Depot:** Leicester (LR)
Purchaser and restorer of ex-BR locomotives for hire to the UK and overseas rail industries

Class 37/9

Vehicle Length: 61ft 6in (18.74m)
Height: 13ft 0¼in (3.96m)
Width: 8ft 11⅝in (2.73m)

Engine: Ruston RK270T
Horsepower: 1,800hp (1,342kW)
Electrical Equipment: English Electric

Number	Depot	Pool	Livery	Owner	Operator
37905	LR	-	-	URL	-
37906	LR	-	-	URL	-

Class 56

Vehicle Length: 63ft 6in (19.35m)
Height: 13ft 0in (3.96m)
Width: 9ft 2in (2.79m)

Engine: Ruston Paxman 16RK3CT
Horsepower: 3,250hp (2,420kW)
Electrical Equipment: Brush

Number	Depot	Pool	Livery	Owner	Operator
56007(S)	LR	MBDL	BLU	URL	-
56009(S)	LR	-	BLU	URL	- (Spares)
56018(S)	P	MBDL		URL	-
56031(S)	LR	MBDL		URL	-
56032(S)	LR	-	-	URL	-
56037(S)	P	WNSO		URL	-
56038(S)	LR	-		URL	-
56060(S)	WH	MBDL	-	URL	-
56065(S)	LR	MBDL	-	URL	-
56069(S)	LR	MBDL		URL	-
56077(S)	P	WNSO		URL	- (Spares)
56081(S)	LR	MBDL	GRY	URL	- (with FLR)
56098(S)	LR	MBDL	GRY	URL	-
56104(S)	LR	WNSO	GRY	URL	-
56106(S)	LR	MBDL		URL	-

Spot hire locos to be introduced; six from the above list should be returned to traffic. Locos will soon be moving to Leicester depot, the new Headquarters for the UK Rail Leasing operation.

Left: New company UK Rail Leasing, the owner of a number of Class 56 heavy haul freight locos, has taken on the lease of the former DB Schenker depot at Leicester, located at the north end of Leicester station. The facility, with covered inspection and workshop building, outside sidings and a fuelling stand, is now the base for a number of locos. **Antony Christie**

Electric Traction Limited

Address: ✉ Woodlands, Manse Road, Inverurie, Aberdeenshire, Scotland, AB51 3UJ
Depot: Long Marston (LM)
Electric Traction Ltd provides spot hire of Class 86 and 87 traction, as well as providing engineering and graphic design services to the rail industry.

Class 86

Vehicle Length: 58ft 6in (17.83m)   *Power Collection: 25kV ac overhead*
Height: 13ft 0⅝in (3.97m)   *Horsepower: 5,900hp (4,400kW)*
Width: 8ft 8¼in (2.64m)   *Electrical Equipment: GEC*

Number		Depot	Pool	Livery	Owner	Operator	Name
86101		WA	ACAC	BLU	ETL	NRL	*Sir William Stanier FRS*
86401		WA	ETLO	NSE	ETL	ETL	*Northampton Town*
86701	(86205) (S)	RU	EPUK	COL	ETL	-	*Orion*
86702	(86260) (S)	WN	EPUK	ETL	ETL	-	*Cassiopeia*

Right: *Electric Traction Limited is one of the smaller spot hire operators and, as its name implies, the company deals with electric main-line locos. Four Class 86s are on its books, which are made available if needed. One loco, No. 86701, the former Class 86/2 No. 86205, is currently painted in Colas Rail Freight livery following a contract with the operator.* **Antony Christie**

Class 87

Vehicle Length: 58ft 6in (17.83m)   *Power Collection: 25kV ac overhead*
Height: 13ft 1¼in (3.99m)   *Horsepower: 7,860hp (5,680kW)*
Width: 8ft 8¼in (2.64m)   *Electrical Equipment: GEC*

Number	Depot	Pool	Livery	Owner	Operator	Name
87002	WN	ETLO	BLU	ETL	NRL	*Royal Sovereign*

Right: *One operational Class 87 is maintained by Electric Traction Ltd, No. 87002, which is fully Network Rail certified and does power charter traffic from time to time. The loco is finished in mid-1970s BR Rail Blue with full yellow warning ends and carries its original BR name* Royal Sovereign. *The loco is seen powering a charter over the East Coast Main Line.* **Peter Squibbs**

Eversholt Rail Group (Previously HSBC Rail)

Address: ✉ PO Box 29499, 1 Eversholt Street, London, NW1 2ZF
✉ info@eversholtrail.co.uk © 0207 380 5040 ⓘ www.eversholtrail.co.uk
Chief Operating Officer: Mary Kenny

Rolling Stock Hire Companies – Electric Traction Ltd, Eversholt

Harry Needle Railroad Company

Address: ✉ Harry Needle Railway Shed, Barrow Hill Roundhouse, Campbell Drive,
Chesterfield, Derbyshire, S43 2PR

Managing Director: Harry Needle

Depot: Barrow Hill (BH)

Harry Needle Railroad Company also operates as a scrap dealer in dismantling locomotives and rolling stock.

Class 01.5

Number	Depot	Pool	Livery	Owner	Operator	
01552 (TH167V)	BH	HNRL	IND	HNR	IND	
01564 (12088)	-	HNRL	BLK	HNR	IND	Preserved at Aln Valley Railway

Class 08 and 09

Vehicle Length: 29ft 3in (8.91m)
Height: 12ft 8⅝in (3.87m)
Width: 8ft 6in (2.59m)
Engine: English Electric 6K
Horsepower: 400hp (298kW)
Electrical Equipment: English Electric

Number	Depot	Pool	Livery	Owner	Operator		Number	Depot	Pool	Livery	Owner	Operator
08389	BH	HNRL	EWS	HNR	HNR		08868	CP	HNRL	LNW	HNR	LNW
08502	BH	HNRL	NOR	HNR	HNR		08892	HE	HNRL	DRS	HNR	HNR
08527	BH	HNRL	JAR	HNR	NOR		08905	BH	HNRL	EWS	HNR	IND
08685	BH	HNRL	EWS	HNR	HNR		08918	BH	HNRL	EWS	HNR	BUR
08700	BH	HNRL	BLU	HNR	HNR		08924	BH	HNRL	HNR	HNR	GBR
08765	BU	HNRL	EWS	HNR	HNR		08929(S)	LM	HNRS	BLK	HNR	-
08786	BH	HNRL	BRD	HNR	HNR		08943	CZ	MBDL	HNR	HNR	NRM
08818	BH	HNRL	HNR	HNR	GBR		08954	PO	HNRS	BLU	HNR	ALS
08834	BH	HNRL	DRS	HNR	OLD		09014	BU	HNRS	EWS	HNR	-
							09018	BU	HNRS	HNR	HNR	LAF

Class 20

Vehicle Length: 46ft 9¼in (14.26m)
Height: 12ft 7⅝in (3.84m)
Width: 8ft 9in (2.66m)
Engine: English Electric 8SVT Mk2
Horsepower: 1,000hp (745kW)
Electrical Equipment: English Electric

Number	Depot	Pool	Livery	Owner	Operator		Number	Depot	Pool	Livery	Owner	Operator
20016(S) ø	BH	HNRS	BLU	HNR	-		20110	BH	HNRL	GRN	HNR	TAT
20056	BH	HNRL	COR	HNR	TAT		20118	BH	GBEE	GRY	HNR	HNR
20066	BH	HNRL	TAT	HNR	TAT		20121(S)	WEN	HNRS	ORG	HNR	HNR
20081(S) ø	LM	HNRS	BLU	HNR	-		20132‡	BH	GBEE	RFG	HNR	HNR
20088(S) ø	LM	HNRS	RFG	HNR	-		20138(S)	LM	HNRS	RFT	HNR	-
20092(S)	BH	HNRS	LAF	HNR	-		20166	WEN	HNRS	ORG	HNR	HNR
20096	BH	GBEE	BLU	HNR	HNR		20168	EA	HNRL	WHT	HNR	LAF
20107‡	BH	GBEE	ORG	HNR	HNR		‡ Main line certified ø Reported for sale					

Left: *A considerable number of the 1950s-design BR Class 20s are still in operation and thankfully, due to the engineering skills of suppliers such as the Harry Needle Railroad Co, a number are still kept main-line certified. In recent years a high demand for the class has been seen to fulfil a GB Railfreight contract to move London Underground 'S' stock between the builder's works in Derby and the LUL network. This view of an 'S' stock transfer move at Tamworth shows the train led by Railfreight grey-liveried No. 20118.* **Antony Christie**

Number		Depot	Pool	Livery	Owner	Operator	Name/Notes
20311	(20102)	BH	GBEE	ORG	HNR	HNR	
20314 ‡	(20117)	BH	GBEE	ORG	HNR	HNR	‡ Allocated number 92 70 0020314-5
20901	(20101)	BH	GBEE	GBN	HNR	HNR	
20903(S)	(20083)	LM	HNRS	DRS	HNR	-	
20904(S)	(20041)	LM	HNRS	DRS	HNR	-	
20905	(20225)	BH	GBEE	GBN	HNR	HNR	
20906	(20219)	LAF	HNRL	WHT	HNR	LAF	

Names applied
20132   *Barrow Hill Depot*
20168   *Sir George Earle*

20056 carries Tata Steel No. 81.
20066 carries Tata Steel No. 82.

Above: *Two former Direct Rail Services Class 20/3s are now on the books of HNRC, with Nos. 20311 and 20314 sporting HNRC orange livery. The two locos are seen working in multiple powering a Bombardier 'S' stock transfer move at Stenson Junction.* **Tim Easter**

Class 37/0

Vehicle Length: 61ft 6in (18.74m)	Engine: English Electric 12CSVT	
Height: 13ft 0¼in (3.96m)	Horsepower: 1,750hp (1,304kW)	
Width: 8ft 11⅝in (2.73m)	Electrical Equipment: English Electric	

Number	Depot	Pool	Livery	Owner	Operator/Notes
37029	BH	HNRS	GRN	HNR	HNR (At Epping & Ongar Railway)
37057(S)	BH	HNRS	BLU	HNR	- (spares)
37165(S) (37374)	CS	HNRS	CIV	HNR	-

Class 47

Vehicle Length: 63ft 6in (19.35m)	Engine: Sulzer 12LDA28C	
Height: 12ft 10⅜in (3.91m)	Horsepower: 2,580hp (1,922kW)	
Width: 9ft 2in (2.79m)	Electrical Equipment: Brush	
Electric Train Heat fitted		

Number		Depot	Pool	Livery	Owner	Operator
47703	(47514)	BH	HNRL	-	HNR	Wabtec
47714	(47511)	OD	HNRL	ANG	HNR	SEC*
47715	(47502)	BH	HNRL	BLK	HNR	HNR
47761	(47038/564)	BH	HNRL	RES	HNR	(Stored)

* Operating at Old Dalby

Nemesis Rail

Address: ✉ Nemesis Rail Ltd, Burton Depot, Burton-on-Trent
📧 enquiries@ nemesisrail.com ✆ 01246 472331 ⓘ www.nemesisrail.com
Formed from the demise of FM Rail
Depot: Burton (BU)

Above: *The former BR depot at Burton-on-Trent is now the home of Nemesis Rail, a major workshop facility for national operators and the preservation sector. The site houses a major workshop which can deal with locomotives and coaching stock. A number of major restoration and overhaul contracts have been carried out at the site. The company also own a number of locos for hire and contract work. This is a general view of the facility from the north end.* **Stuart Hillis**

Class 31/1

			Vehicle Length: 56ft 9in (17.29m) Height: 12ft 7in (3.91m) Width: 8ft 9in (2.65m)		Engine: English Electric 12SVT Horsepower: 1,470hp (1,097kW) Electrical Equipment: Brush		

Number	Depot	Pool	Livery	Owner	Operator	Name
31128	BU	NRLO	BLU	NEM	NYM	*Charybdis*

Class 33/1

			Vehicle Length: 50ft 9in (15.47m) Height: 12ft 8in (3.86m) Width: 9ft 3in (2.81m)		Engine: Sulzer 8LDA28A Horsepower: 1,550hp (1,156kW) Electrical Equipment: Crompton Parkinson		

Number	Depot	Pool	Livery	Owner	Operator	Name
33103	BU	MBDL	BLU	NEM	DAR	*Swordfish*

Class 37/5

			Vehicle Length: 61ft 6in (18.74m) Height: 13ft 0¼in (3.96m) Width: 8ft 11⅝in (2.73m)		Engine: English Electric 12CSVT Horsepower: 1,750hp (1,304kW) Electrical Equipment: English Electric	

Number	Depot	Pool	Livery	Owner	Operator
37679(S) (37123)	BU	MBDL	TGG	NEM	-

Class 45/1

			Vehicle Length: 67ft 11in (20.70m) Height: 12ft 10½in (3.91m) Width: 9ft 1½in (2.78m)		Engine: Sulzer 12LDA28B Horsepower: 2,500hp (1,862kW) Electrical Equipment: Crompton Parkinson		

Number	Depot	Pool	Livery	Owner	Operator	Name
45112	BH	MBDL	BLU	NEM	NEM	*Royal Army Ordnance Corps*

Class 47

Vehicle Length: 63ft 6in (19.35m)			Engine: Sulzer 12LDA28C		
Height: 12ft 10⅜in (3.91m)			Horsepower: 2,580hp (1,922kW)		
Width: 9ft 2in (2.79m)			Electrical Equipment: Brush		
Electric Train Heat fitted to Class 47/4 and 47/7					

Number	Depot	Pool	Livery	Owner	Operator
47375	BU	MBDL	BLU	NEM	NEM
47488	BU	MBDL	GRN	NEM	NEM
47701	BU	MBDL	BLK	NEM	NEM

47744	BU	MBDL	EWS	NEM	NEM

47375/488/701/744 Destined for export to Hungary for Continental Railway Solutions

Porterbrook

Address: ✉ Ivatt House, The Point, Pinnacle Way, Pride Park, Derby, DE24 8ZS
✎ enquiries@porterbrook.co.uk © 01332 285050 ① www.porterbrook.co.uk

Managing Director: Paul Francis
Owned by: ACP, AIMCo, EDF, Hastings Management

Right: *Porterbrook is one of the three main rolling stock owners in the UK, although today some smaller businesses are emerging. Porterbrook is the owner of the FGW Class 158 fleet. Here, set No. 158959, one of the three-car units, departs from Westbury on 23 July 2014 with an evening Cardiff to Portsmouth Harbour service.* **CJM**

Transmart Trains

Address: ✉ Green Farm House, Falfield, Wootton-under-Edge, Gloucestershire, GL12 8DL
Managing Director: Oliver Buxton
Depots: Selhurst (SU), Stewarts Lane (SL). Part of Cambrian Transport

Class 73

‡ At Barry Railway
• Not main-line certified

Vehicle Length: 53ft 8in (16.35m)			Power: 750V dc third rail or English Electric 6K		
Height: 12ft 5⁷⁄₁₆in (3.79m)			Horsepower: electric - 1,600hp (1,193kW)		
Width: 8ft 8in (2.64m)			Horsepower: diesel - 600hp (447kW)		
			Electrical Equipment: English Electric		

Number	Depot	Pool	Livery	Owner	Operator
73118	‡	-	GRY	TTS	TTS
73133•	BM	-	GRN	TTS	SWT

■ Former Gatwick Express Class 488 vehicles Nos. 72505, 72620, 72621, 72629, 72710 from sets 488206 and 488311 are also owned by Transmart Trains.

20189 Ltd

Managing Director: Michael Owen

Class 73

Vehicle Length: 53ft 8in (16.35m)			Power: 750V dc third rail or English Electric 6K		
Height: 12ft 5⁷⁄₁₆in (3.79m)			Horsepower: electric - 1,600hp (1,193kW)		
Width: 8ft 8in (2.64m)			Horsepower: diesel - 600hp (447kW)		
			Electrical Equipment: English Electric		

Number	Depot	Pool	Livery	Owner	Operator	Name
73128	SE	MBEL	GRY	201	GBRF	O V S Bulleid

Class 20 Loco Ltd

Class 20

Vehicle Length: 46ft 9¼in (14.26m)			Engine: English Electric 8SVT Mk2		
Height: 12ft 7⅜in (3.84m)			Horsepower: 1,000hp (745kW)		
Width: 8ft 9in (2.66m)			Electrical Equipment: English Electric		

Number	Depot	Pool	Livery	Owner	Operator
20227	BH	MBDL	LUL	C2L	Victor Railfreight

Rolling Stock Hire Companies – Nemesis, Porterbrook, Transmart, 20189 Ltd

Listings provide details of locomotives and stock authorised for operation on the UK National Rail network and that can be seen operating special and charter services.
Preserved locomotives authorised for main-line operation are found in the preserved section.

Bo'ness & Kinneil Railway

Number	Type	Depot	Livery	Operator	Use
464	AO3/BCK	BT	CAL	BOK	Charter train use
1375 (99803)	AO2/TK	BT	CAL	BOK	Charter train use
3096 (99827)	AD11/FO	BT	MAR	BOK	Charter train use
3115	AD11/FO	BT	MAR	BOK	Charter train use
3150	AD11/FO	BT	MAR	BOK	Charter train use
4831 (99824)	AC21/TSO	BT	MAR	BOK	Charter train use
4832 (99823)	AC21/TSO	BT	MAR	BOK	Charter train use
4836 (99831)	AC21/TSO	BT	MAR	BOK	Charter train use
4856 (99829)	AC21/TSO	BT	MAR	BOK	Charter train use
5028 (99830)	AC21/TSO	BT	CAR	BOK	Charter train use
13229 (99826)	AA11/FK	BT	MAR	BOK	Charter train use
13230 (99828)	AA11/FK	BT	MAR	BOK	Charter train use

Flying Scotsman Railway Ltd

Number	Type	Depot	Livery	Operator	Notes/Name
316 (S) (975608)	AO11/PFK	CS	PUL	FSL	Pullman Magpie
321 (S)	AO11/PFK	CS	PUL	FSL	Pullman Swift
337 (S)	AO11/PSK	CS	PUL	FSL	Pullman Car No. 337

Great Scottish & Western Railway Co

Number	Type	Depot	Livery	Operator	Notes/Name
313 (S) (99964)	AO11/PFK	CS	MAR	GSW	Royal Scotsman - Finch
317 (99967)	AO11/PFK	CS	MAR	GSW	Royal Scotsman - Raven
319 (99965)	AO11/PFK	CS	MAR	GSW	Royal Scotsman - Snipe
324 (99961)	AO11/PFP	CS	MAR	GSW	Royal Scotsman - Amber
329 (99962)	AO11/PFP	CS	MAR	GSW	Royal Scotsman - Pearl
331 (99963)	AO11/PFP	CS	MAR	GSW	Royal Scotsman - Topaz
1999 (99131)	AO10/SAL	CS	MAR	GSW	Royal Scotsman - Lochaber

Hastings Diesels Limited

The following vehicles are owned by Hastings Diesels Ltd and kept at St Leonards. Usually a six-car train is formed which is fitted with central door locking and is main-line certified (original class numbers shown in brackets).
60000 (201), 60019 (202), 60116 (202), 60118 (202), 60501 (201), 60528 (202), 60529 (202), 69337 (422 EMU), 70262 (411 EMU).
In autumn 2014, the set **1001** was formed **60116+60529+70262+69337+60501+60118**

Left: *Hastings Diesels Limited is the owner of nine Class 201, 202, 411 and 422 vehicles, which are usually formed into one six-car 'Hastings' DEMU and based at St Leonards near Hastings. The vehicles are available for charter and hire use and each year make a limited number of outings over Network Rail. Carrying set number 1001, the superbly restored 1950s DEMU is seen at Birmingham New Street.* **Chris Smetham**

Mid-Hants Railway

Number	Type	Depot	Livery	Operator					
1105	AJ41/RG	RL	GRN	MHR	21252	AB31/BCK	RL	GRN	MHR

North Yorkshire Moors Railway

Class 08

Vehicle Length: 29ft 3in (8.91m)
Height: 12ft 8⅝in (3.87m)
Width: 8ft 6in (2.59m)

Engine: English Electric 6K
Horsepower: 400hp (298kW)
Electrical Equipment: English Electric

Number	Depot	Pool	Livery	Owner	Operator	Note
08850	NY	MBDL	BLU	NYM	NYM	Restricted main-line use

Class 25

Vehicle Length: 50ft 6in (15.39m)
Height: 12ft 8in (3.86m)
Width: 9ft 1in (2.76m)

Engine: Sulzer 6LDA28B
Horsepower: 1,250hp (932kW)
Electrical Equipment: Brush

Number	Depot	Pool	Livery	Owner	Operator	Name	Note
25278	NY	MBDL	GRN	NYM	NYM	Sybilia	Restricted main-line use

Coaching Stock

Number	Type	Depot	Livery	Operator
1823	AN21/RMB	NY	MAR	NYM
3860	AC21/TSO	NY	MAR	NYM
3872	AC21/TSO	NY	CAR	NYM
3948	AC21/TSO	NY	CAR	NYM
4198	AC21/TSO	NY	CAR	NYM
4252	AC21/TSO	NY	CAR	NYM
4290	AC21/TSO	NY	MAR	NYM
4455	AC21/TSO	NY	CAR	NYM
4786	AC21/TSO	NY	MAR	NYM
4817	AC21/TSO	NY	CHC	NYM
5000	AC21/TSO	NY	MAR	NYM
5029	AC21/TSO	NY	CHC	NYM
9267	AE21/BSO	NY	CHC	NYM
9274	AE21/BSO	NY	CHC	NYM
16156 (7156)	AA31/CK	NY	MAR	NYM
21100	AB31/BCK	NY	CHC	NYM
35089	AB2I/BSK	NY	MAR	NYM

Railfilms Limited / Statesman Rail

Number	Type	Depot	Livery	Operator	Name
84 (99884)	Mk1 Pantry	CS	PUL	RAF	
310 (99107)	AO11/PFL	BO	PUL	RAF	Pegasus / Trianon Bar
1211 (3305)	AJ1F/RFB	CS	PUL	RAF	
1659 (16509)	AJ41/RBR	CS	PUL	RAF	
3188	AD1D/FO	CS	PUL	RAF	Snowdon (ex-Sovereign)
3231	AD1E/FO	CS	PUL	RAF	Ben Cruachan (ex-Apollo)
3312	AD1E/FO	CS	PUL	RAF	Helvellyn
3438	AD1F/FO	CS	PUL	RAF	
4362	AC21/SO	BU	-	RAF	Ben Lomond
5797	AD2E/TSO	BU	BLG	RAF	
5912	AD2F/TSO	CS	PUL	RAF	
5991	AD2F/TSO	CS	PUL	RAF	
9005	GWR	SDR	GWR	SDR	
13508	AA1B/FK	BU	MAR	RAF	
17080	AO3/BCK	CS	PUL	RAF	
35511 (17130)	AB5C	Shildon	PUL	RAF	
99993	Mk1 TSO	CS	MAR	RAF	

Ridings Railtours

Number	Type	Depot	Livery	Operator					
5520 (S)	AC2C/TSO	SV	PUL	RRS	13581 (S)	AA1D/FK	SV	ICS	RRS
					13583 (S)	AA1D/FK	SV	ICS	RRS

Riviera Trains

Class 08

Vehicle Length: 29ft 3in (8.91m)
Height: 12ft 8⅝in (3.87m)
Width: 8ft 6in (2.59m)

Engine: English Electric 6K
Horsepower: 400hp (298kW)
Electrical Equipment: English Electric

Number	Depot	Pool	Livery	Owner	Operator	Name
08507	CP	RTLO	RIV	RIV	RIV	Hannah
08704	CP	RTLO	BLU	RIV	RIV	Katie

Riviera

Class 47

Vehicle Length: 63ft 6in (19.35m)	Engine: Sulzer 12LDA28C
Height: 12ft 10⅜in (3.91m)	Horsepower: 2,580hp (1,922kW)
Width: 9ft 2in (2.79m)	Electrical Equipment: Brush
Electric Train Heat fitted	

Number	Depot	Pool	Livery	Owner	Operator	Name
47769 (47491)	CP	RTLO	VIR	RIV	RIV	
47812 D1916 (47657)	CP	GBDF	GRN	RIV	GBR	
47815 D1748 (47660)	CP	GBDF	RIV	RIV	RIV	Great Western
47843 (47623)	CP	GBDF	RIV	RIV	GBR	Vulcan
47847 (47577)	CP	GBDF	RIV	RIV	RIV	
47848 (47632)	CP	GBDF	BLU	RIV	RIV	Titan Star

Below: *Crewe-based Riviera Trains is a rolling stock provider to both the national operators and the charter operators. Its fleet is maintained to the highest standards. In 2014 GB Railfreight entered a contract with Riviera for the hire of some Class 47s to power freight services. As its locos were fitted with green-spot multiple operating, the locos were most suitable for this need. On hire to GBRf, Oxford blue No. 47843* Vulcan *pilots green-liveried No. 47812 with a freight on the East Coast Main Line.* **Peter Marsh**

Coaching Stock

Number	Type	Depot	Livery	Operator	Notes/Name
1200 (6459)	AJ1F/RFO	EH	RIV	RIV	Set 04 - The Great Briton - *Amber*
1203 (3291)	AJ1F/RFO	EH	RIV	RIV	
1212 (6453)	AJ1F/RFO	EH	VIR	RIV	Set 05 - The Norfolkman
1651	AJ41/RBR	EH	RIV	RIV	Set 02 - The Royal Scot Set
1657	AJ41/RBR	EH	CHC	RIV	
1671	AJ41/RBR	EH	CHC	RIV	
1683	AJ41/RBR	BH	BLU	RIV	Set 04 - The Great Briton - *Carol*
1691	AJ41/RBR	CP	CCM	RIV	Set 02 - The Royal Scot Set
1692	AJ41/RBR	EH	CHC	RIV	Set 01 - The British Classic Set
1699	AJ41/RBR	CP	BLU	RIV	Set 04 - The Great Briton
1813	AN21/RMB	CP	CHC	RIV	Set 03
1832	AN21/RMB	EH	CCM	RIV	
1863	AN21/RMB	CM	CHC	RIV	Set 01 - The British Classic Set
3066 (99566)	AD11/FO	EH	CCM	RIV	Set 02 - The Royal Scot Set
3068 (99568)	AD11/FO	EH	CCM	RIV	Set 02 - The Royal Scot Set
3069 (99540)	AD11/FO	EH	CCM	RIV	Set 02 - The Royal Scot Set
3097	AD11/FO	EH	CCM	RIV	Set 02 - The Royal Scot Set
3098	AD11/FO	EH	CHC	RIV	Set 01 - The British Classic Set
3100	AD11/FO	EH	CHC	RIV	
3107	AD11/FO	EH	CHC	RIV	Set 01 - The British Classic Set
3110 (99124)	AD11/FO	EH	CHC	RIV	Set 01 - The British Classic Set
3112 (99357)	AD11/FO	EH	CHC	RIV	Set 01 - The British Classic Set
3119	AD11/FO	EH	CCM	RIV	Set 02 - The Royal Scot Set
3120	AD11/FO	EH	CCM	RIV	Set 03
3121	AD11/FO	EH	CHC	RIV	Set 02 - The Royal Scot Set
3122	AD11/FO	EH	CHC	RIV	Set 01 - The British Classic Set
3123	AD11/FO	EH	CHC	RIV	Set 03

3125	AD11/FO	EH	CHC	RIV	
3133 (S) (99192)	AD11/FO	EH	MAR	RIV	
3140	AD11/FO	EH	CHC	RIV	Set 01 - The British Classic Set
3141 (3608)	AD11/FO	EH	MRN	RIV	Set 03
3144 (3602)	AD11/FO	BQ	MRN	RIV	Set 03
3146	AD11/FO	EH	MRN	RIV	Set 03
3147 (3604)	AD11/FO	EH	LNE	RIV	Set 03
3148	AD11/FO	CD	GRN	RIV	
3149	AD11/FO	EH	CCM	RIV	Set 02 - The Royal Scot Set
3181 (S)	AD1D/FO	EH	RIV	RIV	*Topaz*
3223 (S)	AD1E/FO	BU	RIV	RIV	*Diamond*
3227	AD1E/FO	EH	RIV	RIV	
3240 (S)	AD1E/FO	BU	RIV	RIV	*Sapphire*
3277	AD1F/FO	EH	ANG	RIV	Set 05 - The Norfolkman
3278	AD1F/FO	EH	RIV	RIV	
3295	AD1F/FO	EH	ANG	RIV	Set 05 - The Norfolkman
3304	AD1F/FO	EH	VIR	RIV	Set 07 - The West Coast Set
3314	AD1F/FO	EH	VIR	RIV	Set 07 - The West Coast Set
3325	AD1F/FO	EH	VIR	RIV	Set 07 - The West Coast Set
3330	AD1F/FO	EH	RIV	RIV	Set 04 - The Great Briton - *Brunel*
3333	AD1F/FO	EH	VIR	RIV	Set 07 - The West Coast Set
3334	AD1F/FO	EH	ANG	RIV	Set 05 - The Norfolkman
3336	AD1F/FO	CD	RIV	RIV	Set 05 - The Norfolkman
3340	AD1F/FO	EH	VIR	RIV	Set 07 - The West Coast Set
3344	AD1F/FO	EH	RIV	RIV	Set 07 - The West Coast Set
3345	ADIF/FO	EH	VIR	RIV	Set 07 - The West Coast Set
3348	AD1F/FO	EH	RIV	RIV	Set 04 - The Great Briton - *Gainsborough*
3356	AD1F/FO	EH	RIV	RIV	Set 04 - The Great Briton - *Tennyson*
3364	AD1F/FO	EH	RIV	RIV	Set 04 - The Great Briton - *Shakespeare*
3379	AD1F/FO	EH	ANG	RIV	
3384	AD1F/FO	EH	RIV	RIV	Set 04 - The Great Briton - *Dickens*
3386	AD1F/FO	EH	VIR	RIV	Set 07 - The West Coast Set
3390	AD1F/FO	EH	RIV	RIV	Set 04 - The Great Briton - *Constable*
3397	AD1F/FO	EH	RIV	RIV	Set 04 - The Great Briton - *Wordsworth*
3417	AD1F/FO	EH	ANG	RIV	
3426	AD1F/FO	EH	RIV	RIV	Set 04 - The Great Briton - *Elgar*
4927	AC21/TSO	EH	CHC	RIV	Set 01 - The British Classic Set
4946	AC21/TSO	EH	CHC	RIV	
4949	AC21/TSO	EH	CHC	RIV	Set 03
4959	AC21/TSO	ZA	CHC	RIV	
4991	AC21/TSO	EH	CHC	RIV	
4998	AC21/TSO	EH	CHC	RIV	Set 03
5008 (99002)	AC21/TSO	CD	MAN	RIV	
5009	AC21/TSO	EH	CHC	RIV	Set 01 - The British Classic Set
5027 (S)	AC21/TSO	EH	GRN	RIV	
5040	AC21/TSO	EH	CHC	RIV	Set 01 - The British Classic Set
5276	AC2A/TSO	BQ	RIV	RIV	Set 02 - The Royal Scot Set
5292	AC2A/TSO	EH	CHC	RIV	Set 02 - The Royal Scot Set
5309 (S)	AC2A/TSO	EH	CHC	RIV	
5341	AC2A/TSO	EH	CCM	RIV	Set 02 - The Royal Scot Set
5366	AC2A/TSO	EH	CHC	RIV	Set 02 - The Royal Scot Set
5494 (S)	AC2B/TSO	SV	NSE	RIV	
5647 (S)	AC2D/TSO	EH	RIV	RIV	
5910	AC2F/TSO	EH	VIR	RIV	Set 07 - The West Coast Set
5921	AC2F/TSO	EH	RIV	RIV	Set 05 - The Norfolkman
5929	AC2F/TSO	EH	ANG	RIV	Set 05 - The Norfolkman
5937	AC2F/TSO	EH	VIR	RIV	
5945	AC2F/TSO	EH	VIR	RIV	
5950	AC2F/TSO	EH	RIV	RIV	
5952	AC2F/TSO	EH	VIR	RIV	
5955 (S)	AC2F/TSO	EH	VIR	RIV	
5961	AC2F/TSO	EH	VIR	RIV	Set 07 - The West Coast Set
5964	AC2F/TSO	EH	ANG	RIV	
5965	AC2F/TSO	EH	ATW	RIV	
5976	AC2F/TSO	EH	ATW	RIV	
5985	AC2F/TSO	EH	ANG	RIV	Set 05 - The Norfolkman
5987	AC2F/TSO	EH	VIR	RIV	Set 07 - The West Coast Set

Riviera

5998	AC2F/TSO	EH	ANG	RIV	Set 05 - The Norfolkman
6006	AC2F/TSO	CF	ANG	RIV	Set 05 - The Norfolkman
6024 (S)	AC2F/TSO	EH	VIR	RIV	
6027	AC2F/TSO	EH	RIV	RIV	Set 07 - The West Coast Set
6042	AC2F/TSO	EH	ANG	RIV	Set 05 - The Norfolkman
6051	AC2F/TSO	EH	VIR	RIV	Set 07 - The West Coast Set
6054	AC2F/TSO	EH	VIR	RIV	Set 07 - The West Coast Set
6067	AC2F/TSO	EH	VIR	RIV	
6137	AC2F/TSO	EH	ATW	RIV	
6141	AC2F/TSO	EH	RIV	RIV	Set 07 - The West Coast Set
6158	AC2F/TSO	EH	VIR	RIV	Set 07 - The West Coast Set
6176 (S)	AC2F/TSO	EH	VIR	RIV	
6177	AC2F/TSO	EH	RIV	RIV	
6183	AC2F/TSO	EH	ATW	RIV	
6310 (81448)	AX51/GEN	EH	CHC	RIV	
6320	AZ5Z/SAL	SK	MRN	RIV	
6720 (6602)	AN1D/RMBF §		MRN	RIV	§ Stored Fawley
6722 (6611)	AN1D/RMBF	LM	FSW	RIV	
9504	AC2E/BSO	EH	RIV	RIV	Set 07 - The West Coast Set
9507	AC2E/BSO	EH	VIR	RIV	
9509	AE2E/BSO	CP	ATW	RIV	
9520	AE2F/BSO	EH	RIV	RIV	Set 07 - The West Coast Set
9521	AE2F/BSO	EH	ATW	RIV	
9526	AC2F/BSO	EH	RIV	RIV	
9527	AC2F/BSO	EH	ANG	RIV	
9537	AE2F/BSO	EH	ADV	RIV	
9539	AE2F/BSO	EH	ATW	RIV	
17056 (14056)	AB1A/BFK	CD	MAR	RIV	
17077 (14077)	AB1A/BFK	BQ	RIV	RIV	Set 04 - The Great Briton - *Catherine*
17105 (2905)	AX5B/BFK	EH	RIV	RIV	Set 02 - Staff Couchette
21224	AB31/BCK	EH	MAR	RIV	Directors saloon
21245 (99356)	AB31/BCK	EH	MAR	RIV	Set 03
21269	AB31/BCK	EH	CHC	RIV	
21272 (99129)	AB31/BCK	EH	CHC	RIV	Set 01 - The British Classic Set
35469 (99763)	AB21/BSK	EH	CCM	RIV	Set 03
80041 (1690)	AK51/RK	EH	MAR	RIV	Set 03 - Pride of the Nation
80042 (1646)	AJ41/RK	EH	BLG	RIV	
94538 (94426)	BG	EH	RES	DBS	

Below: *Riviera Trains owns and operates a significant number of passenger vehicles which are made available to the charter sector for various types of passenger operations, from VIP days out to bargain enthusiast trains. In the main vehicles are based at either Crewe or Eastleigh and the vast majority are in excellent condition. Mk1 TSO No. 4998 is illustrated painted in chocolate and cream livery.* **Nathan Williamson**

Right: *A number of catering vehicles are operated by Riviera, able to provide a wide selection of service from sit-down luxury land cruise-style dinners to a basic buffet. Painted in chocolate and cream, RBR No. 1671 is illustrated.* **Nathan Williamson**

Scottish Railway Preservation Society

Number	Type	Depot	Livery	Operator
1859 (99822)	AN21/RMB	BT	MAR	SRP
21241	AB31/BCK	BT	MAR	SRP
35185	AB21/BSK	BT	MAR	SRP

Stratford Class 47 Group

Vehicle Length: 63ft 6in (19.35m)
Height: 12ft 10½in (3.91m)
Width: 9ft 2in (2.79m)
Electric Train Heat fitted
Engine: Sulzer 12LDA28C
Horsepower: 2,580hp (1,922kW)
Electrical Equipment: Brush

Number	Depot	Pool	Livery	Owner	Operator	Name
47580 (47732)	MNR	MBDL	LLB	S4G	S4G	*County of Essex*

Right: *The Stratford Class 47 Group owns one loco, Type 4 No. 47580, which when not in use is kept at the Mid Norfolk Railway. The electric train heat fitted loco is painted in BR Rail Blue with full yellow ends and a red buffer beam. In 2013-14 it was in operation with a full height Union Jack flag on the side, recreating the days of two Stratford Class 47s which carried bodyside flags in 1977 to mark the Queen's Jubilee. The loco is seen approaching Northam Junction with a charter.* **Mark V. Pike**

Venice Simplon Orient Express (VSOE)

Number	Name	Type	Depot	Livery	Operator	Notes
213 (99535)	*Minerva*	AO40/PFP	SL	PUL	VSO	
239 (S)	*Agatha*	AO40/PFP	SL	PUL	VSO	
243 (99541)	*Lucille*	AO40/PFP	SL	PUL	VSO	
245 (99534)	*Ibis*	AO40/PFK	SL	PUL	VSO	
254 (99536)	*Zena*	AO40/PFP	SL	PUL	VSO	
255 (99539)	*Ione*	AO40/PFK	SL	PUL	VSO	
261 (S)	Car No. 83	AO40/PTP	SL	PUL	VSO	
264 (S)	*Ruth*	AO40/PCK	SL	PUL	VSO	

Private Train Operators – Riviera, SRPS, Stratford 47 Group, VSOE

VSOE

280 (99537)	Audrey	AO40/PFK	SL	PUL	VSO	
281 (99546)	Gwen	AO40/PFK	SL	PUL	VSO	
283 (S)	Mona	AO40/PFK	SL	PUL	VSO	
284 (99543)	Vera	AO40/PFK	SL	PUL	VSO	
285 (S)	Car No. 85	AO40/PTP	SL	PUL	VSO	
286 (S)	Car No. 86	AO40/PTP	SL	PUL	VSO	
288 (S)	Car No. 88	AO40/PTB	SL	PUL	VSO	
292 (S)	Car No. 92	AO40/PTB	SL	PUL	VSO	
293 (S)	Car No. 93	AO40/PTB	SL	PUL	VSO	
301 (99530)	Perseus	AO41/PFP	SL	PUL	VSO	
302 (99531)	Phoenix	AO41/PFP	SL	PUL	VSO	
307 (S)	Carina	AO41/PFK	SL	PUL	VSO	
308 (99532)	Cygnus	AO41/PFP	SL	PUL	VSO	
325 (2907)		AJ11/RFO	CP	PUL	VSO	
1207 (6422)		AJ11/RFO	CP	-	VSO	
1221 (3371)		AJ11/RFO	CP	-	VSO	
1566		AK51/RKB	CP	VSN	VSO	
1953		AJ41/RBR	CP	VSN	VSO	
3174	Glamis	AD1D/FO	CP	VSN	VSO	
3182	Warwick	AD1D/FO	CP	VSN	VSO	
3232		AD1E/FO	CD	RIV	CAD	
3247	Chatsworth	AD1E/FO	CP	VSN	VSO	
3267	Belvoir	AD1E/FO	CP	VSN	VSO	
3273	Alnwick	AD1E/FO	CP	VSN	VSO	
3275	Harlech	AD1E/FO	CP	VSN	VSO	
6313 (92167)		AX51/GEN	SL	PUL	VSO	
9502		AE2E/BSO	SL	PUL	VSO	
10541 (99968)		AO4G/SSV	CS	MRN	VSO	Royal Scotsman - State Car 5
10556 (99969)		AO4G/SSV	CS	MRN	VSO	Royal Scotsman - Service Car
10569 (S)	Leviathan	AU4G/SLEP	CP	PUL	VSO	
10729	Crewe	AS4G/SLE	CP	VSN	VSO	
10734 (2914)	Balmoral	AS4G/SLE	CP	VSN	VSO	
17167 (14167)	Mow Cop	AB1D/BFK	CP	VSN	VSO	
35466 (99545)		AB21/BSK	SL	PUL	VSO	
92904		NBA	CP	PUL	VSO	

Above: *The VSOE company operates the UK's most luxurious trains, the VSOE 'British Pullman' and 'The Northern Belle'. Pullman car No. 302* Phoenix *is illustrated, a 1952-built first class parlour vehicle used extensively on the Southern Region 'Golden Arrow' service.* **CJM**

Vintage Trains

Class 47

Vehicle Length: 63ft 6in (19.35m)		Engine: Sulzer 12LDA28C		
Height: 12ft 10⅜in (3.91m)		Horsepower: 2,580hp (1,922kW)		
Width: 9ft 2in (2.79m)		Electrical Equipment: Brush		
Electric Train Heat fitted				

Number	Depot	Pool	Livery	Owner	Operator
47773 (47541)	TM	MBDL	GRN	VTN	VTN

Coaching Stock

Number	Type	Depot	Livery	Owner	Operator
335 (99361)	AO11/PSK	TM	PUL	VTN	VTN
349 (99349)	AO11/PSP	TM	PUL	VTN	VTN
353 (99353)	AO11/PSP	TM	PUL	VTN	VTN
1201 (6445)	AJ1F/RFO	TM	CHC	VTN	VTN
3351	AD1F/FO	CS	CHC	VTN	VTN
5157	AC2Z/TSO	TM	CHC	VTN	VTN
5177	AC2Z/TSO	TM	CHC	VTN	VTN
5191	AC2Z/TSO	TM	CHC	VTN	VTN
5198	AC2Z/TSO	TM	CHC	VTN	VTN
5212	AC2Z/TSO	TM	CHC	VTN	VTN
5928	AC2F/TSO	TM	CHC	VTN	VTN
9101 (9398)	AH2Z/BSOT	TM	CHC	VTN	VTN
9496	AE2E/BSO	TM	CHC	VTN	VTN
9711	AF2F/DBSO	TM	CHC	VTN	VTN
17018 (99108)	AB11/BFK	TM	CHC	VTN	VTN
17090	AB1A/BFK	TM	CHC	VTN	VTN
96100 (86374)	GUV	TM	BRN	VTN	VTN

Right: *A very interesting vehicle operated by Vintage Trains is former GUV No. 86374, now steam loco water tanker No. 96100. This coach has been completely rebuilt internally to carry an extra water supply for steam locomotives to avoid having to take on waters en route. The vehicle retains its original outline and doors to fit in with a train formation and looks 'in place' in most train consists.* **CJM**

West Coast Railway Company

Class 03

Vehicle Length: 26ft 3in (7.92m)		Engine: Gardner 8L3		
Height: 12ft 7⁷⁄₁₆in (3.72m)		Horsepower: 204hp (149kW)		
Width: 8ft 6in (2.59m)		Mechanical Equipment: Wilson-Drewry		

Number	Depot	Pool	Livery	Owner	Operator	Name
03196(S)	CS	MBDL	GRN	WCR	WCR	Joyce
D2381(S)	CS	MBDL	BLK	WCR	WCR	

Class 08

Vehicle Length: 29ft 3in (8.91m)		Engine: English Electric 6K		
Height: 12ft 8⅝in (3.87m)		Horsepower: 400hp (298kW)		
Width: 8ft 6in (2.59m)		Electrical Equipment: English Electric		

Number	Depot	Pool	Livery	Owner	Operator	Name
08418	CS	MBDL	EWS	WCR	WCR	
08485	CS	MBDL	BLU	WCR	WCR	
08678(S)	CS	AWCX	GLX	WCR	WCR	Artila

Class 33

Vehicle Length: 50ft 9in (15.47m)				Engine: Sulzer 8LDA28A		
Height: 12ft 8in (3.86m)				Horsepower: 1,550hp (1,156kW)		
Width: 33/0, 9ft 3in (2.81m),				Electrical Equipment: Crompton		
33/2 8ft 8in (2.64m)				Parkinson		

Number	Depot	Pool	Livery	Owner	Operator	Name
33025(S)	CS	AWCX	WCR	WCR	WCR	Glen Falloch
33029	CS	AWCA	WCR	WCR	WCR	
33207	CS	AWCA	WCR	WCR	WCR	Jim Martin

Class 37

			Engine: English Electric 12CSVT
Vehicle Length: 61ft 6in (18.74m)			
Height: 13ft 0¼in (3.96m)			Horsepower: 1,750hp (1,304kW)
Width: 8ft 11⅝in (2.73m)			Electrical Equipment: English Electric

Number	Depot	Pool	Livery	Owner	Operator	Name
37214 (S)	CS	AWCX	WCR	WCR	WCR	Loch Laidon
37516 (S) (37086)	CS	AWCA	WCR	WCR	-	
37517 (S) (37018)	CS	MBDL	LHL	WCR	-	
37518 (37076)	CS	AWCX	ICS	WCR	WCR	Fort William/An Gearasden
37668 (37257)	CS	AWCX	WCR	WCR	WCR	
37669 (37129)	CS	AWCX	WCR	WCR	WCR	
37676 (37126)	CS	AWCA	WCR	WCR	WCR	Loch Rannoch
37685 (37234)	CS	AWCA	WCR	WCR	WCR	Loch Arkaig
37706 (37016)	CS	AWCA	WCR	WCR	WCR	
37710 (S) (37044)	CS	MBDL	LHL	WCR	-	
37712 (37102)	CS	AWCX	WCR	WCR	WCR	

37668, 37669 fitted with Hitachi ETRMS for Cambrian Line duties

Class 47

Vehicle Length: 63ft 6in (19.35m)			Engine: Sulzer 12LDA28C	
Height: 12ft 10⅜in (3.91m)			Horsepower: 2,580hp (1,922kW)	
Width: 9ft 2in (2.79m)			Electrical Equipment: Brush	
Electric Train Heat fitted to Class 47/4, 47/7 and 47/8				

Number	Depot	Pool	Livery	Owner	Operator	Name
47194 (S)	CS	AWCX	TLF	WCR	-	
47237	CS	AWCA	WCR	WCR	WCR	
47245	CS	AWCA	WCR	WCR	WCR	
47270	CS	AWCA	BLU	WCR	WCR	Swift
47355 (S)	CS	AWCX	BLK	WCR	-	
47492	CS	AWCX	RES	WCR	WCR	
47500 (S) (47770)	CS	AWCX	WCR	WCR	-	
47746 (47605)	CS	AWCA	WCR	WCR	WCR	
47760 (47562)	CS	AWCA	WCR	WCR	WCR	
47768 (47490)	CS	AWCX	EWS	WCR	WCR	
47772 (S) (47537)	CS	AWCX	RES	WCR	-	
47776 (47578)	CS	AWCX	RES	WCR	-	
47786 (47821)	CS	AWCA	WCR	WCR	WCR	Roy Castle OBE
47787 (47823)	CS	AWCX	WCR	WCR	WCR	Windsor Castle
47802 (47552)	CS	AWCA	DRS	WCR	WCR	
47804 (47792)	CS	AWCA	WCR	WCR	WCR	
47826 (47637)	CS	AWCA	WCR	WCR	WCR	
47832 (47560)	CS	AWCA	WCR	WCR	WCR	
47851/D1648 (47639)	CS	AWCA	WCR	WCR	WCR	
47854 (47674)	CS	AWCA	WCR	WCR	WCR	Diamond Jubilee

Class 57

Vehicle Length: 63ft 6in (19.38m)			Engine: EMD 645-12E3
Height: 12ft 10⅜in (3.91m)			Horsepower: 2,500hp (1,860kW)
Width: 9ft 2in (2.79m)			Electrical Equipment: Brush

Number	Depot	Pool	Livery	Owner	Operator
57001 (47356)	CS	AWCA	WCR	WCR	WCR
57005 (47350)	CS	AWCX	WCR	WCR	WCR
57006 (47187)	CS	AWCA	WCR	WCR	WCR
57313 (47371)	CS	AWCA	WCR	WCR	ATW
57314 (47372)	CS	AWCA	WCR	WCR	ATW
57315 (47234)	CS	AWCA	WCR	WCR	ATW
57316 (47290)	CS	AWCA	BLU	WCR	ATW
57601 (47825)	CS	AWCA	WCR	WCR	WCR

Above: *Carnforth-based West Coast Railway Co operates a total of eight Class 57s, a mix of Class 57/0, 57/3 and 57/6. Soon after transfer to WCRC, Arriva Trains blue-liveried No. 57313 is illustrated, devoid of its original drop-head 'Dellner' coupling.* **CJM**

Coaching Stock

Number	Name	Type	Depot	Livery	Operator	Notes
159 (99980)		AO10/SAL	CS	MAR	WCR*	LNWR saloon (ex-Q of Scots)
326 (S) (99402)	Emerald	AO11/PFP	CS	PUL	WCR	
347 (99347)	Car No. 347	AO11/PSO	CS	WCR	WCR	
348 (99348)	Car No. 348	AO11/PSP	CS	WCR	WCR	
350 (99350)	Car No. 350	AO11/PSP	CS	GRN	WCR	
351 (99351)	Car No. 351	AO11/PSP	CS	WCR	WCR	
352 (99352)	Amethyst	AO11/PSP	CS	PUL	WCR	
354 (99354)	The Hadrian Bar	AO11/PSP	CS	PUL	WCR	
504 (99678)	Ullswater	AP1Z/PFK	CS	PUL	WCR	
506 (99679)	Windermere	AP1Z/PFK	CS	PUL	WCR	
546 (S) (99670)	City of Manchester	AQ1Z/PFP	CS	PUL	WCR	
548 (99671)	Grasmere	AQ1Z/PFP	CS	PUL	WCR	
549 (99672)	Bassenthwaite	AQ1Z/PFP	CS	PUL	WCR	
550 (99673)	Rydal Water	AQ1Z/PFP	CS	PUL	WCR	
551 (99674)	Buttermere	AQ1Z/PFP	CS	PUL	WCR	
552 (99675)	Ennerdale Water	AQ1Z/PFP	CS	PUL	WCR	
553 (99676)	Crummock Water	AQ1Z/PFP	CS	PUL	WCR	
586 (99677)	Derwent Water	AR1Z/PFB	CS	PUL	WCR	
807 (99881)		AO10/SAL	CS	SPL	WCR*	GNR Saloon (ex-Q of Scots)
1644 (S)		AJ41/RBR	CS	ICS	WCR	
1650 (S)		AJ41/RBR	CS	ICS	WCR	
1652 (S)		AJ41/RBR	CS	ICS	WCR	
1655 (S)		AJ41/RBR	CS	ICS	WCR	
1663 (S)		AJ41/RBR	CS	ICS	WCR	
1666		AJ41/RBR	CS	WCR	WCR	
1670 (S)		AJ41/RBR	CS	ICS	WCR	
1730		AJ41/RBR	CS	WCR	WCR	
1840		AN21/RMB	CS	WCR	WCR	Set - The Green Train
1860		AN21/RMB	CS	WCR	WCR	

WCRC

1861 (99132)		AN21/RMB	CS	WCR	WCR	
1882 (99311)		AN21/RMB	CS	WCR	WCR	
1961		AJ41/RBR	CS	WCR	WCR	Set - The Green Train
2127 (S)		AO11/SLF	CS	MAR	WCR	
3058	Florence	AD11/FO	CS	WCR	WCR	
3093 (977594)	Florence	AD11/FO	CS	WCR	WCR	
3105 (99121)	Julia	AD11/FO	CS	WCR	WCR	
3106 (99122)	Alexandra	AD11/FO	CS	WCR	WCR	
3113 (99125)	Jessica	AD11/FO	CS	WCR	WCR	
3117 (99127)	Christina	AD11/FO	CS	WCR	WCR	
3128 (99371)	Victoria	AD11/FO	CS	WCR	WCR	
3130 (99128)	Pamela	AD11/FO	CS	WCR	WCR	
3136 (3605)	Diana	AD11/FO	CS	WCR	WCR	
3143 (3609)	Patricia	AD11/FO	CS	WCR	WCR	
3313		AD1F/FO	CS	WCR	WCR	
3326		AD1F/FO	CS	WCR	WCR	
3350		AD1F/FO	CS	WCR	WCR	
3352		AD1F/FO	CS	WCR	WCR	
3359		AD1F/FO	CS	WCR	WCR	
3360		AD1F/FO	CS	ICS	WCR	
3362		AD1F/FO	CS	ICS	WCR	
3392 (S)		AD1F/FO	CS	BPM	WCR	Blue Pullman vehicle
3395		AD1F/FO	CS	WCR	WCR	
3431		AD1F/FO	CS	WCR	WCR	
4860 (S) (99193)		AC21/TSO	CS	MAR	WCR	
4905		AC21/TSO	CS	WCR	WCR	
4912 (99318)		AC21/TSO	CS	WCR	WCR	
4931 (99329)		AC21/TSO	CS	WCR	WCR	
4932 (S)		AC21/TSO	CS	BLG	WCR	
4940		AC21/TSO	CS	WCR	WCR	
4951		AC21/TSO	CS	WCR	WCR	
4954 (99326)		AC21/TSO	CS	WCR	WCR	
4958		AC21/TSO	CS	WCR	WCR	
4960		AC21/TSO	CS	WCR	WCR	
4973		AC21/TSO	CS	WCR	WCR	
4984		AC21/TSO	CS	WCR	WCR	
4994		AC21/TSO	CS	WCR	WCR	
4997 (S)		AC21/TSO	CS	BLG	WCR	
5032 (99194)		AC21/TSO	CS	WCR	WCR	
5033 (99328)		AC21/TSO	CS	WCR	WCR	
5035 (99195)		AC21/TSO	CS	WCR	WCR	
5044 (99327)		AC21/TSO	CS	WCR	WCR	
5125 (S)		AC2Z/TSO	BH	GRN	WCR	
5171		AC2Z/TSO	CS	MAR	WCR	
5200		AC2Z/TSO	CS	GRN	WCR	
5216		AC2Z/TSO	CS	MAR	WCR	
5222		AC2Z/TSO	CS	MAR	WCR	
5229	The Green Knight	AC2Z/SO	CS	MAR	WTN	
5236		AC2Z/SO	CS	MAR	WCR	
5237		AD2Z/SO	CS	MAR	WCR	
5239	The Red Knight	AD2Z/SO	CS	MAR	WTN	
5249		AD2Z/SO	CS	MAR	WCR	
5278	Melisande	AC2A/TSO	CS	CHC	WTN	
5419		AC2A/TSO	CS	WCR	WTN	
5756 (S)		AC2E/TSO	CS	WCR	WCR	
6000		AC2F/TSO	CS	WCR	WCR	
6012		AC2F/TSO	CS	WCR	WCR	
6014 (S)		AC2F/TSO	CS	ICS	WCR	At Hellifield
6021		AC3F/TSO	CS	WCR	WCR	
6022		AC2F/TSO	CS	WCR	WCR	
6103		AC2F/TSO	CS	WCR	WCR	
6115 (S)		AC2F/TSO	CS	WCR	WCR	
6135 (S)		AC2F/TSO	CS	ICS	WCR	At Hellifield
6312 (92925)		AX51/GEN	CS	WCR	WCR	
6528 (5592)		AG2C/TSOT	CS	WCR	WCR	
6723		AN1D/RMBF	CS	WCR	WCR	
6724		AN1D/RMBF	CS	WCR	WCR	
9104 (S) (9401)		AH2Z/BSOT	CS	WCR	WCR	
9391	Pendragon	AE2Z/BSO	CS	PUL	WTN	

9392		AE2Z/BSO	CS	WCR	WCR	Set - The Green Train
9440		AE2C/BSO	SH	WCR	WCR	
9448 (S)		AE2C/BSO	CS	WCR	WCR	
9493		AE2D/BSO	CS	WCR	CWR	Blue Pullman vehicle
13227		AA11/FK	CD	WCR	WCR	
13306 (S)		AA11/FK	CS	WCR	WCR	
13320	*Anna*	AA11/FO	CS	WCR	WCR	
13321 (99316)		AA11/FK/RBR	CS	WCR	WCR	
13440 (S)		AA1A/FK	CS	GRN	WCR	Set - The Green Train
17102 (99680)		AB1A/BFK	CS	MAB	WCR	
17168 (S) (99319)		AB1D/BFK	CS	WCR	WCR	
18756 (25756)		AA21/SK	CS	MAR	WCR	
18806 (99722)		AA21/SK	CS	WCR	WCR	
18893 (99712)		Kitchen	CS	WCR	WCR	
19208 (99884)	Car No. 84	AA21/SK	CS	WCR	WCR	
21256 (99304)		AB31/BCK	CS	WCR	WCR	
21266		AB31/BCK	CS	WCR	WCR	
34525 (S) (99966)		AR51/GEN	CS	WCR	WCR	
35407 (99886)		AB21/BSK	CS	MAR	WCR	LNWR livery (Q of Scots)
45018 (99052)		AO10/SAL	CS	QOS	WCR	
45026 (S)		SAL	CS	MAR	WCR	LMS Inspection Saloon
96175		GUV	CS	MAR	WCR	Water carrier
99723 (35459)		AB21/BSK	CS	WCR	WCR	

WCR* - Owned by Scottish Highland Railway Co

Right and Below: *In the main the West Coast Railway passenger fleet is immaculately turned out in the company's maroon house colours, which sadly looks very drab when faded and dirty. On the right is Mk2 SO No. 5249 in immaculate condition, while below is Mk1 RBR No. 1666 looking somewhat weather-worn, but in many ways more representative of its old BR days. Both:* **Antony Christie**

Private Train Operators – WCRC

Most preserved locomotives authorised for main-line operation, either steam or diesel, operate with a support coach conveying owners' representatives, engineering staff and light maintenance equipment. Support coaches can be allocated to a specific locomotive or operate with a pool of locos.

Number	Type	Depot	Livery	Support Coach for
14007 (99782) *Mercator*	AB11/BSK	NY	MAR	61264 or 60163
17013 (14013) *Botaurus*	AB11/BFK	CM	PUL	60019
17015 (14015)	AB11/BFK	TM	CHC	Tyseley
17019 (14019)	AB11/BFK	CS	MAR	61994
17025 (14025)	AB11/BFK	CS	MAR	45690
17096	AB1B/BFK	SL	CHC	35028
21096 (99080)	AB31/BCK	NY	MAR	60007
21232 (99040)	AB31/BCK	SK	MAR	46233
21236 (99120)	AB31/BCK	ZG	GRN	30828
21249	AB21/BCK	BH	CCM	60163
35317	AD21/BSK	BQ	GRN	30850
35322 (99035)	AB21/BSK	CS	MAR	70000 and WCRC traction
35329	AB21/BSK	RL	GRN	Mid Hants fleet
35449 (99241)	AB21/BSK	BQ	MAR	45231
35451	AB21/BSK	MI	GRN	34046
35461 (99720)	AB21/BSK	TM	CHC	5029
35463 (99312)	AB21/BSK	CS	WCR	WCR fleet
35464	AB21/BSK	PR	MAR	Swanage Railway
35465 (99991)	AB21/BSK	BQ	CCM	Jeremy Hosking / 70000
35468 (99953)	AB21/BSK	NY	MAR	NYMR fleet
35470	AB21/BSK	TM	CHC	Vintage Trains fleet
35476 (99041)	AB21/BSK	SK	MAR	46233
35486 (99405)	AB21/BSK	--	MAR	60009 or 61994
35508	AB1C/BSK	BQ	MAR	East Lancs fleet
35517 (17088)	ABIK/BSK	BQ	MAR	East Lancs fleet
35518 (17097)	AB11/BFK	SH	GRN	34067
80204 (35297)	NNX	TN	MAR	61994
80217 (35299)	NNX	CS	MAR	WCRC fleet
80220 (35276)	NNX	NY	MAR	62005

Below: *The main-line operation of preserved steam and to a lesser extent diesel locomotives requires the use of support coaches, where owning staff and equipment spares can be carried. These coaches are usually attached between the loco and train and most of the main operators own and operate several vehicles. Former NNX Royal Mail vehicle No. 80204 is operated by West Coast Railway and is officially the support coach for loco 61994; however, when not required it acts as a general support vehicle or sometimes a barrier coach if West Coast is the providers of traction for coaching stock moves, especially HST stock. The vehicle is shown below coupled between a Class 47 and a FGW HST vehicle.* **CJM**

Locomotives

No locos were off lease at the time of going to press

Diesel Multiple Units

No DMUs were off lease at the time of going to press

Electric Multiple Units

Number	Class	Owner	Location
317708	317	ANG	IL
317709	317	ANG	IL
317710	317	ANG	IL
317714	317	ANG	IL
317719	317	ANG	IL
317723	317	ANG	IL
317729	317	ANG	IL
317732	317	ANG	IL

Coaching Stock - Passenger

Number	Type	Owner	Location
1209 (6457)	RFO	EVL	ZH
1219 (3418)	RFO	EVL	KT
3229	FO	EVL	KT
3434	FO	EVL	OY
5636	TSO	EVL	PM
5888	TSO	EVL	CS
6121	TSO	EVL	KT
6160	TSO	EVL	LM
6164	TSO	EVL	KT
10204 (40502)	RFM	PTR	3M
10206 (40507)	RFM	PTR	LM
10231 (10016)	RFM	PTR	§
10241 (10009)	RFM	PTR	IL
10253 (10026)	RFM	PTR	LM
10256 (10028)	RFM	PTR	YO¶
10260 (10001)	RFM	PTR	YO¶

¶ Instruction vehicle - Yoker
§ Fire Training School

10547	SLE	PTR	IS
10661 Concept vehicle at Wolverton			
10667	SLE	-	LM
10698	SLE	-	LM
10733	SLE	-	MM
11026	FO	PTR	LM
11074	FO	PTR	LM

12008	TSO	PTR	ZB
12022	TSO	PTR	ZB
12029	TSO	PTR	LM
12036	TSO	PTR	LM
12083	TSO	PTR	LM
12092	TSO	PTR	LM
12095	TSO	PTR	LM
12101	TSO	PTR	LM
12144	TSO	PTR	LM
12156	TSO	PTR	LM
12160	TSO	PTR	LM
12163	TSO	PTR	BN

Coaching Stock - HST

Number	Type	Owner	Location
40417 (40017)	TRSB	DBR	ZK
40425 (40025)	TRSB	DBR	ZK

42324 owned by East Midlands Trains now at Birkenshaw Fire Training School

Coaching Stock - NPCCS

Number	Type	Owner	Location
82109	DVT	PTR	ZB
82125	DVT	PTR	LM
82149	DVT	PTR	FC
92159 (81534)	BG	EVL	KT
92901 (92001)	BG	EVL	WB
92931 (92031)	BG	EVL	PY
96139 (93751)	GUV	EVL	WB
96181 (93875)	GUV	EVL	LM

In the foreseeable futures a considerable number of multiple unit trains will be coming off lease and returned to their owners as new stock takes to the rails; this will include HST stock displaced by the introduction of InterCity Express Stock of Class 800 and 801 on both the East Coast and Great Western routes. It is likely that the majority of HST power cars and trailer stock will find new operators, who will take advantage of such quality stock becoming available. The new Scottish franchise is committed to introducing HST sets in the Central belt. The Class 91s and Mk4 sets will also be displaced from their core route, but at this stage it is unclear if these will be used for secondary or additional East Coast services or returned to their owners.

In terms of multiple units, the introduction of electric multiple units on the CrossRail route will displace DMUs of Class 165 and 166 working on the London section of the Great Western route and Class 315s working on the present Greater Anglia Liverpool Street to Shenfield route. The Class 165s and 166s could be cascaded to other Western routes such as Devon and Cornwall, while the 315s could find further use or be scrapped. The Class 313s working on the new Thameslink, Southern and Great Northern franchise are also scheduled for replacement and these sets are likely to be cascaded via refurbishment to new routes. The full introduction of the Class 700 Thameslink stock will see the complete replacement of the Class 319 sets from the London area and these are very likely to find further use in the North East, or even on the Cardiff Valleys electrification.

Class 317s and 321s currently operated by TSGN will be stood down when new stock enters service and again these 'modern' sets will find new operators. Scotland is to benefit from an extra 14 Class 321s. Total refurbishment of stock to virtual new standards is likely in all cases.

The new TSGN franchise also calls for the total replacement of the Class 442s on the London to Gatwick Airport route; when this new 'Electrostar' stock enters service, the Class 442s will be stood down and again a full refurbishment and overhaul is likely to see these quality Mk3 sets emerge as front-line stock with another operator. There is talk of using the vehicles together with HST power cars. ∎

Off-Lease Rolling Stock

Preserved motive power is listed in this section. Those in a red typeface are authorised for main line operation.

Locomotives

Number	Operator/Base	Status

Prototype Locomotives

LMS7050	NRM	STC
LMS7051	MID	OPR
LMS7069	GWR	RES
D0226	KWV	OPR
18000	DID	STC
'Deltic'	NRM	STC

Non-Classified

D2511	KWV	OPR
D2767	BKR	OPR
D2774	STR	RES
DS75	NRS	STC

Class 01

D2953	PRL	OPR
D2956	ELR	OPR

Class 02

D2854	PRL	OPR
D2858	MRC	RES
D2860	NRM	OPR
D2866	PRL	RES
D2867	BAT	OPR
D2868	HST	OPR

Class 03

03018	MFM	RES
03020	LDL	STO
03022	SWI	OPR
D2023	KES	OPR
D2024	KES	STO
03027	PRL	RES
03037	-	OPR
D2041	COL	OPR
D2046	PVR	RES
D2051	NNR	STO
03059	IOW	OPR
03062	ELR	OPR
03063	NNR	OPR
03066	BHR	OPR
03069	GWR	OPR
03072	LHR	OPR
03073	RAC	OPR
03078	TYN	OPR
03079	DER	OPR
03081	MFM	RES
03084	ECC	OPR
03089	MFM	OPR
03090	NRS	OPR
03094	CRT	OPR
03099	PRL	OPR
03112	KES	OPR
03113	PRL	RES
D2117	LHR	OPR
D2118	PRL	RES
03119	EPO	OPR
03120	FHL	OPR
03128	APF	STO
D2133	WSR	OPR
03134	DEE	OPR

D2138	MRC	OPR
D2139	PRL	RES
03141	PRB	RES
03144	WEN	OPR
03145	MOL	OPR
D2148	RIB	OPR
03152	SWI	OPR
03158	LWR	OPR
03162	LAN	OPR
03170	BAT	OPR
D2178	GWI	OPR
03180	PRL	OPR
D2182	GWR	OPR
D2184	COL	OPR
03189	RIB	RES
D2192	PDR	OPR
03197	LDL	RES
D2199	PRL	OPR
03371	ROW	OPR
03399	MFM	OPR

Class 04

D2203	EMB	OPR
D2205	WSR	STO
D2207	NYM	OPR
D2229	PRL	RES
D2245	BAT	STO
D2246	SDR	OPR
D2271	WSR	STO
D2272	PRL	RES
D2279	EAR	OPR
D2280	NNR	RES
D2284	PRL	OPR
D2298	BRC	OPR
D2302	BHR	OPR
D2310	BAT	OPR
D2324	PRL	STO
D2325	MFM	OPR
D2334	CVR	OPR
D2337	PRL	RES

Class 05

05001	IOW	OPR
D2578	BHR	OPR
D2587	HST	RES
D2595	RIB	OPR

Class 06

06003	HST	OPR

Class 07

07001	HST	OPR
07005	GCR	RES
07010	AVR	OPR
07011	SEL	OPR
07012	APF	RES
07013	ELR	RES

Class 08

D3000	PRL	RES
D3002	PVR	OPR
D3014	PDR	OPR
08011	CPR	OPR
08012	CRT	OPR

08015	SVR	OPR
08016	PRL	OPR
08021	BRM	OPR
08022	CWR	OPR
08032	MHR	OPR
08046	CRB	OPR
08054	EMB	OPR
08060	CWR	OPR
08064	NRS	OPR
D3101	GCR	OPR
08102	LWR	OPR
08108	KES	OPR
08114	GCR	OPR
08123	CWR	OPR
08133	SVR	OPR
D3255	CVR	STO
08164	ELR	OPR
08168	BAT	OPR
D3261	SWI	RES
08195	LAN	OPR
08238	DFR	OPR
08266	KWV	OPR
08288	MHR	OPR
08331	MRC	OPR
08359	TSR	OPR
08377	WSR	OPR
08388	NHD	STO
08436	SWN	OPR
08443	BKR	RES
08444	BWR	OPR
08471	SVR	OPR
08473	DFR	STO
08476	SWN	OPR
08479	ELR	OPR
08490	STR	OPR
08528	BAT	OPR
08556	NYM	OPR
08590	MRC	OPR
08598	IND	OPR
08604	DID	OPR
08628	RIB	OPR
08631	MNR	OPR
08635	SVR	RES
08694	GCR	RES
08767	NNR	OPR
08769	SVR	OPR
08772	NNR	OPR
08773	EMB	OPR
08780	SOU	OPR
08825	CPR	OPR
08850	NYM	OPR
D4095	MSR	OPR
08896	SVR	OPR
08911	NRM	OPR
08927	GWR	OPR
08937	DAR	OPR
08944	ELR	OPR

Class 09

09001	PRL	RES
09004	SPV	OPR
09010	SDR	RES
09012	SVR	OPR
09015	PRI	STO

09017	NRM	OPR
09019	WSR	OPR
09024	ELR	RES
09025	SWI	OPR

Class 10

D3452	BWR	OPR
D3489	SPV	OPR
D4067	GCR	OPR
D4092	BHR	RES

Class 11

12052	CRB	STO
12077	MRC	OPR
12082	MHR	OPR
(Runs as 12049)		
12093	CRB	OPR
12099	SVR	OPR
12131	NNR	OPR

Class 12

15224	SPV	OPR

Class 14

D9500	PRL	RES
D9502	PRL	STO
D9504	NVR	OPR
D9513	EMB	OPR
D9516	GWS	OPR
D9518	WSR	OPR
D9520	NVR	OPR
D9521	DFR	OPR
D9523	DVR	OPR
D9524	EHC	RES
D9525	PRL	OPR
D9526	WSR	OPR
D9529	NVR	OPR
D9531	ELR	RES
D9537	ELR	RES
D9539	RIB	OPR
D9551	SVR	OPR
D9553	GWR	STO
D9555	DFR	OPR

Class 15

D8233	ELR	RES

Class 17

D8568	CPR	RES

Class 20

D8000	NRM	OPR
20001	BAR	OPR
20007	GCR	OPR
20020	BKR	RES
20031	KWV	OPR
20035	CVR	STO
20048	MRC	RES
20057	MRC	RES
20059	BRM	RES
20063	GWR	STO
20069	NNR	OPR
20087	ELR	OPR
20098	GCR	RES
20137	GWR	OPR
20154	GCR	OPR
20169	SRC	RES

20177	SVR	STO
20188	SVR	OPR
20205	MRC	RES
20214	LHR	OPR
20228	BIR	OPR

Class 24

24032	NYM	RES
24054	ELR	OPR
24061	NYM	RES
24081	GWR	OPR

Class 25

25035	GCR	OPR
25057	NNR	OPR
25059	KWV	OPR
25067	BAT	OPR
25072	CRB	RES
25083	CRB	RES
25173	EPO	OPR
25185	PDR	OPR
25191	SDR	STO
25235	BKR	RES
25244	EKR	STO
25262	SDR	OPR
25265	GCR	RES
25279	GCR	OPR
25283	DFR	RES
25309	WCR	RES
25313	WEN	RES
25321	MRC	OPR
25322	CVR	RES

Class 26

26001	CRB	OPR
26002	STR	RES
26004	BKR(for sale)	STO
26007	GCR	OPR
26010	LAN	OPR
26011	BHR	RES
26014	CRB	OPR
26024	BKR	OPR
26025	STR	RES
26035	CRB	RES
26038	BKR	RES
26040	MET	RES
26043	GWR	RES

Class 27

27001	BKR	OPR
27005	BKR	STO
27007	MHR	RES
27024	LHR	OPR
27050	STR	RES
27056	GCR	OPR
27059	SVR	RES
27066	DFR	OPR

Class 28

D5705	ELR	RES

Class 31

D5500	NRM	OPR
31101	BAT	RES
31108	MRC	OPR
31119	EMB	OPR
31130	BAT	OPR

31162	EHC	OPR
31163	CPR	OPR
31203	PBR(Nem)	OPR
31206	RST	OPR
31207	NNR	OPR
31210	DFR	RES
31235	MNR	OPR
31255	COL	OPR
31270	PRL	OPR
31271	NVR	OPR
31289	NLR	OPR
31327	STR	OPR
31414	ECC	OPR
31415	BHR	RES
31418	MRC	RES
31435	EMB	OPR
31438	EPO	OPR
31461	NEM	STO
31463	GCR	OPR
31466	DFR	OPR
31530	MNR	RES

Class 33

33002	SDR	OPR
33008	BAT	RES
33012	SWN	OPR
33018	NEM	RES
33019	BAT	OPR
33021	BRM	RES
33030	BAT	RES
33035	ECC	OPR
33046	MRC	STO
33048	WSR	OPR
33052	KES	OPR
33053	MHR	OPR
33057	WSR	RES
33063	SPV	OPR
33065	SPV	RES
33102	CVR	RES
33108	BHR	RES
33109	ELR	OPR
33110	BWR	RES
33111	SWN	OPR
33116	GCR	OPR
33117	ELR	RES
33201	MRC	OPR
33202	MFM	OPR
33208	MHR	OPR

Class 35

D7017	WSR	OPR
D7018	WSR	RES
D7029	SVR	RES
D7076	ELR	OPR

Class 37

D6700	NRM	OPR
37003	MNR	OPR
37009	GCR	RES
37023	ALY	RES
37025	BKR	RES
37032	NNR	RES
37037	MNR	OPR
37042	EVR	OPR
37075	CVR	OPR
37097	CRB	OPR
37108	RAC	OPR

Preserved Motive Power

Preserved Motive Power

37109	ELR	OPR	46035	RAC	STO	55015	BHR	RES
37142	BWR	OPR	46045	MRC	OPR	55016	BHR	OPR
37146	SRC	RES				55019	BHR	OPR
37152	PRL	RES	**Class 47**			55022	ELR	OPR
37188	PRL	RES	47004	EMB	OPR			
37207	PVR	RES	47105	GWR	OPR	**Class 56**		
37215	GWR	OPR	47117	GCR	OPR	56006	BHR	OPR
37216	PBR	OPR	47192	DAR	OPR	56097	GCR	OPR
37227	BAT	RES	47205	NLR	OPR			
37240	LAN	OPR	47292	GCR	OPR	**Class 58**		
37248	GWR	RES	47306	BWR	OPR	58016	BHR	RES
37250	WED	RES	47367	NNR	OPR			
37254	SPV	OPR	47376	GWR	RES	**Class 97**		
37255	GCR	OPR	47401	MRC	OPR	97650	LWR	OPR
37263	DFR	RES	47402	ELR	OPR	97651	STR	OPR
37264	BRM	RES	47417	MRC	RES	97654	PRL	OPR
37275	SDR	OPR	47449	LAN	OPR			
37294	EMB	RES	47484	BHR	RES	**Class 71**		
37308	EHD	RES	47524	CVR	RES	71001	BHR	STO
37314	MRC	OPR	47540	WEN	STO			
37324	GWR	OPR	47596	MNR	RES	**Class 73**		
37372	BHR	RES	47635	BAT	OPR	73001	DFR	OPR
37403	BKR	RES	47640	BAT	OPR	73003	SWI	OPR
37407	CVR	STO	47643	BKR	OPR	73110	GCR	OPR
37413	BOK	RES	47712	RAC	OPR	73114	BAT	OPR
37418	ELR	RES	47763	MFM	OPR	73129	GWR	OPR
37424	CVR	STO	47765	GCR	RES	73130	FIN	OPR
37674	WEN	OPR	47771	COL	RES	73134	BHR	OPR
37679	NLR	RES	47773	BRM	OPR	73140	SPV	OPR
37901	ELR	OPR	47785	ECC	RES	73210	MNR	OPR
			47793	MFM	OPR			
Class 40			47798	NRM/WCR	OPR	**Class 76**		
D200	NRM	RES	47799	EVR	RES	E26020	NRM	STC
40012	MRC	OPR	47840	WST	OPR			
40013	BHR	OPR				**Class 77**		
40106	WAS	OPR	**Class 50**			E27000	MRC	STC
40118	BRM	RES	50002	SDR	RES	E27001	MSM	STC
40135	ELR	OPR	50007	WAS	RES			
40145	ELR	OPR	50008	BOD	OPR	**Class 81**		
			50015	ELR	OPR	81002	BHR	STC
Class 41			50017	BOD	OPR			
HST			50019	MNR	OPR	**Class 82**		
41001	GCN	OPR	50021	BRM	RES	82008	BHR	STC
			50026	EHD	RES			
Class 42			50027	MHR	OPR	**Class 83**		
D821	SVR	OPR	50029	PRL	STO	83012	BHR	STC
D832	WSR	OPR	50030	PRL	RES			
			50031	EHD	RES	**Class 84**		
Class 44			50033	BRM	STO	84001	BHR	STC
D4	MRC	RES	50135	EHD	OPR			
44008	PRL	OPR	50042	BWR	OPR	**Class 85**		
			50044	MRC	OPR	85101	BHR	STC
Class 45			50049	SVR (CF)	OPR			
45015	BAT	STO	50050	YEO	RES	**Class 86**		
45041	MRC	OPR				86213	BHR	OPR
45060	BHR	OPR	**Class 52**			86259	BRM	OPR
45105	BHR	RES	D1010	WSR	OPR			
45108	MRC	RES	D1013	SVR	OPR	**Class 87**		
45118	NLR	RES	D1015	BRM	OPR	87001	NRM	STC
45125	GCR	OPR	D1023	NRM	OPR	87035	RAC	RES
45132	EPO	RES	D1041	ELR	STO			
45133	MRC	RES	D1048	MRC	RES	**Class 89**		
45135	ELR	RES	D1062	SVR	OPR	89001	BHR	STC
45149	GWR	RES						
			Class 55			**London Transport**		
Class 46			55002	NRM	RES	12	LUL	OPR
46010	GCN	OPR	55009	BHR	OPR			

Above: *Mainly due to the high costs of meeting Network Rail Group Standards, there is still only a limited number of ex-BR main line diesel locomotives certified for main-line use. One loco which always causes great attraction is Diesel Traction Group-owned Class 52 'Western' No. D1015* Western Champion. *In this view the loco is seen between Dawlish Warren and Dawlish on 10 May 2014 powering the 'Western Lickeys The Banks' tour, the 07.00 Solihull to Plymouth.* **CJM**

Diesel Units

Number	Base
Number	*Base*
Unclassified	
APT-E	NRS
LEV1	NNR
RB004	TEL
79018	MRC
79612	MRC
79900	ECC
79960	NNR
79962	KWV
79963	NNR
79964	KWV
79976	GCR
79978	COL
Class 100	
56301	MNR
Class 101	
50222	BIR
50256	EKR
50338	BIR
51187	CRT
51188	ECC
51189	KWV
51192	ELR
51205	CRT
51210	WEN
51226	MNR
51228	NNR

Number	Base
51247	WEN
51427	GCR
51432	SWN
51434	MNR
51498	SWN
51499	MNR
51503	MNR
51505	EAR
51511	NYM
51512	CRT
51213	EAR
51803	KWV
53160	MRC
53164	CHS
53170	ECC
53193	GCR
53203	GCR
53204	NYM
53253	MRC
53266	GCR
53321	GCR
53746	WEN
54055	CRT
54062	NNR
54365	EAR
54408	SPV
56343	EKR
56352	ELR
56358	EAR
59117	MNR
59539	NYM

Number	Base
Class 104	
50447	LAN
50454	LAN
50455	TEL
50479	TEL
50494	CVR
50517	CVR
50528	LAN
50531	TEL
50547	CVR
50556	TEL
56182	CVR
59137	CVR
59228	TEL
Class 105	
51485	ELR
56121	ELR
56456	LAN
Class 107	
51990	STR
52005	NVR
52006	AVR
52008	STR
52025	AVR
52030	STR
59791	NVR
Class 108	
50599	EAR
50619	DFR

Number	Base
50632	PBR
50929	KWV
50980	BWR
51562	ELR
51565	KWV
51566	DFR
51567	MRC
51568	KEI
51571	KES
51572	WEN
51907	LAN
51909	MSR
51914	DFR
51919	BVR
51922	ELR
51933	DFR
51941	SVR
51942	PBR
51947	BWR
51950	GWR
51973	MRC
52044	PBR
52048	BVR
52053	KEI
52054	BWR
52062	GWR
52064	SVR
53628	KEI
53645	GCR
53926	GCR
53971	KES
54223	EAR

54270	PBR	59719	SDR	59510	GWR	59609	MRC
54279	LDL	59740	SDR	59513	PDR		
54490	LAN	59761	BRC	59514	SWI	**Class 140**	
54504	SWN			59515	YEO	140001 - 55500/01	KEI
56208	SVR	**Class 116**		59516	SWN		
56224	ECC	51131	BAT	59517	PDR	**Class 141**	
56271	MSR	51138	GCR	59520	PBR	141103	WED
56484	MRC	51151	GCR	59521	MRC	141108	COL
56491	KEI	51321	BAT	59522	CHS	141110	WED
56492	DFR	59003	PDR	59603	CHS	141113	MRC
56495	KLR	59004	PDR				
59245	APF	59444	CHS	**Class 119**		**Class 201, 202 and 203**	
59250	SVR			51073	ECC	60116	HAD
59387	DFR	**Class 117**		51074	SWI	60118	HAD
59389	GCR	51339	GWR	51104	SWI	60501	HAD
		51342	EPO			60529	HAD
Class 109		51346	SWN	**Class 120**		60750	WPH
50416	LAN	51347	GWI	59276	GCR	201001	HAD
56171	LAN	51351	PBR				
		51353	MRC	**Class 121**		**Class 205**	
Class 110		51356	SWN	55019	BRM	60117	PBR
51813	WEN	51359	NLR	55023	CPR	60822	LDL
51842	WEN	51360	ECC	55024	BRM	60828	PBR
52071	LHR	51363	GWR	55028	SWN	60154 X 1101	EKR
52077	LHR	51365	GWR	55029	RST	60800 X 1101	EKR
59701	CVR	51367	STR	55033	COL	70549	ELR
		51372	TIT	54289	ECC	Set 205009	EDR
Class 111		51381	MFM	56287	COL	Set 205025	MHR
59575	MRC	51382	GWR			Set 205028	DAR
		51384	EPO	**Class 122**		Set 1132	DAR
Class 114		51388	SWN	55000	SDR	Set 205033	LDL
50015	MRC	51392	SWN	55001	ELR	Set 205205	EPO
50019	MRC	51395	MRC	55003	GWR		
54057	STR	51397	PBR	55005	BAT	**Class 207**	
56006	MRC	51398	MRC	55006	ECC	60127	SWI
56015	MRC	51400	WEN	55009	MNR	60130 X 207202	ELR
		51401	GWI	55012	SHI	60138	WPH
Class 115		51402	STR			60142	SPV
51655	(BIR)	51405	GWR	**Class 126**		60145	SEL
51663	WSR	51407	GWR	51017	BKR	60149	SEL
51669	SPV	59486	SWN	51043	BKR	60616	SPV
51677	(BIR)	59488	PDR	59404	BKR	60901	SWI
51859	WSR	59492	SWN	79443	BKR	60904 X 207202	ELR
51880	WSR	59494	PDR			60916	SPV
51886	BRC	59500	WEN	**Class 127**			
51887	WSR	59503	PDR	51616	GCR	901001	CVR
51899	BRC	59506	WSR	51618	LAN		
59659	SDR	59507	PDR	51622	GCR		
59664	(BIR)	59508	GWI	55966	MRC		
59678	-	59509	WEN	55976	MRC		

Left: *Former BR Southern Region Class 205 'Hampshire' set No. 1132 (205032) is preserved at the Okehampton Railway in Devon and operates limited passenger services between Okehampton and Meldon. The set is restored to early 1960s BR green livery with small yellow warning ends. It is seen departing from Okehampton bound for Meldon.* **CJM**

Preserved Motive Power

Electric Units

Unclassified	
28249	NRM
29666	MRC
29670	MRC
79998	DEE
79999	DEE

BEL	
85	SOU
87	KEI
91	RAM

BIL	
10656 (2090)	NRS
12123 (2090)	NRS

COR	
10096	EKR
11161	EKR
11179	NRM
11201	BLU
11825	EKR

DD	
13004	NIR

Class 302	
75033	MFM
75250	MFM

Class 303	
303023/032	BKR

Class 306	
306017	EAR

Class 307	
75023	ERM

Class 308	
75881	ERM

Class 309	
309616	COV
309624	COV

Class 405 (SUB)	
S8143S	NRM
4732	COV

Class 411/412 (CEP)	
61742	DAR
61743	DAR
61798	EVR
61799	EVR
61804	EVR
61805	EVR
70229	EVR
70257	GCR
70273	DFR
70284	NIR
70292	SMP
70296	NIR
70354	EVR
70527	WRN
70531	SMP
70539	EVR
70576	SNI
70607	EVR
Set 1198	PBR
Set 7105	EKR

Class 414 (HAP)	
61275	NRM
61287 (4311)	COV
75395	NRM
75407 (4311)	COV

Class 415 (EPB)	
14351 (5176)	NIR
14352 (5176)	NIR
15345	COV
15396 (5176)	NIR

Class 416 (EPB)	
65302	FIN
65304	FIN
65373 (5759)	EKR
77558 (5759)	EKR
14573 (6307)	COV
16117 (6307)	COV
65321 (5791)	COV
77112 (5793)	COV

Class 419 (MLV)	
68001	EKR
68002	EKR
68003	EVR
68004	MNR
68005	EVR
68008	EKR
68009	EKR

Class 421 (CIG)	
62364	DFR
62378	DFR
62887	LWR
69339	GCR
76726	DFR
76740	DFR
76797	DFR
76811	DFR
76812	DAR
Set 1496	DAR
Set 1497	MNR
Set 1498	EPO
Set 1399	PBR

Class 422 (BEP)	
69304	NIR
69310	DAR
69318	COL
69332	DAR
69333	LDL
69337	HAD

Class 423 (VEP)	
(42)3417	BLU/IL
76398 (3905)	DAR
76875	NRM

Class 438 (TC)	
76275 (404)	PRI
76277 (405)	DAR
70589 (412)	PRI
413	MRC
417	DAR
428	LUL

Class 457	
67300	COV

Class 488	
72501	ECC
72617	ECC

Class 489	
68500	ECC
68506	ECC

Class 501	
61183	COV
75186	COV

Class 502	
28361	TEB
29896	TEB

Class 503	
28690	COV
29298	COV
29720	COV

Class 504	
65451	ELR
77172	ELR

Right: *Former Southern Region Waterloo-Weymouth line 4TC set No. 428 formed with vehicles 76297, 71163, 70823 and 76324 is owned by London Transport and usually kept at West Ruislip depot. It is finished in fake wood livery applied by vinyl and retains its push-pull controls for use with a Class 33/1 or 73 loco. The set is seen at Norden on the Swanage Railway.* **Antony Christie**

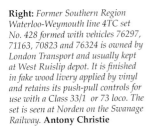

Preserved Motive Power

Ex-BR Industrial Locos

Over the years a number of former BR locomotives have, after withdrawal from normal duties, been taken up for use by industrial operators. The list below represents those which are understood to still be in existence in late 2014. Some locos operated at preservation sites are deemed to be 'industrial' but these are grouped in the preserved section.

Class 03
03179 *Clive*   First Capital Connect, Hornsey Depot

Class 08
08202   The Chasewater Light Railway
08220   Traditional Traction, working at Longport
08375   Hanson Cement, Ketton
08411   LH Group, Burton – owned by Classic Traction
08441   Railway Support Services, Wishaw
08445   Daventry International Railfreight Terminal (DIRFT) – at LH Group, Burton
08447   John G. Russell Transit, Hillington, Glasgow
08460   Railway Support Services, Wishaw
08484 *Captain Nathaniel Darell*   Felixstowe Dock & Railway
08503   Barry Island Railway
08511   RSS Rye Farm, Wishaw
08535   Corus, Shotton Works
08598   Chasewater Light Railway
08600   LH Group Services, Barton-under-Needwood
08613   Hanson Traction, Washwood Heath
08622 (H028) (7)   Hanson, Ketton
08643   Aggregate Industries, Whatley
08648   P D Ports, Teesport No. 20
08652   Hanson Aggregates, Whatley Quarry
08670   RSS, Wishaw
08683   RSS, Wishaw
08699   Weardale Railway
08728   St Modwen Storage, Long Marston
08731   Aggregate Industries, Merehead
08743 *Bryan Turner*   LH Group Services, Barton-under-Needwood
08774 *Arthur Vernon Dawson*   AV Dawson, Middlesbrough
08787   Hanson Aggregates, Machen
08807   AV Dawson, Middlesbrough
08809   Corus, Shotton (at Washwood Heath 12/10)
08818 *Molly*   Faber Prest Ports, Flixborough Wharf
08823 (D3991)   Daventry International Railfreight Terminal
08847   Stored at Norwich Crown Point (Cotswold Rail - for sale)
08870 (H024)   Castle Cement, Ketton
08872   European Metal Reprocessing, Attercliffe
08873   Freightliner Terminal, Southampton
08903 *John W. Antill*   SembCorp Utilities Teesside, Wilton
08912   AV Dawson, Middlesbrough
08913   LH Group Services, Barton-under-Needwood
08915   Stephenson Railway Museum
08933   Aggregate Industries, Merehead
08936   Corus, Shotton Works
08937 *Bluebell Mel*   Aggregate Industries, Meldon Quarry
08947   Aggregate Industries, Knights Rail Services, Eastleigh

Class 09
09022   Boston Docks Co
09023   European Metal Reprocessing, Attercliffe

Class 11
12088   Butterwell

Class 14
D9529 (14029)   Aggregate Industries, Bardon Quarry

Industrial

These lists give details of former UK diesel and electric locos exported for further use overseas and understood to still be operational.

Class 03
D2013	Italy
D2032	Italy
D2033	Italy
D2036	Italy

Class 04
D2216	Italy
D2232	Italy
D2289	Italy
D2295	Italy

Class 08
D3047	Lamco Liberia
D3092	Lamco Liberia
D3094	Lamco Liberia
D3098	Lamco Liberia
D3100	Lamco Liberia

Class 10
D3639	Conakry (Guinea)
D3649	Conakry (Guinea)

Class 14
D9534	Bruges

Class 56
56101	Floyd, Hungary 92 55 0659-001-5
56115	Floyd, Hungary 92 55 0659-002-3
56117	Floyd, Hungary 92 55 0659-003-1

Class 58
58001	ETF France
58004	TSO France
58005	ETF France
58006	ETF France
58007	TSO France
58009	TSO France
58010	TSO France
58011	TSO France
58013	ETF France
58015	Transfesa, Spain
58018	TSO France
58020	Transfesa, Spain
58021	TSO France
58024	Transfesa, Spain
58025	Continental Rail, Spain
58026	TSO France
58027	Continental Rail, Spain
58029	Transfesa, Spain
58030	Transfesa, Spain
58031	Transfesa, Spain
58032	ETF France
58033	TSO France
58034	TSO France
58035	TSO France
58036	ETF France
58038	ETF France
58039	ETF France
58040	TSO France
58041	Transfesa, Spain
58042	TSO France
58043	Transfesa, Spain
58044	ETF France
58046	TSO France
58047	Transfesa, Spain
58049	ETF France
58050	Continental Rail, Spain

Class 66
66010	ECR, France
66022	ECR, France
66026	ECR, France
66032	ECR, France
66036	ECR, France
66038	ECR, France
66042	ECR, France
66045	ECR, France
66049	ECR, France
66052	ECR, France
66064	ECR, France
66072	ECR, France
66073	ECR, France
66123	ECR, France
66146	ECR, Poland
66153	ECR, Poland
66157	ECR, Poland
66159	ECR, Poland
66163	ECR, Poland
66166	ECR, Poland
66173	ECR, Poland
66178	ECR, Poland
66179	ECR, Poland
66180	ECR, Poland
66189	ECR, Poland
66190	ECR, France
66195	ECR, France
66196	ECR, Poland
66202	ECR, France
66203	ECR, France
66205	ECR, France
66208	ECR, France
66209	ECR, France
66210	ECR, France
66211	ECR, France
66212	ECR, France
66214	ECR, France
66215	ECR, France
66216	ECR, France
66217	ECR, France
66218	ECR, France
66219	ECR, France
66220	ECR, Poland
66222	ECR, France
66223	ECR, France
66224	ECR, France
66225	ECR, France
66226	ECR, France
66228	ECR, France
66229	ECR, France
66231	ECR, France
66233	ECR, France
66234	ECR, France
66235	ECR, France
66236	ECR, France
66237	ECR, Poland
66240	ECR, France
66241	ECR, France
66242	ECR, France
66244	ECR, France
66246	ECR, France
66247	ECR, France
66248	ECR, Poland
66411	Freightliner PL, As 66013FPL
66412	Freightliner PL, As 660xxFPL
66417	Freightliner PL, As 66014FPL
66582	Freightliner PL, As 66009FPL
66583	Freightliner PL, As 66010FPL
66584	Freightliner PL, As 66011FPL
66586	Freightliner PL, As 66008FPL
66608	Freightliner PL, As 66603FPL
66609	Freightliner PL, As 66605FPL
66611	Freightliner PL, As 66604FPL
66612	Freightliner PL, As 66606FPL
66624	Freightliner PL, As 66602FPL
66625	Freightliner PL, As 66601FPL

Class 86
86215	Floyd, Hungary 91 55 0450-005-8
86217	Floyd, Hungary 91 55 0450-006-?
86218	Floyd, Hungary 91 55 0450-004-1
86228	Floyd, Hungary 91 55 0450-007-
86233	Bulgaria (spares)
86232	Floyd, Hungary 91 55 0450-003-3
86242	Floyd, Hungary 91 55 0450-008-
86248	Floyd, Hungary 91 55 0450-001-7
86250	Floyd, Hungary 91 55 0450-002-5
86424	Floyd, Hungary

Class 87
87003	BZK Bulgaria 91 52 00 87003-7
87004	BZK Bulgaria 91 52 00 87004-5
87006	BZK Bulgaria 91 52 00 87006-0
87007	BZK Bulgaria 91 52 00 87007-8
87008	BZK Bulgaria
87009	BUL Bulgaria 91 52 00 87009-4
87010	BZK Bulgaria 91 52 00 87010-2
87012	BZK Bulgaria 91 52 00 87012-8
87013	BZK Bulgaria 91 52 00 87013-6
87014	BZK Bulgaria (spares)
87017	BUL Bulgaria 91 52 00 87017-7
87019	BZK Bulgaria 91 52 00 87019-3
87020	BZK Bulgaria 91 52 00 87020-1
87022±	BZK Bulgaria 91 52 00 87022-7
87023	BUL Bulgaria 91 52 00 87023-5
87025	BUL Bulgaria 91 52 00 87025-0
87026	BZK Bulgaria 91 52 00 87026-8
87028	BZK Bulgaria 91 52 00 87028-4
87029	BZK Bulgaria 91 52 00 87029-2
87033	BZK Bulgaria 91 52 00 87033-4
87034	BZK Bulgaria 91 52 00 87034-2

± Out of service - fire damage

Class 92
92001	DBS Romania 91 53 0472-002
92012	DBS Romania 91 53 0472-001
92025	DBS Bulgaria
92027	DBS Bulgaria
92034	DBS Bulgaria

A number of preserved modern traction locomotives have been allocated five-digit Class 89 TOPS numbers to allow their operation either under power or dead over the National Network. The numbers allocated are shown below; not all locos may currently be authorised for use on Network Rail metals.

The first two digits are the class, the third is the power type, while the final two digits are the final two of the original running number. If two locos clash with the same number, the second to be registered will have 1 added to the number.

Class 89 TOPS No.	BR No.	Type	Name
89100	20050	Class 20	-
89101	20001	Class 20	-
89127	20227	Class 20	-
89166	20166	Class 20	-
89188	20188	Class 20	-
89200	31018	Class 31	-
89204	26004	Class 26	-
89210	27059	Class 27	-
89212	LT 12	Met Loco	Sarah Siddons
89223	25173	Class 25	-
89233	25283	Class 25	-
89247	27001	Class 27	-
89254	24054	Class 24	-
89259	25309	Class 25	-
89261	24061	Class 24	-
89262	25262	Class 25	-
89280	31162	Class 31	-
89317	D7017	Class 35	-
89376	D7076	Class 35	-
89400	E27000	Class 77	Electra
89401	47401	Class 47	North Eastern
89402	50002	Class 50	Superb
89403	71001	Class 71	-
89404	44004	Class 44	Great Gable
89405	47105	Class 47	-
89407	50007	Class 50	Sir Edward Elgar
89408	50008	Class 50	Thunderer
89412	40012	Class 40	Aureol
89413	D1013	Class 52	Western Ranger
89415	50015	Class 50	Valiant
89416	D1015	Class 52	Western Champion
89417	50017	Class 50	Royal Oak
89420	45108	Class 45	-
89421:1	D821	Class 42	Greyhound
89421:2	50021	Class 50	Rodney
89423	45125	Class 45	-
89424	D1023	Class 52	Western Fusilier
89427	50027	Class 50	Lion
89431	50031	Class 50	Hood
89432	D832	Class 42	Onslaught
89435	40135	Class 40	-
89440	45133	Class 45	-
89441	D1041	Class 52	Western Prince
89442	47192	Class 47	-
89443	50042	Class 50	Triumph
89444	50044	Class 50	Exeter
89445	40145	Class 40	-
89448	D1048	Class 52	Western Lady
89449	50049	Class 50	Defiance
89453	45041	Class 45	Royal Tank Regiment
89460	45060	Class 45	Sherwood Forester
89462	D1062	Class 52	Western Courier
89466	47449	Class 47	-
89472	46035	Class 46	Ixion
89500	55022	Class 55	Royal Scots Grey
89502	55002	Class 55	The King's Own Yorkshire Light Infantry
89503	81002	Class 81	-
89509	55009	Class 55	Alycidon
89515	55015	Class 55	Tulyar
89516	55016	Class 55	Gordon Highlander
89519	55019	Class 55	Royal Highland Fusilier
89523	DP1	Proto	Deltic
89535	83012	Class 83	-
89561	85101	Class 85	-

Below: *To enable ex-BR locomotives to operate over the National Network, locos are allocated a Class 89 series number. On the left is original 'Peak' Class 44 No. D4 (44004) which is allocated TOPS identity 89404. The loco is seen together with Class 25 No. D7671.* **CJM**

Several preserved steam locomotives have been allocated five-digit TOPS numbers to allow their operation over the National Network. The numbers allocated are shown below; not all locos may currently be authorised for use on Network Rail metals.

TOPS No.	Railway No.	Type	Name
98150	1450	GWR 14xx	
98166	1466	GWR 14xx	
98186	686	0-6-0T	Lady Armaghdale
98212	41312	LMS 2MT	
98219	55189	CR 0-4-4T	
98221	46521	LMS 2MT	
98238	1638	GWR 16xx	
98240	3440	GWR 34xx	City of Truro
98241	46441	LMS 2MT	
98243	46443	LMS 2MT	
98253	30053	SR M7	
98254	58926	LNWR 2F	
98273	65243	NBR J36	Maude
98315	7715	GWR 57xx	
98321	69621	GER N7	A. J. Hill
98372	30072	SR USA	
98400	41000	LMS 4P	
98406	43106	LMS 4MT	
98414	75014	BR 4MT	
98425	7325	GWR 7321	
98426	31625	SR U	
98427	44027	LMS 4F	
98435	80135	BR 4MT	
98455	4555	GWR 45xx	
98457	9600	GWR 8750	
98460	7760	GWR 57xx	
98466	9466	GWR 94xx	
98469	75069	BR 4MT	
98472	5572	GWR 4575	
98476	76079	BR 4MT	
98478	68078	WD 4F	
98479	80079	BR 4MT	
98480	80080	BR 4MT	
98482	3882	0-6-0ST	Barbara
98488	4588	GWR 4575	
98494	65894	LNER J27	
98498	80098	BR 4MT	
98500	45000	LMS 5MT	
98502	7802	GWR 78xx	Bradley Manor
98505	45305	LMS 5MT	Alderman A E Draper
98507	45407	LMS 5MT	Lancashire Fusilier
98510	45110	LMS 5MT	
98512	7812	GWR 78xx	Erlestoke Manor
98519	7819	GWR 78xx	Hinton Manor
98525	45025	LMS 5MT	
98526	30925	SR V	Cheltenham
98529	73129	BR 5MT	
98530	4930	GWR 49xx	Hagley Hall
98531	45231	LMS 5MT	Sherwood Forester
98532	44932	LMS 5MT	
98536	4936	GWR 49xx	Kinlet Hall
98549	4965	GWR 49xx	Rood Ashton Hall
98553	4953	GWR 49xx	Pitchford Hall
98560	6960	GWR 6959	Raveningham Hall
98564	61264	LNER B1	
98565	42765	LMS 5MT	
98567	44767	LMS 5MT	George Stephenson
98568	42968	LMS 5MT	
98571	44871	LMS 5MT	
98572	5972	GWR 49xx	Olton Hall
98577	30777	SR N15	Sir Lamiel
98596	73096	BR 5MT	
98598	6998	GWR 6959	Burton Agnes Hall
98605	62005	LNER K1	
98628	30828	SR S15	
98641	30841	SR S15	
98642	61994	LNER K4	The Great Marquess
98690	45690	LMS 6P5F	Leander
98693	45593	LMS 6P5F	Kolhapur
98696	45596	LMS 6P5F	Bahamas
98699	45699	LMS 6P5F	Galatea
98700	70000	BR 7P	Britannia
98701	34101	SR WC	Hartland
98709	53809	SDJR 7F	
98713	70013	BR 7P	Oliver Cromwell
98715	46115	LMS 7P	Scots Guardsman
98716	34016	SR WC	Bodmin
98727	34027	SR WC	Taw Valley
98728	5029	GWR 4073	Nunney Castle
98729	7029	GWR 4073	Clun Castle
98750	30850	SR LN	Lord Nelson
98751	5051	GWR 4073	Earl Bathurst
98767	34067	SR BB	Tangmere
98771	60800	LNER V2	Green Arrow
98772	34072	SR BB	257 Squadron
98780	5080	GWR 4073	Defiant
98792	34092	SR WC	City of Wells
98800	6000	GWR 60xx	King George V
98801	46201	LMS 8P	Princess Elizabeth
98802	71000	BR 8P	Duke of Gloucester
98803	46203	LMS 8P	Princess Margaret Rose
98805	35005	SR MN	Canadian Pacific
98809	60009	LNER A4	Union of South Africa
98824	6024	GWR 60xx	King Edward I
98828	35028	SR MN	Clan Line
98829	46229	LMS 8P	Duchess of Hamilton
98832	60532	LNER A2	Blue Peter
98834	46233	LMS 8P	Duchess of Sutherland
98851	48151	LMS 8F	
98857	2857	GWR 28xx	
98863	60163	LNER A1	Tornado
98868	60022	LNER A4	Mallard
98872	60103	LNER A3	Flying Scotsman
98873	48773	LMS 8F	
98898	60007	LNER A4	Sir Nigel Gresley
98920	92220	BR 9F	Evening Star

Above: 'New' steam loco A1 Pacific No. 60163 Tornado is allocated TOPS identity 98863. The loco is seen at Bombardier, Derby. **CJM**

Coupling Codes & Couplings

With the introduction of modern traction from the 1950s a number of different methods of multiple operation were introduced, covering the different control principles of locomotives, for example those using electro-pneumatic or electro-magnetic systems.

Six main systems are in operation today:

Blue Star ★ using the electro-pneumatic system and fitted to Classes 20, 25, 31, 33, 37, 40 and 73.

Green Spot ● a unique system installed on some Class 47s operated by the freight sector.

Orange Square ■ an English Electric system used only on the Class 50s.

Red Diamond ♦ a 1970s system developed for the modern freight locos of Classes 56 and 58.

In addition to the above coded systems, the American-developed main-line locos of Classes 59, 66, 67 and 70 use the US standard AAR (Association of American Railroads) system. Direct Rail Services (DRS) has also developed a unique system which is installed on some of the company's Class 20, 37, 47 and 57 locos.

A number of locomotives have either been built with or modified to incorporate Time Division Multiplex (TDM) remote operation equipment, which uses coach lighting-type Railway Clearing House (RCH) nose-end jumper cables.

Some of the surviving first generation DMMU sets carry a **Blue Square** ■ multiple operation system.

Details of the main coupling systems in operation in the UK are included in the accompanying illustrations.

Standard Coupling

Above: *Class 59 and 66 front-end layout (non-DB-S operated). 1-Coupling hook, 2-Coupling shackle, 3-Air brake pipe (red), 4-Main reservoir pipe (yellow), 5-Buffer, 6-Association of American Railroads (AAR) jumper socket. No. 66726 illustrated.* **CJM**

Standard Coupling

Above: *Standard coupling arrangement to be found on many classes of UK loco. 1-Electric Train Supply (ETS) jumper socket, 2-Main reservoir air pipe (yellow), 3-Vacuum brake pipe, 4-Coupling hook and shackle, 5-Air brake pipe (red), 6-Electric Train Supply (ETS) jumper cable. Loco No. 47580 illustrated.* **CJM**

Drop Head Buck-Eye with TDM Coupling

Above: *The unique front-end layout of the Royal Mail Class 325. 1-Brake pipe (red), 2-Main reservoir pipe (yellow), 3-Electric Train Supply (ETS) socket, 4-Time Division Multiplex (TDM) jumper socket, 5-Drop head buck-eye coupling, 6-Electric Train Supply (ETS) cable.* **CJM**

Couplings

Drop Head Dellner Coupling

Above: *Following the introduction of Virgin Trains 'Voyager' and 'Pendolino' stock, a fleet of 16 Class 57/3s was introduced with drop-head Dellner couplers and cabling to provide 'hotel power'. The coupling is seen in this illustration in the raised position. 1-Electric Train Supply (ETS) jumper socket, 2-Main reservoir pipe (yellow), 3-Air brake pipe (red), 4-Coupling hook, 5-Dellner coupling face, 6-Electric Train Supply (ETS) jumper cable.* **CJM**

BSI Coupling

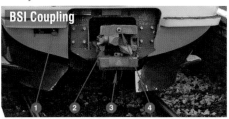

Above: *With the birth of modern multiple unit trains came the Bergische Stahl Industrie (BSI) automatic coupling, first seen in the UK on the Tyne & Wear Metro vehicles in 1978. The modern generation of UK DMUs now concentrates on the Compact BSI coupler with a CK2 coupling interface. The couplers are engaged by the compression of the two coupling faces, which completes a physical connection and also opens a watertight cover to an electrical connection box. The full train air connection is made during the coupling compression process. The coupling is completed by the driver pressing a 'couple' button in the driving cab. 1-Emergency air connection, 2-Coupling face, 3-Electric connection (behind plate), 4-Air connection. The coupling shown is on a Class 166.* **CJM**

Tightlock with Drum Connection

Above: *The Tightlock coupler is a derivative of the Association of American Railroads (AAR) Type H coupler, later under the control of American Public Transportation Association (APTA). A modified Type H coupler was introduced in the UK from the early 1970s and has become a standard fitting on many of the later BR and several post-privatisation EMUs. The UK Tightlock design can be supplied with or without an electrical connection box and with or without a pneumatic connection. This view shows a fully automated version as fitted to the 'Networker' fleet. Attachment is achieved by driving the two vehicles together, which physically connects the vehicles, while a 'roll-cover' box opens to connect electric and pneumatic services. 1-Emergency air connector, 2-Manual release handle, 3-Semi-rotary electric/pneumatic cover, 4-Physical coupler.* **CJM**

Tightlock with Nose End Connections

Above: *The BR Southern Region-designed Class 455 and 456 units have a semi-automatic Tightlock used for physical connections, while air and electrical connections are made by waist-height flexible pipes. 1-Main reservoir pipe (yellow), 2-Control jumper, 3-Tightlock coupler, 4-Couple/Uncouple drum switch, 5-Manual release handle, 6-Control jumper receptacle.* **CJM**

Dellner Coupling with Drum Connector

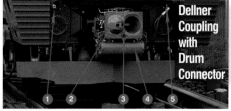

Above: *Dellner couplers have become the standard in the UK and much of Europe; these are fully automatic and come in various forms. 1-Emergency air supply, 2-Dellner coupling plate, 3-Pneumatic connection, 4-Roll-cover to electrical connections, 5-Air supply. Coupling of Class 360 illustrated.* **CJM**

Couplings

Dellner Coupling

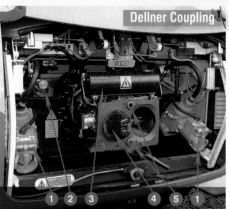

Above: *A large number of different designs of Dellner couplers exist on UK rolling stock. Some feature full automatic operation including pneumatic and electrical connections, while others only provide physical coupling. This view shows a pair of 'Voyager' units coupled together with Dellner couplers. The electrical connection box is above the physical coupler. After trains are 'pushed' together the driver operates a 'couple' button in the cab to complete the attachment. Uncoupling is achieved by the driver pressing an 'uncouple' button and driving the trains apart.* **CJM**

Left: *The Virgin Trains 'Pendolino' stock uses Dellner couplers with a rotary covered electrical connector plate above. These couplers are supplemented by electric train supply connections either side to provide 'hotel power' to Class 390 sets from attached Class 57 locos. 1-Electric Train Supply (ETS) socket, 2-Emergency air connector, 3-Electrical connector plate under semi-rotary cover, 4-Dellner physical coupler, 5-Pneumatic connections. In normal use the Dellner coupler on 'Pendolino' stock is covered by a front fairing.* **CJM**

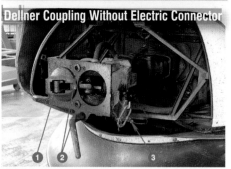

Above: *Under the front-end fairing of the Eurostar Class 373 stock a standard Scharfenberg coupler is located for assistance purposes and shunting. No electrical provision is made and the couplers are seldom used. 1-Scharfenberg coupling face, 2-Pneumatic connections, 3-Manual uncoupling handle.* **CJM**

Above: *In as-installed condition and having never been coupled to another set, a Class 380 Scharfenberg coupler is viewed, showing the auto opening electrical connection box above. 1-Electrical connection box, 2-Coupling face plate, 3-Pneumatic connection.* **CJM**

Couplings

Emergency HST Bar Coupling

Above: *If High Speed Trains are required to be coupled to conventional hook couplings an adaptor coupling is carried on the HST for this purpose. It has to be first attached to the front of the HST by opening the front panel and attaching the aluminium bar to a coupling lug. The other end is then at the right level and length to attach to a standard loco hook coupling without the loco's buffers touching the HST's bodywork. Standard air connection is provided. Locos fitted with swing-head or combination couplers cannot be used to assist HST stock. A Class 59/1 is seen attached to HST power car No. 43150 in this view at Westbury.* **Greg Welsh**

Right: *All DBS Class 66s (except 66001/002) and all Class 67s are fitted with swing-head combination couplers allowing attachment to other like-fitted locos or rolling stock using a knuckle coupling. Two Class 66s are seen here attached using the swing-head coupler. Note that the buffers do not touch and that all traction and braking forces are transmitted through the coupler. Standard buffer beam air connections are provided on one main reservoir and one brake pipe. The auto coupler can be disconnected by using the white uncoupling handle seen on the left.* **Antony Christie**

DBS Combination Coupler

Couplings

Transport for London
London Underground

Address: ✉ Floor 11, Windsor House, 50 Victoria Street, London, SW1H 0TL
📠 pressoffice@tfl.gov.uk
✆ 0845 604 4141
ⓘ www.tfl.gov.uk

Managing Director: Peter Austin

Operations: The London Underground system, now operated by Transport for London (TfL), operates services on 10 lines in and around the capital and uses a mix of surface and tunnel stock.

Bakerloo Line
Tube Line. Operates services between Elephant & Castle and Harrow & Wealdstone.
Rolling Stock: 1972 Mk2, livery - red, white and blue, allocated to Stonebridge Park. Scheduled for replacement in 2018.

Central Line
Tube Line. Operates services between West Ruislip/Ealing and Epping.
Rolling Stock: 1992, livery - red, white and blue, allocated to Hainault.

Circle Line
Sub-Surface Line. Operates circle network in Central London and the branch from Edgware Road to Hammersmith.
Rolling Stock: 'S' stock, introduced 2013-14, livery - red, white and blue, allocated to Hammersmith.

District Line
Sub-Surface Line. Operates services between Wimbledon, Richmond, Ealing, Edgware Road, Kensington Olympia and Upminster.
Rolling Stock: 'S' stock, livery - red, white and blue, allocated to Ealing Common and Upminster.

Jubilee Line
Tube Line. Operates services between Stanmore and Stratford.
Rolling Stock: 1996, livery - red, white and blue, allocated to Wembley Park.

Metropolitan Line
Sub-Surface Line. Operates services from Amersham, Chesham, Watford and Uxbridge to Aldgate.
Rolling Stock: 'S' stock, livery - red, white and blue, allocated to Wembley Park.

Northern Line
Tube Line. Operates services between Morden and Edgware, Mill Hill East and High Barnet.
Rolling Stock: 1995 stock, livery - red, white and blue, allocated to Morden.

Piccadilly Line
Tube Line. Operates services between Heathrow Airport/Uxbridge and Cockfosters.
Rolling Stock: 1973 stock, livery - red, white and blue, allocated to Northfields and Cockfosters. Stock due for replacement in 2014.

Victoria Line
Tube Line. Operates services between Brixton and Walthamstow Central
Rolling Stock: 2009 stock, livery - red, white and blue, allocated to Northumberland Park.

Waterloo & City Line
Tube Line. Operates services between Waterloo and Bank.
Rolling Stock: 1992 stock, livery - red, white and blue, allocated to Waterloo.

Light Rail

Above: *In 2014-15 Bombardier Derby Litchurch Lane has been completing the delivery of 'S' stock in both seven- and eight-car formations for use on the Circle, Hammersmith & City, District and Metropolitan Lines. Two S7 sets, with driving cars Nos. 21471 (left) and 21465 (right) are seen at the Derby construction site in summer 2014.* **CJM**

For space reasons, we are unable in this publication to provide vehicle numbers for London Underground stock. These are available in out sister publication *London Underground Rolling Stock Guide.*

Transport for London Croydon Tramlink

Contact details as London Underground.

CR4000 stock

| | | | | Train Length: 98ft 9in (30.1m) | | Seating: 70 | |
| | | | | Width: 8ft 7in (2.65m) | | Horsepower: 643hp (480kW) | |
				Power Supply: 750V dc overhead		Electrical Equipment: Bombardier	
2530	2533	2536	2539	2542	2545	2548	2551
2531	2534	2537	2540	2543	2546	2549	2552
2532	2535	2538	2541	2544	2547	2550	2553

Stadler Variobahn

| | | | | Train Length: 106ft 2½in (32.37m) | Seating: 70 |
| | | | | Width: 8ft 7in (2.65m) | Horsepower: 650hp (483kW) |
				Power Supply: 750V dc overhead	Electrical Equipment: Stadler
2554	2555	2556	2557	2558	2559

Name applied
2535   *Stephen Parascandolo*
        1980-2007

Right: *Transport for London Croydon Tramlink Stadler Variobahn vehicle 2557 is seen at Mitcham Junction, with one of the older CR4000 vehicles No. 2532 on the right.* **Tim Easter**

Light Rail

Transport for London
Docklands Light Railway

Operated by KeolisAmey Docklands for Transport for London under contract until 2021.

Class B90 (twin)

Train Length: 94ft 5in (28.80m)
Width: 8ft 7in (2.65m)
Power Supply: 750V dc third rail

Seating: 52 + 4 tip-up
Horsepower: 375hp (280kW)
Electrical Equipment: Brush

22	25	28	31	34	37	40	43
23	26	29	32	35	38	41	44
24	27	30	33	36	39	42	

Class B92 (twin)

Train Length: 94ft 5in (28.80m)
Width: 8ft 7in (2.65m)
Power Supply: 750V dc third rail

Seating: 54 + 4 tip-up
Horsepower: 375hp (280kW)
Electrical Equipment: Brush

45	51	57	63	69	75	81	87
46	52	58	64	70	76	82	88
47	53	59	65	71	77	83	89
48	54	60	66	72	78	84	90
49	55	61	67	73	79	85	91
50	56	62	68	74	80	86	

Class B2K (twin)

Train Length: 94ft 5in (28.80m)
Width: 8ft 7in (2.65m)
Power Supply: 750V dc third rail

Seating: 52 + 4 tip-up
Horsepower: 375hp (280kW)
Electrical Equipment: Brush

01	03	05	07	09	11	13	15	92	94	96	98
02	04	06	08	10	12	14	16	93	95	97	99

Class B07 (twin)

Train Length: 94ft 5in (28.80m)
Width: 8ft 7in (2.65m)
Power Supply: 750V dc third rail

Seating: 52 + 4 tip-up
Horsepower: 375hp (280kW)
Electrical Equipment: Bombardier

101	106	111	116	121	126	131	136	141	146	151
102	107	112	117	122	127	132	137	142	147	152
103	108	113	118	123	128	133	138	143	148	153
104	109	114	119	124	129	134	139	144	149	154
105	110	115	120	125	130	135	140	145	150	155

Below: *Four designs of light rail vehicle are to be found operating on the Transport for London Docklands network, with all sets allocated to Poplar depot. Class B92 twin set No. 92 is illustrated at Poplar station. All trains on the Docklands system operate under automatic train control, but each train has an operator on board.* **CJM**

Blackpool Tramway

Address: ✉ Blackpool Transport, Rigby Road, Blackpool, FY1 5DD

📠 jean.cox@blackpooltransport.com

✆ 01253 473001 ⓘ www.blackpooltrams.info

Blackpool Tramway is operated by Blackpool Transport.

Flexity 2

Train Length: 105ft 9in (32.23m)
Width: 8ft 8in (2.65m)
Power Supply: 600V dc overhead

Seating: 74 + 148 standing
Horsepower: 4 x 160hp (120kW) three phase TMs
Electrical Equipment: Bombardier

001	003	005	007	009	011	013	015
002	004	006	008	010	012	014	016

Right: *The modernised Blackpool Tramway operating from Starr Gate (where a new purpose-built depot has been constructed) through to Fleetwood, provides an excellent service on the Lancashire coast. A fleet of 16 Bombardier Flexity 2 five-section trams operates the service. Vehicles are finished in a white and purple livery. Set No. 003 is illustrated.* **CJM**

Edinburgh Tramway

Address: ✉ 55 Annandale Street, Edinburgh, EH7 4AZ

📠 customer@edinburghtrams.com ✆ 0131 475 0177 ⓘhttp://edinburghtrams.com

CAF 7-section

Train Length: 140ft 5in (42.8m)
Width: 8ft 7in (2.65m)
Power Supply: 750V dc overhead

Seating: 78 + 170 standing
Horsepower: 1,287hp (960kW)
Electrical Equipment: CAF

251	255	259	263	267	271	275
252	256	260	264	268	272	276
253	257	261	265	269	273	277
254	258	262	266	270	274	

Right: *The newest UK tram system is that in the city of Edinburgh, Scotland, linking the city centre with Edinburgh Airport. A fleet of 27 seven-section CAF trams operates the system, operating on dedicated tramway sections and on-street running. The service, which commenced in mid-2014, provides an excellent service. Tram No. 261 is seen heading towards Edinburgh city centre at Ingliston Park & Ride.* **CJM**

Light Rail

Glasgow Subway

Address: ✉ SPT, Consort House, 12 West George Street, Glasgow, G2 1HN
- ✍ enquiry@spt.co.uk
- ✆ 0141 332 6811
- ⓘ www.spt.co.uk

Glasgow Subway is operated by Strathclyde Partnership for Transport (SPT).

Single Power Cars

										Length: 42ft 2in (12.81m)	Seating: 36S

Length: 42ft 2in (12.81m) *Width: 7ft 7in (2.34m)* *Power Supply: 600V dc third rail* *Seating: 36S* *Horsepower: 190hp (142.4kW)* *Electrical Equipment: GEC*

101	104	107	110	113	116	119	122	125	128	131
102	105	108	111	114	117	120	123	126	129	132
103	106	109	112	115	118	121	124	127	130	133

Trailer Cars

Length: 41ft 6in (12.70m) *Width: 7ft 7in (2.34m)* *Seating: 40S*

201	202	203	204	205	206	207	208

Right: *Thirty-three power cars and eight trailer cars form the train fleet on the Glasgow Subway, more usually known as the Clockwork Orange. Painted in the line's orange and grey livery, a train is seen at West Street station, led by power car No. 124.*
Robin Ralston

Manchester Metrolink

Address: ✉ Greater Manchester PTE, 2 Piccadilly Gardens, Manchester, M1 3BG
RATP Metrolink, Metrolink House, Queens Road, Manchester, M8 0RY
- ✍ customerservices@metrolink.co.uk
- ✆ 0161 205 2000   ⓘ www.metrolink.co.uk

Metrolink is operated for GMPTE by Metrolink RATP Dev UK Ltd.

M5000 stock

Train Length: 93ft 1in (28.4m) *Width: 8ft 7in (2.65m)* *Power Supply: 750V dc overhead* *Seating: 52 + 8 tip-up* *Horsepower: 643hp (480kW)* *Electrical Equipment: Bombardier*

3001	3015	3029	3043	3057	3071	3085	3099	3113
3002	3016	3030	3044	3058	3072	3086	3100	3114
3003	3017	3031	3045	3059	3073	3087	3101	3115
3004	3018	3032	3046	3060	3074	3088	3102	3116
3005	3019	3033	3047	3061	3075	3089	3103	3117
3006	3020	3034	3048	3062	3076	3090	3104	3118
3007	3021	3035	3049	3063	3077	3091	3105	3119
3008	3022	3036	3050	3064	3078	3092	3106	3120
3009	3023	3037	3051	3064	3079	3093	3107	
3010	3024	3038	3052	3066	3080	3094	3108	
3011	3025	3039	3053	3067	3081	3095	3109	
3012	3026	3040	3054	3068	3082	3096	3110	
3013	3027	3041	3055	3069	3083	3097	3111	
3014	3028	3042	3056	3070	3084	3098	3112	

Right: *Manchester Metrolink is now exclusively operated by M5000 two-vehicle trams, built by Bombardier as part of its Flexity Swift design. A total of 120 vehicles are either in traffic or on order. Set No. 3042 is illustrated in Rochdale Town Centre.* **John Binch**

■ Former T68 trams Nos. 1016, 1022, 1024, 1026 stored at Long Marston.

Midland Metro

Address: ✉ Travel West Midlands, PO Box 3565, Birmingham, B1 3JR
📠 info@travelmetro.co.uk © 0121 254 7272 ⓘ www.travelmetro.co.uk

T-69 Six-axle Stock

Train Length: 108ft 3in (29m)	Seating: 54 + 4 tip-up	
Width: 7ft 9in (2.4m)	Horsepower: 697hp (520kW)	
Power Supply: 750V dc overhead	Builder: Ansaldo/Breda	

01(S)	*Sir Frank Whittle*	07	*Billy Wright*	13	*Anthony Nolan*
02(S)		08	*Joseph Chamberlain*	14	*Jim Eames*
03(S)	*Ray Lewis*	09	*Jeff Astle*	15	*Agenoria*
04		10	*John Stanley Webb*	16	*Gerwyn John*
05	*Sister Dora*	11	*Theresa Stewart*		
06	*Alan Garner*	12			

Urbos 3

Train Length: 108ft 3in (29m)	Seating: 54 + 156 standing	
Width: 8ft 8in (2.65m)	Horsepower: 1,320hp (960kW)	
Power Supply: 750V dc overhead	Builder: CAF	

17	20	23	26	29	32	35
18	21	24	27	30	33	36
19	22	25	28	31	34	

Below: *The first members of the new £40m fleet of CAF 'Urbos 3' trams for the Midland Metro entered service on 5 September 2014, following an official launch ceremony at Wednesbury Depot. On 7 September, set No. 23 is seen at the St. Pauls stop with the 09.30 Birmingham Snow Hill to Priestfield service.* **John Binch**

Nottingham Express Transit

Address: ✉ Transdev Tram UK Ltd, Garrick House, 74 Chiswick High Road, London, W4 1SY
Nottingham City Transport Ltd, Lower Parliament Street, Nottingham, NG1 1GG
📠 info@thetram.net ✆ 0115 942 7777 ⓘ www.thetram.net

Incentro AT6/5	*Train Length: 108ft 3in (29m)* *Width: 7ft 9in (2.4m)* *Power Supply: 750V dc overhead*	*Seating: 54 + 4 tip-up* *Horsepower: 697hp (520kW)* *Electrical Equipment: Bombardier*

201	
202	*DH Lawrence*
203	*Bendigo Thompson*
204	*Erica Beardsmore*
205	*Lord Byron*
206	*Angela Alcock*
207	*Mavis Worthington*
208	*Dinah Minton*
209	*Sid Standard*
210	*Sir Jesse Boot*
211	*Robin Hood*
212	*William Booth*
213	*Mary Potter*
214	*Dennis McCarthy*
215	*Brian Clough*

Above: *A fleet of 15* Incentro AT6/5 *and 22 Citadis 402 trams operate the expanding Nottingham system. In this view at David Lane, Incentro No. 203* Bendigo Thompson *and Citadis 402 No. 218* Jim Taylor *pose side by side showing the obvious design changes.* **Antony Christie**

Citadis 402	*Train Length: 104ft 11¾in (32m)* *Width: 7ft 9in (2.4m)* *Power Supply: 750V dc overhead*	*Seating: 58 + 6 tip-up* *Horsepower: 644hp (480kW)* *EBuilder: Alstom*

216	220	224	228	232	236
217	221	225	229	233	237
218 *Jim Taylor*	222	226	230	234	
219	223	227	231	235	

Sheffield SuperTram

Address: ✉ Stagecoach SuperTram, Nunnery Depot, Woodburn Road, Sheffield, S9 3LS
📠 enquiries@supertram.com, ✆ 0114 272 8282, ⓘ www.supertram.com

Six-axle Stock	*Train Length: 113ft 6in (34.75m)* *Width: 8ft 7in (2.65m)* *Power Supply: 750V dc overhead*	*Seating: 80 + 6 tip-up* *Horsepower: 800hp (596kW)* *Electrical Equipment: Siemens*

101	104	107	110	113	116	119	122	125
102	105	108	111	114	117	120	123	
103	106	109	112	115	118	121	124	

Left: *The Stagecoach-operated Sheffield SuperTram system operates a fleet of 25 three-section trams built by Siemens, each having 80 seats and room for around 250 standing. Set No. 103 is illustrated.* **Antony Christie**

Light Rail

Tyne & Wear Metro

Address: ✉ Tyne & Wear Passenger Transport Executive (NEXUS), Nexus House,
33 St James Boulevard, Newcastle upon Tyne, NE1 4AX
✐ enquiries@nexus.co.uk
✆ 0191 203 3333 ① www.nexus.org.uk

Tyne & Wear Metro stock is allocated TOPS classification 994 for operation over Network Rail metals
between Pelaw and South Hylton.

Six-axle Stock

Train Length: 91ft 3in (27.80m)
Width: 8ft 7in (2.65m)
Power Supply: 1500V dc overhead

Seating: 68 tip-up
Horsepower: 500hp (374kW)
Electrical Equipment: Siemens

4001	4014	4027	4040	4053	4066	4079
4002	4015	4028	4041	4054	4067	4080
4003	4016	4029	4042	4055	4068	4081
4004	4017	4030	4043	4056	4069	4082
4005	4018	4031	4044	4057	4070	4083
4006	4019	4032	4045	4058	4071	4084
4007	4020	4033	4046	4059	4072	4085
4008	4021	4034	4047	4060	4073	4086
4009	4022	4035	4048	4061	4074	4087
4010	4023	4036	4049	4062	4075	4088
4011	4024	4037	4050	4063	4076	4089
4012	4025	4038	4051	4064	4077	4090
4013	4026	4039	4052	4065	4078	

Names applied

4026 *George Stephenson*	4060 *Thomas Bewick*	4077 *Robert Stephenson*
4041 *Harry Cowans*	4073 *Danny Marshall*	4078 *Ellen Wilkinson*

Above: *A fleet of 90 Metro-Cammell two-vehicle six-axle trams operates on the Tyne & Wear Metro system. Set No. 4079 is viewed at Gateshead Metro station with a service bound for Pelaw.* **James Mayl**

Tyne & Wear Metro also operates three battery-electric shunting locomotives at South Gosforth which are registered National Fleet numbers 97901, 97902 and 97903.

Livery Codes

Code	Description
ABL	Arriva Trains - blue
AGI	Aggregate Industries - green, silver and green
AIN	Aggregate Industries - blue
ALS	Alstom Transportation
ANG	Anglia - mid blue
ANN	Anglia - turquoise/white with Greater Anglia branding
ATE	Arriva Trains Executive - turquoise/cream with branding
ATT	Arriva Trains Wales - Welsh Government
ATW	Arriva Trains Wales - turquoise/cream
AWT	Abellio - white Greater Anglia
AXC	Arriva Cross Country - brown, silver, pink
BBR	Balfour Beatty Rail - blue/white
BLG	Blue and grey
BLK	Black
BLL	BR Rail Blue with large logo
BLU	Blue
BLW	Carillion Rail - blue/white
BOM	Bombardier Transportation
BPM	Blue Pullman - Nankin blue and white
BRD	BR Departmental mid grey
BRT	BR Trainload two-tone grey
C2C	c2c - blue/pink
CAL	Caledonian Railway
CAR	Carmine and Cream
CEN	Central Trains - blue and two-tone green
CHC	Chocolate and Cream
CIV	BR Civil Engineers - grey and yellow
COL	Colas - orange, lime green and black
CON	Continental Rail - light/mid blue
COR	Corus Steel - light blue or yellow
COX	Connex - white and yellow
CRG	Chiltern Railways - grey
CRW	Chiltern Railways - white/blue
CTL	Central Trains - blue, green with yellow doors
CWR	Cotswold Rail - silver with branding
DBB	DB Schenker - light blue
DBM	DB Schenker - maroon
DBS	DB Schenker - red
DCG	Devon & Cornwall Railways - green
DCN	Devon & Cornwall Railways - grey
DRB	Direct Rail Services - blue
DRC	Direct Rail Services - blue 'Compass' branding
DRO	Direct Rail Services - Ocean Liner blue
DRS	Direct Rail Services - blue
DRU	Direct Rail Services - unbranded blue
ECG	East Coast - grey
ECR	European Cargo Rail - grey
ECS	East Coast - silver
ECW	East Coast - white
ECT	East Coast - branded National Express livery
EMT	East Midlands Trains, white, blue, swirl cab ends
EPS	European Passenger Services
EPX	Europhoenix - red/silver
ETF	ETF Rail - yellow with green band
EU2	Eurotunnel - Europorte2
EUB	Eurostar new style - blue/grey
EUS	Eurostar - white, yellow and blue
EWE	DBS Executive
EWS	English Welsh Scottish - red with gold band
FCC	First Capital Connect, First Group Urban Lights - mauve/blue with pink, blue and white lower branding
FER	Fertis - grey with branding
FGB	First Great Western - blue
FGF	First Group - GBRf (Barbie)
FGL	First Great Western - local lines
FGS	First Group ScotRail with EWS branding
FGT	First Great Western, Thames/London area branding
FGW	First Great Western - as FST with FGW branding
FHT	First Hull Trains - as FST with Hull Trains branding
FLG	Freightliner - green unbranded
FLP	Freightliner - green/yellow - PowerHaul
FLR	Freightliner - green/yellow - original
FLU	Freightliner - green/yellow - unbranded
FLY	Freightliner - grey
FNA	First livery with National Express East Anglia branding
FOS	Foster Yeoman
FSN	Northern branded First Group
FSP	First ScotRail Strathclyde - carmine and cream (some with turquoise band)
FSR	First ScotRail - as FST with FSR branding
FSS	First ScotRail - blue with white Saltire branding
FST	First Group - dark blue, pink and white swirl
FSW	First Group - green and white with gold branding
FTP	First TransPennine - as FST with FTP branding
GAT	Gatwick Express - white, mid-grey and red with red doors
GBE	GB Railfreight - Europorte branding
GBF	GB Railfreight - swirl
GBM	GB Railfreight - Metronet
GBN	GB Railfreight/Eurotunnel new livery
GBR	GB Railfreight - blue
GBU	GB Railfreight - swirl (no First branding)
GLX	Glaxochem - grey, blue and black
GNE	Great North Eastern Railway - blue
GRN	Green
GRY	Grey
GSW	Great Scottish & Western Railway - maroon
GTL	Grand Central Railway - black
GTO	Grand Central Railway - black with orange
GWG	First Great Western - green
GWR	Great Western Railway - green
HAN	Hanson
HEC	Heathrow Connect - grey, orange
HEL	Heathrow Connect - Terminal 4 'Link'
HEX	Heathrow Express - silver, grey
HNR	Harry Needle Railroad - yellow/grey
HS1	High Speed 1 - blue with powder blue doors

HUN	Hunslet	RTB	Railtrack - blue
IND	Industrial colours of operator	RTK	Railtrack - grey/brown
INT	InterCity - two-tone grey off set with red and white body band	SCE	Stagecoach - white with East Midlands branding
JAR	Jarvis - maroon	SCS	Serco Caledonian Sleeper
KBR	Knorr Bremse Rail - blue, white, green	SCT	ScotRail Caledonian Sleeper - mauve/ white
LAF	Lafarge Aggregates - green/white	SEC	Serco
LHL	Loadhaul Freight - black and orange	SET	South Eastern Trains - white with branding
LLB	Large Logo Blue	SGK	Southern Gatwick Express - blue, white and
LMI	London Midland - grey, green and black		red with swirl ends
LNE	LNER tourist green/cream	SIL	Silver
LOG	London Overground - white and blue with orange doors	SKL	Silverlink London Overground, SLK with London Overground branding
LUL	London Underground red	SLF	Silverlink, with First Great Western branding
MAB	Statesman Pullman - maroon/beige	SLK	Silverlink - mauve, green and white
MAI	MainTrain - blue with branding	SNF	Railfreight grey with SNCF branding
MAL	Malcolm Rail	SNT	SNCF domestic on Eurostar - silver, white and
MAR	Maroon		yellow
MER	Merseyrail - silver and yellow	SOU	Southern - white, black and green
MLF	Mainline Freight - aircraft blue	SPL	Special livery
MLG	Mainline Freight - branded double grey	STN	Stansted Express
MML	Midland Main Line - turquoise/white	STO	Stobart Rail
MSC	Mediterranean Shipping Company	SWM	South West Trains - main-line white and blue
NBP	Northern Belle Pullman - cream/umber	SWO	South West Trains - outer-suburban blue
NE2	National Express with c2c branding	SWS	South West Trains - suburban red
NGE	First Great Eastern - grey/blue with cab end swirl, branded National Express	SWT	South West Trains - blue, red, grey
		TAT	Tata Steel - blue
NOM	Northern Rail - blue Metro branded	TES	Tesco
NOR	Northern Rail - blue, purple, grey	TEX	TransPennine Express - as FST with TPE brand
NOU	Northern Rail - unbranded	TGG	Transrail Grey with 'T' branding
NRL	Network Rail - yellow with branding	THM	Thameslink - blue, white, yellow
NSE	Network SouthEast - red, white and blue	TLF	Trainload Freight - grey
NUB	Northern Rail blue - unbranded ScotRail	TLK	Thameslink new
NWT	North West Trains - dark blue	TLL	Trainload grey with Loadhaul branding
GAR	National Express East Anglia (now Abellio)	TLP	Thameslink promotional multi-coloured
NXE	National Express East Coast		stripes
NXG	National Express East Coast branding on GNER blue livery	TPD	Trans Pennine/Central Trains logo
		TSO	Travaux du Sud Ouest - yellow
NXS	National Express brand on Silverlink	TTG	Two-tone grey
NXU	National Express unbranded white/grey	VAB	Virgin with Abellio Greater Anglia branding
ONE	One Anglia mid-blue (now Abellio)	VIR	Virgin - red/grey
ORA	One Railway with Greater Anglia branding	VSN	VSOE Northern
ORG	HNRC orange	VT1	Virgin - red/grey unbranded
PCL	BR Parcels - red/grey	VWC	Virgin West Coast - silver, red, white and
PTR	Porterbrook		black
PUL	Pullman - umber/cream	WAB	Wabtec Rail - black
QOS	Queen of Scots Pullman	WAG	West Anglia Great Northern - purple
REG	Regional Railways - blue, white	WCR	West Coast Railway - maroon
RES	Rail express systems - red and graphite	WES	Wessex Trains - maroon
RFD	Railfreight Distribution	WET	Wessex Trains - silver, maroon/pink doors
RFE	Railfreight grey with EWS branding	WEX	Wessex Rail Engineering
RFG	Railfreight grey	WHT	White
RFI	Railfreight International	YEL	Yellow
RFP	Railfreight with Petroleum branding		
RFT	BR Railfreight - grey, red and yellow, with large logo and numbers		
RIV	Riviera Trains - maroon		
RML	Royal Mail Limited - red		
ROJ	Royal Diamond Jubilee		
ROY	Royal Train - claret		

Data Tables

Rail Data Tables

Operational Pool Codes

ATLO West Coast Traincare - Locomotives
ATTB West Coast Traincare - Class 57/3 with Dellner
ATZZ West Coast Traincare - Locos for disposal
AWCX West Coast Railway - Stored locos
CDJD Serco Railtest - Shunting locos
COFS Colas Rail - Class 56
COLO Colas Rail - Operational locomotives
COLS Colas Rail - Stored locomotives
COTS Colas Rail - For refurbishment
DFFT Freightliner - Restricted duties
DFGC Freightliner - Class 86/5 trials locomotive
DFGH Freightliner - Heavy Haul Class 70
DFGI Freightliner - Intermodal Class 70
DFGM Freightliner - Intermodal Class 66/5
DFHG Freightliner - Heavy Haul Class 66/5 & 66/6
DFHH Freightliner - Heavy Haul Class 66/5 & 66/6
DFIM Freightliner - Intermodal Class 66/5
DFIN Freightliner - Intermodal - low emission
DFLC Freightliner - Class 90
DFLS Freightliner - Class 08
DFNC Freightliner - Class 86/6
DFRT Freightliner - Class 66 Infrastructure contracts
DFTZ Freightliner - Stored Class 66
DHLT Freightliner - Awaiting repairs
EFOO First Great Western - Class 57
EFPC First Great Western - HST power cars
EFSH First Great Western - Class 08
EHPC CrossCountry Trains - HST power cars
EJLO London Midland - Class 08
EMPC East Midlands Trains - HST power cars
EMSL East Midlands Trains - Class 08
EPXX Europhoenix - Class 86
GBBR Europorte/GBRf - Class 73/9
GBCM Europorte/GBRf - Class 66 commercial contracts
GBED Europorte/GBRf - Class 73/1, 73/2
GBET Europorte/GBRf - Class 92
GBFM Europorte/GBRf - Class 66 modified with RETB
GBMU Europorte/GBRf - Class 66 modified for MU
GBNB Europorte/GBRf - Class 66 new
GBDR Europorte/GBRf - Class 66 new ex DB
GBNL Europorte/GBRf - Class 66 new ex NL
GBRT Europorte/GBRf - Class 66 Infrastructure
GBSD Europorte/GBRf - Class 66 RETB
GBWM Europorte/GBRf - Class 08
GBZZ Europorte/GBRf - Stored locomotives
GCHP Grand Central - HST power cars
GPSS Eurostar UK - Class 08
HNRL Harry Needle Railroad - Class 08, 20 hire locos
HNRS Harry Needle Railroad - Stored locomotives
HTCX Hanson Traction - Class 56
IANA National Express East Anglia - Class 90
IECA National Express East Coast - Class 91
IECP National Express East Coast - HST power cars
INDL Industrial (unofficial code)
MBDL Private operators - Diesel traction
MBED Private operators - Class 73
MRSO Mainline Rail - Class 08
PTXX Eurotunnel - Europorte2 Class 92
QACL Network Rail - Class 86 load banks
QADD Network Rail - Class 31

QCAR Network Rail - HST power cars
QETS Network Rail - Class 97/3
RCZH Railcare Springburn - Class 08
RCZN Railcare Wolverton - Class 08
RFSH Wabtec Rail Doncaster - Class 08
RVLO Rail Vehicle Engineering Derby - Locos
RVLS Rail Vehicle Engineering Derby - Stored locos
SIEM Siemens Transportation - Barriers
TTLS Traditional Traction - Locomotives
WAAC DB Schenker - Class 67
WABC DB Schenker - Class 67 RETB fitted
WACC DB Schenker - Class 67 hire to Chiltern
WAWC DB Schenker - Class 67 hire to Arriva T W
WBAK DB Schenker - Class 66 construction
WBAT DB Schenker - Class 66 general
WBBT DB Schenker - Class 66 RETB fitted
WBLT DB Schenker - Class 66 Lickey banker use
WBRT DB Schenker - Class 66 RHTT general
WBSN DB Schenker - Class 66 RHTT general
WBTT DB Schenker - Class 66 RHTT Tripcock fitted
WCAT DB Schenker - Class 60 standard fuel capacity
WCBT DB Schenker - Class 60 extended fuel capacity
WDAM DB Schenker - Class 59/2
WEAC DB Schenker - Class 90 general
WEDC DB Schenker - Class 90 hire
WFMS DB Schenker - Class 60 Fleet Management
WLAN DB Schenker - Euro Cargo Rail Class 21
WNTS DB Schenker - Stored locos - serviceable
WNXX DB Schenker - Stored locos - unserviceable
WNYX DB Schenker - Stored locos - parts recovery
WNZX DB Schenker - Awaiting disposal
WRLN DB Schenker - Class 08, 09 - North London
WSEN DB Schenker - Euro Cargo Rail - Class 08
WSSA DB Schenker - Class 08, 09 - Axiom Rail
WSSI DB Schenker - Class 08, 09 Industrial
WSSL DB Schenker - Class 08, 09 Logistics
WSSM DB Schenker - Class 08, 09 Energy
WSSK DB Schenker - Class 08, 09 Network/Const'n
WSXX DB Schenker - Class 08, 09 Stored
WFAC DB Schenker - Class 92 general
WFBC DB Schenker - Class 92 HS1 equipped
WFCC DB Schenker - Class 92 HS1 equipped DRS
WFDC DB Schenker - Class 92 Hire DRS
XHAC Direct Rail Services - Class 47
XHCE Direct Rail Services - Class 68 Chiltern
XHCK Direct Rail Services - Class 57
XHNB Direct Rail Services - Northern Belle
XHND Direct Rail Services - Class 37 Network Rail
XHHP Direct Rail Services - Holding Pool
XHIM Direct Rail Services - Class 66 - Intermodal
XHNC Direct Rail Services - Nuclear Traffic
XHSS Direct Rail Services - Stored
XHVE Direct Rail Services - Class 68
XHVT Direct Rail Services - Class 57 Thunderbird
XYPA Mendip Rail - Hanson Group
XYPO Mendip Rail - Foster Yeoman (Aggregate Inds)

■ Pools are given only for locomotive groups which are included in this book. Pool codes for multiple units are not included.

Preserved Site codes

ACL	AC Locomotive Group	MID	Middleton Railway
ALY	Allelys, Studley	MLM	Motorail - Long Marston
APF	Appleby-Frodingham RPS	MNF	Mid-Norfolk Railway
AVR	Avon Valley Railway	MOR	Moreton-on-Lugg
BAT	Battlefield Line	MRC	Middleton Railway Centre
BEL	5Bel Trust Barrow Hill	MSM	Museum of Science & Industry, Manchester
BHR	Barrow Hill Roundhouse	MSR	Midsomer Norton
BIR	Barry Island Railway	NHD	Newton Heath Depot
BKR	Bo'ness & Kinneil Railway	NIR	Northamptonshire Ironstone Railway
BLU	Bluebell Railway	NLR	Northampton & Lamport Railway
BRC	Buckinghamshire Railway Centre	NNR	North Norfolk Railway
BRM	Birmingham Railway Museum, Tyseley	NRM	National Railway Museum, York
BVR	Bridgend Valleys Railway	NRS	National Railway Museum, Shildon
BWR	Bodmin & Wenford Railway	NYM	North Yorkshire Moors Railway
CAN	Canton (Pullman Rail)	PBR	Pontypool & Blaenavon Railway
CHS	Chasewater Railway	PDR	Paignton & Dartmouth Railway
COL	Colne Valley Railway	PRL	Peak Rail
COV	Coventry Electric Railway Museum	PVR	Plym Valley Railway
CPR	Chinnor & Princes Risborough Railway	RAC	Railway Age, Crewe
CRB	Caledonian Railway, Brechin	RAM	Rampart, Derby
CRT	Cambrian Railway Trust	RIB	Ribble Steam Railway
CVR	Churnet Valley Railway	RIP	Rippingdale Station
CWR	Cholsey & Wallingford Railway	ROW	Rowley Mill
DAR	Dartmoor Railway	RST	Rushden Station Transport Museum
DEE	Royal Deeside Railway	SEL	St Leonards Railway Engineering
DER	Derwent Valley Railway	SLN	Stewarts Lane Depot
DFR	Dean Forest Railway	SNI	Snibston Railway
DID	Didcot Railway Centre	SPV	Spa Valley Railway
EAR	East Anglian Railway Museum	SRC	Stainmore Railway Co
ECC	Ecclesbourne Valley Railway	STR	Strathspey Railway
EDR	Eden Valley Railway	SVR	Severn Valley Railway
EHC	Elsecar Heritage Centre	SWI	Swindon & Cricklade Railway
EHD	Eastleigh DBS Depot	SWN	Swanage Railway
EKR	East Kent Railway	TEB	Friends of 502 Group, Tebay
ELR	East Lancashire Railway	TEL	Telford Horsehay Steam Trust
EMB	Embsay Steam Railway	THK	Throckmorton Airfield
EPO	Epping Ongar Railway	TIT	Titley Junction
FHL	Fawley Hall (Private)	TSR	Telford Steam Railway
FIN	Finmere Station, Oxfordshire	TYN	North Tyneside Railway
GCN	Great Central Railway (North)	VOG	Vale of Glamorgan Railway
GCR	Great Central Railway	WAS	Washwood Heath
GKR	Graham Kirk Rail	WCR	West Coast Railway Co
GWI	Gwili Railway	WED	Weardale Railway
GWR	Gloucestershire Warwickshire Railway	WEN	Wensleydale Railway
HAD	Hastings Diesels	WPH	Walthamstow Pump House
IOW	Isle of Wight Railway	WSR	West Somerset Railway
KEI	Keith & Dufftown Railway	XXX	Private unspecified site
KES	Kent & East Sussex Railway	YEO	Yeovil Railway Centre
KIN	MoD Kineton		
KWV	Keighley & Worth Valley Railway	Status	
LAN	Llangollen Railway	OPR	Operational
LDL	Lavender Line	OPR	Operational main-line certified
LHG	LH Group Services, Burton	RES	Under restoration
LHR	Lakeside & Haverthwaite Railway	STC	Static exhibit
LNW	London & North Western, Crewe	STO	Stored
LWR	Lincolnshire Wolds Railway		
MET	Methill (Private)		
MFM	Mangapps Farm Railway Museum		
MHR	Mid Hants Railway		

Data Tables

Depot Codes

Code	Facility	Name	Operator
AB	SD	Aberdeen Guild Street	DBS
AC	CSD	Aberdeen Clayhills	ICE
AD	EMUD	Ashford Hitachi	HIT/SET
AF	T&RSMD	Ashford Chart Leacon	BOM
AH	MoD	Ashchurch	MoD
AK	DMUD	Ardwick	SIE/FTP
AL	DMUD	Aylesbury	CRW
AN	TMD/WRD	Allerton, Liverpool	DBS/NOR
AP	TMD	Ashford Rail Plant	BBR
AS	Store	Allelys	ALL
AT	TMD	Various sites	ALS
AW	SD	Washwood Heath	Hanson
AZ	TMD	Ashford	BBR
AZ	TMD	Alizay (France)	ECR (DBS)
BA	TMD	Crewe Basford Hall	FLR, DBS
BC	MoD	Bicester	MoD
BD	T&RSMD	Birkenhead North	MER
BF	EMUD	Bedford Cauldwell Walk	FCC
BG	SD	Hull Botanic Gardens	NOR
BH	Eng	Barrow Hill Roundhouse	BHE
BI	EMUD	Brighton	SOU
BK	T&RSMD	Barton Hill	LNWR
BM	T&RSMD	Bournemouth	SWT
BN	T&RSMD	Bounds Green	ICE
BO	T&RSMD	Burton	Nemesis
BP	SD	Blackpool CS	NOR
BQ	TMD	Bury	ELR
BR	SD	Bristol Kingsland Road	NRL, FLR
BS	TMD	Bescot	DBS
BT	TMD	Bo'ness	BOK
BW	SD	Barrow-in-Furness	NOR
BZ	T&RSMD	St Blazey	DBS
CA	SD	Cambridge Coldhams Ln	AXI
CB	STORE	Crewe Brook Sidings	DBS
CC	T&RSMD	Clacton	GAR
CD	SD	Crewe Diesel	RIV, DBS
CE	IEMD	Crewe Electric	DBS
CF	DMUD	Cardiff Canton	PUL
CG	TMD	Crewe Gresty Bridge	DRS
CH	DMUD	Chester	ALS, ATW
CJ	SD	Clapham Junction	SWT
CK	DMUD	Corkerhill	FSR
CL	Store	Carlisle Upperby	DBS
CM	SD	Camden	LMI
CO	IEMD	Coquelles (France)	EUR
CP	CARMD	Crewe Carriage Shed	LNW
CQ	T&RSMD	Crewe Railway Age	CHC
CR	SD	Colchester	GAR
CS	T&RSMD	Carnforth	WCR
CT	SD	Cleethorpes	FTP
CV	TMD	Cardiff Canton	ATW
CW	MoD	Caerwent	MoD
CX	Store	Cardiff Tidal	DBS
CY	Store	Crewe Coal/South Yards	DRS
CZ	TMD	Central Rivers	BOM
DD	SD	Doncaster Wood Yard	DBS
DF	T&RSMD	Rail Vehicle Engineering	RVE
DI	Pres	Didcot Railway Centre	GWS
DM	TMD	Dollands Moor	DBS
DO	Store	Donnington Railfreight	-
DT	SD	Didcot Triangle	DBS
DV	SD	Dover	SET
DW	SD	Doncaster West Yard	NRL, WAB
DY	T&RSMD	Derby Etches Park	EMT
EA	SD	Earles Sidings	DBS
EC	T&RSMD	Craigentinny (Edinburgh)	ICE
ED	DMUD	Eastfield	FSR
EF	MPVD	Effingham Junction	AMS
EH	SD	Eastleigh	DBS
EM	EMUD	East Ham	c2c
EN	CARMD	Euston Downside	NRL
EU	SD	Euston Station Sidings	VWC
EZ	DMUD	Exeter	FGW
FB	Store	Ferrybridge	DBS
FC*		Fire College (Moreton-in-Marsh)	
FD	Mobile	Diesel loco	FLR
FE	Mobile	Electric loco	FLR
FF	TRSMD	Forest - Brussels	SNCB, NMBS, EUS
FH	TRACK	Frodingham	GRP
FN	Hire	France	ECR
FP	CSD	Ferme Park	ICE
FR	EMUD	Fratton	SWT
FS	Mobile	Diesel Shunter	FLR
FW	SD	Fort William	DBS
FX	TMD	Felixstowe	FDH
GI	EMUD	Gillingham	SET
GL	TMD	Gloucester	CWR, ADV
GP	SD	Grove Park	SET
GW	EMUD	Glasgow Shields	FSR
HA	TMD	Haymarket	FSR
HD	SD	Holyhead	ATW
HE	EMUD	Hornsey	FCC
HF	SD	Hereford	DBS
HG	Store	Hither Green	DBS
HI	TM	Hitchin	BBR
HJ	SD	Hoo Junction	DBS
HM	SD/WRD	Healey Mills	DBS
HT	T&RSMD	Heaton	NOR, GTL
HY	SD	Oxford Hinksey Yard	NRL
IL	T&RSMD	Ilford	GAR
IM	SD	Immingham	DBS
IP	SD	Ipswich	FLR
IS	TMD	Inverness	FSR
KC	Store	Carlisle Currock WRD	DBS
KD	SD	Kingmoor Yard	DRS
KK	EMUD	Kirkdale	MER
KM	TMD	Carlisle Kingmoor	DRS
KR	T&RSMD	Kidderminster	SVR
KT	MoD	Kineton	MoD
KY	SD/WRD	Knottingley	DBS
LA	T&RSMD	Laira	FGW
LB	Eng	Loughborough	BTL
LD	TMD	Leeds Midland Road	FLR
LE	T&RSMD	Landore	FGW
LG	T&RSMD	Longsight Electric	ALT
LH	Eng	LH Group	LHG
LL	CSD	Liverpool Edge Hill	ALS
LM	Store	Long Marston	MLS
LO	T&RSMD	Longsight Diesel	NOR
LP*	Eng	EMD Longport	EMD

Data Tables

LR	Eng	Leicester	EMD
LT	MoD	Longtown	MoD
LU	MoD	Ludgershall	MoD
LY	T&RSMD	Le Landy (Paris)	SNCF, EUS
MA	CARMD	Manchester International	ALS
MD	TMD	Merehead	MRL
MG	TMD	Margam	DBS
MH	SD	Millerhill	DBS
ML	SD	Motherwell	DRS
MM	Store	Moreton-in-Marsh	-
MN	DMUD	Machynlleth	ATW
MQ	Store	Meldon Quarry	BAR
MR	SD	March	GBR
MW	MoD	Marchwood Military Port	MoD
MY	SD/Store	Mossend Yard	DBS, FLR
NB	SD	New Brighton	MER
NC	T&RSMD	Norwich Crown Point	GAR
ND	Works	NedTrans, Tilburg	NDZ
NG	T&RSMD	New Cross Gate	LOL
NH	DMUD	Newton Heath	NOR
NL	T&RSMD	Neville Hill (Leeds)	EMT, ICE
NM	SD	Nottingham Eastcroft	EMT
NN	EMUD	Northampton, Kings Heath	SIE, LMI
NT	EMUD	Northam	SIE, SWT
NY	T&RSMD	Grosmont	NYM
OD	Eng	Old Dalby	ALS
OH	EMUD	Old Oak Common Electric	SIE
ON	SD	Orpington	SET
OO	HSTMD	Old Oak Common HST	FGW
OX	CSD	Oxford Carriage Sidings	FGW
OY	CARMD	Oxley	ALS
PB	SD	Peterborough	DBS
PC	TRSMD	Polmadie	ALS
PE	SD	Peterborough Nene	FCC
PF	SD	Peak Forest	DBS
PH	SD	Perth	FSR
PM	TRSMD	St Philip's Marsh (Bristol)	FGW
PN	SD	Preston Station	NOR
PN	TMD	Poznan (Poland)	ECR (DBS)
PQ	SD	Harwich Parkeston Quay	DBS
PT	SD	Peterborough	GBR
PY	MoD	Shoeburyness (Pigs Bay)	MoD, KRS
PZ	TRSMD	Penzance (Long Rock)	FGW
RE	EMUD	Ramsgate	SET
RG	DMUD	Reading	FGW
RH	SD	Redhill	DBS
RL	TRSMD	Ropley	MHR
RO	SD	Rotherham Steel	DBS
RU	TMD	Rugby Rail Plant	GRP
RY	EMUD	Ryde	SWT
SA	DMUD	Salisbury	SWT
SB	TMD	Shrewsbury	NOR
SE	TRSMD	St Leonards	SLR
SG	EMUD	Slade Green	SET
SH	CARMD	Southall Railway Centre	WCR
SI	EMUD	Soho	LMI
SJ	TRSMD	Stourbridge Junction	LMI
SK	TRSMD	Swanwick	MRC
SL	TRSMD	Stewarts Lane	DBS, VSO, SOU
SM	SD	Sheffield Station	NOR
SN	SD	Shoeburyness	c2c
SO*		Southend	

SP	CRDC	Springs Branch	DBS
SQ	SD	Stockport	NOR
ST	SD	Southport	MER
SU	TRSMD	Selhurst	SOU
SX	SD	Shrewsbury	ATW
SZ	TMD	Southampton Maritime	FLR
TB	SD	Three Bridges	DBS
TE	TMD	Thornaby/Tees Yard	DBS
TF	SD	Orient Way	GAR
TG	SD	Tonbridge	GBR
TI	TRSMD	Temple Mills	EUS
TJ	TMD	Tavistock Junction	COL
TM	SD	Tyseley Loco Works	BRM
TN	SD	Taunton Fairwater	NRL, FLR
TO	TMD	Toton	DBS
TS	DMUD	Tyseley	LMI
TT	Store	Toton Training Compound	DBS
TY	Store	Tyne Yard	DBS
VI	SD	Victoria	SET
VR	SD	Aberystwyth	ATW
VZ	EMUD	Strawberry Hill	SIE, SWT
WA	SD	Warrington Arpley	DBS
WB	TRSMD	Wembley	ALS
WD	EMUD	East Wimbledon	SWT
WE	SD	Willesden Brent	DBS
WF	SD	Wansford	NVR
WH	Eng	Whatley	MRL
WK	SD	West Kirby	MER
WN	EMUD	Willesden	LOG
WO	TMD	Wolsingham	WER
WP	SD	Worksop	DBS
WS	SD	Worcester	LMI
WW	SD	West Worthing	SOU
WY	SD/CSD	Westbury Yard	DBS
WZ*	TRSMD	Washwood Heath	HAN
XW	TMD	Crofton	BOM
XX	-	Exported	-
YK	DMUD	Siemens York	SIE, FTP
YL	TMD	York Leeman Road	JAR, FLF
YM	Store	National Railway Museum	NRM
YN	SD	York North Yard	DBS
YO	SD	Yoker	FSR
ZA	Eng	RTC Derby	SER, NRL, AEA
ZB	Eng	Doncaster	WAB
ZC	Eng	Crewe	BOM
ZD	Eng	Derby Litchurch Lane	BOM
ZE	Eng	Washwood Heath	COL
ZG	Eng	Eastleigh Works	KRS
ZH	Eng	Glasgow	RCL
ZI	Eng	Ilford	BOM
ZK	Eng	Kilmarnock	BTL
ZL	Eng	Cardiff Canton	PUL
ZN	Eng	Wolverton	RCL
ZS	Eng	Locotech Wakefield	BAR
ZW	Eng	Stoke-on-Trent (Marcroft)	AXI
WZ		Warsaw (Poland)	DBS
3M*		3M Industries, Bracknell	

* Unofficial code

Data Tables

Rail Data Tables

Operator Codes

AFG	Arlington Fleet Group
ALL	Allelys Heavy Haul
ALS	Alstom
AMS	Amec Spie Rail
ATW	Arriva Trains Wales
AXC	Arriva Cross Country
AXI	Axiom Rail
BAR	British American Railway Services
BBR	Balfour Beatty
BHE	Barrow Hill Roundhouse
BOK	Bo'ness & Kinneil
BOM	Bombardier
BRM	Birmingham Railway Museum
BTL	Brush Traction Limited
C2C	c2c Rail
CAR	Carillion
CHS	Crewe Heritage Centre
COL	Colas Rail
CON	Continental Rail (Spain)
COR	Corus Steel
CRW	Chiltern Railways
DBA	DB Arriva
DBR	DB Regio
DBS	DB Schenker West
DRS	Direct Rail Services
ECR	Euro Cargo Rail (DBS)
ELR	East Lancashire Railway
EMT	East Midlands Trains
ETF	ETF Freight (France)
ETL	Electric Traction Ltd
EU2	Eurotunnel Europorte2
EUR	Eurotunnel
EUS	Eurostar
FCC	First Capital Connect
FDH	Felixstowe Dock & Harbour
FGW	First Great Western
FHT	First Hull Trains
FLR	Freightliner
FSL	Flying Scotsman Railway Ltd
FSR	First ScotRail

FTP	First TransPennine
GBR	GB Railfreight
GRP	Grant Rail Plant
GTL	Grand Central Railway
GWS	Great Western Society
HEC	Heathrow Connect
HEX	Heathrow Express
HIT	Hitachi
HNR	Harry Needle Railroad
ICE	Inter City East Coast
IND	Industrial operator
IRY	Ian Riley
JHS	Jeremy Hoskins
KBR	Knorr Bremse Rail
KRS	Knights Rail Services
LAF	Lafarge Aggregates
LMI	London Midland
LNW	L&NWR Railway Co
LOG	London Overground
LUL	London Underground Ltd
MER	Merseyrail
MHR	Mid Hants Railway
MoD	Ministry of Defence
MRC	Midland Railway Centre
MRL	Mendip Rail Ltd
MRS	Motorail Logistics
NDZ	NedTrains
NOR	Northern Rail
NOT	Northumbria Rail
NRL	Network Rail
NRM	National Railway Museum
NVR	Nene Valley Railway
NYM	North Yorkshire Moors Railway
OLD	Old Dalby Test Track
POB	Port of Boston
PUL	Pullman Group
RAF	Railfilms Ltd
RCL	Railcare Ltd
RIV	Riviera Trains
RRS	Ridings Railtours
RVE	Rail Vehicle Engineering
S4G	Stratford 47 Group
SET	SouthEastern Trains
SIE	Siemens
SIL	Stagecoach Island Line
SLR	St Leonards Rail Engineering
SNB	Société Nationale des Chemins de fer Belges
SNF	Société Nationale des Chemins de fer Français
SOU	Southern
SRP	Scottish Railway Preservation Society
SVR	Severn Valley Railway
SWT	South West Trains
TRN	Transfesa
TSO	Travaux du Sud Ouest (France)
TTS	Transmart Trains
VSO	Venice Simplon Orient Express
VTN	Vintage Trains
VWC	Virgin West Coast
WAB	Wabtec
WCR	West Coast Railway Co

Below: *Freightliner Class 70 No. 70017 passes through the middle road at Swindon on 9 September 2014 with the Wentloog to Southampton container service.* **CJM**

Data Tables

Owner Codes

201	20189 Ltd (Michael Owen)	FOS	Foster Yeoman
AEA	AEA Rail Technology	GBR	GB Railfreight
ALS	Alstom	GTL	Grand Central Railway Ltd
ANG	Angel Trains	HAN	Hanson Traction
ATW	Arriva Trains Wales	HEC	Hunslet Engine Co
AUT	Arriva UK Trains	HBS	Halifax-Bank of Scotland
BAA	British Airports Authority	HJA	Howard Johnson Associates
BCC	Bridgend County Council	HNR	Harry Needle Railroad
BEA	Beacon Rail	IRY	Ian Riley
BOM	Bombardier	JAR	Jarvis
BOT	Bank of Tokyo (Mitsubishi)	KBR	Knorr Bremse Rail
BTM	BTMU Capital Corporation	KRS	Knights Rail Services
C20	Class 20 Locomotive Ltd	MAG	Macquarie Group
CBR	CB Rail	NRL	Network Rail
CCC	Cardiff County Council	NYM	North Yorkshire Moors Railway
COL	Colas Rail	PTR	Porterbrook
CRW	Chiltern Railways	QWR	QW Rail Leasing
CWR	Cotswold Rail	RCL	Railcare Limited
DBR	DB Regio	RIV	Riviera Trains
DBS	DB Schenker West	RML	Royal Mail
DBS/T	DB Schenker/Transfesa	RMS	RMS Locotech
DRS	Direct Rail Services	RTR	RT Rail
ECR	Euro Cargo Rail (DBS)	RVE	Rail Vehicle Engineering
ECT	ECT Main Line Rail	S4G	Stratford Class 47 Group
EMT	East Midlands Trains	SEC	Serco
ETL	Electric Traction Ltd	SIE	Siemens
EU2	Eurotunnel Europorte2	SNB	Société Nationale des Chemins de fer Belges
EUR	Eurotunnel	SNF	Société Nationale des Chemins de fer Français
EUS	Eurostar	SOU	Southern (Govia)
EVL	Eversholt Leasing	SWT	South West Trains (Stagecoach)
FGP	First Group	TTS	Transmart Trains
FLF	Fastline Freight	URL	UK Rail Leasing
FLR	Freightliner	VTN	Vintage Trains
		WAB	Wabtec
		WCR	West Coast Railway Co
		WYP	West Yorkshire PTE

Below: *Although the new DB Schenker red and grey livery has been around for some time, only a handful of Class 66s carry the livery. One loco is No. 66097, which on 24 April 2014 is seen passing Barnetby powering the 11.40 Humber Oil Refinery to Kingsbury service.* **CJM**

Data Tables

Rail Data Tables

Station three-letter Codes

Station	Code	Station	Code
Abbey Wood	ABW	Appley Bridge	APB
Aber	ABE	Apsley	APS
Abercynon	ACY	Arbroath	ARB
Aberdare	ABA	Ardgay	ARD
Aberdeen	ABD	Ardlui	AUI
Aberdour	AUR	Ardrossan Harbour	ADS
Aberdovey	AVY	Ardrossan South Beach	ASB
Abererch	ABH	Ardrossan Town	ADN
Abergavenny	AGV	Ardwick	ADK
Abergele & Pensarn	AGL	Argyle Street	AGS
Aberystwyth	AYW	Arisaig	ARG
Accrington	ACR	Arlesey	ARL
Achanalt	AAT	Armathwaite	AWT
Achnasheen	ACN	Arnside	ARN
Achnashellach	ACH	Arram	ARR
Acklington	ACK	Arrochar & Tarbet	ART
Acle	ACL	Arundel	ARU
Acocks Green	ACG	Ascot	ACT
Acton Bridge	ACB	Ascott-u-Wychwood	AUW
Acton Central	ACC	Ash	ASH
Acton Main Line	AML	Ash Vale	AHV
Adderley Park	ADD	Ashburys	ABY
Addiewell	ADW	Ashchurch	ASC
Addlestone	ASN	Ashfield	ASF
Adisham	ADM	Ashford International	AFK
Adlington (Cheshire)	ADC	Ashford (Eurostar)	ASI
Adlington (Lancs)	ADL	Ashford (Surrey)	AFS
Adwick	AWK	Ashley	ASY
Aigburth	AIG	Ashtead	AHD
Ainsdale	ANS	Ashton-under-Lyne	AHN
Aintree	AIN	Ashurst	AHS
Airbles	AIR	Ashurst New Forest	ANF
Airdrie	ADR	Ashwell & Morden	AWM
Albany Park	AYP	Askam	ASK
Albrighton	ALB	Aslockton	ALK
Alderley Edge	ALD	Aspatria	ASP
Aldermaston	AMT	Aspley Guise	APG
Aldershot	AHT	Aston	AST
Aldrington	AGT	Atherstone	ATH
Alexandra Palace	AAP	Atherton	ATN
Alexandra Parade	AXP	Attadale	ATT
Alexandria	ALX	Attenborough	ATB
Alfreton	ALF	Attleborough	ATL
Allens West	ALW	Auchinleck	AUK
Alloa	ALO	Audley End	AUD
Alness	ASS	Aughton Park	AUG
Alnmouth	ALM	Aviemore	AVM
Alresford	ALR	Avoncliff	AVF
Alsager	ASG	Avonmouth	AVN
Althorne	ALN	Axminster	AXM
Althorpe	ALP	Aylesbury	AYS
Altnabreac	ABC	Aylesbury Parkway	AVP
Alton	AON	Aylesford	AYL
Altrincham	ALT	Aylesham	AYH
Alvechurch	ALV	Ayr	AYR
Ambergate	AMB		
Amberley	AMY		
Amersham	AMR		
Ammanford	AMF		
Ancaster	ANC		
Anderston	AND		
Andover	ADV		
Anerley	ANZ		
Angel Road	AGR		
Angmering	ANG		
Annan	ANN		
Anniesland	ANL		
Ansdell & Fairhaven	AFV		
Appleby	APP		
Appledore (Kent)	APD		
Appleford	APF		

Station	Code	Station	Code
Banstead	BAD	Bere Alston	BAS
Barassie	BSS	Bere Ferrers	BFE
Barbican	ZBB	Berkhamsted	BKM
Bardon Mill	BLL	Berkswell	BKW
Bare Lane	BAR	Berney Arms	BYA
Bargeddie	BGI	Berry Brow	BBW
Bargoed	BGD	Berrylands	BRS
Barking	BKG	Berwick	BRK
Barking Underground	ZBK	Berwick-upon-Tweed	BWK
Barlaston	BRT	Bescar Lane	BES
Barming	BMG	Bescot Stadium	BSC
Barmouth	BRM	Betchworth	BTO
Barnehurst	BNH	Bethnal Green	BET
Barnes	BNS	Betws-y-Coed	BYC
Barnes Bridge	BNI	Beverley	BEV
Barnetby	BTB	Bexhill	BEX
Barnham	BAA	Bexley	BXY
Barnhill	BNL	Bexleyheath	BXH
Barnsley	BNY	Bicester North	BCS
Barnstaple	BNP	Bicester Town	BIT
Barnt Green	BTG	Bickley	BKL
Barrhead	BRR	Bidston	BID
Barrhill	BRL	Biggleswade	BIW
Barrow Haven	BAV	Bilbrook	BBK
Barrow upon Soar	BWS	Billericay	BIC
Barrow-in-Furness	BIF	Billingham	BIL
Barry	BRY	Billingshurst	BIG
Barry Docks	BYD	Bingham	BIN
Barry Island	BYI	Bingley	BIY
Barry Links	BYL	Birchgrove	BCG
Barton-on-Humber	BAU	Birchington-on-Sea	BCH
Basildon	BSO	Birchwood	BWD
Basingstoke	BSK	Birkbeck	BIK
Bat & Ball	BBL	Birkdale	BDL
Bath Spa	BTH	Birkenhead Central	BKC
Bathgate	BHG	Birkenhead North	BKN
Batley	BTL	Birkenhead Park	BKP
Battersby	BTT	Birmingham Int	BHI
Battersea Park	BAK	Birmingham Moor St	BMO
Battle	BAT	Birmingham New St	BHM
Battlesbridge	BLB	Birmingham Snow Hill	BSW
Bayford	BAY	Bishop Auckland	BIA
Beaconsfield	BCF	Bishopbriggs	BBG
Bearley	BER	Bishops Stortford	BIS
Bearsden	BRN	Bishopstone	BIP
Bearsted	BSD	Bishopton	BPT
Beasdale	BSL	Bitterne	BTE
Beaulieu Road	BEU	Blackburn	BBN
Beauly	BEL	Blackheath	BKH
Bebington	BEB	Blackhorse Road	BHO
Beccles	BCC	Blackpool North	BPN
Beckenham Hill	BEC	Blackpool P Beach	BPB
Beckenham Junction	BKJ	Blackpool South	BPS
Bedford	BDM	Blackrod	BLK
Bedford St Johns	BSJ	Blackwater	BAW
Bedhampton	BDH	Blaenau Ffestiniog	BFF
Bedminster	BMT	Blair Atholl	BLA
Bedworth	BEH	Blairhill	BAI
Bedwyn	BDW	Blake Street	BKT
Beeston	BEE	Blakedown	BKD
Bekesbourne	BKS	Blantyre	BLT
Belle Vue	BLV	Blaydon	BLO
Bellgrove	BLG	Bleasby	BSB
Bellingham	BGM	Bletchley	BLY
Bellshill	BLH	Bloxwich	BLX
Belmont	BLM	Bloxwich North	BWN
Belper	BLP	Blundellsands & Crosby	BLN
Beltring	BEG	Blythe Bridge	BYB
Belvedere	BVD	Bodmin Parkway	BOD
Bempton	BEM	Bodorgan	BOR
Ben Rhydding	BEY	Bognor Regis	BOG
Benfleet	BEF	Bogston	BGS
Bentham	BEN	Bolton	BON
Bentley	BTY	Bolton-on-Dearne	BTD
Bentley (South Yorks)	BYK	Bookham	BKA

Data Tables

Bootle	BOC	Brora	BRA	Carlisle	CAR	Chorley	CRL
Bootle New Strand	BNW	Brough	BUH	Carlton	CTO	Chorleywood	CLW
Bootle Oriel Road	BOT	Broughty Ferry	BYF	Carluke	CLU	Christchurch	CHR
Bordesley	BBS	Broxbourne	BXB	Carmarthen	CMN	Christs Hospital	CHH
Borough Green	BRG	Bruce Grove	BCV	Carmyle	CML	Church & Oswaldtwistle	CTW
Borth	BRH	Brundall	BDA	Carnforth	CNF	Church Fenton	CHF
Bosham	BOH	Brundall Gardens	BGA	Carnoustie	CAN	Church Stretton	CTT
Boston	BSN	Brunstane	BSU	Carntyne	CAY	Cilmeri	CIM
Botley	BOE	Brunswick	BRW	Carpenders Park	CPK	City Thameslink	CTK
Bottesford	BTF	Bruton	BRU	Carrbridge	CAG	Clacton on Sea	CLT
Bourne End	BNE	Bryn	BYN	Carshalton	CSH	Clandon	CLA
Bournemouth	BMH	Buckenham	BUC	Carshalton Beeches	CSB	Clapham High Street	CLP
Bournville	BRV	Buckley	BCK	Carstairs	CRS	Clapham Junction	CLJ
Bow Brickhill	BWB	Bucknell	BUK	Cartsdyke	CDY	Clapham (Yorkshire)	CPY
Bowes Park	BOP	Bugle	BGL	Castle Bar Park	CBP	Clapton	CPT
Bowling	BWG	Builth Road	BHR	Castle Cary	CLC	Clarbeston Road	CLR
Boxhill & Westhumble	BXW	Bulwell	BLW	Castleford	CFD	Clarkston	CKS
Bracknell	BCE	Bures	BUE	Castleton	CAS	Claverdon	CLV
Bradford Forster Sq	BDQ	Burgess Hill	BUG	Castleton Moor	CSM	Claygate	CLG
Bradford Interchange	BDI	Burley Park	BUY	Caterham	CAT	Cleethorpes	CLE
Bradford-on-Avon	BOA	Burley-in-Wharfedale	BUW	Catford	CTF	Cleland	CEA
Brading	BDN	Burnage	BNA	Catford Bridge	CFB	Clifton	CLI
Braintree	BTR	Burneside	BUD	Cathays	CYS	Clifton Down	CFN
Braintree Freeport	BTP	Burnham	BNM	Cathcart	CCT	Clitheroe	CLH
Bramhall	BML	Burnham-on-Crouch	BUU	Cattal	CTL	Clock House	CLK
Bramley	BLE	Burnley Barracks	BUB	Causeland	CAU	Clunderwen	CUW
Bramley (Hants)	BMY	Burnley Central	BNC	Cefn-y-Bedd	CYB	Clydebank	CYK
Brampton (Cumbria)	BMP	Burnley Manchester Rd	BYM	Chadwell Heath	CTH	Coatbridge Central	CBC
Brampton (Suffolk)	BRP	Burnside	BUI	Chafford Hundred	CFH	Coatbridge Sunnyside	CBS
Branchton	BCN	Burntisland	BTS	Chalfont & Latimer	CFO	Coatdyke	COA
Brandon	BND	Burscough Bridge	BCB	Chalkwell	CHW	Cobham & Stoke d'A'n	CSD
Branksome	BSM	Burscough Junction	BCJ	Chandlers Ford	CFR	Codsall	CSL
Braystones	BYS	Bursledon	BUO	Chapel-en-le-Frith	CEF	Cogan	CGN
Bredbury	BDY	Burton Joyce	BUJ	Chapelton	CPN	Colchester	COL
Breich	BRC	Burton-on-Trent	BUT	Chapeltown	CLN	Colchester Town	CET
Brentford	BFD	Bury St Edmunds	BSE	Chappel & Wakes Colne	CWC	Coleshill Parkway	CEH
Brentwood	BRE	Busby	BUS	Charing	CHG	Collingham	CLM
Bricket Wood	BWO	Bush Hill Park	BHK	Charing Cross (FSR)	CHC	Collington	CLL
Bridge of Allan	BEA	Bushey	BSH	Charlbury	CBY	Colne	CNE
Bridge of Orchy	BRO	Butlers Lane	BUL	Charlton	CTN	Colwall	CWL
Bridgend	BGN	Buxted	BXD	Chartham	CRT	Colwyn Bay	CWB
Bridgeton	BDG	Buxton	BUX	Chassen Road	CSR	Combe	CME
Bridgwater	BWT	Byfleet & New Haw	BFN	Chatelherault	CTE	Commondale	COM
Bridlington	BDT	Bynea	BYE	Chatham	CTM	Congleton	CNG
Brierfield	BRF	Cadoxton	CAD	Chathill	CHT	Conisbrough	CNS
Brigg	BGG	Caergwrle	CGW	Cheadle Hulme	CHU	Connel Ferry	CON
Brighouse	BGH	Caerphilly	CPH	Cheam	CHE	Cononley	CEY
Brighton	BTN	Caersws	CWS	Cheddington	CED	Conway Park	CNP
Brimsdown	BMD	Caldicot	CDT	Chelford	CEL	Conwy	CNW
Brinnington	BNT	Caledonian Rd & Bby	CIR	Chelmsford	CHM	Cooden Beach	COB
Bristol Parkway	BPW	Calstock	CSK	Chelsfield	CLD	Cookham	COO
Bristol Temple Meads	BRI	Cam & Dursley	CDU	Cheltenham Spa	CNM	Cooksbridge	CBR
Brithdir	BHD	Camberley	CAM	Chepstow	CPW	Coombe Halt	COE
British Steel Redcar	RBS	Camborne	CBN	Cherry Tree	CYT	Copplestone	COP
Briton Ferry	BNF	Cambridge	CBG	Chertsey	CHY	Corbridge	CRB
Brixton	BRX	Cambridge Heath	CBH	Cheshunt	CHN	Corby	COR
Broad Green	BGE	Cambuslang	CBL	Chessington North	CSN	Corkerhill	CKH
Broadbottom	BDB	Camden Road	CMD	Chessington South	CSS	Corkickle	CKL
Broadstairs	BSR	Camelon	CMO	Chester	CTR	Corpach	CPA
Brockenhurst	BCU	Canley	CNL	Chester Road	CRD	Corrour	CRR
Brockholes	BHS	Cannock	CAO	Chesterfield	CHD	Coryton	COY
Brockley	BCY	Canonbury	CNN	Chester-le-Street	CLS	Coseley	CSY
Brockley Whins	BNR	Canterbury East	CBE	Chestfield & Swalecliffe	CSW	Cosford	COS
Bromborough	BOM	Canterbury West	CBW	Chetnole	CNO	Cosham	CSA
Bromborough Rake	BMR	Cantley	CNY	Chichester	CCH	Cottingham	CGM
Bromley Cross	BMC	Capenhurst	CPU	Chilham	CIL	Cottingley	COT
Bromley North	BMN	Carbis Bay	CBB	Chilworth	CHL	Coulsdon South	CDS
Bromley South	BMS	Cardenden	CDD	Chingford	CHI	Coventry	COV
Bromsgrove	BMV	Cardiff Bay	CDB	Chinley	CLY	Cowden	CWN
Brondesbury	BSY	Cardiff Central	CDF	Chippenham	CPM	Cowdenbeath	COW
Brondesbury Park	BSP	Cardiff Queen Street	CDQ	Chipstead	CHP	Cradley Heath	CRA
Brookmans Park	BPK	Cardonald	CDO	Chirk	CRK	Craigendoran	CGD
Brookwood	BKO	Cardross	CDR	Chislehurst	CIT	Cramlington	CRM
Broome	BME	Carfin	CRF	Chiswick	CHK	Craven Arms	CRV
Broomfleet	BMF	Cark & Cartmel	CAK	Cholsey	CHO	Crawley	CRW

Data Tables

Rail Data Tables

Station	Code	Station	Code	Station	Code	Station	Code
Crayford	CRY	Denmark Hill	DMK	Durrington-on-Sea	DUR	Exeter St Thomas	EXT
Crediton	CDI	Dent	DNT	Dyce	DYC	Exhibition Centre	EXG
Cressing	CES	Denton	DTN	Dyffryn Ardudwy	DYF	Exmouth	EXM
Cressington	CSG	Deptford	DEP	Eaglescliffe	EAG	Exton	EXN
Creswell	CWD	Derby	DBY	Ealing Broadway	EAL	Eynsford	EYN
Crewe	CRE	Derby Road	DBR	Earlestown	ERL	Failsworth	FLS
Crewkerne	CKN	Derker	DKR	Earley	EAR	Fairbourne	FRB
Crews Hill	CWH	Devonport	DPT	Earlsfield	EAD	Fairfield	FRF
Crianlarich	CNR	Dewsbury	DEW	Earlswood (Surrey)	ELD	Fairlie	FRL
Criccieth	CCC	Didcot Parkway	DID	Earlswood (Midlands)	EWD	Fairwater	FRW
Cricklewood	CRI	Digby & Sowton	DIG	East Boldon	EBL	Falconwood	FCN
Croftfoot	CFF	Dilton Marsh	DMH	East Croydon	ECR	Falkirk Grahamston	FKG
Crofton Park	CFT	Dinas Powys	DNS	East Didsbury	EDY	Falkirk High	FKK
Cromer	CMR	Dinas Rhondda	DMG	East Dulwich	EDW	Falls of Cruachan	FOC
Cromford	CMF	Dingle Road	DGL	East Farleigh	EFL	Falmer	FMR
Crookston	CKT	Dingwall	DIN	East Garforth	EGF	Falmouth Docks	FAL
Cross Gates	CRG	Dinsdale	DND	East Grinstead	EGR	Falmouth Town	FMT
Crossflatts	CFL	Dinting	DTG	East Kilbride	EKL	Fareham	FRM
Crosshill	COI	Disley	DSL	East Malling	EML	Farnborough (Main)	FNB
Crosskeys	CKY	Diss	DIS	East Midlands Parkway	EMD	Farnborough North	FNN
Crossmyloof	CMY	Dockyard	DOC	East Tilbury	ETL	Farncombe	FNC
Croston	CSO	Dodworth	DOD	East Worthing	EWR	Farnham	FNH
Crouch Hill	CRH	Dolau	DOL	Eastbourne	EBN	Farningham Road	FNR
Crowborough	COH	Doleham	DLH	Eastbrook	EBK	Farnworth	FNW
Crowhurst	CWU	Dolgarrog	DLG	Easterhouse	EST	Farringdon	ZFD
Crowle	CWE	Dolwyddelan	DWD	Eastham Rake	ERA	Fauldhouse	FLD
Crowthorne	CRN	Doncaster	DON	Eastleigh	ESL	Faversham	FAV
Croy	CRO	Dorchester South	DCH	Eastrington	EGN	Faygate	FGT
Crystal Palace	CYP	Dorchester West	DCW	Ebbw Vale Parkway	EBV	Fazakerley	FAZ
Cuddington	CUD	Dore	DOR	Eccles	ECC	Fearn	FRN
Cuffley	CUF	Dorking	DKG	Eccles Road	ECS	Featherstone	FEA
Culham	CUM	Dorking Deepdene	DPD	Eccleston Park	ECL	Fellgate	FEG
Culrain	CUA	Dorking West	DKT	Edale	EDL	Felixstowe	FLX
Cumbernauld	CUB	Dormans	DMS	Eden Park	EDN	Feltham	FEL
Cupar	CUP	Dorridge	DDG	Edenbridge	EBR	Feniton	FNT
Curriehill	CUH	Dove Holes	DVH	Edenbridge Town	EBT	Fenny Stratford	FEN
Cuxton	CUX	Dover Priory	DVP	Edge Hill	EDG	Fernhill	FER
Cwmbach	CMH	Dovercourt	DVC	Edinburgh Park	EDP	Ferriby	FRY
Cwmbran	CWM	Dovey Junction	DVY	Edinburgh Waverley	EDB	Ferryside	FYS
Cynghordy	CYN	Downham Market	DOW	Edmonton Green	EDR	Ffairfach	FFA
Dagenham Dock	DDK	Drayton Green	DRG	Effingham Junction	EFF	Filey	FIL
Daisy Hill	DSY	Drayton Park	DYP	Eggesford	EGG	Filton Abbey Wood	FIT
Dalgety Bay	DAG	Drem	DRM	Egham	EGH	Finchley Rd & Frognal	FNY
Dalmally	DAL	Driffield	DRF	Egton	EGT	Finsbury Park	FPK
Dalmarnock	DAK	Drigg	DRI	Elephant & Castle	EPH	Finstock	FIN
Dalmeny	DAM	Droitwich Spa	DTW	Elgin	ELG	Fishbourne (Sussex)	FSB
Dalmuir	DMR	Dronfield	DRO	Ellesmere Port	ELP	Fishersgate	FSG
Dalreoch	DLR	Drumchapel	DMC	Elmers End	ELE	Fishguard Harbour	FGH
Dalry	DLY	Drumfrochar	DFR	Elmstead Woods	ESD	Fiskerton	FSK
Dalston	DLS	Drumgelloch	DRU	Elmswell	ESW	Fitzwilliam	FZW
Dalston Kingsland	DLK	Drumry	DMY	Elsecar	ELR	Five Ways	FWY
Dalton	DLT	Dublin Ferryport	DFP	Elsenham	ESM	Fleet	FLE
Dalwhinnie	DLW	Dublin Port - Stena	DPS	Elstree & Borehamwood	ELS	Flimby	FLM
Danby	DNY	Duddeston	DUD	Eltham	ELW	Flint	FLN
Danescourt	DCT	Dudley Port	DDP	Elton & Orston	ELO	Flitwick	FLT
Danzey	DZY	Duffield	DFI	Ely	ELY	Flixton	FLI
Darlington	DAR	Duirinish	DRN	Emerson Park	EMP	Flowery Field	FLF
Darnall	DAN	Duke Street	DST	Emsworth	EMS	Folkestone Central	FKC
Darsham	DSM	Dullingham	DUL	Enfield Chase	ENC	Folkestone West	FKW
Dartford	DFD	Dumbarton Central	DBC	Enfield Lock	ENL	Ford	FOD
Darton	DRT	Dumbarton East	DBE	Enfield Town	ENF	Forest Gate	FOG
Darwen	DWN	Dumbreck	DUM	Entwistle	ENT	Forest Hill	FOH
Datchet	DAT	Dumfries	DMF	Epsom	EPS	Formby	FBY
Davenport	DVN	Dumpton Park	DMP	Epsom Downs	EPD	Forres	FOR
Dawlish	DWL	Dunbar	DUN	Erdington	ERD	Forsinard	FRS
Dawlish Warren	DWW	Dunblane	DBL	Eridge	ERI	Fort Matilda	FTM
Deal	DEA	Duncraig	DCG	Erith	ERH	Fort William	FTW
Dean	DEN	Dundee	DEE	Esher	ESH	Four Oaks	FOK
Dean Lane	DNN	Dunfermline Q'n Margaret	DFL	Essex Road	EXR	Foxfield	FOX
Deansgate	DGT	Dunfermline Town	DFE	Etchingham	ETC	Foxton	FXN
Deganwy	DGY	Dunkeld & Birnam	DKD	Euxton Balshaw Lane	EBA	Frant	FRT
Deighton	DHN	Dunlop	DNL	Evesham	EVE	Fratton	FTN
Delamere	DLM	Dunrobin Castle	DNO	Ewell East	EWE	Freshfield	FRE
Denby Dale	DBD	Dunston	DOT	Ewell West	EWW	Freshford	FFD
Denham	DNM	Dunton Green	DNG	Exeter Central	EXC	Frimley	FML
Denham Golf Club	DGC	Durham	DHM	Exeter St Davids	EXD	Frinton on Sea	FRI

Data Tables

Station	Code	Station	Code	Station	Code	Station	Code
Frizinghall	FZH	Great Bentley	GRB	Harpenden	HPD	Hexham	HEX
Frodsham	FRD	Great Chesterford	GRC	Harrietsham	HRM	Heyford	HYD
Frome	FRO	Great Coates	GCT	Harringay	HGY	Heysham Port	HHB
Fulwell	FLW	Great Malvern	GMV	Harringay Green Lanes	HRY	High Brooms	HIB
Furness Vale	FNV	Great Missenden	GMN	Harrington	HRR	High St (Glasgow)	HST
Furze Platt	FZP	Great Yarmouth	GYM	Harrogate	HGT	High Street Kensington	ZHS
Gainsborough Central	GNB	Green Lane	GNL	Harrow & Wealdstone	HRW	High Wycombe	HWY
Gainsborough Lea Rd	GBL	Green Road	GNR	Harrow-on-the-Hill	HOH	Higham	HGM
Garelochhead	GCH	Greenbank	GBK	Hartford	HTF	Highams Park	HIP
Garforth	GRF	Greenfaulds	GRL	Hartlebury	HBY	Highbridge & Burnham	HIG
Gargrave	GGV	Greenfield	GNF	Hartlepool	HPL	Highbury & Islington	HHY
Garrowhill	GAR	Greenford	GFD	Hartwood	HTW	Hightown	HTO
Garscadden	GRS	Greenhithe for Bluewater	GNH	Harwich International	HPQ	Hildenborough	HLB
Garsdale	GSD	Greenock Central	GKC	Harwich Town	HWC	Hillfoot	HLF
Garston (Hertfordshire)	GSN	Greenock West	GKW	Haslemere	HSL	Hillington East	HLE
Garswood	GSW	Greenwich	GNW	Hassocks	HSK	Hillington West	HLW
Gartcosh	GRH	Gretna Green	GEA	Hastings	HGS	Hillside	HIL
Garth (Bridgend)	GMG	Grimsby Docks	GMD	Hatch End	HTE	Hilsea	HLS
Garth (Powys)	GTH	Grimsby Town	GMB	Hatfield	HAT	Hinchley Wood	HYW
Garve	GVE	Grindleford	GRN	Hatfield & Stainforth	HFS	Hinckley	HNK
Gathurst	GST	Grosmont	GMT	Hatfield Peverel	HAP	Hindley	HIN
Gatley	GTY	Grove Park	GRP	Hathersage	HSG	Hinton Admiral	HNA
Gatwick Airport	GTW	Guide Bridge	GUI	Hattersley	HTY	Hitchin	HIT
Georgemas Junction	GGJ	Guildford	GLD	Hatton	HTN	Hither Green	HGR
Gerrards Cross	GER	Guiseley	GSY	Havant	HAV	Hockley	HOC
Gidea Park	GDP	Gunnersbury	GUN	Havenhouse	HVN	Hollingbourne	HBN
Giffnock	GFN	Gunnislake	GSL	Haverfordwest	HVF	Hollinwood	HOD
Giggleswick	GIG	Gunton	GNT	Hawarden	HWD	Holmes Chapel	HCH
Gilberdyke	GBD	Gwersyllt	GWE	Hawarden Bridge	HWB	Holmwood	HLM
Gilfach Fargoed	GFF	Gypsy Lane	GYP	Hawkhead	HKH	Holton Heath	HOL
Gillingham (Dorset)	GIL	Habrough	HAB	Haydon Bridge	HDB	Holyhead	HHD
Gillingham (Kent)	GLM	Hackbridge	HCB	Haydons Road	HYR	Holytown	HLY
Gilshochill	GSC	Hackney Central	HKC	Hayes & Harlington	HAY	Homerton	HMN
Gipsy Hill	GIP	Hackney Downs	HAC	Hayes (Kent)	HYS	Honeybourne	HYB
Girvan	GIR	Hackney Wick	HKW	Hayle	HYL	Honiton	HON
Glaisdale	GLS	Haddenham & T Parkway	HDM	Haymarket	HYM	Honley	HOY
Glan Conwy	GCW	Haddiscoe	HAD	Haywards Heath	HHE	Honor Oak Park	HPA
Glasgow Central	GLC	Hadfield	HDF	Hazel Grove	HAZ	Hook	HOK
Glasgow Queen Street	GLQ	Hadley Wood	HDW	Headcorn	HCN	Hooton	HOO
Glasshoughton	GLH	Hag Fold	HGF	Headingley	HDY	Hope (Derbyshire)	HOP
Glazebrook	GLZ	Hagley	HAG	Headstone Lane	HDL	Hope (Flintshire)	HPE
Gleneagles	GLE	Hairmyres	HMY	Heald Green	HDG	Hopton Heath	HPT
Glenfinnan	GLF	Hale	HAL	Healing	HLI	Horley	HOR
Glengarnock	GLG	Halesworth	HAS	Heath High Level	HHL	Hornbeam Park	HBP
Glenrothes with Thornton	GLT	Halewood	HED	Heath Low Level	HLL	Hornsey	HRN
Glossop	GLO	Halifax	HFX	Heathrow Airport T123	HXX	Horsforth	HRS
Gloucester	GCR	Hall Green	HLG	Heathrow Airport T4	HAF	Horsham	HRH
Glynde	GLY	Hall-i'-th'-Wood	HID	Heathrow Terminal 5	HWV	Horsley	HSY
Gobowen	GOB	Hall Road	HLR	Heaton Chapel	HTC	Horton-in-Ribblesdale	HIR
Godalming	GOD	Halling	HAI	Hebden Bridge	HBD	Horwich Parkway	HWI
Godley	GDL	Haltwhistle	HWH	Heckington	HEC	Hoscar	HSC
Godstone	GDN	Ham Street	HMT	Hedge End	HDE	Hough Green	HGN
Goldthorpe	GOE	Hamble	HME	Hednesford	HNF	Hounslow	HOU
Golf Street	GOF	Hamilton Central	HNC	Heighington	HEI	Hove	HOV
Golspie	GOL	Hamilton Square	BKQ	Helensburgh Central	HLC	Hoveton & Wroxham	HXM
Gomshall	GOM	Hamilton West	HNW	Helensburgh Upper	HLU	How Wood	HWW
Goodmayes	GMY	Hammerton	HMM	Hellifield	HLD	Howden	HOW
Goole	GOO	Hampden Park	HMD	Helmsdale	HMS	Howwood (Renfrew)	HOZ
Goostrey	GTR	Hampstead Heath	HDH	Helsby	HSB	Hoylake	HYK
Gordon Hill	GDH	Hampton	HMP	Hemel Hempstead	HML	Hubberts Bridge	HBB
Goring & Streatley	GOR	Hampton Court	HMC	Hendon	HEN	Hucknall	HKN
Goring-by-Sea	GBS	Hampton Wick	HMW	Hengoed	HNG	Huddersfield	HUD
Gorton	GTO	Hampton-in-Arden	HIA	Henley-in-Arden	HNL	Hull Paragon	HUL
Gospel Oak	GPO	Hamstead	HSD	Henley-on-Thames	HOT	Humphrey Park	HUP
Gourock	GRK	Hamworthy	HAM	Hensall	HEL	Huncoat	HCT
Gowerton	GWN	Hanborough	HND	Hereford	HFD	Hungerford	HGD
Goxhill	GOX	Handforth	HTH	Herne Bay	HNB	Hunmanby	HUB
Grange Park	GPK	Hanwell	HAN	Herne Hill	HNH	Huntingdon	HUN
Grange-Over-Sands	GOS	Hapton	HPN	Hersham	HER	Huntly	HNT
Grangetown	GTN	Harlech	HRL	Hertford East	HFE	Hunts Cross	HNX
Grantham	GRA	Harlesden	HDN	Hertford North	HFN	Hurst Green	HUR
Grateley	GRT	Harling Road	HRD	Hessle	HES	Hutton Cranswick	HUT
Gravelly Hill	GVH	Harlington	HLN	Heswall	HSW	Huyton	HUY
Gravesend	GRV	Harlow Mill	HWM	Hever	HEV	Hyde Central	HYC
Grays	GRY	Harlow Town	HWN	Heworth	HEW	Hyde North	HYT
Great Ayton	GTA	Harold Wood	HRO	Heworth Metro	HEZ	Hykeham	HKM

Data Tables

Station	Code	Station	Code	Station	Code	Station	Code
Hyndland	HYN	Kings Nympton	KGN	Lenham	LEN	London Bridge	LBG
Hythe	HYH	Kings Park	KGP	Lenzie	LNZ	London Cannon Street	CST
IBM	IBM	Kings Sutton	KGS	Leominster	LEO	London Charing Cross	CHX
Ifield	IFI	Kingsknowe	KGE	Letchworth Garden City	LET	London Euston	EUS
Ilford	IFD	Kingston	KNG	Leuchars (St Andrews)	LEU	London Fenchurch St	FST
Ilkley	ILK	Kingswood	KND	Levenshulme	LVM	London Fields	LOF
Imperial Wharf	IMW	Kingussie	KIN	Lewes	LWS	London King's Cross	KGX
Ince	INC	Kintbury	KIT	Lewisham	LEW	London Liverpool St	LST
Ince & Elton	INE	Kirby Cross	KBX	Leyland	LEY	London Marylebone	MYB
Ingatestone	INT	Kirk Sandall	KKS	Leyton Midland Road	LEM	London Paddington	PAD
Insch	INS	Kirkby	KIR	Leytonstone High Road	LER	London Road (Brighton)	LRB
Invergordon	IGD	Kirkby-in-Ashfield	KKB	Lichfield City	LIC	London Road (Guildford)	LRD
Invergowrie	ING	Kirkby Stephen	KSW	Lichfield Trent Valley	LTV	London St Pancras	STP
Inverkeithing	INK	Kirkby-in-Furness	KBF	Lidlington	LID	London Victoria	VIC
Inverkip	INP	Kirkcaldy	KDY	Limehouse	LHS	London Waterloo	WAT
Inverness	INV	Kirkconnel	KRK	Lincoln Central	LCN	London Waterloo East	WAE
Invershin	INH	Kirkdale	KKD	Lingfield	LFD	Long Buckby	LBK
Inverurie	INR	Kirkham & Wesham	KKM	Lingwood	LGD	Long Eaton	LGE
Ipswich	IPS	Kirkhill	KKH	Linlithgow	LIN	Long Preston	LPR
Irlam	IRL	Kirknewton	KKN	Liphook	LIP	Longbeck	LGK
Irvine	IRV	Kirkwood	KWD	Liskeard	LSK	Longbridge	LOB
Isleworth	ISL	Kirton Lindsey	KTL	Liss	LIS	Longcross	LNG
Islip	ISP	Kiveton Bridge	KIV	Lisvane & Thornhill	LVT	Longfield	LGF
Iver	IVR	Kiveton Park	KVP	Little Kimble	LTK	Longniddry	LND
Ivybridge	IVY	Knaresborough	KNA	Little Sutton	LTT	Longport	LPT
Jewellery Quarter	JEQ	Knebworth	KBW	Littleborough	LTL	Longton	LGN
Johnston	JOH	Knighton	KNI	Littlehampton	LIT	Looe	LOO
Johnstone	JHN	Knockholt	KCK	Littlehaven	LVN	Lostock	LOT
Jordanhill	JOR	Knottingley	KNO	Littleport	LTP	Lostock Gralam	LTG
Kearsley	KSL	Knucklas	KNU	Liverpool Central	LVC	Lostock Hall	LOH
Kearsney	KSN	Knutsford	KNF	Liverpool James Street	LVJ	Lostwithiel	LOS
Keighley	KEI	Kyle of Lochalsh	KYL	Liverpool Lime Street	LIV	Loughborough	LBO
Keith	KEH	Ladybank	LDY	Liverpool South Parkway	LPY	Loughborough Junction	LGJ
Kelvedon	KEL	Ladywell	LAD	Livingston North	LSN	Lowdham	LOW
Kelvindale	KVD	Laindon	LAI	Livingston South	LVG	Lower Sydenham	LSY
Kemble	KEM	Lairg	LRG	Llanaber	LLA	Lowestoft	LWT
Kempston Hardwick	KMH	Lake	LKE	Llanbedr	LBR	Ludlow	LUD
Kempton Park	KMP	Lakenheath	LAK	Llanbister Road	LLT	Luton	LUT
Kemsing	KMS	Lamphey	LAM	Llanbradach	LNB	Luton Airport Parkway	LTN
Kemsley	KML	Lanark	LNK	Llandaf	LLN	Luxulyan	LUX
Kendal	KEN	Lancaster	LAN	Llandanwg	LDN	Lydney	LYD
Kenley	KLY	Lancing	LAC	Llandecwyn	LLC	Lye	LYE
Kennett	KNE	Landywood	LAW	Llandeilo	LLL	Lymington Pier	LYP
Kennishead	KNS	Langbank	LGB	Llandovery	LLV	Lymington Town	LYT
Kensal Green	KNL	Langho	LHO	Llandrindod	LLO	Lympstone Commando	LYC
Kensal Rise	KNR	Langley	LNY	Llandudno	LLD	Lympstone Village	LYM
Kensington Olympia	KPA	Langley Green	LGG	Llandudno Junction	LLJ	Lytham	LTM
Kent House	KTH	Langley Mill	LGM	Llandybie	LLI	Macclesfield	MAC
Kentish Town	KTN	Langside	LGS	Llanelli	LLE	Machynlleth	MCN
Kentish Town West	KTW	Langwathby	LGW	Llanfairfechan	LLF	Maesteg	MST
Kenton	KNT	Langwith-Whaley Thorns	LAG	Llanfairpwll	LPG	Maesteg (Ewenny Rd)	MEW
Kents Bank	KBK	Lapford	LAP	Llangadog	LLG	Maghull	MAG
Kettering	KET	Lapworth	LPW	Llangammarch	LLM	Maiden Newton	MDN
Kew Bridge	KWB	Larbert	LBT	Llangennech	LLH	Maidenhead	MAI
Kew Gardens	KWG	Largs	LAR	Llangynllo	LGO	Maidstone Barracks	MDB
Keyham	KEY	Larkhall	LRH	Llanharan	LLR	Maidstone East	MDE
Keynsham	KYN	Lawrence Hill	LWH	Llanhilleth	LTH	Maidstone West	MDW
Kidbrooke	KDB	Layton	LAY	Llanishen	LLS	Malden Manor	MAL
Kidderminster	KID	Lazonby & Kirkoswald	LZB	Llanrwst	LWR	Mallaig	MLG
Kidsgrove	KDG	Lea Green	LEG	Llansamlet	LAS	Malton	MLT
Kidwelly	KWL	Lea Hall	LEH	Llantwit Major	LWM	Malvern Link	MVL
Kilburn High Road	KBN	Leagrave	LEA	Llanwrda	LNR	Manchester Airport	MIA
Kildale	KLD	Lealholm	LHM	Llanwrtyd	LNW	Manchester Oxford Rd	MCO
Kildonan	KIL	Leamington Spa	LMS	Llwyngwril	LLW	Manchester Piccadilly	MAN
Kilgetty	KGT	Leasowe	LSW	Llwynypia	LLY	Manchester United FC	MUF
Kilmarnock	KMK	Leatherhead	LHD	Loch Awe	LHA	Manchester Victoria	MCV
Kilmaurs	KLM	Ledbury	LED	Loch Eil Outward Bound	LHE	Manea	MNE
Kilpatrick	KPT	Lee	LEE	Lochailort	LCL	Manningtree	MNG
Kilwinning	KWN	Leeds	LDS	Locheilside	LCS	Manor Park	MNP
Kinbrace	KBC	Leicester	LEI	Lochgelly	LCG	Manor Road	MNR
Kingham	KGM	Leigh (Kent)	LIH	Lochluichart	LCC	Manorbier	MRB
Kinghorn	KGH	Leigh-on-Sea	LES	Lochwinnoch	LHW	Manors	MAS
Kings Langley	KGL	Leighton Buzzard	LBZ	Lockerbie	LOC	Mansfield	MFT
King's Lynn	KLN	Lelant	LEL	Lockwood	LCK	Mansfield Woodhouse	MSW
Kings Norton	KNN	Lelant Saltings	LTS	London Blackfriars	BFR	March	MCH

Data Tables

Station	Code	Station	Code	Station	Code	Station	Code
Marden	MRN	Morden South	MDS	Newport (Essex)	NWE	Paignton	PGN
Margate	MAR	Morecambe	MCM	Newport (S. Wales)	NWP	Paisley Canal	PCN
Market Harborough	MHR	Moreton (Dorset)	MTN	Newquay	NQY	Paisley Gilmour Street	PYG
Market Rasen	MKR	Moreton (Merseyside)	MRT	Newstead	NSD	Paisley St James	PYJ
Markinch	MNC	Moreton-in-Marsh	MIM	Newton Abbot	NTA	Pallion	PAI
Marks Tey	MKT	Morfa Mawddach	MFA	Newton Aycliffe	NAY	Palmers Green	PAL
Marlow	MLW	Morley	MLY	Newton for Hyde	NWN	Pangbourne	PAN
Marple	MPL	Morpeth	MPT	Newton (Lanarks)	NTN	Pannal	PNL
Marsden	MSN	Mortimer	MOR	Newton St Cyres	NTC	Pantyffynnon	PTF
Marske	MSK	Mortlake	MTL	Newton-le-Willows	NLW	Par	PAR
Marston Green	MGN	Moses Gate	MSS	Newtonmore	NWR	Parbold	PBL
Martin Mill	MTM	Moss Side	MOS	Newton-on-Ayr	NOA	Park Lane	CIC
Martins Heron	MAO	Mossley	MSL	Newtown (Powys)	NWT	Park Street	PKT
Marton	MTO	Mossley Hill	MSH	Ninian Park	NNP	Parkstone (Dorset)	PKS
Maryhill	MYH	Mosspark	MPK	Nitshill	NIT	Parson Street	PSN
Maryland	MYL	Moston	MSO	Norbiton	NBT	Partick	PTK
Maryport	MRY	Motherwell	MTH	Norbury	NRB	Parton	PRN
Matlock	MAT	Motspur Park	MOT	Normans Bay	NSB	Patchway	PWY
Matlock Bath	MTB	Mottingham	MTG	Normanton	NOR	Patricroft	PAT
Mauldeth Road	MAU	Mottisfont & Dunbridge	DBG	North Berwick	NBW	Patterton	PTT
Maxwell Park	MAX	Mouldsworth	MLD	North Camp	NCM	Peartree	PEA
Maybole	MAY	Moulsecoomb	MCB	North Dulwich	NDL	Peckham Rye	PMR
Maze Hill	MZH	Mount Florida	MFL	North Fambridge	NFA	Pegswood	PEG
Meadowhall	MHS	Mount Vernon	MTV	North Llanrwst	NLR	Pelaw T&W Metro	PAW
Meldreth	MEL	Mountain Ash	MTA	North Queensferry	NQU	Pemberton	PEM
Melksham	MKM	Muir of Ord	MOO	North Road	NRD	Pembrey & Burry Port	PBY
Melton	MES	Muirend	MUI	North Sheen	NSH	Pembroke	PMB
Melton Mowbray	MMO	Musselburgh	MUB	North Walsham	NWA	Pembroke Dock	PMD
Menheniot	MEN	Mytholmroyd	MYT	North Wembley	NWB	Penally	PNA
Menston	MNN	Nafferton	NFN	Northallerton	NTR	Penarth	PEN
Meols	MEO	Nailsea & Backwell	NLS	Northampton	NMP	Pencoed	PCD
Meols Cop	MEC	Nairn	NRN	Northfield	NFD	Pengam	PGM
Meopham	MEP	Nantwich	NAN	Northfleet	NFL	Penge East	PNE
Merrytown	MEY	Narberth	NAR	Northolt Park	NLT	Penge West	PNW
Merstham	MHM	Narborough	NBR	Northumberland Park	NUM	Penhelig	PHG
Merthyr Tydfil	MER	Navigation Road	NVR	Northwich	NWI	Penistone	PNS
Merthyr Vale	MEV	Neath	NTH	Norton Bridge	NTB	Penkridge	PKG
Metheringham	MGM	Needham Market	NMT	Norwich	NRW	Penmaenmawr	PMW
MetroCentre	MCE	Neilston	NEI	Norwood Junction	NWD	Penmere	PNM
Mexborough	MEX	Nelson	NEL	Nottingham	NOT	Penrhiwceiber	PER
Micheldever	MIC	Neston	NES	Nuneaton	NUN	Penrhyndeudraeth	PRH
Micklefield	MIK	Netherfield	NET	Nunhead	NHD	Penrith	PNR
Middlesbrough	MBR	Nethertown	NRT	Nunthorpe	NNT	Penryn	PYN
Middlewood	MDL	Netley	NTL	Nutbourne	NUT	Pensarn (Gwynedd)	PES
Midgham	MDG	New Barnet	NBA	Nutfield	NUF	Penshurst	PHR
Milfield	MIF	New Beckenham	NBC	Oakengates	OKN	Pentre-Bach	PTB
Milford Haven	MFH	New Brighton	NBN	Oakham	OKM	Pen-y-Bont	PNY
Milford (Surrey)	MLF	New Clee	NCE	Oakleigh Park	OKL	Penychain	BPC
Mill Hill Broadway	MIL	New Cross	NWX	Oban	OBN	Penyffordd	PNF
Mill Hill (Lancashire)	MLH	New Cross Gate	NXG	Ockendon	OCK	Penzance	PNZ
Millbrook (Bedfordshire)	MLB	New Cumnock	NCK	Ockley	OLY	Perranwell	PRW
Millbrook (Hants)	MBK	New Eltham	NEH	Old Hill	OHL	Perry Barr	PRY
Milliken Park	MIN	New Hey	NHY	Old Roan	ORA	Pershore	PSH
Millom	MLM	New Holland	NHL	Old Street	OLD	Perth	PTH
Mills Hill	MIH	New Hythe	NHE	Oldfield Park	OLF	Peterborough	PBO
Milngavie	MLN	New Lane	NLN	Oldham Mumps	OLM	Petersfield	PTR
Milnrow	MLR	New Malden	NEM	Oldham Werneth	OLW	Petts Wood	PET
Milton Keynes Central	MKC	New Mills Central	NMC	Olton	OLT	Pevensey & Westham	PEV
Minffordd	MFF	New Mills Newtown	NMN	Ore	ORE	Pevensey Bay	PEB
Minster	MSR	New Milton	NWM	Ormskirk	OMS	Pewsey	PEW
Mirfield	MIR	New Pudsey	NPD	Orpington	ORP	Pilning	PIL
Mistley	MIS	New Southgate	NSG	Orrell	ORR	Pinhoe	PIN
Mitcham Eastfields	MTC	Newark Castle	NCT	Orrell Park	OPK	Pitlochry	PIT
Mitcham Junction	MIJ	Newark North Gate	NNG	Otford	OTF	Pitsea	PSE
Mobberley	MOB	Newbridge	NBE	Oulton Broad North	OUN	Pleasington	PLS
Monifieth	MON	Newbury	NBY	Oulton Broad South	OUS	Plockton	PLK
Monks Risborough	MRS	Newbury Racecourse	NRC	Outwood	OUT	Pluckley	PLC
Montpelier	MTP	Newcastle	NCL	Overpool	OVE	Plumley	PLM
Montrose	MTS	Newcastle Airport	APN	Overton	OVR	Plumpton	PMP
Moorfields	MRF	Newcastle Metro	NCZ	Oxenholme Lake District	OXN	Plumstead	PLU
Moorgate	ZMG	Newcraighall	NEW	Oxford	OXF	Plymouth	PLY
Moorside	MSD	Newhaven Harbour	NVH	Oxshott	OXS	Pokesdown	POK
Moorthorpe	MRP	Newhaven Town	NVN	Oxted	OXT	Polegate	PLG
Morar	MRR	Newington	NGT	Paddock Wood	PDW	Polesworth	PSW
Morchard Road	MRD	Newmarket	NMK	Padgate	PDG	Pollokshaws East	PWE

Data Tables

Station	Code	Station	Code	Station	Code	Station	Code
Pollokshaws West	PWW	Raynes Park	RAY	Salfords	SAF	Shippea Hill	SPP
Pollokshields East	PLE	Reading	RDG	Salhouse	SAH	Shipton	SIP
Pollokshields West	PLW	Reading West	RDW	Salisbury	SAL	Shirebrook	SHB
Polmont	PMT	Rectory Road	REC	Saltaire	SAE	Shirehampton	SHH
Polsloe Bridge	POL	Redbridge	RDB	Saltash	STS	Shireoaks	SRO
Ponders End	PON	Redcar Central	RCC	Saltburn	SLB	Shirley	SRL
Pontarddulais	PTD	Redcar East	RCE	Saltcoats	SLT	Shoeburyness	SRY
Pontefract Baghill	PFR	Reddish North	RDN	Saltmarshe	SAM	Sholing	SHO
Pontefract Monkhill	PFM	Reddish South	RDS	Salwick	SLW	Shoreham (Kent)	SEH
Pontefract Tanshelf	POT	Redditch	RDC	Sandal & Agbrigg	SNA	Shoreham-by-Sea	SSE
Pontlottyn	PLT	Redhill	RDH	Sandbach	SDB	Shortlands	SRT
Pontyclun	PYC	Redland	RDA	Sanderstead	SNR	Shotton	SHT
Pont-y-Pant	PYP	Redruth	RED	Sandhills	SDL	Shotts	SHS
Pontypool & New Inn	PPL	Reedham (Norfolk)	REE	Sandhurst	SND	Shrewsbury	SHR
Pontypridd	PPD	Reedham (Surrey)	RHM	Sandling	SDG	Sidcup	SID
Poole	POO	Regent Centre (New'le)	REG	Sandown	SAN	Sileby	SIL
Poppleton	POP	Reigate	REI	Sandplace	SDP	Silecroft	SIC
Port Glasgow	PTG	Renton	RTN	Sandwell & Dudley	SAD	Silkstone Common	SLK
Port Sunlight	PSL	Retford	RET	Sandwich	SDW	Silver Street	SLV
Port Talbot Parkway	PTA	Rhiwbina	RHI	Sandy	SDY	Silverdale	SVR
Portchester	PTC	Rhoose Cardiff Int Airport	RIA	Sankey for Penketh	SNK	Singer	SIN
Porth	POR	Rhosneigr	RHO	Sanquhar	SQH	Sittingbourne	SIT
Porthmadog	PTM	Rhyl	RHL	Sarn	SRR	Skegness	SKG
Portlethen	PLN	Rhymney	RHY	Saundersfoot	SDF	Skewen	SKE
Portslade	PLD	Ribblehead	RHD	Saunderton	SDR	Skipton	SKI
Portsmouth & Southsea	PMS	Rice Lane	RIL	Sawbridgeworth	SAW	Slade Green	SGR
Portsmouth Arms	PMA	Richmond	RMD	Saxilby	SXY	Slaithwaite	SWT
Portsmouth Harbour	PMH	Rickmansworth	RIC	Saxmundham	SAX	Slateford	SLA
Possilpark & Parkhouse	PPK	Riddlesdown	RDD	Scarborough	SCA	Sleaford	SLR
Potters Bar	PBR	Ridgmont	RID	Scotscalder	SCT	Sleights	SLH
Poulton-le-Fylde	PFY	Riding Mill	RDM	Scotstounhill	SCH	Slough	SLO
Poynton	PYT	Risca & Pontymister	RCA	Scunthorpe	SCU	Small Heath	SMA
Prees	PRS	Rishton	RIS	Seaburn	SEB	Smallbrook Junction	SAB
Prescot	PSC	Robertsbridge	RBR	Sea Mills	SML	Smethwick Galton Bridge	SGB
Prestatyn	PRT	Roby	ROB	Seaford	SEF	Smethwick Rolfe Street	SMR
Prestbury	PRB	Rochdale	RCD	Seaforth & Litherland	SFL	Smitham	SMI
Preston	PRE	Roche	ROC	Seaham	SEA	Smithy Bridge	SMB
Preston Park	PRP	Rochester	RTR	Seamer	SEM	Snaith	SNI
Prestonpans	PST	Rochford	RFD	Seascale	SSC	Snodland	SDA
Prestwick Int Airport	PRA	Rock Ferry	RFY	Seaton Carew	SEC	Snowdown	SWO
Prestwick Town	PTW	Rogart	ROG	Seer Green & Jordans	SRG	Sole Street	SOR
Priesthill & Darnley	PTL	Rogerstone	ROR	Selby	SBY	Solihull	SOL
Princes Risborough	PRR	Rolleston	ROL	Selhurst	SRS	Somerleyton	SYT
Prittlewell	PRL	Roman Bridge	RMB	Sellafield	SEL	South Acton	SAT
Prudhoe	PRU	Romford	RMF	Selling	SEG	South Bank	SBK
Pulborough	PUL	Romiley	RML	Selly Oak	SLY	South Bermondsey	SBM
Purfleet	PFL	Romsey	ROM	Settle	SET	South Croydon	SCY
Purley	PUR	Roose	ROO	Seven Kings	SVK	South Elmsall	SES
Purley Oaks	PUO	Rose Grove	RSG	Seven Sisters	SVS	South Gosforth	SGH
Putney	PUT	Rose Hill Marple	RSH	Sevenoaks	SEV	South Greenford	SGN
Pwllheli	PWL	Rosyth	ROS	Severn Beach	SVB	South Gyle	SGL
Pyle	PYL	Rotherham Central	RMC	Severn Tunnel Junction	STJ	South Hampstead	SOH
Quakers Yard	QYD	Roughton Road	RNR	Shalford	SFR	South Hylton	SHZ
Queenborough	QBR	Rowlands Castle	RLN	Shanklin	SHN	South Kenton	SOK
Queens Park (Glasgow)	QPK	Rowley Regis	ROW	Shaw & Crompton	SHA	South Merton	SMO
Queens Park (London)	QPW	Roy Bridge	RYB	Shawford	SHW	South Milford	SOM
Queens Road, Peckham	QRP	Roydon	RYN	Shawlands	SHL	South Ruislip	SRU
Queenstown Road	QRB	Royston	RYS	Sheerness-on-Sea	SSS	South Tottenham	STO
Quintrell Downs	QUI	Ruabon	RUA	Sheffield	SHF	South Wigston	SWS
Radcliffe (Notts)	RDF	Rufford	RUF	Shelford	SED	South Woodham Ferrers	SOF
Radlett	RDT	Rugby	RUG	Shenfield	SNF	Southall	STL
Radley	RAD	Rugeley Town	RGT	Shenstone	SEN	Southampton Airport	SOA
Radyr	RDR	Rugeley Trent Valley	RGL	Shepherd's Bush	SPB	Southampton Central	SOU
Rainford	RNF	Runcorn	RUN	Shepherds Well	SPH	Southbourne	SOB
Rainham (Essex)	RNM	Runcorn East	RUE	Shepley	SPY	Southbury	SBU
Rainham (Kent)	RAI	Ruskington	RKT	Shepperton	SHP	Southease	SEE
Rainhill	RNH	Ruswarp	RUS	Shepreth	STH	Southend Central	SOC
Ramsgate	RAM	Rutherglen	RUT	Sherborne	SHE	Southend East	SOE
Ramsgreave & Wilpshire	RGW	Ryde St Johns Road	RYR	Sherburn-in-Elmet	SIE	Southend Victoria	SOV
Rannoch	RAN	Ryde Esplanade	RYD	Sheringham	SHM	Southminster	SMN
Rauceby	RAU	Ryde Pier Head	RYP	Shettleston	SLS	Southport	SOP
Ravenglass for Eskdale	RAV	Ryder Brow	RRB	Shieldmuir	SDM	Southwick	SWK
Ravensbourne	RVB	Rye	RYE	Shifnal	SFN	Sowerby Bridge	SOW
Ravensthorpe	RVN	Rye House	RYH	Shildon	SHD	Spalding	SPA
Rawcliffe	RWC	Salford Central	SFD	Shiplake	SHI	Spean Bridge	SBR
Rayleigh	RLG	Salford Crescent	SLD	Shipley	SHY	Spital	SPI

Data Tables

Station	Code	Station	Code	Station	Code	Station	Code
Spondon	SPO	Stratford (London)	SRA	Thorne South	TNS	Upper Warlingham	UWL
Spooner Row	SPN	Stratford-upon-Avon	SAV	Thornford	THO	Upton	UPT
Spring Road	SRI	Strathcarron	STC	Thornliebank	THB	Upwey	UPW
Springburn	SPR	Strawberry Hill	STW	Thornton Abbey	TNA	Urmston	URM
Springfield	SPF	Streatham	STE	Thornton Heath	TTH	Uttoxeter	UTT
Squires Gate	SQU	Streatham Common	SRC	Thorntonhall	THT	Valley	VAL
St Albans	SAC	Streatham Hill	SRH	Thorpe Bay	TPB	Vauxhall	VXH
St Albans Abbey	SAA	Streethouse	SHC	Thorpe Culvert	TPC	Virginia Water	VIR
St Andrews Road	SAR	Strines	SRN	Thorpe-le-Soken	TLS	Waddon	WDO
St Annes-on-the-Sea	SAS	Stromeferry	STF	Three Bridges	TBD	Wadhurst	WAD
St Austell	SAU	Strood	SOO	Three Oaks	TOK	Wainfleet	WFL
St Bees	SBS	Stroud	STD	Thurgarton	THU	Wakefield Kirkgate	WKK
St Budeaux Ferry Road	SBF	Sturry	STU	Thurnscoe	THC	Wakefield Westgate	WKF
St Budeaux Victoria Rd	SBV	Styal	SYA	Thurso	THS	Walkden	WKD
St Columb Road	SCR	Sudbury	SUY	Thurston	TRS	Wallasey Grove Road	WLG
St Denys	SDN	Sudbury & Harrow Road	SUD	Tilbury Town	TIL	Wallasey Village	WLV
St Erth	SER	Sudbury Hill Harrow	SDH	Tile Hill	THL	Wallington	WLT
St Germans	SGM	Sugar Loaf	SUG	Tilehurst	TLH	Wallyford	WAF
St Helens Central	SNH	Summerston	SUM	Tipton	TIP	Walmer	WAM
St Helens Junction	SHJ	Sunbury	SUU	Tir-Phil	TIR	Walsall	WSL
St Helier	SIH	Sunderland	SUN	Tisbury	TIS	Walsden	WDN
St Ives (Cornwall)	SIV	Sundridge Park	SUP	Tiverton Parkway	TVP	Waltham Cross	WLC
St James Park	SJP	Sunningdale	SNG	Todmorden	TOD	Walthamstow Central	WHC
St James Street	SJS	Sunnymeads	SNY	Tolworth	TOL	Walthamstow Queen's Rd	WMW
St Johns	SAJ	Surbiton	SUR	Ton Pentre	TPN	Walton (Merseyside)	WAO
St Keyne	SKN	Sutton Coldfield	SUT	Tonbridge	TON	Walton-on-the-Naze	WON
St Leonards Warrior Sq	SLQ	Sutton Common	SUC	Tondu	TDU	Walton-on-Thames	WAL
St Margarets (London)	SMG	Sutton Parkway	SPK	Tonfanau	TNF	Wanborough	WAN
St Margarets (Herts)	SMT	Sutton (Surrey)	SUO	Tonypandy	TNP	Wandsworth Common	WSW
St Mary Cray	SMY	Swale	SWL	Tooting	TOO	Wandsworth Road	WWR
St Michaels	STM	Swanley	SAY	Topsham	TOP	Wandsworth Town	WNT
St Neots	SNO	Swanscombe	SWM	Torquay	TQY	Wanstead Park	WNP
St Pancras International	SPX	Swansea	SWA	Torre	TRR	Warblington	WBL
St Peter's	STZ	Swanwick	SNW	Totnes	TOT	Ware	WAR
Stadium of Light	STI	Sway	SWY	Tottenham Hale	TOM	Wareham	WRM
Stafford	STA	Swaythling	SWG	Totton	TTN	Wargrave	WGV
Staines	SNS	Swinderby	SWD	Town Green	TWN	Warminster	WMN
Stallingborough	SLL	Swindon	SWI	Trafford Park	TRA	Warnham	WNH
Stalybridge	SYB	Swineshead	SWE	Trefforest	TRF	Warrington Bank Quay	WBQ
Stamford	SMD	Swinton (Gr Manchester)	SNN	Trefforest Estate	TRE	Warrington Central	WAC
Stamford Hill	SMH	Swinton (Yorks)	SWN	Trehafod	TRH	Warwick	WRW
Stanford-le-Hope	SFO	Sydenham	SYD	Treherbert	TRB	Warwick Parkway	WRP
Stanlow & Thornton	SNT	Sydenham Hill	SYH	Treorchy	TRY	Water Orton	WTO
Stansted Airport	SSD	Syon Lane	SYL	Trimley	TRM	Waterbeach	WBC
Stansted Mountfitchet	SST	Syston	SYS	Tring	TRI	Wateringbury	WTR
Staplehurst	SPU	Tackley	TAC	Troed-y-rhiw	TRD	Waterloo (Merseyside)	WLO
Stapleton Road	SRD	Tadworth	TAD	Troon	TRN	Watford High Street	WFH
Starbeck	SBE	Taffs Well	TAF	Trowbridge	TRO	Watford Junction	WFJ
Starcross	SCS	Tain	TAI	Truro	TRU	Watford North	WFN
Staveley (Cumbria)	SVL	Talsarnau	TAL	Tulloch	TUL	Watlington	WTG
Stechford	SCF	Talybont	TLB	Tulse Hill	TUH	Watton-at-Stone	WAS
Steeton & Silsden	SON	Tal-y-Cafn	TLC	Tunbridge Wells	TBW	Waun-Gron Park	WNG
Stepps	SPS	Tame Bridge Parkway	TAB	Turkey Street	TUR	Wavertree Tech Park	WAV
Stevenage	SVG	Tamworth	TAM	Tutbury & Hatton	TUT	Wedgwood	WED
Stevenston	STV	Taplow	TAP	Twickenham	TWI	Weeley	WEE
Stewartby	SWR	Tattenham Corner	TAT	Twyford	TWY	Weeton	WET
Stewarton	STT	Taunton	TAU	Ty Croes	TYC	Welham Green	WMG
Stirling	STG	Taynuilt	TAY	Ty Glas	TGS	Welling	WLI
Stockport	SPT	Teddington	TED	Tygwyn	TYG	Wellingborough	WEL
Stocksfield	SKS	Teesside Airport	TEA	Tyndrum Lower	TYL	Wellington (Shropshire)	WLN
Stocksmoor	SSM	Teignmouth	TGM	Tyseley	TYS	Welshpool	WLP
Stockton	STK	Telford Central	TFC	Tywyn	TYW	Welwyn Garden City	WGC
Stoke Mandeville	SKM	Templecombe	TMC	Uckfield	UCK	Welwyn North	WLW
Stoke Newington	SKW	Tenby	TEN	Uddingston	UDD	Wem	WEM
Stoke-on-Trent	SOT	Teynham	TEY	Ulceby	ULC	Wembley Central	WMB
Stone	SNE	Thames Ditton	THD	Ulleskelf	ULL	Wembley Stadium	WCX
Stone Crossing	SCG	Thatcham	THA	Ulverston	ULV	Wemyss Bay	WMS
Stonebridge Park	SBP	Thatto Heath	THH	Umberleigh	UMB	Wendover	WND
Stonegate	SOG	The Hawthorns	THW	University	UNI	Wennington	WNN
Stonehaven	STN	The Lakes	TLK	University (Sundl'd)	UNV	West Allerton	WSA
Stonehouse	SHU	Theale	THE	Uphall	UHA	West Brompton	WBP
Stoneleigh	SNL	Theobalds Grove	TEO	Upholland	UPL	West Byfleet	WBY
Stourbridge Junction	SBJ	Thetford	TTF	Upminster	UPM	West Calder	WCL
Stourbridge Town	SBT	Thirsk	THI	Upper Halliford	UPH	West Croydon	WCY
Stowmarket	SMK	Thornaby	TBY	Upper Holloway	UHL	West Drayton	WDT
Stranraer	STR	Thorne North	TNN	Upper Tyndrum	UTY	West Dulwich	WDU

Data Tables

West Ealing	WEA	Whitchurch (Cardiff)	WHT	Winchfield	WNF	Worcester Park	WCP
West Ham	WEH	Whitchurch (Hants)	WCH	Winchmore Hill	WIH	Worcester Shrub Hill	WOS
West Hampstead	WHD	Whitchurch (Shropshire)	WTC	Windermere	WDM	Workington	WKG
West Hampstead T'link	WHP	White Hart Lane	WHL	Windsor & Eton Central	WNC	Worksop	WRK
West Horndon	WHR	White Notley	WNY	Windsor & Eton Riverside	WNR	Worle	WOR
West Kilbride	WKB	Whitecraigs	WCR	Winnersh	WNS	Worplesdon	WPL
West Kirby	WKI	Whitehaven	WTH	Winnersh Triangle	WTI	Worstead	WRT
West Malling	WMA	Whitland	WTL	Winsford	WSF	Worthing	WRH
West Norwood	WNW	Whitley Bridge	WBD	Wishaw	WSH	Wrabness	WRB
West Ruislip	WRU	Whitlocks End	WTE	Witham	WTM	Wraysbury	WRY
West Runton	WRN	Whitstable	WHI	Witley	WTY	Wrenbury	WRE
West St Leonards	WLD	Whittlesea	WLE	Witton	WTT	Wressle	WRS
West Sutton	WSU	Whittlesford Parkway	WLF	Wivelsfield	WVF	Wrexham Central	WXC
West Wickham	WWI	Whitton	WTN	Wivenhoe	WIV	Wrexham General	WRX
West Worthing	WWO	Whitwell	WWL	Woburn Sands	WOB	Wye	WYE
Westbury (Wilts)	WSB	Whyteleafe	WHY	Woking	WOK	Wylam	WYM
Westcliff	WCF	Whyteleafe South	WHS	Wokingham	WKM	Wylde Green	WYL
Westcombe Park	WCB	Wick	WCK	Woldingham	WOH	Wymondham	WMD
Westenhanger	WHA	Wickford	WIC	Wolverhampton	WVH	Wythall	WYT
Wester Hailes	WTA	Wickham Market	WCM	Wolverton	WOL	Yalding	YAL
Westerfield	WFI	Widdrington	WDD	Wombwell	WOM	Yardley Wood	YRD
Westerton	WES	Widnes	WID	Wood End	WDE	Yarm	YRM
Westgate-on-Sea	WGA	Widney Manor	WMR	Wood Street	WST	Yate	YAE
Westhoughton	WHG	Wigan North Western	WGN	Woodbridge	WDB	Yatton	YAT
Weston Milton	WNM	Wigan Wallgate	WGW	Woodgrange Park	WGR	Yeoford	YEO
Weston-super-Mare	WSM	Wigton	WGT	Woodhall	WDL	Yeovil Junction	YVJ
Wetheral	WRL	Wildmill	WMI	Woodhouse	WDH	Yeovil Pen Mill	YVP
Weybridge	WYB	Willesden Junction	WIJ	Woodlesford	WDS	Yetminster	YET
Weymouth	WEY	Williamwood	WLM	Woodley	WLY	Ynyswen	YNW
Whaley Bridge	WBR	Willington	WIL	Woodmansterne	WME	Yoker	YOK
Whalley	WHE	Wilmcote	WMC	Woodsmoor	WSR	York	YRK
Whatstandwell	WTS	Wilmslow	WML	Wool	WOO	Yorton	YRT
Whifflet	WFF	Wilnecote	WNE	Woolston	WLS	Ystrad Mynach	YSM
Whimple	WHM	Wimbledon	WIM	Woolwich Arsenal	WWA	Ystrad Rhondda	YSR
Whinhill	WNL	Wimbledon Chase	WBO	Woolwich Dockyard	WWD		
Whiston	WHN	Winchelsea	WSE	Wootton Wawen	WWW		
Whitby	WTB	Winchester	WIN	Worcester Foregate St	WOF		

Left: *Three-car First Great Western Class 165 set No. 165102 departs from Oxford station to the depot on 29 May 2014 after arriving with a service from Paddington.* CJM

DMU and EMU Vehicle Codes

BDMSO	Battery Driving Motor Standard Open	MFL	Motor First Lavatory
DM	Driving Motor	MPMV	Motor Parcels Mail Van
DMBO	Driving Motor Brake Open	MS	Motor Standard
DMBS	Driving Motor Brake Standard	MSL	Motor Standard Lavatory
DMCL	Driving Motor Composite Lavatory	MSLRB	Motor Standard Lavatory Restaurant Buffet
DMCO	Driving Motor Composite Open	MSO	Motor Standard Open
DMF	Driving Motor First	MSRMB	Motor Standard Restaurant Micro Buffet
DMFLO	Driving Motor First Luggage Open	PTSO	Pantograph Trailer Standard Open
DMRFO	Driving Motor Restaurant First Open	RB	Restaurant Buffet
DMS	Driving Motor Standard	TBFO	Trailer Brake First Open
DMSL	Driving Motor Standard Lavatory	TCO	Trailer Composite Open
DMSO	Driving Motor Standard Open	TFO	Trailer First Open
DTCO	Driving Trailer Composite Open	TPMV	Trailer Parcels Mail Van
DTPMV	Driving Trailer Parcels Mail Van	TSO	Trailer Standard Open
DTSO	Driving Trailer Standard Open	TSRMB	Trailer Standard Restaurant Micro Buffet
MBC	Motor Brake Composite		
MBSO	Motor Brake Standard Open	(A) - A Car	
MC	Motor Composite	(B) - B Car	

Data Tables

Number Cross-Link

This cross number checklist indicates in which section of the ABC Rail Guide 2015 full details of rolling stock can be found.

Number Cross-Link Codes

Code		Code		Code	
3MP	3M Productions	FLR	Freightliner	PRE	Preserved
AFG	Arlington Fleet Group	FSL	Flying Scotsman Railway Ltd	PUL	Pullman Rail
ALS	Alstom	FSR	First ScotRail	RAF	Railfilms
ATW	Arriva Trains Wales	FTP	First TransPennine	RCL	Railcare
AXC	Arriva CrossCountry	GAR	Abellio Greater Anglia	RIV	Riviera Trains
BAR	British American Railway	GBR	GB Railfreight	RRS	Ridings Railtours
BOK	Bo'ness & Kinneil Railway	GSW	Great Scottish & Western Rly	RVE	Rail Vehicle Engineering
BOM	Bombardier Transportation	GTL	Grand Central Railway	S4L	Stratford Class 47 Group
C2C	c2c Railway	HAN	Hanson Traction	SEC	Serco Railtest
COL	Colas	HEC	Heathrow Connect	SET	SouthEastern Trains
CRW	Chiltern Railways	HEX	Heathrow Express	SIE	Siemens
DBR	DB Regio	HNR	Harry Needle Railroad Co	SIL	Stagecoach Island Line
DBS	DB Schenker	ICE	InterCity East Coast	SNF	SNCF (French Railways)
DRS	Direct Rail Services	IND	Industrial	SRP	Scottish Railway Preservation Soc
ECR	Euro Cargo Rail	JHS	Jeremy Hoskins	SUP	Support Coaches
EMT	East Midlands Trains	LMI	London Midland	SWT	South West Trains
EPX	Europhoenix Ltd	LNW	London North Western	TSG	Thameslink, Southern and
ETL	Electric Traction Ltd	LOG	London Overground		Great Northern
EUR	Eurotunnel	MER	Merseyrail	TTS	Transmart Trains
EUR	Europorte2	MHR	Mid Hants Railway	UKL	UK Rail Leasing
EUS	Eurostar UK	MRL	Mendip Rail Ltd	VSO	Venice Simplon Orient Express
EXP	Exported	NEM	Nemesis Rail	VTN	Vintage Trains
FGW	First Great Western	NOR	Northern Railways	VWC	Virgin West Coast
FHT	First Hull Trains	NRL	Network Rail Limited	WAB	Wabtec
		NYM	North Yorkshire Moors Railway	WCR	West Coast Railway
		OLS	Off Lease		

Locomotives – Diesel & Electric

Number	Code	Number	Code	Number	Code	Number	Code	Number	Code
D0226	PRE	D2139	PRE	D2854	PRE	D8000	PRE	E5001	PRE
		D2148	PRE	D2858	PRE				
D4	PRE	D2178	PRE	D2860	PRE	D8233	PRE	E26020	PRE
		D2182	PRE	D2866	PRE			E27000	PRE
		D2184	PRE	D2867	PRE	D8568	PRE	E27001	PRE
12	PRE	D2192	PRE	D2868	PRE				
		D2199	PRE			D9500	PRE	9005	EUR
44	MRL			D2953	PRE	D9502	PRE	9007	EUR
120	MRL	D2203	PRE	D2956	PRE	D9504	PRE	9011	EUR
		D2205	PRE			D9513	PRE	9013	EUR
		D2207	PRE	D3000	PRE	D9516	PRE	9015	EUR
D200	PRE	D2229	PRE	D3002	PRE	D9518	PRE	9018	EUR
		D2245	PRE	D3014	PRE	D9520	PRE	9022	EUR
D821	PRE	D2246	PRE	D3101	PRE	D9521	PRE	9024	EUR
D832	PRE	D2271	PRE	D3255	PRE	D9523	PRE	9026	EUR
		D2272	PRE	D3261	PRE	D9524	PRE	9029	EUR
D1010	PRE	D2279	PRE	D3452	PRE	D9525	PRE	9033	EUR
D1013	PRE	D2280	PRE	D3489	PRE	D9526	PRE	9036	EUR
D1015	PRE	D2284	PRE			D9529	PRE	9037	EUR
D1023	PRE	D2298	PRE	D4067	PRE	D9531	PRE		
D1041	PRE	D2302	PRE	D4092	PRE	D9537	PRE	9701	EUR
D1048	PRE	D2310	PRE	D4095	PRE	D9539	PRE	9702	EUR
D1062	PRE	D2324	PRE			D9551	PRE	9703	EUR
		D2325	PRE	D5500	PRE	D9553	PRE	9704	EUR
D2023	PRE	D2334	PRE			D9555	PRE	9705	EUR
D2024	PRE	D2337	PRE	D5705	PRE			9706	EUR
D2041	PRE					DELTIC	PRE	9707	EUR
D2046	PRE	D2511	PRE	D6700	PRE			9711	EUR
D2051	PRE	D2578	PRE			DS75	PRE	9712	EUR
D2117	PRE	D2587	PRE	D7017	PRE			9713	EUR
D2118	PRE	D2595	PRE	D7018	PRE	LMS7050	PRE	9714	EUR
D2133	PRE	D2767	PRE	D7029	PRE	LMS7051	PRE	9715	EUR
D2138	PRE	D2774	PRE	D7076	PRE	LMS7069	PRE	9716	EUR

Data Tables

Number Cross-Link

9717	EUR	03128	PRE	08410	FGW	08617	ALS	08790	ALS
9718	EUR	03134	PRE	08411	IND	08622	BAR	08795	FGW
9719	EUR	03141	PRE	08417	NRL	08623	DBS	08799	DBS
9720	EUR	03144	PRE	08418	WCR	08624	FLR	08804	DBS
9721	EUR	03145	PRE	08423	BAR	08629	KBR	08805	LMI
9722	EUR	03152	PRE	08436	PRE	08628	PRE	08807	IND
9723	EUR	03158	PRE	08441	IND	08630	DBS	08809	IND
		03162	PRE	08442	LNW	08631	BOM	08810	LNW
9801	EUR	03170	PRE	08443	PRE	08635	PRE	08818	HNR
9802	EUR	03179	IND	08444	PRE	08641	FGW	08822	FGW
9803	EUR	03189	PRE	08445	IND	08643	MRL	08823	IND
9804	EUR	03196	WCR	08447	IND	08644	FGW	08824	DBS
9806	EUR	03197	PRE	08451	ALS	08645	FGW	08825	PRE
9808	EUR	03180	PRE	08454	ALS	08648	BAR	08830	LNW
9809	EUR	03371	PRE	08460	IND	08649	KBR	08834	HNR
9810	EUR	03381	WCR	08471	PRE	08650	MRL	08836	FGW
9812	EUR	03399	PRE	08472	WAB	08652	MRL	08846	BOM
9814	EUR			08473	PRE	08653	DBS	08847	IND
9816	EUR	05001	PRE	08476	PRE	08663	FGW	08850	NYM
9817	EUR			08479	PRE	08669	WAB	08853	WAB
9819	EUR	06003	PRE	08480	DBS	08670	IND	08865	DBS
9820	EUR			08483	FGW	08676	DBS	08868	HNR
9821	EUR	07001	PRE	08484	IND	08678	WCR	08870	BAR
9823	EUR	07005	PRE	08485	WCR	08682	BOM	08871	WAB
9825	EUR	07007	AFG	08490	PRE	08683	IND	08872	IND
9827	EUR	07010	PRE	08495	DBS	08685	HNR	08873	BAR
9828	EUR	07011	PRE	08499	PUL	08690	EMT	08874	BAR
9831	EUR	07012	PRE	08500	DBS	08691	FLR	08877	DBS
9832	EUR	07013	PRE	08502	HNR	08694	PRE	08881	PRE
9834	EUR			08503	IND	08696	ALS	08885	BAR
9835	EUR	08011	PRE	08507	RIV	08699	IND	08886	DBS
9838	EUR	08012	PRE	08511	IND	08700	HNR	08887	ALS
9840	EUR	08015	PRE	08516	LNW	08704	RIV	08891	FLR
		08016	PRE	08523	BAR	08706	DBS	08892	HNR
01509	CRW	08021	PRE	08525	EMT	08709	DBS	08896	PRE
01551	SIE	08022	PRE	08527	HNR	08711	DBS	08899	EMT
01552	HNR	08032	PRE	08528	PRE	08714	DBS	08903	IND
01564	HNR	08046	PRE	08530	FLR	08721	ALS	08905	HNR
		08054	PRE	08531	FLR	08724	WAB	08908	EMT
03018	PRE	08060	PRE	08535	IND	08728	IND	08911	PRE
03020	PRE	08064	PRE	08536	RVE	08730	KBR	08912	IND
03022	PRE	08102	PRE	08556	PRE	08731	MRL	08913	IND
03027	PRE	08108	PRE	08567	DBS	08735	DBS	08915	IND
03037	PRE	08114	PRE	08568	KBR	08737	DBS	08918	HNR
03059	PRE	08123	PRE	08571	WAB	08738	DBS	08922	DBS
03062	PRE	08133	PRE	08573	BAR	08743	IND	08924	IND
03063	PRE	08164	PRE	08575	FLR	08750	BAR	08925	GBR
03066	PRE	08168	PRE	08578	DBS	08754	BAR	08927	PRE
03069	PRE	08195	PRE	08580	DBS	08756	BAR	08929	HNR
03072	PRE	08202	IND	08585	FLR	08757	DBS	08933	IND
03073	PRE	08220	IND	08588	BAR	08762	BAR	08934	GBR
03078	PRE	08238	PRE	08590	PRE	08764	WAB	08936	BAR
03079	PRE	08266	PRE	08593	DBS	08765	HNR	08937	PRE
03081	PRE	08288	PRE	08596	WAB	08767	PRE	08939	DBS
03084	PRE	08308	BAR	08598	IND	08769	PRE	08943	HNR
03089	PRE	08331	PRE	08600	IND	08772	PRE	08944	PRE
03090	PRE	08359	PRE	08602	BOM	08773	PRE	08947	MRL
03094	PRE	08375	IND	08604	PRE	08774	IND	08948	EUS
03099	PRE	08377	PRE	08605	DBS	08780	PRE	08950	EMT
03112	PRE	08388	PRE	08611	ALS	08784	DBS	08954	IND
03113	PRE	08389	HNR	08613	BAR	08785	FLR	08956	NRL
03119	PRE	08393	FLR	08615	WAB	08786	HNR	08993	DBS
03120	PRE	08401	GBR	08616	LMI	08787	IND	08994	DBS

No.	Code	No.	Code	No.	Code	No.	Code	No.	Code
08995	DBS	20154	PRE	25309	PRE	31530	PRE	37218	DRS
		20166	HNR	25313	PRE	31601	BAR	37219	COL
09001	PRE	20168	HNR	25321	PRE	31602	BAR	37227	PRE
09002	GBR	20169	PRE	25322	PRE			37240	PRE
09004	PRE	20177	PRE			33002	PRE	37248	PRE
09006	DBS	20188	PRE	26001	PRE	33008	PRE	37250	PRE
09007	LOG	20189	GBR	26002	PRE	33012	PRE	37254	PRE
09009	GBR	20205	PRE	26004	PRE	33018	PRE	37255	PRE
09010	PRE	20214	PRE	26007	PRE	33019	PRE	37259	DRS
09012	PRE	20227	C2L	26010	PRE	33021	PRE	37261	DRS
09014	HNR	20228	PRE	26011	PRE	33025	WCR	37263	PRE
09015	PRE	20301	DRS	26014	PRE	33029	WCR	37264	PRE
09017	PRE	20302	DRS	26024	PRE	33030	PRE	37275	PRE
09018	HNR	20303	DRS	26025	PRE	33035	PRE	37294	PRE
09019	PRE	20304	DRS	26035	PRE	33046	PRE	37308	PRE
09022	IND	20305	DRS	26038	PRE	33048	PRE	37314	PRE
09023	IND	20308	DRS	26040	PRE	33052	PRE	37324	PRE
09024	PRE	20309	DRS	26043	PRE	33053	PRE	37372	PRE
09025	PRE	20311	HNR			33057	PRE	37401	DRS
09026	TSG	20312	DRS	27001	PRE	33063	PRE	37402	DRS
09106	DBS	20314	HNR	27005	PRE	33065	PRE	37403	PRE
09201	DBS	20901	GBR	27007	PRE	33102	PRE	37405	DRS
09204	LNW	20903	HNR	27024	PRE	33103	NEM	37406	DRS
		20904	HNR	27050	PRE	33108	PRE	37407	PRE
12052	PRE	20905	GBR	27056	PRE	33109	PRE	37409	DRS
12077	PRE	20906	HNR	27059	PRE	33110	PRE	37413	PRE
12082	PRE			27066	PRE	33111	PRE	37418	PRE
12088	IND	21544	ECR			33116	PRE	37419	DRS
12093	PRE	21545	ECR	31101	PRE	33117	PRE	37421	COL
12099	PRE	21546	ECR	31105	NRL	33201	PRE	37422	DRS
12131	PRE	21547	ECR	31106	RVE	33202	PRE	37423	DRS
		21610	ECR	31108	PRE	33207	WCR	37424	PRE
15224	PRE	21611	ECR	31119	PRE	33208	PRE	37425	DRS
				31128	NEM			37502	FLR
18000	PRE	21901	EUR	31130	PRE	37003	PRE	37503	DRS
		21902	EUR	31162	PRE	37009	PRE	37510	DRS
20001	PRE	21903	EUR	31163	PRE	37023	PRE	37516	WCR
20007	PRE	21904	EUR	31190	BAR	37025	PRE	37517	WCR
20016	HNR	21905	EUR	31203	PRE	37029	HNR	37518	WCR
20020	PRE	21906	EUS	31206	PRE	37032	PRE	37521	DRS
20031	PRE	21907	EUS	31207	PRE	37037	PRE	37601	DRS
20035	PRE			31210	PRE	37038	DRS	37602	DRS
20048	PRE	24032	PRE	31233	NRL	37042	PRE	37603	DRS
20056	HNR	24054	PRE	31235	PRE	37057	HNR	37604	DRS
20057	PRE	24061	PRE	31255	PRE	37059	DRS	37605	DRS
20059	PRE	24081	PRE	31270	PRE	37069	DRS	37606	DRS
20063	PRE			31271	PRE	37075	PRE	37607	DRS
20066	HNR	25035	PRE	31285	NRL	37097	PRE	37608	DRS
20069	PRE	25057	PRE	31289	PRE	37108	PRE	37609	DRS
20081	HNR	25059	PRE	31327	PRE	37109	PRE	37610	DRS
20087	PRE	25067	PRE	31414	PRE	37116	COL	37611	DRS
20088	HNR	25072	PRE	31415	PRE	37142	PRE	37612	DRS
20092	HNR	25083	PRE	31418	PRE	37146	PRE	37667	DRS
20096	HNR	25173	PRE	31435	PRE	37152	PRE	37668	WCR
20098	PRE	25185	PRE	31438	PRE	37165	HNR	37669	WCR
20107	HNR	25191	PRE	31452	BAR	37175	COL	37670	DRS
20110	HNR	25235	PRE	31454	BAR	37188	PRE	37674	PRE
20118	HNR	25244	PRE	31459	RVE	37194	DRS	37676	WCR
20121	HNR	25262	PRE	31461	PRE	37198	NRL	37679	NEM
20132	HNR	25265	PRE	31463	PRE	37207	PRE	37682	DRS
20137	PRE	25278	NYM	31465	NRL	37214	WCR	37685	WCR
20138	HNR	25279	PRE	31466	PRE	37215	PRE	37688	DRS
20142	GBR	25283	PRE	31468	RVE	37216	PRE	37703	DRS

Data Tables

❑ 37706	WCR	❑ 43052	EMT	❑ 43152	FGW	❑ 43307	ICE	❑ 47417	PRE
❑ 37710	WCR	❑ 43053	FGW	❑ 43153	FGW	❑ 43308	ICE	❑ 47449	PRE
❑ 37712	WCR	❑ 43054	EMT	❑ 43154	FGW	❑ 43309	ICE	❑ 47484	PRE
❑ 37714	DRS	❑ 43055	EMT	❑ 43155	FGW	❑ 43310	ICE	❑ 47488	NEM
❑ 37716	DRS	❑ 43056	FGW	❑ 43156	FGW	❑ 43311	ICE	❑ 47492	WCR
❑ 37718	DRS	❑ 43058	EMT	❑ 43158	FGW	❑ 43312	ICE	❑ 47500	WCR
❑ 37800	EPX	❑ 43059	EMT	❑ 43159	FGW	❑ 43313	ICE	❑ 47501	DRS
❑ 37884	EPX	❑ 43060	EMT	❑ 43160	FGW	❑ 43314	ICE	❑ 47524	PRE
❑ 37901	PRE	❑ 43061	EMT	❑ 43161	FGW	❑ 43315	ICE	❑ 47526	WCR
❑ 37905	UKL	❑ 43062	NRL	❑ 43162	FGW	❑ 43316	ICE	❑ 47540	PRE
❑ 37906	UKL	❑ 43063	FGW	❑ 43163	FGW	❑ 43317	ICE	❑ 47580	S4G
		❑ 43064	EMT	❑ 43164	FGW	❑ 43318	ICE	❑ 47596	PRE
❑ 40012	PRE	❑ 43066	EMT	❑ 43165	FGW	❑ 43319	ICE	❑ 47635	PRE
❑ 40013	PRE	❑ 43069	FGW	❑ 43168	FGW	❑ 43320	ICE	❑ 47640	PRE
❑ 40106	PRE	❑ 43070	FGW	❑ 43169	FGW	❑ 43321	AXC	❑ 47643	PRE
❑ 40118	PRE	❑ 43071	FGW	❑ 43170	FGW	❑ 43357	AXC	❑ 47701	NEM
❑ 40135	PRE	❑ 43073	EMT	❑ 43171	FGW	❑ 43366	AXC	❑ 47703	HNR
❑ 40145	PRE	❑ 43075	EMT	❑ 43172	FGW	❑ 43367	ICE	❑ 47712	PRE
		❑ 43076	EMT	❑ 43174	FGW	❑ 43378	AXC	❑ 47714	HNR
❑ 41001	PRE	❑ 43078	FGW	❑ 43175	FGW	❑ 43384	AXC	❑ 47715	HNR
		❑ 43079	FGW	❑ 43176	FGW	❑ 43423	GTL	❑ 47727	COL
❑ 43002	FGW	❑ 43081	EMT	❑ 43177	FGW	❑ 43465	GTL	❑ 47739	COL
❑ 43003	FGW	❑ 43082	EMT	❑ 43179	FGW	❑ 43467	GTL	❑ 47744	NEM
❑ 43004	FGW	❑ 43083	EMT	❑ 43180	FGW	❑ 43468	GTL	❑ 47746	WCR
❑ 43005	FGW	❑ 43086	FGW	❑ 43181	FGW	❑ 43480	GTL	❑ 47749	COL
❑ 43009	FGW	❑ 43087	FGW	❑ 43182	FGW	❑ 43484	GTL	❑ 47760	WCR
❑ 43010	FGW	❑ 43088	FGW	❑ 43183	FGW			❑ 47761	HNR
❑ 43012	FGW	❑ 43089	EMT	❑ 43185	FGW	❑ 44008	PRE	❑ 47763	PRE
❑ 43013	NRL	❑ 43091	FGW	❑ 43186	FGW			❑ 47765	PRE
❑ 43014	NRL	❑ 43092	FGW	❑ 43187	FGW	❑ 45015	PRE	❑ 47768	WCR
❑ 43015	FGW	❑ 43093	FGW	❑ 43188	FGW	❑ 45041	PRE	❑ 47769	RIV
❑ 43016	FGW	❑ 43094	FGW	❑ 43189	FGW	❑ 45060	PRE	❑ 47771	PRE
❑ 43017	FGW	❑ 43097	FGW	❑ 43190	FGW	❑ 45105	PRE	❑ 47772	WCR
❑ 43018	FGW	❑ 43098	FGW	❑ 43191	FGW	❑ 45108	PRE	❑ 47773	VTN
❑ 43020	FGW	❑ 43122	FGW	❑ 43192	FGW	❑ 45112	NEM	❑ 47776	WCR
❑ 43021	FGW	❑ 43124	FGW	❑ 43193	FGW	❑ 45118	PRE	❑ 47785	PRE
❑ 43022	FGW	❑ 43125	FGW	❑ 43194	FGW	❑ 45125	PRE	❑ 47786	WCR
❑ 43023	FGW	❑ 43126	FGW	❑ 43195	FGW	❑ 45132	PRE	❑ 47787	WCR
❑ 43024	FGW	❑ 43127	FGW	❑ 43196	FGW	❑ 45133	PRE	❑ 47790	DRS
❑ 43025	FGW	❑ 43128	FGW	❑ 43197	FGW	❑ 45135	PRE	❑ 47793	PRE
❑ 43026	FGW	❑ 43129	FGW	❑ 43198	FGW	❑ 45149	PRE	❑ 47798	PRE
❑ 43027	FGW	❑ 43130	FGW	❑ 43206	ICE			❑ 47799	PRE
❑ 43028	FGW	❑ 43131	FGW	❑ 43207	AXC	❑ 46010	PRE	❑ 47802	WCR
❑ 43029	FGW	❑ 43132	FGW	❑ 43208	ICE	❑ 46035	PRE	❑ 47804	WCR
❑ 43030	FGW	❑ 43133	FGW	❑ 43238	ICE	❑ 46045	PRE	❑ 47805	DRS
❑ 43031	FGW	❑ 43134	FGW	❑ 43239	ICE			❑ 47810	DRS
❑ 43032	FGW	❑ 43135	FGW	❑ 43251	ICE	❑ 47004	PRE	❑ 47811	FLR
❑ 43033	FGW	❑ 43136	FGW	❑ 43257	ICE	❑ 47105	PRE	❑ 47812	RIV
❑ 43034	FGW	❑ 43137	FGW	❑ 43272	ICE	❑ 47117	PRE	❑ 47813	DRS
❑ 43035	FGW	❑ 43138	FGW	❑ 43274	ICE	❑ 47192	PRE	❑ 47815	RIV
❑ 43036	FGW	❑ 43139	FGW	❑ 43277	ICE	❑ 47194	WCR	❑ 47816	FLR
❑ 43037	FGW	❑ 43140	FGW	❑ 43285	AXC	❑ 47205	PRE	❑ 47818	DRS
❑ 43040	FGW	❑ 43141	FGW	❑ 43290	ICE	❑ 47237	WCR	❑ 47826	WCR
❑ 43041	FGW	❑ 43142	FGW	❑ 43295	ICE	❑ 47245	WCR	❑ 47828	DRS
❑ 43042	FGW	❑ 43143	FGW	❑ 43296	ICE	❑ 47270	WCR	❑ 47830	FLR
❑ 43043	EMT	❑ 43144	FGW	❑ 43299	ICE	❑ 47292	PRE	❑ 47832	WCR
❑ 43044	EMT	❑ 43145	FGW	❑ 43300	ICE	❑ 47306	PRE	❑ 47840	PRE
❑ 43045	EMT	❑ 43146	FGW	❑ 43301	AXC	❑ 47355	WCR	❑ 47841	DRS
❑ 43046	EMT	❑ 43147	FGW	❑ 43302	ICE	❑ 47367	PRE	❑ 47843	RIV
❑ 43047	EMT	❑ 43148	FGW	❑ 43303	AXC	❑ 47375	NEM	❑ 47847	RIV
❑ 43048	EMT	❑ 43149	FGW	❑ 43304	AXC	❑ 47376	PRE	❑ 47848	RIV
❑ 43049	EMT	❑ 43150	FGW	❑ 43305	ICE	❑ 47401	PRE	❑ 47851	WCR
❑ 43050	EMT	❑ 43151	FGW	❑ 43306	ICE	❑ 47402	PRE	❑ 47853	DRS

Data Tables

No.	Code	No.	Code	No.	Code	No.	Code	No.	Code
47854	WCR	56312	BAR	58032	DBS	60034	DBS	66007	DBS
		56313	BAR	58033	DBS	60035	DBS	66008	DBS
50002	PRE			58034	DBS	60036	DBS	66009	DBS
50007	PRE	57001	WCR	58035	DBS	60037	DBS	66010	DBS
50008	PRE	57002	DRS	58036	DBS	60038	DBS	66011	DBS
50015	PRE	57003	DRS	58038	DBS	60039	DBS	66012	DBS
50017	PRE	57004	DRS	58039	DBS	60040	DBS	66013	DBS
50019	PRE	57005	WCR	58040	DBS	60041	DBS	66014	DBS
50021	PRE	57006	WCR	58041	DBS	60043	DBS	66015	DBS
50026	PRE	57007	DRS	58042	DBS	60044	DBS	66016	DBS
50027	PRE	57008	DRS	58043	DBS	60045	DBS	66017	DBS
50029	PRE	57009	DRS	58044	DBS	60046	DBS	66018	DBS
50030	PRE	57010	DRS	58046	DBS	60047	COL	66019	DBS
50031	PRE	57011	DRS	58047	DBS	60048	DBS	66020	DBS
50033	PRE	57012	DRS	58048	DBS	60049	DBS	66021	DBS
50135	PRE	57301	DRS	58049	DBS	60051	DBS	66022	DBS
50042	PRE	57302	DRS	58050	DBS	60052	DBS	66023	DBS
50044	PRE	57303	DRS			60053	DBS	66024	DBS
50049	PRE	57304	DRS	59001	MRL	60054	DBS	66025	DBS
50050	PRE	57305	DRS	59002	MRL	60055	DBS	66026	DBS
		57306	DRS	59003	GBR	60056	COL	66027	DBS
55002	PRE	57307	DRS	59004	MRL	60057	DBS	66028	DBS
55009	PRE	57308	DRS	59005	MRL	60059	DBS	66029	DBS
55015	PRE	57309	DRS			60060	DBS	66030	DBS
55016	PRE	57310	DRS	59101	MRL	60061	DBS	66031	DBS
55019	PRE	57311	DRS	59102	MRL	60062	DBS	66032	DBS
55022	PRE	57312	DRS	59103	MRL	60063	DBS	66033	DBS
		57313	WCR	59104	MRL	60064	DBS	66034	DBS
56006	PRE	57314	WCR			60065	DBS	66035	DBS
56007	URL	57315	WCR	59201	DBS	60066	DBS	66036	DBS
56009	URL	57316	WCR	59202	DBS	60067	DBS	66037	DBS
56018	URL	57601	WCR	59203	DBS	60069	DBS	66038	DBS
56031	URL	57602	FGW	59204	DBS	60071	DBS	66039	DBS
56032	URL	57603	FGW	59205	DBS	60072	DBS	66040	DBS
56037	URL	57604	FGW	59206	DBS	60073	DBS	66041	DBS
56038	URL	57605	FGW			60074	DBS	66042	DBS
56049	COL			60001	DBS	60076	COL	66043	DBS
56051	COL	58001	DBS	60002	COL	60077	DBS	66044	DBS
56060	URL	58004	DBS	60003	DBS	60079	DBS	66045	DBS
56065	URL	58005	DBS	60004	DBS	60083	DBS	66046	DBS
56069	URL	58006	DBS	60005	DBS	60084	DBS	66047	DBS
56077	URL	58007	DBS	60007	DBS	60085	COL	66048	DBS
56078	COL	58008	DBS	60009	DBS	60086	DBS	66049	DBS
56081	URL	58009	DBS	60010	DBS	60087	COL	66050	DBS
56087	COL	58010	DBS	60011	DBS	60088	DBS	66051	DBS
56091	BAR	58011	DBS	60012	DBS	60090	DBS	66052	DBS
56090	COL	58012	DBS	60013	DBS	60091	DBS	66053	DBS
56094	COL	58013	DBS	60015	DBS	60092	DBS	66054	DBS
56096	COL	58015	DBS	60017	DBS	60093	DBS	66055	DBS
56097	PRE	58016	PRE	60018	DBS	60094	DBS	66056	DBS
56098	URL	58017	DBS	60019	DBS	60095	COL	66057	DBS
56101	EXP	58018	DBS	60020	DBS	60096	COL	66058	DBS
56103	BAR	58020	DBS	60021	COL	60097	DBS	66059	DBS
56104	URL	58021	DBS	60022	DBS	60099	DBS	66060	DBS
56105	COL	58022	DBS	60024	DBS	60100	DBS	66061	DBS
56106	URL	58023	DBS	60025	DBS	60500	DBS	66062	DBS
56113	COL	58024	DBS	60026	COL			66063	DBS
56115	EXP	58025	DBS	60027	DBS	66001	DBS	66064	DBS
56117	EXP	58026	DBS	60028	DBS	66002	DBS	66065	DBS
56301	EPX	58027	DBS	60029	DBS	66003	DBS	66066	DBS
56302	COL	58029	DBS	60030	DBS	66004	DBS	66067	DBS
56303	BAR	58030	DBS	60032	DBS	66005	DBS	66068	DBS
56311	BAR	58031	DBS	60033	DBS	66006	DBS	66069	DBS

Data Tables

No.		No.		No.		No.		No.	
66070	DBS	66133	DBS	66196	DBS	66412	EXP	66541	FLR
66071	DBS	66134	DBS	66197	DBS	66413	FLR	66542	FLR
66072	DBS	66135	DBS	66198	DBS	66414	FLR	66543	FLR
66073	DBS	66136	DBS	66199	DBS	66415	FLR	66544	FLR
66074	DBS	66137	DBS	66200	DBS	66416	FLR	66545	FLR
66075	DBS	66138	DBS	66201	DBS	66417	EXP	66546	FLR
66076	DBS	66139	DBS	66202	DBS	66418	FLR	66547	FLR
66077	DBS	66140	DBS	66203	DBS	66419	FLR	66548	FLR
66078	DBS	66141	DBS	66204	DBS	66420	FLR	66549	FLR
66079	DBS	66142	DBS	66205	DBS	66421	DRS	66550	FLR
66080	DBS	66143	DBS	66206	DBS	66422	DRS	66551	FLR
66081	DBS	66144	DBS	66207	DBS	66423	DRS	66552	FLR
66082	DBS	66145	DBS	66208	DBS	66424	DRS	66553	FLR
66083	DBS	66146	DBS	66209	DBS	66425	DRS	66554	FLR
66084	DBS	66147	DBS	66210	DBS	66426	DRS	66555	FLR
66085	DBS	66148	DBS	66211	DBS	66427	DRS	66556	FLR
66086	DBS	66149	DBS	66212	DBS	66428	DRS	66557	FLR
66087	DBS	66150	DBS	66213	DBS	66429	DRS	66558	FLR
66088	DBS	66151	DBS	66214	DBS	66430	DRS	66559	FLR
66089	DBS	66152	DBS	66215	DBS	66431	DRS	66560	FLR
66090	DBS	66153	DBS	66216	DBS	66432	DRS	66561	FLR
66091	DBS	66154	DBS	66217	DBS	66433	DRS	66562	FLR
66092	DBS	66155	DBS	66218	DBS	66434	DRS	66563	FLR
66093	DBS	66156	DBS	66219	DBS			66564	FLR
66094	DBS	66157	DBS	66220	DBS	66501	FLR	66565	FLR
66095	DBS	66158	DBS	66221	DBS	66502	FLR	66566	FLR
66096	DBS	66159	DBS	66222	DBS	66503	FLR	66567	FLR
66097	DBS	66160	DBS	66223	DBS	66504	FLR	66568	FLR
66098	DBS	66161	DBS	66224	DBS	66505	FLR	66569	FLR
66099	DBS	66162	DBS	66225	DBS	66506	FLR	66570	FLR
66100	DBS	66163	DBS	66226	DBS	66507	FLR	66571	FLR
66101	DBS	66164	DBS	66227	DBS	66508	FLR	66572	FLR
66102	DBS	66165	DBS	66228	DBS	66509	FLR	66582	EXP
66103	DBS	66166	DBS	66229	DBS	66510	FLR	66583	EXP
66104	DBS	66167	DBS	66230	DBS	66511	FLR	66584	EXP
66105	DBS	66168	DBS	66231	DBS	66512	FLR	66585	FLR
66106	DBS	66169	DBS	66232	DBS	66513	FLR	66586	EXP
66107	DBS	66170	DBS	66233	DBS	66514	FLR	66587	FLR
66108	DBS	66171	DBS	66234	DBS	66515	FLR	66588	FLR
66109	DBS	66172	DBS	66235	DBS	66516	FLR	66589	FLR
66110	DBS	66173	DBS	66236	DBS	66517	FLR	66590	FLR
66111	DBS	66174	DBS	66237	DBS	66518	FLR	66591	FLR
66112	DBS	66175	DBS	66238	DBS	66519	FLR	66592	FLR
66113	DBS	66176	DBS	66239	DBS	66520	FLR	66593	FLR
66114	DBS	66177	DBS	66240	DBS	66522	FLR	66594	FLR
66115	DBS	66178	DBS	66241	DBS	66523	FLR	66595	FLR
66116	DBS	66179	DBS	66242	DBS	66524	FLR	66596	FLR
66117	DBS	66180	DBS	66243	DBS	66525	FLR	66597	FLR
66118	DBS	66181	DBS	66244	DBS	66526	FLR	66598	FLR
66119	DBS	66182	DBS	66245	DBS	66527	FLR	66599	FLR
66120	DBS	66183	DBS	66246	DBS	66528	FLR		
66121	DBS	66184	DBS	66247	DBS	66529	FLR	66601	FLR
66122	DBS	66185	DBS	66248	DBS	66530	FLR	66602	FLR
66123	DBS	66186	DBS	66249	DBS	66531	FLR	66603	FLR
66124	DBS	66187	DBS	66250	DBS	66532	FLR	66604	FLR
66125	DBS	66188	DBS			66533	FLR	66605	FLR
66126	DBS	66189	DBS	66301	DRS	66534	FLR	66606	FLR
66127	DBS	66190	DBS	66302	DRS	66535	FLR	66607	FLR
66128	DBS	66191	DBS	66303	DRS	66536	FLR	66608	EXP
66129	DBS	66192	DBS	66304	DRS	66537	FLR	66609	EXP
66130	DBS	66193	DBS	66305	DRS	66538	FLR	66610	EXP
66131	DBS	66194	DBS			66539	FLR	66611	EXP
66132	DBS	66195	DBS	66411	EXP	66540	FLR	66612	EXP

66613	FLR	66751	GBR	67027	DBS	73003	PRE	77024	ECR
66614	FLR	66752	GBR	67028	DBS	73101	RVE	77025	ECR
66615	FLR	66753	GBR	67029	DBS	73103	PRE	77026	ECR
66616	FLR	66754	GBR	67030	DBS	73107	GBR	77027	ECR
66617	FLR	66755	GBR			73109	201	77028	ECR
66618	FLR	66756	GBR	68001	DRS	73110	PRE	77029	ECR
66619	FLR	66757	GBR	68002	DRS	73114	PRE	77030	ECR
66620	FLR	66758	GBR	68003	DRS	73117	PRE	77031	ECR
66621	FLR	66759	GBR	68004	DRS	73118	TTS	77032	ECR
66622	FLR	66760	GBR	68005	DRS	73119	GBR	77033	ECR
66623	FLR	66761	GBR	68006	DRS	73128	PRE	77034	ECR
66624	EXP	66762	GBR	68007	DRS	73129	PRE	77035	ECR
66625	EXP	66763	GBR	68008	DRS	73130	PRE	77036	ECR
		66764	GBR	68009	DRS	73133	TTS	77037	ECR
66701	GBR	66765	GBR	68010	CRW	73134	PRE	77038	ECR
66702	GBR	66766	GBR	68011	CRW	73136	GBR	77039	ECR
66703	GBR	66767	GBR	68012	CRW	73138	NRL	77040	ECR
66704	GBR	66768	GBR	68013	CRW	73139	RVE	77041	ECR
66705	GBR	66769	GBR	68014	CRW	73140	PRE	77042	ECR
66706	GBR	66770	GBR	68015	CRW	73141	GBR	77043	ECR
66707	GBR	66771	GBR	68016	DRS			77044	ECR
66708	GBR	66772	GBR	68017	DRS	73201	GBR	77045	ECR
66709	GBR			68018	DRS	73202	TSG	77046	ECR
66710	GBR	66846	COL	68019	DRS	73207	GBR	77047	ECR
66711	GBR	66847	COL	68020	DRS	73210	PRE	77048	ECR
66712	GBR	66848	COL	68021	DRS	73212	GBR	77049	ECR
66713	GBR	66849	COL	68022	DRS	73213	GBR	77050	ECR
66714	GBR	66850	COL	68023	DRS	73235	SWT	77051	ECR
66715	GBR			68024	DRS			77052	ECR
66716	GBR	66951	FLR	68025	DRS	73951	RVE	77053	ECR
66717	GBR	66952	FLR			73952	RVE	77054	ECR
66718	GBR	66953	FLR	70001	FLR			77055	ECR
66719	GBR	66954	FLR	70002	FLR	73961	GBR	77056	ECR
66720	GBR	66955	FLR	70003	FLR	73962	GBR	77057	ECR
66721	GBR	66956	FLR	70004	FLR	73963	GBR	77058	ECR
66722	GBR	66957	FLR	70005	FLR	73964	GBR	77059	ECR
66723	GBR			70006	FLR	73965	GBR	77060	ECR
66724	GBR	67001	ATW	70007	FLR	73966	GBR		
66725	GBR	67002	ATW	70008	FLR	73967	GBR	81002	PRE
66726	GBR	67003	ATW	70009	FLR				
66727	GBR	67004	DBS	70010	FLR	77001	ECR	82008	PRE
66728	GBR	67005	DBS	70011	FLR	77002	ECR		
66729	GBR	67006	DBS	70013	FLR	77003	ECR	83012	PRE
66730	GBR	67007	DBS	70014	FLR	77004	ECR		
66731	GBR	67008	DBS	70015	FLR	77005	ECR	84001	PRE
66732	GBR	67009	DBS	70016	FLR	77006	ECR		
66733	GBR	67010	DBS	70017	FLR	77007	ECR	85101	PRE
66735	GBR	67011	DBS	70018	FLR	77008	ECR		
66736	GBR	67012	DBS	70019	FLR	77009	ECR	86101	ETL
66737	GBR	67013	DBS	70020	FLR	77010	ECR	86213	PRE
66738	GBR	67014	DBS			77011	ECR	86215	EXP
66739	GBR	67015	DBS	70801	COL	77012	ECR	86217	EXP
66740	GBR	67016	DBS	70802	COL	77013	ECR	86218	EXP
66741	GBR	67017	DBS	70803	COL	77014	ECR	86226	EPX
66742	GBR	67018	DBS	70804	COL	77015	ECR	86228	EXP
66743	GBR	67019	DBS	70805	COL	77016	ECR	86229	EPX
66744	GBR	67020	DBS	70806	COL	77017	ECR	86231	EPX
66745	GBR	67021	DBS	70807	COL	77018	ECR	86232	EPX
66746	GBR	67022	DBS	70808	COL	77019	ECR	86233	EXP
66747	GBR	67023	DBS	70809	COL	77020	ECR	86234	EPX
66748	GBR	67024	DBS	70810	COL	77021	ECR	86235	EPX
66749	GBR	67025	DBS			77022	ECR	86242	EXP
66750	GBR	67026	DBS	73001	PRE	77023	ECR	86246	EPX

Data Tables

No.	Code	No.	Code	No.	Code	No.	Code	No.	Code
86247	EPX	90001	GAR	91113	ICE	92044	GBR	51073	PRE
86248	EXP	90002	GAR	91114	ICE	92045	GBR	51074	PRE
86250	EXP	90003	GAR	91115	ICE	92046	GBR	51104	PRE
86251	EPX	90004	GAR	91116	ICE			51131	PRE
86259	PRE	90005	GAR	91117	ICE	97301	NRL	51138	PRE
86401	ETL	90006	GAR	91118	ICE	97302	NRL	51151	PRE
86424	EXP	90007	GAR	91119	ICE	97303	NRL	51187	PRE
86501	FLR	90008	GAR	91120	ICE	97304	NRL	51188	PRE
86604	FLR	90009	GAR	91121	ICE			51189	PRE
86605	FLR	90010	GAR	91122	ICE	97650	PRE	51192	PRE
86607	FLR	90011	GAR	91124	ICE	97651	PRE	51205	PRE
86609	FLR	90012	GAR	91125	ICE	97654	PRE	51210	PRE
86610	FLR	90013	GAR	91126	ICE			51226	PRE
86612	FLR	90014	GAR	91127	ICE	323 539-7	AFG	51228	PRE
86613	FLR	90015	GAR	91128	ICE	323 674-2	AFG	51247	PRE
86614	FLR	90016	FLR	91129	ICE			51321	PRE
86622	FLR	90017	DBS	91130	ICE	DH50-1	GBR	51339	PRE
86627	FLR	90018	DBS	91131	ICE	DH50-2	GBR	51342	PRE
86628	FLR	90019	DBS	91132	ICE			51346	PRE
86632	FLR	90020	DBS			8.701	GBR	51347	PRE
86637	FLR	90021	DBS	92001	EXP	8.702	GBR	51351	PRE
86638	FLR	90022	DBS	92002	DBS	8.703	GBR	51353	PRE
86639	FLR	90023	DBS	92003	DBS	8.704	GBR	51356	PRE
86701	ETL	90024	DBS	92004	DBS	8.708	GBR	51359	PRE
86702	ETL	90025	DBS	92005	DBS	8.711	GBR	51360	PRE
		90026	DBS	92006	GBR	8.712	GBR	51363	PRE
87001	PRE	90027	DBS	92007	DBS	8.716	GBR	51365	PRE
87002	ETL	90028	DBS	92008	DBS	8.717	GBR	51367	PRE
87003	EXP	90029	DBS	92009	DBS	8.718	GBR	51372	PRE
87004	EXP	90030	DBS	92010	GRB	8.719	GBR	51381	PRE
87006	EXP	90031	DBS	92011	DBS	8.720	GBR	51382	PRE
87007	EXP	90032	DBS	92012	EXP			51384	PRE
87008	EXP	90033	DBS	92013	DBS	**Diesel Multiple**		51388	PRE
87009	EXP	90034	DBS	92014	GBR	**Units**		51392	PRE
87010	EXP	90035	DBS	92015	DBS	APT-E	PRE	51395	PRE
87012	EXP	90036	DBS	92016	DBS	LEV1	PRE	51397	PRE
87013	EXP	90037	DBS	92017	DBS			51398	PRE
87014	EXP	90038	DBS	92018	GBR	RB004	PRE	51400	PRE
87017	EXP	90039	DBS	92019	DBS			51401	PRE
87019	EXP	90040	DBS	92020	GBR	50015	PRE	51402	PRE
87020	EXP	90041	FLR	92021	GBR	50019	PRE	51405	PRE
87022	EXP	90042	FLR	92022	DBS	50222	PRE	51407	PRE
87023	EXP	90043	FLR	92023	GBR	50256	PRE	51427	PRE
87025	EXP	90044	FLR	92024	DBS	50338	PRE	51432	PRE
87026	EXP	90045	FLR	92025	EXP	50416	PRE	51434	PRE
87028	EXP	90046	FLR	92026	DBS	50447	PRE	51485	PRE
87029	EXP	90047	FLR	92027	EXP	50454	PRE	51498	PRE
87033	EXP	90048	FLR	92028	GBR	50455	PRE	51499	PRE
87034	EXP	90049	FLR	92029	DBS	50479	PRE	51503	PRE
87035	PRE	90050	DBS	92030	DBS	50494	PRE	51505	PRE
				92031	DBS	50517	PRE	51511	PRE
88001	DRS	91101	ICE	92032	GBR	50528	PRE	51512	PRE
88002	DRS	91102	ICE	92033	GBR	50531	PRE	51513	PRE
88003	DRS	91103	ICE	92034	EXP	50547	PRE	51562	PRE
88004	DRS	91104	ICE	92035	DBS	50556	PRE	51565	PRE
88005	DRS	91105	ICE	92036	DBS	50599	PRE	51566	PRE
88006	DRS	91106	ICE	92037	DBS	50619	PRE	51567	PRE
88007	DRS	91107	ICE	92038	GBR	50632	PRE	51568	PRE
88008	DRS	91108	ICE	92039	DBS	50929	PRE	51571	PRE
88009	DRS	91109	ICE	92040	GBR	50980	PRE	51572	PRE
88010	DRS	91110	ICE	92041	DBS			51604	PRE
		91111	ICE	92042	DBS	51017	PRE	51616	PRE
89001	PRE	91112	ICE	92043	GBR	51043	PRE	51618	PRE

No.	Code	No.	Code	No.	Code	No.	Code	No.	Code
51622	PRE	54408	PRE	59514	PRE	121032	CRW	142052	NOR
51655	PRE	54490	PRE	59515	PRE	121034	CRW	142053	NOR
51663	PRE	54504	PRE	59516	PRE			142054	NOR
51669	PRE	55000	PRE	59517	PRE	139001	LMI	142055	NOR
51677	PRE	55001	PRE	59520	PRE	139002	LMI	142056	NOR
51803	PRE	55003	PRE	59521	PRE			142057	NOR
51813	PRE	55005	PRE	59522	PRE	140001	PRE	142058	NOR
51842	PRE	55006	PRE	59539	PRE			142060	NOR
51859	PRE	55009	PRE	59575	PRE	141103	PRE	142061	NOR
51880	PRE	55012	PRE	59603	PRE	141108	PRE	142062	NOR
51886	PRE	55020	CRW	59609	PRE	141110	PRE	142063	NOR
51887	PRE	55023	PRE	59659	PRE	141113	PRE	142064	NOR
51899	PRE	55028	PRE	59664	PRE			142065	NOR
51907	PRE	55029	PRE	59678	PRE	142001	NOR	142066	NOR
51909	PRE	55032	CRW	59701	PRE	142002	ATW	142067	NOR
51914	PRE	55033	PRE	59719	PRE	142003	NOR	142068	NOR
51919	PRE	55034	CRW	59740	PRE	142004	NOR	142069	ATW
51922	PRE	55966	PRE	59761	PRE	142005	NOR	142070	NOR
51933	PRE	55976	PRE	59791	PRE	142006	ATW	142071	NOR
51941	PRE					142007	NOR	142072	ATW
51942	PRE	56006	PRE	60000	HDL	142009	NOR	142073	ATW
51947	PRE	56015	PRE	60019	HDL	142010	ATW	142074	ATW
51950	PRE	56121	PRE	60116	HDL	142011	NOR	142075	ATW
51973	PRE	56171	PRE	60117	PRE	142012	NOR	142076	ATW
51990	PRE	56182	PRE	60118	HDL	142013	NOR	142077	ATW
		56208	PRE	60127	PRE	142014	NOR	142078	NOR
52005	PRE	56224	PRE	60130	PRE	142015	NOR	142079	NOR
52006	PRE	56271	PRE	60138	PRE	142016	NOR	142080	ATW
52008	PRE	56287	PRE	60142	PRE	142017	NOR	142081	ATW
52025	PRE	56301	PRE	60145	PRE	142018	NOR	142082	ATW
52030	PRE	56343	PRE	60149	PRE	142019	NOR	142083	ATW
52044	PRE	56352	PRE	60154	PRE	142020	NOR	142084	NOR
52048	PRE	56358	PRE	60501	HDL	142021	NOR	142085	ATW
52053	PRE	56456	PRE	60528	HDL	142022	NOR	142086	NOR
52054	PRE	56484	PRE	60529	HDL	142023	NOR	142087	NOR
52062	PRE	56491	PRE	60616	PRE	142024	NOR	142088	NOR
52064	PRE	56492	PRE	60750	PRE	142025	NOR	142089	NOR
52071	PRE	56495	PRE	60800	PRE	142026	NOR	142090	NOR
52077	PRE			60822	PRE	142027	NOR	142091	NOR
		59003	PRE	60828	PRE	142028	NOR	142092	NOR
53160	PRE	59004	PRE	60901	PRE	142029	NOR	142093	NOR
53164	PRE	59117	PRE	60904	PRE	142030	NOR	142094	NOR
53170	PRE	59137	PRE	60916	PRE	142031	NOR	142095	NOR
53193	PRE	59228	PRE	69337	HDL	142032	NOR	142096	NOR
53203	PRE	59245	PRE			142033	NOR		
53204	PRE	59250	PRE	70262	HDL	142034	NOR	143601	ATW
53253	PRE	59276	PRE			142035	NOR	143602	ATW
53266	PRE	59387	PRE	70549	PRE	142036	NOR	143603	FGW
53321	PRE	59389	PRE			142037	NOR	143604	ATW
53628	PRE	59404	PRE	79018	PRE	142038	NOR	143605	ATW
53645	PRE	59444	PRE	79443	PRE	142039	NOR	143606	ATW
53746	PRE	59486	PRE	79612	PRE	142040	NOR	143607	ATW
53926	PRE	59488	PRE	79900	PRE	142041	NOR	143608	ATW
53971	PRE	59492	PRE	79960	PRE	142042	NOR	143609	ATW
		59494	PRE	79962	PRE	142043	NOR	143610	ATW
54055	PRE	59500	PRE	79963	PRE	142044	NOR	143611	FGW
54057	PRE	59503	PRE	79964	PRE	142045	NOR	143612	FGW
54062	PRE	59506	PRE	79976	PRE	142046	NOR	143614	ATW
54223	PRE	59507	PRE	79978	PRE	142047	NOR	143616	ATW
54270	PRE	59508	PRE			142048	NOR	143617	FGW
54279	PRE	59509	PRE	121019	PRE	142049	NOR	143618	FGW
54289	PRE	59510	PRE	121020	CRW	142050	NOR	143619	FGW
54365	PRE	59513	PRE	121024	PRE	142051	NOR	143620	FGW

Data Tables

143621	FGW	150133	NOR	150247	FGW	153321	EMT	156405	EMT
143622	ATW	150134	NOR	150248	FGW	153322	GAR	156406	EMT
143623	ATW	150135	NOR	150249	FGW	153323	ATW	156407	GAR
143624	ATW	150136	NOR	150250	ATW	153324	NOR	156408	EMT
143625	ATW	150137	NOR	150251	ATW	153325	FGW	156409	GAR
		150138	NOR	150252	ATW	153326	EMT	156410	EMT
144001	NOR	150139	NOR	150253	ATW	153327	ATW	156411	EMT
144002	NOR	150140	NOR	150254	ATW	153328	NOR	156412	GAR
144003	NOR	150141	NOR	150255	ATW	153329	FGW	156413	EMT
144004	NOR	150142	NOR	150256	ATW	153330	NOR	156414	EMT
144005	NOR	150143	NOR	150257	ATW	153331	NOR	156415	EMT
144006	NOR	150144	NOR	150258	ATW	153332	NOR	156416	GAR
144007	NOR	150145	NOR	150259	ATW	153333	FGW	156417	GAR
144008	NOR	150146	NOR	150260	ATW	153334	LMI	156418	GAR
144009	NOR	150147	NOR	150261	FGW	153335	GAR	156419	GAR
144010	NOR	150148	NOR	150262	ATW	153351	NOR	156420	NOR
144011	NOR	150149	NOR	150263	FGW	153352	NOR	156421	NOR
144012	NOR	150150	NOR	150264	ATW	153353	ATW	156422	GAR
144013	NOR			150265	FGW	153354	LMI	156423	NOR
144014	NOR	150201	NOR	150266	FGW	153355	EMT	156424	NOR
144015	NOR	150202	FGW	150267	ATW	153356	LMI	156425	NOR
144016	NOR	150203	NOR	150268	NOR	153357	EMT	156426	NOR
144017	NOR	150204	NOR	150269	NOR	153358	NOR	156427	NOR
144018	NOR	150205	NOR	150270	NOR	153359	NOR	156428	NOR
144019	NOR	150206	NOR	150271	NOR	153360	NOR	156429	NOR
144020	NOR	150207	NOR	150272	NOR	153361	FGW	156430	FGW
144021	NOR	150208	ATW	150273	NOR	153362	ATW	156431	FSR
144022	NOR	150210	NOR	150274	NOR	153363	NOR	156432	FSR
144023	NOR	150211	NOR	150275	NOR	153364	LMI	156433	FSR
		150213	ATW	150276	NOR	153365	LMI	156434	FSR
150001	FGW	150214	NOR	150277	NOR	153366	LMI	156435	FSR
150002	FGW	150215	NOR	150278	ATW	153367	ATW	156436	FSR
		150216	FGW	150279	ATW	153368	FGW	156437	FSR
150101	FGW	150217	ATW	150280	ATW	153369	FGW	156438	NOR
150102	FGW	150218	NOR	150281	ATW	153370	FGW	156439	FSR
150103	NOR	150219	FGW	150282	ATW	153371	LMI	156440	NOR
150104	FGW	150220	NOR	150283	ATW	153372	FGW	156441	NOR
150105	LMI	150221	FGW	150284	ATW	153373	FGW	156442	FSR
150106	FGW	150222	NOR	150285	ATW	153374	EMT	156443	NOR
150107	LMI	150223	NOR			153375	LMI	156444	NOR
150108	FGW	150224	NOR	150925	FGW	153376	EMT	156445	FSR
150109	LMI	150225	NOR	150926	FGW	153377	FGW	156446	FSR
150110	NOR	150226	NOR			153378	NOR	156447	FSR
150111	NOR	150227	ATW	153301	NOR	153379	EMT	156448	NOR
150112	NOR	150228	NOR	153302	EMT	153380	FGW	156449	FSR
150113	NOR	150229	ATW	153303	ATW	153381	EMT	156450	NOR
150114	NOR	150230	ATW	153304	NOR	153382	FGW	156451	NOR
150115	NOR	150231	ATW	153305	FGW	153383	EMT	156452	NOR
150116	NOR	150232	FGW	153306	GAR	153384	EMT	156453	FSR
150117	NOR	150233	FGW	153307	NOR	153385	EMT	156454	NOR
150118	NOR	150234	FGW	153308	EMT			156455	NOR
150119	NOR	150235	ATW	153309	GAR	155341	NOR	156456	FSR
150120	FGW	150236	ATW	153310	EMT	155342	NOR	156457	FSR
150121	FGW	150237	ATW	153311	EMT	155343	NOR	156458	FSR
150122	FGW	150238	FGW	153312	ATW	155344	NOR	156459	NOR
150123	FGW	150239	FGW	153313	EMT	155345	NOR	156460	NOR
150124	FGW	150240	ATW	153314	GAR	155346	NOR	156461	NOR
150127	FGW	150241	ATW	153315	NOR	155347	NOR	156462	FSR
150128	FGW	150242	ATW	153316	NOR			156463	NOR
150129	FGW	150243	FGW	153317	NOR	156401	EMT	156464	NOR
150130	FGW	150244	FGW	153318	FGW	156402	GAR	156465	FSR
150131	FGW	150245	ATW	153319	EMT	156403	EMT	156466	NOR
150132	NOR	150246	FGW	153320	ATW	156404	EMT	156467	FSR

Data Tables

Number	Code	Number	Code	Number	Code	Number	Code	Number	Code
156468	NOR	158716	FSR	158813	EMT	158884	SWT	165002	CRW
156469	NOR	158717	FSR	158815	NOR	158885	SWT	165003	CRW
156470	EMT	158718	FSR	158816	NOR	158886	SWT	165004	CRW
156471	NOR	158719	FSR	158817	NOR	158887	SWT	165005	CRW
156472	NOR	158720	FSR	158818	ATW	158888	SWT	165006	CRW
156473	EMT	158721	FSR	158819	ATW	158889	SWT	165007	CRW
156474	FSR	158722	FSR	158820	ATW	158890	SWT	165008	CRW
156475	NOR	158723	FSR	158821	ATW	158901	NOR	165009	CRW
156476	FSR	158724	FSR	158822	ATW	158902	NOR	165010	CRW
156477	FSR	158725	FSR	158823	ATW	158903	NOR	165011	CRW
156478	FSR	158726	FSR	158824	ATW	158904	NOR	165012	CRW
156479	NOR	158727	FSR	158825	ATW	158905	NOR	165013	CRW
156480	NOR	158728	FSR	158826	ATW	158906	NOR	165014	CRW
156481	NOR	158729	FSR	158827	ATW	158907	NOR	165015	CRW
156482	NOR	158730	FSR	158828	ATW	158908	NOR	165016	CRW
156483	NOR	158731	FSR	158829	ATW	158909	NOR	165017	CRW
156484	NOR	158732	FSR	158830	ATW	158910	NOR	165018	CRW
156485	FSR	158733	FSR	158831	ATW	158950	FGW	165019	CRW
156486	NOR	158734	FSR	158832	ATW	158951	FGW	165020	CRW
156487	NOR	158735	FSR	158833	ATW	158952	FGW	165021	CRW
156488	NOR	158736	FSR	158834	ATW	158953	FGW	165022	CRW
156489	NOR	158737	FSR	158835	ATW	158954	FGW	165023	CRW
156490	NOR	158738	FSR	158836	ATW	158955	FGW	165024	CRW
156491	NOR	158739	FSR	158837	ATW	158956	FGW	165025	CRW
156492	FSR	158740	FSR	158838	ATW	158957	FGW	165026	CRW
156493	FSR	158741	FSR	158839	ATW	158958	FGW	165027	CRW
156494	FSR	158752	NOR	158840	ATW	158959	FGW	165028	CRW
156495	FSR	158753	NOR	158841	ATW	158960	FGW	165029	CRW
156496	FSR	158754	NOR	158842	NOR	158961	FGW	165030	CRW
156497	EMT	158755	NOR	158843	NOR			165031	CRW
156498	EMT	158756	NOR	158844	NOR	159001	SWT	165032	CRW
156499	FSR	158757	NOR	158845	NOR	159002	SWT	165033	CRW
156500	FSR	158758	NOR	158846	EMT	159003	SWT	165034	CRW
156501	FSR	158759	NOR	158847	EMT	159004	SWT	165035	CRW
156502	FSR	158763	FGW	158848	NOR	159005	SWT	165036	CRW
156503	FSR	158766	FGW	158849	NOR	159006	SWT	165037	CRW
156504	FSR	158770	EMT	158850	NOR	159007	SWT	165038	CRW
156505	FSR	158773	EMT	158851	NOR	159008	SWT	165039	CRW
156506	FSR	158774	EMT	158852	EMT	159009	SWT		
156507	FSR	158777	EMT	158853	NOR	159010	SWT	165101	FGW
156508	FSR	158780	EMT	158854	EMT	159011	SWT	165102	FGW
156509	FSR	158782	FSR	158855	NOR	159012	SWT	165103	FGW
156510	FSR	158783	EMT	158856	EMT	159013	SWT	165104	FGW
156511	FSR	158784	NOR	158857	EMT	159014	SWT	165105	FGW
156512	FSR	158785	EMT	158858	EMT	159015	SWT	165106	FGW
156513	FSR	158786	FSR	158859	NOR	159016	SWT	165107	FGW
156514	FSR	158787	NOR	158860	NOR	159017	SWT	165108	FGW
		158788	EMT	158861	NOR	159018	SWT	165109	FGW
158701	FSR	158789	FSR	158862	EMT	159019	SWT	165110	FGW
158702	FSR	158790	NOR	158863	EMT	159020	SWT	165111	FGW
158703	FSR	158791	NOR	158864	EMT	159021	SWT	165112	FGW
158704	FSR	158792	NOR	158865	EMT	159022	SWT	165113	FGW
158705	FSR	158793	NOR	158866	EMT			165114	FGW
158706	FSR	158794	NOR	158867	FSR	159101	SWT	165116	FGW
158707	FSR	158795	NOR	158868	FSR	159102	SWT	165117	FGW
158708	FSR	158796	NOR	158869	FSR	159103	SWT	165118	FGW
158709	FSR	158797	NOR	158870	FSR	159104	SWT	165119	FGW
158710	FSR	158798	FGW	158871	FSR	159105	SWT	165120	FGW
158711	FSR	158799	EMT	158872	NOR	159106	SWT	165121	FGW
158712	FSR			158880	SWT	159107	SWT	165122	FGW
158713	FSR	158806	EMT	158881	SWT	159108	SWT	165123	FGW
158714	FSR	158810	EMT	158882	SWT			165124	FGW
158715	FSR	158812	EMT	158883	SWT	165001	CRW	165125	FGW

Data Tables

Number	Code	Number	Code	Number	Code	Number	Code	Number	Code
165126	FGW	170107	AXC	170426	FSR	171721	TSG	175004	ATW
165127	FGW	170108	AXC	170427	FSR	171722	TSG	175005	ATW
165128	FGW	170109	AXC	170428	FSR	171723	TSG	175006	ATW
165129	FGW	170110	AXC	170429	FSR	171724	TSG	175007	ATW
165130	FGW	170111	AXC	170430	FSR	171725	TSG	175008	ATW
165131	FGW	170112	AXC	170431	FSR	171726	TSG	175009	ATW
165132	FGW	170113	AXC	170432	FSR	171727	TSG	175010	ATW
165133	FGW	170114	AXC	170433	FSR	171728	TSG	175011	ATW
165134	FGW	170115	AXC	170434	FSR	171729	TSG		
165135	FGW	170116	AXC	170450	FSR	171730	TSG	175101	ATW
165136	FGW	170117	AXC	170451	FSR	171801	TSG	175102	ATW
165137	FGW	170201	GAR	170452	FSR	171802	TSG	175103	ATW
		170202	GAR	170453	FSR	171803	TSG	175104	ATW
166201	FGW	170203	GAR	170454	FSR	171804	TSG	175105	ATW
166202	FGW	170204	GAR	170455	FSR	171805	TSG	175106	ATW
166203	FGW	170205	GAR	170456	FSR	171806	TSG	175107	ATW
166204	FGW	170206	GAR	170457	FSR			175108	ATW
166205	FGW	170207	GAR	170458	FSR	172001	LOG	175109	ATW
166206	FGW	170208	GAR	170459	FSR	172002	LOG	175110	ATW
166207	FGW	170270	GAR	170460	FSR	172003	LOG	175111	ATW
166208	FGW	170271	GAR	170461	FSR	172004	LOG	175112	ATW
166209	FGW	170272	GAR	170470	FSR	172005	LOG	175113	ATW
166210	FGW	170273	GAR	170471	FSR	172006	LOG	175114	ATW
166211	FGW	170301	FTP	170472	FSR	172007	LOG	175115	ATW
166212	FGW	170302	FTP	170473	FSR	172008	LOG	175116	ATW
166213	FGW	170303	FTP	170474	FSR				
166214	FGW	170304	FTP	170475	FSR	172101	CRW	180101	GTL
166215	FGW	170305	FTP	170476	FSR	172102	CRW	180102	FGW
166216	FGW	170306	FTP	170477	FSR	172103	CRW	180103	FGW
166217	FGW	170307	FTP	170478	FSR	172104	CRW	180104	FGW
166218	FGW	170308	FTP					180105	GTL
166219	FGW	170309	FTP	170501	LMI	172211	LMI	180106	FGW
166220	FGW	170393	FSR	170502	LMI	172212	LMI	180107	GTL
166221	FGW	170394	FSR	170503	LMI	172213	LMI	180108	FGW
		170395	FSR	170504	LMI	172214	LMI	180109	FHT
168001	CRW	170396	FSR	170505	LMI	172215	LMI	180110	FHT
168002	CRW	170397	AXC	170506	LMI	172216	LMI	180111	FHT
168003	CRW	170398	AXC	170507	LMI	172217	LMI	180112	GTL
168004	CRW	170401	FSR	170508	LMI	172218	LMI	180113	FHT
168005	CRW	170402	FSR	170509	LMI	172219	LMI	180114	GTL
		170403	FSR	170510	LMI	172220	LMI		
168106	CRW	170404	FSR	170511	LMI	172221	LMI	185101	FTP
168107	CRW	170405	FSR	170512	LMI	172222	LMI	185102	FTP
168108	CRW	170406	FSR	170513	LMI			185103	FTP
168109	CRW	170407	FSR	170514	LMI	172331	LMI	185104	FTP
168110	CRW	170408	FSR	170515	LMI	172332	LMI	185105	FTP
168111	CRW	170409	FSR	170516	LMI	172333	LMI	185106	FTP
168112	CRW	170410	FSR	170517	LMI	172334	LMI	185107	FTP
168113	CRW	170411	FSR	170518	AXC	172335	LMI	185108	FTP
		170412	FSR	170519	AXC	172336	LMI	185109	FTP
168214	CRW	170413	FSR	170520	AXC	172337	LMI	185110	FTP
168215	CRW	170414	FSR	170521	AXC	172338	LMI	185111	FTP
168216	CRW	170415	FSR	170522	AXC	172339	LMI	185112	FTP
168217	CRW	170416	FSR	170523	AXC	172340	LMI	185113	FTP
168218	CRW	170417	FSR	170630	LMI	172341	LMI	185114	FTP
168219	CRW	170418	FSR	170631	LMI	172342	LMI	185115	FTP
		170419	FSR	170632	LMI	172343	LMI	185116	FTP
170101	AXC	170420	FSR	170633	LMI	172344	LMI	185117	FTP
170102	AXC	170421	FSR	170634	LMI	172345	LMI	185118	FTP
170103	AXC	170422	FSR	170635	LMI			185119	FTP
170104	AXC	170423	FSR	170636	AXC	175001	ATW	185120	FTP
170105	AXC	170424	FSR	170637	AXC	175002	ATW	185121	FTP
170106	AXC	170425	FSR	170638	AXC	175003	ATW	185122	FTP
				170639	AXC				

Data Tables

Number	Code	Number	Code	Number	Code	Number	Code	Number	Code
185123	FTP	220024	AXC	222007	EMT	61799	PRE	76812	PRE
185124	FTP	220025	AXC	222008	EMT	61804	PRE	76875	PRE
185125	FTP	220026	AXC	222009	EMT	61805	PRE		
185126	FTP	220027	AXC	222010	EMT			77172	PRE
185127	FTP	220028	AXC	222011	EMT	62364	PRE		
185128	FTP	220029	AXC	222012	EMT	62384	NRL	79998	PRE
185129	FTP	220030	AXC	222013	EMT	62378	PRE	79999	PRE
185130	FTP	220031	AXC	222014	EMT	62887	PRE		
185131	FTP	220032	AXC	222015	EMT	65302	PRE	303032	PRE
185132	FTP	220033	AXC	222016	EMT	65304	PRE		
185133	FTP	220034	AXC	222017	EMT	65451	PRE	306017	PRE
185134	FTP			222018	EMT				
185135	FTP	221101	VWC	222019	EMT	67300	PRE	309616	PRE
185136	FTP	221102	VWC	222020	EMT			309624	PRE
185137	FTP	221103	VWC	222021	EMT	68001	PRE		
185138	FTP	221104	VWC	222022	EMT	68002	PRE	313018	TSG
185139	FTP	221105	VWC	222023	EMT	68003	PRE	313024	TSG
185140	FTP	221106	VWC			68004	PRE	313025	TSG
185141	FTP	221107	VWC	222101	EMT	68005	PRE	313026	TSG
185142	FTP	221108	VWC	222102	EMT	68008	PRE	313027	TSG
185143	FTP	221109	VWC	222103	EMT	68009	PRE	313028	TSG
185144	FTP	221110	VWC	222104	EMT	68500	PRE	313029	TSG
185145	FTP	221111	VWC			68506	PRE	313030	TSG
185146	FTP	221112	VWC	**Electric Multiple**				313031	TSG
185147	FTP	221113	VWC	**Units**		69304	PRE	313032	TSG
185148	FTP	221114	VWC	85	PRE	69310	PRE	313033	TSG
185149	FTP	221115	VWC	87	PRE	69318	PRE	313035	TSG
185150	FTP	221116	VWC	91	PRE	69332	PRE	313036	TSG
185151	FTP	221117	VWC	2090	PRE	69333	PRE	313037	TSG
		221118	VWC	4732	PRE	69337	PRE	313038	TSG
202202	PRE	221119	AXC	5176	PRE	69339	PRE	313039	TSG
		221120	AXC	5759	PRE			313040	TSG
205009	PRE	221121	AXC	5791	PRE	70229	PRE	313041	TSG
205025	PRE	221122	AXC	5793	PRE	70257	PRE	313042	TSG
205028	PRE	221123	AXC	6307	PRE	70273	PRE	313043	TSG
205032	PRE	221124	AXC	7105	PRE	70284	PRE	313044	TSG
205033	PRE	221125	AXC	8143	PRE	70292	PRE	313045	TSG
205101	PRE	221126	AXC			70296	PRE	313046	TSG
205205	PRE	221127	AXC	10096	PRE	70354	PRE	313047	TSG
		221128	AXC	11161	PRE	70527	PRE	313048	TSG
220001	AXC	221129	AXC	11179	PRE	70531	PRE	313049	TSG
220002	AXC	221130	AXC	11201	PRE	70539	PRE	313050	TSG
220003	AXC	221131	AXC	11825	PRE	70576	PRE	313051	TSG
220004	AXC	221132	AXC			70607	PRE	313052	TSG
220005	AXC	221133	AXC	13004	PRE			313053	TSG
220006	AXC	221134	AXC			72501	PRE	313054	TSG
220007	AXC	221135	AXC	15345	PRE	72617	PRE	313055	TSG
220008	AXC	221136	AXC					313056	TSG
220009	AXC	221137	AXC	28249	PRE	75023	PRE	313057	TSG
220010	AXC	221138	AXC	28361	PRE	75033	PRE	313058	TSG
220011	AXC	221139	AXC	28690	PRE	75186	PRE	313059	TSG
220012	AXC	221140	AXC	29298	PRE	75250	PRE	313060	TSG
220013	AXC	221141	AXC	29666	PRE	75395	PRE	313061	TSG
220014	AXC	221142	VWC	29670	PRE	75407	PRE	313062	TSG
220015	AXC	221143	VWC	29720	PRE	75881	PRE	313063	TSG
220016	AXC	221144	VWC	29896	PRE			313064	TSG
220017	AXC					76398	PRE		
220018	AXC	222001	EMT	61183	PRE			313121	NRL
220019	AXC	222002	EMT	61275	PRE	76726	PRE	313122	TSG
220020	AXC	222003	EMT	61287	PRE	76740	PRE	313123	TSG
220021	AXC	222004	EMT	61742	PRE	76746	PRE	313134	TSG
220022	AXC	222005	EMT	61743	PRE	76797	PRE		
220023	AXC	222006	EMT	61798	PRE	76811	PRE	313201	TSG

Data Tables

Number	Code
313202	TSG
313203	TSG
313204	TSG
313205	TSG
313206	TSG
313207	TSG
313208	TSG
313209	TSG
313210	TSG
313211	TSG
313212	TSG
313213	TSG
313214	TSG
313215	TSG
313216	TSG
313217	TSG
313219	TSG
313220	TSG
314201	FSR
314202	FSR
314203	FSR
314204	FSR
314205	FSR
314206	FSR
314207	FSR
314208	FSR
314209	FSR
314210	FSR
314211	FSR
314212	FSR
314213	FSR
314214	FSR
314215	FSR
314216	FSR
315801	GAR
315802	GAR
315803	GAR
315804	GAR
315805	GAR
315806	GAR
315807	GAR
315808	GAR
315809	GAR
315810	GAR
315811	GAR
315812	GAR
315813	GAR
315814	GAR
315815	GAR
315816	GAR
315817	GAR
315818	GAR
315819	GAR
315820	GAR
315821	GAR
315822	GAR
315823	GAR
315824	GAR
315825	GAR
315826	GAR
315827	GAR
315828	GAR
315829	GAR
315830	GAR
315831	GAR
315832	GAR
315833	GAR
315834	GAR
315835	GAR
315836	GAR
315837	GAR
315838	GAR
315839	GAR
315840	GAR
315841	GAR
315842	GAR
315843	GAR
315844	GAR
315845	GAR
315846	GAR
315847	GAR
315848	GAR
315849	GAR
315850	GAR
315851	GAR
315852	GAR
315853	GAR
315854	GAR
315855	GAR
315856	GAR
315857	GAR
315858	GAR
315859	GAR
315860	GAR
315861	GAR
317337	TSG
317338	TSG
317339	TSG
317340	TSG
317341	TSG
317342	TSG
317343	TSG
317344	TSG
317345	TSG
317346	TSG
317347	TSG
317348	TSG
317501	GAR
317502	GAR
317503	GAR
317504	GAR
317505	GAR
317506	GAR
317507	GAR
317508	GAR
317509	GAR
317510	GAR
317511	GAR
317512	GAR
317513	GAR
317514	GAR
317515	GAR
317649	GAR
317650	GAR
317651	GAR
317652	GAR
317653	GAR
317654	GAR
317655	GAR
317656	GAR
317657	GAR
317658	GAR
317659	GAR
317660	GAR
317661	GAR
317662	GAR
317663	GAR
317664	GAR
317665	GAR
317666	GAR
317667	GAR
317668	GAR
317669	GAR
317670	GAR
317671	GAR
317672	GAR
317708	GAR
317709	OLS
317710	OLS
317714	OLS
317719	OLS
317722	GAR
317723	OLS
317729	GAR
317732	OLS
317881	GAR
317882	GAR
317883	GAR
317884	GAR
317885	GAR
317886	GAR
317887	GAR
317888	GAR
317889	GAR
317890	GAR
317891	GAR
317892	GAR
318250	FSR
318251	FSR
318252	FSR
318253	FSR
318254	FSR
318255	FSR
318256	FSR
318257	FSR
318258	FSR
318259	FSR
318260	FSR
318261	FSR
318262	FSR
318263	FSR
318264	FSR
318265	FSR
318266	FSR
318267	FSR
318268	FSR
318269	FSR
318270	FSR
319001	TSG
319002	TSG
319003	TSG
319004	TSG
319005	TSG
319006	TSG
319007	TSG
319008	TSG
319009	TSG
319010	TSG
319011	TSG
319012	TSG
319013	TSG
319214	TSG
319215	TSG
319216	TSG
319217	TSG
319218	TSG
319219	TSG
319220	TSG
319361	NOR
319362	NOR
319363	NOR
319364	NOR
319365	NOR
319366	TSG
319367	TSG
319368	TSG
319369	TSG
319370	TSG
319371	TSG
319372	TSG
319373	TSG
319374	TSG
319375	TSG
319376	TSG
319377	TSG
319378	TSG
319379	TSG
319380	NOR
319381	TSG
319382	TSG
319383	TSG
319384	TSG
319385	TSG
319386	TSG
319421	TSG
319422	TSG
319423	TSG
319424	TSG
319425	TSG
319426	TSG
319427	TSG
319428	TSG
319429	TSG
319430	TSG
319431	TSG
319432	TSG
319433	TSG
319434	TSG
319435	TSG
319436	TSG
319437	TSG
319438	TSG
319439	TSG
319440	TSG
319441	TSG
319442	TSG
319443	TSG
319444	TSG
319445	TSG
319446	TSG
319447	TSG
319448	TSG
319449	TSG
319450	TSG
319451	TSG
319452	TSG
319453	TSG
319454	TSG
319455	TSG
319456	TSG
319457	TSG
319458	TSG
319459	TSG
319460	TSG
320301	FSR
320302	FSR
320303	FSR
320304	FSR
320305	FSR
320306	FSR
320307	FSR
320308	FSR
320309	FSR
320310	FSR
320311	FSR
320312	FSR
320313	FSR
320314	FSR
320315	FSR
320316	FSR
320317	FSR
320318	FSR
320319	FSR
320320	FSR
320321	FSR
320322	FSR
321301	GAR
321302	GAR
321303	GAR
321304	GAR
321305	GAR
321306	GAR

Data Tables

❏ 321307	GAR	❏ 321403	TSG	❏ 323207	LMI	❏ 332010	HEX	❏ 350101	LMI
❏ 321308	GAR	❏ 321404	TSG	❏ 323208	LMI	❏ 332011	HEX	❏ 350102	LMI
❏ 321309	GAR	❏ 321405	TSG	❏ 323209	LMI	❏ 332012	HEX	❏ 350103	LMI
❏ 321310	GAR	❏ 321406	TSG	❏ 323210	LMI	❏ 332013	HEX	❏ 350104	LMI
❏ 321311	GAR	❏ 321407	TSG	❏ 323211	LMI	❏ 332014	HEX	❏ 350105	LMI
❏ 321312	GAR	❏ 321408	TSG	❏ 323212	LMI			❏ 350106	LMI
❏ 321313	GAR	❏ 321409	TSG	❏ 323213	LMI	❏ 333001	NOR	❏ 350107	LMI
❏ 321314	GAR	❏ 321410	TSG	❏ 323214	LMI	❏ 333002	NOR	❏ 350108	LMI
❏ 321315	GAR	❏ 321411	LMI	❏ 323215	LMI	❏ 333003	NOR	❏ 350109	LMI
❏ 321316	GAR	❏ 321412	LMI	❏ 323216	LMI	❏ 333004	NOR	❏ 350110	LMI
❏ 321317	GAR	❏ 321413	LMI	❏ 323217	LMI	❏ 333005	NOR	❏ 350111	LMI
❏ 321318	GAR	❏ 321414	LMI	❏ 323218	LMI	❏ 333006	NOR	❏ 350112	LMI
❏ 321319	GAR	❏ 321415	LMI	❏ 323219	LMI	❏ 333007	NOR	❏ 350113	LMI
❏ 321320	GAR	❏ 321416	LMI	❏ 323220	LMI	❏ 333008	NOR	❏ 350114	LMI
❏ 321321	GAR	❏ 321417	LMI	❏ 323221	LMI	❏ 333009	NOR	❏ 350115	LMI
❏ 321322	GAR	❏ 321418	TSG	❏ 323222	LMI	❏ 333010	NOR	❏ 350116	LMI
❏ 321323	GAR	❏ 321419	TSG	❏ 323223	NOR	❏ 333011	NOR	❏ 350117	LMI
❏ 321324	GAR	❏ 321420	TSG	❏ 323224	NOR	❏ 333012	NOR	❏ 350118	LMI
❏ 321325	GAR	❏ 321421	GAR	❏ 323225	NOR	❏ 333013	NOR	❏ 350119	LMI
❏ 321326	GAR	❏ 321422	GAR	❏ 323226	NOR	❏ 333014	NOR	❏ 350120	LMI
❏ 321327	GAR	❏ 321423	GAR	❏ 323227	NOR	❏ 333015	NOR	❏ 350121	LMI
❏ 321328	GAR	❏ 321424	GAR	❏ 323228	NOR	❏ 333016	NOR	❏ 350122	LMI
❏ 321329	GAR	❏ 321425	GAR	❏ 323229	NOR			❏ 350123	LMI
❏ 321330	GAR	❏ 321426	GAR	❏ 323230	NOR	❏ 334001	FSR	❏ 350124	LMI
❏ 321331	GAR	❏ 321427	GAR	❏ 323231	NOR	❏ 334002	FSR	❏ 350125	LMI
❏ 321332	GAR	❏ 321428	GAR	❏ 323232	NOR	❏ 334003	FSR	❏ 350126	LMI
❏ 321333	GAR	❏ 321429	GAR	❏ 323233	NOR	❏ 334004	FSR	❏ 350127	LMI
❏ 321334	GAR	❏ 321430	GAR	❏ 323234	NOR	❏ 334005	FSR	❏ 350128	LMI
❏ 321335	GAR	❏ 321431	GAR	❏ 323235	NOR	❏ 334006	FSR	❏ 350129	LMI
❏ 321336	GAR	❏ 321432	GAR	❏ 323236	NOR	❏ 334007	FSR	❏ 350130	LMI
❏ 321337	GAR	❏ 321433	GAR	❏ 323237	NOR	❏ 334008	FSR		
❏ 321338	GAR	❏ 321434	GAR	❏ 323238	NOR	❏ 334009	FSR	❏ 350231	LMI
❏ 321339	GAR	❏ 321435	GAR	❏ 323239	NOR	❏ 334010	FSR	❏ 350232	LMI
❏ 321340	GAR	❏ 321436	GAR	❏ 323240	LMI	❏ 334011	FSR	❏ 350233	LMI
❏ 321341	GAR	❏ 321437	GAR	❏ 323241	LMI	❏ 334012	FSR	❏ 350234	LMI
❏ 321342	GAR	❏ 321438	GAR	❏ 323242	LMI	❏ 334013	FSR	❏ 350235	LMI
❏ 321343	GAR	❏ 321439	GAR	❏ 323243	LMI	❏ 334014	FSR	❏ 350236	LMI
❏ 321344	GAR	❏ 321440	GAR			❏ 334015	FSR	❏ 350237	LMI
❏ 321345	GAR	❏ 321441	GAR	❏ 325001	DBS	❏ 334016	FSR	❏ 350238	LMI
❏ 321346	GAR	❏ 321442	GAR	❏ 325002	DBS	❏ 334017	FSR	❏ 350239	LMI
❏ 321347	GAR	❏ 321443	GAR	❏ 325003	DBS	❏ 334018	FSR	❏ 350240	LMI
❏ 321348	GAR	❏ 321444	GAR	❏ 325004	DBS	❏ 334019	FSR	❏ 350241	LMI
❏ 321349	GAR	❏ 321445	GAR	❏ 325005	DBS	❏ 334020	FSR	❏ 350242	LMI
❏ 321350	GAR	❏ 321446	GAR	❏ 325006	DBS	❏ 334021	FSR	❏ 350243	LMI
❏ 321351	GAR	❏ 321447	GAR	❏ 325007	DBS	❏ 334022	FSR	❏ 350244	LMI
❏ 321352	GAR	❏ 321448	GAR	❏ 325008	DBS	❏ 334023	FSR	❏ 350245	LMI
❏ 321353	GAR			❏ 325009	DBS	❏ 334024	FSR	❏ 350246	LMI
❏ 321354	GAR	❏ 321901	NOR	❏ 325011	DBS	❏ 334025	FSR	❏ 350247	LMI
❏ 321355	GAR	❏ 321902	NOR	❏ 325012	DBS	❏ 334026	FSR	❏ 350248	LMI
❏ 321356	GAR	❏ 321903	NOR	❏ 325013	DBS	❏ 334027	FSR	❏ 350249	LMI
❏ 321357	GAR			❏ 325014	DBS	❏ 334028	FSR	❏ 350250	LMI
❏ 321358	GAR	❏ 322481	NOR	❏ 325015	DBS	❏ 334029	FSR	❏ 350251	LMI
❏ 321359	GAR	❏ 322482	NOR	❏ 325016	DBS	❏ 334030	FSR	❏ 350252	LMI
❏ 321360	GAR	❏ 322483	NOR			❏ 334031	FSR	❏ 350253	LMI
❏ 321361	GAR	❏ 322484	NOR	❏ 332001	HEX	❏ 334032	FSR	❏ 350254	LMI
❏ 321362	GAR	❏ 322485	NOR	❏ 332002	HEX	❏ 334033	FSR	❏ 350255	LMI
❏ 321363	GAR			❏ 332003	HEX	❏ 334034	FSR	❏ 350256	LMI
❏ 321364	GAR	❏ 323201	LMI	❏ 332004	HEX	❏ 334035	FSR	❏ 350257	LMI
❏ 321365	GAR	❏ 323202	LMI	❏ 332005	HEX	❏ 334036	FSR	❏ 350258	LMI
❏ 321366	GAR	❏ 323203	LMI	❏ 332006	HEX	❏ 334037	FSR	❏ 350259	LMI
		❏ 323204	LMI	❏ 332007	HEX	❏ 334038	FSR	❏ 350260	LMI
❏ 321401	TSG	❏ 323205	LMI	❏ 332008	HEX	❏ 334039	FSR	❏ 350261	LMI
❏ 321402	TSG	❏ 323206	LMI	❏ 332009	HEX	❏ 334040	FSR	❏ 350262	LMI

❏ 350263	LMI	❏ 357036	C2C	❏ 360202	HEC	❏ 373018	EUS	❏ 374002	EUS
❏ 350264	LMI	❏ 357037	C2C	❏ 360203	HEC	❏ 373019	EUS	❏ 374003	EUS
❏ 350265	LMI	❏ 357038	C2C	❏ 360204	HEC	❏ 373020	EUS	❏ 374004	EUS
❏ 350266	LMI	❏ 357039	C2C	❏ 360205	HEC	❏ 373021	EUS	❏ 374005	EUS
❏ 350267	LMI	❏ 357040	C2C			❏ 373022	EUS	❏ 374006	EUS
		❏ 357041	C2C	❏ 365501	TSG	❏ 373101	EUS	❏ 374007	EUS
❏ 350368	LMI	❏ 357042	C2C	❏ 365502	TSG	❏ 373102	EUS	❏ 374008	EUS
❏ 350369	LMI	❏ 357043	C2C	❏ 365503	TSG	❏ 373103	EUS	❏ 374009	EUS
❏ 350370	LMI	❏ 357044	C2C	❏ 365504	TSG	❏ 373104	EUS	❏ 374010	EUS
❏ 350371	LMI	❏ 357045	C2C	❏ 365505	TSG	❏ 373105	EUS	❏ 374011	EUS
❏ 350372	LMI	❏ 357046	C2C	❏ 365506	TSG	❏ 373106	EUS	❏ 374012	EUS
❏ 350373	LMI	❏ 357201	C2C	❏ 365507	TSG	❏ 373107	EUS	❏ 374013	EUS
❏ 350374	LMI	❏ 357202	C2C	❏ 365508	TSG	❏ 373108	EUS	❏ 374014	EUS
❏ 350375	LMI	❏ 357203	C2C	❏ 365509	TSG	❏ 373201	EUS	❏ 374015	EUS
❏ 350376	LMI	❏ 357204	C2C	❏ 365510	TSG	❏ 373202	EUS	❏ 374016	EUS
❏ 350377	LMI	❏ 357205	C2C	❏ 365511	TSG	❏ 373203	EUS	❏ 374017	EUS
		❏ 357206	C2C	❏ 365512	TSG	❏ 373204	EUS	❏ 374018	EUS
❏ 350401	FTP	❏ 357207	C2C	❏ 365513	TSG	❏ 373205	EUS	❏ 374019	EUS
❏ 350402	FTP	❏ 357208	C2C	❏ 365514	TSG	❏ 373206	EUS	❏ 374020	EUS
❏ 350403	FTP	❏ 357209	C2C	❏ 365515	TSG	❏ 373207	EUS	❏ 374021	EUS
❏ 350404	FTP	❏ 357210	C2C	❏ 365516	TSG	❏ 373208	EUS	❏ 374022	EUS
❏ 350405	FTP	❏ 357211	C2C	❏ 365517	TSG	❏ 373209	EUS	❏ 374023	EUS
❏ 350406	FTP	❏ 357212	C2C	❏ 365518	TSG	❏ 373210	EUS	❏ 374024	EUS
❏ 350407	FTP	❏ 357213	C2C	❏ 365519	TSG	❏ 373211	EUS	❏ 374025	EUS
❏ 350408	FTP	❏ 357214	C2C	❏ 365520	TSG	❏ 373212	EUS	❏ 374026	EUS
❏ 350409	FTP	❏ 357215	C2C	❏ 365521	TSG	❏ 373213	EUS	❏ 374027	EUS
❏ 350410	FTP	❏ 357216	C2C	❏ 365522	TSG	❏ 373214	EUS	❏ 374028	EUS
		❏ 357217	C2C	❏ 365523	TSG	❏ 373215	EUS	❏ 374029	EUS
❏ 357001	C2C	❏ 357218	C2C	❏ 365524	TSG	❏ 373216	EUS	❏ 374030	EUS
❏ 357002	C2C	❏ 357219	C2C	❏ 365525	TSG	❏ 373217	EUS	❏ 374031	EUS
❏ 357003	C2C	❏ 357220	C2C	❏ 365527	TSG	❏ 373218	EUS	❏ 374032	EUS
❏ 357004	C2C	❏ 357221	C2C	❏ 365528	TSG	❏ 373219	EUS	❏ 374033	EUS
❏ 357005	C2C	❏ 357222	C2C	❏ 365529	TSG	❏ 373220	EUS	❏ 374034	EUS
❏ 357006	C2C	❏ 357223	C2C	❏ 365530	TSG	❏ 373221	EUS		
❏ 357007	C2C	❏ 357224	C2C	❏ 365531	TSG	❏ 373222	EUS	❏ 375301	SET
❏ 357008	C2C	❏ 357225	C2C	❏ 365532	TSG	❏ 373223	EUS	❏ 375302	SET
❏ 357009	C2C	❏ 357226	C2C	❏ 365533	TSG	❏ 373224	EUS	❏ 375303	SET
❏ 357010	C2C	❏ 357227	C2C	❏ 365534	TSG	❏ 373225	EUS	❏ 375304	SET
❏ 357011	C2C	❏ 357228	C2C	❏ 365535	TSG	❏ 373226	EUS	❏ 375305	SET
❏ 357012	C2C			❏ 365536	TSG	❏ 373227	EUS	❏ 375306	SET
❏ 357013	C2C	❏ 360101	GAR	❏ 365537	TSG	❏ 373228	EUS	❏ 375307	SET
❏ 357014	C2C	❏ 360102	GAR	❏ 365538	TSG	❏ 373229	EUS	❏ 375308	SET
❏ 357015	C2C	❏ 360103	GAR	❏ 365539	TSG	❏ 373230	EUS	❏ 375309	SET
❏ 357016	C2C	❏ 360104	GAR	❏ 365540	TSG	❏ 373231	EUS	❏ 375310	SET
❏ 357017	C2C	❏ 360105	GAR	❏ 365541	TSG	❏ 373232	EUS		
❏ 357018	C2C	❏ 360106	GAR			❏ 373301	EUS	❏ 375601	SET
❏ 357019	C2C	❏ 360107	GAR	❏ 373001	EUS	❏ 373302	EUS	❏ 375602	SET
❏ 357020	C2C	❏ 360108	GAR	❏ 373002	EUS	❏ 373303	EUS	❏ 375603	SET
❏ 357021	C2C	❏ 360109	GAR	❏ 373003	EUS	❏ 373304	EUS	❏ 375604	SET
❏ 357022	C2C	❏ 360110	GAR	❏ 373004	EUS	❏ 373305	EUS	❏ 375605	SET
❏ 357023	C2C	❏ 360111	GAR	❏ 373005	EUS	❏ 373306	EUS	❏ 375606	SET
❏ 357024	C2C	❏ 360112	GAR	❏ 373006	EUS	❏ 373307	EUS	❏ 375607	SET
❏ 357025	C2C	❏ 360113	GAR	❏ 373007	EUS	❏ 373308	EUS	❏ 375608	SET
❏ 357026	C2C	❏ 360114	GAR	❏ 373008	EUS	❏ 373309	EUS	❏ 375609	SET
❏ 357027	C2C	❏ 360115	GAR	❏ 373009	EUS	❏ 373310	EUS	❏ 375610	SET
❏ 357028	C2C	❏ 360116	GAR	❏ 373010	EUS	❏ 373311	EUS	❏ 375611	SET
❏ 357029	C2C	❏ 360117	GAR	❏ 373011	EUS	❏ 373312	EUS	❏ 375612	SET
❏ 357030	C2C	❏ 360118	GAR	❏ 373012	EUS	❏ 373313	EUS	❏ 375613	SET
❏ 357031	C2C	❏ 360119	GAR	❏ 373013	EUS	❏ 373314	EUS	❏ 375614	SET
❏ 357032	C2C	❏ 360120	GAR	❏ 373014	EUS			❏ 375615	SET
❏ 357033	C2C	❏ 360121	GAR	❏ 373015	EUS	❏ 373999	EUS	❏ 375616	SET
❏ 357034	C2C			❏ 373016	EUS			❏ 375617	SET
❏ 357035	C2C	❏ 360201	HEC	❏ 373017	EUS	❏ 374001	EUS	❏ 375618	SET

Data Tables

375619	SET	375904	SET	377102	TSG	377201	TSG	377419	TSG
375620	SET	375905	SET	377103	TSG	377202	TSG	377420	TSG
375621	SET	375906	SET	377104	TSG	377203	TSG	377421	TSG
375622	SET	375907	SET	377105	TSG	377204	TSG	377422	TSG
375623	SET	375908	SET	377106	TSG	377205	TSG	377423	TSG
375624	SET	375909	SET	377107	TSG	377206	TSG	377424	TSG
375625	SET	375910	SET	377108	TSG	377207	TSG	377425	TSG
375626	SET	375911	SET	377109	TSG	377208	TSG	377426	TSG
375627	SET	375912	SET	377110	TSG	377209	TSG	377427	TSG
375628	SET	375913	SET	377111	TSG	377210	TSG	377428	TSG
375629	SET	375914	SET	377112	TSG	377211	TSG	377429	TSG
375630	SET	375915	SET	377113	TSG	377212	TSG	377430	TSG
		375916	SET	377114	TSG	377213	TSG	377431	TSG
375701	SET	375917	SET	377115	TSG	377214	TSG	377432	TSG
375702	SET	375918	SET	377116	TSG	377215	TSG	377433	TSG
375703	SET	375919	SET	377117	TSG			377434	TSG
375704	SET	375920	SET	377118	TSG	377301	TSG	377435	TSG
375705	SET	375921	SET	377119	TSG	377302	TSG	377436	TSG
375706	SET	375922	SET	377120	TSG	377303	TSG	377437	TSG
375707	SET	375923	SET	377121	TSG	377304	TSG	377438	TSG
375708	SET	375924	SET	377122	TSG	377305	TSG	377439	TSG
375709	SET	375925	SET	377123	TSG	377306	TSG	377440	TSG
375710	SET	375926	SET	377124	TSG	377307	TSG	377441	TSG
375711	SET	375927	SET	377125	TSG	377308	TSG	377442	TSG
375712	SET			377126	TSG	377309	TSG	377443	TSG
375713	SET	376001	SET	377127	TSG	377310	TSG	377444	TSG
375714	SET	376002	SET	377128	TSG	377311	TSG	377445	TSG
375715	SET	376003	SET	377129	TSG	377312	TSG	377446	TSG
		376004	SET	377130	TSG	377313	TSG	377447	TSG
375801	SET	376005	SET	377131	TSG	377314	TSG	377448	TSG
375802	SET	376006	SET	377132	TSG	377315	TSG	377449	TSG
375803	SET	376007	SET	377133	TSG	377316	TSG	377450	TSG
375804	SET	376008	SET	377134	TSG	377317	TSG	377451	TSG
375805	SET	376009	SET	377135	TSG	377318	TSG	377452	TSG
375806	SET	376010	SET	377136	TSG	377319	TSG	377453	TSG
375807	SET	376011	SET	377137	TSG	377320	TSG	377454	TSG
375808	SET	376012	SET	377138	TSG	377321	TSG	377455	TSG
375809	SET	376013	SET	377139	TSG	377322	TSG	377456	TSG
375810	SET	376014	SET	377140	TSG	377323	TSG	377457	TSG
375811	SET	376015	SET	377141	TSG	377324	TSG	377458	TSG
375812	SET	376016	SET	377142	TSG	377325	TSG	377459	TSG
375813	SET	376017	SET	377143	TSG	377326	TSG	377460	TSG
375814	SET	376018	SET	377144	TSG	377327	TSG	377461	TSG
375815	SET	376019	SET	377145	TSG	377328	TSG	377462	TSG
375816	SET	376020	SET	377146	TSG			377463	TSG
375817	SET	376021	SET	377147	TSG	377401	TSG	377464	TSG
375818	SET	376022	SET	377148	TSG	377402	TSG	377465	TSG
375819	SET	376023	SET	377149	TSG	377403	TSG	377466	TSG
375820	SET	376024	SET	377150	TSG	377404	TSG	377467	TSG
375821	SET	376025	SET	377151	TSG	377405	TSG	377468	TSG
375822	SET	376026	SET	377152	TSG	377406	TSG	377469	TSG
375823	SET	376027	SET	377153	TSG	377407	TSG	377470	TSG
375824	SET	376028	SET	377154	TSG	377408	TSG	377471	TSG
375825	SET	376029	SET	377155	TSG	377409	TSG	377472	TSG
375826	SET	376030	SET	377156	TSG	377410	TSG	377473	TSG
375827	SET	376031	SET	377157	TSG	377411	TSG	377474	TSG
375828	SET	376032	SET	377158	TSG	377412	TSG	377475	TSG
375829	SET	376033	SET	377159	TSG	377413	TSG		
375830	SET	376034	SET	377160	TSG	377414	TSG	377501	TSG
		376035	SET	377161	TSG	377415	TSG	377502	TSG
375901	SET	376036	SET	377162	TSG	377416	TSG	377503	TSG
375902	SET			377163	TSG	377417	TSG	377504	TSG
375903	SET	377101	TSG	377164	TSG	377418	TSG	377505	TSG

Data Tables

377506	TSG	378143	LOG	379013	GAR	387105	TSG	390039	VWC
377507	TSG	378144	LOG	379014	GAR	387106	TSG	390040	VWC
377508	TSG	378145	LOG	379015	GAR	387107	TSG	390141	VWC
377509	TSG	378146	LOG	379016	GAR	387108	TSG	390042	VWC
377510	TSG	378147	LOG	379017	GAR	387109	TSG	390043	VWC
377511	TSG	378148	LOG	379018	GAR	387110	TSG	390044	VWC
377512	TSG	378149	LOG	379019	GAR	387111	TSG	390045	VWC
377513	TSG	378150	LOG	379020	GAR	387112	TSG	390046	VWC
377514	TSG	378151	LOG	379021	GAR	387113	TSG	390047	VWC
377515	TSG	378152	LOG	379022	GAR	387114	TSG	390148	VWC
377516	TSG	378153	LOG	379023	GAR	387115	TSG	390049	VWC
377517	TSG	378154	LOG	379024	GAR	387116	TSG	390050	VWC
377518	TSG			379025	GAR	387117	TSG	390151	VWC
377519	TSG	378201	LOG	379026	GAR	387118	TSG	390152	VWC
377520	TSG	378202	LOG	379027	GAR	387119	TSG	390153	VWC
377521	TSG	378203	LOG	379028	GAR	387120	TSG	390154	VWC
377522	TSG	378204	LOG	379029	GAR	387121	TSG	390155	VWC
377523	TSG	378205	LOG	379030	GAR	387122	TSG	390156	VWC
		378206	LOG			387123	TSG	390157	VWC
377601	TSG	378207	LOG	380001	FSR	387124	TSG		
377602	TSG	378208	LOG	380002	FSR	387125	TSG	395001	SET
377603	TSG	378209	LOG	380003	FSR	387126	TSG	395002	SET
377604	TSG	378210	LOG	380004	FSR	387127	TSG	395003	SET
377605	TSG	378211	LOG	380005	FSR	387128	TSG	395004	SET
377606	TSG	378212	LOG	380006	FSR	387129	TSG	395005	SET
377607	TSG	378213	LOG	380007	FSR			395006	SET
377608	TSG	378214	LOG	380008	FSR	390001	VWC	395007	SET
377609	TSG	378215	LOG	380009	FSR	390002	VWC	395008	SET
377610	TSG	378216	LOG	380010	FSR	390103	VWC	395009	SET
377611	TSG	378217	LOG	380011	FSR	390104	VWC	395010	SET
377612	TSG	378218	LOG	380012	FSR	390005	VWC	395011	SET
377613	TSG	378219	LOG	380013	FSR	390006	VWC	395012	SET
377614	TSG	378220	LOG	380014	FSR	390107	VWC	395013	SET
377615	TSG	378221	LOG	380015	FSR	390008	VWC	395014	SET
377616	TSG	378222	LOG	380016	FSR	390009	VWC	395015	SET
377617	TSG	378223	LOG	380017	FSR	390010	VWC	395016	SET
377618	TSG	378224	LOG	380018	FSR	390011	VWC	395017	SET
377619	TSG	378225	LOG	380019	FSR	390112	VWC	395018	SET
377620	TSG	378226	LOG	380020	FSR	390013	VWC	395019	SET
377621	TSG	378227	LOG	380021	FSR	390114	VWC	395020	SET
377622	TSG	378228	LOG	380022	FSR	390115	VWC	395021	SET
377623	TSG	378229	LOG			390016	VWC	395022	SET
377624	TSG	378230	LOG	380101	FSR	390117	VWC	395023	SET
377625	TSG	378231	LOG	380102	FSR	390118	VWC	395024	SET
377626	TSG	378232	LOG	380103	FSR	390119	VWC	395025	SET
		378233	LOG	380104	FSR	390020	VWC	395026	SET
377701	TSG	378234	LOG	380105	FSR	390121	VWC	395027	SET
377702	TSG	378255	LOG	380106	FSR	390122	VWC	395028	SET
377703	TSG	378256	LOG	380107	FSR	390123	VWC	395029	SET
377704	TSG	378257	LOG	380108	FSR	390124	VWC		
377705	TSG			380109	FSR	390125	VWC	411198	PRE
377706	TSG	379001	GAR	380110	FSR	390126	VWC		
377707	TSG	379002	GAR	380111	FSR	390127	VWC	421399	PRE
377708	TSG	379003	GAR	380112	FSR	390128	VWC	421496	PRE
		379004	GAR	380113	FSR	390129	VWC	421497	PRE
378135	LOG	379005	GAR	380114	FSR	390130	VWC	421498	PRE
378136	LOG	379006	GAR	380115	FSR	390131	VWC	432417	PRE
378137	LOG	379007	GAR	380116	FSR	390132	VWC		
378138	LOG	379008	GAR			390134	VWC	442401	TSG
378139	LOG	379009	GAR	387101	TSG	390135	VWC	442402	TSG
378140	LOG	379010	GAR	387102	TSG	390136	VWC	442403	TSG
378141	LOG	379011	GAR	387103	TSG	390137	VWC	442404	TSG
378142	LOG	379012	GAR	387104	TSG	390138	VWC	442405	TSG

Data Tables

❏ 442406	TSG	❏ 444044	SWT	❏ 450089	SWT	❏ 450566	SWT	❏ 455814	TSG
❏ 442407	TSG	❏ 444045	SWT	❏ 450090	SWT	❏ 450567	SWT	❏ 455815	TSG
❏ 442408	TSG			❏ 450091	SWT	❏ 450568	SWT	❏ 455816	TSG
❏ 442409	TSG	❏ 450001	SWT	❏ 450092	SWT	❏ 450569	SWT	❏ 455817	TSG
❏ 442410	TSG	❏ 450002	SWT	❏ 450093	SWT	❏ 450570	SWT	❏ 455818	TSG
❏ 442411	TSG	❏ 450003	SWT	❏ 450094	SWT			❏ 455819	TSG
❏ 442412	TSG	❏ 450004	SWT	❏ 450095	SWT	❏ 455701	SWT	❏ 455820	TSG
❏ 442413	TSG	❏ 450005	SWT	❏ 450096	SWT	❏ 455702	SWT	❏ 455821	TSG
❏ 442414	TSG	❏ 450006	SWT	❏ 450097	SWT	❏ 455703	SWT	❏ 455822	TSG
❏ 442415	TSG	❏ 450007	SWT	❏ 450098	SWT	❏ 455704	SWT	❏ 455823	TSG
❏ 442416	TSG	❏ 450008	SWT	❏ 450099	SWT	❏ 455705	SWT	❏ 455824	TSG
❏ 442417	TSG	❏ 450009	SWT	❏ 450100	SWT	❏ 455706	SWT	❏ 455825	TSG
❏ 442418	TSG	❏ 450010	SWT	❏ 450101	SWT	❏ 455707	SWT	❏ 455826	TSG
❏ 442419	TSG	❏ 450011	SWT	❏ 450102	SWT	❏ 455708	SWT	❏ 455827	TSG
❏ 442420	TSG	❏ 450012	SWT	❏ 450103	SWT	❏ 455709	SWT	❏ 455828	TSG
❏ 442421	TSG	❏ 450013	SWT	❏ 450104	SWT	❏ 455710	SWT	❏ 455829	TSG
❏ 442422	TSG	❏ 450014	SWT	❏ 450105	SWT	❏ 455711	SWT	❏ 455830	TSG
❏ 442423	TSG	❏ 450015	SWT	❏ 450106	SWT	❏ 455712	SWT	❏ 455831	TSG
❏ 442424	TSG	❏ 450016	SWT	❏ 450107	SWT	❏ 455713	SWT	❏ 455832	TSG
		❏ 450017	SWT	❏ 450108	SWT	❏ 455714	SWT	❏ 455833	TSG
❏ 444001	SWT	❏ 450018	SWT	❏ 450109	SWT	❏ 455715	SWT	❏ 455834	TSG
❏ 444002	SWT	❏ 450019	SWT	❏ 450110	SWT	❏ 455716	SWT	❏ 455835	TSG
❏ 444003	SWT	❏ 450020	SWT	❏ 450111	SWT	❏ 455717	SWT	❏ 455836	TSG
❏ 444004	SWT	❏ 450021	SWT	❏ 450112	SWT	❏ 455718	SWT	❏ 455837	TSG
❏ 444005	SWT	❏ 450022	SWT	❏ 450113	SWT	❏ 455719	SWT	❏ 455838	TSG
❏ 444006	SWT	❏ 450023	SWT	❏ 450114	SWT	❏ 455720	SWT	❏ 455839	TSG
❏ 444007	SWT	❏ 450024	SWT	❏ 450115	SWT	❏ 455721	SWT	❏ 455840	TSG
❏ 444008	SWT	❏ 450025	SWT	❏ 450116	SWT	❏ 455722	SWT	❏ 455841	TSG
❏ 444009	SWT	❏ 450026	SWT	❏ 450117	SWT	❏ 455723	SWT	❏ 455842	TSG
❏ 444010	SWT	❏ 450027	SWT	❏ 450118	SWT	❏ 455724	SWT	❏ 455843	TSG
❏ 444011	SWT	❏ 450028	SWT	❏ 450119	SWT	❏ 455725	SWT	❏ 455844	TSG
❏ 444012	SWT	❏ 450029	SWT	❏ 450120	SWT	❏ 455726	SWT	❏ 455845	TSG
❏ 444013	SWT	❏ 450030	SWT	❏ 450121	SWT	❏ 455727	SWT	❏ 455846	TSG
❏ 444014	SWT	❏ 450031	SWT	❏ 450122	SWT	❏ 455728	SWT	❏ 455847	SWT
❏ 444015	SWT	❏ 450032	SWT	❏ 450123	SWT	❏ 455729	SWT	❏ 455848	SWT
❏ 444016	SWT	❏ 450033	SWT	❏ 450124	SWT	❏ 455730	SWT	❏ 455849	SWT
❏ 444017	SWT	❏ 450034	SWT	❏ 450125	SWT	❏ 455731	SWT	❏ 455850	SWT
❏ 444018	SWT	❏ 450035	SWT	❏ 450126	SWT	❏ 455732	SWT	❏ 455851	SWT
❏ 444019	SWT	❏ 450036	SWT	❏ 450127	SWT	❏ 455733	SWT	❏ 455852	SWT
❏ 444020	SWT	❏ 450037	SWT			❏ 455734	SWT	❏ 455853	SWT
❏ 444021	SWT	❏ 450038	SWT			❏ 455735	SWT	❏ 455854	SWT
❏ 444022	SWT	❏ 450039	SWT	❏ 450543	SWT	❏ 455736	SWT	❏ 455855	SWT
❏ 444023	SWT	❏ 450040	SWT	❏ 450544	SWT	❏ 455737	SWT	❏ 455856	SWT
❏ 444024	SWT	❏ 450041	SWT	❏ 450545	SWT	❏ 455738	SWT	❏ 455857	SWT
❏ 444025	SWT	❏ 450042	SWT	❏ 450546	SWT	❏ 455739	SWT	❏ 455858	SWT
❏ 444026	SWT	❏ 450071	SWT	❏ 450547	SWT	❏ 455740	SWT	❏ 455859	SWT
❏ 444027	SWT	❏ 450072	SWT	❏ 450548	SWT	❏ 455741	SWT	❏ 455860	SWT
❏ 444028	SWT	❏ 450073	SWT	❏ 450549	SWT	❏ 455742	SWT	❏ 455861	SWT
❏ 444029	SWT	❏ 450074	SWT	❏ 450550	SWT	❏ 455750	SWT	❏ 455862	SWT
❏ 444030	SWT	❏ 450075	SWT	❏ 450551	SWT			❏ 455863	SWT
❏ 444031	SWT	❏ 450076	SWT	❏ 450552	SWT	❏ 455801	TSG	❏ 455864	SWT
❏ 444032	SWT	❏ 450077	SWT	❏ 450553	SWT	❏ 455802	TSG	❏ 455865	SWT
❏ 444033	SWT	❏ 450078	SWT	❏ 450554	SWT	❏ 455803	TSG	❏ 455866	SWT
❏ 444034	SWT	❏ 450079	SWT	❏ 450555	SWT	❏ 455804	TSG	❏ 455867	SWT
❏ 444035	SWT	❏ 450080	SWT	❏ 450556	SWT	❏ 455805	TSG	❏ 455868	SWT
❏ 444036	SWT	❏ 450081	SWT	❏ 450557	SWT	❏ 455806	TSG	❏ 455869	SWT
❏ 444037	SWT	❏ 450082	SWT	❏ 450558	SWT	❏ 455807	TSG	❏ 455870	SWT
❏ 444038	SWT	❏ 450083	SWT	❏ 450559	SWT	❏ 455808	TSG	❏ 455871	SWT
❏ 444039	SWT	❏ 450084	SWT	❏ 450560	SWT	❏ 455809	TSG	❏ 455872	SWT
❏ 444040	SWT	❏ 450085	SWT	❏ 450561	SWT	❏ 455810	TSG	❏ 455873	SWT
❏ 444041	SWT	❏ 450086	SWT	❏ 450562	SWT	❏ 455811	TSG	❏ 455874	SWT
❏ 444042	SWT	❏ 450087	SWT	❏ 450563	SWT	❏ 455812	TSG		
❏ 444043	SWT	❏ 450088	SWT	❏ 450564	SWT	❏ 455813	TSG	❏ 455901	SWT
				❏ 450565	SWT				

Data Tables

455902 SWT	458519 SWT	465045 SET	465243 SET	466020 SET
455903 SWT	458520 SWT	465046 SET	465244 SET	466021 SET
455904 SWT	458521 SWT	465047 SET	465245 SET	466022 SET
455905 SWT	458522 SWT	465048 SET	465246 SET	466023 SET
455906 SWT	458523 SWT	465049 SET	465247 SET	466024 SET
455907 SWT	458524 SWT	465050 SET	465248 SET	466025 SET
455908 SWT	458525 SWT		465249 SET	466026 SET
455909 SWT	458526 SWT	465151 SET	465250 SET	466027 SET
455910 SWT	458527 SWT	465152 SET		466028 SET
455911 SWT	458528 SWT	465153 SET	465901 SET	466029 SET
455912 SWT	458529 SWT	465154 SET	465902 SET	466030 SET
455913 SWT	458530 SWT	465155 SET	465903 SET	466031 SET
455914 SWT	458531 SWT	465156 SET	465904 SET	466032 SET
455915 SWT	458532 SWT	465157 SET	465905 SET	466033 SET
455916 SWT	458533 SWT	465158 SET	465906 SET	466034 SET
455917 SWT	458534 SWT	465159 SET	465907 SET	466035 SET
455918 SWT	458535 SWT	465160 SET	465908 SET	466036 SET
455919 SWT	458536 SWT	465161 SET	465909 SET	466037 SET
455920 SWT		465162 SET	465910 SET	466038 SET
	465001 SET	465163 SET	465911 SET	466039 SET
456001 SWT	465002 SET	465164 SET	465912 SET	466040 SET
456002 SWT	465003 SET	465165 SET	465913 SET	466041 SET
456003 SWT	465004 SET	465166 SET	465914 SET	466042 SET
456004 SWT	465005 SET	465167 SET	465915 SET	466043 SET
456005 SWT	465006 SET	465168 SET	465916 SET	
456006 SWT	465007 SET	465169 SET	465917 SET	483002 SIL
456007 SWT	465008 SET	465170 SET	465918 SET	483004 SIL
456008 SWT	465009 SET	465171 SET	465919 SET	483006 SIL
456009 SWT	465010 SET	465172 SET	465920 SET	483007 SIL
456010 SWT	465011 SET	465173 SET	465921 SET	483008 SIL
456011 SWT	465012 SET	465174 SET	465922 SET	483009 SIL
456012 SWT	465013 SET	465175 SET	465923 SET	
456013 SWT	465014 SET	465176 SET	465924 SET	489102 NRL
456014 SWT	465015 SET	465177 SET	465925 SET	489105 NRL
456015 SWT	465016 SET	465178 SET	465926 SET	489106 NRL
456016 SWT	465017 SET	465179 SET	465927 SET	
456017 SWT	465018 SET	465180 SET	465928 SET	507001 MER
456018 SWT	465019 SET	465181 SET	465929 SET	507002 MER
456019 SWT	465020 SET	465182 SET	465930 SET	507003 MER
456020 SWT	465021 SET	465183 SET	465931 SET	507004 MER
456021 SWT	465022 SET	465184 SET	465932 SET	507005 MER
456022 SWT	465023 SET	465185 SET	465933 SET	507006 MER
456023 SWT	465024 SET	465186 SET	465934 SET	507007 MER
456024 SWT	465025 SET	465187 SET		507008 MER
	465026 SET	465188 SET	466001 SET	507009 MER
458501 SWT	465027 SET	465189 SET	466002 SET	507010 MER
458502 SWT	465028 SET	465190 SET	466003 SET	507011 MER
458503 SWT	465029 SET	465191 SET	466004 SET	507012 MER
458504 SWT	465030 SET	465192 SET	466005 SET	507013 MER
458505 SWT	465031 SET	465193 SET	466006 SET	507014 MER
458506 SWT	465032 SET	465194 SET	466007 SET	507015 MER
458507 SWT	465033 SET	465195 SET	466008 SET	507016 MER
458508 SWT	465034 SET	465196 SET	466009 SET	507017 MER
458509 SWT	465035 SET	465197 SET	466010 SET	507018 MER
458510 SWT	465036 SET		466011 SET	507019 MER
458511 SWT	465037 SET	465235 SET	466012 SET	507020 MER
458512 SWT	465038 SET	465236 SET	466013 SET	507021 MER
458513 SWT	465039 SET	465237 SET	466014 SET	507023 MER
458514 SWT	465040 SET	465238 SET	466015 SET	507024 MER
458515 SWT	465041 SET	465239 SET	466016 SET	507025 MER
458516 SWT	465042 SET	465240 SET	466017 SET	507026 MER
458517 SWT	465043 SET	465241 SET	466018 SET	507027 MER
458518 SWT	465044 SET	465242 SET	466019 SET	507028 MER

Data Tables

507029 MER	700030 TSG	700132 TSG	335 VTN	1953 VSO
507030 MER	700031 TSG	700133 TSG	337 FSL	1961 WCR
507031 MER	700032 TSG	700134 TSG	347 WCR	1999 GSW
507032 MER	700033 TSG	700135 TSG	348 WCR	
507033 MER	700034 TSG	700136 TSG	349 VTN	2127 WCR
	700035 TSG	700137 TSG	350 WCR	
508103 MER	700036 TSG	700138 TSG	352 WCR	2903 NRL
508104 MER	700037 TSG	700139 TSG	353 VTN	2904 NRL
508108 MER	700038 TSG	700140 TSG	354 WCR	2915 NRL
508110 MER	700039 TSG	700141 TSG	464 BOK	2916 NRL
508111 MER	700040 TSG	700142 TSG	504 WCR	2917 NRL
508112 MER	700041 TSG	700143 TSG	506 WCR	2918 NRL
508114 MER	700042 TSG	700144 TSG	546 WCR	2919 NRL
508115 MER	700043 TSG	700145 TSG	548 WCR	2920 NRL
508117 MER	700044 TSG	700146 TSG	549 WCR	2921 NRL
508120 MER	700045 TSG	700147 TSG	550 WCR	2922 NRL
508122 MER	700046 TSG	700148 TSG	551 WCR	2923 NRL
508123 MER	700047 TSG	700149 TSG	552 WCR	
508124 MER	700048 TSG	700150 TSG	553 WCR	3058 WCR
508125 MER	700049 TSG	700151 TSG	586 WCR	3066 RIV
508126 MER	700050 TSG	700152 TSG	807 WCR	3068 RIV
508127 MER	700051 TSG	700153 TSG		3069 RIV
508128 MER	700052 TSG	700154 TSG	1105 MHR	3093 WCR
508130 MER	700053 TSG	700155 TSG		3096 BOK
508131 MER	700054 TSG		1200 RIV	3097 RIV
508134 MER	700055 TSG	901001 PRE	1201 VTN	3098 RIV
508136 MER	700056 TSG		1203 RIV	3100 RIV
508137 MER	700057 TSG	**Coaching Stock**	1207 VSO	3105 WCR
508138 MER	700058 TSG	84 RAF	1209 OLS	3106 WCR
508139 MER	700059 TSG	159 WCR	1211 RAF	3107 RIV
508140 MER	700060 TSG		1212 RIV	3110 RIV
508141 MER		213 VSO	1219 OLS	3112 RIV
508143 MER	700101 TSG	239 VSO	1221 VSO	3113 WCR
	700102 TSG	243 VSO	1254 DRS	3115 BOK
700001 TSG	700103 TSG	245 VSO	1256 NRL	3117 WCR
700002 TSG	700104 TSG	254 VSO	1375 BOK	3119 RIV
700003 TSG	700105 TSG	255 VSO	1566 VSO	3120 RIV
700004 TSG	700106 TSG	261 VSO	1644 WCR	3121 RIV
700005 TSG	700107 TSG	264 VSO	1650 WCR	3122 RIV
700006 TSG	700108 TSG	280 VSO	1651 RIV	3123 RIV
700007 TSG	700109 TSG	281 VSO	1652 WCR	3124 RIV
700008 TSG	700110 TSG	283 VSO	1655 WCR	3125 RIV
700009 TSG	700111 TSG	284 VSO	1657 RIV	3127 RIV
700010 TSG	700112 TSG	285 VSO	1659 RAF	3130 WCR
700011 TSG	700113 TSG	286 VSO	1663 WCR	3133 RIV
700012 TSG	700114 TSG	288 VSO	1666 WCR	3136 WCR
700013 TSG	700115 TSG	292 VSO	1670 WCR	3140 RIV
700014 TSG	700116 TSG	293 VSO	1671 RIV	3141 RIV
700015 TSG	700117 TSG	301 VSO	1683 RIV	3143 WCR
700016 TSG	700118 TSG	302 VSO	1691 RIV	3144 RIV
700017 TSG	700119 TSG	307 VSO	1692 RIV	3146 RIV
700018 TSG	700120 TSG	308 VSO	1699 RIV	3147 RIV
700019 TSG	700121 TSG	310 RAF	1730 WCR	3148 RIV
700020 TSG	700122 TSG	313 GSW	1800 WCR	3149 RIV
700021 TSG	700123 TSG	316 FSL	1813 RIV	3150 BOK
700022 TSG	700124 TSG	317 GSW	1823 NYM	3174 VSO
700023 TSG	700125 TSG	319 GSW	1832 RIV	3181 RIV
700024 TSG	700126 TSG	321 FSL	1840 WCR	3182 VSO
700025 TSG	700127 TSG	324 GSW	1859 SRP	3188 RAF
700026 TSG	700128 TSG	325 VSO	1860 WCR	3223 RIV
700027 TSG	700129 TSG	326 WCR	1861 WCR	3227 RIV
700028 TSG	700130 TSG	329 GSW	1863 RIV	3229 OLS
700029 TSG	700131 TSG	331 GSW	1882 WCR	3231 RAF

Data Tables

No.		No.		No.		No.		No.	
3232	VSO	4362	RAF	5494	RIV	6139	DBR	9539	RIV
3240	RIV	4455	NYM	5520	RRS	6141	RIV	9704	BAR
3247	VSO	4786	NYM	5631	DBS	6152	DBR	9705	DRS
3267	VSO	4817	NYM	5632	DBS	6158	RIV	9707	DRS
3273	VSO	4831	BOK	5636	OLS	6160	OLS	9709	BAR
3275	VSO	4832	BOK	5647	RIV	6164	OLS	9710	BAR
3277	RIV	4836	BOK	5657	DBS	6173	DRS	9711	VTN
3278	RIV	4856	BOK	5756	WCR	6176	RIV	9800	FSR
3279	DBS	4860	WCR	5797	RAF	6177	RIV	9801	FSR
3292	DBS	4905	WCR	5810	DRS	6183	RIV	9802	FSR
3295	RIV	4912	WCR	5888	OLS	6310	RIV	9803	FSR
3304	RIV	4927	RIV	5910	RIV	6311	DBR	9804	FSR
3312	RAF	4931	WCR	5912	RAF	6312	WCR	9805	FSR
3313	WCR	4932	WCR	5919	DRS	6313	VSO	9806	FSR
3314	RIV	4940	WCR	5921	RIV	6320	RIV	9807	FSR
3318	DBR	4946	WCR	5922	DBS	6528	WCR	9808	FSR
3325	RIV	4949	RIV	5924	DBS	6700	FSR	9809	FSR
3326	WCR	4951	WCR	5928	VTN	6701	FSR	9810	FSR
3330	RIV	4954	WCR	5929	RIV	6702	FSR		
3331	DBR	4958	WCR	5937	RIV	6703	FSR	10200	GAR
3333	RIV	4959	RIV	5945	RIV	6704	FSR	10201	DBR
3334	RIV	4960	WCR	5950	RIV	6705	FSR	10202	DBR
3336	RIV	4973	WCR	5952	RIV	6706	FSR	10203	GAR
3340	RIV	4984	WCR	5954	DBS	6707	FSR	10204	3MP
3344	RIV	4991	RIV	5955	RIV	6708	FSR	10206	OLS
3345	RIV	4994	WCR	5959	DBS	6720	RIV	10211	DBS
3348	RIV	4997	WCR	5961	RIV	6722	RIV	10212	GAR
3350	WCR	4998	RIV	5964	RIV	6723	WCR	10214	GAR
3351	VTN			5965	RIV	6724	WCR	10215	DBS
3352	WCR	5000	NYM	5971	DRS			10216	GAR
3356	RIV	5008	RIV	5976	RIV	9005	RAF	10217	GAR
3358	DBS	5009	RIV	5981	NRL	9101	VTN	10219	FGW
3359	WCR	5027	RIV	5985	RIV	9104	WCR	10222	DBS
3360	WCR	5028	BOK	5987	RIV	9267	NYM	10223	GAR
3362	WCR	5029	NYM	5991	RAF	9274	NYM	10225	FGW
3364	RIV	5032	WCR	5995	DRS	9391	WCR	10226	DBS
3366	DRS	5033	WCR	5998	RIV	9392	WCR	10228	GAR
3374	DRS	5035	WCR			9419	DRS	10229	GAR
3375	DBS	5040	RIV	6000	WCR	9428	DRS	10231	OLS
3379	RIV	5044	WCR	6001	DRS	9440	WCR	10232	FGW
3384	RIV	5125	WCR	6006	RIV	9448	WCR	10233	DBS
3386	RIV	5157	VTN	6008	DRS	9481	NRL	10235	DBR
3388	DBS	5171	WCR	6012	WCR	9488	DRS	10237	DBS
3390	RIV	5177	VTN	6014	WCR	9493	WCR	10241	OLS
3392	WCR	5191	VTN	6021	WCR	9494	DBR	10242	DBR
3395	WCR	5198	VTN	6022	WCR	9496	VTN	10246	DBR
3397	RIV	5200	WCR	6024	RIV	9502	VSO	10247	GAR
3399	DBS	5212	VTN	6027	RIV	9504	RIV	10249	ATW
3400	DBS	5216	WCR	6036	DBR	9506	DBS	10250	DBS
3417	RIV	5222	WCR	6042	RIV	9507	RIV	10253	OLS
3424	DBS	5229	WCR	6046	DRS	9508	DRS	10256	OLS
3426	RIV	5236	WCR	6051	RIV	9509	RIV	10257	DBS
3431	WCR	5237	WCR	6054	RIV	9516	NRL	10259	ATW
3434	OLS	5239	WCR	6064	DRS	9520	RIV	10260	OLS
3438	RAF	5249	WCR	6067	RIV	9521	RIV	10271	CRW
3766	WCR	5276	RIV	6103	WCR	9522	DBR	10272	CRW
3860	NYM	5278	WCR	6110	DBR	9523	NRL	10273	CRW
3872	NYM	5292	RIV	6115	WCR	9525	DRS	10274	CRW
3948	NYM	5309	RIV	6117	DRS	9526	RIV	10300	ICE
		5341	RIV	6121	OLS	9527	RIV	10301	ICE
4198	NYM	5366	RIV	6122	DRS	9529	DBR	10302	ICE
4252	NYM	5419	WCR	6135	WCR	9531	DBR	10303	ICE
4290	NYM	5482	DBS	6137	RIV	9537	RIV	10304	ICE

❑ 10305	ICE	❑ 10563	FGW	❑ 11039	DBS	❑ 11299	ICE	❑ 12005	GAR

❑ 10305	ICE	❑ 10563	FGW	❑ 11039	DBS	❑ 11299	ICE	❑ 12005	GAR
❑ 10306	ICE	❑ 10565	FSR	❑ 11044	DBR	❑ 11301	ICE	❑ 12008	OLS
❑ 10307	ICE	❑ 10569	VSO	❑ 11046	DBR	❑ 11302	ICE	❑ 12009	GAR
❑ 10308	ICE	❑ 10580	FSR	❑ 11048	GAR	❑ 11303	ICE	❑ 12011	GAR
❑ 10309	ICE	❑ 10584	FGW	❑ 11054	DBR	❑ 11304	ICE	❑ 12012	GAR
❑ 10310	ICE	❑ 10589	FGW	❑ 11066	GAR	❑ 11305	ICE	❑ 12013	GAR
❑ 10311	ICE	❑ 10590	FGW	❑ 11067	GAR	❑ 11306	ICE	❑ 12015	GAR
❑ 10312	ICE	❑ 10594	FGW	❑ 11068	GAR	❑ 11307	ICE	❑ 12016	GAR
❑ 10313	ICE	❑ 10596	FGW	❑ 11069	GAR	❑ 11308	ICE	❑ 12019	GAR
❑ 10315	ICE	❑ 10597	FSR	❑ 11070	GAR	❑ 11309	ICE	❑ 12021	GAR
❑ 10317	ICE	❑ 10598	FSR	❑ 11072	GAR	❑ 11310	ICE	❑ 12022	OLS
❑ 10318	ICE	❑ 10600	FSR	❑ 11073	GAR	❑ 11311	ICE	❑ 12024	GAR
❑ 10319	ICE	❑ 10601	FGW	❑ 11074	OLS	❑ 11312	ICE	❑ 12026	GAR
❑ 10320	ICE	❑ 10605	FSR	❑ 11075	GAR	❑ 11313	ICE	❑ 12027	GAR
❑ 10321	ICE	❑ 10607	FSR	❑ 11076	GAR	❑ 11314	ICE	❑ 12029	OLS
❑ 10323	ICE	❑ 10610	FSR	❑ 11077	GAR	❑ 11315	ICE	❑ 12030	GAR
❑ 10324	ICE	❑ 10612	FGW	❑ 11078	GAR	❑ 11316	ICE	❑ 12031	GAR
❑ 10325	ICE	❑ 10613	FSR	❑ 11079	DBR	❑ 11317	ICE	❑ 12032	GAR
❑ 10326	ICE	❑ 10614	FSR	❑ 11080	GAR	❑ 11318	ICE	❑ 12034	GAR
❑ 10328	ICE	❑ 10616	FGW	❑ 11081	GAR	❑ 11319	ICE	❑ 12035	GAR
❑ 10329	ICE	❑ 10617	FSR	❑ 11082	GAR	❑ 11320	ICE	❑ 12036	OLS
❑ 10330	ICE	❑ 10648	FSR	❑ 11085	GAR	❑ 11321	ICE	❑ 12037	GAR
❑ 10331	ICE	❑ 10650	FSR	❑ 11087	GAR	❑ 11322	ICE	❑ 12040	GAR
❑ 10332	ICE	❑ 10661	OLS	❑ 11088	GAR	❑ 11323	ICE	❑ 12041	GAR
❑ 10333	ICE	❑ 10666	FSR	❑ 11090	GAR	❑ 11324	ICE	❑ 12042	GAR
❑ 10401	GAR	❑ 10667	OLS	❑ 11091	GAR	❑ 11325	ICE	❑ 12046	GAR
❑ 10402	GAR	❑ 10675	FSR	❑ 11092	GAR	❑ 11326	ICE	❑ 12047	DRS
❑ 10403	GAR	❑ 10680	FSR	❑ 11093	GAR	❑ 11327	ICE	❑ 12049	GAR
❑ 10404	GAR	❑ 10681	DBR	❑ 11094	GAR	❑ 11328	ICE	❑ 12051	GAR
❑ 10405	GAR	❑ 10682	DBS	❑ 11095	GAR	❑ 11329	ICE	❑ 12056	GAR
❑ 10406	GAR	❑ 10683	FSR	❑ 11096	GAR	❑ 11330	ICE	❑ 12057	GAR
❑ 10501	FSR	❑ 10688	FSR	❑ 11097	DBR	❑ 11401	ICE	❑ 12060	GAR
❑ 10502	FSR	❑ 10689	FSR	❑ 11098	GAR	❑ 11402	ICE	❑ 12061	GAR
❑ 10504	FSR	❑ 10690	FSR	❑ 11099	GAR	❑ 11403	ICE	❑ 12062	GAR
❑ 10506	FSR	❑ 10693	FSR	❑ 11100	GAR	❑ 11404	ICE	❑ 12063	DRS
❑ 10507	FSR	❑ 10698	OLS	❑ 11101	GAR	❑ 11405	ICE	❑ 12064	GAR
❑ 10508	FSR	❑ 10699	FSR	❑ 11201	ICE	❑ 11406	ICE	❑ 12065	DRS
❑ 10513	FSR	❑ 10703	FSR	❑ 11219	ICE	❑ 11407	ICE	❑ 12066	GAR
❑ 10516	FSR	❑ 10706	FSR	❑ 11229	ICE	❑ 11408	ICE	❑ 12067	GAR
❑ 10519	FSR	❑ 10710	DBR	❑ 11237	ICE	❑ 11409	ICE	❑ 12073	GAR
❑ 10520	FSR	❑ 10714	FSR	❑ 11241	ICE	❑ 11410	ICE	❑ 12078	GAR
❑ 10522	FSR	❑ 10718	FSR	❑ 11244	ICE	❑ 11411	ICE	❑ 12079	GAR
❑ 10523	FSR	❑ 10719	FSR	❑ 11273	ICE	❑ 11412	ICE	❑ 12081	GAR
❑ 10526	FSR	❑ 10722	FSR	❑ 11277	ICE	❑ 11413	ICE	❑ 12082	GAR
❑ 10527	FSR	❑ 10723	FSR	❑ 11278	ICE	❑ 11414	ICE	❑ 12083	OLS
❑ 10529	FSR	❑ 10729	VSO	❑ 11279	ICE	❑ 11415	ICE	❑ 12084	GAR
❑ 10531	FSR	❑ 10731	DBR	❑ 11280	ICE	❑ 11416	ICE	❑ 12087	DRS
❑ 10532	FGW	❑ 10733	OLS	❑ 11281	ICE	❑ 11417	ICE	❑ 12089	GAR
❑ 10534	FGW	❑ 10734	VSO	❑ 11282	ICE	❑ 11418	ICE	❑ 12090	GAR
❑ 10540	DBR			❑ 11283	ICE	❑ 11419	ICE	❑ 12091	GAR
❑ 10541	VSO	❑ 11005	DBR	❑ 11284	ICE	❑ 11420	ICE	❑ 12092	OLS
❑ 10542	FSR	❑ 11006	DRS	❑ 11285	ICE	❑ 11421	ICE	❑ 12093	GAR
❑ 10543	FSR	❑ 11007	GAR	❑ 11286	ICE	❑ 11422	ICE	❑ 12095	OLS
❑ 10544	FSR	❑ 11011	DRS	❑ 11287	ICE	❑ 11423	ICE	❑ 12097	GAR
❑ 10546	DBR	❑ 11013	DBR	❑ 11288	ICE	❑ 11424	ICE	❑ 12098	GAR
❑ 10547	OLS	❑ 11018	GAR	❑ 11289	ICE	❑ 11425	ICE	❑ 12099	GAR
❑ 10548	FSR	❑ 11019	DBR	❑ 11290	ICE	❑ 11426	ICE	❑ 12100	FGW
❑ 10551	FSR	❑ 11026	OLS	❑ 11291	ICE	❑ 11427	ICE	❑ 12101	OLS
❑ 10553	FSR	❑ 11028	DBR	❑ 11292	ICE	❑ 11428	ICE	❑ 12103	GAR
❑ 10554	DBR	❑ 11029	DBR	❑ 11293	ICE	❑ 11429	ICE	❑ 12105	GAR
❑ 10556	VSO	❑ 11030	DBR	❑ 11294	ICE	❑ 11430	ICE	❑ 12107	GAR
❑ 10561	FSR	❑ 11031	DBS	❑ 11295	ICE	❑ 11998	ICE	❑ 12108	GAR
❑ 10562	FSR	❑ 11033	DBR	❑ 11298	ICE	❑ 11999	ICE	❑ 12109	GAR

Data Tables

No.	Code	No.	Code	No.	Code	No.	Code	No.	Code
12110	GAR	12214	ICE	12417	ICE	12486	ICE	17105	RIV
12111	GAR	12215	ICE	12419	ICE	12488	ICE	17159	DRS
12114	GAR	12216	ICE	12420	ICE	12489	ICE	17167	VSO
12115	GAR	12217	ICE	12421	ICE			17168	WCR
12116	GAR	12218	ICE	12422	ICE	12513	ICE	17173	FGW
12118	GAR	12219	ICE	12423	ICE	12514	ICE	17174	FGW
12120	GAR	12220	ICE	12424	ICE	12515	ICE	17175	FGW
12122	GAR	12222	ICE	12425	ICE	12518	ICE		
12125	GAR	12223	ICE	12426	ICE	12519	ICE	18756	WCR
12126	GAR	12224	ICE	12427	ICE	12520	ICE	18806	WCR
12129	GAR	12225	ICE	12428	ICE	12522	ICE	18893	WCR
12130	GAR	12226	ICE	12429	ICE	12526	ICE		
12132	GAR	12227	ICE	12430	ICE	12533	ICE	19208	WCR
12133	GAR	12228	ICE	12431	ICE	12534	ICE		
12134	DRS	12229	ICE	12432	ICE	12538	ICE	21096	SUP
12137	GAR	12230	ICE	12433	ICE			21100	NYM
12138	GAR	12231	ICE	12434	ICE	12602	CRW	21224	RIV
12139	GAR	12232	ICE	12436	ICE	12603	CRW	21232	SUP
12141	GAR			12437	ICE	12604	CRW	21236	SUP
12142	FGW	12300	ICE	12438	ICE	12605	CRW	21241	SRP
12143	GAR	12301	ICE	12439	ICE	12606	CRW	21245	RIV
12144	OLS	12302	ICE	12440	ICE	12607	CRW	21249	SUP
12146	GAR	12303	ICE	12441	ICE	12608	CRW	21252	MHR
12147	GAR	12304	ICE	12442	ICE	12609	CRW	21256	WCR
12148	GAR	12305	ICE	12443	ICE	12612	CRW	21266	WCR
12150	GAR	12307	ICE	12444	ICE	12613	CRW	21269	RIV
12151	GAR	12308	ICE	12445	ICE	12614	CRW	21272	RIV
12153	GAR	12309	ICE	12446	ICE	12615	CRW		
12154	GAR	12310	ICE	12447	ICE	12616	CRW	34525	WCR
12156	OLS	12311	ICE	12448	ICE	12617	CRW		
12159	GAR	12312	ICE	12449	ICE	12618	CRW	35089	NYM
12160	OLS	12313	ICE	12450	ICE	12619	CRW	35185	SRP
12161	FGW	12315	ICE	12452	ICE	12621	CRW	35290	DBR
12163	OLS	12316	ICE	12453	ICE	12623	CRW	35317	SUP
12164	GAR	12317	ICE	12454	ICE	12625	CRW	35322	SUP
12166	GAR	12318	ICE	12455	ICE	12627	CRW	35329	SUP
12167	GAR	12319	ICE	12456	ICE			35407	WCR
12170	GAR	12320	ICE	12457	ICE	13227	WCR	35449	SUP
12171	GAR	12321	ICE	12458	ICE	13229	BOK	35451	SUP
12176	ATW	12322	ICE	12459	ICE	13230	BOK	35461	SUP
12177	ATW	12323	ICE	12460	ICE	13306	WCR	35463	SUP
12178	ATW	12324	ICE	12461	ICE	13320	WCR	35464	SUP
12179	ATW	12325	ICE	12462	ICE	13321	WCR	35465	SUP
12180	ATW	12326	ICE	12463	ICE	13440	WCR	35466	VSO
12181	ATW	12327	ICE	12464	ICE	13508	RAF	35468	SUP
12182	ATW	12328	ICE	12465	ICE	13581	RRS	35469	RIV
12183	ATW	12329	ICE	12466	ICE	13583	RRS	35470	SUP
12184	ATW	12330	ICE	12467	ICE			35476	SUP
12185	ATW	12331	ICE	12468	ICE	14007	SUP	35486	SUP
				12469	ICE			35508	SUP
12200	ICE			12470	ICE	16156	NYM	35511	RAF
12201	ICE	12400	ICE	12471	ICE			35517	SUP
12202	ICE	12401	ICE	12472	ICE	17013	SUP	35518	SUP
12203	ICE	12402	ICE	12473	ICE	17015	SUP		
12204	ICE	12403	ICE	12474	ICE	17018	VTN	40101	FGW
12205	ICE	12404	ICE	12476	ICE	17019	SUP	40102	FGW
12207	ICE	12405	ICE	12477	ICE	17025	SUP	40103	FGW
12208	ICE	12406	ICE	12478	ICE	17056	RIV	40104	FGW
12209	ICE	12407	ICE	12480	ICE	17077	RIV	40106	FGW
12210	ICE	12409	ICE	12481	ICE	17080	RAF	40107	FGW
12211	ICE	12410	ICE	12483	ICE	17090	VTN	40108	FGW
12212	ICE	12411	ICE	12484	ICE	17096	SUP	40109	FGW
12213	ICE	12414	ICE	12485	ICE	17102	WCR	40110	FGW
		12415	ICE						

No.	Code	No.	Code	No.	Code	No.	Code	No.	Code
40111	FGW	40752	FGW	41075	EMT	41170	ICE	42050	FGW
40112	FGW	40753	EMT	41076	EMT	41176	FGW	42051	AXC
40113	FGW	40754	EMT	41077	EMT	41180	FGW	42052	AXC
40114	FGW	40755	FGW	41079	EMT	41182	FGW	42053	AXC
40115	FGW	40756	EMT	41083	ICE	41183	FGW	42054	FGW
40116	FGW	40757	FGW	41084	EMT	41185	ICE	42055	FGW
40117	FGW			41087	ICE	41186	FGW	42056	FGW
40118	FGW	40801	FGW	41088	ICE	41187	FGW	42057	ICE
40119	FGW	40802	FGW	41089	FGW	41189	FGW	42058	ICE
		40803	FGW	41090	ICE	41190	ICE	42059	ICE
40204	FGW	40805	ICE	41091	ICE	41192	FGW	42060	FGW
40205	FGW	40806	FGW	41092	ICE	41193	AXC	42061	FGW
40207	FGW	40807	FGW	41094	FGW	41194	AXC	42062	FGW
40210	FGW	40808	FGW	41095	ICE	41195	AXC	42063	ICE
40221	FGW	40809	FGW	41097	ICE	41201	GTL	42064	ICE
40231	FGW	40810	FGW	41098	ICE	41202	GTL	42065	ICE
		40811	FGW	41099	ICE	41203	GTL	42066	FGW
40402	DBR			41100	ICE	41204	GTL	42067	FGW
40403	DBR	40900	FGW	41102	FGW	41205	GTL	42068	FGW
40416	DBR	40901	FGW	41103	FGW	41206	GTL	42069	FGW
40417	OLS	40902	FGW	41104	FGW			42070	FGW
40419	OLS	40903	FGW	41106	FGW	42003	FGW	42071	FGW
40424	GTL	40904	FGW	41108	FGW	42004	FGW	42072	FGW
40425	OLS			41110	FGW	42005	FGW	42073	FGW
40426	GTL	41004	FGW	41111	EMT	42006	FGW	42074	FGW
40433	GTL	41006	FGW	41112	EMT	42007	FGW	42075	FGW
40434	DBR	41008	FGW	41113	EMT	42008	FGW	42076	FGW
		41010	FGW	41115	ICE	42009	FGW	42077	FGW
40700	EMT	41012	FGW	41116	FGW	42010	FGW	42078	FGW
40701	ICE	41016	FGW	41117	EMT	42012	FGW	42079	FGW
40702	ICE	41018	FGW	41118	ICE	42013	FGW	42080	FGW
40703	FGW	41020	FGW	41120	ICE	42014	FGW	42081	FGW
40704	ICE	41022	FGW	41122	FGW	42015	FGW	42083	FGW
40705	ICE	41024	FGW	41124	FGW	42016	FGW	42085	FGW
40706	ICE	41026	AXC	41126	FGW	42019	FGW	42087	FGW
40708	ICE	41028	FGW	41128	FGW	42021	FGW	42089	FGW
40710	FGW	41030	FGW	41130	FGW	42023	FGW	42091	ICE
40711	ICE	41032	FGW	41132	FGW	42024	FGW	42092	FGW
40713	FGW	41034	FGW	41134	FGW	42025	FGW	42093	FGW
40715	FGW	41035	AXC	41135	FGW	42026	FGW	42094	FGW
40716	FGW	41038	FGW	41136	FGW	42027	FGW	42095	FGW
40718	FGW	41039	ICE	41137	FGW	42028	FGW	42096	FGW
40720	ICE	41040	ICE	41138	FGW	42029	FGW	42097	AXC
40721	FGW	41041	EMT	41140	FGW	42030	FGW	42098	FGW
40722	FGW	41043	ICE	41142	FGW	42031	FGW	42099	FGW
40727	FGW	41044	ICE	41144	FGW	42032	FGW	42100	EMT
40728	EMT	41046	EMT	41146	FGW	42033	FGW	42101	FGW
40730	EMT	41052	FGW	41149	FGW	42034	FGW	42102	FGW
40732	ICE	41056	FGW	41150	ICE	42035	FGW	42103	FGW
40733	FGW	41057	EMT	41151	ICE	42036	AXC	42105	FGW
40734	FGW	41058	ICE	41152	ICE	42037	AXC	42106	ICE
40735	ICE	41059	FGW	41154	ICE	42038	AXC	42107	FGW
40737	ICE	41061	EMT	41156	EMT	42039	FGW	42108	FGW
40739	FGW	41062	ICE	41158	FGW	42040	FGW	42109	ICE
40740	ICE	41063	EMT	41159	ICE	42041	FGW	42110	ICE
40741	EMT	41064	EMT	41160	FGW	42042	FGW	42111	EMT
40742	ICE	41066	ICE	41161	FGW	42043	FGW	42112	EMT
40743	FGW	41067	EMT	41162	FGW	42044	FGW	42113	EMT
40746	EMT	41068	EMT	41164	ICE	42045	FGW	42115	FGW
40748	ICE	41069	EMT	41165	ICE	42046	FGW	42116	ICE
40749	EMT	41070	EMT	41166	FGW	42047	FGW	42117	ICE
40750	ICE	41071	EMT	41167	FGW	42048	FGW	42118	FGW
40751	EMT	41072	EMT	41169	FGW	42049	FGW	42119	EMT

Data Tables

No.	Code	No.	Code	No.	Code	No.	Code	No.	Code
42120	EMT	42188	ICE	42256	FGW	42335	ICE	42507	FGW
42121	EMT	42189	ICE	42257	FGW	42337	EMT	42508	FGW
42123	ICE	42190	ICE	42258	FGW	42339	EMT	42509	FGW
42124	EMT	42191	ICE	42259	FGW	42340	ICE	42510	FGW
42125	ICE	42192	ICE	42260	FGW	42341	EMT	42511	FGW
42126	FGW	42193	ICE	42261	FGW	42342	AXC	42512	FGW
42127	ICE	42194	EMT	42263	FGW	42343	FGW	42513	FGW
42128	ICE	42195	FGW	42264	FGW	42344	FGW	42514	FGW
42129	FGW	42196	FGW	42265	FGW	42345	FGW	42515	FGW
42130	ICE	42197	FGW	42266	FGW	42346	FGW	42516	FGW
42131	EMT	42198	ICE	42267	FGW	42347	FGW	42517	FGW
42132	EMT	42199	ICE	42268	FGW	42348	FGW	42518	FGW
42133	EMT	42200	FGW	42269	FGW	42349	FGW	42519	FGW
42134	ICE	42201	FGW	42271	FGW	42350	FGW	42520	FGW
42135	EMT	42202	FGW	42272	FGW	42351	FGW	42551	FGW
42136	EMT	42203	FGW	42273	FGW	42352	ICE	42552	FGW
42137	EMT	42204	FGW	42275	FGW	42353	ICE	42553	FGW
42138	FGW	42205	ICE	42276	FGW	42354	ICE	42554	FGW
42139	EMT	42206	FGW	42277	FGW	42355	ICE	42555	FGW
42140	EMT	42207	FGW	42279	FGW	42356	FGW	42556	FGW
42141	EMT	42208	FGW	42280	FGW	42357	ICE	42557	FGW
42143	FGW	42209	FGW	42281	FGW	42360	FGW	42558	FGW
42144	FGW	42210	ICE	42283	FGW	42361	FGW	42559	FGW
42145	FGW	42211	FGW	42284	FGW	42362	FGW	42560	FGW
42146	ICE	42212	FGW	42285	FGW	42363	ICE	42561	FGW
42147	ICE	42213	FGW	42286	ICE	42364	FGW	42562	FGW
42148	EMT	42214	FGW	42287	FGW	42365	FGW	42563	FGW
42149	EMT	42215	ICE	42288	FGW	42366	AXC	42564	FGW
42150	ICE	42216	FGW	42289	FGW	42367	AXC	42565	FGW
42151	EMT	42217	FGW	42290	AXC	42368	AXC	42566	FGW
42152	EMT	42218	FGW	42291	FGW	42369	AXC	42567	FGW
42153	EMT	42219	ICE	42292	FGW	42370	AXC	42568	FGW
42154	ICE	42220	EMT	42293	FGW	42371	AXC	42569	FGW
42155	EMT	42221	FGW	42294	FGW	42372	AXC	42570	FGW
42156	EMT	42222	FGW	42295	FGW	42373	AXC	42571	FGW
42157	EMT	42224	FGW	42296	FGW	42374	AXC	42572	FGW
42158	ICE	42225	EMT	42297	FGW	42375	AXC	42573	FGW
42159	ICE	42226	ICE	42299	FGW	42376	AXC	42574	FGW
42160	ICE	42227	EMT	42300	FGW	42377	AXC	42575	FGW
42161	ICE	42228	ICE	42301	FGW	42378	AXC	42576	FGW
42163	ICE	42229	EMT	42302	FGW	42379	AXC	42577	FGW
42164	EMT	42230	EMT	42303	FGW	42380	AXC	42578	FGW
42165	EMT	42231	FGW	42304	FGW	42381	FGW	42579	FGW
42166	FGW	42232	FGW	42305	FGW	42382	FGW	42580	FGW
42167	FGW	42233	FGW	42306	ICE	42383	FGW	42581	FGW
42168	FGW	42234	AXC	42307	ICE	42384	EMT	42582	FGW
42169	FGW	42235	ICE	42308	FGW			42583	FGW
42171	ICE	42236	FGW	42310	FGW	42401	GTL		
42172	ICE	42237	ICE	42315	FGW	42402	GTL	44000	FGW
42173	FGW	42238	ICE	42317	FGW	42403	GTL	44001	FGW
42174	FGW	42239	ICE	42319	FGW	42404	GTL	44002	FGW
42175	FGW	42240	ICE	42321	FGW	42405	GTL	44003	FGW
42176	FGW	42241	ICE	42322	ICE	42406	GTL	44004	FGW
42177	FGW	42242	ICE	42323	ICE	42407	GTL	44005	FGW
42178	FGW	42243	ICE	42325	FGW	42408	GTL	44007	FGW
42179	ICE	42244	ICE	42326	ICE	42409	GTL	44008	FGW
42180	ICE	42245	FGW	42327	EMT			44009	FGW
42181	ICE	42247	FGW	42328	EMT	42501	FGW	44010	FGW
42182	ICE	42250	FGW	42329	EMT	42502	FGW	44011	FGW
42183	FGW	42251	FGW	42330	ICE	42503	FGW	44012	AXC
42184	FGW	42252	FGW	42331	EMT	42504	FGW	44013	FGW
42185	FGW	42253	FGW	42332	FGW	42505	FGW	44014	FGW
42186	ICE	42255	FGW	42333	FGW	42506	FGW	44015	FGW

Number	Op	Number	Op	Number	Op	Number	Op	Number	Op
44016	FGW	44081	FGW	99311	WCR	**NPCCS Stock**		82116	DBR
44017	AXC	44083	FGW	99312	SUP	6260	NRL	82118	GAR
44018	FGW	44085	EMT	99316	WCR	6261	NRL	82120	DBR
44019	ICE	44086	FGW	99318	WCR	6262	NRL	82121	GAR
44020	FGW	44088	GTL	99319	WCR	6263	NRL	82122	DBR
44021	AXC	44089	GTL	99326	WCR	6264	NRL	82123	DBR
44022	FGW	44090	FGW	99327	WCR	6330	FGW	82124	NRL
44023	FGW	44091	FGW	99328	WCR	6336	FGW	82125	OLS
44024	FGW	44093	FGW	99329	WCR	6338	FGW	82126	GAR
44025	FGW	44094	ICE	99348	WCR	6340	ICE	82127	GAR
44026	FGW	44097	FGW	99349	VTN	6344	ICE	82129	NRL
44027	EMT	44098	ICE	99350	WCR	6346	ICE	82132	GAR
44028	FGW	44100	FGW	99353	VTN	6348	FGW	82133	GAR
44029	FGW	44101	FGW	99354	WCR	6352	ICE	82136	GAR
44030	FGW			99361	VTN	6353	ICE	82137	DBR
44031	ICE	45001	AXC	99371	WCR	6354	ICE	82138	DBR
44032	FGW	45002	AXC	99402	WCR	6355	ICE	82139	GAR
44033	FGW	45003	AXC	99405	SUP	6358	ICE	82140	KBR
44034	FGW	45004	AXC			6359	ICE	82141	DBR
44035	FGW	45005	AXC	99530	VSO	6376	COL	82143	GAR
44036	FGW	45018	WCR	99531	VSO	6377	COL	82145	NRL
44037	FGW	45020	DBR	99532	VSO	6378	COL	82146	DBS
44038	FGW	45026	WCR	99534	VSO	6379	COL	82148	DBR
44039	FGW			99535	VSO	6392	EMT	82149	OLS
44040	FGW	46001	FGW	99536	VSO			82150	DBR
44041	EMT	46002	FGW	99537	VSO	9393	ICE	82152	GAR
44042	FGW	46003	FGW	99539	VSO	9394	ICE		
44043	FGW	46004	FGW	99541	VSO			82200	ICE
44044	EMT	46005	FGW	99543	VSO	9701	NRL	82201	ICE
44045	ICE	46006	FGW	99545	VSO	9702	NRL	82202	ICE
44046	EMT	46007	FGW	99546	VSO	9703	NRL	82203	ICE
44047	EMT	46008	FGW	99678	WCR	9708	NRL	82204	ICE
44048	EMT	46009	FGW	99679	WCR	9713	NRL	82205	ICE
44049	FGW	46010	FGW	99670	WCR	9714	NRL	82206	ICE
44050	ICE	46011	FGW	99671	WCR			82207	ICE
44051	EMT	46012	FGW	99672	WCR	62384	NRL	82208	ICE
44052	AXC	46013	FGW	99673	WCR			82209	ICE
44054	EMT	46014	FGW	99674	WCR	64664	AFG	82210	ICE
44055	FGW	46015	FGW	99675	WCR	64707	AFG	82211	ICE
44056	ICE	46016	FGW	99676	WCR			82212	ICE
44057	ICE	46017	FGW	99677	WCR	72612	NRL	82213	ICE
44058	ICE	46018	FGW	99680	WCR	72616	NRL	82214	ICE
44059	FGW			99706	WCR	72630	NRL	82215	ICE
44060	FGW	80041	RIV	99710	WCR	72631	NRL	82216	ICE
44061	ICE	80042	RIV	99712	WCR	72639	NRL	82217	ICE
44063	ICE			99713	WCR			82218	ICE
44064	FGW	99035	SUP	99717	WCR	80204	SUP	82219	ICE
44065	GTL	99040	SUP	99718	WCR	80217	SUP	82220	ICE
44066	FGW	99041	SUP	99721	WCR	80220	SUP	82222	ICE
44067	FGW	99080	SUP	99722	WCR			82223	ICE
44068	FGW			99723	WCR	82101	DRS	82224	ICE
44069	FGW	99108	VTN	99782	SUP	82102	GAR	82225	ICE
44070	EMT	99120	SUP	99792	SUP	82103	GAR	82226	ICE
44071	EMT	99121	WCR	99884	WCR	82105	GAR	82227	ICE
44072	AXC	99125	WCR			82106	DBR	82228	ICE
44073	ICE	99127	WCR	99953	SUP	82107	GAR	82229	ICE
44074	FGW	99128	WCR	99966	WCR	82109	OLS	82230	ICE
44075	ICE	99132	WCR	99968	VSO	82110	DBR	82231	ICE
44076	FGW	99193	WCR	99969	VSO	82111	NRL	82301	CRW
44077	ICE	99194	WCR			82112	GAR	82302	CRW
44078	FGW	99195	WCR	99991	SUP	82113	DBR	82303	CRW
44079	FGW	99241	SUP	99993	RAF	82114	GAR	82304	CRW
44080	ICE	99304	WCR	99995	SUP	82115	NRL	82305	CRW

Data Tables

❏ 82306	ATW		❏ 96606	COL		❏ 977337	NRL
❏ 82307	ATW		❏ 96607	COL		❏ 977868	NRL
❏ 82308	ATW		❏ 96608	COL		❏ 977869	NRL
❏ 82309	CRW		❏ 96609	COL		❏ 977969	NRL
						❏ 977974	NRL
❏ 92114	NRL		❏ 99666	NRL		❏ 977983	NRL
❏ 92159	OLS					❏ 977984	NRL
			Service Stock			❏ 977985	NRL
❏ 92901	OLS		❏ 950001	NRL		❏ 977986	NRL
❏ 92904	VSO		❏ 960014	CRW		❏ 977993	NRL
❏ 92931	OLS		❏ 960301	CRW		❏ 977994	NRL
❏ 92939	NRL					❏ 977995	NRL
❏ 94538	RIV		❏ 971001	NRL		❏ 977997	NRL
❏ 96100	VTN		❏ 971002	NRL			
❏ 96139	OLS		❏ 971003	NRL		❏ 999508	NRL
❏ 96175	WCR		❏ 971004	NRL		❏ 999550	NRL
❏ 96181	OLS					❏ 999602	NRL
❏ 96371	DRS		❏ 975025	NRL		❏ 999605	NRL
❏ 96372	DRS		❏ 975081	NRL		❏ 999606	NRL
❏ 96373	DRS		❏ 975091	NRL			
❏ 96374	WAB		❏ 975280	NRL			
❏ 96375	DRS		❏ 975464	NRL			
❏ 96602	COL		❏ 975486	NRL			
❏ 96603	COL		❏ 975814	NRL			
❏ 96604	COL		❏ 975984	NRL			
❏ 96605	COL						

Below: *Four-car Class 220 CrossCountry 'Voyager' set No. 220015 passes through Eastleigh on 9 April 2014 forming the 06.37 Nottingham to Bournemouth service.* **CJM**

Data Tables

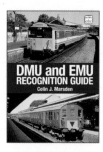
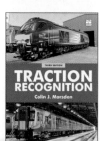